# Human Capital
# Population Economics in the Middle East

# HUMAN CAPITAL
## Population Economics in the Middle East

Edited by

Ismail Sirageldin

I.B.Tauris *Publishers*
LONDON • NEW YORK

in association with the
Economic Research Forum
for the Arab Countries, Iran and Turkey

Published in 2002 by I.B.Tauris & Co. Ltd.
6 Salem Road, London W2 4BU
175 Fifth Avenue, New York, NY 10010
*www.ibtauris.com*

In the United States of America and in Canada distributed by Palgrave Macmillan,
a division of St. Martins Press, 175 Fifth Avenue, New York, NY 10010

Published by arrangement with
The American University in Cairo Press
113 Sharia Kasr el Aini, Cairo, Egypt
*www.aucpress.com*

in association with
The Economic Research Forum for the Arab Countries, Iran and Turkey
7 Boulos Hanna Street, Dokki, 11123 Cairo
*www.erf.org.eg*



ISBN 1 86064 795 2

A full CIP record for this book is available from the British Library
A full CIP record for this book is available from the Library of Congress

Printed in Egypt

# Contents

# Contributors

**Ali A. Ali,** Economic Advisor, Arab Planning Institute, Kuwait.

**Ragui Assaad,** Associate Professor of Planning and Public Affairs at the Humphrey Institute of Public Affairs, University of Minnesota, USA.

**Ibrahim A. Elbadawi,** Lead Economist, Development Economics Research Group (DECRG), World Bank, Washington, DC.

**Yousef Al-Ebraheem,** Minister of Finance, Minister of Planning, and Minister of State for Administrative Development Affairs, Kuwait.

**Nicholas P. Glytsos,** Senior Research Economist and Head of the Labour Economics Division, Centre of Planning and Economic Research (KEPE), Athens, Greece.

**Anne Valia Goujon,** Researcher, Institute for Demography (IFD), Austrian Academy of Sciences, Vienna, Austria.

**Fatma El-Hamidi,** Adjunct Professor, Graduate School of Public and International Affairs, University of Pittsburg, USA.

**Jalaleddin Jalali,** Professor of Economics, Institute for Research in Planning and Development, Tehran, Iran.

**Zeinab Khadr,** Research Assistant Professor, Social Research Center, American University in Cairo, and Assistant Professor, Faculty of Economics and Political Science, Cairo University, Egypt.

**İsmet Koç,** Associate Professor, Hacettepe University Institute of Population Studies, Ankara, Turkey.

**Barry McCormick,** Professor of Economics, Department of Economics, University of Southampton, United Kingdom.

**Hoda Rashad,** Research Professor and Director, Social Research Center, American University in Cairo, Egypt.

**Farzaneh Roudi,** Policy Analyst, Population Reference Bureau, Washington, DC.

**Djavad Salehi-Isfahani,** Professor of Economics, Virginia Polytechnic Institute and State University, USA.

**Ismail Sirageldin,** Professor Emeritus, Economics, Population Dynamics and International Health, Johns Hopkins University, USA.

**Aysıt Tansel,** Professor, Department of Economics, Middle East Technical University, Ankara, Turkey.

**Ali C. Tasiran,** Associate Professor, Department of Statistics, Gothenburg University, Sweden.

**İnsan Tunalı,** Associate Professor, Department of Economics, College of Administrative Sciences and Economics, Koc University, Istanbul, Turkey.

**Jackline Wahba,** Lecturer, Department of Economics, University of Southampton, United Kingdom.

**Jeffrey G. Williamson,** Laird Bell Professor of Economics, Department of Economics, Harvard University, USA.

**Tarik M. Yousef,** Assistant Professor of Economics, School of Foreign Service, Georgetown University, USA.

# Preface

This volume contains a selection of papers originally presented at a conference entitled "Population Challenges in the Middle East and North Africa: Toward the Twenty-first Century," convened by the Economic Research Forum for the Arab Countries, Iran and Turkey in Cairo in November 1998. The conference provided a rare opportunity for a wide-ranging group of experts—political scientists, sociologists, and economists, as well as population specialists—to come together to examine the developmental consequences of demographic change and to explore the ability of policy makers to incorporate these effects into their socioeconomic development strategies. It is the interdisciplinary nature of the present volume that gives it a particularly valuable dimension.

The papers that originated in the 1998 conference have since been thoroughly reworked for inclusion in the book, and new ones from other ERF venues have been added to complete the scope of the coverage. While the data inevitably refers to the 1980s and mid-1990s, the findings and analyses are based on highly innovative methodologies, which make important contributions to scholarship in their own right. The chapters that follow thus provide new and sophisticated treatments and interpretations of specific population issues in the Middle East and North Africa, as well as contributing substantively to our knowledge of the sociodemographic and economic development processes in the region.

Much effort has gone into the production of this volume. Aside from the contributing authors, numerous colleagues and anonymous referees provided suggestions to improve the presentation and content. The volume could never have been completed without the support of Abda El-Mahdi and the publication staff of the Economic Research Forum, especially Maureen Moynihan, Gillian Potter, and Pauline Wickham. The able editorial and production work of Hugh Hughes and the AUC Press, and the editorial assistance of Rabab El-Mahdi of McGill University, Canada, who carefully reviewed all the chapters and made valuable editorial and substantive suggestions, is very much appreciated.

Ismail Sirageldin
November 2001

# Introduction

*Ismail Sirageldin*

As they enter the twenty-first century, the countries of the Middle East and North Africa (MENA) region—the Arab countries, Iran, and Turkey—are experiencing major socioeconomic and political changes, with demographic change playing a fundamental role. Prospects for development in the region, for the twenty-first century, depend to a large extent on the awareness of policy makers of the developmental consequences of demographic change and their ability to incorporate these effects into their socioeconomic development strategies, with negative externalities minimized and positive ones maximized. These are complex interdisciplinary dynamics. The purpose of this book is to examine the patterns of demographic change in the region and elucidate some of the pathways of the demographic processes that influence socioeconomic performance and outcomes.

In this introduction we present a general statement of the determinants and developmental consequences of demographic change and the necessary conditions for positive socioeconomic outcomes. The chapters in the volume attempt to cover a wide spectrum of determinants and consequences of demographic change in the region. However, some important socioeconomic consequences of demographic change are not represented in the book. The role of demand for labor, the effect of population aging on intergenerational transfers and pension schemes, and the environmental impact of population growth and its distribution are three such missing issues. Although there are similarities among the countries of the region, they differ significantly in their resource endowment, economic structures, and demographic parameters. The chapters attempt to capture some of these diversities. The book is divided into four parts: demography and development, human capital, labor markets, and migration and urbanization. A brief overview of the chapters is presented in the last section of this introduction.

## Demography and Development

Demographic processes such as population growth, spatial distribution, and age structure play a pivotal role in development. They shape the destiny of development prospects through their consequences, while themselves being shaped by development processes and outcomes. There is more agreement on the causes of mortality decline than on the determinants of fertility. Medical technology and public health measures that made possible the development of effective means of disease control and prevention, combined with effective social organization and better nutritional status, are largely credited for the health revolution that took place in the second half of the twentieth century. They made parents' decisions to invest in the health of their children more informed, effective, and economical. The decline in infant and child mortality, given the prevailing young age structures, has been remarkable in almost all countries of the region, although a large variance in health status persists (see Mosley and Chen, 1984; Hill, 1992). Differentials in health status and mortality are now seen as being associated with socioeconomic status, parental education, and lack of public health infrastructures or access to such facilities.

The case of fertility determinants is less clear. On the one extreme, there are those who believe that the birth rate is socially determined. Throughout the history of humanity, "the long-run birth rate was kept as low as possible consistent with survival—as low, that is, as death rate. Why? The answer seems to be that the hominids were exploring a unique evolutionary niche by relying on culture, learning, and social organization as their mode of adaptation" (Davis, 1986: 49–50; see also Carr-Saunders, 1922, for an early statement). The Davis and Carr-Saunders paradigm implies the presence of a macro-micro feedback system that provides signals for disequilibria that promote learning and effective actions on both the micro and the macro levels of societies. These disequilibria include not only the environmental notion of 'carrying capacity,' but also the negative effect of improved infant and child survival on desired fertility. That general framework, outlined by Kingsley Davis, allowed for varied disciplinary interpretations of the determinants of fertility. Sociologists and anthropologists highlighted the role of culture, values, and norms in fertility behavior, while economists emphasized the role of markets, relative prices, and the allocation of household resources over the life cycle (Khan, 1979). Others emphasized the role of new contraceptive technology and its diffusion, in the second half of the twentieth century, through national and international population programs, combined with the role of mass education, mass media, and effective communication, as major causes of fertility transition in the developing countries. They reduced the market cost of effective fertility control as well as changing the value system that influences reproductive behavior, and accordingly reduced the perceived social cost of fertility control while increasing the age at marriage (see Bhushan and Sirageldin, 1996). This last is mainly a result of increased education among females and their labor force participation. What is apparent, however, is that most of these forces are currently operative in the region and their combined effects are exerting a downward pressure on fertility. Fertility has started a sustained decline, with significant developmental effects on age structure, labor force participation, and geographic and occupational mobility.

### *The Onset of the Demographic Transition*

After decades of declining mortality and high fertility, almost all the Arab countries, Iran, and Turkey are entering the final phase of the demographic transition. Fertility has started a secular decline in the region. The fact that current levels of fertility remain high in some of these countries is a reflection of disparities in health status and of the initial high level of fertility and later timing of change. However, a significant process of convergence is taking place among the late comers. For example, Libya, Sudan, and Syria have been experiencing a record pace of fertility decline, with total fertility rates (TFR) declining by between 2.0 and 2.5 children per woman in the few years between the late 1980s and early 1990s. Fertility decline is largely a result of five proximate factors: nuptiality (age at marriage and marriage rates), contraception behavior, pregnancy termination, breastfeeding behavior, and given natural fecundity; this last is determined primarily by genetic factors and health status. In many countries of the region, especially the Arab countries, fertility decline has been closely associated more with delayed marriage rather than a decline in marital fertility. The experience of Abu Dhabi in the United Arab Emirates, for example, is representative of that of many countries in the region. Age at marriage has played a major role in the present phase of fertility decline in the Emirate. Between 1975 and 1985, according to census data, the proportion of nationals in Abu Dhabi who never married increased from about 19 percent to 32 percent of the adult population, a significant 65 percent increase, and the trend has been continuing in the late 1990s. Delayed marriage among young men and women is partly a result of females' increased years of education and their labor force participation. Higher age at marriage is also part of the process of cultural change associated with increased modernity, urbanization, and openness to global information and cultures. However, changes in nuptiality patterns without associated socioeconomic and institutional changes could have consequences on the status of women that are not necessarily positive, and could lead to intergenerational transmission of poverty. The region is experiencing a social revolution with both positive and negative results. How fertility declines is an important social question that requires careful assessment and follow-up.

As a result of the fertility transition, the high rates of population growth in the countries of the region are expected to decline in the coming decades. This is due mainly to the decline in fertility that has been building upon young age structures as a consequence of generations of high fertility, but also to the earlier and rapid decline in mortality. As the age structure gets older, the crude death rates increase even in the absence of changes in age-specific death rates, with the result that population growth declines even faster. There are other characteristics of the change in the age structure that have significant developmental consequences, the most important of which is the change in the natural growth rates of the various cohorts, with migration being considered an outcome. The working-age population is expected to grow at a high rate, faster than that of the population as a whole, and especially higher than the growth rates of the younger generations. The cohorts of working age are expected to maintain these high rates of growth for at least a generation, while the older cohorts will gain significantly in relative size in the coming decades. These known demographic patterns and changes are certain to materialize in the MENA region. Differences among countries in their demographic parameters are only a matter of timing and expected cohort sizes at the stationary state, and not in the pattern of change itself. However, these differences could generate intercountry differentials in capital-intensive techniques that may generate pressure for labor migration.

For all practical purposes, in the present phase of the demographic transition, demography as an accounting science is largely exogenous to the region. The decline of fertility could be sustained or accelerated through socioeconomic and population policies, especially in countries or areas where fertility levels continue to be high. But such policies, although important in their own right and context, should not be the main focus of integrated population-development policies for the countries of the region. Rather, the policy focus should be on how to capitalize on the potentials of the present phase of the demographic transition, especially its socioeconomic externalities, to enhance the potential for sustained development.

## *A Window of Opportunity for Development*

It is now fashionable in the population-economic growth literature to indicate that this final stage of the demographic transition provides a window of development opportunities. The window opens to positive development as a result of enhanced saving potential, reduced demographic dependency, a reorientation of investment toward capital widening, and the potential for enhancing labor quality, through investment in the quality of education and in health. It must be emphasized that the 'window of opportunity' opens at the last stage of the demographic transition, when fertility starts its secular decline converging toward low mortality and population growth decline, while the working-age population continues to grow at high rates. However, as the term indicates, it is only an opportunity. The older term—labor replacement (see Farooq, 1975)—implies that the average quality of the labor force will increase at a fast pace through better health and education. The converse is evidently true. The acceleration in the improvement of the labor force is a consequence of the young age structure that prevails at the onset of the fertility decline. But that positive effect was also a potential, and so it was with the Coale and Hoover (1958) framework that started the modeling of these economic-demographic relations more than a generation ago. It all depends on how the potential for saving, generated by the demographic window, has been channeled into productive investment in human capital and the promotion of its demand. The window of opportunity could be as negative as it could be positive. As Samir Radwan succinctly observed (Radwan, 1998: 3): "The decline of fertility in the region cannot be separated from the low equilibrium trap (it is not for example a response to significant improvement in education)." Furthermore, "The relative abundance of the labor component of this opportunity has been with us for some time but has been squandered through limited human capital accumulation and unemployment (including underemployment)."

The window of opportunity framework provides a useful policy framework. An integrated population-development policy should identify and minimize the effects of the negative forces and enhance the positive ones that maximize the development prospects associated with the presence of the 'window of opportunity.' At this stage of development in the Arab region, these forces are only partly demographic and mainly socioeconomic and political. They may be grouped into supply-side factors, demand-side factors, and factors that enhance and sustain social welfare. The most obvious factor on the supply side in the Arab region is human resource development (HRD). The demand side includes the factors necessary for the productive utilization of human resources, the promotion of economic growth, and the minimization of unemployment and poverty. In the present environment of the global economy, the window of opportunity may be viewed as a shift from micro reproductive regimes toward a regime of social reform.

## *Human Resource Development: Supply Side*

Two dimensions of HRD in the region require attention: the quantity and the quality of the labor force. We already mentioned the quantity dimension of human resources in the region: the population of working age is expected to grow at high rates for decades to come. As to the quality dimension, which refers to the motivational aspects of human development, two factors are essential for enhanced productivity: education and health. Indeed, human resource development includes more than enhancing productivity in the labor market. Associated with the onset of fertility decline in the region, average years of education, especially that of females, has increased greatly. However, almost all studies of educational achievement indicate that the region lags in the quality dimension of education, especially at the basic level of education as well as in mathematics and the sciences. Even countries that are leaders in the region in their education effort such as Jordan, or with high per pupil expenditure such as Kuwait, are lagging, according to standardized international educational achievement tests. The situation at the higher levels of education and in the research and development field (R&D), although improving, is similarly lagging by international standards (UNESCO, 1995). Furthermore, the synergy among health status, socioeconomic status, and educational achievement presents a potential for intergenerational continuity of lower educational quality for population groups in the region. The labor force in MENA will continue to grow at high rates for decades to come, but for sizable segments of the population its quality is constrained by the presence of low-quality basic education, uncertain health outcomes, and poverty.

The qualitative dimension of human resource development has to do with motivation. An achievement motivation, the ability to envision opportunities, a sense of discipline, a work ethic commitment, and a sense of self-esteem that is transmitted from one generation to the next: these are some of the elements that define a motivated and progressive society.[1] These qualities have been highly strained in the region as a result of decades of various types of socialism, as well as by the distribution pattern of oil revenue in the oil economies, which have provided both free education and social benefits, combined with guaranteed public employment and generous pensions. The large majority of the citizen labor force in MENA countries is employed in the public sector, protected from market competition. The sheltering pattern was not confined to citizens of the oil countries, however, since a large segment of regional labor from the non-oil economies was similarly employed in the oil economies. As a result, a generation of human resources developed a culture of dependency. At present, with the opening of global competition and the decline of the real price of oil, a major motivational adjustment is taking place. The causes, nature, and direction of this adjustment should be understood and shaped by fiscal and social policies (Sirageldin, 1999).

### *Human Resource Development: Demand Side*

The demographic window of opportunity depends on more than supply-side considerations. The presence of a strong and growing demand for labor is a prerequisite. The role of demand is not examined in this volume. There are pessimistic views of growth prospects in the region. In a recent assessment (ESCWA Secretariat, 1996: 99), it was indicated that:

> ESCWA member countries have weak manufacturing structures, high illiteracy rates, limited industrial skills, poor saving ratios, a low level of manufacturing exports, inadequate R&D, high indebtedness, small companies with limited international experience, limited regional cooperation and trade, heavy dependence on government, inefficient bureaucracies, limited private sector participation, and above all [a] hostile international economic environment.

Pessimism has not been universal, however. In a World Bank (1995: 2–3) report, it was indicated that, during the period 1960–85, the region outperformed all other regions except East Asia, in income growth, low levels of poverty, and the equality of income distribution. The World Bank assessment included the oil economies and the period of the oil boom. Many changes have taken place since then, including the decline in the real price of oil and the debt crisis that ignited various structural adjustment programs. Although some of the economic parameters mentioned in the ESCWA assessment have improved, internal demand has not gained enough strength to provide opportunities for the growing labor supply in most countries of the region. Nor have the fundamental factors of labor quality, transparency in governance, and modern infrastructure improved sufficiently to attract international investment in high technology industries in the present globalization environment. The situation in the oil economy (Gulf Cooperation Council or GCC) countries seems equally alarming (Askari, Bazzari, and Tyler, 1998). The challenge on the demand-side may not be resolved by simply opening the economies of the region to global competition and hoping that both labor efficiency and institutional quality will improve. There are social and economic internal reforms that need to be undertaken first. As discussed elsewhere (Sirageldin, 1999), these internal reforms include the development of human resources, equality of opportunities, transparency in governance, strong local demand, and a sustainable environment.

### *Labor Mobility*

Another important factor in the twilight of supply and demand considerations is labor mobility and migration. The past pattern of high rates of temporary labor migration to, within, and outside the region, with such significant socioeconomic consequences as remittances and changed consumption behavior, has faded out greatly in the 1990s. This has been primarily a result of reduced oil prices, regional internal conflict, and the emergence of the European Union. On the other hand, the emerging processes of globalization reduce the need for labor movement to the extent that the mobility of capital is enhanced. It must be emphasized, however, that current knowledge about linkages between globalization or regionalization and migration is not well established. In a recent critical review of the evidence, Assous (2000: 66) concludes:

> Even if regional integration does lead to a decrease in migration flows, it may not necessarily be for the reasons established by standard trade theory. Other factors could include: (i) a reduction in the demand for foreign labor; (ii) the existence of significant cultural barriers to assimilation which discourage many potential migrants; and (iii) a stable political situation and effective economic management in sending countries which, even if the economy has not yet generated much employment, could instill confidence in its citizens by offering them the hope of a rapid improvement in their living standards.

Globalization, however, increases labor mobility for the highly skilled and motivated segments of the labor force. This pattern introduces a development challenge in the region, especially with the presence of a large and growing unskilled segment of the labor force, with low educational levels and poor-quality skills. The acceleration of education quality at the basic level is a must and it needs to be combined with extensive on-the-job and other types of training.

### *Support for the Elderly*

The populations of the MENA region have begun the aging process. That process, combined with urbanization and the adoption of modern life styles, has implications for the traditional patterns of intergenerational transfers from the working cohort to the dependent young and older cohorts. Many countries of the region have established social security programs that have non-sustainable benefits in the medium term. Some pension programs, as the case of Turkey illustrates, are facing severe financial crisis, mainly a result of program design. If the program maintains the current structure of coverage and benefits, the deficit is expected to accelerate as the aging of the population reaches its peak early in the twenty-first century (Sayan and Kenc, 1998). Other programs in the region have fundamental structural problems. The oil economies of the GCC countries have instituted generous social security (SS) programs, but their financing is based mainly on non-renewable oil revenue. These programs cannot be sustained without the development of sustainable non-oil sectors (see Sirageldin and Al-Rahmani, 1999). The MENA countries should examine their present SS programs in anticipation of the increasing future demands of older age cohorts. This is especially important, since the present market-oriented economies, and the openness of the globalization process, will eventually erode traditional sources of support for the elderly.

### *Policy Priorities*

The preceding discussion indicates that the MENA pattern of population dynamics seems to be set for at least a generation. The policy challenge is how to deal with the externalities of these dynamics in order to maximize the potential for growth and development in the region. This is a difficult challenge, especially as unemployment and poverty are emerging and will become important policy issues in the coming decades. In the context of the present phase of demographic transition, inequality and poverty could lead to segmentation in the social system, transmitted through generations. In this sociodemographic environment, social fund programs may act as temporary remedial measures but not as long-term prevention. An in-depth understanding of the intergenerational dynamics of poverty and income distribution is necessary for effective policies (see Sirageldin, 1975).

Three sets of policy issues are emerging in the region in the context of this final phase of the demographic transition. They comprise improving the quality of the supply of human resources, enhancing the demand potential for human resources, and, most fundamental of all, launching a program of internal reform in order to be better equipped in the openness of the globalization era.

## An Overview of the Volume

Part I of this volume, which consists of four chapters, examines issues in population and development. It highlights major challenges facing the region in the present phase of demographic transition. A window of development opportunity seems to have opened. However, the processes of demographic change have presented challenges to development which, combined with changes in the global environment, seem to lead to unemployment, inequality, and the growth of poverty in the region. Furthermore, the continuing reliance on non-renewable resources as the main source of revenue presents additional challenges in capturing the positive opportunities of the transition in the oil economies.

Chapter 1, by Williamson and Yousef, presents the analytic foundation of the demographic window of opportunity. This framework highlights the consequences to economic growth of the demographic transition when it moves from high fertility and mortality to lower levels in the later phase of the transition. It emphasizes that each phase of demographic transition is associated with an age structure that has different age-specific growth rates and different dependency ratios, and consequently a different impact on economic growth performance. In their empirical application, the authors estimated that the early unfavorable demographic characteristics in the region, including the persistence of high demographic dependency, were one reason that the region lagged behind East Asia in economic performance. They estimated that this unfavorable demographic pattern was responsible for one-third of the difference between the growth of the region and the higher growth rates of East Asia during the past three decades. The authors are careful to caution that benefits from the demographic window of opportunity are not automatic but require the presence of significant financial, legal, and political institutional reform.

In Chapter 2, Rashad and Khadr document the robustness of the fertility transition that is taking place in the Arab region. Fertility is declining regardless of differentials in per capita income or levels of resource endowment and is proceeding at a fast pace. The authors examine the mechanisms of the decline and find that nuptiality is playing a major role in fertility transition. They conclude that, as a result, the region is experiencing a major process of social change. Women's status and their socioeconomic roles are changing, but the welfare outcome is uncertain. Female labor force participation is expected to increase, but so will gender inequality and poverty in the absence of socioeconomic policies that promote overall employment opportunities and enhance gender equality. The findings of the chapter invite important areas for research and policy analysis.

In Chapter 3, Ali and Elbadawi review the evidence on poverty in the region as it interacts with inequality and growth. Is poverty an outcome of the pattern of growth in the region or a result of income inequality? If the latter, a second question arises as to whether inequality is a transitional phenomenon that disappears as income grows in the region, *a la* Kuznets. Ali and Elbadawi attempted to investigate these complex questions empirically. They developed a model with two-components: growth and poverty. They tested their model on six Arab countries (Algeria, Egypt, Jordan, Morocco, Mauritania, and Tunisia) that had data on both income distribution and poverty. The findings indicate that in the period 1975–96, initial high levels of inequalities led, with the exception of Egypt and Mauritania, to lower growth, since they generated social conflict, which exacerbated the effects of external shocks. The findings also indicate that the dynamics of poverty and its reduction vary among the six Arab countries. For example, with the exception of Egypt, both growth and distribution were required to alleviate poverty, although in varying degrees. For Egypt, growth alone was the major factor constraining the reduction of poverty. None of the GCC countries were included in the analysis, partly for lack of data and partly due to the unique structure of their resource endowment.

In Chapter 4, Al-Ebraheem and Sirageldin examine the potential for human resource development in the special case of the oil economies of the GCC countries, where oil, a non-renewable resource, is the major source of finance and the public sector is pivotal in the economic and social domains. They observed that the government budget should be the main focus of the analysis of human resource development in these countries. The prime reason is that public finance dominates economic activities and is being dominated by revenue from oil, a non-renewable resource. They developed a budget statement that incorporates the rate of depletion of oil reserves as well as indicators to monitor success in building a renewable non-oil production sector. The difference between oil revenue and government revenue based on a hypothetical tax system, levied on the non-oil renewable production sector, is labeled the 'renewable resource gap' and is presented as a main indicator of development in these oil economies. The main policy goal is to reduce and ultimately eliminate the renewable resource gap. Closing the gap is important, since the vast majority of the national labor force in the GCC countries is employed in the public sector: i.e., their wage bill and other benefits are being paid from oil revenue. This situation generates dependency and lack of competitiveness, inhibits the evolution of democratic institutions, and, given the high rates of growth of national labor, may not be sustained as long as the renewable resource gap persists. Furthermore, high population growth complicates the potential to close the gap. The chapter presents estimates of the gap. Its size has not declined over time and has even increased in some GCC countries. The authors conclude that, in the absence of socio-economic reform that closes the renewable resource gap, the GCC countries are living today at the expense of tomorrow.

Part II focuses on human capital and has three chapters. As discussed above, development in the region depends on the ability to utilize potential savings to enhance human capital as the window of opportunity opens in the last phase of the demographic transition. Meanwhile, education affects fertility levels, with progress in education, especially for females, accelerating fertility transition. How fertility and education interact and affect the future growth of population and human capital accumulation in the Arab countries of the region is examined in Chapter 5 by Goujon. First, the author reviewed the evolution of fertility and education in the Arab region within the last 10–15 years. There has been evident progress in educational achievement, especially among females, and in fertility decline. Next, using a multi-state population projection method that divides the population by levels of educational attainment with different mortality and fertility schedules, Goujon was able to project, through the mid-2000s, population growth, age structures, and educational attainment for a sample of countries in the region. Rapid population growth is certain in Jordan, Syria, and Palestine. On the whole, population growth will be slower under a rapid development scenario with high education and low fertility and mortality. Projection results are influenced by the built-in momentum of educational attainment and its diffusion through progressive education policies, and in particular by the ability to close the gender gap in education.

The issue of the accumulation of human capital as fertility declines is examined in depth in Chapter 6 by Salehi-Isfahani for the case of Iran, where the goal of the population program has been: fewer children but better children. Salehi-Isfahani illustrates that demographic development in Iran provided for a favorable age structure, which enhances the saving potential that frees resources to invest in improving the quality of children's education and health, on both the macro and the household levels. The latter depends on the shift from child quantity to child quality that is associated with parental education and the expected returns from education and training in the marketplace. Parents in Iran are better educated, but market signals lack incentives for the quantity-quality shift, according to the author. The chapter highlights the importance of developing an adequate measure of educational quality and allowing for the control of cultural factors.

In Chapter 7, Tasiran, the last contributor in Part II, presents an econometric analysis of fertility dynamics in Turkey, which has been experiencing a demographic transition accompanied by economic growth since the 1950s. The study is pioneering to the extent it is using a dynamic approach that takes into consideration time-level effects in the study of fertility. The relation of age to the risk of first birth is shown to be non-linear, and there are significant differentials according to education, ethnicity, and migration status.

Part III focuses on labor markets in the region and consists of four contributions. Jalali and Roudi, in Chapter 8, survey the evidence on the relation between globalization and unemployment in the MENA region. They argue that the process of economic globalization is proceeding quickly in terms of increased cross-border transactions of goods, services, and finance, but that MENA economies have low participation in the process. They speculate that one reason for the region's hesitation to be fully integrated in the globalization process is the fear of increased unemployment, a result of downsizing or closure of inefficient firms in the early stages of economic liberalization. That fear is well founded, according to the authors, since MENA has the highest unemployment rate of all geographic areas, as the chapter documents. The authors conclude, however, that although short-term unemployment is to be expected, there will in the long term be a growth benefit from the globalization process, resulting from the necessity to absorb the expected high growth rate of labor in the region.

In Chapter 9, Assaad and El-Hamidi use an econometric methodology to focus on factors affecting female labor supply in Egypt. The chapter examines how female participation and hours of work in both the public and the private sectors respond to wages and other individual characteristics. Results indicate that education and predicted wages are important determinants of participation, with high estimated response. Furthermore, the findings support the known pattern that large family size acts as a constraint on female participation in wage employment, more so than in non-wage employment.

Chapter 10, by Koç, provides a well-documented descriptive analysis of three gender-related issues in Turkey: How impoverished are female-headed households? What is the pattern of their income sources and consumption expenditures? Do female-headed households require government support? The findings indicate that the majority of female-headed households are poor and economically vulnerable. The pattern of sources of their resources, and their allocation, is different than that of male-headed households, indicating the presence of an Engle-expenditure pattern. They rely more heavily on non-earned income and allocate a much larger share of their resources to food, clothing, and other necessities. The chapter concludes that the social consequences of the present status of female-headed households are alarming, especially in the light of the increase in this trend in Turkey.

In Chapter 11, the last in Part III, Tansel examines differentials in returns to general versus high school training in Turkey. Investment in vocational training is an important issue in human capital analysis and policy in Turkey (and in MENA in general), where policy makers have been emphasizing that the number of vocational high schools should be increased and that students should be streamlined to vocational high school training. Findings from studies on the subject are divided between the two systems. Some indicate that the rates of return to investments in general curricula are much higher than in vocational programs, while others stress the relative social profitability of general and vocational schooling in developing countries. For the analysis, Tansel applied a three-way logit model to a recent national household expenditure survey. The findings reinforce the conclusions of other studies in developing countries. When controlled for observed characteristics and sample selection, the wages for men of the vocational high school graduates are higher than the wages of the general high school graduates. Although not as robust, the conclusions for women were similar. The author concludes that vocational high schools are superior to general high schools in terms of several indicators of efficacy in enhancing labor market outcomes in Turkey.

Part IV, the concluding section, discusses issues in migration and urbanization. The MENA region is characterized by large inter- and intra-country migration flows, both temporary and permanent. Why people migrate, and what the consequences of their move are, is an important question. In Chapter 12, Tunalı develops a model of rationality in migration decision and applies it to a micro data set from Turkey. After careful correction for selectivity, the findings support the rationality hypothesis. Both migrants and non-migrants chose the options with the highest yield, given their circumstances. However, gains are not realized except for a small minority. Tunalı concludes that migration may be viewed as a lottery of sorts: individuals are willing to invest in a proposition that has a high probability of yielding negative returns, since a large payoff is possible—a pattern that seems a variant on the Todaro (1968) model of migration. The socioeconomic and policy consequences of these findings are important and require careful follow-up.

Glytsos, in Chapter 13, presents a quantitative analysis of the effect of migrant remittances on the economies of Algeria, Egypt, Greece, Jordan, Morocco, Portugal, Syria, and Tunisia. Using a demand-oriented dynamic econometric model, the author focused on the long- and short-run effects of remittances on consumption, investment, imports, and outputs in each country. Findings, although instructive, are not uniform across countries. The study, although tentative in its conclusions, provides some interesting observations. The effects of remittances are not independent of the channels through which they were transferred. On the whole, both the flow of remittances and their impact on consumption, investment, and growth are relatively unstable temporally and inter-country. Whether remittances promote growth in the MENA countries continues to be an open question.

In the final chapter, McCormick and Wahba review, in the case of Egypt, the evidence on migration to big cities. The authors examine whether internal migration has contributed to the growth of Egypt's three largest cities—Cairo, Giza, and Alexandria—and whether migration has altered the skill and human capital composition of the labor force of these cities. Using the 1988 Labor Force Sample Survey, they estimated two binomial logit models. Their findings indicate that net internal migration of male workers to large cities has been almost zero in the decade of the 1980s. Education has a positive effect on the likelihood of migration to big cities to small towns, but not back to rural areas. Those who migrate to big cities at a young age tend to stay longer—until they reach their mid-30s, when the probability of their move increases. The result was that in the 1980s, the average age of populations in big cities declined, while the size of these urban populations did not increase.

## Notes

1 John Atkinson (1964) defines the achievement motive as the "propensity to strive for success in situations involving an evaluation of one's performance in relation to some standard of excellence." This underlies a "capacity for taking pride in accomplishment where success at one or another activity is achieved." For an empirical application, see Morgan, Sirageldin, and Baerwaldt, 1966.

## References

Askari, H., M. Bazzari, and W. Tyler. 1998. "Policies and Economic Potential in the Countries of the Gulf Cooperation Council," in N. Shafik (ed.), *Economic Challenges Facing Middle Eastern and North African Countries: Alternative Futures*, pp. 225–55. London and New York: Macmillan and St. Martin's Press, in association with Economic Research Forum for the Arab Countries, Iran and Turkey.

Assous, Laurence. 2000. *Globalization, Migration and Development*, Social Issues/Employment, OECD Proceedings, pp. 59–72. Paris: Organization for Economic Co-operation and Development.

Atkinson, John W. 1964. *An Introduction to Motivation*. Princeton, NJ: D. Van Nostrand.

Bhushan, Indu, and Ismail Sirageldin. 1996. "Education, Fertility Desires, and the Perceived Cost of Contraception," in *Research in Human Capital and Development*, Vol. 9, pp. 103–32. Greenwich, CT: JAI Press.

Carr-Saunders, A. M. 1922. *The Population Problem: A Study in Human Evolution*. Oxford: Clarendon Press.

Coale, Ansley J., and Edgar M. Hoover. 1958. *Population Growth and Economic Development in Low-Income Countries: A Case Study of India's Prospects*. Princeton, NJ: Princeton University Press.

Davis, Kingsley. 1986. "Low Fertility in Evolutionary Perspective," in Kingsley Davis, Mikhail S. Barnstam, and Rita Ricardo-Campbell (eds.), *Below Replacement Fertility in Industrial Societies: Causes, Consequences, Policies*, supplement to Vol. 12, *Population and Development Review*, pp. 48–65. New York: Population Council.

ESCWA Secretariat. 1996. "Overview: Industrial Strategies and Policies in the ESCWA Region Within the Context of a Changing International and Regional Environment," *Industrial Strategies and Policies for Management and Entrepreneurial Skills under Conditions of Global and Regional Change,* Selected Proceedings, Expert Group Meeting, Bahrain, 20–23 November 1995. Amman: ESCWA, FES, and ERF.

Farooq, Ghazi, 1976. "Population Growth, Manpower, and Employment," in Warren Robinson (ed.), *Population and Development Planning*, pp. 45–68. New York: Population Council.

Hill, Kenneth (ed.). 1992. *Child Health Priorities for the 1990s*. Baltimore, MD: The Johns Hopkins University, Institute for International Programs.

Khan, M. Ali. 1979. "Relevance of Human Capital Theory to Fertility Research: Comparative Findings for Bangladesh and Pakistan," *Research in Human Capital and Development*, Vol. 1, pp. 3–44. Greenwich, CT: JAI Press.

Morgan, James N., Ismail Sirageldin, and Nancy Baerwaldt. 1996. *Productive Americans: A Study of How Individuals Contribute to Economic Progress*. Ann Arbor, MI: The University of Michigan, Institute for Social Research.

Mosley, Henry, and Lincoln Chen. 1984. "An Analytical Framework for the Study of Child Survival in Developing Countries," in Henry Mosley and Lincoln Chen (eds.), *Child Survival Strategies for Research, Population and Development Review*, Supplement to Vol. 10. New York: Population Council.

Radwan, Samir. 1998. "Demographic Transition and Welfare: A Window of Opportunity for the MENA Region," *Forum*, Newsletter of the Economic Research Forum, Vol. 5, No. 4: 1–3. December 98/January 99. Cairo, Egypt: Economic Research Forum.

Sayan, S., and T. Kenc. 1998. "Long-term Consequences of Rehabilitating a Financially Troubled Pension System: An Overlapping Generation, General Equilibrium Analysis of Turkey," paper presented at Fifth ERF Annual Conference. Gammath, Tunisia, 31 August–2 September.

Sirageldin, Ismail. 1975. "The Demographic Aspects of Income Distribution," in Warren Robinson (ed.), *Population and Development Planning*, pp. 153–87. New York: Population Council.

———.1998. "Globalization, Regionalization and Recent Trade Agreements: Impact on Arab Economies—Rapid Exogenous Change—Slow Endogenous Response," in Ahmed Al-Kawaz (ed.), *New Economic Developments and their Impact on Arab Economies*, pp. 15–56. Amsterdam: North-Holland.

———, and Eqbal Al-Rahmani. 1999. "Elderly Support in Oil Economies: How Sustainable Is the 21st Century, with Illustrations from Kuwait," paper presented at Kuwait Economic Society Annual Conference. Kuwait, 27–29 April.

Todaro, M. 1968. "An Analysis of Industrialization. Employment and Unemployment in Less Developed Countries," *Yale Economic Essays*, 8: 331–402.

UNESCO. 1995. *The Higher Education System in the Arab States: Development of S&T Indicators*, report prepared for UNESCO by Subhi Qasem. Cairo: UNESCO.

World Bank. 1995. *Claiming the Future: Choosing Prosperity in the Middle East and North Africa.* Washington, DC: The World Bank.

# Part I

# Demography and Development

# 1

# Demographic Transitions and Economic Performance in the Middle East and North Africa

*Jeffrey G. Williamson and Tarik M. Yousef*

## Introduction

The populations of the Middle East and North Africa (MENA) have grown very rapidly in the post-World War II period, faster than all regions in the world except sub-Saharan Africa (Table 1.1).[1] The total population of the region in the 1950s was estimated at 100 million, by 1995 it had reached 300 million, and by 2025 it is projected to climb to over 500 million (United Nations, 1996). These demographic trends go hand in hand with increased urbanization, rapid rural-urban migration, and a rising gap in food self-sufficiency. Yet, for much of the post-independence era, population growth was a concern only of demographers. MENA's economies were undergoing rapid structural transformation and economic growth, while the state expanded its role as employer and producer under the auspices of the import-substitution model of development (Richards and Waterbury, 1996).

**Table 1.1: Population Growth and Fertility, 1970–98**

| | Population Growth (annual %) | | | Fertility Rates (children/female) | | |
|---|---|---|---|---|---|---|
| | 1970–79 | 1980–89 | 1990–98 | 1970–80 | 1980–90 | 1990–98 |
| East Asia & Pacific | 2.04 | 1.59 | 1.40 | 4.18 | 2.76 | 2.30 |
| South Asia | 2.41 | 2.21 | 1.94 | 5.63 | 4.74 | 3.83 |
| Latin America | 2.42 | 2.01 | 1.75 | 4.71 | 3.59 | 3.00 |
| Sub-Saharan Africa | 2.85 | 2.95 | 2.80 | 6.62 | 6.39 | 5.82 |
| Middle income | 1.95 | 1.65 | 1.34 | 4.07 | 2.92 | 2.43 |
| Low income | 2.43 | 2.29 | 2.09 | 5.65 | 4.91 | 4.16 |
| **MENA** (region) | 2.90 | 3.17 | 2.59 | 6.43 | 5.59 | 4.35 |
| Algeria | 3.06 | 2.94 | 2.34 | 7.18 | 5.71 | 4.06 |
| Egypt | 2.12 | 2.50 | 2.11 | 5.46 | 4.62 | 3.75 |
| Jordan | 3.80 | 3.75 | 5.28 | 7.30 | 6.11 | 4.92 |
| Morocco | 2.39 | 2.16 | 1.89 | 6.30 | 4.72 | 3.73 |
| Syria | 3.31 | 3.31 | 3.10 | 7.56 | 6.74 | 4.68 |
| Tunisia | 2.16 | 2.47 | 1.97 | 5.86 | 4.36 | 3.07 |
| Iran | 3.17 | 3.31 | 1.70 | 6.59 | 6.00 | 3.99 |
| Turkey | 2.33 | 2.32 | 1.62 | 4.76 | 3.62 | 2.81 |

*Source:* World Bank (2000).

So why have MENA's concerns for demographic performance become increasingly central to policy thinking and economic research in recent years? To a large extent, worries about rapid population growth in MENA have coincided with the region's poor economic performance since the mid-1980s (World Bank, 1995). Economic growth has deteriorated in the past decade, labor productivity has declined, and unemployment rates have risen sharply. In the wake of policy efforts to stabilize, liberalize, and generate growth, concerns that rapid population growth might account for poor economic performance have emerged even in the absence of clear pro-Malthusian evidence linking the two.

The goal of this chapter is to provide an analytical framework for understanding the impact of population growth and demographic dynamics on economic growth in MENA. We focus on the role of demographic transitions in enhancing and/or retarding growth performance. Utilizing a comparative empirical growth framework, we show how demographic changes help account for MENA's relative growth performance over the period 1960–90. We identify the channels through which demography has conditioned growth in the past and is likely to do so in the future.

## Demography and Economic Growth

### *Economic Realities and Policy Thinking on Demography*

El Badry (1965) was the first to call to attention the rapid rise in MENA's population and its potential impact on economic development. Back in the 1960s, only Egypt and Turkey had conducted comprehensive population censuses on a regular and systematic basis; elsewhere, demographers were busy assembling scanty data to document demographic trends. Nevertheless, the available information was sufficient for Shultz (1970) to warn that "rapid population growth has emerged as an impediment to the future development of many low-income countries in the Middle East."[2] His analysis had focused on the implications of population growth on government spending, urban crowding, and agricultural productivity. Subsequent warnings by demographers in and outside the region were largely ignored by policy makers, who in many instances adopted a pro-natal population growth stance (Omran and Roudi, 1993). In part, the economic state of the region in the early 1970s alleviated fears of any impending economic crisis. MENA was in the middle of an economic boom following the oil shock; unemployment rates were low and continued to decline as a result of rapid labor migration to the oil-exporting countries and Europe (Birks and Sinclair, 1980). Meanwhile, capital inflows in the form of worker remittances and official financing softened fiscal deficits and external resource imbalances in the non-oil economies of the region.

Things had changed by the end of the 1980s. The once booming regional economy had come to a sudden halt following the oil bust in the mid-1980s. Again, economic conditions were paramount in influencing official and academic thinking in MENA. For example, labor economists have expressed concern about rapid labor force growth at a time when the region's labor markets already have high levels of unemployment, diminished emigration possibilities abroad, and limited work opportunities outside the public sector (Al-Qudsi *et al.*, 1995; Diwan, 1995). Indeed, in just a few years before the year 2000, MENA's labor markets had to absorb about 30 million more adults of working age, and by 2025 it will have to absorb another 160 million. Similarly, governments have become anxious about the anticipated financial burdens entailed by further population growth in the face of large cuts in development expenditures, limited resources for public infrastructure and health, and the anticipated compression of existing food, employment, and educational subsidies (World Bank, 1994).

## *Demography and Economic Growth: An Elusive Link*

What consequences has rapid population growth had on economic performance in MENA? The question turns on various issues, ranging from the impact of demographic pressures on development expenditures, poverty, and income inequality to their sectoral influences on land productivity, rural-urban migration, and human capital formation (Simon, 1996). What concerns us in this chapter is the impact of population growth on long-run per capita gross domestic product (GDP) growth.[3] The first generation of postwar studies on the relationship between population and economic growth has yielded ambiguous correlations, as the scatter plot in Figure 1.1 illustrates (Kelley, 1988). Similarly, more sophisticated cross-country comparisons that condition for other variables have offered inconclusive findings on the impact of population growth on GDP per capita growth; results tended to hinge on the sample, the time period, and the choice of explanatory variables (Kelley and Schmidt, 1994).

The revival of the life-cycle model, and its incorporation into empirical studies of cross-country growth, have renewed interest in the link between demography and economic growth (Bloom and Williamson, 1997; Radelet, Sachs, and Lee, 1997). More promising

**Figure 1.1: Population Growth and GDP per Capita Growth, 1965–90**

*Sources:* Penn World Table (5.6) and World Bank (1997).

results have emerged linking demographic changes to observed trends in capital and labor accumulation and ultimately growth performance, especially in the high-performing Asian economies.[4] These studies have emphasized the importance of demographic transitions, the process of moving from pre-industrial conditions of high fertility and high mortality to the post-industrial conditions of low fertility and low mortality (Figure 1.2). Accordingly, what matters for economic growth is not the rate of population growth *per se*, but rather the changing age distribution of populations as countries pass through demographic transitions.[5]

As the stylized version in Figure 1.2 indicates, the demographic transition gives rise to a cycle in population growth and in age structure, the latter measured here as the share of the population working. Each phase of the transition is associated with an age structure and, consequently, a different impact on economic growth.[6] Thus, when a large share of the population is dependent, non-working, and under the age of 14 or over 65, an economy carries a demographic burden that lowers labor input per capita, depresses the savings

**Figure 1.2: Demographic Transition**

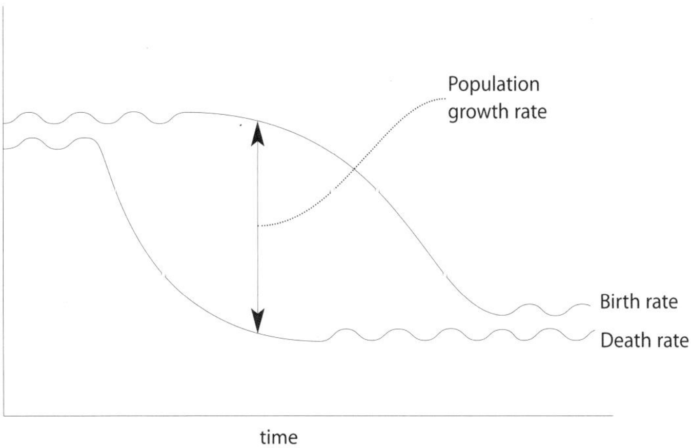


**Population Growth and the Age Structure**

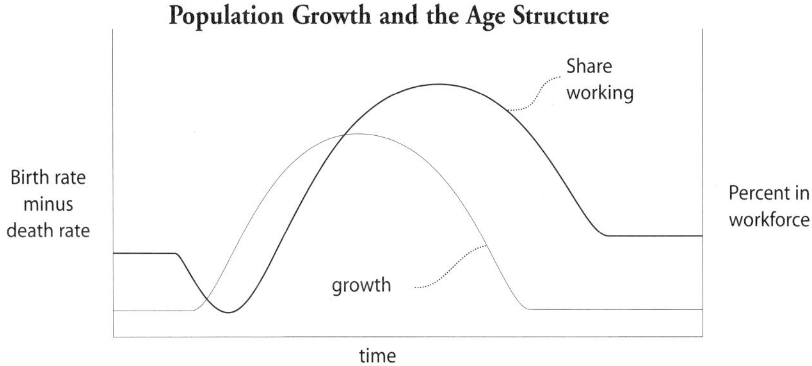


*Source:* Bloom and Williamson (1998).

rate, and reduces the rate of GDP per capita growth. This was the case in Asia and Latin America in the 1950s and 1960s (Higgins and Williamson, 1997; Taylor, 1995). Conversely, countries are endowed with a demographic gift when a larger share of the population is economically active (between the ages 15 and 64), thereby raising the labor force per capita, capital accumulation, and GDP per capita growth, as was the case in Asia, and East Asia in particular, during the miracle years of the 1970s and 1980s.[7]

## The Demographic Transition in MENA

The impact of demographic change on growth, therefore, is conditioned by the age distribution of the population during the transition. More specifically, whether a country carries a demographic burden or receives a demographic gift depends on the relative shares of dependent and economically active in the total population. Indeed, it is this aspect of MENA's demographic transition that is most striking even in comparison to other developing regions. MENA's economically active population grew by an impressive annual rate of 2.88 percent in 1965–90, more than any other region in the world. However, the dependent population also grew at a fast rate, 2.37 percent. The result was a net annual difference of only 0.51 percent, smaller than Latin America's net difference of 0.87 percent, and much smaller than East and Southeast Asia's net difference of 1.96 percent and 1.29 percent, respectively (Table 1.2). Only slow-growing South Asia had a net difference comparable with MENA's, 0.56 percent.

**Table 1.2: MENA's Demographic Transition in an International Perspective, 1965–1990**

(% annual growth)

| | Total Population | Economically Active Population[(a)] | Economically Dependent Population[(b)] | Net Demographic Impact[(c)] |
|---|---|---|---|---|
| East Asia | 1.58 | 2.39 | 0.25 | 2.14 |
| Southeast Asia | 2.36 | 2.90 | 1.66 | 1.24 |
| South Asia | 2.27 | 2.51 | 1.95 | 0.56 |
| Latin America | 2.25 | 2.64 | 1.77 | 0.87 |
| Sub-Saharan Africa | 2.81 | 2.78 | 2.85 | -0.07 |
| | | | | |
| MENA (sample) | 2.73 | 2.88 | 2.37 | 0.51 |
| Algeria | 2.96 | 2.90 | 2.74 | 0.16 |
| Egypt | 2.32 | 2.67 | 1.93 | 0.74 |
| Jordan | 2.86 | 2.76 | 2.75 | 0.01 |
| Morocco | 2.53 | 2.77 | 2.08 | 0.69 |
| Syria | 3.42 | 3.52 | 3.24 | 0.28 |
| Tunisia | 2.28 | 2.52 | 1.59 | 0.93 |
| Iran | 3.18 | 3.21 | 3.02 | 0.19 |
| Turkey | 2.34 | 2.71 | 1.64 | 1.07 |

*Notes:* (a) Economically Active Population = population in the age group 15–64.
(b) Economically Dependent Population = population in the age groups 0–14 and 65+.
(c) Net Demographic Impact = Economically Active Population - Economically Dependent Population.
*Sources:* United Nations (1993).

**Figure 1.3a: Crude Birth Rates by Region, 1950–2020**

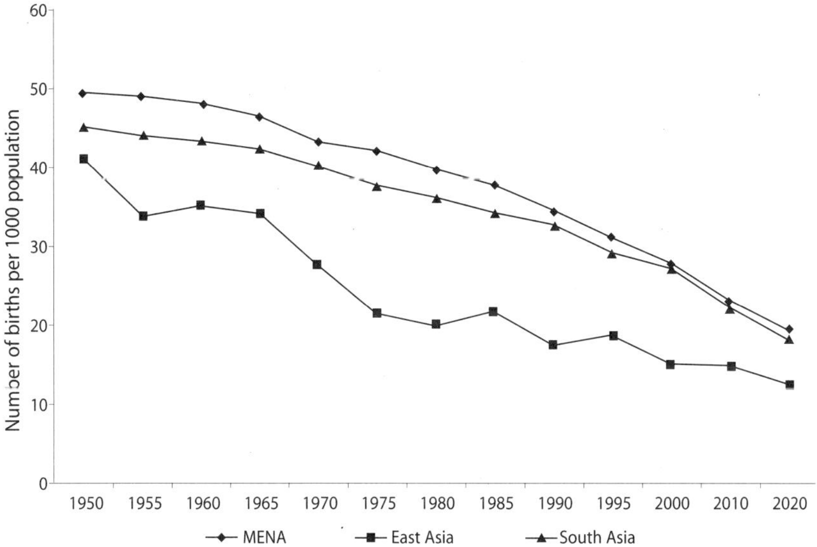


**Figure 1.3b: Crude Death Rates by Region, 1950–2020**

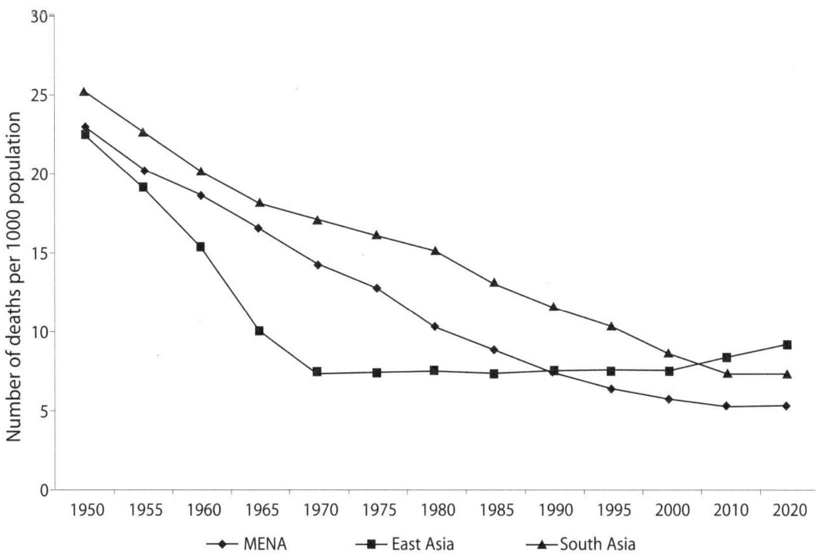


*Source:* United Nations (1993).

What accounts for MENA's small demographic gift? The explanation must lie in the trends in fertility and (child) mortality, since jointly they determine the rate of population growth, changing age distribution, and speed of demographic transition. Like the rest of the developing world, MENA's transition was set in motion by the transfer of health improvements and technology when the newly independent states increased development expenditures in the post-World War II era (El Badry, 1965).[8] The typical result was an acceleration in the population growth rate reflecting the fast fall in mortality rates (Figures 1.3a and 1.3b). However, those most influenced by improved survival rates were infants and children: it was the decline in child mortality that led the way, thus starting a transition where at first there was a glut of children. As a result, MENA's populations in the 1950s and 1960s experienced a rapid increase in the share of the young and the dependency rates increased from a low of 36 percent in 1950 to a high of 46 percent in 1970. Omran (1984) has elaborated on how this process worked in Egypt in the 1950s, when mortality rates fell sharply in response to concerted policy efforts to eradicate epidemics affecting the young (Figure 1.4). Similar patterns in epidemic recession and mortality declines have been recorded throughout the rest of MENA, with success depending on the population size and the extent of resource allocation to public health.

**Table 1.3: Dependency Rates in MENA, 1950–90**

(% shares in the population)

| | Peak Young [a] | Young 0–14 | Prime 25–59 | Old 65+ | Δ From Peak[b] |
|---|---|---|---|---|---|
| MENA | | | | | |
| Algeria | 1970 | 48.4 | 27.8 | 4.1 | -4.7 |
| | 1990 | 43.6 | 29.8 | 3.6 | |
| Morocco | 1970 | 47.6 | 29.5 | 4.2 | -7.1 |
| | 1990 | 40.5 | 33.3 | 5.3 | |
| Tunisia | 1970 | 46.2 | 29.9 | 3.8 | -8.2 |
| | 1990 | 38.0 | 35.2 | 3.9 | |
| Egypt | 1965 | 43.5 | 32.9 | 4.1 | -4.2 |
| | 1990 | 39.3 | 35.9 | 3.9 | |
| Jordan | 1980 | 49.4 | 26.6 | 3.1 | -4.9 |
| | 1990 | 44.4 | 29.2 | 2.7 | |
| Syria | 1970 | 48.9 | 27.7 | 4.4 | -0.6 |
| | 1990 | 48.3 | 28.3 | 2.6 | |
| Iran | 1965 | 45.8 | 30.5 | 3.7 | -1.9 |
| | 1990 | 43.8 | 30.7 | 3.7 | |
| Turkey | 1965 | 42.0 | 34.6 | 4.1 | -7.4 |
| | 1990 | 34.6 | 37.9 | 4.2 | |
| East Asia | 1960 | 40.7 | 36.8 | 3.65 | -17.6 |
| | 1990 | 23.1 | 47.2 | 7.83 | |
| Southeast Asia | 1965 | 43.9 | 32.9 | 3.04 | -9.8 |
| | 1990 | 34.0 | 39.8 | 4.24 | |
| South Asia | 1970 | 43.3 | 33.2 | 3.48 | -3.62 |
| | 1990 | 39.8 | 35.1 | 3.76 | |

*Notes:* (a) Peak young refers to the date when the share of the young reached its peak from 1950. (b) Δ from peak refers to the change from the date when the dependency ratio reached its peak and 1990.

*Sources:* United Nations (1993); Higgins and Williamson (1997).

**Figure 1.4: Diseases of Epidemic Importance in Egypt, 1920–60**

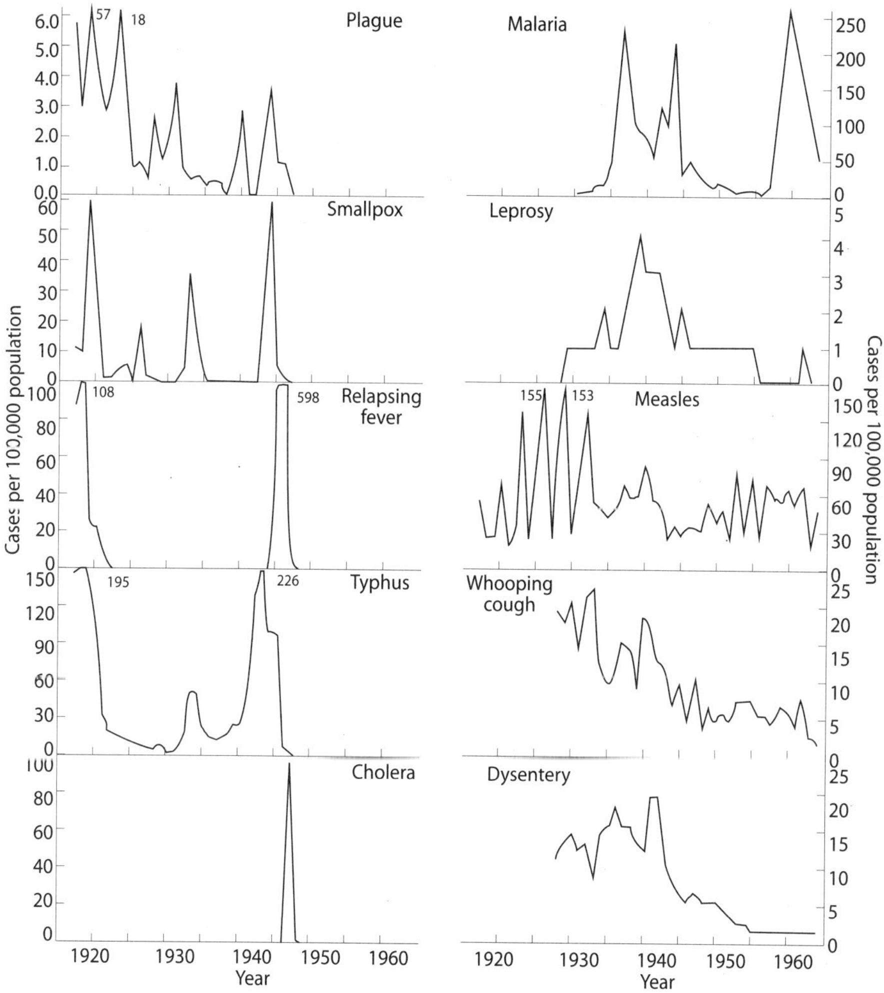


*Source:* Omran (1984).

While the fall in MENA's mortality was not as great as in East Asia, the onset of the fertility decline occurred much later (Figures 1.3a and 1.3b). Up to the mid-1980s, MENA's birth rates had been persistently higher than those in lower- and middle-income countries and only slightly below the world's poorest countries.[9] After reaching their peak, the dependency shares in MENA fell by a modest 4 percent in 1990 compared with an enormous 18 percent fall in East and Southeast Asia, where the peak was reached in the 1960s. Only Morocco, Tunisia, and Turkey came close to Southeast Asia, and none of the MENA countries came close to East Asia. In other words, the fast-growing Asian economies managed to compress their demographic transition into half the time it has taken MENA

(Table 1.3). The extended decline in child mortality and slow decline in fertility since 1950 ensured that MENA's population would exhibit a persistently large share of the dependent population and a slow rate of demographic transition (Figure 1.5).[10]

**Figure 1.5: Ratio of Working Age Population to Dependent Population**

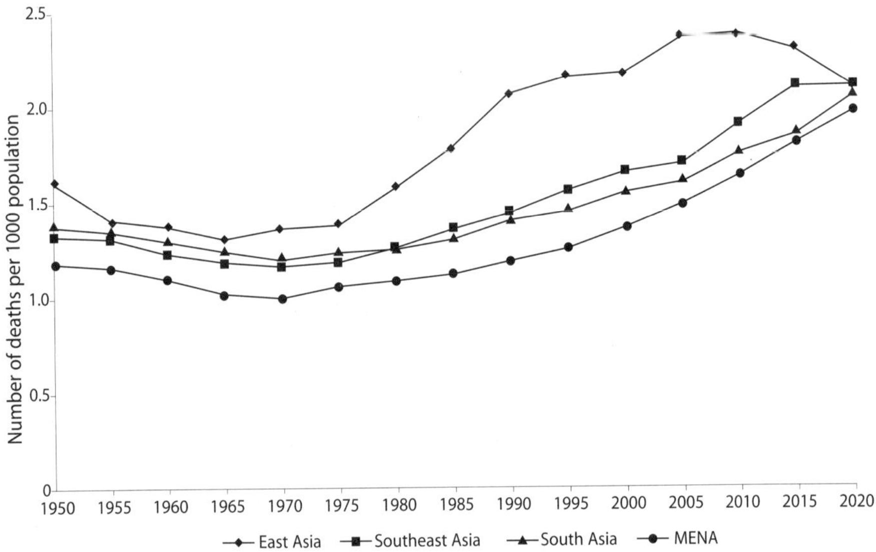


*Source:* United Nations (1993).

## Demography and Growth: Empirical Findings

### *Demography and Economic Performance in the Past*

Can demography help account for differences in growth performance and, more specifically, for MENA's record relative to the rest of the developing world? Recent theoretical and empirical contributions to the study of economic growth have identified a matrix of economic, political, institutional, and endowment factors driving the growth process (Barro and Sala-I-Martin, 1995). Thus, simple correlations will not be useful: instead, the question we seek to answer is how much did demography matter in the past, once we have controlled for other relevant variables? This has been the approach followed by the second-generation studies.

The empirical specification we employ was developed by Radelet, Sachs, and Lee (1997) and has been used by Bloom and Williamson (1998) and Yousef (1998) to analyze the impact of demography on economic growth over the period 1965–90. This approach is particularly useful, since it provides a synthesis of classical and neoclassical theories of long-run growth.[11] Thus, in addition to traditional neoclassical variables—initial conditions, measures of physical and human capital, economic openness and political stability—the empirical model includes variables that control for natural resource intensity, economic geography, government policy, the quality of institutions, and, finally, demographic transitions (see Appendix Table 1.A1 for variable definitions). Table 1.4 provides a regional summary of the average values of the variables used in the estimation, covering MENA, East Asia, South Asia, Southeast Asia, Latin America, sub-Saharan Africa, and the OECD.[12] Throughout, the dependent variable is real GDP per capita growth.

**Table 1.4: Summary of Key Variables by Region**

| | All Countries | East Asia | Southeast Asia | South Asia | Latin America | Sub-Saharan Africa | MENA |
|---|---|---|---|---|---|---|---|
| Real GDP per capita growth (annual avg., 1965–90) | 1.9 | 6.7 | 3.8 | 1.7 | 0.8 | 0.6 | 2.30 |
| **Initial Conditions** | | | | | | | |
| Real GDP per capita in 1965 | 3,163 | 2,010 | 1,161 | 996 | 2,611 | 826 | 1,732 |
| Avg. yrs. of secondary schooling in 1965 | 0.8 | 1.5 | 0.5 | 0.5 | 0.6 | 0.2 | 0.24 |
| **Resources and Geography** | | | | | | | |
| Natural resource intensity | 0.11 | 0.01 | 0.17 | 0.05 | 0.16 | 0.16 | 0.10 |
| Tropics | 0.53 | 0.63 | 1 | 0.40 | 0.91 | 0.79 | 0.19 |
| Landlocked | 0.17 | 0 | 0 | 0 | 0.47 | 0.10 | 0 |
| Coastline distance / land area | 0.29 | 2.83 | 0.43 | 0.07 | 0.17 | 0.02 | 1.12 |
| **Policy and Choice Variables** | | | | | | | |
| Openness (0 to 1; 1=most open) | 0.43 | 0.97 | 0.73 | 0.06 | 0.17 | 0.08 | 0.18 |
| Government savings rate (% of GDP) | 1.6 | 5.6 | 3.5 | 1.0 | 1.2 | 3.0 | 1.0 |
| Quality of institutions (1–10; 10 = best) | 5.99 | 7.79 | 4.95 | 4.23 | 4.37 | 4.72 | 4.29 |
| **Demography** | | | | | | | |
| Growth of the economically active population (annual avg., 1965–90) | 2.23 | 2.39 | 2.90 | 2.51 | 2.64 | 2.78 | 2.88 |
| Growth of the total population (annual avg., 1965–90) | 1.81 | 1.58 | 2.36 | 2.27 | 2.06 | 2.81 | 2.73 |

*Notes:* See Appendix Table 1.A1 for variable definitions and data sources.

Table 1.5 presents the empirical results using Ordinary Least Squares (OLS). The impact of demography on economic growth is examined in column 1 by the inclusion of the population growth rate variable by itself. Its coefficient is small and statistically insignificant, as expected. In the long run, the rate of economic growth is not affected: demography exerts its influence on growth only during the transition by changing the shares of the working adults and the young in the population.[13] This is confirmed in columns 2 and 3, where the growth rate of the economically active population joins the population growth rate; the coefficient on the latter variable is positive and statistically significant. A one percent increase in the growth rate of the economically active population is associated with a 1.46 percent to 1.95 percent increase in GDP per capita. Furthermore, with the rate of growth of the economically active population in the regression, the total population growth rate now has a big negative impact.

To further highlight the transitional nature of demography's impact on economic growth, in column 4 we restrict the coefficients on the two demographic variables to be equal in magnitude and opposite in sign, as would be the case in the steady state. The coefficient is big, positive, and significant. Thus, where the growth rate of the economically active population exceeds that of the total population in our sample, higher GDP growth has appeared. Equivalently, where the middle of the age distribution (ages 15–64) grows faster than the tails (ages 15 and below and 65 and above), GDP per capita grows faster. The opposite is true if the growth rate of the total population exceeds that of the economically active. This finding applies uniformly across all regions in the world including MENA, since the sign and significance of the demographic variables when interacted with regional dummy variables produce essentially the same results as reported above.[14]

**Table 1.5: Demography and Economic Growth, 1965–90**

(dependent variable: growth rate of real GDP per capita, 1965–90)

| **Independent Variables** | **OLS Estimates** | | | |
|---|---|---|---|---|
| | **(1)** | **(2)** | **(3)** | **(4)** |
| Constant | -2.11 | -2.46 | -19.5 | -14.3 |
| | (0.92) | (0.79) | (4.3) | (4.1) |
| GPOP6590 | 0.16 | -1.87 | -1.03 | — |
| | (0.20) | (0.43) | (0.40) | — |
| GEAP6590 | — | 1.95 | 1.46 | — |
| | — | (0.38) | (0.34) | — |
| GEAP6590–GPOP6590 | — | — | — | 1.68 |
| | — | — | — | (0.35) |
| Log GDP per capita in 1965 | -1.50 | -1.36 | -2.00 | -1.97 |
| | (0.25) | (0.21) | (0.21) | (0.22) |
| Log years of schooling in 1965 | 0.82 | 0.50 | 0.22 | 0.28 |
| | (0.18) | (0.16) | (0.14) | (0.14) |
| Natural resource abundance | -4.68 | -4.86 | -2.35 | -2.57 |
| | (1.35) | (1.2) | (1.0) | (1.1) |
| Access to ports | -0.68 | -0.35 | -0.64 | -0.40 |
| | (0.39) | (0.34) | (0.27) | (0.27) |
| Openness | 2.23 | 2.06 | 1.92 | 1.72 |
| | (0.47) | (0.40) | (0.32) | (0.33) |
| Government savings rate | 0.18 | 0.14 | 0.12 | 0.13 |
| | (0.04) | (0.03) | (0.03) | (0.03) |
| Quality of institutions | 0.21 | 0.23 | 0.20 | 0.15 |
| | (0.10) | (0.08) | (0.07) | (0.07) |
| Located in the tropics | — | — | -1.31 | -1.20 |
| | — | — | (0.30) | (0.31) |
| Ratio of coastline distance to land area | — | — | 0.24 | 0.23 |
| | — | — | (0.11) | (0.12) |
| $R^2$ | 0.69 | 0.76 | 0.86 | 0.85 |

*Note:* Standard errors are reported in parentheses below coefficient estimates.

Are demographic forces exogenous to economic growth? If not, then it could be argued that demographic changes are simultaneously driven by the growth of GDP per capita and, hence, that the estimated coefficients are not unbiased. *A priori*, the literature has argued that fertility and mortality rates respond to changes in income (Shultz, 1981). To deal with this potential endogeneity problem, we re-estimated our specifications in Table 1.6 using instrumental variables (IV).[15] The implied coefficients and their statistical significance are consistent with those using OLS, indicating the robustness of our earlier conclusions. Similarly, our conclusions are also not sensitive to the definition of the dependent population and the combination of demographic variables in the regression; thus, including the age group (64 and above) in the definition of dependent population, or estimating the model with the growth rates of the dependent and economically active populations jointly, does not change any of the reported results.[16]

**Table 1.6: Instrumental Variables Estimation of the Effects of Population Growth on Economic Growth**

(dependent variable: growth rate of real GDP per capita, 1965–90)

| Independent Variables | | Specification 2 | Specification 3 | Specification 3 Constrained |
|---|---|---|---|---|
| GEAP6590 | IV | 3.83 | 1.37 | — |
| | | (0.82) | (1.71) | — |
| | OLS | 1.95 | 1.41 | — |
| | | (0.40) | (0.37) | — |
| GPOP6590 | IV | -4.19 | -0.92 | — |
| | | (0.96) | (2.12) | — |
| | OLS | -1.93 | -0.97 | — |
| | | (0.45) | (0.43) | — |
| GEAP6590 - GPOP6590 | IV | — | — | 3.43 |
| | | — | — | (0.98) |
| | OLS | — | — | 1.60 |
| | | — | — | (0.38) |
| Hausman specification Test (Chi Square w/df) | | 7.13 (10 df) | 0.00 (13 df) | 4.14 (12 df) |

*Note:* The specifications above correspond to columns 2–4 in Table 1.5. Instruments from first-stage regression include average growth of the population in 1950–60, percentage of urbanized population in 1965, population policy variables, and dummy variables where the main religion was Muslim or Judeo-Christian.

*Source:* See Bloom and Williamson (1998) for full details.

With the empirical specification in hand, we are now able to provide magnitudes on the impact of demographic pressures on MENA's growth performance. In Table 1.7, we quantify the contribution of each explanatory variable to the observed growth performance and isolate those that are due solely to demographic forces, whether they are gifts or burdens. These calculations for MENA and other regions in the world use the East and Southeast Asian economies as a benchmark for comparison. While illustrative, these calculations imply a big role for demography on MENA's past growth performance. In particular, 33 percent of MENA's growth gap with the high-performing Asian economies is accounted for by demographic differences between the two regions. Put differently, had MENA's demographic transition been as fast as that of East and Southeast Asia, its economic growth rate would have increased from 2.3 percent to 3.3 percent per annum, raising its per capita income in 1990 to US$3,900 instead of US$3,044. For other regions, demography accounts for between 15 percent and 30 percent of the growth gap.[17]

**Table 1.7: Variable Contributions to the Difference in Annual Per Capita GDP Growth Relative to East and Southeast Asia, 1965–90**

(% annual average)

| | South Asia | Latin America | Sub-Saharan Africa | MENA |
|---|---|---|---|---|
| Initial conditions | 0.4 | -0.8 | 0.4 | -0.5 |
| Resources | 0.0 | -1.4 | -1.0 | 0.1 |
| Policy variables | -2.3 | -2.0 | -2.2 | -1.9 |
| Demography | -1.0 | -0.7 | -1.5 | 1.0 |
| Predicted difference in GDP per capita growth (1965–90) | -2.86 | -4.90 | -4.23 | -3.35 |
| Actual difference in growth in GDP per capita growth (1965–90) | -3.55 | -4.45 | -4.65 | -2.95 |

*Note:* The economies of South and Southeast Asia in the sample are Hong Kong, China, Korea, Singapore, Thailand, Malaysia, Indonesia, and the Philippines; the MENA group includes Algeria, Egypt, Jordan, Morocco, Syria, Tunisia, Iran, and Turkey. The calculations used the data in Table 1.4 and the empirical specifications in Table 1.5.
*Source:* Authors' calculations. See Yousef (1998) for full details.

### *Demography and Economic Growth in the Future*

What role will demography play in shaping MENA's economic growth in the future? UN projections over the next 25 years predict a gradual shift in MENA's age structure in favor of the economically active population as a result of sustained decline in fertility rates. By the year 2020, the age distribution of MENA's population will begin to resemble that of East Asia in the 1970s and Southeast Asia in the 1980s (Figure 1.5). We forecast the growth impact of these demographic projections in Table 1.8, based on the coefficients of our estimated model.

**Table 1.8: Contribution of Demography to Future Economic Growth, 1990–2025**

| | Projected Growth of Pop. 1990–25 | Projected Growth of Economically Active Pop. 1990–25 | Projected Growth Rate of Dependent Pop. 1990–25 | Estimated Contribution to GDP P/Capita Growth, 1990–25 (1) | (2) |
|---|---|---|---|---|---|
| MENA | 2.06 | 3.07 | 1.12 | 2.14 | 2.36 |
| East Asia | 0.43 | 0.20 | 0.87 | -0.41 | -0.15 |
| Southeast Asia | 1.29 | 1.66 | 0.63 | 0.82 | 1.09 |
| South Asia | 1.65 | 2.11 | 0.90 | 1.03 | 1.38 |
| Africa | 2.40 | 2.78 | 1.88 | 0.93 | 1.59 |
| South America | 1.50 | 1.87 | 0.94 | 0.84 | 1.19 |
| Europe | 0.17 | -0.004 | 0.48 | -0.33 | -0.18 |

*Note:* The regression coefficients used to calculate the economic growth impact in columns 1 and 2 are drawn from the specifications in columns 2 and 3 in Table 1.5, respectively. Population projections are drawn from UN (1993).

If demography is allowed to have its impact, the future will look very different for MENA and other developing regions in the world. In contrast to the past, GDP per capita growth attributable to demographic influences is projected to accelerate between 1990 and 2025. If nothing happens to offset them, demographic events will induce a 2.1 to 2.4 percentage point rise in MENA's GDP per capita growth. This future growth potential applies to all countries in MENA. Similarly, Africa, Southeast and South Asia, and Latin America stand to gain from demographic events in the future. On the other hand, East Asia, which enjoyed the biggest demographic gift in 1965–90, is likely to experience a growth retardation, again based only on future demographic trends. As MENA's demographic transition catches up with that of East Asia, it creates the possibility for rapid economic convergence. But this is merely a potential, whose realization depends on the features of the economic, social, and political environment.[18]

## Possible Channels of Impact from Demography to Economic Growth

The previous section demonstrated the importance of demographic transitions in accounting for MENA's growth performance. But we have yet to identify the channels through which demography has transmitted its effects. Here, we focus exclusively on the effects of demographic transitions on the accumulation of labor and capital.[19]

### *The Impact of Demography on Labor Force Growth*

The demographic transition in MENA had produced a population age structure dominated by the young and economically dependent until the late 1980s. How much impact did this have on the accumulation of labor inputs? Following Bloom and Williamson (1997), labor inputs per person (working hours per capita or H/P) can be decomposed into three parts: changing hours worked per worker (H/L); changing labor participation rates among the working age population (L/WAP); and changing shares of the population of working age (WAP/P) - the pure demographic effect. Thus, per capita hours worked can be written as H/P = (H/L) (L/WAP) (WAP/P).

**Table 1.9: Per Capita Labor Input Growth**

| | Per Capita Labor Input (% annual growth rate) | Input per Worker % Contribution | Participation Contribution % | Working Age Contribution % |
|---|---|---|---|---|
| East Asia | 0.84 | 0.03 | -0.32 | 1.13 |
| Southeast Asia | 0.62 | 0.28 | -0.28 | 0.62 |
| South Asia | -0.16 | -0.07 | -0.42 | 0.33 |
| Latin America | 0.26 | -0.28 | -0.01 | 0.55 |
| Africa | -0.16 | 0.07 | -0.25 | 0.02 |
| OECD | 0.27 | -0.18 | 0.13 | 0.32 |
| MENA | | | | |
| Egypt | -0.16 | 0.01 | -0.31 | 0.14 |
| Turkey | -0.09 | 0.03 | -0.27 | 0.15 |

*Note:* See the text for an explanation of the derivation of these numbers.
*Sources:* Bloom and Williamson (1997) and International Labor Organization (ILO) Yearbook (various years).

Table 1.9 presents evidence on the sources of growth of labor inputs per capita for various regions in the world, including our MENA sample, over the period 1975–90.[20] In general, the pure demographic effects on the growth of labor input per person are smallest in regions that experienced the slowest demographic transition. In East Asia, where the working age population grew the fastest, the pure demographic effects made a significant positive contribution to the growth of labor input per person and, by extension, economic performance. MENA exhibits demographic effects that are significantly below the high-performing Asian economies and only above those in Africa. These pure demographic forces were offset in all cases by declining participation rates between 1975 and 1990. Such declines in MENA were partly due to the migration of labor to the Gulf economies and Europe (Al-Qudsi *et al.*, 1995).

### *The Impact of Demography on Savings and Investment*

What about the impact of demography on savings, investment, and the accumulation of capital? Ever since Coale and Hoover (1958) proposed their famous dependency hypothesis, economists have elaborated models incorporating their simple but powerful intuition. Standard formulations of their thesis predict that rapid population growth resulting from falling infant and child mortality and rising fertility swells the ranks of the dependent young, increasing consumption requirements at the expense of savings and economic growth.[21] Eventually, the youth dependency burden evolves into a young adult glut and the resulting savings boom contributes to rapid economic growth.[22]

**Table 1.10: National Savings and Investment, 1970–1993**

(% shares of GNP, annual averages)

| | National Savings Rate | | | National Investment Rate | | |
|---|---|---|---|---|---|---|
| | 1970–79 | 1980–89 | 1990–93 | 1970–79 | 1980–89 | 1990–93 |
| East Asia | 27.7 | 34.5 | 36.6 | 29.7 | 32.6 | 35.8 |
| South Asia | 24.2 | 25.3 | 27.8 | 25.9 | 27.9 | 29.2 |
| Southeast Asia | 9.3 | 11.6 | 12.3 | 15.6 | 20.4 | 19.8 |
| Latin America | 18.2 | 13.2 | 10.5 | 22.2 | 20.2 | 19.5 |
| Sub-Saharan Africa | 11.8 | 7.6 | 5.8 | 20.6 | 18.9 | 20.3 |
| MENA | 20.9 | 16.2 | 18.2 | 26.1 | 25.4 | 25.4 |
| MENA (ex. Algeria and Iran) | 15.1 | 12.1 | 14.1 | 23.7 | 24.1 | 25.1 |
| Algeria | 35.0 | 35.4 | 32.1 | 41.6 | 33.9 | 30.0 |
| Egypt | 11.6 | 13.2 | 9.3 | 23.1 | 25.9 | 19.3 |
| Iran | 36.5 | 21.8 | 28.4 | 22.7 | 24.4 | 22.9 |
| Jordan | — | -5.8 | 3.9 | 24.9 | 22.7 | 31.6 |
| Morocco | 14.1 | 15.9 | 17.5 | — | 25.3 | 31.0 |
| Syria | 12.1 | 9.4 | 11.4 | 23.2 | 21.6 | 15.9 |
| Tunisia | 21.4 | 20.7 | 21.1 | 26.2 | 26.9 | 27.9 |
| Turkey | 16.3 | 19.1 | 21.5 | 21.0 | 22.3 | 24.7 |

*Source:* World Bank (1997).

Almost all recent analysis of macro data confirm the Coale-Hoover effects, especially for Asia and Latin America (Edwards, 1997; Kelley and Schmidt, 1996; Higgins and Williamson, 1997; Taylor, 1995). Yousef (1998) examined the dependency hypothesis in the context of MENA; the results obtained are consistent with the international evidence and help explain why the countries in the region with the highest dependency ratios since 1970 tended also to have the smallest savings rates (Table 1.3 and Table 1.10). To the extent that the savings rate and GDP per capita growth are linked, these findings identify another important channel of effects from demographic transitions to economic performance.

The changing age structure of the population has also played an important role in determining the levels and composition of investment in Asia and MENA (Higgins and Williamson, 1997; Yousef, 1998). MENA's investments in the past were provided mainly by the public sector and were concentrated predominantly in the population-sensitive categories—housing, infrastructure, and education—owing to the high dependency rates. In contrast, East Asia's spectacular investment rates during the miracle years were driven by the rapid growth in the labor force and the resulting high investment demand for capital widening.[23] Thus, investment demand and capital accumulation moved in line with the cycle in age structure associated with the demographic transition, rising with increase in the economically dependent population but expanding much more rapidly with the growth of the labor force.

## Conclusions

This chapter has explored the link between population growth and past economic performance in MENA. We demonstrated that demographic transitions have conditioned cross-country growth performance and that MENA conforms to this international pattern. MENA's demographic burden accounts for a significant proportion of its lower GDP per capita growth relative to the high-performing Asian economies. On the basis of future demographic projections alone, MENA will have an opportunity to raise its GDP per capita growth through increased savings, investment, and per capita labor input growth. To realize this potential, MENA will have to devote considerable attention to strengthening its financial, legal, and political institutions while simultaneously adopting a coherent set of long-term economic policies.

## Appendix

### Table 1.A1: Variable Definitions and Data Sources

| Variable Name | Definition (source) | Mean | Standard Deviation |
|---|---|---|---|
| GPOP6590 | Growth rate of the total population, 1965–90 *Source:* UN (1993) | 1.88 | 1.00 |
| GEAP6590 | Growth rate of economically active population, 1965–90. *Source:* UN (1993) | 2.17 | 1.03 |
| GDP per capita growth, 1965–90 | Average real GDP per capita growth, 1965–90. *Source:* Penn World Table (5.6) | | |
| GDP per capita in 1965 | Ratio of GDP per capita and the US in 1965. *Source:* Penn World Table (5.6) | -1.65 | 0.91 |
| Schooling in 1965 | Average years of secondary schooling for population 15+ in 1965. *Source:* Barro and Lee (1994) | -0.70 | 1.15 |
| Natural resource abundance | Share of primary product exports in GDP in 1971. *Source:* World Bank (1997) | 0.10 | 0.09 |
| Access to ports | Dummy variable indicating if country is landlocked. *Source:* Sachs and Warner (1995). | 0.13 | 0.34 |
| Openness | The fraction of years between 1965 and 1990 that a country was considered open. *Source:* Sachs and Warner (1995) | 0.45 | 0.45 |
| Government savings rate | Average government savings rate as share of GDP, 1970–90. *Source:* World Bank (1997) | 1.44 | 3.43 |
| Quality of institutions | Index of the quality of governmental institutions. *Source:* Knack and Keefer (1995) | 6.11 | 2.42 |
| Located in the tropics | Dummy variable indicating if the country is between the tropics. *Source:* Sachs and Warner (1995) | 0.51 | 0.48 |
| Ratio of coastline to land area | *Source:* Radelet et al. (1997) | 0.30 | 0.96 |

## Notes

1 Throughout this chapter, the term MENA will refer to the entire region encompassing the countries of the Middle East and North Africa. However, to facilitate cross-regional comparisons and quantitative analysis, data measuring our MENA variables are taken from Algeria, Egypt, Iran, Jordan, Morocco, Tunisia, Syria, and Turkey. These countries account for two thirds of MENA's population (where the latter includes Turkey).

2 In the past, a great deal was written about the political and social consequences of rapid population growth in MENA, especially as the latter coincided with an increased trend of urbanization. More recently, analysts have addressed the socioeconomic factors driving population growth and family planning policies in MENA (Obermeyer, 1995). There is also a growing literature linking the heightened internal political instability in MENA in the 1990s to the rapid growth in the numbers of the young and unemployed and the expected future pressures on labor markets (Gilbar, 1997; Maynes, 1998).

3 By and large, studies that have specifically analyzed MENA's demographic trends have focused on the determinants of fertility and mortality without exploring the long-term impact on growth and development (Omran, 1984; Sirageldin and Al-Rahmani, 1996).

4 References to the high-performing Asian economies will be used interchangeably with East Asia (China, Hong Kong, Japan, and South Korea) and Southeast Asia (Indonesia, Malaysia,

Philippines, Singapore, and Thailand). South Asia refers to Bangladesh, India, Pakistan, and Sri Lanka.

5 In focusing on the impact of the changing age distribution of the population on economic growth, we are building on a recent promising line of research that has disaggregated the impact of population growth into its components of fertility and mortality effects on economic growth (Barlow, 1994; Brander and Dowrick, 1994; Kelley and Schmidt, 1995).

6 The theoretical basis of this argument relies on examining the impact of changes in the age distribution on the transitional dynamics of GDP per capita growth in a standard neoclassical growth model. The full explanation can be found in Bloom and Williamson (1998).

7 Bloom and Williamson (1997) have identified demography as the most important factor distinguishing the high performing East and Southeast Asian economies from the slower-growing economies in South Asia. On the basis of demography alone, they attributed one half to two thirds of East Asia's superior growth performance in 1965–90 to its favorable demographic structure.

8 Even in Egypt and Turkey, where the state began to address the needs of the public health system as early as the 1920s, the transition was very slow until the 1950s. For example, the proportion of Egypt's population under the age of 14 was constant between 1927 and 1947, rising thereafter to reach 43 percent by 1960.

9 In 1950, the crude birth rate was the highest in the world at 50 per 1000. The decline in the rate between 1950 and 1990 was only half of what took place for the less developed countries (LDCs) as a whole. Omran and Roudi (1993) have linked the recent decline in fertility to the growth of family planning policies in MENA.

10 The determinants of fertility are a matter of controversy in the literature, with researchers divided over the relative importance of economic conditions, population policy, the prevalence of contraception methods, female education, and the socioeconomic status of women (Boulier, 1986; Pritchett, 1994; Shultz, 1981). See Olmsted (1999) for an extensive review of the literature on fertility in MENA. Among the facts that have received attention in MENA is the excess of fertility rates over what would be predicted by levels of income and education, a stylized fact that applies to both the oil-exporting and the non-oil-exporting countries of the region.

11 Previous analyses of cross-country growth determinants include, among others, Barro (1991), Barro and Sala-I-Martin (1995), and Mankiw, Romer, and Weil (1992). Cohen and Hammour (1994) and Page (1998) specifically address MENA's growth record; the former examines the 1965–85 period, while the latter investigates the sources of MENA's decline after 1985.

12 For a theoretical justification of the empirical framework used and its relationship to previous work on cross-country growth, consult the paper by Radelet, Sachs, and Lee (1997).

13 To be more precise, the demographic variables measure the potential pool of working adults who may or may not be working because of low female participation rates or high unemployment among young adults, as has been the case in several MENA countries in the 1980s. Adjusting our demographic variables for this would lower the share of the working age population in MENA, implying an even bigger demographic burden and growth effect for the region.

14 The regressions that allow for dummy variables and region-specific coefficients are not reported here but can be found in Bloom and Williamson (1998) and Yousef (1998).

15 Only the growth rate of the total population is instrumented for, since we believe that the growth rate of the economically active population is exogenous, having been determined by fertility and mortality patterns prior to the period from which we draw our sample.

16 Other conclusions are also supported by the empirical results: economic growth is positively driven by: human capital levels, measured by the average years of secondary schooling of the

adult population; the extent of integration with the global economy, measured by the fraction of years a country was considered open to trade between 1965 and 1990; the quality of institutions; and where government budgetary policies led to a high public savings rate. On the other hand, growth was slower in countries that are landlocked, located in the tropics, or abundant with natural resources. See Radelet *et al.* (1997) for a full elaboration on these results and their policy implications. Finally, once all variables are taken into account, poorer countries tended to grow faster than richer countries: i.e., there is evidence for catch-up or convergence

17 Openness to the world economy is the only variable that explains more of MENA's growth gap than demography—about 45 percent. The rest of MENA's gap with the high-performing Asian economies is accounted for by disadvantages in the initial GDP level, the quality of its institutions, and the low level of schooling.

18 For a discussion of needed financial and fiscal reforms to realize the future demographic gift in MENA, see Yousef (1998).

19 Thus, we do not address the potentially important relationship between demography and human capital accumulation. The link between the accumulation of inputs (labor and capital) and growth has been well established in recent theoretical and empirical research. For example, Krugman (1994), Kim and Lau (1994), and Young (1995) have suggested that the high growth rates in East Asia have been driven primarily by rapid rates of accumulation of factors of production as opposed to the previously assumed high total productivity growth (World Bank, 1993). A frequently noted observation about MENA is the low savings rates by international standards and the bias of investments away from physical capital (Cohen and Hammour, 1994).

20 Due to data limitations, the estimates assume that the trend of hours worked in Egypt's manufacturing sector applies to other industries and countries in MENA, a big but unavoidable assumption.

21 We must note that the effects of population growth on the savings rate and the rate of per capita income only during the transition but not in the long run (steady state). Thus, the relationship between demography and growth in this essay and similar work focuses on transitional dynamics, which may persist for several decades given the slow speed of convergence to the steady state (Barro and Sala-I-Martin, 1995).

22 See Kelley and Schmidt (1996) for a review of the potential channels through which demographic dependency influences savings rates in developing countries.

23 Bloom and Williamson (1997) suggest that one half of East Asia's rapid accumulation rates were due to the capital widening requirements for the growing labor force.

## References

Al-Qudsi, S., R. Assaad, and R. Shaban. 1995. "Labor Markets in the Arab Countries," *International Labor Review*, 134: 65–81.

Barlow, R. 1994. "Population Growth and Economic Growth: Some More Correlations," *Population and Development Review*, 20: 153–65.

El-Badry, M.A. 1965. "Trends in the Components of Population Growth in the Middle East: A Survey of Present Information," *Demography*, 2: 140–86.

Barro, R. 1991. "Economic Growth in a Cross Section of Countries," *Quarterly Journal of Economics*, 106: 407–43.

———, and J.W. Lee. 1994. "Sources of Economic Growth," *Carnegie-Rochester Conference Series on Public Policy*, 40: 1–46.

———, and X. Sala-I-Martin. 1995. *Economic Growth*. New York: McGraw Hill.

Birks, J., and C. Sinclair. 1980. *International Migration and Development in the Arab Region*. Geneva: International Labor Organization.

Bloom, D., and J. Williamson. 1998. "Demographic Transitions and Economic Miracles in Emerging Asia," *World Bank Economic Review*, 12: 419–55.

———. 1997. "Demographic Change and Human Resource Development," in *Emerging Asia: Changes and Challenges*, pp. 141–97. Manila: Asian Development Bank.

Boulier, B. 1986. "Family Planning Programs and Contraceptive Availability: Their Effects on Contraceptive Use and Fertility," in N. Birdsall *et al.* (eds.), *The Effects of Family Planning Programs on Fertility in the Developing World.* World Bank Staff Working Paper No. 677. Washington DC.

Brander, J., and S. Dowrick. 1994. "The Role of Fertility and Population in Economic Growth: Empirical Results from Aggregate Cross-National Data," *Journal of Population Economics*, 7: 1–25.

Coale, A., and E. Hoover. 1958. *Population Growth and Economic Development in Low Income Countries.* Princeton, NJ: Princeton University Press.

Cohen, D., and M. Hammour. 1994. "Economic Growth in the Middle East and North Africa: An International Perspective." ERF Working Paper No. 9403. Cairo, Egypt: Economic Research Forum.

Diwan, I. 1995. *Will Arab Workers Prosper or Be Left Out in the Twenty-First Century?* Washington, DC: World Bank.

Edwards, S. 1997. "Why Are Latin America's Savings Rates So Low?" *Journal of Development Economics*, 51: 5–44.

Gilbar, G. 1997. *Population Dilemmas in the Middle East.* London: Frank Cass.

Higgins, M. 1998. "Demography, National Savings, and International Capital Flows," *International Economic Review*, 39: 343–69.

———, and J. Williamson. 1997. "Asian Demography and Foreign Capital Dependence," *Population and Development Review*, 23: 261–93.

International Labor Organization. *Yearbook*, various years. Geneva: International Labor Organization.

Kelley, A.C. 1988. "Economic Consequences of Population Growth in the Third World," *Journal of Economic Literature*, 27: 1685–728.

Kelley, A., and R. Schmidt. 1994. "Population and Income Change: Recent Evidence," World Bank Discussion Paper No. 249. Washington DC: World Bank.

———. 1995. "Aggregate Population and Economic Growth Correlations: The Role of the Components of Demographic Change," *Demography*, 3: 543–55.

———. 1996. "Savings, Dependency and Development," *Journal of Population Economics*, 9: 365–86.

Kim, J., and L. Lau. 1994. "The Sources of Economic Growth of the East Asian Newly Industrialized Countries," *Journal of the Japanese and International Economics*, 8: 235–71.

Knack, S. and P. Keefer. 1995. "Institutions and Economic Performance: Cross-Country Tests Using Alternative Institutional Measures," *Economics and Politics*, 7: 207–27.

Krugman, P. 1994. "The Myth of Asia's Miracle," *Foreign Affairs*, 73: 62–78.

Mankiw, G., D. Romer, and D. Weil. 1992. "A Contribution to the Empirics of Economic Growth," *Quarterly Journal of Economics*, 107: 407–37.

Maynes, C. 1998. "The Middle East in the Twenty-first Century," *Middle East Journal*, 52: 9–16.

Obermeyer, C. (ed.). 1995. *Family, Gender, and Population in the Middle East: Policies in Context.* Cairo: The American University in Cairo Press.

Olmsted, J. 1999. "Reexamining the Fertility Puzzle in the Middle East and North Africa," forthcoming in E. Doumato and M. Pripstein (eds.), *Middle Eastern Women in the Age of Globalization: Gender, Jobs and Activism*. Westview.

Omran, A. 1984. *Population Problems and Prospects in the Arab World.* New York: United Nations.

———, and F. Roudi. 1993. "The Middle East Population Puzzle," *Population Bulletin*, 48: 1–35.

Page, J. 1998. "From Boom to Bust – And Back? The Crisis of Economic Growth in the Middle East and North Africa," in N. Shafik (ed.), *Prospects for Middle Eastern and North African Economies: From Boom to Bust and Back?*, London and New York: Macmillan and St. Martin's Press.

Pritchett, L. 1994. "Desired Fertility and the Impact of Population Policies," *Population and Development Review*, 20: 1–55.

Radelet, S., J. Sachs, and J. Lee. 1997. "Economic Growth in Asia," in *Emerging Asia: Changes and Challenges*. Manila: Asian Development Bank.

Richards, A., and J. Waterbury. 1996. *A Political Economy of the Middle East*. Boulder, CO: Westview Press.

Sachs, J. and A. Warner. 1995. "Economic Reform and the Process of Global Integration," *Brookings Papers on Economic Activity*, 1: 1–118.

Shultz, T.P. 1970. *Fertility Patterns and Their Determinants in the Arab Middle East*. Santa Monica, CA: The Rand Corporation.

———. 1981. *Economics of Population*. Reading, MA: Addison-Wesley.

Simon, J. 1996. *The Ultimate Resource*. Princeton: Princeton University Press.

Sirageldin, I., and E. Al-Rahmani. 1996. *Population and Development Transformation in the Arab World*. Greenwich, CT: JAI Press.

Taylor, A. 1995. "Debt, Dependence and the Demographic Transition: Latin America into the Next Century," *World Development*, 23: 869–79.

United Nations. various years. *The Sex and Age Distribution of the World Populations*. New York: United Nations.

World Bank. 1993. *The East Asian Miracle: Economic Growth and Public Policy*. Oxford: Oxford University Press for the World Bank.

———. 1994. *A Population Perspective on Development: The Middle East and North Africa*. Baltimore, MD: Johns Hopkins University Press for the World Bank.

———. 1995. *Claiming the Future: A Long-Term Prospective Study of the Middle East and North Africa*. Washington, DC: World Bank.

———. 1997 and 2000. *World Development Indicators*. Washington, DC: World Bank.

Young, A. 1995. "The Tyranny of Numbers: Confronting the Statistical Realities of the East Asian Growth Experience," *Quarterly Journal of Economics*, 110: 641–80.

Yousef, T. 1998. "Demography, Capital Dependency and Growth in MENA." ERF Working Paper No. 9801. Cairo, Egypt: Economic Research Forum.

# 2

# The Demography of the Arab Region: New Challenges and Opportunities

*Hoda Rashad and Zeinab Khadr**

## Introduction

The current profile of the Arab region is one of diversity and demographic change. The 1970s and 1980s witnessed major improvements in health status, particularly in the chances of survival, and the decade of the 1990s marked an important movement on the fertility front. Two features of the current fertility transition are of particular relevance to the future. The first is the magnitude and pace of fertility decline and its linkages to age structural effects. The second relates to the nature of this decline and the fact that it is shaped by profound changes in family formation patterns.

This chapter investigates these two features and highlights their possible consequences on the well-being of individuals. It is divided into four sections. The first summarizes recent fertility changes and the contribution of nuptiality to this change; the second examines the nature and magnitude of nuptiality change and its link to the well-being of women; the third links fertility change to population aging as a new concern; and the last summarizes the main findings of the chapter.

## Fertility Change and the Contribution of Nuptiality

### *Fertility Transition*

Recent fertility levels in the Arab region range from a total fertility rate (TFR) of as low as 2.5 (Lebanon) to as high as 7.6 (Yemen). The picture of a homogenous, high-fertility region with a TFR in the neighborhood of 7.0 during the early 1950s has been replaced by that of a varied, dynamic region experiencing appreciable fertility change. The countries of the region have markedly different patterns of fertility change with respect to onset timing, pace, and magnitude of long-term decline and the main forces sustaining change.

For the purposes of this chapter, the Arab countries are divided into two sub-regions: North Africa, comprising Egypt, Libya, Tunisia, Algeria, Morocco, and Sudan; and West Asia, consisting of Jordan, Lebanon, Syria, Iraq, Saudi Arabia, Kuwait, United Arab Emirates, Qatar, Bahrain, Oman, and Yemen. These sub-regions represent two distinct groups in this study. North African countries tended to start their transition earlier (as early as the 1960s for Tunisia and Egypt), experienced larger declines, and after clear divergence are currently reclustering between a TFR within 3.0 and 4.0. On the other hand, decline in West Asia—with the obvious exception of Lebanon and a number of the smaller Gulf countries—did not start until the 1970s in most of the countries and as late as the

1980s for Saudi Arabia and Kuwait. Currently, these West Asian countries are experiencing a TFR within a wider range of between 4.0 and 7.0.

A detailed analysis of the fertility transition experience of Arab countries is provided in Rashad (2001).[1] In brief, the profile of change, as illustrated in Figure 2.1, may be divided into four distinct groups in terms of estimated TFR levels during 1990–94 (for more details, see Appendix Tables 2.A1 and 2.A2):

- The first group, comprising Lebanon and Tunisia, has the lowest current TFR levels (<3.5), the largest long-term declines (over 50 percent between the mid-1950s and the mid-1990s), and a smooth regular decline that started early—in the 1960s—and retained its pace or gradually picked up speed over time.
- The second group closely follows the first and includes Bahrain, Algeria, Morocco, Syria, Qatar, and Egypt. These countries have moderate current TFR levels (between 3.5 and 4.0) and quite large declines (between 47 percent and 50 percent) except for Egypt (with only 43 percent). Their pattern of decline has varied. Bahrain, Morocco, and Qatar—like countries in the first group—experienced constant or gradual decline; the remaining three countries proceeded erratically. Egypt's decline—despite an early start—abruptly slowed during the 1970s (around a third of its initial pace) and hence required 21 years to complete a 30 percent relative decline. Algeria's transition started much later, in 1970, with a moderate decline, and speeded up to more than triple the original during the 1980s. Syria is the third country that experienced a marked change of pace, its relative decline in just five years (1989–94) surpassing the ten-year relative declines for almost all other countries.

  These abrupt changes for Algeria, Syria, and Egypt are clearly affected by major period forces that interrupted or accelerated the expected pattern. These period effects allowed Algeria and Syria, despite later dates for the onset of decline and an early modest pace, to catch up with nations with earlier and stronger starts. In contrast, these forces prevented Egypt—one of the earliest and a strong leader in TFR decline—from earning its expected leading position with the lowest regional fertility level.[2]
- The third group—Emirates, Sudan, Libya, and Jordan—have current fertility levels of between 4.0 and 5.0. Two countries in the group have particularly interesting patterns of change: Sudan and Libya, which experienced the latest decline, managed within a period of ten years (1984–94) to almost catch up with declines that started 15 to 25 years earlier. They needed only nine years to reach a 30 percent decline; moreover, the bulk of this decline was reached between 1985–89 and 1990–94.
- The last group—Iraq, Saudi Arabia, Yemen, Kuwait, and Oman—shows TFRs of over 5.0 and some as high as 7.4. These countries reflect the smallest long-term changes, with Iraq possibly poised to move quickly to the lower level of TFR (their latest survey estimate of 1985–89 provides good support for this expectation). Oman and Yemen are presently moving down from the extreme TFR levels of above 10.0 that are hypothetically possible but seldom observed in human populations. These high levels have been a result of a combination of early marriage and low celibacy, low practice of contraceptive use, and a reduction of the inhibiting

effects of breast-feeding. These countries, while not reflecting long-term decline, may be just starting their transitions.

Two observations on the transition experienced by Arab countries are worth noting:

- All Arab countries have joined the onset of transition—although they have joined the path of fertility transitions at different stages. The fact that the current levels remain high in some of these countries is a reflection of the initial high level and later timing of change as well as diverse period forces.
- Many late starters are experiencing an unprecedented pace of change. Libya, Sudan, and Syria—whose declines in TFR between 1985–89 and 1990–94 are as high as 2.4, 1.9, and 2.5, respectively—are exceptional cases.[3] Very few countries in the world managed to reach comparable magnitudes of decline in a period of up to 15 years.

**Table 2.1: Levels of Current Fertility and Contraceptives Prevalence for Arab Countries**

| CPR | (modern) | TFR (reference period) | Country | (date of survey) |
|---|---|---|---|---|
| 61.0 | (37.2) | 2.53 (c) | Lebanon | (MCHS95) |
| 62.1 | (30.3) | 3.13 (a) | Bahrain | (FHS95) |
| 59.7 | (49.4) | 3.21 (c) | Tunisia | (MCHS94) |
| 50.3 | (42.4) | 3.31 (b) | Morocco | (DHS95) |
| 47.9 | (45.5) | 3.63 (b) | Egypt | (DHS95) |
| 45.1 | (25.6) | 4.22 (b) | Libya | (MCHS95) |
| 39.6 | (28.3) | 4.22 (b) | Syria | (MCHS93) |
| 50.7 | (42.9) | 4.39 (b) | Algeria | (MCHS92) |
| 26.2 | (24.3) | 4.49 (b) | Qatar* | (CHS87) |
| 9.9 | (6.9) | 4.57 (c) | Sudan | (MCHS93) |
| 27.5 | (23.6) | 4.75 (a) | UAE* | (CHS87) |
| 18.0 | (10.3) | 5.25 (b) | Iraq | (CHS89) |
| 40.0 | (26.9) | 5.57 (b) | Jordan | (DHS90) |
| — | — | 6.46 (a) | S. A.* | (CHS87) |
| 34.6 | (31.7) | 6.51 (a) | Kuwait* | (CHS87) |
| 23.8 | (18.3) | 6.65 (a) | Oman* | (FHS95) |
| 9.7 | (6.1) | 7.60 (c) | Yemen | (DMCHS91/92) |

*Notes:* (a) 12 months preceding the survey. (b) 0–2 years preceding the survey. (c) 0–4 years preceding the survey.

*For nationals only.

*Maternal and Child Health Surveys* (MCHS), conducted under the framework of the Pan Arab Project for Child Development (PAPCHILD).

*Demographic and Health Surveys* (DHS), conducted as part of the Demographic and Health Surveys Program.

*Child Health Surveys* (CHS) and *Family Health Surveys* (FHS), conducted under the auspices Gulf Surveys Program.

*Demographic and Maternal Child Health Survey* (DMCHS), conducted jointly by PAPCHILD and DHS

*Source:* Farid (1996).

**Figure 2.1: Profile of Fertility Change in Arab Countries**

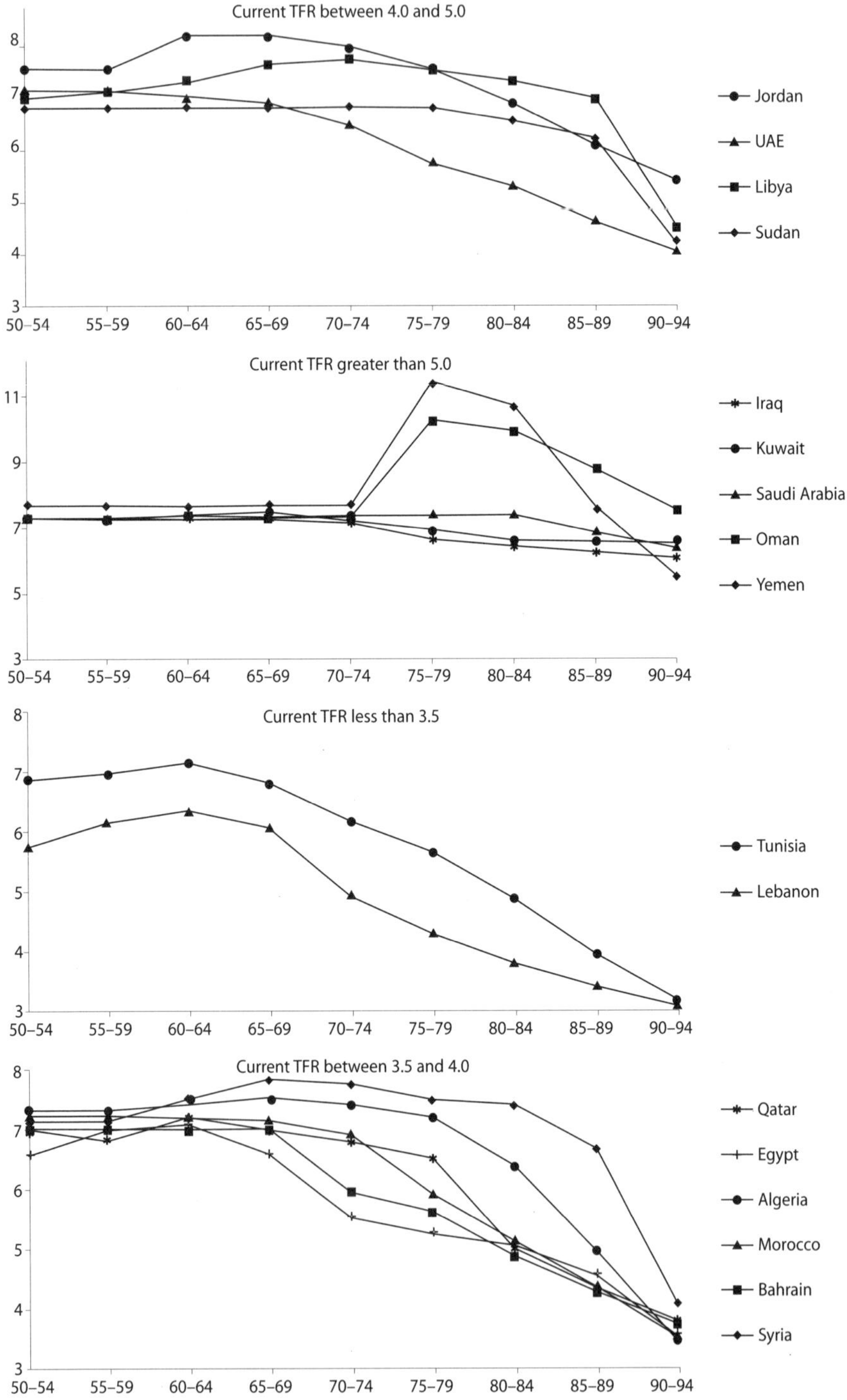

*Nuptiality: The Lead Player*

Fertility changes in the Arab region, as in other developing areas, have occurred during periods of significant advances in contraceptive technology and an explicit/implicit environment of legitimization of family planning programs, as well as a motivational and ideological reconsideration of the desirability of larger families. Clearly, the increase in the use of contraceptives has had a direct impact on the decline in fertility. Table 2.1 provides a summary of contraceptive prevalence rates (CPR) during the early 1990s and demonstrates the important role played by contraceptives in bringing down recent fertility rates.

While the role of contraceptives is widely appreciated and has been carefully monitored over time, very few studies have documented and acknowledged the key role played by marriage. Adlakha *et al.* (1991) and Rashad (1998) have attempted to investigate the determinants of fertility changes across time between the early 1980s and early 1990s. According to Adlakha *et al* (1991: 953),

> Overall, in all countries, changes in marital status are responsible for some reduction in recent fertility. However, in countries of sub-Saharan Africa and North Africa marriage is the dominant factor responsible for most or all of the fertility decline. In Ghana, and Sudan, and to some extent in Morocco, the marital status contribution was greater than the observed decline in TFR. In these three countries, there was a rise in the marital fertility of women. The rise in marital fertility may be a result of the 'catching up effect' (McDonald et al.). It is also important to note that in Morocco, as indicated earlier, contraceptive use by women increased between the surveys. Either this increase was not sufficient to completely negate the rise in marital fertility, or there are some problems with the data.

Table 2.2, extracted from Rashad (1998), adds Tunisia to other Arab countries, where change in patterns of marriage have been the main factor in fertility decline between the early 1980s and 1990s.

**Table 2.2: Decomposition of Factors Responsible for the Change in TFR**

(between WFS and recent years)

| | Egypt | Sudan | Tunisia | Syria |
|---|---|---|---|---|
| TFR at Base Year | 5.27 | 6.20 | 5.90 | 7.30 |
| Source | WFS,80 | WFS,79 | WFS,78 | WFS,78 |
| TFR at End Year | 3.90 | 4.60 | 4.50 | 4.20 |
| Source | DHS,92 | MCHS,93 | DHS,88 | MCHS,93 |
| Distribution of Change Attributed to Various Factors (%)* | | | | |
| Cm (marriage) | -26.15 | -71.72 | -114.71 | -52.20 |
| Ci (breastfeeding) | 34.12 | -32.68 | -12.23 | -11.50 |
| Cc (contraception) | -133.50 | -23.60 | -48.90 | -56.82 |
| TF | 46.15 | 20.79 | 91.82 | 4.16 |
| Interaction | -20.62 | 7.21 | -15.98 | 16.36 |
| **Total** | 100 | 100 | 100 | 100 |

*Note:* * Calculated using the decomposition model presented in Bongaarts, 1983 (see endnote 4).
*Source: World Fertility Surveys* (WFS).

Both Adlakha *et al* (1991) and Rashad (1998) were constrained by the availability of data and have been able to describe the components of fertility change only for those countries that were already several years into their fertility transition.[5]

The current analysis attempts to provide a longer-term picture of the role played by nuptiality in decreasing fertility. The method used is very simple: it calculates an adjusted total fertility for recent years using the age-specific marital fertility for the recent year and the proportion ever married ('ever married' refers to women with a marriage experience and includes currently married, widows, and divorced women) in different age groups corresponding to a base year. The base year is chosen as early as possible to capture nuptiality patterns during a pre-transitional period. The difference between the recent TFR and that of a base year is decomposed to the change in fertility attributed to a change in marital fertility (difference between base TFR and adjusted TFR), and a change in marital status (difference between adjusted TFR and recent TFR). Table 2.3 provides relevant details, while the detailed bases for calculation are provided in Appendix 2.A3.

Table 2.3 shows that among the five countries with appreciable changes in fertility—Algeria, Egypt, Morocco, Syria, and Tunisia—marriage has been the key force of change in three of them. In Tunisia and Morocco, marriage changes have accounted for two thirds of the decline; and in Algeria marriage accounts for all the long-term change. While both data quality and the approximate procedure adopted suggest that the estimated contributions are simply an order of magnitude rather than exact measures, Table 2.3 indicates that nuptiality changes are the lead players in reducing fertility in the Arab countries.

**Table 2.3: Decomposition of Long-Term Fertility Decline to the Contribution of Changes in Martial Status and Marital Fertility**

| | Base Year–Recent Year | Percent Contribution of Changes in | | Decline in TFR |
|---|---|---|---|---|
| | | Marital Status | Marital Fertility | |
| Algeria | Census 77 – MCHS 92 | 100 | 0 | 3.02 |
| Egypt | Census 60 – DHS 95 | 36 | 63 | 3.08 |
| Morocco | Survey 61/63 – DHS 95 | 65 | 35 | 3.59 |
| Sudan | Census 73 – MCHS 93 | 292 | -192 | 0.83* |
| Tunisia | Registration 66 – DHS 88 | 61 | 39 | 2.76 |
| Jordan | Census 61 – DHS 90 | 81 | 19 | 1.8 |
| Kuwait** | Census 70 – CHS 87 | 130 | -31 | 0.71 |
| Syria | Census 70 – MCHS 93 | 30 | 70 | 3.98 |
| Yemen | WFS79 – DMCHS 91/92 | 315 | -215 | 0.4 |

*Notes:* *Census data for Sudan appear to be underestimating the level of TFR during the early 1970s. **For nationals.
*Source:* See Appendix 2.A3, where details of calculations are also given.

The minor contribution of marital fertility change to total change in TFR does not refute the earlier observation that contraceptive practices have played an important role in lowering fertility. Rather, it simply implies that the contraceptive role has been offset by changes in breast-feeding practices and/or other biological factors. The role of marriage in bringing down fertility suggests that profound changes have affected, and are affecting, family formation in Arab countries. An understanding of the Arab fertility transition cannot be confined to understanding changes in reproductive strategies among married women, but must include a discussion of nuptiality change and changes in other (than contraceptive) proximate determinants of marital fertility. The next section highlights some of the important nuptiality changes and their consequences.

## Nuptiality Changes and the Well-being of Women

The first aspect of nuptiality that has undergone significant change is the proportion of women who never marry. Table 2.4 indicates that during the 1960s and 1970s, in a number of Arab countries, between 15 percent and 26 percent of women aged 15–49 never married. These figures increased considerably in the 1990s (ranging between 24 percent to 61 percent, except for Oman, where the proportion is 18 percent) and reached at least 40 percent in half of the Arab countries. Thus, for many of these countries, two out of every five women in the age group 15–49 have never been married. Libya is an extreme example that calls for further confirmation, where two thirds of women 15–49 have not married. If we include ever married women who were not at the time married—adding divorced and widowed women—the proportion reaches 50 percent or more in three Arab countries.

These large percentages are not simply a product of later marriages. Column 5 of Table 2.4 indicates that for many Arab countries (11 out of 16) a proportion between 7 percent and 21 percent remain never married by age 30–39. Although Table 2.4, column 6, suggests that only a small proportion of women aged 40–49 never married (in only three countries does this proportion exceed 5 percent), it is expected—particularly from the experience of the cohort aged 30–39—that Arab societies with near universal marriages will soon become the exception rather than the norm.

**Table 2.4: Percentage of Women Never Married or Not Currently Married in Different Years**

| | Year | | Never Married 15–49 | | Not Currently Married 15–49 | Never Married 30–39 | | Never Married 40–49 | |
|---|---|---|---|---|---|---|---|---|---|
| | Base | Recent | Base | Recent | Recent | Base | Recent | Base | Recent |
| Algeria | — | 1992[2] | — | 46.4 | 50.1 | — | 10.0 | — | 2.60 |
| Egypt | 1960[1] | 1995[3] | 15.4 | 29.9 | 34.9 | 2.50 | 3.87 | 1.50 | 1.55 |
| Libya | 1973[4] | 1995[2] | 15.7 | 61.2 | 69.3 | 0.80 | 20.6 | 0.50 | 2.30 |
| Morocco | — | 1995[3] | — | 42.5 | 47.8 | — | 16.5 | — | 3.50 |
| Sudan | 1973[1] | 1993[2] | 15.1 | 39.3 | 45.1 | 2.30 | 11.7 | 1.80 | 2.41 |
| Tunisia | — | 1988[3] | — | 41.4 | 43.8 | — | 8.51 | — | 5.65 |
| Bahrain | — | 1989[5] | — | 41.9 | 46.0 | — | 12.4 | — | 3.55 |
| Iraq | 1977[4] | 1987[4] | 26.5 | 34.5 | 40.0 | 6.50 | 8.00 | 3.40 | 4.20 |
| Jordan | 1961[1] | 1990[3] | 26.4 | 43.8 | 46.4 | 4.40 | 8.54 | 2.80 | 2.37 |
| Kuwait | 1970[1] | 1987[5] | 23.6 | 32.0 | 35.4 | 2.60 | 3.87 | 0.80 | 2.11 |
| Lebanon | — | — | — | — | — | — | — | — | — |
| Oman | — | 1988/89[5] | — | 17.9 | 22.5 | — | 2.10 | — | 0.20 |
| Qatar | — | 1987[5] | — | 42.0 | 46.8 | — | 21.1 | — | 6.40 |
| S. Arabia | — | 1987[5] | — | 33.0 | 37.9 | — | 7.40 | — | 2.40 |
| Syria | 1970[1] | 1993[2] | 25.7 | 44.2 | 55.8 | 4.7 | 13.3 | 2.85 | 5.80 |
| UAE | — | 1987[5] | — | 35.3 | 40.4 | — | 7.28 | — | 1.95 |
| Yemen | 1979[6] | 1991/92[3] | — | 23.9 | 28.4 | — | 1.76 | — | 0.11 |

*Sources:* 1: Various censuses. 2: *Maternal and Child Health Surveys.* 3: *Demographic and Health Surveys.* 4: *UN Demographic Yearbooks.* 5: *Child Health Surveys* in Gulf countries. 6: *World Fertility Surveys.*

Age at first marriage, another important aspect of nuptiality, has also changed considerably in recent years. Table 2.5 shows that 25 years earlier, three quarters of Arab countries had between 73 percent and 86 percent of their female population aged 20–24 married by age 20. By the year of the survey, only between 29 percent and 48 percent of these women are married by age 20. In other words, the median age of this cohort has not yet been defined.

The marked changes in nuptiality can also be gauged by comparing the increase in median age at first marriage across time. More than one third of the Arab countries considered have experienced an increase in the median age of marriage for cohort 25–29 from between 4.7 and 7.7 years over a 20-year span.

The singulate mean age at marriage (SMAM) is another relevant indicator providing a synthetic period measure for the number of years spent in the single state for those who ever marry. Table 2.5 indicates that SMAM at base year (spanning periods from 1960 to 1978) are more clustered. They range from 16.9 to 21.1, with the majority of countries (8 out of 10) between 18.7 and 21.0. The range for recent years is much wider: from 19.2 to 29.2. Arab countries are now clustered around two ranges: the first within 21.7 to 22.9 (5 countries out of 15); and the second (7 countries out of 15) within 24.0 and 26.3, reflecting extremely high SMAM.

**Table 2.5: Age at First Marriage**

| Country | (Survey) | Proportion of Women 20–24 Married by Age 20[1] | | Median Age at First Marriage for Cohort 25–29 For Different Periods[2] | | | Singulate Mean Age at Marriage | | Year of Survey |
|---|---|---|---|---|---|---|---|---|---|
| | | 25 years ago | Recent | 1967–75 | 1977–85 | 1987–95 | Base | Recent | |
| Algeria | (MCHS93) | 85.6 | 23.6 | 16.3 | 18.3 | 21.9 | 21.1 | 25.6 | (1977)[a] |
| Egypt | (DHS95) | 64.8 | 41.4 | 18.0 | 19.2 | 20.2 | 19.8 | 22.3 | (1960)[a] |
| Libya | (MCHS95) | — | | 16.0 | 17.7 | — | 18.7 | 29.2 | (1973)[b] |
| Morocco | (DHS95) | 73.5 | 31.4 | 17.5 | 19.6 | 23.8 | 17.5 | 26.3 | (1960) |
| Sudan | (MCHS93) | 83.6 | 35.7 | 14.8 | 15.6 | 19.5 | 18.7 | 25.4 | (1973)[a] |
| Tunisia | (DHS88) | — | — | 19.9 | 20.0 | 23.2 | 20.9 | 25.0 | (1966) |
| Bahrain | (CHS89) | 87.7 | 23.3 | 14.8 | 17.9 | 22.5 | — | 25.4 | |
| Jordan | (DHS90) | 62.0 | 29.7 | 18.9 | 18.8 | 21.2 | 20.4 | 24.0 | (1961)[a] |
| Kuwait | (CHS87) | 78.9 | 44.2 | 17.1 | 18.0 | 19.1 | 19.8 | 21.7 | (1970)[a] |
| Oman | (CHS88/89) | 88.8 | 76.2 | 14.7 | 15.2 | 15.7 | — | 19.2 | |
| Qatar | (CHS87) | — | — | 15.9 | 16.6 | 21.4 | — | 22.9 | |
| S. Arabia | (CHS87) | 75.0 | 48.4 | 16.3 | 16.4 | 20.5 | — | 21.8 | |
| Syria | (MCHS93) | — | — | 18.0 | 18.0 | 20.1 | 20.7 | 24.5 | (1970)[a] |
| UAE | (CHS87) | 83.0 | 46.8 | 16.2 | 16.3 | 17.7 | — | 22.9 | |
| Yemen | (DMCHS91/92) | 79.3 | 62.0 | 15.7 | 15.7 | 16.2 | 16.9 | 20.9 | (1979)[c] |

*Sources:* Farid (1996); Khalifa (1997). (a): Various censuses. (b): *UN Demographic Yearbooks.* (c): *World Fertility Surveys.*

Countries with significant changes in the timing of marriage are Algeria, Libya, Morocco, Sudan, Tunisia, Bahrain, Jordan, and Syria. These are also the countries that reflect a very high percentage (between 8.5 percent and 20.6 percent) of women remaining single within the age group 30–39. For these countries, it is clear that the proportion of time spent by women in the not-married status is large indeed. (See Table 2.6).

**Table 2.6: Period Estimates of the Average Number[(a)] and Percentage of Years a Female Spends in a Non-married State in the 35 Years between Ages 15 and 50**

| Country (Year of Survey) | Years Never Married | | Years Not Currently Married | |
|---|---|---|---|---|
| | Number | Percentage | Number | Percentage |
| Algeria (93) | 11.31 | 32.3 | 13.08 | 37.4 |
| Egypt (95) | 8.09 | 23.1 | 9.89 | 28.3 |
| Libya (95) | 14.42 | 41.2 | 16.06 | 45.9 |
| Morocco (95) | 9.41 | 26.9 | 13.76 | 39.3 |
| Sudan (93) | 10.54 | 30.1 | 13.13 | 37.5 |
| Tunisia (88) | 10.87 | 31.1 | 12.04 | 34.4 |
| Bahrain (89) | 10.94 | 31.3 | 13.05 | 37.3 |
| Jordan (90) | 9.58 | 27.4 | 10.98 | 31.4 |
| Kuwait (87) | 7.52 | 21.5 | 9.23 | 26.4 |
| Oman (88/89) | 4.31 | 12.3 | 6.33 | 18.1 |
| Qatar (87) | 11.47 | 32.8 | 13.69 | 39.1 |
| Saudi Arabia (87) | 7.75 | 22.1 | 9.99 | 28.5 |
| Syria (93) | 10.58 | 30.2 | 11.72 | 33.5 |
| UAE (87) | 8.63 | 24.7 | 11.32 | 32.3 |
| Yemen (91/92) | 5.87 | 16.8 | 7.65 | 21.9 |

*Note:* (a) Calculated by adding the proportions of single females in each age group up to and including that for the age group 45–49 and multiplying the sum by five.
*Source:* Authors' calculations.

In nearly half of the Arab countries, a female spends around a third of her prime 35 years of life in the unmarried state. If this period is extended to include older ages—with much higher prevalence of widowhood and divorce—the average number of years spent in the unmarried state may reach as high as 20 years between ages 15 and 70. Thus, the nature of the nuptiality changes occurring in Arab countries implies that more women are spending longer spans of their lives in non-marital living arrangements and that some women may live in permanent celibacy. The implication of these changes on the well-being of individual Arab women is closely linked to their unique traits and resources, familial and societal support systems, and opportunities for self fulfillment beyond the role of mother and wife.

The family as a unit is central in Arab societies. Societal recognition and support systems appear to revolve around the roles of women as wives and mothers. A working mother is offered opportunities for leave without pay and early retirement. Some countries with high unemployment rates are reconsidering the values of women working and are highlighting the familial benefits of non-working mothers. The importance of careers for the fulfillment of women is given second place, and the burden of combining a career with parenthood is solely that of women. Societal mechanisms for alleviating the double burden of dual functions and allowing mothers to better perform their productive non-familial roles are indeed the exceptions.

In this social context, the non-married woman and her psychological and economic well-being is totally ignored. The preceding section illustrated that such women constitute a large portion of the population and that its relative weight and sheer size will continue to increase. Hence, the profile of single women—their level of dependency and their support networks—are features of well-being that call for further investigation. The very limited data provided in Table 2.7 suggest a high level of dependency in terms of personal educational characteristics and ability to earn a living.

**Table 2.7: Profile of Never Married Women in the Age Group 15–49**

| Country | (Survey) | Prop. with Primary Education or Less (no schooling) | Percent Working | Percent Working for Cash |
|---|---|---|---|---|
| Algeria | (MCHS 93) | 62.4 (19.9) | 7.5 | 6.6 |
| Egypt | (DHS 95) | 29.4 (16.4) | 13.3 | 12.25 |
| Sudan | (MCHS 93) | 62.3 (40.7) | 13.0 | 9.97 |
| Yemen | (MDHS 91/92) | 84.6 (71.2) | 4.6 | 2.99 |

*Source:* Authors' calculations.

It is interesting to note that the decrease in prospects of marriage is affecting both educated and uneducated women. For example, the proportion of never-married among Sudanese women with less than primary education increased from 19.6 percent in 1979 to 29.1 in 1993 and that of women with at least primary education increased from 41.0 percent to 67.6 percent. These comparable increases contradict the prevalent wisdom that the delay in marriage is primarily attributable to the spread of education. Economic difficulties and societal changes have resulted in a rise in the marriage age and in the proportion unmarried of all women.

For women with access to higher education and paid employment, the delay in marriage is not necessarily a negative development and is probably allowing better career opportunities. It is uneducated and unemployed women who are shouldering the burden of the nuptiality transition. The future challenge for single women—and also for married women whose reduced fertility implies a reduction in number of years devoted to childbearing and child rearing—is to have both fulfilling lives and the means for self and family support.

Trends in female educational achievements are indeed pointing to major improvements in this dimension of well-being.[6] It should be pointed out, though, that for some countries of the region the prospects for universal education remain very slim, while in others the improvement in education has not been combined with better opportunities for gainful and fulfilling employment. Women's empowerment and access to wage-earning work is an economic and emotional necessity for single women and also for more and more families.

Fertility reduction in many developing countries has generally been equated with progress and development. For such progress to be equally shared by members of society and to result in improving the quality of people's lives, societal concerns with reduction of population size should be paralleled with equal investment in women's needs. Investment should be made to empower women, upgrade their resources, expand their choices in life, and foster more balanced gender relations.

## Population Aging and Policy Implications

### *Aging in Arab Countries*

As has been the case of many developing countries, the population of Arab countries has until recently been considered too young to justify a focused attention on aging. Table 2.8 shows that the median age for most Arab countries has not reached 20. Half of Arab countries have less than 5 percent of their population in the age group 60+.[7] Clearly, many Arab countries follow the standard definition of young populations—populations with medians under 20 and aged proportions (65 and older) under 5 percent. Very few Arab populations are on the point of surpassing this young age structure and starting to mature (a mature population is defined as a population with median age between 20 and 29 and proportion 65+ between 6 and 10 percent). Table 2.8 also suggests that West Asian countries are more likely to be younger than those of North Africa.

While the current picture may explain the lukewarm attitude to aging as an issue of concern, the existing momentum for aging should not be overlooked. The momentum for aging usually derives largely from the magnitude and pace of decline in fertility, as well as survival improvements at older ages. The relationship between fertility declines and changes in the age structure of a population is straightforward. With fertility declines, the number and proportion of children under age 15 decreases, which contributes to an increase in the proportions of other age groups. Furthermore, rapid fertility decline is associated with rapid aging, since this decline can be interpreted to mean an entrance of smaller successive birth cohorts to the age structure, which in turn increases the proportion of adults and older persons in the total population.

The effects of mortality decline on the age structure, however, depend primarily on the age pattern of the decline. Survival gains during the early stages of the mortality decline benefit all population groups, and are more substantial and pronounced among young persons and women in reproductive ages. These gains contribute, consequently, to the youth of the population. However, with medical advances and improved public health measures, these gains extend benefits to older persons and contribute to the survival of larger proportions of successive cohorts into advanced age. Hence, while fertility decline sets the pace for population aging, mortality decline can have diminishing power on the aging effects of fertility at some points in time, while at other points it acts as an accelerating force based on the age pattern of the decline.

Continued high levels of fertility, accompanied by sustained declines in mortality levels, have contributed to the youth of Arab populations. However, diversity in demographic experience among the Arab countries, and the recent substantial declines in fertility, suggest different future age structures. The more recent and quite rapid transition for some Arab countries will eventually lead to the rapid aging of the region's populations. The dynamics of fertility decline, together with survival gains that have greatly extended life expectancies in Arab countries, indicate movement toward the hypothesized accelerating aging populations. Thus, we can argue that the mechanisms of population aging are currently operating in some countries in the Arab region and that their populations are progressing toward an older age structure, while other countries in the region still maintain their young age structure.

Table 2.8 presents the United Nations' estimates for current and projected aged (60+) population proportions for the Arab countries. It confirms the findings indicated by recent surveys that in 1990 most of the region's countries had not yet aged. However, in a period of 20 years, it is projected that this proportion will substantially increase, and by the year 2030 many Arab countries will have more than 10 percent of their populations over age 60.

As indicated, the three Gulf countries of Bahrain, Qatar, and United Arab Emirates reflect both a strong and an exceptionally fast movement toward aging. Within only 20 years, the proportions aged 60+ will have increased between two- and over five-fold. By the year 2030, the proportion aged 60+ will be at least 21 percent of the whole population. These are populations that experienced very high life expectancies (above 70 years) and moderate fertility levels in the 1990s (a TFR of less than or in the neighborhood of 4.0). Many other countries' populations will also be considered old by the year 2030. Algeria, Egypt, Morocco, Tunisia, Kuwait, and Lebanon are expected to have a proportion aged 60+ between 12 percent and 16.4 percent. Saudi Arabia and Syria, similarly, are projected by the UN to have an appreciable proportion at older ages—around 10 percent.

**Table 2.8: Some Measures of Aging for Arab Countries and Selected Others**

| | Recent Data | | | Source | Proportion 60+ Projected (UN, 1996) & (calculated)[b] | | |
|---|---|---|---|---|---|---|---|
| | Median Age | Proportion (60+) | Gender Ratio | | 1990 | 2010 | 2030 |
| **North Africa** | | | | | | | |
| Algeria | 19.1 | 6.7 | 110 | MCHS92 | 5.5 | 6.1 | 12.0 |
| Egypt | 19.4 | 6.2 | 98 | DHS95 | 6.3 | 6.7 | 13.1 |
| Libya | 19.7 | 6.0 | 108 (103)[a] | MCHS95 | 4.1 (6.0) | 5.4 (5.8) | 6.8 (9.8) |
| Morocco | 20.4 | 6.0 | 118 (101)[a] | DHS95 | 6.1 | 7.3 | 14.7 |
| Sudan | 18.5 | 7.3 | 128 | MCH93 | 4.6 | 5.8 | 8.8 |
| Tunisia | 20.3 | 7.5 | 112 | DHS88 | 6.4 | 7.5 | 15.1 |
| **West Asia** | | | | | | | |
| Bahrain [n] | 20.0 | 5.7 | 120 (116)[a] | CHS89 | 3.9 | 7.9 | 21.0 |
| Iraq | 22.1 | 5.1 | (87)[a] | | 4.5 | 5.5 | 9.1 |
| Jordan | 17.3 | 4.3 | 114 (111)[a] | DHS90 | 4.2 | 4.8 | 8.3 |
| Kuwait [n] | 13.9 | 3.3 | 126 (106)[a] | CHS87 | 2.1 | 7.2 | 16.4 |
| Lebanon | | | | | 8.1 | 8.2 | 14.9 |
| Oman | 14.3 | 4.4 | 150 | CHS88/89 | 3.8 | 4.2 | 5.1 |
| Qatar [n] | 20.6 | 4.2 | 159 | CHS87 | 2.1 | 11.4 | 22.5 |
| Saudi Arabia [n] | 15.4 | 4.3 | 117 | CHS87 | 4.0 | 5.9 | 9.0 |
| Syria | 18.2 | 5.7 | 134 (106)[a] | MCHS93 | 4.4 (5.7) | 4.8 (6.6) | 9.0(11.5) |
| UAE [n] | 16.7 | 4.9 | 122 | CHS87 | 2.5 | 11.3 | 22.0 |
| Yemen | 14.1 | 7.0 | 120 (111)[a] | MCHS91 | 4.1 | 3.5 | 5.1 |
| **Other Nations** | | | | | | | |
| Indonesia | 87.3 | 6.3 | 24.0[c] | | 6.3 | 8.6 | 14.8 |
| Malaysia | 85.4 | 6.7 | 23.0[c] | | 5.8 | 8.0 | 14.1 |
| South Korea | 67.1 | 6.1 | 30.0[c] | | 7.7 | 13.3 | 24.5 |
| Sweden | 38.7 | 22.8 | 78.0[c] | | 22.8 | 24.8 | 28.8 |
| United Kingdom | 35.7 | 20.8 | 74.0[c] | | 20.8 | 22.9 | 28.7 |
| United States | 32.8 | 16.6 | 73.3[c] | | 16.6 | 18.5 | 25.7 |
| Japan | 37.2 | 28.5 | 74.3[c] | | 17.4 | 28.5 | 33.1 |

*Notes and sources:*

(n): These figures and proportions are for national citizens.

(a): The parentheses contain gender ratios according to the latest published censuses.

(b): The parentheses contain the projected figures estimated using population parameters (age distribution and fertility) according to recent surveys.

(c): Median age from Kinsella and Taeuber (1994); proportion 60+ and gender ratio from United Nations (1996).

The pace of aging is another crucial factor that should be taken into consideration when evaluating the aging experience. For example, in the United States, an increase in the proportion aged 65 and above from 4 percent to 11 percent occurred over a period of 80 years. Similar increases are expected to happen in just 35 years in Morocco, and 40 years in Tunisia and Egypt.[8] If we note the exceptional pace of decline in fertility in countries like Libya, Syria, and Sudan, we expect the actual pace of aging in these countries to be even faster than that reflected in the UN projections.

In actuality, the UN projections shown in Table 2.8 are believed to be an underestimate of the aging experience in many Arab countries. The reasons for this can be summarized in the fact that the UN Base Year estimates for the proportions aged 60+ in some Arab countries are lower than those portrayed in recent surveys. This is clear for Algeria, Libya, Sudan, Tunisia, Bahrain, Kuwait, Qatar, Syria, UAE, and Yemen. Furthermore, the United Nations' fertility assumptions do not capture the very recent and fast-paced decline in some countries. For example, in Libya a projection starting with a 60+ proportion of 6 percent rather than 4 percent of the total population, together with a lower base fertility, resulted in altering future projections. By the year 2030, the projected proportion in Libya is expected to reach as high as 10 percent rather than the under 7 percent projected by the United Nations. Similar results can be seen for Syria—where a starting point of 5.7 percent leads to a proportion of more than 11 percent rather that 9 percent in 2030 (calculated figures are provided in Table 2.8).

Clearly, the aging process in the Arab region, although it has not yet begun, is building rapid momentum for the coming three decades. Furthermore, if one considers the large population base in countries such as Egypt, these projected proportions reflect not only older persons' share in the population but also the large population size. For example, it is expected that by the year 2030 Egypt will have more than 13 million aged 60 and over. This growth in the numbers and proportions of older persons in the population poses a variety of new challenges to Arab countries—challenges concerning not only older persons, but also the overall effects on the population as a whole. The next subsection discusses some of these challenges concerning older persons' economic, social, and physical well-being and their policy implications.

### *Aging in the Arab Region and Its Policy Implications*

The expected rapid pace of population aging in the Arab countries in the near future delineates an important social, economic, and political issue that warrants substantial consideration among researchers and policy makers. Efficient planning to accommodate this rapidly growing segment of the population is an urgent policy issue. The sheer numbers of the future elderly can create tremendous pressure on the services provided to them and to others as well. An objective and comprehensive understanding of the needs of this age group and their surroundings is therefore essential. Equally important is a careful examination and adaptation of other countries' experiences in this area. Future plans, moreover, should be multidimensional—incorporating a variety of considerations as well as taking into account those whose lives are affected by them.

The economic well-being of older persons can be defined as the ability of older persons to support themselves and contribute significantly to their community. This definition encompasses a broad set of factors. Two such are income in old age and the participation of the elderly in the labor force. Limited data are available on old age income in the Arab world. However, most Arab countries adopt old age social security policies, which are tied primarily to employment in the government. Some policies extend their coverage to include other categories (US Department of Health and Human Services, 1994). In both cases, the benefits of these policies are extremely limited and not sufficient to secure the economic well-being of older persons as a group. Tadros (1984) pointed out that in Egypt more than 52 percent of the social security beneficiaries reported the inadequacy of pensions and other social security benefits to meet their needs. They indicated that they depend on family, loans, and pursuit of income-producing activities to supplement their income. Furthermore, Khadr (1997) in her study[9] of the aged in Egypt indicated that there is a positive relationship between poverty and aging regardless of how poverty is measured—as, for example, by income level or by self evaluation of current income defined as subjective poverty. Tadros (1984) attributed this relationship to the inadequacy of pensions and the emergence of health needs that consume a proportionate share of older persons' income.

Nonexistent or limited social security policies in developing countries encourage older persons to extend their working life beyond retirement age (Kinsella, 1994). Table 2.9 compares economic activity rates among older persons in some Arab countries with other developing and developed countries. It shows high labor force participation among older men in developing countries in general. It also reveals that although activity rates differ substantially among the Arab countries, almost two fifths of men aged 60 and older in the Arab countries continue to participate in the labor market compared with less than one fourth in developed countries—except for Japan.

Table 2.9 also highlights the low levels of female participation in the labor force in the Arab region, with less than 9 percent economically active at age 60 and older. Such low levels are not necessarily an indication of high economic security among females but more likely a sign of high economic dependability. In Egypt, more than 25 percent of older women reported their children as the basic source of income (Khadr, 1997). Noting the significant changes in nuptiality patterns and the profile of unmarried women discussed earlier, the future is likely to see a large number of unmarried, uneducated, and economically dependent female elders.

**Table 2.9: Percentage of Economically Active Population Aged 60+**

| | Economically Active Population (60 +) | |
|---|---|---|
| | Male | Female |
| Algeria | 36.0 | 2.0 |
| Egypt | 45.0 | 7.0 |
| Jordan | 40.0 | 1.0 |
| Morocco | 38.0 | 9.0 |
| Tunisia | 40.0 | 5.0 |
| Indonesia | 68.0 | 30.0 |
| Malaysia | 22.0 | 9.0 |
| South Korea | 53.0 | 28.0 |
| Sweden | 23.0 | 14.0 |
| United Kingdom | 21.0 | 8.0 |
| United States | 27.0 | 14.0 |
| Japan | 51.0 | 23.0 |

*Source:* National Institute of Aging (NIA), 1996.

The social well-being of older persons includes numerous dimensions of their life, such as their integration and active participation in the social network surrounding them. Cowgill (1972) argued that urbanization and the invasion of modern attitudes substantially affect older persons' social networks. Modern attitudes lead to the replacement of traditional familial support with an institutionalized type of support (United Nations, 1991). Urbanization and modernization tend to undermine the status of older persons and in some cases increase their isolation.

Limiting our attention to only one aspect of the lives of the elderly, namely their living arrangements, we find that family studies in the Arab region have extensively reported the high prevalence of extended and multigenerational living arrangements. In a study of living arrangements of the older population in seven developing countries, Hashimoto (1991) examined a sample in one of Cairo's neighborhoods—Met Ockoba. It was found that more than 73 percent of the older persons in the sample were living with family members of direct descent, with almost 43 percent living with unmarried children in a nuclear family household. In addition, more than 17 percent of the sample had a child living in the same apartment block or within the same area of the city as their parents. These figures show that almost 90 percent of the aged in this sample are being cared for by their children, either through co-residence or through proximity of residence. Hashimoto also showed that the likelihood of living in a multigenerational household with married children increased with age and with being female. Furthermore, wealthy older persons are more likely to co-reside with unmarried children, and the poor more likely to co-reside with married children, as a strategy for pooling family resources. Childless older persons are more likely to live in single or conjugal households. Khadr (1997) has also found that a son rather than a daughter is the preferred child for co-residence.

Ongoing social changes and their effects on Arab family systems are expected to introduce significant changes to these traditional living arrangements. The tendency toward more nuclear living arrangements among the young generation will decrease the prevalence of extended family living arrangements that secure continuous care and guardianship for older family members. Khadr (1997), in her study of the older population in Egypt, showed a similar pattern of living arrangements to that observed by Hashimoto. Of her sample, 77 percent lived with someone of direct descent. However, her examination of older persons' living arrangements in Egypt by place of residence highlights the effects of modernization (as presented by urban residence) on traditional living arrangements. Table 2.10 points to the high prevalence of solitary living arrangements of the urban sample, with almost 10 percent living alone and slightly more than 10 percent living with spouse only. While for the rural sample, only a little more than 5 percent were shown as living alone and 7 percent lived with spouse only. The aggregate figures for living alone or with spouse only, of 20 percent and 12 percent respectively, highlight the difference in urban-versus-rural older population trends.

From a policy perspective, these changes in the living arrangements of older persons are expected to have significant implications and require substantial planning—planning in which sufficient and efficient social institutions can extend their services to solitary-living older persons and provide them with needed care. Detailed examination of the factors underlying older persons' choice of living arrangements is necessary. Examining the nature of their social relationships with their children, relatives, and friends, as well as the effects of the community on these relationships, can enhance our understanding of the social context of older persons and provide a comprehensive base for efficient future planning.

**Table 2.10: Living Arrangements of Older Persons (60+) in Egypt**

| Living Arrangement | Urban % | Rural % | Total % |
|---|---|---|---|
| Living alone | 9.8 | 5.2 | 7.2 |
| Living with spouse only | 10.3 | 7.0 | 8.4 |
| Living with non-married children | 43.1 | 18.5 | 29.4 |
| Living with married children | 27.4 | 64.8 | 48.1 |
| Living with others | 6.5 | 3.9 | 5.1 |

*Source:* Khadr (1997).

Finally, the physical well-being of older persons has to do primarily with their health status, and with the relationship between mortality declines and levels of morbidity among older persons. The essence of this relationship has been a controversial issue in the literature. On one hand, Fries (1983) argued that a healthy lifestyle and modern medicine tend to decrease old-age mortality levels and to compress morbidity into a short time period preceding death. On the other hand, Manton (1982) argued that modern medicine can contribute to prolong disability by reducing the severity of illnesses and delaying disease progression. If an attempt is to be made to predict impending health needs, we need to assess both these lines of argument and their implications on health policies and services. This can be done only by careful examination of the current health status of older persons and that of the future older cohort. Khadr (1997) showed that more than 13.1 percent of the population aged 60 and older self-evaluate their current health as poor. Further, more than 26 percent reported their inability to cook for themselves, and more than 12 percent were unable to carry on their household chores. More than 29 percent reported experiencing at least two illnesses in the preceding six months that affected the activities of their daily lives. Table 2.11 shows an increase in the morbidity and disability levels by age among older persons.

**Table 2.11: Health Indices for Older Persons (60+) in Egypt (%)**

| Health Indices | Males | | | Females | | | Total | | | |
|---|---|---|---|---|---|---|---|---|---|---|
| | 60–64 | 65–69 | 70+ | 60–64 | 65–69 | 70+ | 60–64 | 65–69 | 70+ | All ages |
| Self-report poor health | 12.3 | 13.1 | 16.5 | 5.5 | 12.5 | 19.9 | 8.8 | 12.8 | 18.0 | 13.1 |
| Disability[a] | 5.1 | 6.2 | 12.3 | 8.2 | 7.8 | 31.0 | 6.7 | 7.0 | 21.0 | 12.0 |
| Inability to cook | 26.8 | 33.8 | 43.8 | 12.3 | 10.2 | 31.7 | 19.4 | 22.7 | 38.2 | 26.0 |
| Experience of 2+ diseases[b] | 21.0 | 31.7 | 27.4 | 23.3 | 34.3 | 42.1 | 22.2 | 33.0 | 34.2 | 29.0 |

*Notes:* (a): Disability is measured in terms of having disability in four or more of the activities of daily living.
(b): Diseases that affect daily activities.
*Source:* Khadr (1997).

A forthcoming study[10] provides further evidence of the higher levels of morbidity and disability being experienced by aged persons in Egypt. It also highlights the effects of low-income levels on accessing health services among the elderly.

The gender differential in health status in older age is yet another significant area of inquiry. Researchers have indicated that women tend to outlive men, but that women are more likely to experience higher levels of morbidity in their old age (Verburgge, 1984). This pattern can be observed in the case of Egypt in Table 2.11.

In addition to the well-being of the elderly, there should be a concern for the impact of the aging process on the younger generations that carry the responsibilities of caring for their aged parents and older family members. While declines in fertility imply a decline in the youth dependency ratio, aging means a rising old-age dependency ratio. Furthermore, aging means that those in the middle generations have a longer period of caring for their young children while at the same time providing support for their elderly parents or family members. Watkins *et al.* (1987) highlighted the effects of population aging on the middle-aged segment of the population. She found that the increase in the likelihood of having a living parent among middle-aged women in the United States during the 1980s prolonged the time interval during which these women would be obligated to care simultaneously for their young children (<18 years) and for their elderly parents (>65 years). This overloaded obligation would have substantial effects not only on middle-aged women but also on all family members due to the consequent excessive demand on family resources such as income, time, and space.

## Summary and Conclusions

High population growth has been central to international and national demographic agendas. Demography as a science remains dominated by a search to reduce high fertility and attempts to explain determinants of change. Many Arab countries, including some of those with no explicit population policies, share this concern over high fertility. While appreciable changes have been documented on the fertility front, the decline in fertility has not yet fully responded to macro-societal goals and reproductive/child health concerns. Thus, the focus on high fertility is likely to continue for some time to come.

This chapter argues that the nature and magnitude of recent fertility changes are introducing two new areas of concern. The first relates to the well-being of women whose prospects of marriage are being reduced without there being enough comparable improvements in their ability to lead independent and fulfilling lives. The chapter suggests that in the absence of serious efforts to address constrained resources among women and biased gender relations, the success in reducing population growth will not translate into an improved quality of life. The second challenge relates to the fact that the age structural changes in the Arab region have acquired enough momentum to introduce aging as a new area of concern. The limited available data on the economic, social, and physical well-being of today's elderly confirm that the future will bring increased pressures on national resources. In addition, it will generate a variety of new challenges that need to be met if the well-being of older persons, as well as that of other family members involved in their care, is to be ensured.

## Appendix

### Table 2.A1: Total Fertility Rates for Arab Countries

| Arab Countries (size of pop. in thousands during 1990–95 ) | Years | | | | | | | | | Latest Survey Adjusted 90–94** |
|---|---|---|---|---|---|---|---|---|---|---|
| | 50–54 | 55–59 | 60–64 | 65–69 | 70–74 | 75–79 | 80–84 | 85–89 | 90–94 | |
| **North Africa** | | | | | | | | | | |
| Simple average | 6.90 | 7.01 | 7.10 | 7.02 | 6.70 | 6.34 | 5.83 | 5.14 | 3.74 | 3.90 |
| Weighted average | 6.82 | 7.00 | 7.08 | 6.85 | 6.33 | 5.99 | 5.55 | 4.89 | 3.67* | 3.89* |
| Algeria (24935) | 7.28 | 7.28 | 7.38 | 7.48 | 7.38 | 7.17 | 6.35 | 4.97 | 3.47[a] | 3.64 |
| Egypt (56312) | 6.56 | 6.97 | 7.07 | 6.56 | 5.53 | 5.27 | 5.06 | 4.58 | 3.58[a] | 3.99 |
| Libya (4545) | 6.87 | 6.97 | 7.17 | 7.48 | 7.58 | 7.38 | 7.17 | 6.87 | 4.44[a] | 4.55 |
| Morocco (24334) | 7.17 | 7.17 | 7.15 | 7.09 | 6.89 | 5.90 | 5.10 | 4.40 | 3.55[a] | 3.69 |
| Sudan (25585) | 6.67 | 6.67 | 6.67 | 6.67 | 6.67 | 6.67 | 6.42 | 6.10 | 4.19[a] | 4.15 |
| Tunisia (8080) | 6.87 | 6.97 | 7.17 | 6.83 | 6.15 | 5.66 | 4.88 | 3.94 | 3.18[b] | 3.37 |
| **West Asia** | | | | | | | | | | |
| Simple average | 7.04 | 7.06 | 7.21 | 7.20 | 6.89 | 7.19 | 6.70 | 5.92 | 5.08 | 4.87 |
| Weighted average | 7.18* | 7.20* | 7.33* | 7.37* | 7.27* | 7.67* | 7.39* | 6.52* | 5.49* | 5.29* |
| Bahrain (490) | 6.97 | 6.79 | 7.17 | 6.97 | 5.94 | 5.62[c] | 4.90[c] | 4.29[c] | 3.76[c] | 3.57 |
| Iraq (18078) | 7.17 | 7.17 | 7.17 | 7.17 | 7.11 | 6.56 | 6.35 | 6.15 | 5.97[b] | 5.25(85–89) |
| Jordan (4259) | 7.38 | 7.38 | 7.99 | 7.99 | 7.79 | 7.38 | 6.76 | 6.00 | 5.33[b] | 4.56 |
| Kuwait (2143) | 7.21 | 7.21 | 7.31 | 7.41 | 7.14[d] | 6.83[d] | 6.53[d] | 6.50[d] | 6.47[d] | 6.47 |
| Lebanon (2555) | 5.74 | 6.15 | 6.35 | 6.05 | 4.92 | 4.30 | 3.79 | 3.42 | 3.09[b] | 2.53(91–95) |
| Oman (1751) | 7.20 | 7.20 | 7.20 | 7.20 | 7.20 | 10.13[c] | 9.82[c] | 8.70[c] | 7.46[c] | 7.42 |
| Qatar (485) | 6.97 | 6.97 | 6.97 | 6.97 | 6.76 | 6.49[c] | 5.02[c] | 4.37[c] | 3.80[c] | 3.70 |
| S. A. (16048) | 7.17 | 7.17 | 7.26 | 7.26 | 7.30 | 7.28 | 7.28 | 6.80 | 6.35[b] | 6.35 |
| Syria (12348) | 7.09 | 7.09 | 7.46 | 7.79 | 7.69 | 7.44 | 7.38 | 6.66 | 4.13[a] | 3.69 |
| UAE (1671) | 6.97 | 6.97 | 6.87 | 6.76 | 6.35 | 5.66 | 5.23 | 4.60 | 4.05[b] | 4.05 |
| Yemen (11311) | 7.61 | 7.61 | 7.61 | 7.61 | 7.60 | 11.36[c] | 10.60[c] | 7.62[c] | 5.49[c] | 5.49 |
| **Total** | | | | | | | | | | |
| Simple average | 6.99 | 7.04 | 7.17 | 7.13 | 6.82 | 6.89 | 6.39 | 5.65 | 4.6 | 4.48 |
| Weighted average | 6.95* | 7.07* | 7.16* | 7.04* | 6.68* | 6.58* | 6.19* | 5.45* | 4.27* | 4.31* |

*Notes:* For TFR 1990–94: (a) The relative decline in the last two periods preceding the most recent health survey is used to extrapolate 1985–89 UN measures. (b) TFR was estimated using UN measures and assuming the relative decline prevailing between 1980–84 and 1985–89 applies to between 85–89 and 90–94. (c) The last survey estimates replacing UN measures for 1975 to 1989 and extrapolated for 1990–94. (d) Using vital registration data until 1985–89 and extrapolated for 1990–94.

* Weighted using population size (UN, 1994).

** Adjusted to correspond to 1990–94 using the last two fertility measures from the latest survey when two measures are available, or the latest survey estimate if lower than extrapolated (Iraq, Lebanon). Otherwise, the extrapolated measures for 1990–94 are retained (Kuwait, S.A., UAE).

*Source:* United Nations (1995) for population size and TFR during 1950–89, unless otherwise indicated.

## Table 2.A2: Profile of Changes in Fertility for Arab Countries

| Current Level TFR During 1990–94[a] | Countries in Ascending Order of TFR | Year Change Began [b] | TFR at Year of Onset of Decline | Long-term Trend % Decline 1955–60 to 1990–95[a] | Percent Decline for Consecutive 10-Year Periods Following Onset of Decline | | | Number of Years to Achieve 30 % Decline FromOnset |
|---|---|---|---|---|---|---|---|---|
| | | | | | 1 | 2 | 3 | |
| 2.5 to 3.49 | Lebanon | 1960 | 6.35 | 0.579 | 0.225 | 0.230 | 0.185 | 14 |
| | Tunisia | 1960 | 7.17 | 0.512 | 0.142 | 0.207 | 0.348 | 19 |
| 3.5 to 3.99 | Bahrain | 1960 | 7.17 | 0.474 | 0.172 | 0.175 | 0.233 | 19 |
| | Algeria | 1970 | 7.38 | 0.500 | 0.140 | 0.454 | | 14 |
| | Morocco | 1965 | 7.09 | 0.485 | 0.168 | 0.254 | | 16 |
| | Syria | 1975 | 7.44 | 0.480 | 0.105 | 0.380[c] | | 13 |
| | Qatar | 1970 | 6.76 | 0.469 | 0.257 | 0.243 | | 12 |
| | Egypt | 1960 | 7.07 | 0.428 | 0.218 | 0.085 | 0.292 | 21 |
| 4.0 to 4.99 | UAE | 1965 | 6.67 | 0.419 | 0.163 | 0.187 | | 19 |
| | Sudan | 1980 | 6.42 | 0.378 | 0.347 | | | 9 |
| | Libya | 1980 | 7.17 | 0.347 | 0.381 | | | 9 |
| | | | | | (0.05[c], 0.313[c]) | | | |
| | Jordan | 1970 | 7.79 | 0.425 | 0.132 | 0.212 | | 19 |
| | | | | | (0.042[c], 0.354[c]) | | | |
| 5.0 to 7.7 | Iraq | 1970 | 7.11 | 0.268 | 0.107 | 0.060 | | |
| | S. Arabia | 1980 | 7.28 | 0.114 | 0.066 | | | |
| | Yemen | 1975 | 11.36 | 0.155 | 0.329 | 0.280[c] | | 9 |
| | Kuwait | 1980 | 6.53 | 0.103 | -0.019 | | | |
| | Oman | 1975 | 10.13 | -0.018 | 0.141 | 0.143[c] | | |

*Notes.* (a): Using adjusted survey estimates provided in Table 2.4.
(b): The year of onset of decline is the date followed by a decrease in TFR of at least 0.7 over a period of 10 years, or if such a precipitous decline has not occurred, it is the year in which a fall of 10 percent in fertility from its pre-transitional maximum occurred.
(c): The relative decline during five years only.
*Source:* Based on Table 2.4.

## Appendix 2.A3: Basis for Decomposing the Change in Fertility to a Change in Marital Fertility and a Change in Marital Status

Method:

TFR base – TFR recent =
difference due to change in marital fertility +
difference due to change in marital status.
= (TFR base – adjusted TFR) + (adjusted TFR – TFR recent)

Adjusted TFR =
$\sum$ (Age-specific marital fertility rates in recent years
× prop. ever married in base year by age groups)

Difference due to changes in marital fertility=
$\sum$ (a. m. f. r. (1) × prop. mar (1)) × 5 - $\sum$ (a. m. f. r. (2) × prop. mar (1)) × 5

Difference due to changes in marital fertility=
$\sum$ (a. m. f. r. (2) × prop. mar (1)) × 5 - $\sum$ (a. m. f. r. (2) × prop. mar (2)) × 5

Where (1) and (2) refer to base year, and recent year respectively and,
TFR: Total fertility rates
a. m. f. r. (x): Age-specific marital fertility rates in years (x)
Prop. mar (x): proportion ever married by age group in year (x).

### Table 2.A4: Illustrative Calculations for Egypt

| Age | a.s.f rates | | Prop. Ever Married | | a.m.f. Rates - Recent | Adjusted a.s.f Rates |
|---|---|---|---|---|---|---|
| | Base (1) | Recent (2) | Base (3) | Recent (4) | (5)=(2)/(4) | (3) × (5) |
| 15–19 | 45 | 61 | 34 | 14.3 | 427 | 145 |
| 20–24 | 229 | 200 | 77.1 | 48.1 | 416 | 321 |
| 25–29 | 378 | 210 | 93.3 | 86.6 | 242 | 226 |
| 30–34 | 396 | 140 | 96.7 | 94.9 | 148 | 143 |
| 35–39 | 211 | 81 | 98.1 | 97.4 | 83 | 82 |
| 40–44 | 61 | 27 | 98.2 | 98.1 | 28 | 27 |
| 45–49 | 21 | 7 | 98.8 | 98.8 | 7 | 7 |
| TFR | 6.71 | 3.63 | | | | 4.75 |

*Notes:* TFR base: TFR recent = 6.71–3.63 = 3.08. Difference due to change in marital fertility = 6.71–4.75 = 1.96. Difference due to change in marital status = 4.75–3.63 = 1.12. Percent contribution of change in marital fertility = 1.96/3.08 = 64 percent. Percent contribution of change in marital status = 1.12/3.08 = 36 percent.
*Source:* Authors' calculations.

*Data used and their sources:*

**Table 2.A5: Age-specific Fertility Rates for Selected Arab Countries**

| Age | Algeria | | Egypt | | Jordan | | Kuwait | | Morocco | | Sudan | | Syria | | Tunisia | | Yemen | |
|---|---|---|---|---|---|---|---|---|---|---|---|---|---|---|---|---|---|---|
| | Census 1977 | MCHS 1992 | Census 1960 | DHS 95 | Census 1961 | DHS 90 | Census 1970 | CHS 87 | 61–63 | DHS 95 | Census 1973 | MCHS 93 | Census 1970 | MCHS 93 | 1966 | DHS 88 | WFS 78 | DHS 90 |
| 15–19 | 97 | 21 | 45 | 61 | 108 | 49 | 121 | 42 | 93 | 35 | 109 | 53 | 153 | 61 | 77 | 30 | 170 | 102 |
| 20–24 | 285 | 143 | 229 | 200 | 328 | 219 | 339 | 255 | 300 | 125 | 259 | 167 | 318 | 164 | 293 | 167 | 244 | 283 |
| 25–29 | 342 | 214 | 378 | 210 | 382 | 296 | 375 | 326 | 317 | 138 | 273 | 215 | 380 | 225 | 343 | 249 | 341 | 315 |
| 30–34 | 336 | 220 | 396 | 140 | 361 | 264 | 315 | 300 | 289 | 146 | 213 | 210 | 339 | 189 | 311 | 225 | 303 | 284 |
| 35–39 | 267 | 164 | 211 | 81 | 213 | 188 | 225 | 231 | 184 | 117 | 150 | 162 | 260 | 129 | 239 | 134 | 199 | 258 |
| 40–44 | 129 | 92 | 61 | 27 | 77 | 79 | 59 | 103 | 106 | 82 | 55 | 74 | 135 | 64 | 120 | 62 | 197 | 172 |
| 45–49 | 27 | 23 | 21 | 7 | 19 | 19 | 16 | 43 | 92 | 18 | 28 | 33 | 45 | 11 | 35 | 13 | 76 | 120 |
| TFR | 7.41 | 4.39 | 6.71 | 3.63 | 7.4 | 5.6 | 7.21 | 6.5 | 6.9 | 3.31 | 5.4 | 4.57 | 8.2 | 4.22 | 7.1 | 4.34 | 8.1 | 7.7 |

**Table 2.A6: Proportion Ever Married for Selected Arab Countries**

| Age | Algeria | | Egypt | | Jordan | | Kuwait | | Morocco | | Sudan | | Syria | | Tunisia | | Yemen | |
|---|---|---|---|---|---|---|---|---|---|---|---|---|---|---|---|---|---|---|
| | Census 1977 | MCHS 1992 | Census 1960 | DHS 95 | Census 1961 | DHS 90 | Census 1970 | CHS 87 | 1960 | DHS 95 | Census 1973 | MCHS 93 | Census 1970 | MCHS 93 | 1966 | DHS 88 | WFS 78 | DHS 90 |
| 15–19 | 46.0 | 3.6 | 34 | 14.3 | 28.0 | 10.6 | 29.8 | 11.7 | 58.8 | 10.5 | 43.1 | 10.6 | 22.3 | 13.9 | 18.5 | 4.4 | 61.0 | 24.7 |
| 20–24 | 79.0 | 29.6 | 77.1 | 48.1 | 73.3 | 45.2 | 80.0 | 59.9 | 94.0 | 39.8 | 85.0 | 39.9 | 70.2 | 42.3 | 71.1 | 35.9 | 93.0 | 71.8 |
| 25–29 | 93.0 | 65.2 | 93.3 | 86.6 | 88.8 | 73.7 | 94.8 | 89.7 | 97.7 | 60.2 | 95.4 | 67.2 | 89.0 | 69.5 | 88.5 | 70.1 | 97.0 | 90.9 |
| 30–34 | 97.0 | 86.8 | 96.7 | 94.9 | 94.4 | 89.1 | 98.3 | 95.5 | 98.4 | 79.2 | 97.3 | 83.5 | 94.3 | 83.0 | 92.4 | 88.6 | 98.0 | 97.5 |
| 35–39 | 98.0 | 93.6 | 98.1 | 97.4 | 96.9 | 94.6 | 99.2 | 96.9 | 98.7 | 88.4 | 98.2 | 93.0 | 96.3 | 91.2 | 91.9 | 95.4 | 100 | 98.0 |
| 40–44 | 99.0 | 96.9 | 98.2 | 98.1 | 97.2 | 97.3 | 99.4 | 97.6 | 98.6 | 94.4 | 98.2 | 96.7 | 96.8 | 93.7 | 87.9 | 96.6 | 98.0 | 99.8 |
| 45–49 | 99.0 | 98.1 | 98.8 | 98.8 | 97.2 | 98.0 | 99.6 | 98.4 | 98.5 | 99.4 | 98.3 | 98.4 | 97.5 | 94.8 | 81.8 | 91.6 | 99.0 | 100 |

## Notes

* This chapter is produced within the framework of a project entitled "New Demography of the Arab Region." The project is a collaborative effort between Arab scholars and national and international institutions. It is coordinated by by the Social Research Center of the American University in Cairo and supported by the Mellon, Hewlett, and Ford Foundations.

1 The analysis reconstructed the long-term fertility trends by reconciling the measures of TFR provided in United Nations (1995) and different recent survey measures. It also provided an adjusted/extrapolated estimate of TFR for 1990–94 for all Arab countries. For each Arab country, it calculated (a) the date of the onset of fertility transition (defined as the date followed by a decrease in TFR of at least 0.7 over a period of 10 years, or if such a precipitous decline had not occurred, the year in which a fall of 10 percent in fertility from its pre-transitional maximum occurred); and (b) the long-term relative decline in TFR between 1950 and 1954 and 1990 and 1994, as well as the number of years needed to reach 30 percent in TFR from the onset of fertility decline. Appendix Table 2.A1 provides the TFR measures used in the analysis.

2 The period checks on Egyptian decline are clearly associated with hiccups brought about by the dynamics of wars, external political and economic pressures, and internal inefficiencies that curtailed the great ambitions of the early 1950s.

3 Based on Table 2.A.1 and using the extrapolated rates for 1990–94.

4 Adlakha *et al.* (1991: 953) provides the following description of Bongaart's decomposition model: "The Bongaart model is a useful way of quantifying the relative importance of intermediate or proximate determinants that control fertility. The model is a multiplicative one in which each component is expressed as an index. According to the model, the actual level of fertility or the total fertility rate (TFR) can be written as follows: TFR = Cm x Cc x Ca x Ci x TF, where Cm is the index of marriage, Cc, the index of contraception, Ca, the index of abortion, Ci, the index of infecundability, and TF the potential fertility or total fertility—the total number of children a woman would bear if there were no inhibiting effects. In the analysis that follows for the WFS and DHS surveys, the component of abortion Ca, as in most studies, is not considered because data to compute it were not available. Thus, the model is reduced to three components. Theoretically each index can range from zero to one but such extreme values are generally not found. The differences of each index from one can be interpreted as a proportionate reduction attributable to a particular component." For details on the model, see Bongaart (1982) and Casterline *et al.* (1984).

5 Both studies used as their base year the WFS surveys that were conducted in Arab countries during the early 1980s, while the year of comparison used different DHS and MCHS surveys.

6 The Arab region has recently witnessed an impressive stride in female education. For example, the percentage of females enrolled in secondary schools for Oman has jumped from a meager 7 percent in 1980 to 64 percent in 1995—thereby joining the movements in all other Gulf countries toward eliminating the educational gender gap. The ratio of female enrollment in secondary school per 100 males during 1995 is above 100 for half the Gulf countries (Bahrain, Qatar, and UAE), is above 93 for another two (Oman and Kuwait), and is 87 in Saudi Arabia (PRB, 1997).

7 Ages 60+ and 65+ are the most commonly used age groups to identify the 'aged.' However, research in aging in developing countries relies on 60+ more, since life expectancy in these countries hovers around age 60. Furthermore, age 60 corresponds to retirement and to withdrawal from active working life to a less structured period.

8 This time estimate is based on United Nations (1996) projections of those aged 65+ in the Arab countries.

9 The study is based on a survey carried out by the Social Research Center in Collaboration with the United Nations Office in Vienna titled "The Developmental Implication of Demographic Changes: Global Aging in 1994." The survey was fielded in three governorates in Egypt: Cairo, Menoufia, and Giza. The sample was designed to represent the older population resident in villages and cities.

10 This study is a nationally representative study carried out during 1995 by the Social Research Center titled "Poverty, Social Stratification, and Mobility."

## References

Abdel-Azeem, F., S. Farid, and A. Khalifia (eds.). 1993. *Egypt Maternal and Child Health Survey 1991.* Cairo: Central Agency for Public Mobilization and Statistics and PAPCHILD/League of Arab States.

Adlakha, A., M. Ayad, and S. Kumar. 1991. "The Role of Nuptiality in Fertility Decline: A Comparative Analysis," in *Proceedings of the Demographic and Health Surveys World Conference,* pp. 947–64. Colombia, MD: Macro International Inc.

Al-Mazrou, Y., and S. Farid (eds.). 1991. *Saudi Arabia Child Health Survey.* Riyadh: Ministry of Health.

Al-Muhaideb, A., A. Abdul-Ghafour, and S. Farid (eds.). 1991. *United Arab Emirates Child Health Survey.* Abu Dhabi: Ministry of Health.

Aloui, T., M. Ayad, and H. Fourati. 1989. *Enquête Démographique et de Santé en Tunisie 1988.* Tunis: Office National de la Famille et de la Population, and Columbia, MD: IRD/Macro Systems Inc.

Al-Rashoud, R., and S. Farid. 1991. *Kuwait Child Health Survey.* Kuwait: Ministry of Health.

Azelmat, M., M. Ayad, and H. Belhachmi. 1989. *Enquête Nationale sur la Planification Familiale, la Fécondité et la Santé de la Population au Maroc 1987.* Rabat: Ministère de la Santé Publique, Service des l'Information Sanitaire, and Columbia, MD: Institute for Resource Development/Westinghouse.

———, and E. Housni. 1993. *Maroc: Enquête Nationale sur la Population et la Santé 1992.* Rabat: Ministère de la Santé Publique, and Columbia, MD: Macro International Inc.

Bongaarts, J., and P.G. Potter. 1983. *Fertility, Biology, and Behavior: An Analysis of the Proximate Determinants.* New York, NY: Academic Press.

Casterline, J., S. Singh, and H. Ashurt. 1984. "The Proximate Determinants of Fertility." *World Fertility Survey Comparative Studies,* No. 39. Voorburg, The Netherlands: International Statistical Institute.

Central Bureau of Statistics (in collaboration with the World Fertility Survey). 1982. *Syria Fertility Survey 1977.* Damascus.

Central Bureau of Statistics. 1995. *Syria Maternal and Child Health Survey 1993.* Damascus; and PAPCHILD/League of Arab States, Cairo.

Central Planning Organization, Department of Statistics (in collaboration with the World Fertility Survey). 1983. *Yemen Arab Republic Fertility Survey 1979.* Sana'a.

Central Statistical Organization. 1994. *Yemen Demographic and Maternal and Child Health Survey 1991/92.* Sana'a; PAPCHILD/League of Arab States, Cairo; and Macro International Inc., Columbia, MD.

Cowgill, D.O., and L.D. Holmes (eds). 1972. *Aging and Modernization.* New York: Appleton-Century-Crofts.

Department of Statistics. 1976. *Jordan Fertility Survey 1975.* Amman, Hashemite Kingdom of Jordan.

Department of Statistics. 1991. *Sudan Demographic and Health Survey 1989/90.* Khartoum; and Macro International Inc., Columbia, MD.

El-Zanaty, F., H. Sayed, H. Zaky, and A.Way. 1993. *Egypt Demographic and Health Survey 1992.* Cairo: National Population Council, and Calverton, MD: Macro International Inc.

Farid, S. 1996. "Transitions in Demographic and Health Patterns in the Arab Region," in *Proceedings of the Arab Regional Population Conference,* IUSSP, Cairo, Vol. 1, pp. 435–65. Cairo: CDC Press.

Federal Ministry of Health. 1995. *Sudan Maternal and Child Health Survey 1993.* Khartoum, and PAPCHILD/League of Arab States, Cairo.

Fries, J.F. 1983. "The Compression of Morbidity," *Milbank Memorial Fund Quarterly /Health and Society,* 61: 397–419.

General Committee for Health and Social Security. 1996. *Libya Maternal and Child Health Survey 1995: Preliminary Report.* Tripoli, and PAPCHILD/League of Arab States, Cairo.

Hallouda, A.M., S.Z. Amin, and S. Farid (eds.). 1983. *The Egyptian Fertility Survey,* Vol. 2. Cairo: Central Agency for Public Mobilization and Statistics.

Hashimoto, A. 1991. "Living Arrangements of the Aged in Seven Developing Countries: A Preliminary Analysis," *Journal of Cross Cultural Gerontology,* 6: 359–81.

Khadr, Z.A. 1997. *Living Arrangement and Social Support of Older Population in Egypt.* Ph.D. Dissertation, Population Studies Center, University of Michigan, Ann Arbor, MI.

Khalifa, M. 1997. "Age at First Marriage in Selected Arab Countries: A Reproductive Health Approach." Background paper presented in the Specialist Workshop on "Reproductive Health in Arab Countries." Jointly organized by the Social Research Center of the American University in Cairo and Harvard School of Public Health. Cairo, 16–25 March.

Kinsella, K., and C.M. Taeuber. 1994. "An Aging World II," in US Bureau of the Census, *International Population Report,* pp. 25, 92–3. Washington, DC.

Manton, K.G. 1982. "Changing Concepts of Morbidity and Mortality in the Elderly Population," *Milbank Memorial Fund Quarterly /Health and Society,* 60: 183–244.

McDonald, P.F., L. T. Ruzicka, and J.C. Caldwell. 1980. "Interpretations Between Nuptiality and Fertility: The Evidence from the World Fertility Survey," in *Proceedings of the World Fertility Survey Conference,* Vol. 2. London: WFS.

Ministère de la Santé Publique, Direction des Affaires Téchniques, Service d'Exploitation Mécanographique. 1979–80. *Enquête Nationale sur la Fécondité et la Planification Familiale au Maroc 1978.* Rabat.

Ministry of Health. 1990. *Iraq Child Health Survey 1989: Preliminary Report.* Baghdad.

Ministry of Health. 1996. *Lebanon Maternal and Child Health Survey 1995: Preliminary Report.* Beirut, and PAPCHILD/League of Arab States, Cairo.

Ministry of Health. 1996. *Tunisia Maternal and Child Health Survey 1994/95.* Tunis, and PAPCHILD/League of Arab States, Cairo.

Ministry of National Planning, Department of Statistics. 1979. *Sudan Fertility Survey 1977.* Khartoum.

National Institute of Aging. 1996. *Global Aging into the 21st Century.* US Bureau of the Census Wallchart Washington, DC.

National Office of Statistics. 1994. *Algeria Maternal and Child Health Survey.* Algiers, and PAPCHILD/League of Arab States, Cairo.

National Population Council. 1996. *Egypt Demographic and Health Survey 1995: Preliminary Report.* Cairo, and Macro International Inc., Calverton, MD.

Rashad, H. 1998. "Arab Countries in Transition: An Overview and a Search for Explanations." The Social Research Center of the American University in Cairo Working Papers Series, No. 1. Cairo: American University in Cairo.

———. 2001. "A Comparative Analysis of Fertility in Arab Countries: Explaining the Anomalies," in Basia Zaba and John Blacker (eds), *Brass Tacks: Essays in Medical Demography.* London: Athlone Press.

Sayed, H., M. Osman, F. El-Zanaty, and A. Way. 1989. *Egypt Demographic and Health Survey 1988.* Cairo: National Population Council, and Columbia, MD: Institute for Resource Development/Macro Systems, Inc.
Suleiman, M., A. Al-Ghassany, and S. Farid (eds.). 1992. *Oman Child Health Survey 1992.* Muscat: Ministry of Health.
Tadros, H. 1984. "Social Security and the Family in Egypt." *The Cairo Papers in Social Science,* Vol. 7, Monograph 1.
United Nations. 1991. *Aging and Urbanization: Proceedings of the United Nations International Conference on Aging Populations in the Context of Urbanization.* New York.
———. 1995. *World Population Prospects:* 1994 Revision. New York.
———. 1996. *The Age and Sex Distribution of the World Population*: 1996 Revision. New York.
US Department of Health and Human Services. 1994. *Social Security Programs Throughout the World: 1993.* Social Security Administration: Office of Research and Statistics: SSA Publication No. 13–11805, Research Report #63. Washington, DC.
Verburgge, L.M. 1984. "Longer Life but Worsening Health? Trends in Health and Mortality of Middle Aged and Older Persons," *Milbank Memorial Fund Quarterly /Health and Society,* 62: 475–519.
Watkins, S.C., J.A. Menken, and J. Bongaart. 1987. "Demographic Foundation of Family Change," *American Sociological Review,* 52: 346–58.
Yacoub, I., and S. Farid (eds.). 1992. *Bahrain Child Health Survey.* Manama: Ministry of Health.

# 3

# Poverty in the Arab World: The Role of Inequality and Growth

*Ali A. Ali and Ibrahim A. Elbadawi**

## 1. Introduction

The Arab countries that belong to North Africa and the Middle East region (MENA)[1] have distinguished themselves by their relatively high achievements in human development over the past 40 years or so. In particular, the region is characterized by low poverty and a notable equality of income distribution. According to a World Bank (1995: 2–3) report, "during 1960–85 the MENA region outperformed all other regions except East Asia in income growth and the equality of income distribution." The report then points out that these achievements have made it possible for the region to realize enormous social benefits: "infant mortality more than halved, and life expectancy rose by more than ten years. Primary school enrollment shot up from 61 percent in 1965 to 98 percent in 1991. And adult literacy improved from 34 percent in 1970 to 53 percent in 1990, with particular progress made in the oil-exporting countries." The report also credits the region's governments for effectively reducing poverty: "by 1990 only 5.6 percent of the population in MENA lived on less than US$1 a day—the global benchmark for absolute poverty—compared with 14.7 percent in East Asia and 28.8 percent in Latin America. And whatever the wealth, poverty was lower in MENA countries than elsewhere." Finally, the report, in our view correctly, attributes these achievements to both accelerated growth (in the 1970s and early 1980s) and distribution, with the latter being in terms of "generous transfers to large parts of the population."

In this chapter a simple dynamic model of poverty, growth, and distribution will be presented and used to explore the experience of six Arab countries in poverty reduction. The countries concerned are Algeria, Egypt, Jordan, Mauritania, Morocco, and Tunisia. More importantly, the model will be utilized to motivate future strategies for further poverty reductions in the six countries, based on their economic performance during 1975–96. The model allows poverty and growth to depend on distribution in the short to longer run. In the short run, the model also accounts for the joint effects on growth of shocks, social conflicts, and a society's capacity for mediating conflicts among social groups within its own structure. However, in a much longer horizon, distribution is assumed to be endogenous to growth via a Kuznets curve. We take the view that the Kuznets hypothesis is meant to describe a long transformation process, during which not only production structures change, but also institutions. In short periods of time, different economies may find themselves on either side of the Kuznets curve, assuming that it exists. The side on which economies find themselves will have an important implication for the reduction of poverty. This feature of the model, together with the growth and poverty equations, allows dynamic interactions between growth and distribution. This is one of the key areas recommended for future research by Alesina and Rodrik (1994) in their seminal paper on this literature. Moreover, this feature permits our model to have a further important policy implication, in that it makes possible a broad classification of countries according to whether sustained reduction of poverty would require acceleration of growth, redistributive measures, or both.

Before proceeding with the analysis, it may be worth underscoring an important feature of the Arab countries as a group. This feature has to do with the relatively high economic diversity among the countries of the region. To highlight this diversity, we follow ERF (1998) and group the countries of the region in four broad categories: mixed oil producers (MOP: Algeria, Iran, and Iraq); Gulf Cooperation Council (GCC: Bahrain, Kuwait, Oman, Qatar, Saudi Arabia, and UAE); diversified economies (DE: Egypt, Jordan, Morocco, Syria, Tunisia, and Turkey); and, lastly, primary producers (PP: Mauritania, Sudan, and Yemen).[2] The 1996 distribution of population and GDP over these categories was such that DE accounted for 49 percent of population and 39 percent of GDP; MOP's share in population was equal to its GDP share at 31 percent; PP's population share was 12 percent, while its share of GDP was only 2 percent; and GCC's population share was only 7 percent and its GDP share 29 percent. Excluding Iran and Turkey, the two non-Arab countries in ERF's definition of MENA, it is an easy matter to show that the Arab countries display a similar distribution to that of larger MENA. Thus, Arab DE had a population weight of 48 percent and a GDP share of 2 percent; MOP, a population share of 21 percent and a GDP share of 24 percent; PP, a population share of 20 percent but a GDP share of only 3 percent; and GCC, a population share of 11 percent and a GDP share of 46 percent.

The region's economic diversity is likewise captured by differences in per capita GDP. Not surprisingly, GCC ranks top on the scale with a per capita GDP of US$9045 in 1996, followed by MOP (US$2478). DE ranks third with a per capita GDP of US$1280, while PP's per capita GDP amounted to only US$276. The production structure of the four groups differs as well. Thus, in 1996 the agricultural sector accounted for 24 percent and 23 percent of GDP in PP and MOP respectively, and for 16.2 percent in DE, and only 2.4 percent of GDP in GCC. The manufacturing sector accounted for 14.4 percent of GDP in DE, 11 percent in MOP and GCC, and 9 percent in PP. Thus, none of the country groups of the region could be considered industrialized (defining this stage in terms of a manufacturing sector contribution of 20 percent of GDP). Extractive industry, however, contributed fairly large shares in GCC (35 percent of GDP) and MOP (27 percent of GDP).

Another important feature to note about the region has to do with its recent growth performance, which is generally judged to have been below potential (ERF, 1998). Thus, over the period 1991–95 the best-performing group was PP with an average growth rate of GDP of 3.8 percent per annum, followed by DE (3.4 percent GDP growth rate). GCC recorded a growth rate of 2.9 percent, while MOP's growth rate was a mere 0.8 percent. Given population growth rates for the respective groups, only PP and DE recorded marginal improvements in GDP per capita over the period (at a rate of 0.7 percent per annum). Therefore, aside from the performance of the economically marginal

PP group, current per capita growth in the region is either negative or zero. With such conditions of economic stagnation but low inequality, it has been argued that even modest growth will have a dramatic effect on poverty (as measured by US$1 per person per day). According to some estimates (e.g., World Bank, 1995: 8), "moving from zero growth to 1 percent annual growth in the MENA region would reduce the number of poor in the region by 8 million over the next decade." On the other hand, the report also estimates that, "without the higher growth that the reform can bring, the number of poor (those living on less than US$1 a day) would rise to 15 million by 2010." We hasten to point out, however, that a strategy for poverty reduction that is exclusively centered on growth—such as the one described above—can be successful only in the context of the limited development objective of dealing with *abject* poverty. This concept of poverty, which assumes a fixed poverty line relative to mean income, has been coming under intense pressure from labor movements, NGOs, and other stake-holders in developing countries. Also, recent contributions to the development literature support the view that the poverty line should be responsive to growth in mean income (for a review, see Ali and Elbadawi, 1999).

If a broader view of poverty is taken, the analysis of this chapter will show that with initial conditions of low inequality and faltering growth in the region, a strategy for poverty reduction based on growth alone may not be successful. This is because the model predicts the level of Gini ($\tilde{G}$) consistent with stationary or declining poverty to be negatively related to the long-term rate of growth. Therefore, despite fairly low initial inequality (as measured by the Gini index: G), inequality may still be a constraint on poverty reduction if growth is not sufficiently strong. Depending on the envisaged growth performance in the MENA region during the next decade, this analysis may have important implications for future strategies for poverty reduction in the region.

These points noted, the remainder of the chapter is organized as follows. The poverty, growth, and distribution model is presented and discussed in section 2, as well as in Appendix 3.A8. Section 3 contains a brief description of the estimation results of the Kuznets relationship, which emphasizes the reverse endogeneity of distribution relative to growth as a byproduct of at least some, if not all, development processes. The section also includes discussions of the estimation results of the growth and poverty specifications of section 2. The Appendix tables provide detailed calculations of the model's structural parameters, using the parameter estimates of section 3. The computed parameters were subsequently used to analyze the factors determining the dynamics of poverty and growth in the Arab world and other regions (section 4) as well as to identify policy strategies for poverty reductions in the six Arab countries under discussion (section 5). Section 6 concludes.

In view of data limitations, further analysis will be confined to the six Arab countries under review, which throughout this chapter will be liberally referred to as the 'Arab world.' For the remainder of this section, we discuss briefly some aspects of diversity in the MENA and the Arab regions. To motivate the policy implications of our model for the potential roles of growth and distribution in poverty reduction, we also briefly examine the appropriate strategy for dealing with poverty in the Arab world during the current economic slump, which has been impacting the region since the second half of the 1980s.

## 2. A Model of Growth, Distribution, and Poverty

We posit below a simple model of growth, poverty, and distribution. While focusing on the role of inequality in the joint determination of the first two variables, the model also accounts for other non-distributional fundamentals of growth and of the direct effect of growth on poverty. In addition, we posit a formulation of the Kuznets relationship specifying inequality as an additive function of mean income and other time-varying fixed effects. The steady-state solution of the model allows derivation of the rate of growth consistent with stationary poverty, and the level of inequality consistent with both stationary poverty and zero rate of acceleration of growth (i.e. constant long-term rate of growth). Departure from the steady state, on the other hand, permits analysis of the phase dynamics of poverty and growth around the steady state.

### *2.i The Basic Model*

$$g^* = g(G,F) = -\beta_0 G + \beta' F = -\beta_0 G + g_F \tag{1}$$

$$\dot{g} = -\lambda_1 \tau G(1 - I) + \lambda_2 (g^* - g)_0 + \lambda_3' \,(Policy - Policy_0) \tag{2}$$

$$\hat{P} = -(1 - \varepsilon)\eta g + \theta \hat{G} \tag{3}$$

$$\hat{G} = v\hat{\mu} + v_0 = vg + v_0 \tag{4}$$

where $g$ is the rate of real growth; $g^*$ is long-term steady-state growth; G is a measure of inequality; $F$= vector of other growth fundamentals (policy variables, human capital, institutions, initial income, etc.); $\lambda_1$, $\lambda_2$ are scalars, and $\lambda_3$ is a vector of parameters reflecting the effect due to the change in the vector of policy variables ($Policy - Policy_0$); $\tau$ is a measure of exogenous shocks; $I$ is an index of the effectiveness of institutions for resolving social conflicts; $P$ is an index of poverty; $\mu$ = mean income; $z$ = poverty line; $\varepsilon$ = elasticity of poverty line with respect to mean income; $-\eta$ = elasticity of poverty index with respect to $\mu$; $\theta$ is the elasticity of $P$ relative to G, $\dot{x} = dx$ is absolute change over time, and $\hat{x}$ indicates a rate of change $\frac{dx}{x}$.

The above model has two major components: a growth component (equations 1 and 2) and a poverty component (equations 3 and 4). We discuss these in turn.

*The growth component*

Under the growth component, equation 1 specifies long-run target growth as being determined by the degree of income inequality and a host of other fundamentals—reflecting policy variables, external factors, and initial conditions. Following Alesina and Rodrik (1994), we assume growth to be negatively associated with the initial degree of inequality (Gini). At the theoretical level, Alesina and Rodrik formally establish this negative link by showing that less equal societies are more prone to distributive polices, which reduces growth by introducing economic distortion. They also empirically corroborate the prediction of their model using global cross-country data. More recently, Rodrik (1998a) formally justifies the link between growth and the more general concept of "distributional conflicts." Such conflicts, Rodrik (1998a: 2) argues, can "diminish the productivity with which a society's resources are utilized in a number of ways: by delaying needed adjustment in fiscal policies and key relative prices (such as the real exchange rate or real wages), by generating uncertainty in economic environment, and by diverting activities from the productive sphere to the redistributive one."

Equation 2 is an error-correction extension of the specification proposed by Rodrik (1998a) in which growth persistence is disrupted by external shocks in an environment of high social conflicts (G) and weak institutions (1-*I*). The variable ($\tau\, G(1 - I)$) accounts for the interactions of "latent" social conflict (in our case taken to be the degree of inequality) with external shocks on one hand, and with domestic institutions of conflict management on the other. Rodrik shows these interactions to be the main factor behind the persistence of growth in East Asia, and its collapse everywhere else in the developing world, following the external shocks of the late 1970s. Equation 2 expresses growth persistence as a weighted function of this effect, an "error correction effect," and the impact effects of changes in the policy fundamentals of growth. More formally, this equation can be shown to be consistent with optimizing behavior, if we assume that the government pursues a *moving* growth target by minimizing the following two-period error-correction loss function:

$$l(g) = \zeta_1(g - g_0{}^*)^2 + \zeta_2[(g - g_0)^2 + (\varphi'\Delta h)^2] + \zeta_3'\Delta h(g - g_0),$$

where $\Delta h = (\Delta Policy, \tau G(1 - I))$ is a vector of determinants of the dynamics of growth, which include changes in the policy fundamentals of growth in addition to the conflict variable. It is straightforward to show that equation 2 is a direct result of the above minimization problem.[3]

*The poverty component*

Under the poverty component, equation 3 is derived from the standard general specification of poverty index, P, as a function of the standard of living and an inequality measure, such as the Gini coefficient. Most commonly used poverty measures satisfy the requirement of being homogeneous of degree zero in the poverty line ($z$) and mean income ($\mu$). Plausible restrictions on the poverty index are that (a) its partial with respect to mean income is negative, implying that, for a given inequality, an increase (reduction) in mean income (the poverty line) will be expected to lead to a reduction in poverty, and (b) its partial with respect to the inequality index is positive, implying that an increase in inequality, for a given mean income, will be expected to lead to an increase in poverty (see, e.g. Ali, 1998).[4]

Total logarithmic differentiation of this generally formulated poverty index gives rise to equation 3, which decomposes a poverty change into a growth component and a distribution component, where $\eta$ is the absolute value of the elasticity of the poverty index with respect to mean income and $\theta$ is its elasticity with respect to the distribution parameter:

$$\frac{dP}{P} = -\eta(\frac{\mu}{z}, G)[\frac{d\mu}{\mu} - \frac{dz}{z}] + \theta(\frac{\mu}{z}, G)\frac{dG}{G}.$$

Under appropriate assumptions about the behavior of the poverty line, this equation can be regarded as a complete decomposition of a change in poverty between a growth component and a distribution component. Until recently, the dominant approach has been to assume that the poverty line is constant (i.e. $\frac{dz}{z} = 0$) and to add a residual component $R(\mu/z, G)$.[5]

If the poverty line is assumed to change, however, the equation could *not* be taken as a complete decomposition of poverty changes, without modeling the elasticity of the poverty line with respect to mean income as well.[6] Recent work has confirmed that it is indeed reasonable to assume that the poverty line is a function of mean income (see, for example, Ali, 1998; Foster, 1998; and Atkinson, 1998). Under such a procedure, equation 3 posits a complete decomposition of the change in poverty over time, conditional on the size of the income elasticity of the poverty line ($\varepsilon$). As can be seen from equation 3, for a constant degree of inequality, growth will to lead to a reduction in poverty only if the poverty line is inelastic with respect to mean income (i.e. $\varepsilon < 1$).

Equation 4 is a general specification of the inequality-development relationship (i.e. the Kuznets curve). For empirical purposes, Anand and Kanbur (1993a, 1993b) proposed the following format as consistent with the original formulation of the hypothesis: $G = \phi_0 - \phi_1\mu - \phi_2 \frac{1}{\mu}$. For the purposes of empirical estimation we add a term that depends on time to capture a time trend.

## *2.ii Steady-state Equilibrium and Phase Dynamics*

Using equation 4 in equation 3 gives the ultimate reduced-form expression for the rate of change in poverty, which decomposes the change in the poverty index into a "growth effect" net of the distributional effect through the growth channel ($-\alpha = -(1 - \varepsilon)\eta + \theta v$) and a "trend distributional effect" ($\alpha_0 = \theta v_0$).

$$\hat{P} = -\alpha g + \alpha_0, \tag{5}$$

For given G and $g_F$, steady-state levels of $g$ and P (i.e. consistent with $\dot{g} = \hat{P} = 0 = \tau$) can be obtained from (1) - (2) and (5):

$$g = g^* = -\beta_0 G + \beta' F = -\beta_0 G + g_F \tag{6}$$

(from 1 and 2), and

$$g^\circ = \frac{\alpha_0}{\alpha} \quad \text{(from 5)} \tag{7}$$

The intersection of equations 6 and 7 in the $(g, G)$ plane solves for the stationary level of inequality ($\tilde{G}$) consistent with constant rate of long-term growth ($\dot{g} = 0$) and stationary rate of poverty growth ($\hat{P} = 0$):

$$\tilde{G} = \frac{1}{\alpha\beta_0}(\alpha\tilde{g}_F - \alpha_0) \tag{8}$$

The above expression suggests that a stationary level of poverty (i.e. $\hat{P} = 0$) is not necessarily inconsistent with a high steady-state level of inequality ($\tilde{G}$), provided that the absolute rate of reduction in poverty due to non-distributional growth fundamentals ($\alpha g_F$) is higher than the rate of change (increase) in poverty due to non-growth factors ($\alpha_0$) and that the effect of inequality on the rate of change of poverty through the growth channel ($\alpha\beta_0$) is small. If, on the other hand, the latter is actually large, or the differences between the two components of the rate of change in poverty are small, a much smaller steady-state level of inequality may be required to prevent poverty from rising. Analysis of the phase dynamics around the steady state in the (g,G) plane is provided in Appendix 3.A8.

## 3. Income Distribution, Poverty, and Growth

In this section we estimate the key specifications of growth, distribution, and poverty of section 2 required for calculating the structural parameters of the model. First, we estimate long-term growth as well as persistence of growth (equations 1 and 2 of section 2), using global panel data drawn from 62 countries. Second, we estimate three indexes of poverty and a Kuznets relationship, which permit calculation of the various elasticities underlying equations 3 and 4 of section 2.

### *3.i The Growth Estimation Results*

*Long-term growth*

We estimate an endogenous growth model for a panel of 62 developing countries over six period-averages: 1970–74, 1975–79, 1980–84, 1985–89, 1990–92, and 1993–96. Given the emphasis on the effect of income distribution on growth, the pivotal variable in the model is the Gini coefficient. However, our model also controls for other growth fundamentals suggested in the literature. The estimated model is stated in equation 9 below, where t-statistics are in parentheses:

$$g = 4.308 + \underset{(2.050)}{0.511} \ln l - \underset{(-2.652)}{0.0711} \ln G_{t-1} + \underset{(3.241)}{0.1156} invest - \underset{(-2.359)}{9.362} gcon \qquad (9)$$

*Notes:*
$R^2 = 19.34$ Wald Test $\chi 2 = 35.57 N = 236$
*Period of estimation:* 1965–69, 1970–74, 1975–79, 1980–89, 1990–92, 1993–96
Where $g$ is the real growth per capita, $l$ is labour force growth net of population growth, $G$ is the Gini coefficient, *invest* is investment to GDP ratio, *gcon* is government consumption to *GDP* ratio.

The reported regression is a random-effects model, which produces more plausible estimates than the fixed-effects model (not reported).[7] The results suggest that income inequality is negatively and significantly associated with growth, with a parameter value of –0.07.[8] In addition to initial inequality, the above regression accounts for two pivotal macroeconomic growth variables (investment and government consumption) and a demographic variable, given by the growth of labor force relative to population growth.[9] The two macroeconomic variables could, arguably, account for, or at least reflect, all the macroeconomic effects that matter for growth. To the extent that instrumentation of the investment variables has successfully addressed its potential endogeneity, the effects of investment could be interpreted to account for overall economic reforms. However, in the presence of the other macroeconomic variables, investment may be capturing the effects of other structural reforms, such as the privatization of public enterprises, the resolution of debt-overhang problems, or liberalization of foreign direct investment regimes (Easterly, Loayza, and Montiel, 1996).[10]

*Persistence of growth*

Using the estimated long-run growth model of equation 9, we estimate the determinants of growth persistence before and after 1975, which marked the beginning of major episodes of external shocks that affected most of the developing world. The regression was based on the error-correction persistence model of equation 2. The estimation results are reported in equation 10 below:

$$\dot{g} = 0.85866 - 0.00069 conf4 - 15.8839 policy + 0.72405 ecm \quad (10)$$
$$(-3.403) \quad (-2.540) \quad (7.211)$$
$$Adj\ R^2 = 55.48 \quad F\text{-}test = 22.18 \quad N = 52$$

*Notes:*
$\dot{g}$ is defined as average annual rate of growth in 1975–96 minus average annual rate of growth for 1965–74.
*confl4* is defined as the std deviation of $\Delta\ln(TOT)_{70-79} \times openness_{70-79} \times gini_{65-74} \times democracy_{70s}$.
*policy* is defined as the "instrumented" change in government consumption as a ratio of GDP in 1975–96 relative to 1965–74.
*ecm* is defined as the predicted growth in 1964–74 period minus actual growth in the same period.

Following Rodrik (1998a), the key variable in this regression is 'Conflict,' which reflects the capacity (or, rather, the inability) of a society for managing external shocks.[11] External shocks can be economically costly when social divisions run deep (due, for example, to high income-inequality) and the society's institutions for conflict management are weak. Therefore, this variable suggests that the combination of deep social conflicts and weak social and political institutions tends to magnify the effects of external shocks on growth, by leading to growth-retarding policies (the precise definition of 'Conflict' is provided in the notes to equation 10). The estimated coefficient for Conflict was highly significant at -0.00069.[12] The above model also accounts for error-correction effects, which suggest that growth in the current period must accelerate, if growth in the previous period was lower than the rate consistent with long-term equilibrium growth. The estimated error-correction effect (at 0.72) was found to be highly significant as well as consistent with theoretical predictions. In addition to these two effects, the model accounts for the potential role of changes in policy in the dynamics of growth, by adding the change in government consumption to the set of explanatory variables. The latter variable could be interpreted as an indicator for recent macroeconomic reforms adopted by many countries, following the external shocks of the second half of the 1970s. The effect due to the change in government consumption (at -15.9) was, as expected, negatively and significantly associated with acceleration of growth.[13]

For the remainder of this section, we briefly analyze the poverty and distribution parameters that will be used, together with growth parameters, in computing the structural parameters and quantifying the policy predictions of the model of section 2.

### *3.ii Income Distribution and Poverty*

As is well known, high-quality data sets, permitting comparison of inequality across countries and regions, has only recently become available. The currently accepted criteria for high quality require that observations be based on comprehensive household surveys that comprehensively cover the whole population and use a comprehensive measure of income, including consumption out of own production. For the MENA region, only a limited sample is reported to have high-quality data sets. This is a limitation on this study as well. Thus the MENA countries in this chapter exclude both Iran and Turkey (with a combined weight of 34.4 percent of the population and 38.6 percent of the GDP of the region) owing to the lack of recent high-quality data. Excluded for the same reason are the countries in the GCC category (with a weight of 7.2 percent of the population and 28.6 percent of the GDP of the region) in addition to Iraq, which has been in a rather abnormal economic condition since the Gulf war. Of the remaining Arab countries, the sample used represents 68 percent of the population and 92.6 percent of GDP.

Given income distribution information, poverty results can be generated using appropriately specified poverty lines. Recent literature on the measurement of poverty revisited the issue of relative and absolute poverty lines (see, for example, Foster, 1998; and Atkinson, 1998). The motivation for this seems to be the established practice of estimating a poverty line on the basis of the basic needs approach (CBN) and of keeping such a line constant over time and across countries, as was done for the USA poverty studies until very recently. In contrast, European practice has been exclusively relative, in that it specifies the poverty line as a fixed proportion of the standard of living (e.g. 50 percent of median or mean income). Both practices have serious implications for the behavior of poverty over time. If the poverty line is allowed to change with income, the elasticity of the poverty line with respect to income becomes an important parameter in the behavior of poverty. This is the approach we follow here, given our concern with the dynamic relationship between growth, distribution, and poverty (see, for example, Ali and Thorbecke, 1998). In consequence, we use the following estimated poverty line equation (where figures between brackets are t-values):

$$\underset{(56.8)}{\text{Log } z = 1.3719} + \underset{(11.0)}{0.00303\, u} - \underset{(-5.3)}{0.000001886\, u^2}\ ;\ R^2 = 0.97 \qquad (11)$$

To generate the poverty results, we use the high-quality expenditure and distribution data of Deininger and Squire (1996) and the World Bank (1998). A summary of our results is reported in Table 3.1 for the four world regions with which we are dealing. For inequality we report the Gini coefficients, while for poverty we report the three standard measures: headcount ratio (H: to measure incidence or spread), the poverty-gap ratio (P1: to measure depth), and the squared poverty-gap ratio (P2: to measure severity). The reported results are averages over the results of individual countries generated by Povcal (a program used for grouped data: t-statistics are shown in brackets). We hasten to note that these are intended to be illustrative results for the purposes of making our dynamic model operational.

If we look first at expenditure distribution, we note that Latin America boasts the highest degree of inequality in the distribution of income, as reflected by a Gini coefficient of about 50 percent. Next highest in reported inequality is sub-Saharan Africa, with a Gini of 48 percent. The lowest inequality is reported for Asia, with a Gini coefficient of 37 percent, and the second lowest is MENA, with a Gini of about 39 percent. These results are in conformity with the generally accepted ranking among world regions. However, we note also that most of the distribution data for Latin America is based on income, whereas for other developing regions it is based on expenditure. Deininger and Squire (1996: 582) established the result that the Gini coefficients based on expenditure distribution are usually lower than those based on income by about 6.6 percentage points, and they therefore advise researchers to do the adjustment prior to drawing conclusions on ranking. On the basis of this adjustment, we see that the ranking above will remain intact, save for Africa and Latin America, which change places in terms of the highest inequality. MENA's inequality becomes moderate rather than on the low side.

**Table 3.1: Inequality and Poverty in a Sample of Countries by World Regions**

| Region | No. of Countries | Mean Expenditure* (US$) | Poverty Line* (US$) | Gini Coefficient (%) Fine | Head-Count Ratio (%)Fine | Poverty-Gap Ratio (%Fine) | Squared Poverty-Gap Ratio (% Fine) |
|---|---|---|---|---|---|---|---|
| MENA | 6 | 115.3 | 50.8 | 38.95 | 21.52 | 6.51 | 3.38 |
| | | (45.1) | (13.7) | (3.61) | (8.80) | (5.83) | (4.91) |
| Africa | 18 | 75.0 | 41.9 | 48.0 | 52.10 | 23.04 | 13.21 |
| | | (70.4) | (24.2) | (10.07) | (13.78) | (8.06) | (5.87) |
| Asia | 8 | 97.67 | 45.84 | 37.03 | 24.72 | 6.99 | 2.95 |
| | | (45.62) | (13.37) | (7.18) | (12.22) | (4.25) | (2.03) |
| Latin America | 16 | 172.7 | 73.6 | 50.38 | 34.83 | 14.40 | 7.94 |
| | | (82.0) | (32.7) | (6.69) | (8.57) | (5.04) | (3.59) |
| Overall | 48 | 109.1 | 52.0 | 45.83 | 37.96 | 15.42 | 8.51 |
| | | (78.6) | (27.8) | (9.39) | (16.33) | (9.10) | (6.08) |

*Note:* * Per person per month.
*Source:* Own calculations.

As indicated by the standard deviation, there exists variation among countries in the degree of inequality. In the MENA sample that we are using, the lowest inequality is reported for Egypt, with a Gini coefficient of 30 percent in 1991 (i.e. a Gini of 37 percent for income distribution), followed by Morocco and Algeria with a Gini of about 39 percent each. The highest inequality is reported for Mauritania with a Gini coefficient of 42.5 percent, followed by Jordan (40.7 percent) and Tunisia (40 percent).

Given our method of estimating the poverty line, the table shows that MENA can claim the lowest poverty for all measures except for the severity of poverty. Asia follows in second place as the region with lowest poverty in terms of incidence and depth, but ranks first in terms of severity. Africa is the highest poverty region for all poverty measures, followed by Latin America. Thus, according to the above results, about 22 percent of MENA population were living below a poverty line of US$51 per person per month in the early 1990s. At the other extreme, 52 percent of Africa's population were living below a poverty line of US$42 per person per month. Among MENA countries, the highest incidence of poverty in the sample is recorded for Mauritania, where 39 percent of the population lived below a poverty line of US$33 per person per month. On the other hand, the lowest incidence of poverty is recorded for Egypt, with 14 percent of the population living below a poverty line of US$42 per person per month.

Similar results can be read for the depth and severity of poverty as recorded by the poverty-gap and the squared poverty-gap measures, respectively. Using Table 3.1, we can easily calculate the average income of the poor, where this is shown to be US$34 per person per month in MENA, compared with US$23 per person per month in Africa, and US$44 for Latin America. Among MENA countries, the lowest average income for the poor of US$18 per person per month is recorded for Mauritania.

For the purposes of our model, the sensitivity of poverty with respect to growth (changes in per capita consumption expenditure or income) and distribution (changes in the Gini coefficient) is important. Table 3.2 reports a summary of the elasticity of the various poverty measures to growth and distribution. We also report the elasticity of the poverty line with respect to income. These elasticities, together with the elasticity of the Gini coefficient with respect to income, will be combined to arrive at the overall growth elasticity of poverty. For ease of reference, the elasticity with respect to income will be denoted by -η(y), while that for the Gini coefficient will be denoted by , where the argument y denotes the poverty measure (H, P1, and P2). The elasticity of the poverty line with respect to income will be denoted by ε.

**Table 3.2: The Sensitivity of Poverty to Growth and Distribution: Summary Elasticities**

| Region | -η(H) | -η(P1) | -η(P2) | θ(*H*) | θ(*P*1) | θ(*P*2) | ε |
|---|---|---|---|---|---|---|---|
| MENA | -2.29 | -3.20 | -4.00 | 2.83 | 6.21 | 9.48 | 0.29 |
| | (0.77) | (1.48) | (2.36) | (1.14) | (2.14) | (3.28) | (0.10) |
| Africa | -0.98 | -1.43 | -1.76 | 0.64 | 2.43 | 4.17 | 0.19 |
| | (0.47) | (0.60) | (0.76) | (0.77) | (1.37) | (1.92) | (0.14) |
| Asia | -2.44 | -3.42 | -4.28 | 2.54 | 5.65 | 8.66 | 0.25 |
| | (1.12) | (2.13) | (3.26) | (1.63) | (3.18) | (4.82) | (0.10) |
| Latin | -1.17 | -1.52 | -1.92 | 1.52 | 4.32 | 7.04 | 0.39 |
| America | (0.37) | (0.59) | (0.86) | (0.59) | (0.96) | (1.37) | (0.14) |
| Sample | -1.45 | -2.01 | -2.51 | 1.52 | 4.07 | 6.54 | 0.26 |
| | (0.86) | (1.37) | (1.94) | (1.25) | (2.24) | (3.26) | (0.15) |

*Source:* Own calculations (standard deviations in parentheses).

The table, further, indicates that the pattern of sensitivity of poverty is similar in MENA and Asia, where it is seen that poverty is responsive both to growth and to distribution and where sensitivity to distribution is consistently higher than that to growth. The sensitivity of poverty to growth is marginally higher in Asia than in MENA, while the reverse is true for distribution. Thus, for example, a percentage point increase in per capita consumption expenditure will be expected to reduce poverty by 2.3 and 2.4 percentage points in MENA and Asia, respectively. A percentage point decline in the Gini coefficient, on the other hand, will be expected to reduce poverty by 6.2 and 5.7 percentage points in MENA and Asia, respectively. By contrast, the sensitivity of poverty to growth and distribution is lowest in Africa, followed by Latin America. However, the sensitivity of poverty to changes in the distribution of income in Latin America is almost double that of Africa.

To obtain the growth elasticity of poverty after allowing for changes in the distribution of income over time and for the functional dependence of the poverty line on mean income would require specifying the way in which distribution changes with income. The most celebrated result in this respect is that of Kuznets (1955), where it is argued that in the early stages of development inequality tends to increase before it declines.[14] Such a relationship is seen as reflecting a long-term transformation process during which production structures as well as institutions change. Owing to a lack of long time-series observations on inequality measures, the empirical testing of the Kuznets' hypothesis proceeded on the basis of cross-section estimation. Anand and Kanbur (1993) subjected the hypothesis to in-depth scrutiny both theoretical and empirical. As a result of this investigation, they argued that the most suitable format for testing the hypothesis, using the Gini coefficient as the indicator of inequality, is to regress it on income per capita and its reciprocal. On the basis of such an estimate, a Kuznets elasticity can be calculated. For the purposes of applying our model, we estimated such a relationship for our sample of countries where the income variable is taken as real per capita consumption in 1987 prices. We included in the estimation the year of observation to capture any time trend. The results of the estimation is reported in equation 12 below, where figures in parentheses are t-values:[15]

$$\text{Gini} = \underset{(21.3)}{0.0267\,T} - \underset{(-5.7)}{0.002\,u} - \underset{(-3.9)}{2486.7\,(1/u)};\ R^2 = 0.44 \qquad (12)$$

It should be easy to calculate the turning point on the above Kuznets curve as about US$1111 of private per capita consumption in 1987 prices. Thus countries with per capita consumption lower than this turning point would be expected to experience increasing inequality as their economies transform, other things being the same. Beyond the turning point, countries are experiencing declining inequality. This is the sense in which a Kuznets relationship is useful in the context of the dynamic interaction between growth, inequality, and poverty.

On the basis of the above estimated equation, the Kuznets elasticity, $\kappa$, is given by:

$$\kappa = [-0.0020155\ u + 2486.7/u]\ (1/\text{Gini}) \qquad (13)$$

Using the country information, we see that the average Kuznets elasticity for the MENA region is 0.05, with a standard deviation of 0.06. Higher average elasticities are recorded for Africa (0.161, with a standard deviation of 0.174) and Asia (0.244, with a standard deviation of 0.148). The average Kuznets elasticity for Latin America is 0.01, with a standard deviation of 0.04. Not surprisingly, most of the developing countries in the sample were found to be below the turning point, except for 14 out of the 48 countries covered by the sample (see Appendix Table 3.A2). This last group includes only two Arab countries: Algeria and Jordan, with mean per capita consumption of US$1243 and US$1352, respectively.

## 4. The Dynamics of Growth and Poverty in the Arab World and Other Regions

In the model of section 2, dynamic behavior obtains if $\hat{p}$ and $\dot{g}$ are not assumed to be equal to zero. The analysis is based on equations 14 and 15 below, which are, respectively, generated by substituting (5), (7), and -(8) in (2), and (7) in (5):

$$\dot{g} = -\lambda_1 \tau G(1 - I)G + \lambda_2(\beta_0(\tilde{G}_0 - G_0) + \frac{1}{\alpha}\hat{p}_0] + \lambda_3\ (Policy - Policy_0) \qquad (14)$$

$$\hat{p} = -\alpha g + \alpha_0 = \alpha(g^\circ - g) = \alpha\beta_0(G - \tilde{G}) + \alpha(\tilde{g}_F - g_F)^{16} \qquad (15)$$

Equation 14 suggests that the dynamic path of growth (persistence) is accounted for by four influences. First, acceleration of growth is negatively influenced by the external shock effect, with the extent of inequality and ineffectiveness of institutions determining the magnification effect of the shock. This effect is obvious and was sufficiently motivated by Rodrik (1998a). Second, it is positively influenced by the extent to which the initial steady-state level of inequality $\tilde{G}_0$ (consistent with $\dot{g} = \hat{p} = 0$) is larger than actual levels of inequality in the initial period ($G_0$), with the effect weighted by (the absolute value of) the elasticity of inequality on growth ($\beta_0$). This effect suggests that when inequality in the initial period was lower than the level consistent with zero rate of growth acceleration, the latter must be positive in the current period before a new steady state with higher growth and a lower level of poverty is reached. Third, growth acceleration is also positively affected by the rate of change of poverty in the previous period weighted by the inverse elasticity of poverty on growth ($\frac{1}{\alpha}$). This effect is consistent with a welfare function that targets a zero or negative change in poverty, which suggests that for any given level of inequality in the initial period, a rise in poverty in the initial period requires acceleration of growth in the current period to address the poverty problem. The fourth effect suggests that a change in policy (say, an improvement in policy) between the two periods should lead to acceleration of growth. The last three channels are all generated by the error-correction extension to Rodrik's model.

Finally, equation 15 suggests that when growth rates in the initial period fall short of the rate consistent with a stationary level of poverty, poverty will worsen in the current period. How far poverty rises will depend on the extent of the growth shortfall and on the size of the net growth effect on the rate of change of poverty ($\alpha$). Similarly, poverty worsens in the current period when initial inequality exceeds the level consistent with a stationary level of poverty. For a given wedge between the two levels of initial inequality, the rise in poverty depends on the product $\alpha\beta$, where the latter is the negative of the effect of inequality on long-term growth. Moreover, the net change in poverty can be expressed as an outcome of a pure income effect (negative for positive growth rates) plus a pure (positive) distributional effect.

Appendix Table 3.A2 provides estimates of the poverty line, three measures of poverty as well as the elasticities for poverty, the poverty line, and the Kuznets curve. Appendix Tables 3.A4, 3.A5, and 3.A6 compute the key structural parameters and indexes of the model, based on the poverty-gap ratio (P1). Further analysis will be confined to this index of poverty. The computations of these tables provide the estimates for the structural parameters of equations 14 and 15. This allows us to illustrate some of the key predictions of the theoretical model. First, we undertake a decomposition analysis of the factors that led to the collapse of growth in the post-1975 period across the developing world, except in Asia. The post-1975 era has been characterized with various episodes of massive external shocks, primarily in terms of negative trade shocks, but in terms of spells of positive shocks as well. Second, we undertake a similar analysis of the behavior of poverty since 1975. In both cases we also analyze the country-specific dynamic behavior of growth and poverty in the six Arab countries.

## *4.i The Post-1975 Collapse of Growth in the Arab World*

Persistence of growth (average annual rate of growth in 1975–96 minus the rate for 1965–74) is explained by four potential determinants (equation 14): the capacity of a society to manage the impact of exogenous shocks (both negative or positive: see note 10), represented by the variable 'Conflict'; the change in macroeconomic policy, perhaps due to economic reforms in response to shocks; the extent to which society is equal relative to the level consistent with steady-state equilibrium (stationary poverty and zero acceleration/deceleration of growth); and the extent of poverty in the initial period. The results by regional median are shown in Figure 3.1. Appendix Table 3.A5 contains detailed country-by-country results.

We begin by analyzing the median growth performance at the regional level inside and outside the Arab world. Notwithstanding possible country-specific anomalies, the main regional story bodes quite well with other stylized facts on cross-regional performances.

First, between the two periods, median annual rates of growth decelerated by -1.6 percent in the Arab world, -2.0 percent in Sub-Saharan Africa (SSA), and -1.7 percent in Latin America and the Caribbean (LAC), while growth accelerated by 0.4 percent in Asia. By and large, the observed rates of changes were explained by the four channels identified above, where the differences between the actual and the predicted change in the rates of growth are less than 40 percent for any of the three regions.

Second, the role of the capacity for managing conflicts following external shocks was one of the main factors behind this outcome in the Arab world, SSA, and to a lesser extent LAC and Asia. The failures of the Arab world, SSA, and LAC in this area contribute -1.0 percent, -1.1, and -0.5 percent, respectively, to the collapse of growth in the two regions; while it would have decelerated growth by -0.1 percent in Asia, if other factors had remained at their 1965–74 levels.

Third, the nature of income distribution in the preceding period plays the most dominant role in setting Asia apart from the other two regions. This factor could be interpreted as the 'absolute conflict' effect. A more equitable initial income distribution (relative to levels consistent with steady state) in Asia has had a partial contribution of 0.8 percent per

**Figure 3.1: Determinants of Growth Dynamics in Arab Countries and Other Regions in 1975–96 Relative to 1965–74 (average annual % change)**

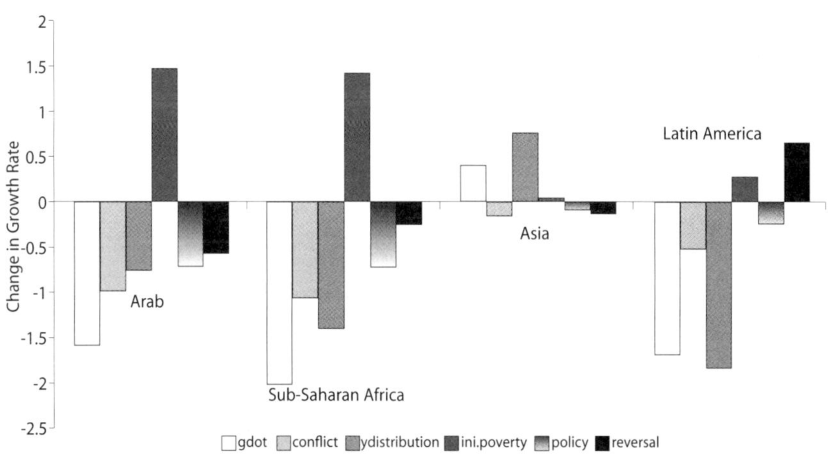


*Notes:* gdot = average annual rate of growth in 1975–96 minus average annual rate of growth in 1965–74.
Conflict ≡ component of change due to conflict (*confl4* is used: see Ali and Elbadawi, 1999, notes to Table 4.2).
Inequality ≡ component of change due to initial inequality (lagged Gini).
Ini.poverty ≡ component of change due to behavior of poverty in the initial period (rate of change of poverty in 1965–74).
Policy ≡ annual average rate of change in government consumption between the two periods.
*Source:* Appendix Table 3.A5.

annum to subsequent growth acceleration in the post-1975 period. On the other hand, less equitable initial income distributions (as in SSA and LAC), or low initial inequality but still higher than steady-state levels (as in the Arab world), have, respectively, accounted for -0.8 percent, -1.4, and -1.9 percent of the deceleration of growth in the three regions during the post-1975 era.

Fourth, rising poverty in the preceding period appears to matter, as a trigger factor, for generating concerns about the need to accelerate growth in the current period. The motivation for policy makers, for example, to be concerned about growth when poverty is high or rising could be justified by altruistic political motives on the part of the ruling elites. This effect would have led to acceleration of growth by about 1.4 percent in the Arab world and SSA, if other factors remained at their initial levels. However, the effects of this factor were small for the other two regions: about 0.3 percent for LAC and a negligible 0.01 percent for Asia. The results for Asia appear consistent with the sustained growth acceleration and relatively better performance of poverty over time.

Fifth, the direct effect of change in policy was generally of a lesser order of magnitude compared with the others. However, while it accounted for only a miniscule part of growth in Asia (-0.09 percent) and only a small fraction in LAC (-0.3 percent), a worsening policy environment would have had caused a higher growth-reducing effect in both the Arab world and SSA (at -0.7 percent).

Finally, diversity abounds, even among the limited number of countries considered from the Arab region (Jordan is not considered for lack of data). For example, unlike the median performance of the group, Egypt and Mauritania have actually experienced growth acceleration rather than deceleration. In the case of Egypt, the observed growth acceleration (at an annual average rate of 2.4 percent) was substantially accounted for by the four channels—where the combined positive effects due to equitable initial income distribution, initial poverty, and macroeconomic policy improvement (at 3.8 percent) more than compensated for the negative effects due to shocks and social conflicts (at -1.0 percent). For the case of Mauritania, however, the model predicts growth deceleration rather than the observed growth acceleration. In this case, the positive effects on growth of initial poverty (at 1.5 percent) were dominated by the combined negative effects of the other three factors (at -3.6). The model also fails to predict the actual deceleration of growth in Morocco (-1.6 percent) and Tunisia (-2.0), where it predicts acceleration driven by the initial poverty effects. However, as in the case of Egypt, the model accurately predicts growth deceleration in Algeria (at -2.5 percent), where the positive effect due to initial poverty was substantially dominated by the combined negative impact of the remaining three factors. The model also predicts shocks and social conflicts to have strong and deleterious effects on growth in Algeria, Egypt, and Mauritania, while these were predicted to have much less effect in the cases of Morocco and Tunisia. This prediction is strongly corroborated by stylized facts about the five countries.

### *4.ii The Behavior of Poverty in the Arab World since 1975*

The behavior of poverty over time (estimated average annual rate of change in poverty during 1975–96) is explained by the net effects on poverty of growth and distribution (equation 15). The results, by regional median, are shown in Figure 3.2. Appendix Table 3.A6 contains detailed country-by-country results.

Starting with the analysis of the median regional change in poverty, we note that as in the case of growth—and notwithstanding some possible country-specific anomalies—the main regional story bodes quite well for the future in the light of other stylized facts on cross-regional performances. First, between the two periods, median poverty rose by about 0.8 percent for the Arab world, 1.3 percent for SSA, and 1.9 percent for LAC, while it declined by -2.3 percent for Asia.

Second, the income-invariant distributional effect would have led to a rise in poverty in all regions: by 4.4 percent for the Arab world, 1.4 percent for SSA, 2.3 percent for LAC, and 3.3 percent for Asia. However, unlike the other three regions, the 'pure' growth effect in Asia substantially dominated the distributional effect. While, for unchanged distribution, sustained growth acceleration would have reduced poverty in Asia by about -5.6 percent, growth was rather inconsequential in two of the remaining three regions (it would have reduced poverty by -0.1 per cent for SSA and -0.5 percent for LAC). On the other hand, while the growth effect in the Arab region was substantial (at -3.6 percent), the estimated distributional effect was even higher (at 4.4 percent). Therefore, it is not surprizing that Asia experienced an overall decline in poverty, while the reverse happened in the other three regions.

Third, the results for Asia appear to support the Kuznets thesis, where growth was associated with rising inequality, even though the former was sufficiently deep to lead to overall poverty reduction despite worsening income distribution. On the other hand, the results of the other three regions describe cases of either high but not sufficient growth (Arab world) or a combination of decelerating growth and worsening income distribution, with the latter determining the net effect on poverty (SSA and LAC).

**Figure 3.2: Dynamics of Poverty in Arab Countries and Other Regions (predicted annual average change in poverty for 1975–96)**

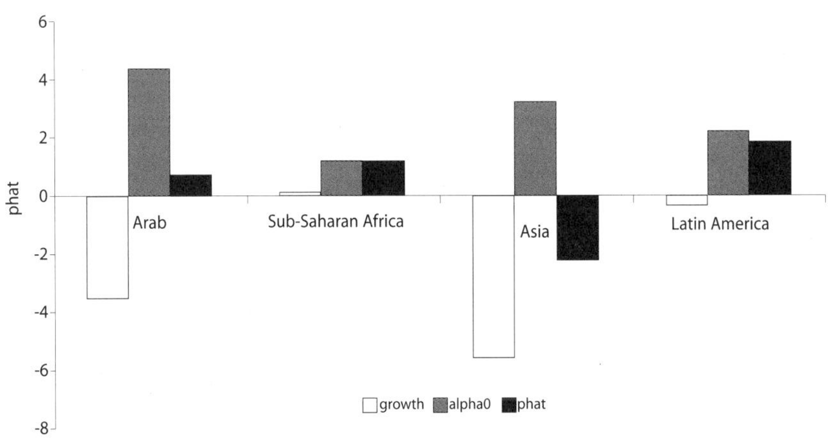


*Notes:* Growth: component of change in poverty due to growth.
alpha0: component of change due to distribution.
phat: net change in poverty.
*Source:* Appendix Table 3.A6.

Finally, the predicted performance of poverty also reveals a diverse set of experiences among the six Arab countries. For example, unlike the group median behavior, poverty in Egypt and Jordan was predicted to have declined during the period, where the poverty-reducing growth effect dominated the distribution effect. On the other hand, for Morocco and Tunisia the growth effect was strong, but not strong enough to dominate the very substantial distributional effects. However, unlike the former two counties, the remaining two cases of Algeria and Mauritania are fairly straightforward, where the growth effects were marginal.

## 5. Strategies for Poverty Reduction in the Arab World

In section 4, we discussed the dynamic behavior of inequality, poverty, and growth around the steady state, where six phases were identified, two of which give rise to stable paths toward the steady state (Appendix Figure 3.A1). Based on average growth, poverty, and distribution performance (Appendix Table 3.A7), Table 3.3 classifies the six Arab countries according to the phase they are likely to be associated with during the 1975–96 period. We discuss below this classification and the implied strategy for poverty reduction in these countries.[17]

First, in the case of Algeria during 1975–96, economic performance was characterized by rising poverty, decelerating growth, and higher levels of inequality than are consistent with the steady state. According to our model, Algeria was located in Phase VI, which produces a 'transitional low equilibrium trap,' driven by an unstable path of rising poverty. For this country, both low growth and bad distribution are constraints on sustainable poverty reduction. However, redistributive measures are particularly important to move the Algerian economy to Phase IV (to the left of the $G = \widetilde{G}$ schedule: Appendix Figure 3.A1), where the rise in poverty will come to a halt at the steady state along a stable path. Moreover, a combination of growth acceleration and efficient distributional measures could push the country further to Phase III, where poverty declines continuously along a transitional unstable path of 'super-performance.'

Second, Phase V contains two Arab countries (Mauritania and Morocco) that have similar initial economic indicators as those of Algeria, except that they were able—on average—to accelerate growth. Nevertheless, these countries will eventually diverge to Phase VI and therefore are likely to be located in the region characterized by the 'transitional low equilibrium trap.' Even though growth may be less of a constraint for these countries, they would need the same redistributive measures recommended for Algeria.

Third, in terms of overall average performance during 1975–96, the Egyptian economy was one of equitable income distribution (relative to steady-state levels) and declining poverty, despite decelerating economic growth. Based on this performance, the Egyptian economy is located in Phase II, which diverges into an unstable path of continuously declining poverty. This is probably the phase consistent with the good side of the Kuznets curve, where only growth matters for simultaneously reducing poverty and improving distribution over time. This would happen if this phase also produces a relatively sustained era of 'transitional super-performance.' However, and as the recent Asian crisis attests, it appears that the real challenge for maintaining this 'potentially' unstable phase as long as possible is maintaining high growth, and especially avoiding growth collapse.

**Table 3.3: Strategies for Poverty Reduction in the Arab World**

(based on average performance in 1975–96)

| Countries | Phases | Performance post-1975 (Appendix Table 3.A7) | Predicted Performance/ Recommended Strategy |
|---|---|---|---|
| Jordan, Tunisia | Phase I<br>$G > \tilde{G}$<br>$\hat{P} < 0$<br>$\dot{g} < 0$ | 1. Declining poverty<br>2. Decelerating growth<br>3. Inequality higher than levels consistent with steady-state | 1. Poverty would decline at a decreasing rate along a stable path toward the steady state.<br>2. Avoiding growth collapse and achieving more equitable distribution would prolong the cycle of declining poverty (shift to Phase III). |
| Egypt | Phase II<br>$G < \tilde{G}$<br>$\hat{P} < 0$<br>$\dot{g} < 0$ | 1. Declining poverty<br>2. Decelerating growth<br>3. Inequality lower than steady-state levels | 1. Divergent phase into an unstable path of continuously declining poverty.<br>2. Distribution is not a constraint. Accelerating growth, especially avoiding growth collapse(East Asia recent experience), should be the key element of the strategy. |
| Mauritania, Morocco | Phase V<br>$G > \tilde{G}$<br>$\hat{P} > 0$<br>$\dot{g} > 0$ | 1. Rising poverty<br>2. Accelerating growth<br>3. Inequality higher than steady-state levels | 1. Divergent phase of continuously rising poverty: 'transitional low equilibrium trap'<br>2. Growth is not an immediate constraint, but redistributive measures will be required to shift the economy to Phase IV, and possibly Phase III. |
| Algeria | Phase VI<br>$G > \tilde{G}$<br>$\hat{P} > 0$<br>$\dot{g} < 0$ | 1. Rising poverty<br>2. Decelerating growth<br>3. Inequality higher than steady-state levels | 1. Unstable path toward continuously rising poverty: 'transitional low equilibrium trap.'<br>2. Both growth and distribution are constraints, but redistributive measures will be required to shift the economy to phase IV, and possibly Phase III. |

*Source:* Appendix Table 3.A7

Finally, two more countries (Jordan and Tunisia) were located in Phase I, where growth was decelerating, inequality was higher than steady-state levels, yet poverty was declining. This last could be accounted for by high and efficient, though decelerating, growth rates. However, for this group, poverty is predicted to decline at a decreasing rate along a stable path and will, therefore, come to a halt at the steady state. For this group, both distribution and growth are important. For example, a collapse of growth (negative rates of real growth) might push these countries into a transitional 'low equilibrium trap,' where poverty rises over time (as seems to be the case of Jordan since the late 1980s). On the other hand, more equitable distribution and positive growth could move these countries into a 'transitional super-performance' phase, and hence produce a more sustained era of declining poverty.

To recapitulate: the central tenets of the recommended strategies are that—with the exception of Egypt, where only growth was the constraint—both distribution and growth are constraints. For the cases of Jordan and Tunisia, both measures would be required to prolong the phase of poverty decline, and hence bring down poverty to acceptable levels at the steady state when poverty becomes stationary. Moreover, for the cases of Algeria, Mauritania, and Morocco, both measures would be required before the three countries could escape the dire consequences of a possibly lingering, though transitional, 'low equilibrium trap' of rising poverty. Admittedly, the above analysis depends on the estimated (or assumed) initial performance of the countries in terms of growth acceleration and changes in poverty and distribution. The simulated strategies for dealing with poverty are, therefore, contingent on the choice of the initial period. However, we do not anticipate the central thesis—that both growth and distribution would be required for sustainable reduction of poverty—to change. If anything, with lower growth, the emphasis on the centrality of both measures is likely to be strengthened rather than weakened.[18]

## 6. Conclusions

In this chapter an attempt was made to explore the dynamic interaction between economic growth, distribution of income, and poverty in the context of a simple model. The analysis highlighted the factors that led to the growth collapse as well as the rise in poverty in the Arab world and other developing regions, except Asia, during the 1975–96 period. The model also suggests tentative country-specific strategies for dealing with poverty in the six Arab countries under scrutiny.

To identify these broad strategies, indicators of country performance during 1975–96—in terms of the rate of acceleration of growth, changes in poverty, and the extent of inequality—were used. The recommended strategies suggest that for Egypt only growth was the major constraint and that growth acceleration and, especially avoidance of growth collapse, would position this country on an unstable, though possibly prolonged, path of declining poverty. For all remaining five countries, both growth and distribution would be required for achieving a lasting impact on poverty. In the cases of Jordan and Tunisia, both would be required to prolong the phase of poverty declines, and hence bring down poverty to acceptable levels at the steady state when poverty becomes stationary. Moreover, for the cases of Algeria, Mauritania, and Morocco, both measures would be required before the three countries could escape the severe consequences of a possibly rather long, though transitional, 'low equilibrium trap' of rising poverty. Moreover, the recommended strategies would still be valid, in our view, should we confine the initial performance period to 1986–96, which witnessed an overall economic slowdown in the region. If anything, with lower growth, the emphasis on the centrality of both measures is likely to be strengthened rather than weakened.

## Appendix

### Table 3.A1: Mean Expenditure and Gini Coefficients for a Sample of Countries

(mean expenditure in 1987 PPP dollars and Gini coefficients in percentages)

| Country (year) | Mean Exp. $/pers./yr | Gini Coeff. (%) | Country (year) | Mean Exp. $/pers./yr | Gini Coeff. (%) | Country (year) | Mean Exp. $/pers./yr | Gini Coeff. (%) |
|---|---|---|---|---|---|---|---|---|
| Bolivia (90) | 1034.3 | 42.04 | Bangladesh (89) | 630.2 | 26.92 | Spain (88) | 4576.9 | 28.16 |
| Brazil (85) | 1474.8 | 59.54 | India (83) | 322.0 | 32.2 | Australia (85) | 7939.3 | 37.83 |
| Chile (89) | 1590.4 | 57.88 | Nepal (85) | 474.2 | 30.06 | UK (88) | 7752.4 | 39.83 |
| Colombia (88) | 2462.6 | 53.11 | Pakistan(91) | 797.0 | 31.15 | Italy (86) | 7220.7 | 34.03 |
| Costa Rica (89) | 1168.4 | 46.07 | Sri Lanka (90) | 585.5 | 32.47 | Netherlands (88) | 6880.8 | 28.78 |
| Dom. Rep. (89) | 1148.3 | 50.46 | Botswana (86) | 929.2 | 54.21 | Canada (87) | 9275.0 | 34.59 |
| Guatemala (87) | 527.9 | 58.26 | Cote d'Ivoire (85) | 839.5 | 44.63 | Belgium (79) | 7034.9 | 28.08 |
| Honduras (89) | 539.4 | 59.49 | Ethiopia (82) | 568.2 | 35.90 | Finland (81) | 6241.8 | 31.91 |
| Jamaica (90) | 1540.4 | 43.16 | Ghana (88) | 875.5 | 36.74 | France (89) | 7179.9 | 36.05 |
| Mexico (84) | 1158.6 | 50.71 | Kenya (92) | 703.3 | 57.46 | Germany (88) | 6806.2 | 33.29 |
| Panama (89) | 1313.9 | 56.57 | Lesotho (87) | 722.4 | 56.02 | USA (85) | 12195.4 | 37.35 |
| Peru (86) | 937.7 | 45.72 | Mauritania (88) | 663.0 | 42.53 | Norway (79) | 7338.2 | 30.92 |
| Venezuela (89) | 1003.7 | 44.08 | Senegal(92) | 550.0 | 54.12 | Denmark (81) | 7241.3 | 33.62 |
| China (85) | 888.2 | 32.96 | Tanzania (91) | 873.6 | 59.01 | Sweden (81) | 6690.4 | 29.19 |
| Indonesia (84) | 537.0 | 34.15 | Zambia (91) | 242.8 | 43.51 | Japan (79) | 6898.1 | 28.70 |
| Philippines (88) | 792.6 | 40.68 | Zimbabwe (90) | 939.6 | 56.83 | Switzerland (82) | 10096.9 | 38.99 |
| Thailand (88) | 1210.4 | 43.81 | New Zealand (82) | 6165.0 | 39.50 | Average | 3151.6 | 41.67 |

*Source:* Chen, Datt, and Ravallion (1993) and World Bank (1994).

## Table 3.A2: Poverty Line, Inequality and Poverty Measures,

| | Country | Year | $\mu$ | PRC | Z | G | H | P1 | P2 |
|---|---|---|---|---|---|---|---|---|---|
| 1 | Algeria | 88 | 118.00 | 1243.76 | 50.40 | 39.281 | 16.870 | 4.210 | 1.710 |
| 2 | Botswana* | 86 | 53.67 | 472.10 | 33.81 | 54.209 | 54.460 | 25.630 | 15.020 |
| 3 | Cote d'Ivoire | 88 | 65.00 | 612.08 | 36.38 | 36.893 | 30.100 | 8.860 | 3.520 |
| 4 | Egypt | 91 | 88.77 | 659.49 | 42.27 | 32.006 | 13.880 | 2.080 | 0.420 |
| 5 | Gabon | 77 | 133.04 | 2621.09 | 55.16 | 62.872 | 46.220 | 21.640 | 12.710 |
| 6 | Guinea | 95 | 28.42 | 299.73 | 28.61 | 46.870 | 63.680 | 34.430 | 23.360 |
| 7 | Guinea Bissau | 91 | 37.27 | 143.24 | 30.35 | 56.168 | 61.860 | 34.810 | 24.430 |
| 8 | Kenya | 92 | 49.95 | 232.65 | 33.00 | 57.891 | 59.400 | 28.420 | 17.020 |
| 9 | Lesotho | 87 | 80.79 | 331.00 | 40.21 | 56.011 | 45.770 | 21.790 | 13.160 |
| 10 | Madagascar | 93 | 31.72 | 183.84 | 29.25 | 43.459 | 65.480 | 27.970 | 15.100 |
| 11 | Mauritania | 88 | 51.00 | 363.90 | 33.23 | 42.535 | 38.720 | 18.190 | 13.330 |
| 12 | Mauritius | 91 | 278.79 | 1352.70 | 117.50 | 36.555 | 16.010 | 4.240 | 1.750 |
| 13 | Morocco | 91 | 110.77 | 691.00 | 48.35 | 39.200 | 21.340 | 4.970 | 1.540 |
| 14 | Niger | 92 | 32.40 | 211.88 | 29.38 | 36.243 | 61.060 | 21.590 | 10.150 |
| 15 | Nigeria | 93 | 62.85 | 139.57 | 35.88 | 44.893 | 40.030 | 17.530 | 10.010 |
| 16 | Rwanda | 83 | 36.34 | 329.57 | 30.17 | 29.066 | 50.030 | 13.120 | 4.570 |
| 17 | Senegal | 91 | 63.04 | 487.82 | 35.93 | 54.117 | 49.660 | 22.670 | 13.080 |
| 18 | South Africa | 93 | 229.20 | 1401.39 | 92.75 | 61.060 | 45.610 | 23.500 | 14.970 |
| 19 | Tanzania | 93 | 26.00 | 125.54 | 28.15 | 38.102 | 70.950 | 30.500 | 16.340 |
| 20 | Tunisia | 90 | 184.24 | 784.44 | 73.47 | 40.001 | 19.140 | 5.320 | 1.990 |
| 21 | Uganda | 93 | 30.18 | 445.99 | 28.95 | 40.740 | 67.420 | 27.640 | 14.120 |
| 22 | Zambia | 76 | 52.13 | 208.27 | 33.48 | 51.998 | 52.420 | 24.240 | 14.190 |
| 23 | Zimbabwe | 90 | 58.52 | 317.20 | 34.89 | 56.834 | 57.560 | 26.070 | 14.270 |
| | **Africa** | **Average** | **82.70** | **593.84** | **43.55** | **45.96** | **45.55** | **19.54** | **11.16** |
| | | **$\sigma$** | **66.96** | **581.34** | **22.45** | **9.84** | **18.03** | **10.18** | **6.90** |
| 1 | Bangladesh | 86 | 45.45 | 143.00 | 32.04 | 38.976 | 41.670 | 12.860 | 5.900 |
| 2 | China | 92 | 132.06 | 169.90 | 54.85 | 37.256 | 18.750 | 7.260 | 3.910 |
| 3 | India | 92 | 44.21 | 238.59 | 31.78 | 32.044 | 40.840 | 10.370 | 3.650 |
| 4 | Indonesia | 93 | 107.72 | 361.12 | 47.47 | 31.688 | 10.680 | 1.190 | 0.180 |
| 5 | Jordan | 91 | 139.09 | 1352.86 | 57.13 | 40.656 | 19.190 | 4.260 | 1.270 |
| 6 | Malaysia | 89 | 182.51 | 1121.98 | 72.79 | 48.351 | 28.430 | 9.370 | 4.060 |
| 7 | Pakistan | 91 | 80.29 | 238.94 | 40.09 | 31.143 | 15.130 | 3.420 | 1.300 |
| 8 | Philippines | 88 | 104.00 | 418.95 | 46.41 | 46.665 | 29.310 | 9.230 | 4.080 |
| 9 | Sri Lanka | 90 | 85.10 | 321.75 | 41.31 | 30.098 | 12.940 | 2.180 | 0.510 |
| | **Asia** | **Average** | **102.27** | **485.23** | **47.10** | **37.43** | **24.10** | **6.68** | **2.76** |
| | | **$\sigma$** | **44.85** | **439.15** | **13.06** | **6.83** | **11.58** | **4.07** | **1.98** |
| 1 | Bolivia | 90 | 71.57 | 559.90 | 37.94 | 42.038 | 34.460 | 11.500 | 5.040 |
| 2 | Brazil | 89 | 282.15 | 1254.23 | 119.31 | 60.662 | 48.050 | 23.420 | 13.930 |
| 3 | Chile | 94 | 226.66 | 1538.71 | 91.57 | 56.493 | 38.100 | 14.950 | 7.530 |
| 4 | Columbia | 91 | 226.43 | 786.69 | 91.47 | 50.293 | 28.340 | 11.810 | 6.680 |
| 5 | Costa Rica | 89 | 191.14 | 1020.60 | 76.23 | 46.116 | 25.690 | 10.420 | 5.700 |
| 6 | Dom. Rep. | 89 | 124.93 | 651.40 | 52.60 | 50.789 | 32.800 | 11.900 | 5.730 |
| 7 | El Salvador | 77 | 91.97 | 1073.20 | 43.11 | 47.462 | 39.720 | 13.440 | 5.650 |
| 8 | Guatemala | 89 | 155.93 | 719.53 | 62.88 | 59.899 | 40.840 | 20.510 | 13.220 |
| 9 | Honduras | 92 | 77.12 | 640.73 | 39.30 | 51.752 | 41.050 | 16.940 | 9.410 |
| 10 | Jamaica | 93 | 120.71 | 1126.84 | 51.31 | 37.916 | 17.630 | 4.020 | 1.240 |
| 11 | Mexico | 89 | 300.86 | 1230.72 | 129.66 | 55.278 | 38.200 | 16.450 | 9.340 |
| 12 | Nicaragua | 93 | 59.83 | 692.82 | 35.19 | 50.072 | 47.020 | 19.820 | 10.720 |
| 13 | Panama | 89 | 140.35 | 1378.10 | 57.54 | 56.822 | 38.190 | 19.870 | 13.410 |
| 14 | Peru | 94 | 155.22 | 2613.93 | 62.63 | 45.106 | 24.860 | 8.210 | 3.750 |
| 15 | Trinidad** | 81 | 233.12 | 1618.46 | 94.57 | 41.565 | 24.350 | 11.740 | 7.650 |
| 16 | Venezuela | 90 | 304.78 | 1127.06 | 131.88 | 53.836 | 38.050 | 15.390 | 8.020 |
| | **L. America** | **Average** | **172.67** | **743.22** | **73.58** | **50.38** | **34.83** | **14.40** | **7.94** |
| | | **$\sigma$** | **82.01** | **515.16** | **32.66** | **6.69** | **8.57** | **5.04** | **3.59** |
| | **Overall** | **Average** | **109.05** | **751.21** | **52.003** | **45.833** | **37.958** | **15.416** | **8.513** |
| | | **$\sigma$** | **78.64** | **591.16** | **27.75** | **9.39** | **16.33** | **9.10** | **6.08** |

*Notes:* $\mu$ = mean income

PRC = per capita private consumption

Z = poverty line, based on below equation

G = measure of inequality

H = an index of poverty (head count ratio)

P1: an index of poverty

P2: an index of poverty

$-\eta_H$ = elasticity of poverty index (H) relative to mean income

(based on regression 2 of Table 3.1)

Poverty Line Estimation Equation: $\text{Log}Z_i = 1.3719 + 0.00303\mu_i - 0.000001886(\mu_i \times \mu_i)$;

(56.76) (10.96) (-5.25 )

## and Associated Elasticities

| $-\eta_H$ | $-\eta_{P1}$ | $-\eta_{P2}$ | $\theta_H$ | $\theta_{P1}$ | $\theta_{P2}$ | $\varepsilon$ | v | $v_0$ |
|---|---|---|---|---|---|---|---|---|
| -2.670 | -3.000 | -2.930 | 3.570 | 6.350 | 8.590 | 0.305 | -0.013 | 0.0007 |
| -0.750 | -1.120 | -1.410 | 0.440 | 2.250 | 4.000 | 0.152 | 0.080 | 0.0005 |
| -1.740 | -2.400 | -3.030 | 1.370 | 3.670 | 5.960 | 0.181 | 0.077 | 0.0007 |
| -3.540 | -5.670 | -7.840 | 3.900 | 8.340 | 12.820 | 0.239 | 0.076 | 0.0008 |
| -0.800 | -1.140 | -1.400 | 1.130 | 4.020 | 6.810 | 0.336 | -0.069 | 0.0004 |
| -0.650 | -0.850 | -0.950 | 0.000 | 0.999 | 1.980 | 0.083 | 0.164 | 0.0006 |
| -0.620 | -0.780 | -0.850 | 0.140 | 1.410 | 2.650 | 0.108 | 0.304 | 0.0005 |
| -0.740 | -1.090 | -1.340 | 0.380 | 2.070 | 3.710 | 0.142 | 0.177 | 0.0005 |
| -0.820 | -1.100 | -1.310 | 0.830 | 3.120 | 5.340 | 0.220 | 0.122 | 0.0005 |
| -0.820 | -1.340 | -1.700 | 0.070 | 1.200 | 2.310 | 0.092 | 0.303 | 0.0006 |
| -1.260 | -1.130 | -0.730 | 0.670 | 2.140 | 3.460 | 0.145 | 0.143 | 0.0006 |
| -2.390 | -2.770 | -2.840 | 3.280 | 6.180 | 8.640 | 0.552 | 0.024 | 0.0007 |
| -2.130 | -3.290 | -4.440 | 2.750 | 6.540 | 10.320 | 0.289 | 0.056 | 0.0007 |
| -1.130 | -1.830 | -2.250 | 0.120 | 1.290 | 2.440 | 0.094 | 0.312 | 0.0007 |
| -1.010 | -1.280 | -1.500 | 0.760 | 2.720 | 4.630 | 0.176 | 0.391 | 0.0006 |
| -1.670 | -2.810 | -3.740 | 0.340 | 1.780 | 3.170 | 0.105 | 0.237 | 0.0009 |
| -0.840 | -1.190 | -1.470 | 0.630 | 2.650 | 4.610 | 0.176 | 0.076 | 0.0005 |
| -0.680 | -0.940 | -1.140 | 1.000 | 3.860 | 6.620 | 0.496 | -0.017 | 0.0004 |
| -0.740 | -1.330 | -1.730 | 0.060 | 0.820 | 1.710 | 0.076 | 0.513 | 0.0007 |
| -1.860 | -2.600 | -3.340 | 2.810 | 6.430 | 10.050 | 0.430 | 0.040 | 0.0007 |
| -0.800 | -1.440 | -1.910 | 0.030 | 1.100 | 2.170 | 0.088 | 0.115 | 0.0007 |
| -0.830 | -1.160 | -1.430 | 0.460 | 2.200 | 3.900 | 0.148 | 0.222 | 0.0005 |
| -0.670 | -1.210 | -1.650 | 0.460 | 2.450 | 4.480 | 0.164 | 0.127 | 0.0005 |
| **-1.27** | **-1.80** | **-2.21** | **1.10** | **3.20** | **5.23** | **0.21** | **0.148** | **0.0006** |
| **0.78** | **1.14** | **1.57** | **1.24** | **2.15** | **3.05** | **0.13** | **0.144** | **0.0001** |
| -2.050 | -2.240 | -2.360 | 0.860 | 2.360 | 3.830 | 0.130 | 0.439 | 0.0007 |
| -1.470 | -1.580 | -1.720 | 2.080 | 4.630 | 7.230 | 0.334 | 0.384 | 0.0007 |
| -1.930 | -2.940 | -3.680 | 0.760 | 2.540 | 4.220 | 0.127 | 0.310 | 0.0008 |
| -4.590 | -8.010 | -11.450 | 5.820 | 12.440 | 19.070 | 0.283 | 0.194 | 0.0008 |
| -2.280 | -3.510 | -4.730 | 3.260 | 7.460 | 11.650 | 0.348 | -0.022 | 0.0007 |
| -1.420 | -2.030 | -2.610 | 2.140 | 5.570 | 8.950 | 0.427 | -0.001 | 0.0006 |
| -3.120 | -3.420 | -3.250 | 3.120 | 5.430 | 7.260 | 0.219 | 0.319 | 0.0009 |
| -1.640 | -2.180 | -2.520 | 2.040 | 4.940 | 7.610 | 0.274 | 0.109 | 0.0006 |
| -3.300 | -4.930 | -6.630 | 3.500 | 7.290 | 11.140 | 0.231 | 0.235 | 0.0009 |
| **-2.42** | **-3.43** | **-4.33** | **2.62** | **5.85** | **9.00** | **0.26** | **0.219** | **0.0007** |
| **1.05** | **1.99** | **3.05** | **1.54** | **3.04** | **4.62** | **0.10** | **0.163** | **0.0001** |
| -1.380 | -1.200 | -2.560 | 1.220 | 3.660 | 6.040 | 0.198 | 0.079 | 0.0006 |
| -0.670 | -1.050 | -1.360 | 0.920 | 3.800 | 6.590 | 0.555 | 0.009 | 0.0004 |
| -1.070 | -1.550 | -1.970 | 1.570 | 4.760 | 7.860 | 0.493 | -0.026 | 0.0005 |
| -1.250 | -1.400 | -1.540 | 1.840 | 4.540 | 7.220 | 0.493 | 0.031 | 0.0005 |
| -1.270 | -1.470 | -1.660 | 1.910 | 4.720 | 7.510 | 0.441 | 0.008 | 0.0006 |
| -1.270 | -1.760 | -2.160 | 1.740 | 4.790 | 7.720 | 0.320 | 0.049 | 0.0005 |
| -1.060 | -1.950 | -2.760 | 1.210 | 4.350 | 7.400 | 0.247 | 0.003 | 0.0006 |
| -0.830 | -0.990 | -1.100 | 1.230 | 3.950 | 6.590 | 0.381 | 0.033 | 0.0004 |
| -1.120 | -1.420 | -1.600 | 1.070 | 3.330 | 5.470 | 0.211 | 0.050 | 0.0005 |
| -2.300 | -3.390 | -4.480 | 3.120 | 6.930 | 10.760 | 0.311 | -0.002 | 0.0007 |
| -1.030 | -1.320 | -1.520 | 1.360 | 4.070 | 6.650 | 0.570 | -0.008 | 0.0005 |
| -0.970 | -1.370 | -1.700 | 0.680 | 2.660 | 4.590 | 0.168 | 0.044 | 0.0005 |
| -0.840 | -0.920 | -0.960 | 1.210 | 3.770 | 6.260 | 0.351 | -0.017 | 0.0005 |
| -1.550 | -2.030 | -2.380 | 2.300 | 5.480 | 8.470 | 0.379 | -0.096 | 0.0006 |
| -1.080 | -1.070 | -1.070 | 1.580 | 4.040 | 6.500 | 0.501 | -0.042 | 0.0006 |
| -1.050 | -1.470 | -1.840 | 1.380 | 4.240 | 7.030 | 0.573 | 0.007 | 0.0005 |
| **-1.17** | **-1.52** | **-1.92** | **1.52** | **4.32** | **7.04** | **0.39** | **0.007** | **0.0005** |
| **0.37** | **0.59** | **0.86** | **0.59** | **0.96** | **1.37** | **0.14** | **0.042** | **0.0001** |
| **-1.452** | **-2.014** | **-2.511** | **1.523** | **4.070** | **6.541** | **0.263** | **0.114** | **0.0006** |
| **0.86** | **1.37** | **1.94** | **1.25** | **2.24** | **3.26** | **0.15** | **0.146** | **0.0001** |

$-\eta_{P1}$=elasticity of poverty index (P1) relative to mean income;
$-\eta_{P2}$= elasticity of poverty index (P2) relative to mean income;
$\theta_H$= elasticity of poverty index (H) relative to income distribution;
$\theta_{P1}$= elasticity of poverty index (P1) relative to Income distribution;
$\theta_{P2}$= elasticity of poverty index (P2) relative to income distribution;
$\varepsilon$ = elasticity of poverty line with respect to mean income (based on the equation below);
v = Elasticity of Gini Index to per capita private consumption (based on regression 2 of Table 3.1);
$v_0$ = component of the rate of change in Gini that doe not depend on income (or consumption) level

R square = 0.97, adj. R Square = 0.96; and $\varepsilon = [0.00303\mu - 0.000003772(\mu \times \mu)]$

## Table 3.A3: Persistence of Growth Regression

(rate of growth in 1975–96 minus rate of growth for 1965–74)

| | *Confl1* | *Confl11* | *Confl2* | *Confl21* | *Confl3* | *Confl31* | Error Correction Term | Macro Policy | Constant | Adjusted $R^2$ | F-test | N |
|---|---|---|---|---|---|---|---|---|---|---|---|---|
| A1 | -0.0004 | | | | | | | | -0.9073 | 9.27 | 7.54 | 65 |
| | (-2.746) | | | | | | | | | | | |
| B1 | | -0.0004 | | | | | | | -1.0193 | 0.0703 | 5.84 | 65 |
| | | (-2.416) | | | | | | | (-2.386) | | | |
| C1 | | | -0.0005 | | | | | | -0.9264 | 0.1107 | 8.22 | 59 |
| | | | (-2.867) | | | | | | (-2.175) | | | |
| D1 | | | | -0.0004 | | | | | -1.0181 | 0.0797 | 6.02 | 59 |
| | | | | (-2.454) | | | | | (-2.336) | | | |
| E1 | | | | | -0.0004 | | | | -1.1698 | 0.0699 | 5.51 | 61 |
| | | | | | (-2.347) | | | | (-2.927) | | | |
| F1 | | | | | | -0.0003 | | | -1.2877 | 0.0423 | 3.65 | 61 |
| | | | | | | (-1.910) | | | (-2.927) | | | |
| A2 | -0.0003 | | | | | | 0.6126 | | 0.0819 | 0.4396 | 22.96 | 57 |
| | (-2.539) | | | | | | (5.909) | | (0.213) | | | |
| B2 | | -0.0003 | | | | | 0.6223 | | 0.0863 | 0.4641 | 23.38 | 57 |
| | | (-2.637) | | | | | (6.054) | | (0.227) | | | |
| C2 | | | -0.0004 | | | | 0.5860 | | 0.1101 | 0.4546 | 23.50 | 55 |
| | | | (-2.928) | | | | (5.728) | | (0.288) | | | |
| D2 | | | | -0.0004 | | | 0.6124 | | 0.1846 | 0.4664 | 24.60 | 55 |
| | | | | (-3.149) | | | (6.105) | | (0.480) | | | |
| E2 | | | | | -0.0003 | | 0.6128 | | 0.0171 | 0.4324 | 21.95 | 56 |
| | | | | | (-2.566) | | (5.932) | | (0.044) | | | |
| F2 | | | | | | -0.0004 | 0.6389 | | 0.2016 | 0.4469 | 23.22 | 56 |
| | | | | | | (-2.854) | (6.275) | | (0.493) | | | |
| A3 | -0.0003 | | | | | | .7017 | -15.981 | 0.5370 | 0.5145 | 19.02 | 52 |
| | (-2.576) | | | | | | (6.637) | (-2.447) | (1.308) | | | |
| B3 | | -0.0003 | | | | | 0.7144 | -16.854 | 0.5725 | 0.5230 | 19.64 | 52 |
| | | (-2.759) | | | | | (6.856) | (-2.605) | (1.405) | | | |
| C3 | | | -0.0005 | | | | 0.7303 | -18.981 | 0.8685 | 0.5785 | 23.87 | 51 |
| | | | (-3.950) | | | | (7.368) | (-2.692) | (2.174) | | | |
| D3 | | | | -0.0005 | | | 0.7589 | -19.615 | 0.8966 | 0.5780 | 23.83 | 51 |
| | | | | (-3.941) | | | (7.647) | (-2.776) | (2.221) | | | |
| E3 | | | | | -0.0004 | | 0.7601 | -20.584 | 0.8387 | 0.5585 | 22.50 | 52 |
| | | | | | (-3.476) | | (7.594) | (-3.255) | (2.021) | | | |
| F3 | | | | | | -0.0005 | 0.7896 | -21.359 | 0.9028 | 0.5651 | 23.09 | 52 |
| | | | | | | (-3.604) | (7.884) | (-3.384) | (2.159) | | | |

*Notes: Confl*1: standard deviation of $\Delta \ln(\text{TOT})_{70-79} \times openness_{70-79} \times gini_{65-74} \times democracy_{70s}$.
*Confl*11: is defined as *confl*1 with the measure of democracy in the 1980s rather than in the 1970s.
*Confl*2: is defined as std deviation of $\Delta \ln(\text{TOT})_{70-74} \times openness_{70-74} \times gini_{65-74} \times democracy_{70s}$; *Confl*21: is defined as *confl*2 with the measure of democracy in the 1980s rather than in 1970s.
*Confl*3: is defined as std deviation of $\Delta \ln(\text{TOT})_{70-89} \times openness_{70-79} \times gini_{65-74} \times democracy_{70s}$.
*Confl*31: is defined as *confl*3 with the measure of democracy in the 1980s rather than in the 1970s.
Error correction term = predicted annual rate of growth (1965–74) - actual average annual rate of growth (1965–74);
Macro policy = is defined as the 'instrumented' change in government consumption as a ratio of GDP in 1975–96 relative to 1965–74.

## Table 3.A4: Structural Parameters and Variables

| Country | $\alpha_0$ | $\alpha$ | $\beta_0$ | g | $g_0$ | $g_{F0}$ | G | $\tilde{G}_0$ | $G_0$ | $\dot{g}$ | $\hat{p}_0$ | $\hat{p}$ | *Confl4* | *gċon* |
|---|---|---|---|---|---|---|---|---|---|---|---|---|---|---|
| Algeria | 4.344 | 2.167 | 0.071 | 0.045 | 2.571 | 2.7479 | 39.281 | 22.486 | 38.00 | -2.5260 | -1.226 | 4.248 | 2672 | 0.079 |
| Botswana* | 1.115 | 0.771 | 0.071 | 5.293 | 11.708 | 9.1350 | 54.209 | 28.040 | 54.00 | -6.4151 | -7.911 | -2.965 | 1026 | na |
| Cote d'Ivoire | 2.673 | 1.684 | 0.071 | -1.200 | 4.162 | 1.7312 | 36.893 | 28.040 | 41.21 | -5.3623 | -4.336 | 4.695 | 3633 | 0.020 |
| Egypt | 7.003 | 3.677 | 0.071 | 3.673 | 1.305 | 6.3768 | 32.006 | 28.040 | 38.00 | 2.3687 | 2.205 | -6.506 | 1478 | -0.072 |
| Gabon | 1.718 | 1.034 | 0.071 | -0.774 | 8.496 | 3.7205 | 62.872 | 22.486 | 63.18 | -9.2698 | -7.063 | 2.519 | 4850 | 0.041 |
| Guinea | 0.573 | 0.615 | 0.071 | 1.299 | na | 4.1479 | 46.870 | 37.433 | 40.04 | na | na | -0.227 | na | na |
| Guinea Bissau | 0.675 | 0.267 | 0.071 | 0.730 | 0.591 | 4.7226 | 56.168 | 37.433 | 56.12 | 0.1394 | 0.517 | 0.479 | na | 0.007 |
| Kenya | 0.961 | 0.570 | 0.071 | 0.480 | 4.454 | 4.3493 | 57.891 | 37.433 | 54.39 | -3.9741 | -1.577 | 0.687 | 4459 | 0.043 |
| Lesotho | 1.497 | 0.476 | 0.071 | 2.983 | 5.852 | 6.9680 | 56.011 | 28.040 | 56.02 | -2.8693 | -1.291 | 0.076 | 4528 | 0.086 |
| Madagascar | 0.742 | 0.853 | 0.071 | -2.198 | 1.101 | 0.8922 | 43.459 | 37.433 | 43.44 | -3.2995 | -0.197 | 2.617 | 413 | 0.007 |
| Mauritania | 1.352 | 0.660 | 0.071 | 0.320 | 0.996 | 2.7060 | 42.535 | 28.040 | 42.53 | 0.6764 | 2.009 | 1.563 | 1796 | 0.045 |
| Mauritius | 4.543 | 1.392 | 0.071 | 4.310 | 2.155 | 7.3456 | 36.555 | 22.486 | 42.67 | 2.1545 | 1.542 | -1.458 | 274 | 0.009 |
| Morocco | 4.484 | 1.970 | 0.071 | 2.089 | 3.681 | 4.8775 | 39.200 | 28.040 | 39.19 | -1.5918 | -2.768 | 0.367 | 411 | 0.064 |
| Niger | 0.957 | 1.255 | 0.071 | -1.894 | -3.902 | 0.6740 | 36.243 | 37.433 | 36.10 | 2.0079 | 5.854 | 3.334 | 1416 | 0.144 |
| Nigeria | 1.628 | -0.007 | 0.071 | -0.311 | 3.576 | 2.3226 | 44.893 | 37.433 | 37.02 | -3.8867 | 1.654 | 1.626 | 2223 | 0.055 |
| Rwanda | 1.646 | 2.093 | 0.071 | 0.132 | 2.026 | 2.1883 | 29.066 | 28.040 | 28.90 | -1.8941 | -2.596 | 1.369 | 1638 | 0.068 |
| Senegal | 1.316 | 0.779 | 0.071 | -0.037 | -1.503 | 3.8133 | 54.117 | 28.040 | 54.12 | 1.4659 | 2.487 | 1.345 | 1553 | 0.018 |
| South Africa | 1.699 | 0.540 | 0.071 | -0.567 | 3.246 | 3.8650 | 61.060 | 22.486 | 62.30 | -3.8132 | -0.053 | 2.005 | 504 | 0.052 |
| Tanzania | 0.578 | 0.808 | 0.071 | 0.120 | na | na | 38.102 | 37.433 | 38.10 | na | na | 0.481 | na | na |
| Tunisia | 4.320 | 1.226 | 0.071 | 2.469 | 4.492 | 5.5282 | 40.001 | 28.040 | 43.00 | -2.0232 | -1.188 | -0.0367 | 593 | 0.016 |
| Uganda | 0.726 | 1.187 | 0.071 | 1.405 | na | 3.7523 | 40.740 | 28.040 | 33.00 | na | na | -0.942 | na | na |
| Zambia | 1.137 | 0.501 | 0.071 | -2.793 | 0.591 | 0.8350 | 51.998 | 37.433 | 51.00 | -3.3843 | 0.841 | 2.537 | 3954 | -0.002 |
| Zimbabwe | 1.158 | 0.701 | 0.071 | -0.707 | 3.262 | 3.0211 | 56.834 | 28.040 | 52.40 | -3.9689 | -1.127 | 1.654 | 1557 | 0.161 |
| Bangladesh | 1.627 | 0.913 | 0.071 | 2.055 | -0.814 | 4.5599 | 38.976 | 37.433 | 35.21 | 2.8688 | 2.371 | -0.250 | na | 0.000 |
| China | 3.340 | 0.725 | 0.071 | 8.028 | 3.189 | 10.1720 | 37.256 | 37.433 | 30.14 | 4.8387 | 5.651 | -2.194 | 143 | -0.013 |
| India | 2.130 | 1.780 | 0.071 | 3.217 | 1.731 | 5.4418 | 32.044 | 37.433 | 31.28 | 1.4852 | -0.951 | -3.595 | 120 | 0.020 |
| Indonesia | 10.55 | 3.329 | 0.071 | 5.349 | 4.275 | 7.6643 | 31.688 | 28.040 | 32.54 | 1.0744 | -3.680 | -7.256 | 277 | 0.029 |
| Jordan | 4.931 | 2.450 | 0.071 | 2.940 | na | 5.6461 | 40.656 | 22.486 | 38.04 | na | na | -2.271 | na | na |
| Malaysia | 3.096 | 1.168 | 0.071 | 4.815 | 4.325 | 8.2424 | 48.351 | 28.040 | 48.18 | 0.4899 | -1.954 | -2.526 | 217 | 0.014 |
| Pakistan | 4.686 | 0.940 | 0.071 | 2.711 | 2.362 | 5.0000 | 31.143 | 37.433 | 32.18 | 0.3483 | 2.464 | -0.7391 | 183 | 0.007 |
| Philippines | 2.845 | 1.043 | 0.071 | 0.624 | 2.109 | 3.8902 | 46.665 | 28.040 | 45.91 | -1.4849 | 0.645 | 2.194 | 505 | 0.004 |
| Sri Lanka | 6.509 | 2.079 | 0.071 | 3.224 | 2.979 | 6.4380 | 30.098 | 28.040 | 45.18 | 0.2449 | 0.317 | -0.192 | 523 | -0.029 |
| Bolivia | 2.340 | 0.675 | 0.071 | 0.106 | -0.892 | 3.0969 | 42.038 | 28.040 | 42.04 | 0.9986 | 2.942 | 2.268 | 1067 | 0.015 |
| Brazil | 1.683 | 0.502 | 0.071 | 0.956 | 7.454 | 5.0058 | 60.662 | 22.486 | 56.93 | -6.4987 | -2.057 | 1.204 | 529 | -0.005 |
| Chile | 2.264 | 0.911 | 0.071 | 3.537 | 0.754 | 7.7020 | 56.493 | 22.486 | 58.55 | 2.7831 | 1.578 | -0.958 | 1484 | -0.022 |
| Colombia | 2.426 | 0.568 | 0.071 | 2.064 | 3.209 | 5.8238 | 50.293 | 28.040 | 52.85 | -1.1445 | 0.603 | 1.254 | 337 | 0.018 |
| Costa Rica | 2.751 | 0.782 | 0.071 | 0.934 | 3.878 | 4.1185 | 46.116 | 28.040 | 44.77 | -2.9449 | -0.284 | 2.020 | 300 | -0.007 |
| Dom. Rep. | 2.535 | 0.961 | 0.071 | 1.446 | 5.335 | 4.7801 | 50.789 | 28.040 | 46.86 | -3.8882 | -2.593 | 1.144 | 766 | 0.001 |
| El Salvador | 2.463 | 1.455 | 0.071 | 0.235 | 1.093 | 3.6780 | 47.462 | 28.040 | 48.40 | -0.8578 | 0.874 | 2.121 | 1549 | 0.020 |
| Guatemala | 1.772 | 0.481 | 0.071 | 0.190 | 3.345 | 4.0449 | 59.899 | 28.040 | 54.19 | -3.1548 | 0.164 | 1.681 | 544 | 0.016 |
| Honduras | 1.729 | 0.953 | 0.071 | 0.513 | 1.371 | 4.6524 | 51.752 | 28.040 | 58.18 | -0.8574 | 0.422 | 1.240 | 2439 | 0.007 |
| Jamaica | 4.912 | 2.348 | 0.071 | -0.318 | 1.367 | 2.8077 | 37.916 | 28.040 | 43.94 | -1.6849 | 1.703 | 5.659 | 261 | 0.057 |
| Mexico | 1.979 | 0.601 | 0.071 | 1.085 | 3.658 | 4.8394 | 55.278 | 22.486 | 52.78 | -2.5730 | -0.220 | 1.327 | 561 | 0.017 |
| Nicaragua | 1.428 | 1.024 | 0.071 | -3.504 | 1.693 | 0.0757 | 50.072 | 28.040 | 50.32 | -5.1973 | -0.306 | 5.015 | 2156 | 0.115 |
| Panama | 1.783 | 0.662 | 0.071 | 1.421 | 4.043 | 5.1186 | 56.822 | 22.486 | 51.97 | -2.6212 | -0.892 | 0.842 | na | 0.177 |
| Peru | 3.265 | 1.784 | 0.071 | -0.260 | 1.269 | 3.0157 | 45.106 | 22.486 | 46.05 | -1.5295 | 1.000 | 3.729 | 1524 | 0.024 |
| Trinidad** | 2.612 | 0.701 | 0.071 | 0.325 | 2.238 | 3.2925 | 41.565 | 22.486 | 41.72 | -1.9130 | 1.043 | 2.384 | 940 | 0.040 |
| Venezuela | 2.117 | 0.600 | 0.071 | -0.478 | 0.425 | 2.6335 | 53.836 | 22.486 | 43.73 | -0.9027 | 1.862 | 2.403 | 750 | 0.011 |

*Notes:* See p.87

## Table 3.A5: Determinants of Growth Dynamics in the Arab World and Other Regions

(annual average in 1975–96 relative to 1965–74)

| Country/Region | (1) $\dot{g} = g - g_0$ | (2) Effect due to Shock and Social Conflict | (3) Effect due to Equitable Initial Income Distribution | (4) Effect due to Initial Poverty | (5) Effect due to Macroeconomic Policy | (6) Residual |
|---|---|---|---|---|---|---|
| **Algeria** | **2.5260** | **1.8384** | **1.4193** | **1.4329** | **1.2546** | **0.5533** |
| Egypt | 2.3687 | -1.0164 | 1.2809 | 1.3694 | 1.1362 | -0.4014 |
| Mauritania | 0.6764 | -1.2354 | -1.7157 | 1.4915 | -0.7224 | 2.8585 |
| Morocco | -1.5918 | -0.2826 | -0.1350 | 1.6212 | -1.0183 | -1.7771 |
| Tunisia | -2.0232 | -0.4080 | -0.7633 | 2.5186 | -0.2539 | -3.1166 |
| **Arab (Median)** | **-1.5918** | **-1.0164** | **-0.7633** | **1.4915** | **-0.7224** | **-0.5811** |
| Cote d'Ivoire | -5.3623 | -2.4989 | -2.0185 | 1.1192 | -0.3108 | -1.6532 |
| Gabon | -9.2698 | -3.3360 | -1.7641 | 1.1421 | -0.6493 | -4.6626 |
| Kenya | -3.9741 | -3.0673 | -0.8734 | 1.1887 | -0.6830 | -0.5390 |
| Lesotho | -2.8693 | -3.1149 | -0.1151 | 2.2323 | -1.3706 | -0.5010 |
| Madagascar | -3.2995 | -0.2843 | -2.2214 | 0.6219 | -0.1156 | -1.3002 |
| Mauritania | 0.6764 | -1.2354 | -1.7157 | 1.4915 | -0.7224 | 2.8585 |
| Mauritius | 2.1545 | -0.1884 | 0.7580 | 2.3471 | -0.1454 | -0.6167 |
| Niger | 2.0079 | -0.9742 | -1.9233 | 0.5801 | -2.2827 | 6.6080 |
| Rwanda | -1.8941 | -1.1266 | -0.4735 | 0.5546 | -1.0843 | 0.2356 |
| Senegal | 1.4659 | -1.0683 | -1.2497 | 1.2339 | -0.2854 | 2.8354 |
| South Africa | -3.8132 | -0.3468 | -2.6892 | 2.2551 | -0.8271 | -2.2052 |
| Zambia | -3.3843 | -2.7199 | -3.6647 | 1.6381 | 0.0282 | 1.3340 |
| Zimbabwe | -3.9689 | -1.0713 | -1.7088 | 1.1735 | -2.5645 | 0.2022 |
| **Sub Saharan Africa (median)** | **-2.0232** | **-1.0713** | **-1.4193** | **1.4329** | **-0.7224** | **-0.2432** |
| China | 4.8387 | -0.0984 | 9.0749 | -4.5905 | 0.2048 | 0.2479 |
| India | 1.4852 | -0.0828 | 1.4756 | -2.2287 | -0.3163 | 2.6374 |
| Malaysia | 0.4899 | -0.1495 | 1.5664 | 0.2093 | -0.2182 | -0.9181 |
| Pakistan | 0.3483 | -0.1256 | -1.6443 | 2.0803 | -0.1138 | 0.1517 |
| Philippines | -1.4849 | -0.3471 | -1.6087 | -0.1820 | -0.0649 | 0.7178 |
| Sri Lanka | 0.2449 | -0.3597 | 0.0670 | 0.4431 | 0.4600 | -0.3655 |
| **Asia (median)** | **0.4191** | **-0.1376** | **0.7713** | **0.0137** | **-0.0894** | **-0.1390** |
| Bolivia | 0.9986 | -0.7342 | -2.4346 | -2.8858 | -0.2333 | 7.2865 |
| Brazil | -6.4987 | -0.3636 | -1.9376 | 1.8834 | 0.0829 | -6.1639 |
| Chile | 2.7831 | -1.0210 | 0.7970 | -0.5235 | 0.3460 | 3.1845 |
| Columbia | -1.1445 | -0.2319 | -1.5450 | 0.2842 | -0.2803 | 0.6284 |
| Costa Rica | -2.9449 | -0.2066 | -1.9765 | -1.3170 | 0.1166 | 0.4386 |
| Dom. Rep. | -3.8882 | -0.5272 | -0.9541 | 1.1181 | -0.0186 | -3.5064 |
| El Salvador | -0.8578 | -1.0652 | -1.0076 | -1.1957 | -0.3239 | 2.7346 |
| Guatemala | -3.1548 | -0.3743 | -2.5953 | 1.6763 | -0.2483 | -1.6132 |
| Honduras | -0.8574 | -1.6776 | -0.8715 | 0.3237 | -0.1176 | 1.4856 |
| Jamaica | -1.6849 | -0.1794 | -1.6278 | -1.1337 | -0.9118 | 2.1679 |
| Mexico | -2.5730 | -0.3862 | -1.8535 | 1.1568 | -0.2652 | -1.2249 |
| Nicaragua | -5.1973 | -1.4834 | -3.5341 | -1.9172 | -1.8286 | 3.5660 |
| Peru | -1.5295 | -1.0485 | -1.5797 | -0.2951 | -0.3891 | 1.7829 |
| Trinidad** | -1.9130 | -0.6469 | -2.4540 | 2.3891 | -0.6425 | -0.5587 |
| Venezuela | -0.9027 | -0.5158 | -2.9010 | 0.7346 | -0.1786 | 1.9581 |
| **Latin America (median)** | **-1.68485** | **-0.5272** | **-1.8535** | **0.2842** | **-0.24833** | **0.6600** |

*Notes to Table 3.A4:*

$\alpha_0 = \theta v_0$ where $v_0$ is multiplied by 1000 so that $\alpha$ and $\alpha_0$ are comparable in scale; $\alpha = (1 - \varepsilon)\eta - \theta v$, where estimates of $\theta v_0$, $\varepsilon$, $\eta$, and v are obtained from Appendix Table 3.A2 (column for P1).

1. Estimates for $\beta 0$ is obtained from the coefficient of G of regression 6 of Table 4.1 in Ali and Elbadawi (1999).
2. g = average annual per capita GDP growth rate in the 1975–96 period.
3. $g_0$ = average annual per capita GDP growth rate in the 1965–74 period.
4. G ≡ level of inequality in the 1975–96 period.
5. $G_0$= level of inequality in the 1965–74 period.
6. $g_{F0} = g_0 + \beta_0 G_0$, where $g_{F0}$ = average growth explained by non-distributional fundamentals in the 1965–74 period.
7. $\tilde{G}_0 = \frac{1}{\alpha\beta_0}(\alpha g_{F0} - \alpha_0)$; initial level of inequality (1965–74) consistent with steady-state equilibrium ($\hat{g} = \hat{p} = 0$). The data in the column reflect the median value 37.43 for the lower quartile, 28.04 for the second and third quartile, and 22.486 is the fourth quartile (classification according to mean consumption).
8. $\dot{g} = g - g_0$
9. $\hat{p} = -\alpha g + \alpha_0$, where g is the average growth rate in the 1975–96 period.
10. $\hat{p} = -\alpha g_0 + \alpha_0$ where $g_0$ is the average growth rate in 1965–74 period.
11. *Confl4* = conflict variable (see note to Table 4.2 in Ali and Elbadawi, 1999).

    $g\dot{c}on = (gcon_{75-96} - gcon_{65-74})$

*Notes to Table 3.A5:*

(1) g = average annual per capita growth rate in the 1975–96 period.
(2) $g_0$ = average annual per capita growth rate in 1965–74.
(3) Effect due to shocks and social conflicts = $-\lambda_1 \tau(1 - I)G = -\lambda_1$
(4) **confl4* (see notes to Table 4.2 in Ali and Elbadawi, 1999), where $\lambda_1$=0.00069.
(5) Effect due to equitable initial income distribution = $\beta_0\lambda_2(\tilde{G}_0 - G_0)$, where $\tilde{G}_0$ is given by the appropriate median for the country in question (see Appendix Table 3.A4), where $\beta_0$=0.071 and $\lambda_2$=0.72405.
(6) Effect due to poverty dynamics in the initial period = $\lambda_2 \frac{1}{\alpha} \hat{P}_0$ where $\alpha$ and $\hat{P}_0$ are as in Appendix Table 3.A4.
(7) Effect due to macroeconomic policy = $\lambda_3 \times g\dot{c}on$, where $\lambda_3$ = -15.88385 and $g\dot{c}on$ as in Appendix Table 3.A4.

*Source:* Ali and Elbadawi (1999a, Table 4.2); Appendix Table 3.A4, equation 9.

## Appendix Table 3.A6: Dynamics of Poverty in the Arab World and Other Regions

(predicted annual average change in poverty for 1975–96)

| Country | Growth = $-\alpha g$ | $\alpha_0$ | $\hat{P}$ |
|---|---|---|---|
| Algeria | -0.0966 | 4.3443 | 4.2477 |
| Egypt | -13.5084 | 7.0028 | -6.5056 |
| Jordan | -7.2025 | 4.9311 | -2.2714 |
| Mauritania | 0.2108 | 1.3521 | 1.5629 |
| Morocco | -4.1162 | 4.4835 | 0.3674 |
| Tunisia | -3.0273 | 4.3199 | 1.2926 |
| **Arab (median)** | **3.5717** | **4.4139** | **0.8422** |
| Botswana | -4.0807 | 1.1154 | -2.9652 |
| Cote d'Ivoire | 2.0218 | 2.6734 | 4.6952 |
| Gabon | 0.8002 | 1.7183 | 2.5185 |
| Guinea | -0.7997 | 0.5728 | -0.2269 |
| Guinea Bissau | -0.1953 | 0.6746 | 0.4793 |
| Kenya | -0.2735 | 0.9609 | 0.6874 |
| Lesotho | -1.4212 | 1.4970 | 0.0758 |
| Madagascar | 1.8751 | 0.7421 | 2.6172 |
| Mauritania | 0.2108 | 1.3521 | 1.5629 |
| Mauritius | -6.0009 | 4.5434 | -1.4575 |
| Niger | 2.3773 | 0.9565 | 3.3338 |
| Nigeria | -0.0022 | 1.6283 | 1.6260 |
| Rwanda | -0.2770 | 1.6458 | 1.3688 |
| Senegal | 0.0287 | 1.3160 | 1.3446 |
| South Africa | 0.3061 | 1.6989 | 2.0050 |
| Uganda | -1.6673 | 0.7256 | -0.9417 |
| Zambia | 1.4001 | 1.1370 | 2.5371 |
| Zimbabwe | 0.4951 | 1.1585 | 1.6536 |
| **Sub Saharan Africa (Median)** | **-0.0132** | **1.2372** | **1.2505** |
| Bangladesh | -1.8772 | 1.6272 | -0.2499 |
| China | 5.8174 | 3.3398 | 9.1572 |
| India | -5.7249 | 2.1302 | -3.5947 |
| Indonesia | -17.8060 | 10.5502 | -7.2558 |
| Jordan | -7.2025 | 4.9311 | -2.2714 |
| Malaysia | -5.6219 | 3.0959 | -2.5260 |
| Pakistan | -2.5494 | 4.6857 | 2.1363 |
| Philippines | -0.6510 | 2.8449 | 2.1939 |
| Sri Lanka | -6.7010 | 6.5091 | -0.1919 |
| **Asia (Median)** | **-5.6219** | **3.3398** | **-2.2822** |
| Bolivia | -0.0716 | 2.3398 | 2.2681 |
| Brazil | -0.4796 | 1.6834 | 1.2039 |
| Chile | -3.2220 | 2.2644 | -0.9576 |
| Columbia | -1.1724 | 2.4260 | 1.2536 |
| Costa Rica | -0.7304 | 2.7506 | 2.0202 |
| Dom. Rep. | -1.3903 | 2.5345 | 1.1443 |
| El Salvador | -0.3416 | 2.4631 | 2.1215 |
| Guatemala | -0.0912 | 1.7722 | 1.6809 |
| Honduras | -0.4895 | 1.7292 | 1.2397 |
| Jamaica | 0.7472 | 4.9118 | 5.6590 |
| Mexico | -0.6521 | 1.9787 | 1.3266 |
| Nicaragua | 3.5869 | 1.4276 | 5.0145 |
| Panama | -0.9405 | 1.7830 | 0.8425 |
| Peru | 0.4645 | 3.2649 | 3.7294 |
| Trinidad | -0.2276 | 2.6121 | 2.3845 |
| Venezuela | ·0.2863 | 2.1165 | 2.4029 |
| **Latin America (Median)** | **-0.4106** | **2.3021** | **1.8915** |

*Notes to Table 3.A6:*
1. $\alpha = (1 - \varepsilon)\eta - \theta v$ reflect the elasticity of the growth effect on poverty net of the influence of inequality operating through the growth channel (Appendix Table 3.A4).
2. $\alpha_0$ = component of change in poverty due to distribution (Appendix Table 3.A4);
3. g = average annual growth rate in 1975–96 (Appendix Table 3.A4). $\hat{P} = -\alpha g + \alpha_0$(from Appendix Table 3.A4).
*Source:* Appendix Table 3.A4 and equation 10.

## Table 3.A7: Predicted Performance in the Post-1975 Period: Behavior of Poverty, Growth, and Distribution

| Country | $\dot{g}$ | G | $g_F$ | $\tilde{G}$ | $\hat{P}$ | $\dot{g}>0$ | $\dot{g}<0$ | $G>\tilde{G}$ | $G<\tilde{G}$ | $\hat{P}>0$ | $\hat{P}<0$ |
|---|---|---|---|---|---|---|---|---|---|---|---|
| Algeria | -0.0186 | 39.2813 | 3.0870 | 24.26 | 2.155 | | X | X | | X | |
| Botswana | 0.4380 | 54.2085 | 9.5349 | 36.90 | -3.025 | X | | X | | | X |
| Cote d'Ivoire* | -0.0498 | 36.8926 | 1.6108 | 22.62 | 3.685 | | X | X | | X | |
| Egypt | -0.1791 | 32.0057 | 6.0978 | 36.90 | -1.351 | | X | | X | | X |
| Gabon | -0.6891 | 62.8718 | 4.2314 | 24.26 | 2.815 | | X | X | | X | |
| Guinea | 0.3354 | 46.8700 | 4.9185 | 40.93 | 0.124 | X | | X | | X | |
| Guinea Bissau | -0.0461 | 56.1678 | 4.6553 | 40.93 | 0.529 | | X | X | | X | |
| Kenya | 0.2112 | 57.8910 | 4.6197 | 40.93 | 0.707 | X | | X | | X | |
| Lesotho | 1.2555 | 56.0109 | 7.2812 | 36.90 | -0.638 | X | | X | | | X |
| Madagascar | 0.0189 | 43.4587 | 1.1146 | 40.93 | 2.613 | X | | X | | X | |
| Mauritania | 0.4499 | 42.5346 | 2.6514 | 36.90 | 2.775 | X | | X | | X | |
| Mauritius** | 0.2400 | 36.5548 | 6.8509 | 96.25 | -1.284 | X | | | X | | X |
| Morocco | 0.2878 | 39.2002 | 5.0707 | 36.90 | 0.285 | X | | X | | X | |
| Niger | 0.2673 | 36.2425 | 0.8220 | 40.93 | 2.397 | X | | | X | X | |
| Nigeria | 0.5518 | 44.8928 | 2.3346 | 40.93 | 1.270 | X | | X | | X | |
| Rwanda | 0.5904 | 29.0658 | 2.9101 | 36.90 | 2.308 | X | | | X | X | |
| Senegal | -0.0781 | 54.1173 | 3.7643 | 36.90 | 2.483 | | X | X | | X | |
| South Africa | 0.0954 | 61.0600 | 3.7731 | 24.26 | 2.648 | X | | X | | X | |
| Tanzania | 0.0680 | 38.1023 | 2.8305 | 40.93 | 0.481 | X | | | X | X | |
| Tunisia | 0.0255 | 40.0013 | 5.1804 | 36.90 | -0.107 | X | | X | | | X |
| Uganda*** | 0.1965 | 40.7400 | 5.2394 | 40.93 | 0.993 | X | | | X | X | |
| Zambia | 0.4443 | 51.9982 | 1.3863 | 40.93 | 3.037 | X | | X | | X | |
| Zimbabwe | 0.4730 | 56.8337 | 3.9649 | 36.90 | 3.175 | X | | X | | | |
| Bangladesh | 0.3301 | 38.9758 | 4.8540 | 40.93 | -0.413 | X | | | X | | X |
| China | 0.1331 | 37.2560 | 10.2844 | 40.93 | -4.664 | X | | | X | | X |
| India | -0.0603 | 32.0436 | 5.5540 | 40.93 | -1.240 | | X | | X | | X |
| Indonesia | 0.1130 | 31.6877 | 7.4742 | 36.90 | -3.083 | X | | | X | | X |
| Jordan | -0.0956 | 40.6564 | 5.4433 | 24.26 | -0.180 | | X | X | | | X |
| Malaysia** | 0.3634 | 48.3505 | 7.9309 | 111.44 | -2.531 | X | | | X | | X |
| Pakistan | 0.0569 | 31.1428 | 5.2660 | 40.93 | -0.880 | X | | | X | | X |
| Philippines | 0.0261 | 46.6650 | 4.0926 | 36.90 | 1.800 | X | | X | | X | |
| Sri Lanka | -0.0845 | 30.0980 | 5.4566 | 36.90 | -0.887 | | X | | X | | X |
| Bolivia | 0.2426 | 42.0378 | 2.4412 | 36.90 | 2.335 | X | | X | | X | |
| Brazil | -0.0660 | 60.6624 | 5.7386 | 24.26 | 1.420 | | X | X | | X | |
| Chile** | 0.8983 | 56.4927 | 7.6817 | 107.94 | -0.661 | X | | | X | | X |
| Columbia | 0.0091 | 50.2926 | 5.5090 | 36.90 | 0.312 | X | | X | | X | |
| Costa Rica | -0.0670 | 46.1160 | 4.1034 | 36.90 | 1.480 | | X | X | | X | |
| Dom. Rep. | 0.1349 | 50.7888 | 5.2577 | 36.90 | 0.950 | X | | X | | X | |
| El Salvador | -0.0396 | 47.4619 | 3.2543 | 36.90 | 2.202 | | X | X | | X | |
| Guatemala | 0.0481 | 59.8991 | 4.6342 | 36.90 | 2.248 | X | | X | | X | |
| Honduras | 0.0575 | 51.7519 | 4.3309 | 36.90 | 1.914 | X | | X | | X | |
| Jamaica | -0.0343 | 37.9159 | 2.1540 | 36.90 | 2.773 | | X | X | | X | |
| Mexico | 0.1347 | 55.2783 | 4.8068 | 24.26 | 1.316 | X | | X | | X | |
| Nicaragua | 1.3335 | 50.0717 | 0.8606 | 36.90 | 6.065 | X | | X | | X | |
| Panama | 0.0919 | 56.8215 | 4.9116 | 24.26 | 1.045 | X | | X | | X | |
| Peru | 0.0045 | 45.1065 | 2.9385 | 24.26 | 2.400 | X | | X | | X | |
| Trinidad | -0.0771 | 41.5652 | 4.5341 | 24.26 | 1.929 | | X | X | | X | |
| Venezuela | -0.0917 | 53.8359 | 3.0181 | 24.26 | 2.575 | X | | X | | X | |

*Notes to Table 3.A7:*

g = average annual growth, 1975–96

$\dot{g}$ = average annual change for the rate of growth for 1975–96.

G = level of inequality in 1975–76.

$g_F = g + \beta_0 G$ is the average annual growth explained by non-distributional fundamentals (1975–96);

$\widetilde{G} = \frac{1}{\alpha\beta_0}(\alpha g_F - \alpha_0)$, where the parameters are obtained from Appendix Table 3.A4.

The data in the column reflects the median value 24.26 for fourth quartile, 36.9 for second quartile, and 40.93 for the lower quartile (classification according to mean consumption).

* Since $G \cong \widetilde{G}$ (median), in this case G is compared to the country-specific $\widetilde{G}$, which is smaller at about 23.

** Actual G's are compared to country-specific $\widetilde{G}$'s rather than to the corresponding quartile median $\widetilde{G}$'s. This is because for those countries individual $\widetilde{G}$'s are much larger than the median $\widetilde{G}$'s: Mauritius (96); Malaysia(111); and Chile (108), perhaps due to this very high share of growth explained by non-distributional fundamentals ($\widetilde{G}$ is positively associated with $g_F$)

*** For Uganda, actual G is compared to the median for the lower quartile rather than the middle quartile, as the computed mean consumption would suggest. This is because the latter is not consistent with classification based on mean income.

## Appendix 3.A8: Phase Dynamics

Using equations 6, 7, and 8 of section 2, the dynamic behavior of inequality, poverty, and growth around the steady state can be analyzed with the help of a phase diagram (Appendix Figure 3.Al). The diagram suggests six phases, two of which (I, IV) give rise to a stable path toward the steady state; two of which (III, VI) are unstable; and the remaining two (II, V) diverge to unstable phases. The six phases are generated by superimposing the curve $G = \tilde{G}$ (equation 8) on the phase diagram defined by equations 6 and 7. Therefore, strictly speaking, there should be only four phases (I, III, IV, VI), where what we consider as Phase II (Phase V) is in fact a divergent region of Phase I (IV). However, by adhering to this loose notion in defining the phases, we can unambiguously identify the regions according to whether they are likely to lead to stable or divergent paths.

**Figure 3.A1: Phase Diagram of Poverty, Growth, and Distribution**

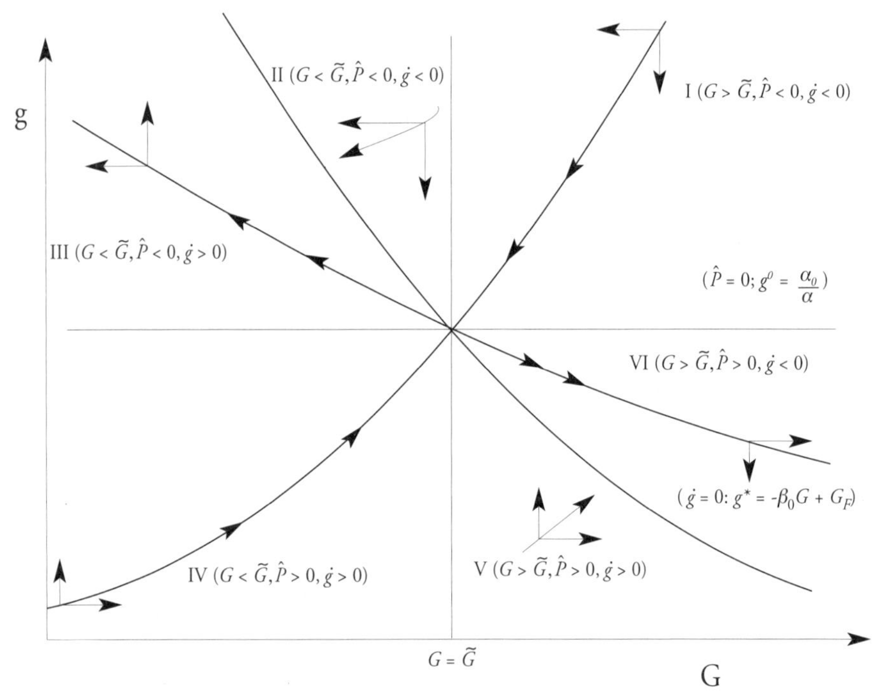


*Notes:*

P= index of poverty
G= Gini coefficient
$g^0$= level of g consistent with $\hat{P} = 0$
g = rate of per capita GDP growth;
$g^*$ = level of g consistent with ;
$\tilde{G}$ = level of G consistent with $\dot{g} = \hat{p} = 0$

First, in Phase I $(G > \tilde{G}, \hat{P} < 0, \dot{g} < 0)$ the highest social benefits are derived from more equitable distribution rather than from further acceleration of growth. Therefore, this phase suggests a stable path, where, en route toward the steady-state, $(G, g)$ decline, while the rate of change of poverty $(\hat{P})$ converges to zero at the steady state.

Second, Phase IV ($G < \tilde{G}, \hat{P} > 0,\ \dot{g} > 0$) suggests that the highest social benefits are derived from accelerated growth rather than from more equitable distribution, where, en route toward the steady state, growth accelerates, distribution worsens, and the rate of change of poverty ($\hat{P}$) converges to zero at the steady state.

Third, Phase III ($G < \tilde{G}, \hat{P} < 0, \dot{g} > 0$) and Phase VI ($G > \tilde{G}, \hat{P} > 0, \dot{g} < 0$) are both unstable. In Phase III, poverty will continuously decline, since all the combinations are right: growth rises over time and inequality—already lower than steady level—continuously declines. Exactly the opposite happens in Phase VI, where poverty rises due to a combination of decelerating growth and worsening inequality, which is already higher than steady-state levels. Both phases, however, are unstable, although they could produce a relatively sustained stint of 'transitional super-performance' (e.g. Phase III: East Asia since the 1960s) or a 'transitional low equilibrium trap' (e.g. Phase VI: Sub-Saharan Africa since the 1970s).

Fourth, Phase II ($G < \tilde{G}, \hat{P} < 0, \dot{g} < 0$) and V ($G > \tilde{G}, \hat{P} > 0, \dot{g} > 0$) are divergent, in that they revert to the unstable path. In Phase II, improving distribution dominates the force of decelerating growth to lead to continuously declining poverty along an unstable path. On the other hand, in Phase V worsening inequality dominates accelerating growth, leading to continuously rising poverty over time along the unstable path.

## Notes

*A condensed version of this chapter, using a non-technical framework, appears in Handoussa and Tzannatos, eds. (2002).

1 Our definition of the MENA region includes the two Arab countries of Sudan and Mauritania, which are not considered part of this region according to the World Bank, for example.

2 Libya and Lebanon are excluded owing to a lack of data.

3 See Domowitz and Elbadawi (1987) for an application of this framework in the demand for money literature.

4 See also Datt and Ravallion (1992), Kakwani (1993), and Ali (1996).

5 The functional dependence of the poverty line on mean income is noted by Ravallion, Datt, and van de Walle (1991: 347, 349), who found, from a survey of local poverty lines from 33 developing countries, that there is a clear "tendency for the local poverty line to increase with mean consumption" and that "the cross-country evidence does suggest that the real poverty lines will tend to increase with growth."

6 For example, a semi-logarithmic linear poverty line such as: $\text{Log}z = a + b_1\mu - b_2\mu^2$ has an associated elasticity $\varepsilon = b_1\mu - 2b_2\mu^2$, where a and b are coefficients.

7 For primary education, initial income, and income squared, one-period lags were used. Therefore, these variables, together with the external shock variable, are assumed to be exogenous. All macroeconomic fundamentals were instrumented. However, available data on Gini poses some problems. There is a group of countries for which data is available for the early 1980s and 1970s; for this group reverse causation from growth to inequality is not likely, given that the effective regression sample covers 1986–89, 1990–93, 1994–96. For the majority of countries, however, reliable inequality data (see Deininger and Squire, 1996) is available only for the second half of the 1980s or the 1990s. Moreover, for most countries, only one or very few data points are available for the entire 1970–96 period. To address these problems, we use instrumented one-period lagged averages of Gini (or just averages for those countries with data available for only one period), where two-period lags of other variables in the regres-

sion were used as instruments. Alesina and Rodrik (1994), for example, also chose instrumentation as one option for addressing reverse causation from growth to inequality.

8 Moreover, using six regressions, Ali and Elbadawi (1999: Table 4.1) find the parameter estimate of the inequality effect to be fairly stable around a median of –0.07.

9 Bloom and Sachs (1998) recommended adding this variable as an explanatory variable in empirical growth regressions, when, as is usually the case, per capita GDP growth, rather than the theoretically consistent GDP per worker growth rate, was used as a dependent variable.

10 Other growth fundamentals not found to be significantly associated with growth include initial income, initial primary school enrollment, external shocks, and financial depth.

11 The measure of external shock we use is the standard deviation of the first log-difference of the terms of trade multiplied by the average share of total trade in GDP in the initial period. This measure captures the unexpected component of the volatility of the streams of income associated with foreign trade. Assuming that the terms of trade follow a random walk (possibly with a drift), Rodrik (1998b) shows that this measure is the theoretically appropriate measure of external volatility. Moreover, Rodrik argues that the fact that this measure treats positive terms-of-trade shocks identically as negative shocks is justified, since positive income shocks could also trigger the same kind of distributional conflicts that obtain under negative shocks.

12 In Ali and Elbadawi (1999), we construct six versions of the Rodrik-type index of conflicts (Conflict). Our results corroborate the earlier findings by Rodrik in that the conflict variable is negatively and robustly associated with growth persistence. In all of the six regressions reported in Table 4.2 (and the 18 regressions of Appendix Table 3.A3 of Ali and Elbadawi, 1999), the effect of 'Conflict' falls within a range of (-0.0007, -0.0001) and has a P value of 0.06 or less.

13 We chose not to assign this interpretation to changes in investment, because, unlike government consumption, it is not a direct policy instrument.

14 See Ali and Elbadawi (1999) for a review of the literature on the Kuznets debate.

15 Cross-country regression results presented in Ali and Elbadawi (1999: Table 3.1) confirm the robust existence of a Kuznets curve using several specifications.

16 However, in subsequent applications we drop the last terms, assuming that the component of growth due to non-distributional fundamentals remains close to its equilibrium values.

17 Ali and Elbadawi (1999) undertakes this exercise for 47 developing countries.

18 This is because the lower the average growth rates during the period, the lower will be the steady-state levels of inequality. Sustainable poverty reduction in this case would require countries to undertake immediate redistributive measures in addition to growth-enhancing policies.

## References


Alesina, A., and D. Rodrik. 1994. "Distributive Politics and Economic Growth," *Quarterly Journal of Economics*, Vol. 109, No. 2.

Ali, A.A.G. 1998. *Dealing with Poverty and Income Distribution Issues in Developing Countries: Cross regional Experience*. Nairobi: AERC.

———. 1996. *Structural Adjustment Programs and Poverty in Sub-Saharan Africa.*, Dakar: CODESRIA.

———, and I. Elbadawi. 1999. "Inequality and the Dynamics of Poverty and Growth," unpublished mimeo. Nairobi: AERC.

———, and E. Thorbecke. 1998. "Poverty in Sub-Saharan Africa: Magnitudes and Characteristics," unpublished mimeo. Nairobi: AERC.

Anand, S., and R. Kanbur. 1993a. "Inequality and Development: A Critique," *Journal of Development Economics*, 41: 19–43.

———. 1993b. "The Kuznets Process and the Inequality-Development Relationship," *Journal of Development Economics*, 40: 25–52.
Atkinson, A. B. 1998. *Poverty in Europe.* Oxford: Blackwell.
Banerjee, A., and A. Newman. 1998. "Information, the Dual Economy and Development," *Review of Economic Studies*, 65: 631–53.
Bloom, D., and J. Sachs. 1998. "Geography, Demography and Economic Growth in Africa," *Brookings Papers on Economic Activity*, 2.
Chen, S., G. Datt, and M. Ravallion, (1993), "Is Poverty Increasing in the Developing World?" Policy Research Working Paper No. 1146, World Bank, Washington DC.
Datt, G., and M. Ravallion. 1992. "Growth and Redistribution Components of Changes in Poverty Measures: A Decomposition with Applications to Brazil and India in the 1980s," *Journal of Development Economics*, Vol. 38, No. 2.
Deininger, K., and L. Squire. 1996. "A New Data Set Measuring Income Inequality," *World Bank Economic Review*, 10: 565–91.
Domowitz, I., and I. Elbadawi. 1987. "An Error Correction Approach to Money Demand: The Case of the Sudan," *Journal of Development Economics*, 2: 257–75.
Easterly, W., N. Loayza, and P. Montiel. 1996. "Has Latin America's Post-Reform Growth Been Disappointing?" Policy Research Working Paper. Washington, DC: The World Bank.
Economic Research Forum (ERF). 1998. *Economic Trends in the MENA Region.* Cairo: Economic Research Forum.
Foster, J.E. 1998. "Absolute versus Relative Poverty," *American Economic Review*, Papers and Proceedings, 88: 335–41.
Handoussa, Heba, and Zafiris Tzannatos (eds.). 2002. *Employment Creation and Social Protection in the Middle East and North Africa.* Cairo: American University in Cairo Press.
Kakwani, N. 1993. "Statistical Inference in the Measurement of Poverty," *Review of Economics and Statistics*, 75: 632–39.
Kuznets, S. 1955. "Economic Growth and Income Inequality," *American Economic Review*, 45: 1–28.
Ravallion, M., G. Datt, and D. van de Walle. 1991. "Quantifying Absolute Poverty in the Developing World," *Review of Income and Wealth*, series 37, no. 4, pp. 345–61.
Rodrik, D. 1998a. "Where Did All the Growth Go? External Shocks, Social Conflict, and Growth Collapses." Cambridge, MA: Harvard University, John F. Kennedy School of Government, mimeo.
———. 1998b. "Why Do More Open Economies Have Bigger Governments?" *Journal of Political Economy*, October.
World Bank. 1995. *Claiming the future: Choosing Prosperity in the Middle East and North Africa.* Washington, DC: The World Bank.
———. 1998. *African Development Indicators 1998/99.* Washington, DC: The World Bank.

# 4

# Budget Deficit, Renewable Resource Gap, and Human Resource Development in Oil Economies

*Yousef Al-Ebraheem and Ismail Sirageldin*[*]

## Introduction: Importance of the Issue

Oil, a non-renewable resource, is the main source of revenue in 'oil economies.'[1] In these economies, oil revenue is controlled by the state and represents the main source of government revenue. The responsibility of the state as the major engine for growth and development, therefore, is well established in practice and cannot be underestimated. A common development objective, one that has been stated in all the development plans of these countries for many decades, is to diversify the economy away from oil. To reach this goal, governments in oil economies have committed a vast amount of resources to strengthen both the supply and the demand sides of human resource development through a free education system and the building of a modern infrastructure.

The goal of diversifying the economy toward a production system that is independent of oil revenue, and that productively engages the national labor force in a competitive market environment, cannot be achieved without extensive public support, at least in the initial stages. Such a development goal, which depends entirely on public finance, should be reflected in the structure of the state budget statement: in the sources of revenue and the pattern of government outlays. In oil economies, the rate of oil depletion, the growth of tax revenue based on non-oil production, and the productive utilization of the national labor force are three key factors that indicate to what extent this development goal has been successfully achieved. It is a puzzle that these three main indicators are in fact neither reflected in the state budget statement, nor used as an evaluation criterion in its formulation.

The present chapter attempts to do just that: incorporate the concept of a renewable resource gap in the budget statement so as to link the rate of oil depletion with the development of tax revenue based on non-oil production and the effective utilization of the national labor force. The chapter also attempts to demonstrate that the conventional financial budget deficit, which has been increasing in recent years, should not be the yardstick by which the development of oil economies is judged. The absence of the concept of a 'renewable resource gap' from the budget statement focuses policy questions on closing the 'financial budget deficit,' while reducing the developmental content of these statements, especially those pertaining to the development of human resources—an aspect of development that we emphasize.[2] The current concern with budget deficit in the oil economies and the recommended policy prescriptions illustrate this trend.

The recent appearance of financial budget deficits in the 'oil economies' has created concern and, concurrently, urgent calls for various remedial actions. Table 4.1 illustrates recent trends in the financial budget deficits of the Gulf Cooperation Council (GCC) countries for the period 1985–2000 For these countries, the budget deficit started more than a decade ago and has persisted through the 1990s, although preliminary estimates indicate a surplus in 2000, a result of increased oil prices. As a percentage of total revenue, it has fluctuated between 32 percent in 1985, 70 percent in 1986, 29 percent in 1989, and up again to 38 percent in 1993. Furthermore, although government revenue is projected to decline in 1997 and 1998, expenditure is not expected to decline at the same rate. Projections of budget deficit for 1997 and 1998 continue to be large in both absolute and relative terms. There are significant differences among the GCC countries. The deficit in Kuwait, for example, accounted for 54 percent and 42 percent of the total GCC deficit in 1997 and 1998, respectively, as Table 4.2 illustrates. The case of Kuwait is partly a result of high defense expenditures. Proposed remedial actions to reduce the budget deficit cover an array of fiscal, income, and monetary policies and institutional reforms that are often proposed as components of structural adjustment policy packages.

**Table 4.1: GCC Public Finance (US$ b)**

| Year | Total Revenue | Total Expenditure | Budget Deficit | Deficit as Percent of Total Revenue | Deficit as Percent of Oil Revenue |
|---|---|---|---|---|---|
| | $b | $b | $b | % | % |
| 1985 | 61.052 | 80.564 | -19.512 | 32 | 46 |
| 1986 | 39.338 | 66.785 | -27.447 | 70 | 109 |
| 1987 | 47.617 | 76.152 | -28.535 | 60 | 88 |
| 1988 | 44.892 | 66.451 | -21.560 | 48 | 73 |
| 1989 | 52.768 | 67.911 | -15.144 | 29 | 44 |
| 1990 | 69.600 | 92.362 | -22.762 | 33 | 43 |
| 1991 | 68.858 | 102.966 | -34.108 | 50 | 68 |
| 1992 | 78.021 | 96.150 | -18.129 | 23 | 31 |
| 1993 | 70.832 | 90.722 | -19.890 | 28 | 39 |
| 1994 | 65.475 | 81.915 | -16.440 | 25 | 36 |
| 1995 | 74.345 | 82.122 | -7.777 | 10 | 16 |
| 1996 | 76.646 | 91.563 | -14.917 | 19 | 29 |
| 1997 | 80.660 | 88.490 | -7.830 | 10 | 11 |
| 1998 | 74.320 | 86.730 | -12.410 | 17 | 27 |
| 1999 | 71.505 | 95.232 | -23.727 | 33 | NA |
| 2000* | 118.465 | 108.447 | 10.018 | 8.4 | NA |

*Sources: IMF Staff Reports* (various issues). GCC: Economic Report No. 10-1995.
* Estimated; based on data published in *The Gulf Economy* [Al-Khaleeg El-Eqtisadi], March 1, 1998, pp. 36–37, Abu Dhabi, UAE.

Many of the proposed policies deal with the shorter-term determinants and consequences of the budget deficit; more often than not, they ignore the more basic determinants of these deficits and their longer-term developmental consequences. Determinants and consequences that are specific to the nature of oil economies must be considered within this context. In the following section, the conventional budget deficit statement is examined.

Next, the concept of a renewable resource gap, and the role of population dynamics in the budgetary framework, are introduced. The issue of an optimal budget statement is examined in this part of the chapter. The following section presents a brief empirical illustration, followed by a discussion of the implication of the analyses and findings for human resource development in oil economies. The chapter ends with a summary and conclusions.

**Table 4.2: Projected Budget Deficit for the GCC Countries, 1997–98 (US$ b)**

| Year | 1997 | | | 1998 | | | 2000 | | |
|---|---|---|---|---|---|---|---|---|---|
| Finance / Country | Govt. Revenue ($b) | Govt. Spend ($b) | Budget Deficit ($b) | Govt. Revenue ($b) | Govt. Spend ($b) | Budget Deficit ($b) | Govt. Revenue ($b) | Govt. Spend ($b) | Budget Deficit ($b) |
| Bahrain | 1.620 | 1.820 | 0.200 | 1.660 | 1.860 | 0.200 | 1.521 | 1.941 | 0.420 |
| Kuwait | 10.350 | 14.600 | 4.250 | 10.720 | 15.920 | 5.200 | 17.084 | 13.071 | -4.013 |
| Oman | 5.270 | 5.960 | 0.690 | 5.290 | 6.70 | 0.780 | 5.758 | 6.087 | 0.302 |
| Qatar | 3.680 | 4.500 | 0.820 | 3.850 | 4.800 | 0.950 | 5.043 | 4.862 | -0.181 |
| Saudi Arabia | 54.400 | 56.000 | 1.600 | 47.460 | 52.260 | 4.800 | 68.909 | 60.487 | -8.422 |
| UAE | 5.340 | 5.610 | 0.270 | 5.340 | 5.820 | 0.480 | 20.123 | 21.999 | 1.876 |
| **Total GCC** | **80.660** | **88.490** | **7.830** | **74.320** | **86.730** | **12.410** | **118.465** | **108.447** | **-10.018** |

*Source:* Based on data published in *The Gulf Economy* [Al-Khaleeg El-Eqtisadi], March 1, 1998, page 37, Abu Dhabi, UAE. For 2000, the data is taken from Arab Unified Report 2001, Arab Monetary Fund. Negative sign indicates surplus.

## The Budget Deficit in Oil Economies

We start by linking the budget deficit statement to macroeconomic imbalances. This linkage is important, since macroeconomic adjustment policies and programs are called for as a result of these imbalances, and the policy packages are viewed as part of long-term development strategies. In general, macro imbalances may be summarized in terms of an identity relating the Current Account Balance (CAB) to Net Domestic Saving:[3]

$$CAB = [PS - PI] + [GR - (GC + GI)] \quad (1)$$

Where

(PS) = [Private Saving] = [Aggregate Output (Y) + International Transfers (InTr) - Government Revenue (GR) - Private Consumption (PC)].

(PI) = Private Investment.

(GC) and (GI) = Public Consumption and Investment, respectively.

The identity in equation 1 implies that imbalances in CAB are a result of imbalances in either the private or the public economy. A negative CAB implies that aggregate spending exceeds income. If international transfers are not sufficient and international borrowing is no longer available, a macroeconomic imbalance occurs. If there were no net saving in the private sector [the private economy is in balance, i.e., (PS - PI) = 0], then it follows that the public economy is not in balance, i.e., a budget deficit exists. It also implies that the fiscal deficit is exactly equal to the current account deficit. In such cases, structural adjustment policies are called into place.[4]

## Toward a Consistent Accounting

First, we will examine the implications of the budget deficit component in equation 1 for an oil economy. The second term in the right-hand side of equation 1, [GR - (GC + GI)], provides a general definition of the 'budget deficit.' The fiscal deficit in equation 1 is defined as the difference between government revenue from all sources and government consumption and investment expenditure. Although apparently straightforward, its operationalization is not so simple. All revenue and expenditure components must be conceptually and empirically consistent, and have the same time reference. These operational issues are important in public finance accounting. However, they are not the main focus of the present discussion.[5] Rather, the focus is on analyzing the policy relevance of this budgetary framework in the context of oil economies. First, we examine more closely the components of government revenue (GR) and of government expenditure (GE = GC + GI) in order to assess the need for alternative specification.

Equation 1 indicates that a government's Operational Budget Deficit/Surplus (OBD/S) is the difference between government revenue (GR) and government expenditure (GE). The second term of the right-hand side of equation 1 may be stated as follows:

$$OBD/S = [GR - GE] = [GR - (GC + GI)] \qquad (2)$$

In oil economies, government revenue (GR) includes three categories, namely:

1. Revenue from the non-renewable resource, oil ($GR_{oil}$),
2. Revenue from financial investment abroad ($GR_{finv}$), and
3. Taxes on returns from accumulated non-oil productive capacity ($GR_{tax}$).

On the expenditure side, aside from government consumption, government investment includes:

1. Investment in infrastructure ($GI_{infra}$),
2. Direct investment in the productive capacity ($GI_{prodc}$), and
3. Government foreign investment ($GI_{finv}$).[6]

Equation 2 may be re-written as follows:

$$OBD/S = [GR_{oil} + GR_{finv} + GR_{tax}] - [GC + GI_{infra} + GI_{prodc} + GI_{finv}] \qquad (3)$$

Table 4.3 presents historical data on sources of government revenue in the GCC countries. In most of these countries, oil revenue continues to be the major source of government revenue. Between 1985 and 1998, it provided between 64 percent and 77 percent of government revenue. Over the years, non-oil revenue has not shown the expected upward trend. In 1985, its value was about US$18.8 billion, stabilized around US$20 billion in 1991–4, and increased to US$25 billion in 1995–6. However, as a percentage of total government revenue, non-oil revenue was stable over the years. Non-oil revenue seems to be closely linked to the value of oil revenue. They both move in the same direction.

Oil revenue, by contrast, is basically the value of the annual depletion of oil reserves [$\delta OR \times P_{oil}$]. The value of the annual depletion is composed of three terms: the annual rate of oil reserves depletion ($\delta$), which is an increasing function of time; the estimated size of oil reserves in physical units (OR), which is a declining function of time; and the price of oil per barrel ($P_{oil}$), which is set exogenously.

**Table 4.3: Sources of Government Revenue in GCC Countries (US$ b)**

| Year | Total Revenue ($b) | Oil Revenue ($b) | Non-oil Revenue ($b) | Oil Revenue as Percent of TTL Revenue (%) |
|---|---|---|---|---|
| 1985 | 61.052 | 42.217 | 18.835 | 69 |
| 1986 | 39.338 | 25.281 | 14.057 | 64 |
| 1987 | 47.617 | 32.244 | 15.373 | 68 |
| 1988 | 44.892 | 29.565 | 15.327 | 66 |
| 1989 | 52.768 | 34.132 | 18.636 | 65 |
| 1990 | 69.600 | 53.343 | 16.257 | 77 |
| 1991 | 68.858 | 49.843 | 19.016 | 72 |
| 1992 | 78.021 | 57.828 | 20.193 | 74 |
| 1993 | 70.832 | 51.193 | 19.640 | 72 |
| 1994 | 65.475 | 49.843 | 19.566 | 70 |
| 1995 | 74.345 | 49.884 | 24.461 | 67 |
| 1996 | 76.646 | 51.009 | 25.636 | 67 |
| 1997 | 94.718 | 70.399 | 24.319 | 74 |
| 1998* | 63.666 | 46.101 | 17.566 | 72 |

*Source:* See references cited in Table 21. Estimate for 1998* is based on Oman, Kuwait, Saudi Arabia, and Qatar.

We start with the simplifying assumption that oil revenue ($\delta OR \times P_{oil}$) is the only source of revenue available to the government and ignore other sources of revenue for the time being.[7] In this 'pure' oil economy, government revenue (GR) equals oil revenue ($\delta OR \times P_{oil}$), and government expenditure is reduced to:

$$GE = [\delta OR \times P_{oil}] + [\text{Government Net Borrowing (GNB)}] \quad (4)$$

Accordingly, the operational budget deficit/surplus (OBD/S) may be written as follows:

$$OBD/S = [\delta OR \times P_{oil}] - [\delta OR \times P_{oil} + GNB] \quad (5)$$

This simplified formulation brings into focus the basic logic and shortcomings of present policies dealing with budget deficits in oil economies: increase $P_{oil}$ and/or reduce GE, i.e., government net borrowing, through improved efficiency, privatization, or the more fundamental development objective of diversifying the economy away from oil. However, the budgetary framework presented in equation 5 is not equipped to serve as a base to assess development objectives in oil economies. The equation requires additional specification.

## Budget Deficit and the Renewable Resource Gap

In essence, equation 5 presents an incomplete accounting statement. It does not take into account the depletion of the country's main asset: non-renewable oil. The costs of oil depletion have been likened to those incurred by environmental pollution. Yet, accounting for oil depletion is relatively simpler, conceptually and empirically, than accounting for environmental degradation. In the latter case, the concept of user cost has been developed.[8] Conceptually, in the case of environmental analysis, user cost is incorporated as part of the national account statement to illustrate that estimates of aggregate income should be lower than in the conventional national account system. Moreover, it illustrates that net investment should be lower, since environmental degradation, which requires conservation efforts and additional maintenance costs, is a direct loss or an accelerated depreciation of social capital. Nonetheless, inadequate knowledge about causes and consequences as well as the synergetic nature of the environment renders estimation of user cost for environmental degradation difficult conceptually and empirically.

In the case of oil economies, estimating the user cost for oil comprises two components:

a. The environmental impact, where the policy question is how to account for negative externalities; and
b. The exhaustion of a non-renewable resource, where the policy question is how to substitute the income from the non-renewable resource with a more sustainable income stream.

In the first case, the environmental impact of oil production and consumption processes—which ranges from air pollution and greenhouse effects to in-shore and offshore oil spills, among others—is a complex subject. It is an integral part of environmental accounting, which will not be discussed in this chapter.

Our focus, rather, is on the second component of user cost: the use of oil as a non-renewable resource. In this case, the task of estimating user cost is far less of a challenge. Indeed, it is relatively simple. As a non-renewable resource, user cost is simply the annual depletion of oil.[9] In value terms in the illustrative 'pure oil economy,' it is equal to government revenue ($GR = \delta OR \times P_{oil}$) as indicated in equation 5. To include the loss of social capital (user cost) in the budgetary framework, equation 5 should be rewritten as follows[10] where NOBD/S represents the 'Operational Budget' Net of 'User Cost':

$$NOBD/S = [\delta OR \times P_{oil}] - [\delta OR \times P_{oil} + GNB] - [\text{User Cost} \cong \delta OR \times P_{oil}] \qquad (6)$$

Equation 6 states the obvious. By the very nature of oil economies, the user cost of oil reserves equals government revenue (GR), which is equal to its expenditure (GE), given the assumption that oil revenue is the sole source of government revenue. In this case, if GNB = 0, then the government operational budget deficit (OBD) will be exactly equal to the value of oil depletion. The OBD/S will always be negative in the framework of equation 6, provided that no other sources of revenue, based on returns from non-renewable resources, are forthcoming.[11] We label the wider definition of deficit implied in equation 6 the *renewable resource gap*.[12] In the case of a 'pure oil economy,' the renewable resource gap is equal to user cost, which in this illustrative case is also equal to oil revenue. The definition of the renewable resource gap in the context of public finance analysis in the case of oil economies is given below in equation 7a. It is this 'renewable resource gap' that must be made explicit in the budget statement and in budgetary analyses. The narrowing, and eventual closing, of the renewable resource gap should be the guiding criterion for the evaluation of budget performance if oil economies are to attain sustainable development. The financial deficit becomes a policy tool as opposed to a policy target in the case of these economies.

There are various routes to the reduction of the budget deficit; not all of them lead to the reduction of the renewable resource gap. These include: an increase in oil revenue ($\delta OR \times P_{oil}$), an increase in the returns from government investment abroad ($iK_{finv}$), an increase in the tax revenue from non-oil production ($tO_3$), an increase in government net borrowing (GNB), and a reduction in government spending ($GC + GIK_{finv} + GIK_3$). Equation 7 presents a more elaborate budgetary framework that incorporates these factors:

$$NOBD/S = [(\delta OR \times P_{oil}) + (iK_{finv}) + (tO_3)] + [GNB] - [(GC) + (GIK_{finv} + GIK_3)] - [\delta OR \times P_{oil}] \quad (7)$$

Where:

| | |
|---|---|
| $\delta OR \times P_{oil}$ | Government revenue from oil in the accounting year, |
| $OR \times P_{oil}$ | Present value of oil reserves, |
| $\delta$ | Rate of oil depletion, |
| *I* | Rate of return on the stock of government investment abroad, $K_{finv}$, |
| t | Tax rate on aggregate output ($O_3$), originating from production based on the accumulated stock of non-oil capital $K_3$. |

Attempts to manipulate the parameters of oil revenue may reduce the budget deficit in equation 5 but not necessarily the renewable resource gap in equation 6. Increasing the oil depletion rate ($\delta$) or the price of oil ($P_{oil}$) are obvious examples. This increase will appear, equally, in both the oil revenue and the user cost terms, leaving the renewable resource gap invariable. Reliance on returns from investments abroad, although not as obvious, is another example of a policy that reduces the budget deficit but not necessarily the renewable resource gap. Investments abroad transform the oil resource, which is highly capital-intensive, into a resource that is highly *foreign*-labor-intensive. The accumulation of assets abroad provides for security against uncertainties, and its returns may supplement the development of a modern infrastructure, thus encouraging direct foreign investment. However, as discussed below, the optimality of this process requires careful analysis. Similarly, attempts to reduce government expenditure by rehabilitating government consumption may reduce the budget deficit but *not necessarily* the renewable resource gap. It is a conclusion of this study that the only viable sustainable option is the development of a tax system levied on non-oil production that engages the national labor force.[13]

To reduce the renewable resource gap, a transformation from oil to a non-oil economy is necessary. The transformation implies that tax revenue from non-oil production, $tO_3$, must exceed and eventually replace $\delta OR \times P_{oil}$. Accordingly, the renewable resource gap may be defined operationally as:

$$\text{Renewable resource gap} = [tO_3] - [\delta OR \times P_{oil}] \quad (7a)$$

The development of $tO_3$ can be achieved by increasing government investment ($GIK_3$) to enhance the economy's non-oil productive capacity $K_3$, which, thereby, increases government revenue from taxes levied on income derived from non-oil production $O_3$. The statement is not new. What is novel is the attempt to link the development of a non-oil production base with the renewable resource gap, and incorporate both concepts into a budgetary framework that has a built-in evaluation criterion. It follows that a financial budget deficit may be tolerated if it reduces the renewable resource gap.

As mentioned earlier, increasing $iK_{finv}$ through an increase in government investment abroad $GIK_{finv}$ will not by itself generate the necessary transformation. The optimality criterion for government investment abroad has been based, historically, on its utility in reducing uncertainties in the economic and political spheres. Reduction of uncertainties is conducive to a better development environment. In oil economies, however, the role of government investment abroad, as part of a development strategy, has not been articulated.[14] Moreover, there is no optimality criterion for the rate of oil depletion ($\delta$). In practice, ($\delta$) may be considered exogenous to national policy formulation in oil economies. Oil production quotas for individual oil-producing countries have been set and strictly enforced by the oil cartels for more than two decades now. The expanded budgetary framework presented in equation 7 may provide insight into the issue of optimality.

## The Role of Population and HRD in an Optimal Budget Statement

The budgetary framework in equation 7 is an attempt to incorporate explicitly the nature and depletion of the stock of oil—a non-renewable category of social capital that is the main source of government revenue. The proposed framework also highlights the importance of monitoring the impact of government expenditure on the development of a non-oil tax base. Such monitoring may require additional data and analysis.

Although expanded in scope, the budgetary framework in equation 7 lacks the effect of an important factor that characterizes the oil economies: namely, the high rate of population growth that is common to the GCC countries. Without accounting for population growth, it is difficult to develop an optimal budgetary statement, particularly in oil economies. In these economies, population growth has direct and indirect effects on the government wage bill, the capital-labor ratio, and the oil depletion rate per capita. In this section we attempt, briefly, to link population growth to the budgetary framework of equation 7. The underlying concept is that of optimum population.[15]

The present discussion follows closely the presentation of Pitchford (1974). Optimum population is a broad term with a wide range of interpretation given to it. In most cases analyses start with an aggregate welfare function (W) of the form:

$$W = Nu(c) \tag{8}$$

Where N is the level of population, c is the consumption per head, u(c) is the utility function of a typical consumer with the usual concavity properties. It is assumed that there is a level of subsistence $c_0>0$, for which $u(c_0) = 0$.[16] Assuming further an aggregate production function with constant returns to scale:

$$\Phi(N, K) \tag{9}$$

Where N is population (labor) and K is the capital stock.

In this case the optimal population *for a given capital stock* is determined by:

$$u(c) = (c - \Phi N)u'(c) \tag{10}$$

Where $\Phi N$ is the marginal product of labor, u(c) is the added utility of consumption.

Equation 10 provides a cost-benefit framework for the evaluation of the welfare contribution of an addition to the population. If the marginal product of the added member is lower than his/her consumption, then the utility derived from the added consumption will increase welfare. The welfare of society, however, declines as a result of that person being subsidized. We note that the marginal product of an added worker depends on the quantity and quality of the capital stock. In the case of oil economies, the capital that contributes the bulk of the revenue is a non-renewable resource (oil) that utilizes a very small fraction of the labor force in its production (extraction) process. It is this linkage between labor and capital in an oil economy that requires further attention.

To link optimal population analysis with the budgetary framework of equation 7, we re-specify the capital stock in equation 9 similar to that in equation 7:

$$\underline{\Phi}\ (N, [OR \times P_{oil}, K_{finv}, K_3]) \tag{11}$$

The production function in equation 11 may look similar to $\Phi$ in equation 9, but in fact they are fundamentally different. The stock of oil reserves ($OR \times P$) in $\underline{\Phi}$ represents the stock of the non-renewable resource, oil, that is being extracted/depleted at the rate $\delta$. It is the main source of social 'revenue.' The contribution of $\delta OR \times P_{oil}$ to the 'distribution branch' of public finance is much greater than its contribution to the production process.[17] Furthermore, as mentioned earlier, the labor content in the production of oil $\delta OR \times P_{oil}$ is insignificant. It is less than one percent of the total labor force.[18] The presence of $OR \times P_{oil}$ in the production function may be questioned on conceptual grounds. In contrast, $OR \times P_{oil}$ is a minor part of K in $\Phi$ of equation 9. On the other hand, $OR \times P_{oil}$, as a non-renewable resource, declines over time, given $P_{oil}$. The reduction in the stock of oil reserves accelerates over time for two reasons. First, given the high rates of population growth in the oil countries, concurrent increases in the level of government expenditure GE and in the rate of oil resource depletion will be required to maintain a constant level of entitlements per head. Second, to maintain the same level of oil revenue $\delta OR \times P_{oil}$, given oil prices, $P_{oil}$, and known reserves, $OR_t$, the depletion rate $\delta<1$ must increase over time, since, as a non-renewable resource, the current stock of oil, $OR_t$, must decline annually: $OR_t = (1-\delta)OR_{t-1}$.

In essence, in oil economies, the depletion rate of oil reserves, $\delta$, is an increasing function of time in the absence of alternative sources of non-oil revenue. It follows that the stability and viability of the social system itself may be called into question when the role of population dynamics is introduced into the analysis. If no alternative sources of income are forthcoming, i.e., no increase in $tO_3$, the government will be able to afford the same level of expenditure (GC) required to meet its social contract commitment. Per capita welfare u(c) will decline over time. Government legitimacy may be questioned if it does not meet its 'perceived' social contract obligations. Concomitantly, in the absence of $tO_3$, the renewable resource gap will widen and the financial deficit will increase if the government attempts to meet the social contract obligations through borrowing—a postponement of certain crisis. At the extreme, given high rates of population growth, per capita consumption, c, for some segments of the population, may fall below the minimum requirement, $c_0$ (i.e., $c < c_0$). If $OR \times P_{oil}$ is the only source of government revenue, optimal population will decline over time—a non-sustainable situation with uncertain sociopolitical consequences (see Sirageldin and Al-Khaled, 1996).

The budgetary framework of equation 7, along with the optimal population analysis in equations 10 and 11, provides a framework for evaluating progress toward sustainable development in the oil economies.

## An Empirical Illustration

The purpose of the present section is to estimate the renewable resource gap for the GCC oil economies and examine its trend over time. The necessary data for such analysis is not available, however. Accordingly, the empirical examples here presented should be considered illustrative of the issues examined in the chapter. A full empirical analysis must wait for the necessary data and should include concrete policy recommendations to develop a Sustainable Government Revenue (SGR) based on non-oil tax base ($tO_3$). The illustrative examples used in this section are for Saudi Arabia (1972–80) and for the GCC countries (selected years). They are presented in Tables 4.4 and 4.5, respectively. The Saudi Arabia illustration is based on data from Stauffer and Lennox (1984) for the period 1972–80.

The data in Stauffer and Lennox are basically an attempt to estimate non-oil GDP for Saudi Arabia. Many assumptions must be made to estimate the renewable resource gap. We hypothesized an average tax rate of 20 percent levied on non-oil production ($O_3$) to estimate non-oil government revenue ($tO_3$). We used the two estimates of oil revenue presented in Stauffer and Lennox: with and without refining. The findings are presented in Table 4.4. During the 1970s, the renewable resource gap increased significantly, especially in the second half of the decade. The Saudi Arabia renewable resource gap, in current prices, increased from SR 9.5b in 1972 to SR 214.4b in 1980 when revenue from refining was not included. When the latter value is included, the renewable resource gap jumped to SR 20.6b and SR 302.8b for 1972 and 1980, respectively. This estimate could be an upper bound, since the hypothesized tax rate is high. It is evident that the total reliance on oil revenue, for public finance, did not change during this period.

**Table 4.4: Renewable Resource Gap in Saudi Arabia, 1972–80 (SR b)**

| Year | GDP | Non-Oil GDP | Tax Revenue | Oil Revenue I | Oil Revenue II | Renewable Resource Gap I | Renewable Resource Gap II |
|---|---|---|---|---|---|---|---|
| 1972 | 33.2 | 8.4 | 1.7 | 11.2 | 22.3 | -9.5 | -20.6 |
| 1973 | 65.5 | 10.7 | 2.1 | 24.5 | 51.3 | -22.4 | -49.2 |
| 1974 | 117.5 | 17.4 | 3.5 | 64.2 | 95.2 | -60.7 | -91.7 |
| 1975 | 151.6 | 30.7 | 6.1 | 93.9 | 112.9 | -87.8 | -106.8 |
| 1976 | 185.7 | 40.9 | 8.2 | 107.9 | 125.7 | -99.7 | -117.5 |
| 1977 | 216.1 | 55.3 | 11.1 | 117.3 | 133.3 | -106.2 | -122.2 |
| 1978 | 239.2 | 76.3 | 15.3 | 114.6 | 135.8 | -99.3 | -120.5 |
| 1979 | 331.3 | 82.7 | 16.5 | 156.6 | 206.6 | -140.1 | -190.1 |
| 1980 | 472.9 | 88.2 | 17.6 | 232.0 | 320.4 | -214.4 | -302.8 |

*Note on estimation:* 1. Estimates for GDP, non-oil GDP, and oil revenue are based on Stauffer and Lennox (1984). 2. Tax revenue is based on an average tax rate of 20 percent of estimated non-oil GDP. 3. Renewable resource gap is calculated as [Sustainable Government Revenue] – [Government Oil Revenue]. Sustainable government revenue is estimated to equal a hypothetical 20 percent tax rate levied on non-oil value added.

Estimates of the renewable resource gap for the GCC countries are presented in Table 4.5 for selected years. These estimates are based on two scenarios. In the first, we assume that the size of non-oil production is 40 percent of reported GDP (scenario 1). In the second, we assume that non-oil value added is 60 percent of GDP (scenario 2).[19] In both scenarios, we assume that government revenue from taxes levied on non-oil production, the concept relevant to the calculation of the 'renewable resource gap,' is equal to an average 20 percent tax rate levied on non-oil value added. The tax revenue on non-oil GDP is the basis for what we call 'sustainable government revenue' (SGR) in the GCC countries. The estimated renewable resource gap in Table 4.5 continues to be sizable for the GCC region as a whole. For three decades, public spending, the main engine for economic activities in the GCC countries, did not narrow the renewable resource gap. The implications for sustainable development and the development of a competitive human resource base are evident and serious.

**Table 4.5: Estimates of Renewable Resource Gap in GCC Countries**

| Year | GDP ($b) | Non-oil GDP S1 (40%) | Non-oil GDP S2 (60%) | Tax Revenue S1 (20%) | Tax Revenue S2 (20%) | Oil Revenue | Resource Gap S1 | Renewable Resource Gap S2 |
|---|---|---|---|---|---|---|---|---|
| 1985 | 153.5 | 61.4 | 92.10 | 12.28 | 18.42 | 42.22 | 29.94 | 23.80 |
| 1990 | 174.3 | 64.72 | 104.58 | 13.94 | 20.92 | 53.34 | 39.40 | 32.42 |
| 1995 | 217.4 | 86.96 | 130.44 | 17.39 | 26.09 | 49.88 | 32.49 | 23.79 |
| 1996 | 239.3 | 95.72 | 143.58 | 19.14 | 28.72 | 51.01 | 31.87 | 22.24 |
| 1997 | 248.2 | 99.28 | 148.92 | 19.86 | 29.78 | 59.02 | 39.16 | 29.24 |
| 1998 | 232.9 | 93.16 | 139.74 | 18.632 | 27.948 | 50.17 | 29.562 | 19.318 |
| 1999 | 256.1 | 102.44 | 153.66 | 20.488 | 30.73 | 50.05 | 29.562 | 19.318 |
| 2000 | 312.9 | 125.16 | 187.74 | 25.032 | 37.548 | 82.9 | 57.868 | 45.352 |

*Notes:* All value in current prices; S1: non-oil GDP = 0.4 × GDP; S2: non-oil GDP = 0.6 × GDP; Non-oil tax revenue = 0.2 × non-oil GDP; Renewable resource gap = non-oil tax revenue – oil revenue

*Sources:* See previous tables.

## Renewable Resource Gap and Human Resource Development in the GCC Countries

The framework presented in this chapter has important implications for human resource development in the region. The previous discussion indicates that oil revenue, a non-renewable resource, is the main source of government revenue. Government revenue is the main force in the GCC economies. This is the case because the government and public sector enterprises employ the bulk of the national labor force in the GCC countries (between 80 percent and 96 percent). The generated demand from government employment has multiplier effects that generate economic activities across the various sectors and branches of the economy. Public expenditure goes beyond its sizable employment of national and expatriate workers. It also provides social services, builds infrastructures, and invests directly in the productive capacity of the economy. Directly or indirectly, public finance policies shape the development of the non-oil sector. Given the depletion nature of oil, if no non-oil sources of revenue are forthcoming, government revenue cannot be sustained for long, and the present system of public finance will eventually collapse. The result could be a steep decline in the standard of living, to levels far below the present one. The linkages between public finance and human resource development in the GCC countries may be illustrated schematically as follows.

A chain of causation, starting with the budget statement, vibrates into the economy, the labor market, and human resource development. Government revenue is dominated by proceeds from oil sales. Revenue from taxes and duties are relatively minor and are based on economic activities generated by the spending of public revenue from oil and its immediate derivatives. Government spending generates the bulk of citizen employment. The latter generates economic activities in the private sector that derives the demand for labor, mainly expatriates. The process depicts an almost one-way causation. This is so, since no tax revenue based on non-oil value added is forthcoming. The chain of causation may be illustrated as follows:

> [Oil revenue] → [(≅60–80%) of Government revenue] → [Government spending] → [Government employment (≅80–96 percent of) national/citizen labor] → [National/citizen labor income] → [Spending pattern of national/citizen labor] → [Economic activities in the private sector] → [Demand for expatriate labor] → [Spending pattern of expatriate labor] → [Additional demand for expatriate labor] → [Additional demand on oil revenue].

Indeed, the effect of public expenditures on economic and social activities, and its derived demand for labor, becomes negative when oil revenue declines. In the absence of sustainable non-oil revenue, the causation is almost one-to-one, allowing for some time lags.

The implications to human resource development (HRD) could be examined using the concepts of net operation budget (OB) and renewable resource gap. The equation may be rewritten as follows (the implied *labor demand* is indicated below the equation terms as minimal or max.):

$$\begin{aligned} OB = \ & \{\underset{\text{[minimal]}}{[\delta OR \times P_{oil}]} + \underset{\text{(max.)}}{[(tO_3) - (\delta OR \times P_{oil})]} + \underset{\text{[Oil dep.]}}{[t + d\,(VA_{oil})]} + \underset{\text{[Foreign]}}{[iK_{finv}]}\} \\ & + [GNB] - [(GC) + (GIK_{finv} + GIK_3)] \qquad (12) \end{aligned}$$

The first term on the right-hand side of equation 12 is oil production. It is highly capital-intensive—labor demand in that sector is minimal and declines as oil reserves decline. The second term is taxes levied on non-oil value added. It is mainly in the private sector and should be the basis for a sustainable demand for labor and government revenue. Taxes and dues levied on oil-dependent value added [$t+d\,(VA_{oil})$] are derived from employment that is mainly in the public sector and highly dependent on public support. It is not viable in the absence of oil revenue. The last part of government revenue is returns from investment abroad. It depends on foreign labor abroad. It is the second term on the right-hand side of equation 12 and represents the renewable resource gap that should be the focus of public policy. Closing that gap should be the primary development target in oil economies. Equation 12 presents that focus within a budgetary framework.

It is evident that public finance is a critical factor in development in general, and in the design of sustainable human resource development in the GCC countries in particular. A long-term strategy for human resource development must examine, in some detail, the system of public finance, especially its impact on the development of sustainable government revenue derived from non-oil production. The development of a base for non-oil production depends to a large degree on the allocation of the budget between investment to develop non-oil production and other government expenditure.

How much of these allocations result in the development of a sustainable non-oil production that engages the national/citizen labor force? This is a vital question for the development of human resources in the GCC countries, but it cannot be answered *a priori*. In this chapter, we have developed the concept of a 'renewable resource gap' as a criterion to evaluate the success of public finance in achieving this goal. Our analysis indicates that the present pattern of labor demand, an inevitable outcome of the structure of these economies, is by far the most critical factor in the development of human resources in oil economies in general and in the GCC countries in particular. For the past three decades, almost all policy recommendations and program efforts have focused on the supply side of human resource development—i.e., education and training—without adequate attention to the role of demand. These efforts have succeeded on the quantity side of education and training but apparently failed on the quality and motivation side. The latter are essential for competitiveness in the present global environment. The present structure of labor demand is, to a large degree, responsible for this apparent failure (Shafik, 1994; Sirageldin and Al-Khaled, 1996).

Most of the national/citizen labor force is employed in the public sector. Public sector employment offers citizens higher salaries, as well as better benefits and security, especially in the shape of a generous pension scheme, than is obtained in the private sector or by expatriate workers. There are negative consequences to this pattern of employment. Aside from the obvious fact that its effective needs and the eventual decline of oil revenue eventually limit the absorptive capacity of the public sector, the bulk of the national force is protected from market competition. Indeed, a large number of citizens act as owners or sponsors of private sector business activities. But very few citizens are on the payroll of private sector establishments. The result is segmented motivation toward work and risk-taking. In the present pattern of state employment, citizen commitment and motivation in the marketplace are not adequately tested.

The labor markets of the GCC economies are segmented in at least three significant ways: public/private, national/expatriate, and male/female. In essence, although small in size, these separate labor markets are composed of many small markets—some overlapping, others not. Each has its own *modus operandi*, culture, and clearance mechanism. However, although these 'mini' labor markets may not add up to a coherent development force, the same force is driving them: the economic power of the state and the spending behavior of the national population. It is the rate of growth of the national/citizen labor force, the growth of non-oil employment, and the rate of growth of non-oil tax revenue that should be the primary focus of any sustainable HRD in the GCC economies. The demand for expatriate labor is derived from the spending behavior of the national/citizen labor force. The latter is derived from the statement of public finance and budget allocation. This simple truth should be the guiding force in the design and evaluation of budget allocations.

## Summary and Conclusions

In this chapter, we have made the case that *assessment* of the growth and relative contribution of non-oil capital ($K_3$) to non-oil output ($O_3$) and to government revenue, through taxing non-oil production ($tO_3$), and independently of oil revenue transfers, should be an essential element of budgetary analysis.[20] Monitoring the growth of $tO_3$ relative to $\delta OR \times P_{oil}$ should be the main focus of budgetary analysis. Furthermore, the introduction of population growth in the analysis makes it clear that the transformation is vital. The time dimension of the transformation becomes evident when the present consumption levels per capita are linked to population growth, to the inevitable increase in the depletion rate of oil ($\delta$), and to the growth of government revenue from non-oil production (tK3). Indeed, the sociopolitical repercussions could be serious if average consumption per capita (c), whether for society as a whole or for major segments of the population, falls below the minimum set by the implied social contract in the oil states. This danger is illustrated by the lack of growth of non-oil revenue both in absolute terms and relative to oil revenue. Furthermore, the concept of non-oil revenue, as used in the standard National Accounts, does not correspond to our concept of non-oil tax revenue, tO3. The former includes other sources of revenue, such as returns on investment abroad or taxes on transfer payments that do not necessarily reduce the renewable resource gap. The effectiveness of all government expenditure, whether on consumption (GC) or on investment (GI), should be monitored and evaluated with respect to its contribution to the growth of tO3.[21]

The present analysis was made possible by formulating a consistent budget statement for oil economies. In that framework, the cost of using the non-renewable resource oil and the concept of the *renewable resource gap* ($tO3 - \delta OR \times P_{oil}$) were introduced explicitly into the budgetary framework. Conventional analysis of the budget deficit, by ignoring the nature of the renewable resource gap in oil economies and relying on an incomplete budget statement, has tended to confuse short-term with long-term signals. The budgetary framework presented in this chapter should alert policy makers in the oil economies to the longer-term development consequences of budgetary and public finance strategies and practice.

An important long-term policy concern is the development of human resources. Governments of the GCC countries have committed large resources for developing the supply of human resources through education and training. The present analysis, however, brings into focus the importance of development on the demand side of human resources. In oil economies, the role of governments in generating demand is substantial and is not necessarily positive. The analysis provides guidelines for both the design and the evaluation of budget allocations.

A conclusion, derived from our analysis, that may seem counter-intuitive is that conventional budget deficits may be tolerated, and even recommended, in theory and practice if they lead to the reduction of the renewable resource gap. This statement is practicable only if the criteria for evaluating the impact of the 'deficit' on the renewable resource gap are well articulated. The present study is only a beginning; refinement of the framework suggested here, and in the data sources and analysis, is still required.

## Notes

* Earlier drafts of this chapter were presented to the Middle East Economic Strategy Group, US Council on Foreign Relations, NY meeting, September 10–11, 1997, and at a World Bank "Brainstorming Session on Development in the GCC Countries," December 9, 1998. We are grateful for the various comments and suggestions received.

1 Oil economies refer to countries in which the oil sector and its immediate derivatives provide the main source of government revenue, typically more than 60 percent, while employing less than one percent of the labor force. In these economies, the government is the major economic force (Sirageldin and Khorshid, 1996, and references cited therein).

2 Human resource development (HRD) has been defined in various ways. In this chapter, we define it as the optimal utilization of human resources leading to increased per capita welfare and its fair distribution within and across generations in the competitive environment of the global era (Sirageldin and Al-Khaled 1996: 4). In this definition, the factors that influence the supply and demand for labor, as well as the efficiency of labor market performance, are included. This wider definition of HRD is important in the context of oil economies. As we attempt to demonstrate, it is the inadequacy of demand that constitutes a major handicap in the sustainable development of human resources in these countries.

3 Structural adjustments are promoted as a result of the presence of macroeconomic imbalances. A simple framework illustrates the situation (for details, see Scobie 1989: 19–33; and Sirageldin and Al-Khaled 1996: 26). In an open economy, it could be shown that, as an identity, the balance of trade (X - M) is equal to the gap between national income Y (the aggregate supply) and domestic absorption [total spending by domestic residents (A) = spending by the private sector (AP) + spending by the public sector (AG)], or:

$$X - M = Y - (AP + AG) \tag{1}$$

Adding international transfers ( InTr ) to both sides of (1), we get the Current Account Balance (CAB):

$$CAB = X + InTr - M = Y + InTr - (AP + AG) \tag{2}$$

A negative CAB equals the excess of spending of domestic residents (AP + AG) over their income—i.e., the country is living beyond its means. If (InTr) is not sufficient to cover the deficit in CAB, and international borrowing is no longer available, a macroeconomic imbalance occurs. In this case (AP + AG) must fall, or (X - M) or Y must rise. Structural adjustment policies are called into place. The scope of these policies may be clarified further by making use of the identity: [domestic absorption (AP + AG) is equal to spending on consumption (PC + GC) + spending on investment (PI + GI)]. Equation 2 can be written as:

$$CAB = Y + InTr - \{(PC + PI) + (GC + GI)\} \tag{3}$$

By introducing government revenue (GR) and defining {Y + InTr - GR - PC} as private saving (PS), we obtain:

$$CAB = (PS-PI) + \{GR-(GC+GI)\} = \text{Net Domestic Saving } \{(\text{Private})+(\text{Public})\} \tag{4}$$

$$CAB = \text{change in the stock of claims on the rest of the world} = (dNFA) \tag{4a}$$

4 The literature on structural adjustment policies varies in its emphasis on form, effectiveness, or social consequences. The following references are illustrative: Holmes (1987), Bell and Reich (1988), Guth (1988), Blejer and Chu (1988), Scobie (1989), World Bank (1990), Standing and Tokman (1991), Sirageldin, Wouters, and Diop (1994), and Richards (1995), as well as many publications by the World Bank, the IMF, and the ILO.

5 A budget statement should be consistent in its use of a flow or an asset management framework. For example, a budget deficit may be viewed within a financial transaction framework or a capital account framework. In the latter view, care must be given not to account for 'all' investment outlays as spending and not to confuse change in inventories with the depreciation of social capital. It should also be consistent in the valuation of the various components. For a discussion, see, for example, Leonard *et.al.*, 1988.

6 In some oil economies, e.g., Kuwait, government disposable revenue (GDR) excludes income from investment abroad.

7 The assumption that oil revenue is the only source of revenue in oil economies approximates the

economic reality of these economies in the early 1970s, especially for the case of the Arab Gulf countries. Recent trends seem not to change the situation significantly, however (Table 4.1).

8 For details, see El-Serafy (1992). Earlier, Stauffer and Lennox (1984) attempted to develop a methodology to account for 'wasting assets' in oil and mineral-exporting rentier states. The Stauffer-Lennox framework will be used in the empirical illustration below. More recently, Askari, Bazzari, and Tyler (1998) examined the issue of non-oil production in the GCC countries from a different perspective. Their focus was not on the development of an evaluative mechanism for the budget statement.

9 There are uncertainties, however, in the measurement of user cost of oil depletion. Estimates of total reserves change with new discoveries and new technologies for extraction. Oil prices are not stable, depending on the development of substitutes for oil, changes in input charges, on fluctuations in the demand for oil products—a result of business cycles, politics, or conservation efforts. However, on a flow basis, annual oil depletion is probably a sound estimate of user cost in the oil economies.

10 Our labeling of oil revenue as 'social capital' is to emphasize its common wealth property. Our use of the term should not be confused with the recent use of 'social capital' in the sociological literature. This latter use is in an early evolutionary stage. It lacks definitional and conceptual clarity. See Portes and Landolt (1996) for a critical review, and Coleman (1988) for an early statement.

11 The introduction of returns from foreign investments and government net borrowing will not change this basic conclusion as discussed below in the text.

12 This is why Sirageldin and Khorshid (1996) stated that the budget deficit was born with the birth of the oil economies. However, the idea of a 'renewable resource gap' was not fully developed in Sirageldin and Khorshid (1996) or Sirageldin and Al-Khaled (1996). The present discussion expands and formalizes their analysis, which does not provide for a complete accounting of oil economies.

13 Taxes on non-oil production, $tO_3$, discussed in the text, are different from those levied on incomes that are highly subsidized by oil revenue in the oil economies. The latter are basically taxes on transfer payments. Furthermore, the definition of 'non oil' production given in this chapter is not equivalent to the 'non-oil sector' as defined in the conventional classification of the national account. This conventional classification, in the case of oil economies, does not take into account the high dependency of 'non-oil production' on the distribution of oil revenue that heavily subsidizes both production and consumption. As Table 4.2 illustrates, non-oil revenue is highly related to oil revenue. Although deficient, these conventional definitions of the non-oil sector inform economic models devised to monitor the growth of the non-oil economy, from which arise significant policy conclusions and recommendations. See for example, Dahel and Sirageldin (1997), especially the review by Kawaz. Hoque and Al-Mutairi in the same volume present an econometric model of Kuwait's non-oil GDP based on the conventional classification. In this chapter, we question the validity of policy conclusions based on such definitions. The contribution of Stauffer and Lennox (1984), mentioned above (n. 8), is an exception. They attempted to re-estimate GDP for oil- and mineral-exporting rentier states, adjusting for the exhaustion of resources. Our focus is different, in that we attempt to introduce the concept of a 'renewable resource gap' in budgetary analysis.

14 In the early stages of the oil boom, foreign investment was a necessity because of the limited absorptive capacity of the oil economies at that time. However, in recent years, public spending on defense, public employment, and social and welfare services has accelerated, partly a result of high rates of population growth and partly because of an uncertain international political environment. The result is the appearance of budget deficit in recent years.

15 For more details, see Sirageldin and Al-Khaled (1996) and references cited therein.

16 In most of the oil economies, a generous entitlement system has significantly raised average consumption above the subsistence level $c_o$. This higher level of 'entitlement consumption' ($c_e > c_o$) is being viewed as normal with declining utility for lower standards, approaching zero at $c_o$. A reduction in the entitlement level of consumption is met with resentment and could have serious sociopolitical consequences. For a discussion of these issues, see Sirageldin (1996a and 1996b).

17 The contribution of oil revenue ($dOR \times P_{oil}$) to the distribution branch of public finance is well documented in the development plans and budget statements of the GCC countries.

18 Notice the absence in the discussion of the role of expatriate labor in oil economies. This absence is deliberate. Our focus is on the fundamental causes of disequilibria in the oil economies, and we view the presence of expatriate labor as a symptom rather than a cause of the disequilibria in these economies.

19 These are the assumptions used by Askari, Bazzari, and Tyler, 1998. We feel however, that the 40 percent assumption is closer to reality. It might even overestimate non-oil value added, especially if the effects of consumer subsidies, mainly dependent on oil revenue, are taken into account.

20 We do not imply, however, that the government becomes the owner or manager of a non-oil sector K3. The goal of government spending on investment ($GI_3$) is to develop a sustainable economy. That goal is better served when these expenditures are limited to the development of social capital, legislation, and infrastructure. This last includes the information and knowledge base necessary for the development of an environment that is efficient and conducive to the development of a competitive non-oil productive capacity in the private sector. This much is known and accepted in policy. What is missing, however, is the presence of an operational evaluation criterion.

21 Tax revenue $_tO_3$ should not be confused with taxes levied on income that is highly dependent on oil revenue. These latter taxes, popularly advocated in adjustment programs, do not in themselves contribute to the narrowing of the renewable resource gap in oil economies.

## References


Al-Ebraheem, Y. H. 1995. "Budget Deficit: Public Finance in Kuwait—Present, Expectations, and Possible Strategies." In Arabic. Kuwait: Dar Qurtas.

———. 1996. "Kuwait's Economic Travails," *Middle East Quarterly*. September, pp. 17–23.

Askari, H., M. Bazzari, and W. Tyler. 1998. "Policies and Economic Potential in the Countries of the Gulf Cooperation Council," in N. Shafik (ed.), *Economic Challenges Facing Middle Eastern and North African Countries: Alternative Futures*, pp. 225–55. London and New York: Macmillan and St. Martin's Press, in association with Economic Research Forum for the Arab Countries, Iran and Turkey.

Bell, D. E., and M. R. Reich (eds.). 1988. *Health, Nutrition, and Economic Crises: Approaches to Policies in the Third World*. Dover, MA: Auburn House Publishing Company.

Blejer, M.I., and K-Y. Chu (eds.) 1988. *Measurement of Fiscal Impact: Methodological Issues*. Occasional Paper 59, June. Washington, DC: International Monetary Fund.

Coleman, J. S. 1988. "Social Capital in the Creation of Human Capital," *American Journal of Sociology*, Vol. 94, Supplement S95–S120.

Dahel, R., and I. Sirageldin (eds.). 1997. *Models for Economic Policy Evaluation*. Greenwich, CT: JAI Press.

Guth, W. (ed.). 1988. *Economic Policy Coordination*. Washington, DC: International Monetary Fund and HWWA-Institute fur Wirtschaftsforschung-Hamburg.

Hoque, A., and N. Al-Mutairi. 1997. "An Economic Model of Kuwait's Non-Oil GDP," in R. Dahel and I. Sirageldin (eds.), pp. 351–66.

Holmes, F. (ed.). 1987. *Economic Adjustment: Policies and Problems.* Washington, DC: International Monetary Fund.

Kawaz, A. 1997. "Survey of some of the Policy Policy-Oriented Macroeconomic Models in the Arab Countries," in R. Dahel and I. Sirageldin (eds.), pp. 135–70.

Leonard, H. B., with J. Crowley, Y. H. Al-Ebraheem, S. A. Salih, and F. Weston. 1988. "Memo on Alternative Definitions of the Budget Deficit." Kuwait: Kuwait Institute for Scientific Research. June.

Portes, A., and P. Landolt. 1996. "The Down Side of Social Capital," *The American Prospect*, 26: 18–26, 94.

Pitchford, J. D. 1974. *Population in Economic Growth.* New York: Elsevier Publishing Company.

Richards, Alan. 1995. "The Impact of Structural Adjustment on Agricultural Development in the Near East Region." Working Paper No. 9525. Cairo: Economic Research Forum for the Arab Countries, Iran and Turkey.

Scobie, G. M. 1989. *Macroeconomic Adjustments and the Poor: Toward a Research Strategy.* Ithaca, NY: CFNPP, Cornell University.

Serafy, S. El. 1992. "Sustainability, Income Measures and Growth," in R. Goodland, H.E. Daly, and S. El Serafy (eds.), *Population Technology and Lifestyle: The Transition to Sustainability*, pp. 63–79. Washington, DC: Island Press for the World Bank and UNESCO.

Shafik, N. 1994. "Big Spending, Small Returns: The Paradox of Human Resource Development in the Middle East." Paper presented at the *Workshop on Labor Markets*, December 16–18, 1994. Cairo: Economic Research Forum for the Arab Countries, Iran and Turkey.

Sirageldin, I. 1996. "Population Dynamics, Environment and Conflict," in I. Sirageldin and E. Al-Rahmani (eds.), pp. 185–218.

———. 1996. "Islam, Society and Economic Policy," in I. Sirageldin and E. Al-Rahmani (eds.), pp. 219–41.

———, and R. Al-Khaled. 1996. *The Challenges of Globalization and Human Resources Development in the Arab World: Myth and Reality.* Liege: International Union for the Scientific Study of Population (IUSSP).

———, and Al-Rahmani (eds.). 1996. *Population and Development Transformations in the Arab World*, pp. 219–41. Greenwich, CT: JAI Press.

———, Wouters, A., and Diop, F. 1994. "The Role of Government Policy in Health: Equity versus Efficiency or Poverty versus Fiscal Vulnerability," in A. Sorkin and I. Sirageldin (eds.), *Nutrition, Food Policy and Development*, 8: 3–24. Greenwich, CT: JAI Press.

———, and M. Khorshid. 1996. "Human Resources Development and the Structure of Oil Economies: Critical Issues with Illustrations from Kuwait," in I. Sirageldin and E. Al-Rahmani (eds.), pp. 49–78.

Standing, G., and Tokman, V. (eds.). 1991. *Toward Social Adjustment.* Geneva: International Labor Organization.

Stauffer, T., and F. Lennox. 1984. "Accounting for 'Wasting Assets': Income Measurement for Oil and Mineral-Exporting Rentier States." Pamphlet Series: OPEC Countries and the New International Economic Order, No. 25. Vienna: The OPEC Fund for International Development.

World Bank. 1990. *Making Adjustment Work for the Poor: A Framework for Policy Reform in Africa.* Washington, DC: World Bank.

# Part II

# Human Capital

# 5

# Population and Education Prospects in the Arab Region

*Anne Valia Goujon*

## Introduction

This chapter considers the demographic and educational prospects in seven countries of the MENA region: Egypt, Jordan, Lebanon, Morocco, Sudan, Syria, and the West Bank and Gaza Strip.[1] In the past few years, the European Mediterranean countries have experienced extremely low patterns of fertility—actually below replacement level. Women in Greece, Italy, Portugal, and Spain have, on average, less than 1.5 children, sometimes less than 1.2 children. There is little doubt among demographers that sub-replacement fertility in the European Mediterranean area is a significant and lasting phenomenon which is unlikely to disappear in the near future (Lutz, 1998).

In contrast, the MENA region has been regarded as one of the most fertile areas in the world and is still regarded as such, albeit wrongly for most of the area. Fertility began to decline in the late 1970s in Northern Africa—Egypt, Morocco, and Tunisia—and has continued in a steady downward trend ever since. There has also been an abrupt decline in Algeria in the past few years, and even Sudan and Libya show sure signs of a decline. In the Middle East region, too, recent declines in fertility have been observed in Jordan, Syria, Saudi Arabia, and Yemen, while Lebanon has already attained low levels (see Rashad and Khadr, Chapter 2 in this volume). The only area experiencing an increase in fertility levels at this time was the West Bank and Gaza, where the rate of natural increase in 1997 was 3.4 percent and 4.6 percent, respectively (Population and Reference Bureau, 1997).

However, even if the general trend is toward lower levels of fertility, the question is: At what speed will the decline fall to below replacement level? The pace of fertility decline is seen as an important issue in both the north and the south Mediterranean. Europe, dominated by sub-replacement fertility and an aging population, sees the rate of population growth in the areas around the Mediterranean as a potential indirect factor of migration intensification. The population dynamics in the Palestinian territories could also have repercussions on the surrounding MENA areas—particularly Jordan, Syria, and Lebanon, not to mention Israel, if the rate of natural increase among the Palestinians is perpetuated in the coming years.

Despite the importance of fertility levels and their effects on the entire region, realistic projections of population growth and fertility decline in MENA are not generally available. It is, therefore, the object of this research to explore different possible outcomes. In doing so, I decided to disaggregate populations further than only age and gender, adding education as an explanatory parameter. It is generally accepted that education is intrinsically linked to fertility decline, as evidenced by the fact that the average Arab woman with some education has fewer children than the one with no education. Thus, education is seen as a factor of heterogeneity capable of influencing many variables of population change, such as fertility decline and the momentum of population growth. This study, then, combines a conservative approach to the projection of populations with a special focus on education.

Although many demographic variables seem to be influenced by a person's level of educational attainment, the correlation between education and fertility has been the most studied. The evidence of a negative relationship is overwhelming, as shown by the results of large fertility surveys.[2] Many social and economic factors (income, husband's education, types of egalitarian or non-egalitarian settings in the society, etc.) are also associated with differentials in marital fertility. However, only the 'place of residence' (rural/urban) factor comes anywhere near the significance of education (Jejeebhoy, 1995; Cleland and Hobcraft, 1985; Cleland and Scott, 1987).

**Table 5.1: Differentials in Total Fertility Rates by Levels of Educational Attainment in Ten Arab Areas, 1975–95**

| | | | Educational Levels | | |
|---|---|---|---|---|---|
| **Country** | **Year** | No Schooling | Primary | Secondary | Tertiary |
| Algeria | 1987 | 5.7 | 4.7 | 4.2 | 3.3 |
| | 1992 | 5.6 | 3.8 | 3.3 | 2.5 |
| Egypt | 1988/89 | 5.8 | 5.1 | 4.0 | 3.4 |
| | 1992 | 5.0 | 4.0 | 3.0 | 2.9 |
| Jordan | 1975/76 | 9.0 | 6.1 | 3.2 | 2.4 |
| | 1990 | 6.9 | 6.0 | 5.4 | 4.1 |
| Lebanon | 1995 | 3.5 | 2.8 | 1.6 | 1.4 |
| Libya | 1984 | 7.3 | 6.3 | 5.6 | 4.5 |
| | 1995 | 5.2 | 4.2 | 3.7 | 3.4 |
| Morocco | 1982 | 6.4 | 5.3 | 4.7 | 3.7 |
| | 1995 | 4.0 | NA | 2.4 | 1.9 |
| Sudan | 1983 | 7.1 | 6.1 | 5.4 | 4.3 |
| | 1993 | 5.4 | 4.7 | 4.3 | 3.7 |
| Syria | 1978 | 8.6 | 4.3 | 3.2 | NA |
| | 1993 | 5.3 | 4.3 | 3.5 | 2.6 |
| Tunisia | 1984 | 5.0 | 4.0 | 3.6 | 2.9 |
| | 1994 | 4.6 | 3.0 | 2.3 | NA |
| West Bank and Gaza | 1995 | 7.0 | 6.8 | 6.0 | 4.7 |

*Sources:* For Algeria (1987), Libya (1984), Morocco (1982), Sudan (1983), Tunisia (1984): Yousif, Goujon, and Lutz, 1996.
For Algeria (1992), Egypt (1988, 1992), Libya (1995), Morocco (1995), Sudan (1993), Syria (1993): El-Khorazaty, 1996.
For Jordan (1975): Department of Statistics, 1979.
For Syria (1978): Central Bureau of Statistics, 1982.
For Jordan (1990): Department of Statistics, 1992.
For Tunisia (1994): Yaakoubd, 1996.
For West Bank and Gaza Strip (1995): Palestinian Central Bureau of Statistics, 1996.
For Lebanon (1995): Goujon, 1997.

It is important to note that most of the linkages between education and fertility are complex. The only direct causal link between an advanced education and a lower fertility level operates through delaying the age at marriage and therefore the entrance of women into their reproductive years. As mentioned by Lutz *et al.* (1999),

> Other links operate through changing values. Schooling improves the information of little girls about the outside world, beyond the household level and the expectations of their parents, giving them more confidence in their capacities and potentials. In turn, their opinions will be more respected and they will have a greater say in household decisions, concerning expenses, family planning, and the education of children. Being educated generally provides women with the opportunity of employment outside the household or family circle; this would in turn limit their fertility because of the opportunity cost associated with children (Jejeebhoy 1995; Macgrath 1976; Noor 1981; Oppong 1987).

In countries where at least two rounds of demographic surveys are available,[3] all figures point to the existence of a differential in fertility levels according to mothers' level of education (Table 5.1). A comparison of this differential between the two data sets shows that it is a dynamic phenomenon that changes size with the overall fertility decrease and levels of school enrollment. As shown in Table 5.1, the differential in fertility level existing between the highest and the lowest level of education has increased in the cases of Algeria, Egypt, Morocco, and Tunisia, while it has decreased in the cases of Jordan, Libya, Sudan, and Syria. In the 1990s, women with a tertiary education bore between 31 percent (Sudan) and 61 percent (Lebanon) fewer children than women with no education. In Algeria and Tunisia, women with some primary education already had more than 30 percent fewer children than uneducated women.

**Figure 5.1: Infant and Child Mortality Rates in the Arab Region in the 1990s by Mother's Level of Education**

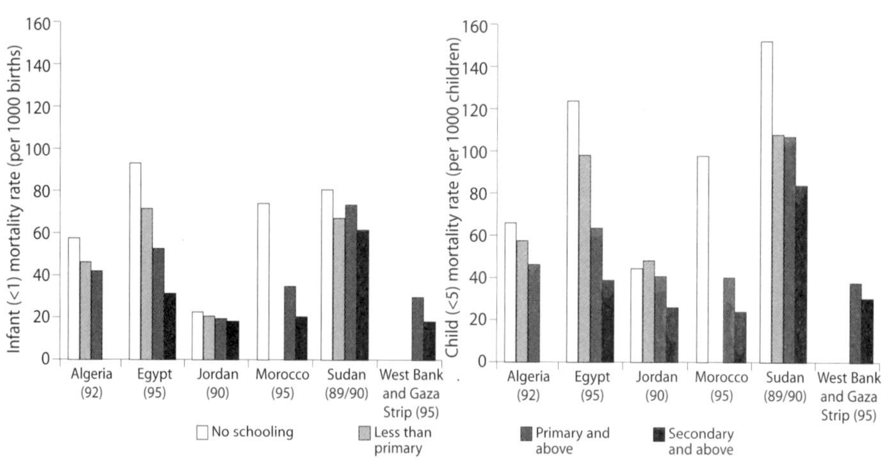


*Sources:* For Algeria (1992), Jordan (1990): El-Khorazaty, 1996. For Egypt (1995): El-Zanaty et al., 1996. For Morocco (1995): Azelmat et al., 1996. For Sudan (1989–1990): Department of Statistics, 1991. For West Bank and Gaza Strip (1995): Palestinian Central Bureau of Statistics, 1996.

Women's education appears to influence not only fertility but also child mortality. Infant and child mortality rates according to the mother's level of education are plotted in Figure 5.1 for selected countries. This reveals the existence of large differentials in all countries. On average, child mortality has been declining as mothers' education increases. There are a few exceptions, such as Sudan in 1989–90, where children born to women with a primary education were more likely to die within their first year of life than children born to mothers with no education.

Figure 5.2 represents female enrollment ratios at primary, secondary, and tertiary levels of education in ten Arab areas in 1980–81 and 1991–95. It shows that school enrollment of girls has increased at all levels, with the exception of Morocco and Sudan. The jump to higher ratios of school enrollment has, however, been stronger at the primary and secondary levels, while female enrollment ratios at tertiary level are significantly lower and have not shown a substantial change in the past 10–15 years. Despite some common features, these figures show that the region is not homogenous and that demographic patterns vary by country. However, they do point to a generalized radical transformation within the last 10–15 years, with the region evolving from levels of high fertility and low education to relative levels of low fertility and high education.

These changes in the levels of educational attainment have affected and will continue to affect the educational structure of the population. The present cohorts of better educated female pupils will most likely adopt different fertility- and mortality-causing patterns—most probably at lower levels than did the older cohorts. Thus, the implications in terms of population growth rates will be significant.

In spite of the positive impact of increased women's schooling having reverse effects on

**Figure 5.2: Female Enrollment Ratios, Primary, Secondary, and Tertiary Levels, 1980–95, Ten Arab Areas**

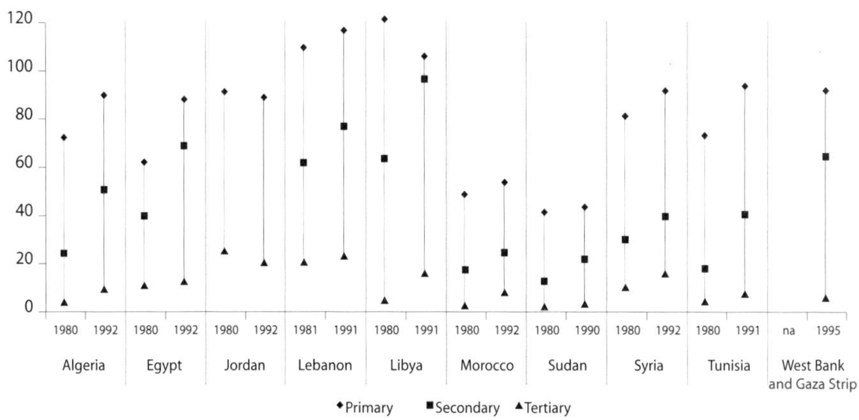


*Notes:* For Algeria, Morocco, Syria, Tunisia, the West Bank and Gaza Strip: enrollment rates at primary and secondary levels are net. For Egypt, Jordan, Lebanon, Libya, Sudan: enrollment rates at primary and secondary levels are gross. For all areas, tertiary enrollment rates are gross.

*Sources:* For all: UNESCO, 1995, except UNESCO, 1990, for Lebanon 1981.

population growth by decreasing the number of children born and increasing their chances of survival; it is likely that the global net effect on population growth will be negative. Based on a sample of 68 countries, Schultz (1994: 257) estimates that the increase of women's schooling by 2.2 years is associated with aggregated lower birth and child death rates of 4.7 percent and 2.0 percent, respectively, for a net effect of population growth reduction of 2.8 percent. Figures would, of course, vary for the Arab countries under study, but it may be assumed that the general negative effect of education on population growth would be borne out for the MENA region as well.

For population projections, there are two ways to proceed: either to implicitly or to explicitly consider education in the definition of fertility and mortality assumptions. Both methods are certainly valid. Most projections include education implicitly, meaning that the fertility and mortality assumptions are based on considerations pertaining to future educational levels, among other factors. The United Nations, for instance, define the target fertility period—the period at which the assumed fertility decline will pause—"by taking into account a range of socioeconomic factors, such as population policies and programmes, adult literacy, school enrollment levels" (United Nations, 1995).

However, I believe that an explicit consideration of educational levels would improve the results of this projection exercise. Therefore, not only does education enter the exercise of assumption definition, it is also present at every stage of the projection work. The population to be projected is disaggregated into several educational categories. For each of these, assumptions are made on the future fertility and mortality of peoples, as well as on the relative weight of the categories in the total population. Goujon and Wils (1996), in a study of the impact of educational fertility differentials on population projections, make several general points about the likely impact of future enrollment levels on fertility and population size. Their main point is that in the case where there are fertility decreases within education groups, these decreases are compounded by a continued increase in the education profile of the adult population. They compare aggregate (no education categories) population projections with multi-state (population disaggregated into several educational categories) projections. They found that the combined presence in a country of massive increases in enrollment rates and large fertility differentials by education could result in a significant difference between the aggregate and the multi-state population. This was verified for Sudan and Tunisia. It would be worth further work to formalize this intuitive generalization.

This chapter is based partly on two studies conducted in 1996 and 1997 at the International Institute for Applied Systems Analysis (IIASA) in Laxenburg, Austria. The first study looked at the demographic and education trends in North Africa (Yousif, Goujon, and Lutz, 1996), while the second concentrated on Jordan, Lebanon, Syria, and the West Bank and Gaza (Goujon, 1997). For the North African report, we chose at that time to base the population and education projections of the six countries on census data relating primarily to the 1980s. For the purpose of this chapter, I have updated the projections for Egypt, Morocco, and Sudan with trends in fertility, child mortality, and levels of education as reflected by new data. The chapter is an attempt to provide a picture of the seven countries under study in the middle of the twenty-first century.

## Methodology

A multi-state population projection method is used.[4] It allows not only for projection of the population as a whole, but also for consideration of heterogeneity by dividing the population into groups—in this case levels of educational attainment (see Appendix 5.A1).

Specific sets of assumptions are applied to these educational groups regarding their fertility and mortality patterns. These assumptions are derived from a thorough analysis of past and present population, fertility, mortality, migration, and education trends (Yousif *et al.*, 1996, and Goujon, 1997). Infants and children under five are affected by different mortality differentials according to their mothers' level of education. No other mortality differential by education was considered.

The weight of each of the educational categories can be changed by increasing or decreasing rates of transition between categories. The study divides the population into four educational categories: low, medium, high, or advanced education.[5] No international migration has been assumed.

The starting year for Jordan, Lebanon, Syria, and the West Bank and Gaza projections is 1994, which corresponds to the year of the latest Economic and Social Commission for Western Asia (ESCWA) country estimates of population age and gender structures at the time of the survey (ESCWA, 1995). The projections for the North Africa group of countries start in 1995 and are based on the United Nations latest estimates of population age and gender structures (United Nations, 1997). All seven countries are projected for a period of 50 years, i.e. ending in 2044–5.

## Scenario Assumptions

Three scenarios were defined for all four educational categories in each of the seven countries. The three scenarios combine low, central, and high assumptions for fertility, mortality, and education. The base-year parameters of each country remain the same in all three scenarios. The main assumptions are summarized in Table 5.2.

### *Rapid Development Scenario*

This scenario combines low fertility, low mortality, and high education, this last meaning the highest levels of enrollment that can be foreseen. All children of the countries concerned would complete the final grade of primary school by 2014–20. Major improvements are also witnessed for all areas at higher levels of schooling: 50 percent of children would receive a secondary education and 40 percent would go into third-level studies. The gender gap—that is, lower levels of enrollment for girls than for boys—would disappear in all cases.

According to the rapid development scenario, total fertility rates (TFR) reach low levels by the end of the projection period. The yearly decrease for the period 1994–2045 is 1.5–1.8 percent for Egypt, Jordan, Sudan, and the West Bank and Gaza, with 1.0–1.2 percent for Lebanon, Morocco, and Syria. This brings the overall fertility level below replacement level (TFR below 1.7) by 2039–45 for all countries except the West Bank and Gaza, which are slightly above replacement level at 2.2. The fertility of women with the highest level of educational attainment would be very low: between 1.1 and 1.9. This assumption of high fertility decline is consistent with the assumptions of higher levels of enrollment and would reflect the efforts realized in most countries during the last decade in terms of female enrollment (Figure 5.B2). Fast-declining fertility rates and fast-increasing enrollment rates are suggestive of rapid improvements in the socioeconomic well-being of the populations concerned. This is also consistent with a rapid decline in mortality rates, with both men and women gaining three years of life expectancy per decade.

**Table 5.2: Main Assumptions of Projections (%)**

| | **Rapid Scenario: Low fertility, low mortality, high education** | **Central Scenario: Central fertility, mortality, and education** | **Stagnation Scenario: High fertility, high mortality, low education** |
|---|---|---|---|
| **Enrollment** | By 2015 | By 2045 | Constant |
| Primary | 100 | 100 | 1995 level |
| Secondary | 50 | 55 | 1995 level |
| Tertiary | 40 | 30 | 1995 level |
| | No differences between male and female levels of enrollment by end of projection period | No difference between male and female levels of enrollment by end of projection period | Differentials in enrollment rates between male and female children kept at 1995 level |
| **TFR in 2044–5** | | | |
| Egypt | 1.5 | 2.0 | 3.1 |
| Jordan | 1.7 | 2.6 | 3.6 |
| Lebanon | 1.5 | 1.8 | 2.7 |
| Morocco | 1.2 | 1.8 | 2.7 |
| Sudan | 1.6 | 2.3 | 4.1 |
| Syria | 1.5 | 2.4 | 4.1 |
| West B. & Gaza | 2.2 | 2.9 | 3.7 |
| **Life expectancy gain per decade** | **3 years** | **2 years** | **1 year** |

*Source:* Author's calculations.

### *Central Scenario*

This scenario combines central assumptions of fertility, mortality, and education. The central path combines assumptions that are considered the most likely if current trends persist over the next 50 years. This means that school enrollment will increase substantially, as in the rapid development scenario; however, to differentiate the central from the rapid development scenario, it was assumed that it will take the whole projection period to reach full intake in primary school, and levels of enrollment in secondary and tertiary school were assumed to be lower than those in the rapid development scenario. No gender gap was assumed, except for Syria, where women will not have achieved full intake in primary by 2044.

The central fertility path would lead to a fertility decline at an average annual rate of 0.5 to 1.5 percent in the seven countries. By 2039–45, the TFR at the national level is assumed to be between 2.9 for the West Bank and Gaza, 2.6 for Jordan, 2.4 for Syria, 2.3 for Sudan, 2.0 for Egypt, and 1.8 in Lebanon and Morocco. The most important decline would take place in the West Bank and Gaza, where the national TFR would drop from

6.2 in 1994 to 2.9 in 2044. Women who have achieved tertiary level education in Egypt, Lebanon, Morocco, and Syria would have a TFR below replacement level, while women with the lowest educational category would have a TFR level of between 2.4 and 4.0 at the end of the projection period.

This central variant assumes a two-year improvement per decade of the average life expectancy at birth for both males and females and for all countries.

### *Stagnation Scenario*

This scenario assumes high levels of fertility and mortality and a low level of education. This would imply a deterioration of the present situation in a number of areas. Educational transition rates are assumed to be kept constant at their 1994–5 levels. This assumption gives countries the benefit of their educational efforts in the recent past. Egypt, Jordan, Lebanon, and the West Bank and Gaza are left with enrollment levels that would translate during the projection period to high levels of educational attainment. In the case of Morocco, Sudan, and Syria, lower levels of education that were prevalent in the base year would be reflected in the future educational attainment of the population.

We assume that fertility remains high, although lower than in the base year, with the exception of Lebanon and Syria, where fertility rates in 1994 were already quite low (2.5 and 4.3 respectively) and a slight increase was implemented. Mortality declines slightly; the life expectancy at birth increases moderately, by one year per decade of average life expectancy.

## Results

### *Population Growth*

Rapid population growth is certain for the Middle East group (Table 5.3). The stagnation, central, and rapid development scenarios show a total population of 82, 67, 58 million persons, respectively, for the four countries—Lebanon, Jordan, Syria, the West Bank and Gaza—in 2044 as compared to an aggregate population of 24 million in 1994. Thus, under all assumptions envisaged by the three scenarios, the projections point to a range of population increases of double and triple proportions within the next 50 years for these four countries. The aggregated regional population results, however, hide some major national differences in terms of population growth. Among the four countries considered, Lebanon would be the only country under all three scenarios where no doubling of the population is forecast, while the population of Jordan and Syria would grow by factors of 2.6–3.6 under all scenarios. For the West Bank and Gaza, the three scenarios show at least a quadrupling of the population, and, under the stagnation scenario, very possibly a five-fold increase, to 11.3 million in 2044.

Population growth will be slower in the North Africa group—Egypt, Morocco, and Sudan—as compared to the Middle East group. Under stagnation assumptions, the aggregate population of the three countries would be multiplied, at most, by 2.4 between 1995 and 2045. These countries would more than double their population under the central scenario—from 115 million in 1995 to 233 million in 2045—while the rapid development scenario would result in a slightly lower projection of 216 million in 2045. The three countries are more homogenous than those in the Middle East group, with very little difference between them in the rates of population growth.

**Table 5.3. Population in 1994–5 and 2044–5: Rapid, Central, and Stagnation Scenarios (in 1,000)**

| | 1994–5 Population | 2044–5 Population | | |
|---|---|---|---|---|
| | | Rapid | Central | Stagnation |
| **North Africa**[a] | | | | |
| Egypt | 62,091 | 118,101 | 127,130 | 151,002 |
| Morocco | 26,531 | 46,061 | 48,972 | 55,897 |
| Sudan | 26,870 | 51,758 | 57,062 | 73,412 |
| **Region Total** | **115,492** | **215,920** | **233,164** | **280,311** |
| **Middle East**[b] | | | | |
| Jordan | 4,058 | 10,655 | 12,194 | 13,880 |
| Lebanon | 3,481 | 5,756 | 6,007 | 6,767 |
| Syria | 13,734 | 32,583 | 39,088 | 50,116 |
| West B. & Gaza | 2,239 | 9,207 | 10,146 | 11,322 |
| **Region Total** | **23,512** | **58,201** | **67,435** | **82,085** |

*Notes:*
[a] Base year and end year, respectively, are 1995 and 2045.
[b] Base year and end year, respectively, are 1994 and 2044.
Rapid development scenario: low fertility / low mortality / high education.
Central scenario: central fertility / central mortality / central education.
Stagnation scenario: high fertility / high mortality / low education.
*Source:* 1994 figures for Jordan, Lebanon, Syria, and the West Bank and Gaza Strip: ESCWA, 1995; 1995 figures for Egypt, Morocco, and Sudan: United Nations, 1997; 2044–5 population figures: author's calculations.

The rapid development scenario gives the lowest population results. As Table 5.4 shows, the population of Jordan and Syria would grow at an annual rate of under 2 percent during the 50-year projection period; between 1.1 and 1.3 percent for the populations of Egypt, Morocco, and Sudan; one percent for Lebanon; and 2.9 percent for the West Bank and Gaza. The population momentum is such that even if fertility had fallen abruptly to an average of two children per woman in 1994–99, the population would still almost double within the next 50 years. This 'certainty' of increase in population growth could have tremendous economic, social, and environmental implications for these countries. It is also of importance for the neighboring countries, especially Israel and Jordan, as well as Lebanon, on account of the potential migration associated with such population growth. Under less favorable conditions, i.e. under the central and stagnation scenarios, the rate of growth is, of course, even more significant.

The lowest population increases occur in Lebanon and Morocco. The annual rates of population growth oscillate between 1.0–1.1 percent in the rapid development scenario, 1.1–1.2 percent in the central scenario, and 1.3–1.5 percent in the stagnation scenario. Lebanon experienced dramatic fertility reductions in the 1970s, combined with high levels of enrollment for both male and female children. For Morocco, the trend toward lower fertility levels has been continuous since the early 1980s, which went hand in hand with a small but constant out-migration, leading to an annual population growth of 2.0 percent in 1995.

**Table 5.4: Average Annual Rate of Population Growth over the Period 1994–5 to 2044–5 under the Rapid Development, Central, and Stagnation Scenarios (%)**

| | Average annual rate of population growth | | | |
|---|---|---|---|---|
| | 1990–95 | 2044–5 | | |
| | | Rapid | Central | Stagnation |
| **North Africa**[a] | | | | |
| Egypt | 2.3[c] | 1.3 | 1.4 | 1.8 |
| Morocco | 2.2[c] | 1.1 | 1.2 | 1.5 |
| Sudan | 3.0[c] | 1.3 | 1.5 | 2.0 |
| **Middle East**[b] | | | | |
| Jordan | 3.3[c] | 1.9 | 2.2 | 2.5 |
| Lebanon | 2.0[c] | 1.0 | 1.1 | 1.3 |
| Syria | 3.5[c] | 1.7 | 2.1 | 2.6 |
| West Bank | 3.4[c] | | | |
| and | | 2.9 | 3.1 | 3.3 |
| Gaza | 4.6[c] | | | |

*Notes:* Rapid scenario: low fertility / low mortality / high education.
Central scenario: central fertility / central mortality / central education.
Stagnation scenario: high fertility / high mortality / low education.
[a] Base year and end year, respectively, are 1995 and 2045.
[b] Base year and end year, respectively, are 1994 and 2044.
[c] Rate of natural increase in 1995 (PRB, 1995).
*Source:* 1990–95 figures: Population and Reference Bureau, 1995; 1994–95 to 2044–5 figures: author's calculations.

Although the population of the seven countries will continue to increase over the next 40 years, it will grow at a slower pace than in the past. Even under the most pessimistic (stagnation) scenario, the average annual rate of population growth in 2039–45 would be below the annual rate of growth in 1994–5 (Table 5.4). The decrease is quite dramatic in the case of Sudan, where the population that had grown at a rate of 3.0 percent in 1995 grows at a rate of 1.5 percent until 2045 under the central scenario, and at a rate of 1.3 percent under the rapid development scenario. Similar important reductions in the rates of population growth can be observed in the case of Jordan and Syria, especially under the rapid development scenario.

### *Age Structure*

Table 5.5 shows that the pattern of the under-15 age group continues to dominate the age structure of most of the populations studied. For Egypt, Jordan, Sudan, Syria, and the West Bank and Gaza, the proportion of the population in the 0–15 age group remains around 30 percent under the stagnation scenario and above 20 percent under the central scenario. The same age group would comprise more than 37 percent of the population under the stagnation scenario in Syria, and the West Bank and Gaza. The central scenario for the West Bank and Gaza gives a figure of 32 percent for the population under 15 years of age. For the two Palestinian territories, even under the rapid scenario for population aging (low fertility and low mortality), 28 percent of the population would still be under

15 years of age by 2044. Under this scenario, the other countries show a lesser proportion of the population in the youngest age group, most of all in Egypt, Lebanon, and Morocco—all below 18 percent. The populations of Lebanon and Morocco will age at a faster rate than in the other countries, with proportions of under 15 years of age equal to 15–25 percent under all three scenarios by 2044–5.

**Table 5.5: Percentage Population below 15 Years of Age; Percentage Population above 60 Years of Age: 1994–5 and 2044–5; Rapid, Central, and Stagnation Scenarios**

| | Ratio 1994–5 | Percent of 0–14 age group in total population in 2044–5 | | |
|---|---|---|---|---|
| | | Rapid Scenario | Central Scenario | Stagnation Scenario |
| **North Africa**[a] | | | | |
| Egypt | 38.0 | 17.6 | 21.7 | 29.6 |
| Morocco | 36.3 | 14.4 | 18.7 | 25.4 |
| Sudan | 41.1 | 20.2 | 25.5 | 35.6 |
| **Middle East**[b] | | | | |
| Jordan | 41.4 | 21.5 | 28.1 | 34.1 |
| Lebanon | 33.2 | 14.5 | 17.2 | 23.9 |
| Syria | 49.1 | 19.4 | 27.0 | 37.2 |
| West Bank & Gaza | 47.5 | 28.1 | 32.3 | 37.2 |
| | **Ratio 1994–5** | **Percent of 60+ age group in total population in 2044–5** | | |
| **North Africa**[a] | | | | |
| Egypt | 6.5 | 20.8 | 17.6 | 13.4 |
| Morocco | 6.3 | 24.6 | 21.1 | 16.8 |
| Sudan | 5.0 | 15.7 | 13.0 | 9.0 |
| **Middle East**[b] | | | | |
| Jordan | 4.2 | 15.3 | 12.1 | 9.4 |
| Lebanon | 7.8 | 29.4 | 25.9 | 20.7 |
| Syria | 6.4 | 15.4 | 11.7 | 8.2 |
| West Bank & Gaza | 5.5 | 10.2 | 8.4 | 7.0 |

*Notes:* Rapid scenario: low fertility / low mortality / high education.
Central scenario: central fertility / central mortality / central education.
Stagnation scenario: high fertility / high mortality / low education.
[a] Base year and end year, respectively, are 1995 and 2045.
[b] Base year and end year, respectively, are 1994 and 2044.
*Source:* Same as for Table 5.3.

Consequently, as Table 5.5 shows, Morocco in the North Africa group and Lebanon in the Middle East group are countries in which relative rapid aging of the population is a certainty under the assumptions of this study. By 2044–5, under the rapid development and central scenarios, the proportion of elderly—above 60 years of age—is forecast at 21–25 percent in Morocco and 26–29 percent in Lebanon. The latter was the only country in which the proportion under 15 years was below 40 percent in 1994. Even under the stagnation scenario, the above-60 population is almost 17 percent and 21 percent for Morocco and Lebanon, respectively. For all the other areas, aging of the population will be very slow, especially in Middle East group. It is even more amazing to see that under the rapid development scenario, only 15 percent of the population of Jordan, Sudan, and Syria and 10 percent of the population of the West Bank and Gaza would be above 60 years of age by 2045.

### *Education*

Comparison across countries regarding the level of educational attainment is difficult because of the lack of information on the quality of national education systems. However, it is still possible to draw some conclusions on future educational prospects in the Arab region.

The level of education of the population increases in all areas considered and under all scenarios. The increase is always stronger for women than for men, with Lebanon and Syria showing the most impressive improvements for both men and women (Table 5.6).

In the Middle East group of countries, the three scenarios entail a substantial decline in the percentage of the population with low schooling in all areas except Syria, where an appreciable decline is envisaged only under rapid development assumptions. According to this scenario, the proportion of the Syrian population with the lowest level of schooling declines from 40 percent for males and 65 percent for females in 1994–5 to near 6 percent and 13 percent, respectively, in 2044–5. For the other countries, reductions are more substantial. In 1994–5, almost a quarter of the male population and almost a third of the female population had attained only the lowest level of education in Jordan, Lebanon, and the West Bank and Gaza. the proportion is only 2–7 percent by 2044 in the rapid development and central scenarios, and 6–11 percent under the stagnation scenario, for both genders.

Another important result is that gender disparities in education narrow considerably at all levels of education and in all countries. It is especially true of the rapid development scenario, where a closing of the gender gap is envisaged by the year 2014–20. Morocco and Syria maintain the highest gender gap in the population with no schooling. There is 7–11 percentage points difference between male and female under the rapid development scenario, and 12–15 percentage points under the central scenario (Table 5.6). The gender gap is almost non-existent in the rapid development and central scenarios in all other countries.

The momentum of education diffusion influences projection results. This can be seen on several levels: (a) the gender gap, (b) the level of educational attainment under the rapid development scenario, and (c) the level of educational attainment under the stagnation scenario.

(a) Although female enrollment rates increase under the central and rapid development scenarios for all areas and the gender gap is reduced considerably, the improvements do not reach the whole adult female population. For instance, in Syria, there will still be 4 percent more men with a primary education than women under the rapid development scenario. More markedly, in Egypt under the central scenario there will still be 6 percentage points difference between the proportion of men and women with advanced education.

(b) The education momentum shows, as well, in the time necessary to translate school enrollment rates into education rates. For example, the high education scenario (rapid development) for most countries implements a full primary school intake for both genders within the next 20 years. In 2039–45, these areas will still comprise between 2 percent and 10 percent of the male population with the lowest level of education; and between 3 percent and 21 percent of the female population. Thus, there is a long time lag between beginning an effort to educate the youth and the effect of having an adult population—and consequently a labor force—which is well educated.

**Table 5.6: Population over 15 Years of Age by Level of Education (%), 1994–5 and 2044–5, Rapid, Central, and Stagnation Scenarios**

| | | Male | | | | Female | | | |
|---|---|---|---|---|---|---|---|---|---|
| | School Levels | 1994–5 | Scenarios –2044–5 Rapid | Central | Stagnation | 1994–5 | Scenarios –2044–5 Rapid | Central | Stagnation |
| **North Africa** [a] | | | | | | | | | |
| Egypt | A | 39.2 | 8.4 | 11.9 | 21.1 | 60.7 | 14.0 | 19.5 | 34.0 |
| | B/C | 24.8 | 49.1 | 47.2 | 27.9 | 16.7 | 47.8 | 45.7 | 25.9 |
| | D | 36.1 | 42.4 | 40.9 | 51.1 | 22.6 | 38.3 | 34.9 | 40.1 |
| Morocco | A | 45.0 | 9.9 | 13.3 | 21.5 | 69.8 | 21.0 | 28.6 | 47.4 |
| | B | 25.2 | 19.3 | 25.9 | 34.2 | 14.2 | 14.6 | 19.1 | 22.6 |
| | C | 25.4 | 45.4 | 45.9 | 38.9 | 14.1 | 40.7 | 39.1 | 26.5 |
| | D | 4.4 | 25.3 | 15.0 | 5.3 | 1.9 | 23.8 | 13.3 | 3.6 |
| Sudan | A | 46.7 | 8.5 | 14.2 | 31.0 | 64.4 | 12.4 | 20.2 | 42.5 |
| | B | 10.6 | 11.2 | 14.9 | 14.7 | 8.6 | 11.1 | 14.7 | 14.5 |
| | C | 16.1 | 43.2 | 37.4 | 15.8 | 10.9 | 42.2 | 36.6 | 14.8 |
| | D | 26.6 | 37.2 | 33.5 | 38.5 | 16.2 | 34.3 | 28.6 | 28.2 |
| **Middle East** [b] | | | | | | | | | |
| Jordan | A | 19.6 | 2.6 | 2.2 | 6.1 | 30.4 | 4.0 | 3.5 | 11.4 |
| | B | 21.2 | 13.1 | 16.4 | 18.8 | 18.2 | 12.5 | 15.9 | 16.5 |
| | C | 40.4 | 51.1 | 54.7 | 50.0 | 36.5 | 50.2 | 53.8 | 45.9 |
| | D | 18.8 | 33.2 | 26.6 | 25.1 | 14.9 | 33.4 | 26.9 | 26.3 |
| Lebanon | A | 31.0 | 4.9 | 5.3 | 6.9 | 35.8 | 6.8 | 6.9 | 8.1 |
| | B | 44.0 | 30.7 | 41.6 | 61.2 | 41.1 | 29.6 | 39.2 | 55.9 |
| | C | 16.7 | 39.2 | 36.2 | 21.4 | 15.4 | 39.5 | 38.6 | 27.2 |
| | D | 8.3 | 25.2 | 16.9 | 10.6 | 7.7 | 24.1 | 15.4 | 8.8 |
| Syria | A | 40.2 | 5.7 | 8.0 | 15.2 | 65.3 | 12.6 | 20.1 | 33.3 |
| | B | 29.7 | 21.2 | 31.0 | 49.0 | 17.7 | 17.6 | 25.9 | 39.1 |
| | C | 22.4 | 45.5 | 44.9 | 30.3 | 13.7 | 43.3 | 39.4 | 23.9 |
| | D | 7.7 | 27.6 | 16.2 | 5.6 | 3.3 | 26.5 | 14.6 | 3.8 |
| West Bank & Gaza | A | 21.1 | 2.1 | 1.8 | 8.2 | 33.6 | 2.6 | 2.2 | 7.6 |
| | B | 22.9 | 13.2 | 16.9 | 24.0 | 20.9 | 14.1 | 17.7 | 29.6 |
| | C | 43.8 | 54.0 | 57.4 | 60.7 | 38.3 | 53.5 | 56.8 | 57.9 |
| | D | 12.2 | 30.7 | 23.9 | 7.1 | 7.1 | 29.9 | 23.3 | 4.9 |

*Notes:* School levels A, B, C, and D correspond, respectively, to the categories low education, medium education, high education, and advanced education.
Rapid development scenario: low fertility / low mortality / high education.
Central scenario: central fertility / central mortality / central education.
Stagnation scenario: high fertility / high mortality / low education.
[a] Base year and end year, respectively, are 1995 and 2045.
[b] Base year and end year, respectively, are 1994 and 2044.
*Sources:* 1995 figures for Egypt estimated from (a) El-Zanaty et al., 1996, and (b) United Nations, 1997.
1995 figures for Morocco estimated from: (a) Azelmat et al., 1993, (b) Azelmat et al., 1996, and (c) United Nations, 1997.
1994 figures for Sudan estimated from: (a) Department of Statistics, Sudan, 1991, (b) PAPCHILD Sudan, 1995, and (c) United Nations, 1997.
1994 figures for Jordan, Lebanon, Syria, West Bank and Gaza Strip: (a) Goujon, 1997, and (b) ESCWA, 1995.
2044–5 figures: author's calculations. A large proportion of the adult population of the North Africa grouping is in the low education groups. More than 39 percent of men (47 percent in Sudan) and more than 61 percent of women (70 percent in Morocco) had only a primary education or less in 1994–5. This disadvantage will take a long time to overcome. Under the central scenario, the male population over 15 years of age in the low education group remains above 12 percent in Egypt, Morocco, and Sudan, and above 20 percent for women by 2045.

(c) The education momentum has a decisive role in slowing the impact of a decline of enrollment rates—e.g. under the implementation of a structural adjustment policy—on the overall level of educational attainment of the population. Once an individual exits school, he/she will keep his/her educational level all his/her lifetime (except for adult schooling and for the loss of literacy skills in older ages, for example, and in certain debilitating diseases). It cannot be taken away, whatever educational policies are put in place. The stagnation scenario implements a stagnation of enrollment rates at 1994–5 levels. This pessimistic scenario shows that some improvements still occur as a result of past educational efforts reaching precedent cohorts. This is evident in countries that have put a great deal of stress on education in the past, such as Egypt, Jordan, Lebanon, and Syria. For instance, in Egypt, the proportion of the female population with an advanced education still increases from 23 percent in 1994–5 to 40 percent in 2044–5 despite stagnation in enrollment levels.

The last main point is the impact of changes in enrollment levels on the overall level of fertility. In all scenarios and for all areas, the overall fertility rate declines at a higher rate than the decrease rate—of fertility—applied to each educational category. The difference is striking, especially in the case of Syria, where, in the rapid development scenario, an annual rate of decrease of 1.0 percent is applied to each educational category: the overall fertility declines at a rate of 2.1 percent per year. The central scenario for Morocco implements a 0.5 percent annual decrease to the fertility of each educational group. As a result, the overall fertility rate declines at a rate of 1.3 percent over the period. The difference stems from the significant increase in female school enrollment between 1994 and 2014–19 in the rapid development and central scenarios. The transition of more and more women to these highly educated groups will influence the relative weight of each educational category and trigger lower national fertility rates than were expected.

## Conclusions

Despite the specificities of each of the studied areas, we find a very high level of coherence in the results of the population projections. With the exception of Lebanon, the momentum built by many years of high fertility will give the other areas more years of high population growth.

The important efforts that are being made toward higher levels of school enrollment in the Arab region may induce fertility rates to decline faster than expected. Educational policies and future levels of enrollment will be decisive in shaping future population composition and growth.

This chapter, it is hoped, will not only encourage further research into the relationships between population dynamics and educational levels, but also assist policy makers to project the outcomes of decisions made. First, the study shows the importance of simultaneously studying population and education trends. In particular, population projections of Arab areas will benefit from the inclusion of education as a defining indicator, not only to determine future levels of population growth (quantitative results) under related scenarios for fertility, mortality, and education, but also to foresee the educational levels (qualitative results) of the total population and, above all, of the working-age population according to these different scenarios. (See Appendix 5.A2, Figures 5.A2(i) – 5.A2(xiv) for graphic evidence using the central scenario as an example.)

Second, further thought should be given to the patterns of change in fertility and mortality levels that are produced by education. A major drawback of projections is to keep fertility and mortality differentials by education groups constant over time. Many studies have shown that these differentials change over time, depending on the overall level of education and fertility, as well as on country conditions.

Third, more research needs to be done so as to extend the projections one step further, with a view to defining specifically the labor force profile associated with the projected levels of educational attainment and to forecasting the possible consequences of the explored paths on economic development.

## Appendix 5.A1: Technical Note on Methodology for Population Projection with Multiple Educational States

The following is an excerpt from Wils and Goujon (1998): "Impact of Educational Fertility Differentials on Population Projections: An Exploration Using the Examples of Sudan and Tunisia."

> The simulations for education diffusion and fertility decline are made using a population projection method. The method is a combination of the discrete time cohort component projection used for single-state populations (Leslie, 1945) and an adapted form of the multi-state population projection method that was first compiled in complete form by Rogers (1975) and Rogers and Wilson (1980).
>
> In the population projection method formalized by Leslie, the population is subject only to births, deaths, and external (net) migration. An age- and gender-specific population vector is pre-multiplied by the so-called Leslie Matrix, which has scalars for the birth, death, and net migration rates. In the multi-state projection method, the age- and gender-specific population is divided into further categories—such as marital status, educational achievement, place of residence—and the transitions between these are included in the projection. These transitions are specific to each age and gender group, and are represented by age- and gender-specific transition matrices. These transition matrices can replace the age- and gender-specific birth, death, and net migration scalars in the Leslie Matrix. The population vector is also extended to include the population by-states. The matrix is arranged as the original one-state Leslie Matrix, but now each scalar in the matrix has been replaced by a small transition matrix, and each scalar in the population vector is a small vector of the population states.
>
> The multi-state projection requires data on the fertility, mortality, and migration for each individual state. It also requires data on the transition from one category to another, and, in the case of educational categories, from one level of school to another.

# Appendix 5.A2: Population Pyramids

## Figure 5.A2(i): Population of Jordan, 1994

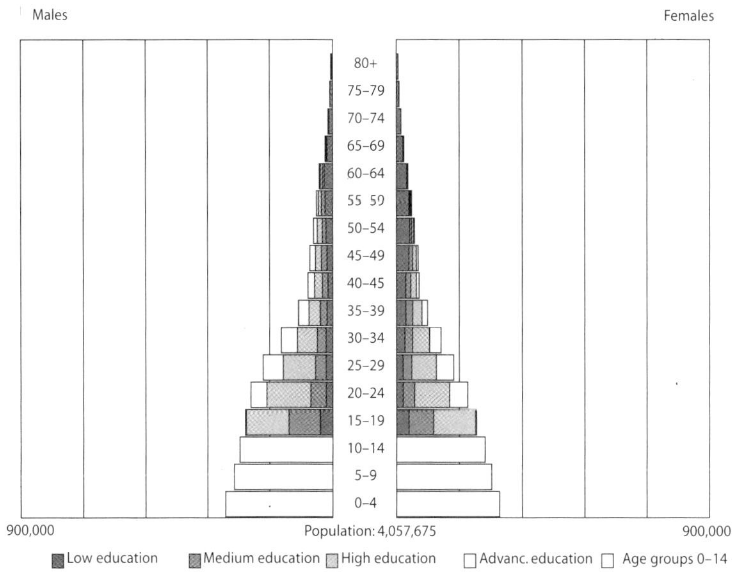


*Source:* As for Table 5.6.

## Figure 5.A2(ii): Population Projection for Jordan, Central Scenario: Central Fertility, Mortality, and Education, 2044

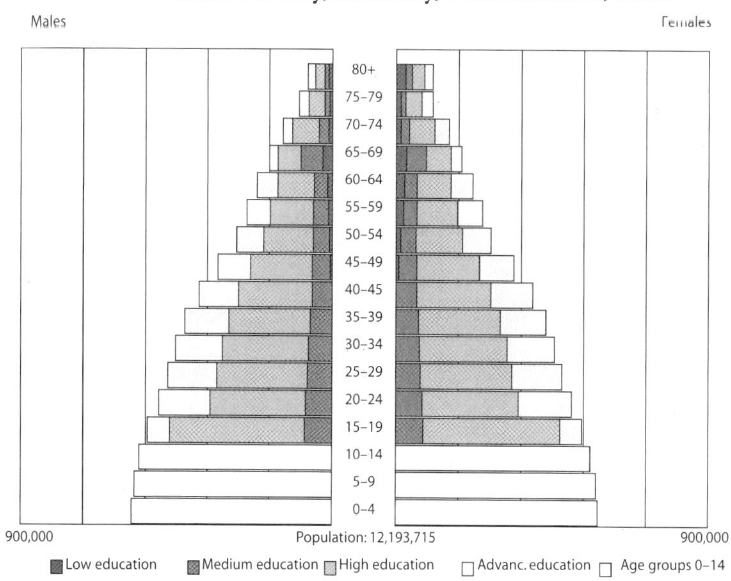


*Source:* Author's calculations.

## Figure 5.A2(iii): Population of Lebanon, 1994

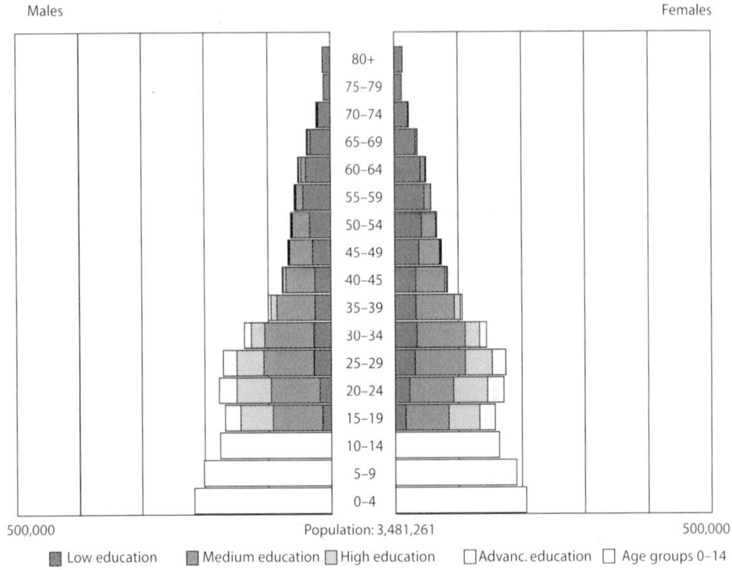


*Source:* As for Table 5.6.

## Figure 5.A2(iv): Population Projection for Lebanon, Central Scenario, Central Fertility, Mortality, and Education, 2044

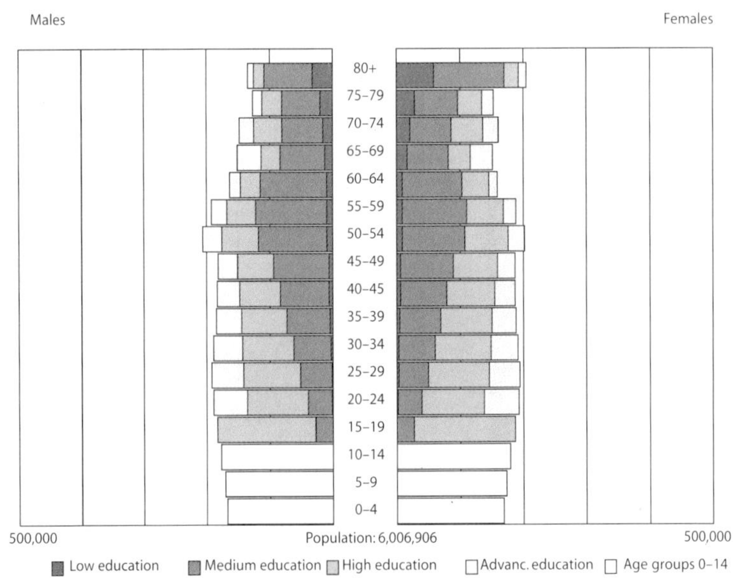


*Source:* Author's calculations.

**Figure 5.A2(v): Population of Syria, 1994**

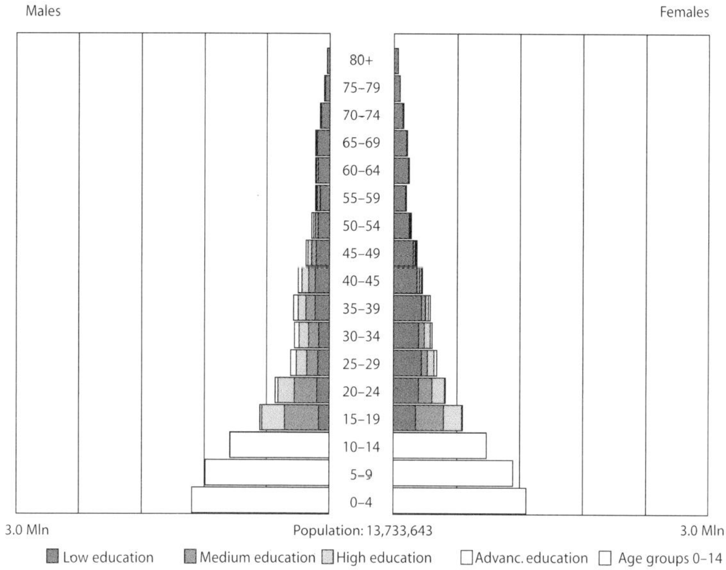


*Source:* As for Table 5.6.

**Figure 5.A2(vi): Population Projection for Syria, Central Scenario, Central Fertility, Mortality, and Education, 2044**

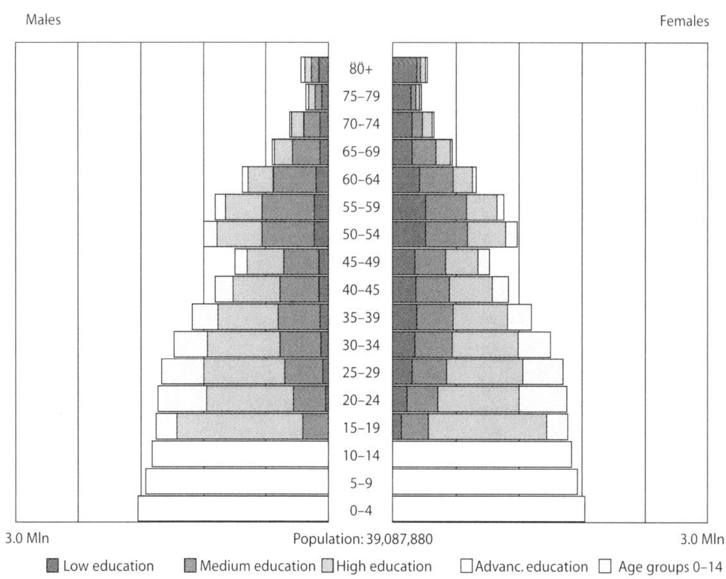


*Source:* Author's calculations.

**Figure 5.A2(vii): Population of the West Bank and Gaza Strip, 1994**

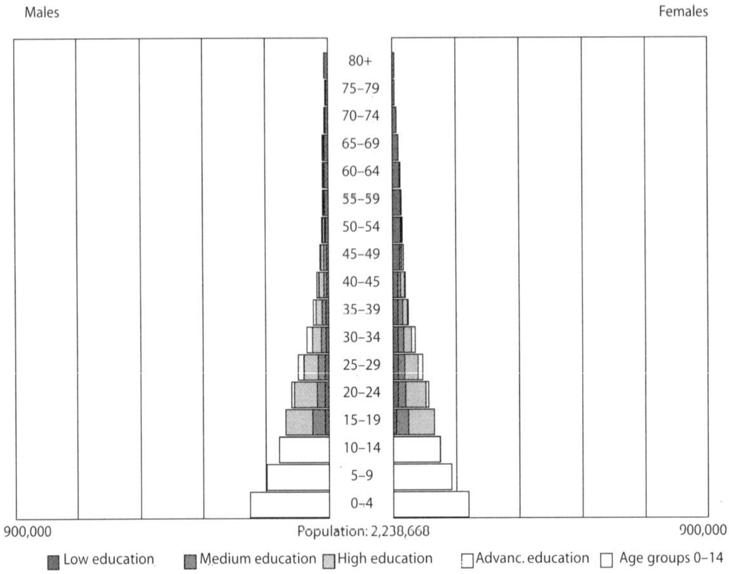


*Source:* As for Table 5.6.

**Figure 5.A2(viii): Population Projection for the West Bank and Gaza Strip, Central Scenario Fertility, Mortality, and Education, 2044**

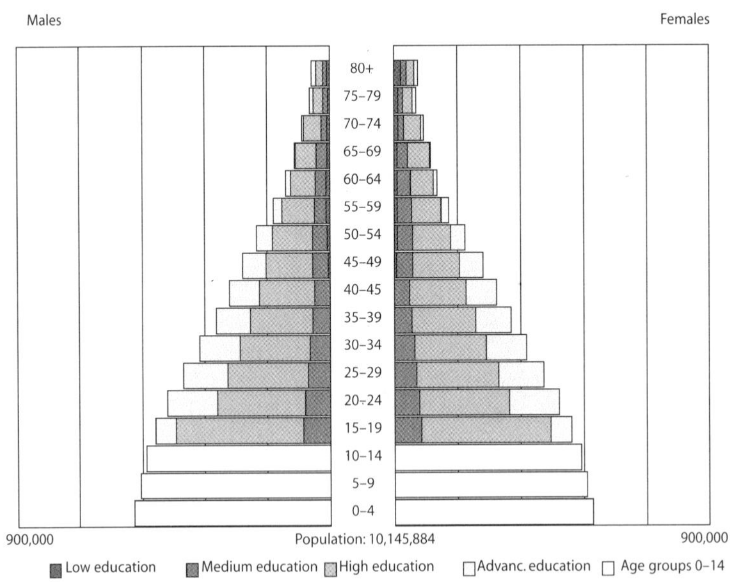


*Source:* Author's calculations.

**Figure 5.A2(ix): Population of Egypt, 1995**

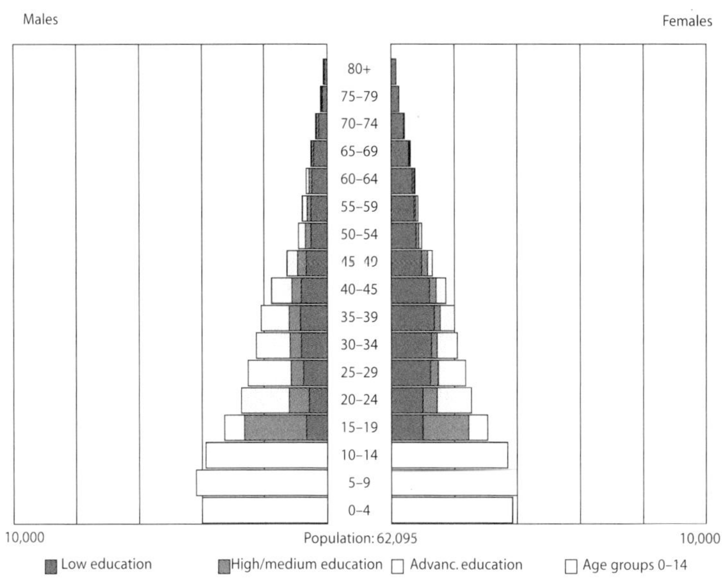


*Source:* As for Table 5.6.

**Figure 5.A2(x): Population Projection for Egypt, Central Scenario, Central Fertility, Mortality, and Education, 2045**

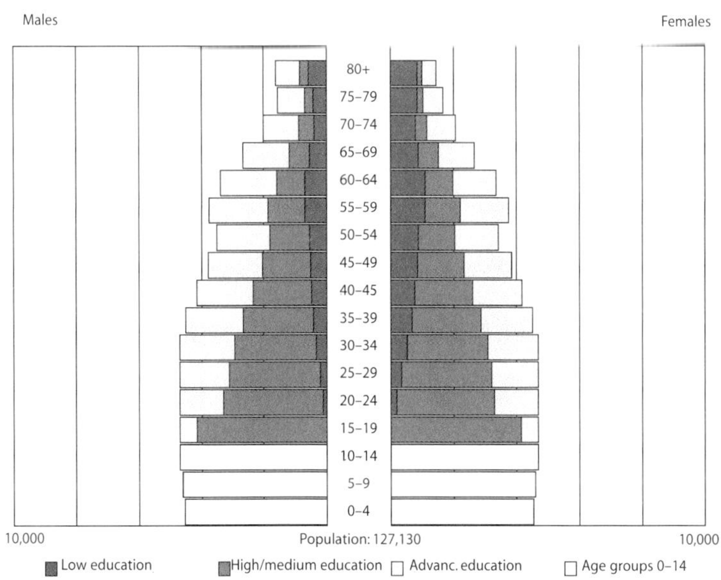


*Source:* Author's calculations.

## Figure 5.A2(xi): Population of Morocco, 1995

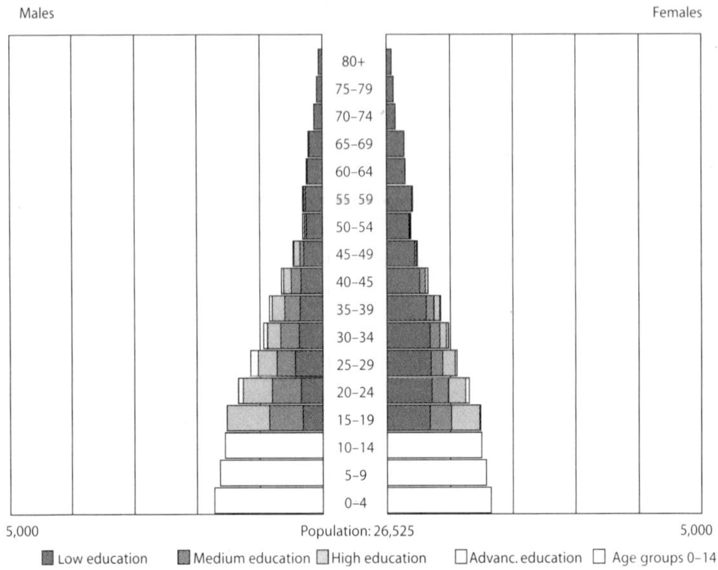


*Source:* As for Table 5.6.

## Figure 5.A2(xii): Population Projection for Morocco, Central Scenario, Central Fertility, Mortality, and Education, 2045

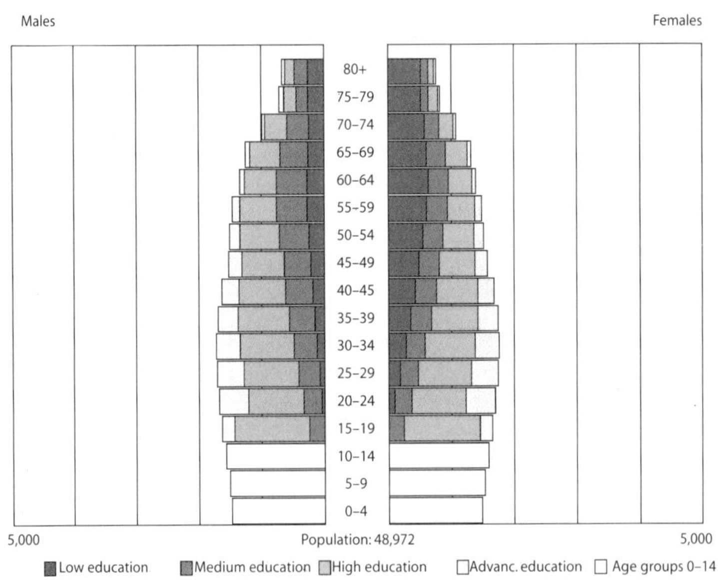


*Source:* Author's calculations.

## Figure 5.A2(xiii): Population of Sudan, 1995

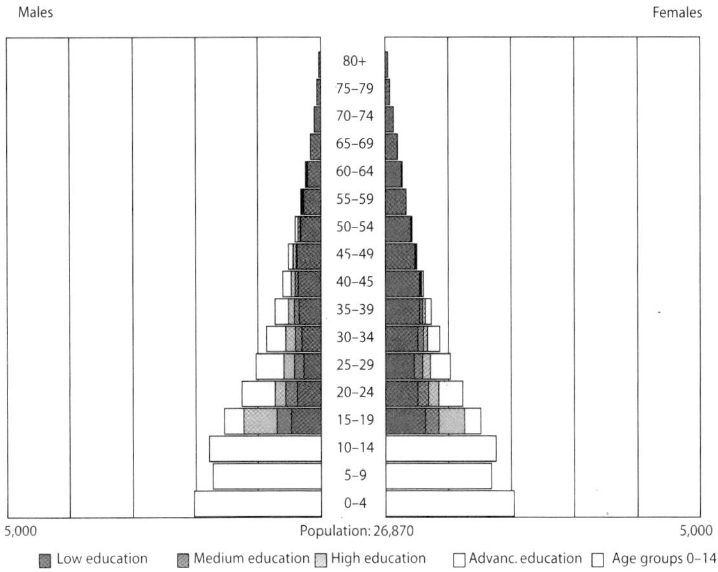


*Source:* As for Table 5.6.

## Figure 5.A2(xiv): Population Projection for Sudan, Central Scenario Central Fertility, Mortality, and Education, 2045

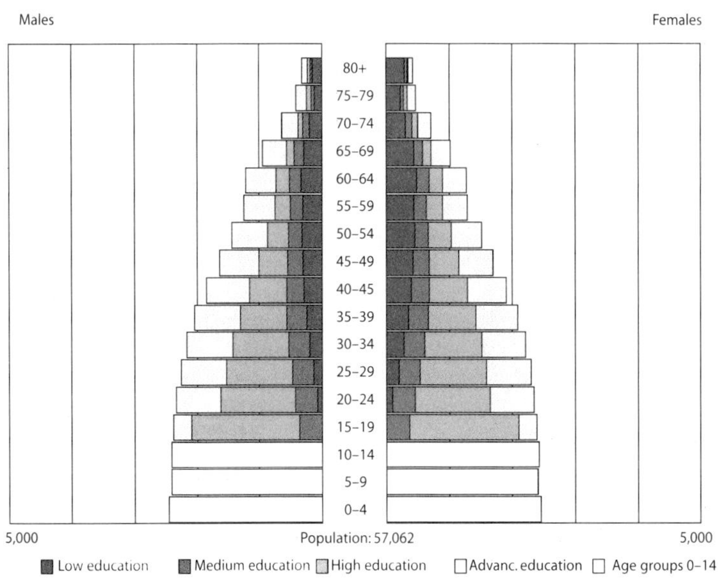


*Source:* Author's calculations.

## Notes

1 For the purposes of this study, I have grouped the countries as follows: North Africa—Egypt, Morocco, Sudan; Middle East—Jordan, Lebanon, Syria, West Bank and Gaza.
2 World Fertility Surveys [WFS] in the 1970s, and Demographic and Health Surveys [DHS] as well as Pan Arab Population and Child Development Surveys [PAPCHILD] in the 1980s and 1990s.
3 In the case of Lebanon and the West Bank and Gaza Strip, the absence of two items of data prevents comparison.
4 Software is the PDE Population Projections, produced at IIASA. This software has been developed by IIASA's population project to be used as population module in multi-sector Population-Development-Environment (PDE) analysis. This tool can also be used independently of PDE analysis for simple and multi-state population projections—in the case of several states that interact with each other (Dippolt *et al.,* 1998). The software can be downloaded free of charge at the following address: http://www.iiasa.ac.at/Research/POP/models/index.html.
5 Definition of the four educational categories: low education, those who have never attended school or have never completed the final grade at the first level of education; medium education, those who have completed the final grade at the first level of education and those who have entered the second level of education but have never completed the preparatory cycle; high education, those who have completed at the second level the final grade of preparatory cycle or of the final cycle; and advanced education, those who have undertaken third-level studies regardless of whether they have completed the course.

## References


Azelmat, Mustapha, M. Ayad, and E.A. Housni. 1993. *Enquête Nationale sur la Population et la Santé (ENPS-II) 1992.* Ministère de la Santé Publique, Rabat, Morocco, and Macro International Inc., Columbia, MD.

———. 1996. *Enquête de Panel sur la Population et la Santé (EPPS), 1995.* Ministère de la Santé Publique. Rabat, Morocco, and Calverton, MD: Macro International Inc.

Cleland, John, and J. Hobcraft (eds.). 1985. *Reproductive Change in Developing Countries: Insights from the World Fertility Survey.* New York: Oxford University Press.

Cleland, John, and C. Scott. 1987. *The World Fertility Survey: An Assessment.* New York: Oxford University Press.

Dippolt, Martina, A. Goujon, and A. Wils. 1998. *Software for Population-Development-Environment (PDE) Analysis, PDE Population Projections, A Population Projection Model with Interacting States, User's Manual.* International Institute for Applied Systems Analysis, Laxenburg, Austria.

El-Khorazaty, M. N. 1996. "Characterization and Determinants of Reproductive Patterns in the Arab World: 1976–1995." Paper presented at the International Union for the Scientific Study of Population (IUSSP), Arab regional conference, Cairo, 8–12 December. Vol. 1, pp. 375–434. IUSSP, Liege, Belgium.

El-Zanaty, Fatma, E.M. Hussein, and G.A. 1996. *Egypt Demographic and Health Survey, 1995.* National Population Council. Cairo, Egypt, and Calverton, MD: Macro International Inc.

Economic and Social Commission for Western Asia (ESCWA). 1994. *Demographic and Related Socio-Economic Data Sheets for Countries of the Economic and Social Commission for Western Asia as Assessed in 1994,* Vol. 8. Amman, Jordan: UNESCWA.

Goujon, Anne. 1997. "Population and Education Prospects in the Western Mediterranean Region." Interim Report IR-97-046/July. International Institute for Applied Systems Analysis, Laxenburg, Austria.

———, and A. Wils. 1996. *The Importance of Education in Future Population: Global Trends and Case Studies on Cape Verde, Sudan, and Tunisia.* International Institute for Applied Systems Analysis (IIASA), Working Paper WP-96-138. Laxenburg, Austria: IIASA.

Jejeebhoy, Shireen J. 1995. *Women's Education, Autonomy and Reproductive Behavior.* Oxford: Clarendon Press.

Jordanian Department of Statistics. 1979. *Jordan Fertility Survey 1976.* Amman, Jordan.

———. 1992. *Jordan Population and Family Health Survey 1990.* Columbia, MD: IRD/Macro International Inc.

Leslie, P.H. 1945. [1975] "On the Use of Matrices in Certain Population Mathematics," *Biometrika,* Vol. 33 (1975): 183–212.

Lutz, Wolfgang. 1998. "Social and Economic Policy Responses to Low Fertility." Paper presented at International Symposium on Population and Development Policies in Low Fertility Countries: Challenges of Changing Age Structures. Seoul, South Korea, 7–12 May.

———, A. Goujon, and G. Doblhammer-Reiter. 1998. "Adding Education to Age And Sex," in Wolfgang Lutz, J.W. Vaupel, and D.A. Ahlburg (eds.), *Frontiers of Population Forecasting.* Population and Development Review, A supplement to Vol. 24, pp. 42–58.

McGrath, Patricia L. 1976. *The Unfinished Assignment: Education for Women.* Washington, DC: Worldwatch Institute.

Noor, Abdoun. 1981. "Education and Basic Human Needs." World Bank Staff Working Paper No. 450. Washington, DC: World Bank.

Oppong, Christine. 1987. *Sex Roles, Population and Development in West Africa.* London: James Currey.

PAPCHILD. *Sudan Maternal and Child Health Survey.* 1992/93, 1995. Federal Ministry of Health, Khartoum, Sudan, and Pan Arab Project for Child Development, League of Arab States, Cairo, Egypt.

Palestinian Central Bureau of Statistics (PCBS). 1996. *The Demographic Survey in the West Bank and Gaza Strip: Preliminary Report.* Ramallah, Palestine: PCBS.

Population and Reference Bureau (PRB). 1995. *Population Data Sheet 1995.* Washington, DC: PRB.

———. 1997. *Population Data Sheet 1997.* Washington, DC: PRB.

Rogers, Andrei. 1975. Introduction to Multi-Regional Mathematical Demography. New York, N.Y.: Wiley & Sons.

———, and A.G. Wilson (eds.). 1980. "Essays in Multi-State Mathematical Demography," Environment and Planning issue, *International Journal of Urban and Regional Research,* Vol. 12, No. 5. London: Pion.

Schultz, T. Paul. 1994. "Human Capital, Family Planning and their Effects on Population Growth." *American Economic Review,* Vol. 84: No. 2.

Syrian Central Bureau of Statistics. 1982. *Syria Fertility Survey 1978. Principal Report. Volume 1.* Damascus, Syrian Arab Republic.

Sudanese Department of Statistics. 1991. *Sudan Demographic and Health Survey 1989/1990.* Columbia, MD, and Institute for Resource Development/Macro International, Inc.

United Nations (UN). 1995. *World Population Prospects: The 1994 Revision.* Department for Economic and Social Information and Policy Analysis. New York, N.Y.: United Nations.

———. 1997. *World Population Prospects: The 1996 Revision.* Department for Economic and Social Information and Policy Analysis. New York, N.Y.: United Nations.

United Nations Educational, Scientific and Cultural Organization (UNESCO). 1990. *Statistical Yearbook.* Paris, France: UNESCO

———. 1995. *Statistical Yearbook.* Paris, France: UNESCO.

Wils, Annababette, and A. Goujon. 1998. "Impacts of Educational Fertility Differentials on Population Projections: An Exploration Using the Examples of Sudan and Tunisia."

Unpublished paper, International Institute for Applied Systems Analysis, Laxenburg, Austria. Copy available from authors on request.

Yaakoubd, Abdel-Ilah. 1996. "La Fécondité dans le Monde Arabe: Tendances et Facteurs d'Evolution (1960–1995)." Paper presented at the International Union for the Scientific Study of Population (IUSSP) Arab regional conference, Cairo, 8–12 December, Vol. 3, pp.164–85. IUSSP, Liege, Belgium.

Yousif, Hassan M., A. Goujon, and W. Lutz. 1996. "Future Population and Education Trends in the Countries of North Africa." Research Report RR-96-11. Laxenburg, Austria: International Institute for Applied Systems Analysis.

# 6

# Population, Human Capital, and Economic Growth in Iran*

*Djavad Salehi-Isfahani*

## Introduction

In 1989 the government of the Islamic Republic of Iran reversed its pro-natal policy to launch an ambitious family planning program with the slogan, "Fewer children, better life." Less than ten years later, the program had delivered on its first promise: fertility had declined by one-third. The promise of a "better life," however, still eludes the average Iranian family, whose income has not risen in the intervening years. Although economic theory suggests a strong link between the decline in fertility and economic growth, the latter does not automatically follow the decline. It is a potential that can be fulfilled only if investment in physical and human capital responds positively to the decline in fertility. In this chapter I examine the potential created by fertility decline in Iran for an increase in human capital. I show, first, that if the lower fertility level endures, the age structure will change dramatically, such that the number of adults per child will at least double in the next twenty years. The greater adult-child ratio represents the potential that has been historically associated with take-off into long-term growth. Barlow (1994) calls this potential the "demographic window of opportunity". (see also Tunalı, 1996), and Bloom and Williamson (1998) label it the "demographic gift"(see also Tunalı 1996 and Salehi-Isfahani 2000). They emphasize the consequences of the changing age structure for labor force growth and savings. In light of the importance of human capital for growth, it seems only natural to consider the effect of age structure on human capital accumulation as well.

Secondly, I examine the conditions that would help Iran take advantage of the demographic window of opportunity. How Iran will spend its demographic gift is crucial to its economic growth during the next twenty years. As far as the accumulation of human capital is concerned, a positive outcome depends on whether the government and families are willing to increase their investment in children. The government's response to the decrease in the number of pupils in the last few years has not been encouraging. Where student numbers have fallen, rather than increase school quality, it has made a proportionate reduction in education expenditures. A much greater potential for human capital accumulation exists in the response of the families to lower fertility. Proper incentives may induce them to use their increased resources, especially time, to invest in the human capital of their children, i.e., substitute quality for quantity. I argue that distortions in the incentives provided by the educational system and the labor market pose serious obstacles to human capital accumulation. This perspective not only presents old policy issues in labor market and educational reform in a new light; it adds urgency to their implementation. Provided the right incentives are put into place, in addition to increased savings and labor supply, a favorable age structure would contribute to growth through the accumulation of human capital as parents and schools increase expenditures of time and resources per child. If not, the historic opportunity will be lost. With this in mind, I discuss the reforms that are needed to increase the efficiency of human capital accumulation in families and schools.

Looking back at the last forty years, the overriding impression that one gets from the record of economic growth in Iran is one of boom and bust rather than steady growth. There was a period of steady growth between 1959 and 1976, which has not been repeated since (Figure 6.1). The last twenty years have seen a 35 percent decline in per capita income, which occurred during 1976–80, followed by zero growth during 1980–98. This is a very poor performance even in comparison to the sluggish MENA region (see Shafiq, 1997), and one that is beaten by only a few African countries. There have been growth spells, but all have followed a rise in oil income. In view of the poor prospects for a dramatic turnaround in the world oil market, for its future growth Iran must rely on a more fundamental source, human capital.[1] Calls for reducing dependence on oil, most recently echoed in President Khatami's "Plan for Economic Reorganization" of 1998 (Plan and Budget Organization, 1998), recognize the limited role that oil has played in fostering economic growth in Iran. Against this background of dimmed prospects for oil-based growth, thanks to the recent decline in fertility a bright spot has emerged which offers a new prospect for expansion of human capital and, in turn, long-term growth. Iranian couples who married in the 1990s have on average half as many children as their parents did in the 1970s, enabling them to substantially increase their investment in the human capital of their children.

Inside the Iranian family, women play a key role in child rearing. Therefore, how they use the time saved from childbearing will greatly influence the rate of accumulation of

**Figure 6.1: GDP, Non-oil GDP and Value Added from Oil (constant 1982/83 billion rials)**

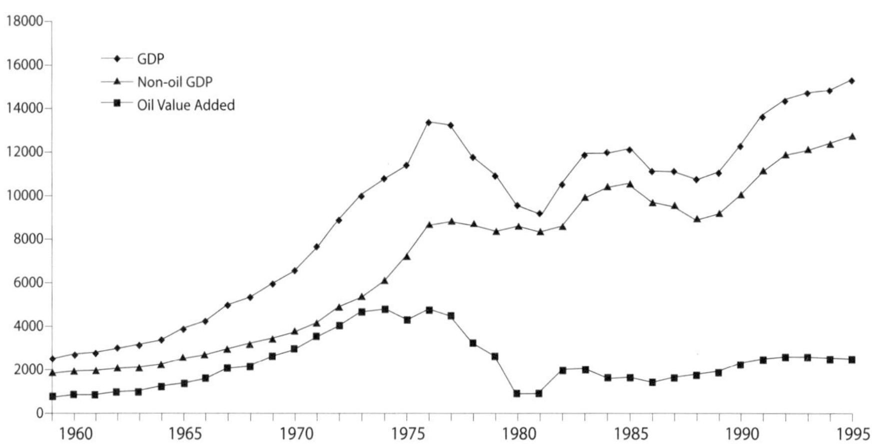


*Source*: Bank Markazi of the Islamic Republic of Iran, Annual Reports, various years.

human capital in Iran. They face three choices: The first is to work outside the home. This is the option that most women in other countries have been inclined to choose, and it has been responsible for a large share of the input-based growth all over the world. However, in Iran, except for the most highly educated group, it may not be viable because of the limited job opportunities for women and the cultural stigmas. If women are unable to work outside the home, they will increase their leisure or time in home production. They may choose more traditional home activities (homemaking) or invest in the human capital (health, nutrition, and education) of their children. For those who are unable to take advantage of outside opportunities, the choice to invest in their children offers the greatest potential for economic growth. Good policies can affect their choice to achieve the best results. Whether or not young mothers choose to spend more time educating their children, and what types of skills they choose to foster, depends on the incentives they are given. Because these incentives are generated primarily in the labor market and shaped by the formal education system, they are at present highly distorted, and there is a risk that parental time will not be used optimally. To take advantage of its demographic window of opportunity, Iran must remove distortions that impede investment in human capital and provide incentives that induce parents to teach their children not the habits and skills that serve them in the present distorted environment, but those that are truly productive.

The chapter is organized as follows. The next section is a brief review of the theoretical underpinnings of the link between population, human capital, and long-term growth. In section 2, I review the evidence pertaining to the decline in fertility, and, in section 3 I analyze the effect this has on the age structure, using a simple demographic projection model. In section 4, I examine labor force participation of women, and in section 5 the role of family in Iran in production of human capital. In sections 6 and 7, I describe the incentives that parents encounter in the present system of formal education and the labor market, respectively, and discuss the role of public policy in shaping incentives that affect family investment in human capital. Section 8 concludes.

## 1. Population, Human Capital, and Long-run Growth

New empirical evidence and theoretical developments in the economics of growth support the view presented in this chapter that Iran can benefit from shifting its main source of growth from hydrocarbons to human capital. Sachs and Warner (1995) present cross-country evidence to show that the performance of resource-exporting countries as a group lags behind that of other developing countries with comparable economic standing. At a theoretical level, new growth theory has emphasized human capital over physical capital as a source of growth (Lucas, 1988; Barro, 1990; Becker, Murphy, and Tamura, 1999; Mankiw, Romer, and Weil, 1992). Thus, the oil boom of the 1970s, which created a period of intense physical capital accumulation without concurrent changes in the human resource situation, most importantly decline in fertility, could not last beyond the oil boom itself.

The shift in emphasis from physical to human capital has dramatically altered the way in which economists view the role of population in long-run growth. Whereas in the traditional growth theory (Solow, 1956) population figured as an exogenous factor that impeded capital deepening, new growth models grant a central role to population (Becker, Murphy, and Tamura, 1990; Galore and Weil, 1996) and emphasize the intergenerational transfer of human capital and its accumulation. Becker's work, summarized in Becker (1992), provides the most direct link between population and economic growth: lower fertility provides an opportunity to increase human capital, which in turn helps sustain lower fertility. This view places family decisions regarding fertility and child education at the heart of the development process. For example, in Becker, Murphy, and Tamura (1990), the choice between raising a large family or having fewer children and investing more in each child is critical for long-term growth. Each generation's level of human capital plays a crucial role in this choice. The more educated the parents are, the more likely they opt for smaller families because not only do they have a higher opportunity cost of time, but also they can teach their children more effectively. Thus, in this scheme, high levels of human capital can sustain long-term growth because they cause low fertility and high investment in human capital.

The traditional approach to the link between demographic transition and economic growth emphasizes the role of increased savings and labor supply (Barlow, 1994; Tunalı, 1996). The human capital approach offers a richer dynamic, leading to the possibility of multiple equilibria. One equilibrium, well known in the development literature as the low-level equilibrium trap, exists because high fertility (and mortality) prevents human capital accumulation, which in turn helps sustain high fertility. A higher equilibrium is made possible by the 'benevolent circle' of low fertility and high human capital, as described above. The incorporation of human capital into the dynamics of population and growth introduces a new rationale for public action. Governments should not only initiate and assist the control of fertility; they should also provide the necessary incentives for parental investment in human capital accumulation. The success achieved by East Asian countries in entering a phase of sustained growth has been attributed to favorable demographics as well as a favorable policy environment (Cinotta and Engelman, 1997).

## 2. The Rise and Fall of Fertility in Iran

Immediately after the revolution period fertility increased, but only temporarily, as it resumed its course of decline in the mid-1980s (Aghajanian, 1991, 1995; Mehryar 1995). A rise followed by a sharp decline in fertility provides Iran with the most advantageous age structure for accumulation of human capital and growth for the next twenty years. The ratio of parents to children (or teacher to student) was important to the past and will be to the future course of fertility. In this section, I examine the data on past levels of fertility and discuss its future course.

The rise and fall in fertility is in part due to the changing rates of population growth. The inter-censal rate fell from 3.1 percent during 1956–66 to 2.7 percent in 1966–76, but unexpectedly increased to 3.9 percent during 1976–86 (see also Table 6.1 below). The last census (1996) revealed a much lower rate of growth, just below 2 percent per year. A similar pattern is visible in the percentage of 0–4 year-olds in the population, which fell from 17.6 percent in 1966 to 16.1 percent in 1976, increased to 18.2 percent in 1986,[2] only to fall to a mere 10.3 percent in 1996. Annual surveys conducted by the Ministry of Health show much of the drop to have happened in the 1990s, from 2.7 percent per year in 1992 to 1.75 percent in 1995.

Estimates of the Total Fertility Rate (TFR) present a similar pattern of in terms of rise and fall (Figure 6.2). According to these figures, TFR started its decrease sometime in the

**Figure 6.2: Total Fertility Rate, 1955–95**

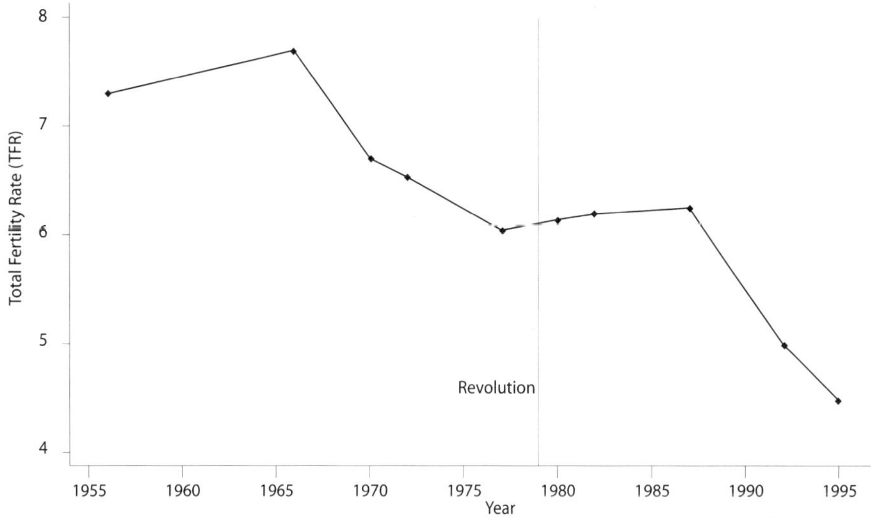


*Source:* World Bank, World Development Indicators, 1997.

1960s and continued until the late 1970s, when the revolution interrupted its course and it began increasing for a few years. In the late 1980s, coinciding with the end of the war with Iraq, the beginning of the reconstruction period under President Rafsanjani, and the resumption of the family planning program, fertility resumed its course of decline once again. This time the pace was fast, as the TFR dropped from 6.2 in 1987 to 4.5 in 1995. Kenneth Hill (1994), who carefully examined the 1986 and 1991 population data, also supports the view of an increase in the birth rate in the early 1980s, followed by a sharp drop—of as much as 40 percent—from around 1986 to the early 1990s. There is evidence that the recent decline in fertility is broadly based, among women of all ages and in both rural and urban areas. Figures 6.3a and 6.3b depict age-specific fertility rates computed from the 1987 and 1992 integrated household surveys. The largest drop appears to be in the 30–39 age category.

Despite overwhelming evidence pointing to a transition in fertility in Iran, predicting fertility for the future is difficult. In projecting fertility for the next twenty years, we should use the current and past levels of fertility with caution for two reasons. First, there is no agreement among demographers as to the current level of fertility. The Ministry of Health estimates, calculated from its own surveys, show TFRs of 4.2 and 2.7 for rural and urban women, respectively, which are considered too low by many demographers in Iran. Second, even a consistent secular trend is not an adequate indication of the future levels of fertility, much less a fluctuating pattern as observed in post-revolution Iran. The fact that the most recent fertility decline was preceded by a rise complicates the prediction of future trends. If the decline were in some way a compensation for the rise, then it may overstate the future trend in lifetime fertility. There are two reasons why the rise and fall may have been connected to each other. First, the rise and fall in period fertility may have been relat-

**Figure 6.3a: Age-specific Fertility Rates for Urban Areas, 1986 and 1991**

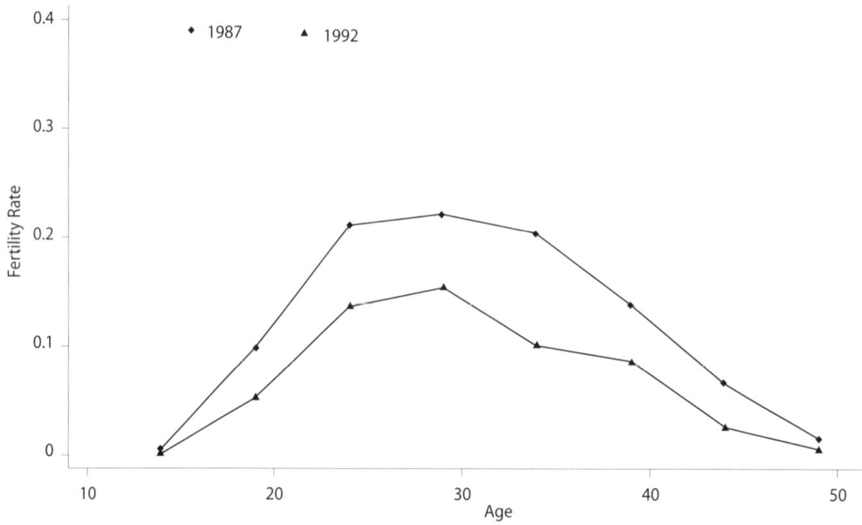


*Source:* Computed by the author from "Socioeconomic Characteristics of Households in Iran," 1987 and 1992.

**Figure 6.3b: Age-specific Fertility Rates for Rural Areas, 1986 and 1991**

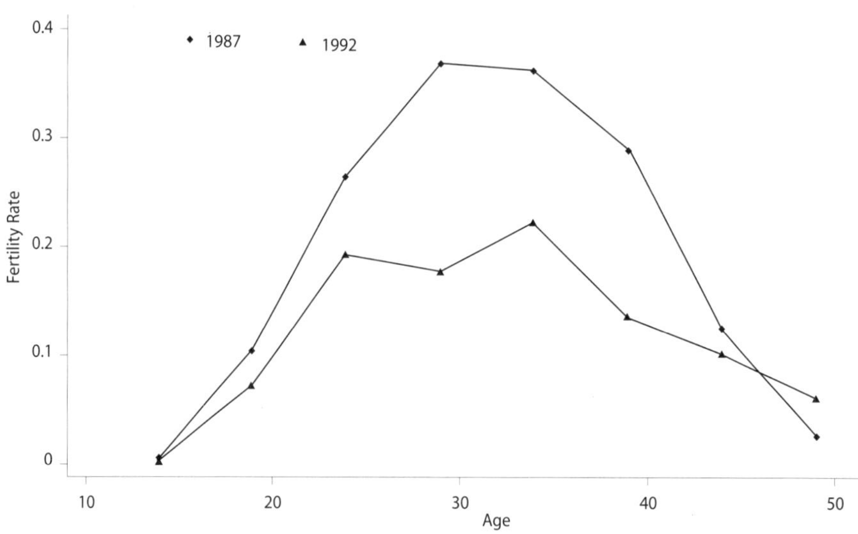


*Source:* Computed by the author from "Socioeconomic Characteristics of Households in Iran," 1987 and 1992.

ed via birth timing. In response to the pro-natal atmosphere of the 1980s couples may have increased fertility without desiring larger families. This could happen if for one reason or another they perceived the pro-natal environment to be temporary. In this case, the rise and fall in period fertility would be the result of an intertemporal substitution of births between the 1980s and 1990s. Second, in response to the same set of incentives, couples may have increased their lifetime fertility. In this case, the rise in the period rate reflects increase in lifetime fertility. Policy changes in the late 1980s would have taken these couples by surprise and caused them to cut their fertility sharply as they tried to adjust to a lower desired family size. Such a scenario could explain how the aggregate period rates, such as the TFR, could have fallen beyond what one would expect based on changes in desired family size. If either of these scenarios is correct, the TFR could increase in the near future to a level consistent with lifetime fertility. Salehi-Isfahani and Tandon (1998) present evidence to this effect.

### *Changes in Age Structure*

The rise and fall of fertility induce wide fluctuations in the age structure of population for many decades. The broad outlines of these changes are well known and easily derived from simulations of the age structure. The relatively large cohort born in the early 1980s will first increase the growth rate of the labor force and later that of the elderly population. In terms of the allocation of family time and public resources, the ratio of adults to children is of great importance. This ratio is akin to the more widely used dependency ratio, which includes the elderly in the denominator, and is used in the analysis of savings and social security. In my projections, assuming that urban and rural fertility and mortality rates stay constant at their early 1990s level, the ratio of dependent to working population will fall from 0.48 in 1986 to 0.36 in 2006, and then rise to 0.39 in 2016. The population of working age and dependent groups that during 1966–86 had been growing at 3.5 percent and 3.2 percent, respectively, will grow at 2.6 percent and 1.6 percent only during 1996–2016.

Because the main concern of this chapter is human capital accumulation, I focus on the adult-child ratio. To determine the range of possibilities for this ratio in the next twenty years, I present two scenarios, one assuming that fertility stays the same,[3] and the other assuming it will continue to decline. Fertility levels between rural and urban areas are different enough to warrant separate projections. For the base projections, I use age-specific fertility rates that are estimated from the 1992 household survey collected by the Statistical Center of Iran (SCI). These rates yield TFRs of 2.8 and 4.8 for urban and rural areas, respectively, which are slightly higher than those obtained three years later from a Ministry of Health survey (2.7 and 4.2) and reported in Malekafzali (1995). For more optimistic projections, I allow the urban TFR to decline gradually to 2.0 in the year 2016 and rural fertility to 2.8. These are indeed not unreasonable expectations, given the success in fertility reduction in the last 10 years, but they assume that current period rates reflect current desired lifetime fertility. In all projections, I use the age-specific mortality rates estimated for 1991 by Taheripour (1996). I keep mortality rates unchanged throughout the projection period. The projected age structure is much less sensitive to assumptions regarding mortality than fertility.

The constant fertility scenario results in an annual (natural) population growth rate of 1.7 percent for the urban and 2.7 percent for rural households.[4] The reduced fertility sce-

**Figure 6.4a: Population Projections, Urban (constant fertility)**

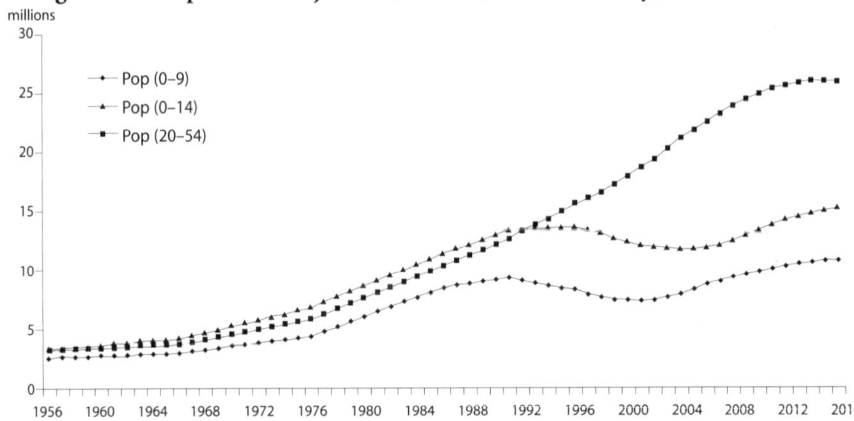


**Figure 6.4b: Population Projections, Urban, (reduced fertility)**

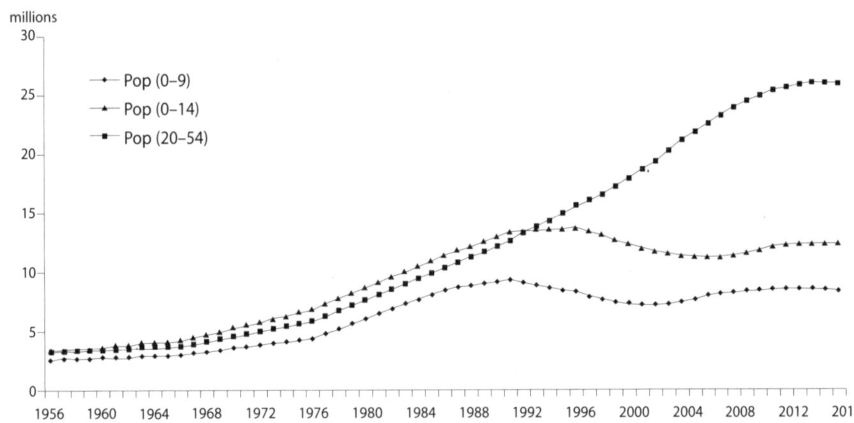


*Source:* Author's projections (both figures).

nario produces growth rates of 1.4 percent for urban and 2.1 percent for rural households. Evidently, there is considerable momentum in the population for growth, so that even when the urban fertility is down to replacement, population continues to increase at the rate of 1.4 percent per year. It will take a long time after families have reached replacement-level fertility for the growth rate to drop to zero.

To begin with urban households, the projection results show a remarkable shift in the adult-child ratio, especially in the reduced fertility scenario (Figures 6.4a and 6.4b).[5] Having remained constant throughout the last 40 years, the ratio of adults (20–54 years) to children (0–9 years) will rise from 1.0 in 1996 to 2.6 in 2016. If urban fertility declines by 29 percent in 2016 from its 1992 level, from a TFR of 2.8 to 2.0, the adult-child ratio will increase to 3.2! In other words, there will be more than three times as many adults per child in 2016 as there have been in the last 40 years. The implications of such a change for the education of the young in urban areas are immense. Projections for rural areas are less dramatic (Figures 6.5a and 6.5b). If fertility were to stay at its 1996 level (constant fertil-

Figure 6.5a: Population Projections, Rural (constant fertility)

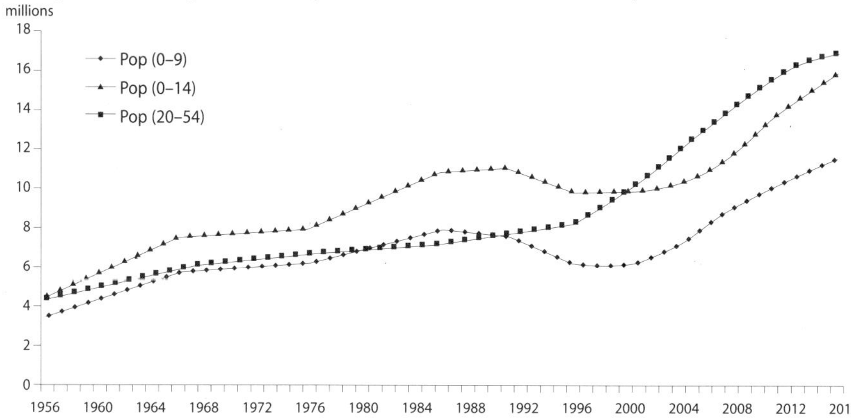


Figure 6.5b: Population Projections, Rural (reduced fertility)

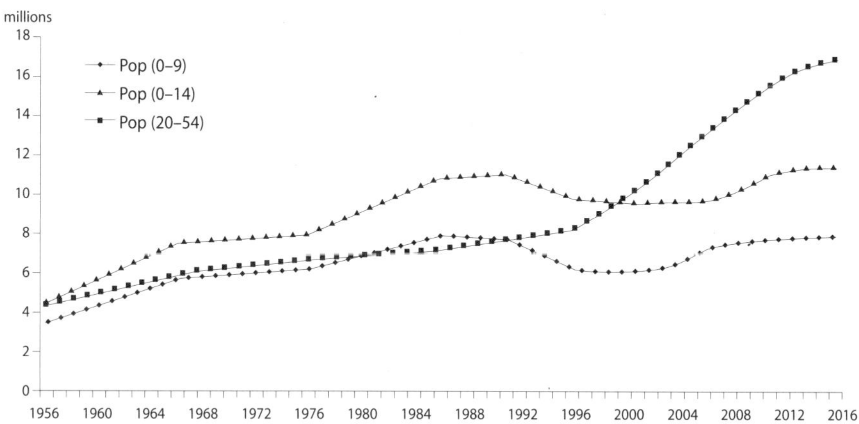


*Source:* Author's projections (both figures).

ity scenario), the adult-child ratio would rise to only 1.5, which is less than 60 percent of the projected ratio for the urban households. If fertility were to drop to 2.8, equal to the present urban TFR, the adult-child ratio will climb to over 2.0.

The comparison between rural and urban age structures warns of a possible widening in regional disparities as a result of differential fertility levels. It also underlines the importance of fertility decline for a favorable age structure. Rural youths, already at a disadvantage because of lower school quality and parental education, face a widening gap due to differential fertility. Put together, these factors depict a troubling picture in which the rural-urban gap in education widens rather than disappears in the future.

## 4. Employment and Participation of Women in the Workforce

As in other countries of the Middle East, the levels of employment and labor force participation of women in Iran are far below those of countries with similar per capita income (Karshenas, 2001). In Iran, after the revolution, employment and participation of women in the labor force decreased until the mid-1980s, after which it reversed itself. According to census data, the rate of participation fell from 12.9 percent in 1976 to 8.2 percent in 1986 and then increased again to 9.1 percent in 1996 (Table 6.1). However, the fluctuations seen in the overall female activity rate were primarily a rural phenomenon, as the urban rate continued to fall, at a slow pace, from 9.0 percent in 1976 to 8.1 percent in 1996. The urban employment rate decreased from 8.5 percent in 1976 to 5.1 percent in 1986, then went back up to 7.1 percent. The rural activity rate fell by more than half, from 16.6 to 7.9 percent, during the same period. No obvious reason can be found for this drastic decline, but a change in the definition of who is 'active' cannot be ruled out as a possibility (see Tabatai and Salehi-Isfahani, 2001).

**Table 6.1: Participation and Employment of Women in Iran, 1976–96 (%)**

| | | 1976 | 1986 | 1996 |
|---|---|---|---|---|
| Active | Total | 12.9 | 8.2 | 9.1 |
| | Urban | 9.0 | 8.3 | 8.1 |
| | Rural | 16.6 | 7.9 | 10.7 |
| Employed | Total | 10.8 | 6.1 | 8.7 |
| | Urban | 8.5 | 5.1 | 7.1 |
| | Rural | 13.0 | 6.3 | 9.6 |

*Source:* Statistical Center of Iran, *Yearbook*, various years.

Can female employment substantially increase to match the full effect of the decline in fertility? The answer is that it is very unlikely, for economic and cultural reasons. A quick look at the balance of supply and demand is not encouraging. According to the constant fertility projections reported above, assuming constant participation rates, the workforce will grow at a rate of nearly 3 percent for the period 1996–2006, and a bit lower during 2006–2016. To accommodate this increase, the economy must create an additional half a million new jobs.[6] If the response of Iranian women to fertility decline is similar to that of women in Malaysia following their fertility decline, female labor force participation could increase to as much as 40 percent. In this case, the rate of job creation would also have to increase by about 40 percent, to about 800,000 jobs per year, which is highly unlikely given the present sluggish state of demand for labor. By most accounts, unemployment has been increasing in the last five years, even without much of an increase in female participation rates, with the new job seekers faring the worst. In 1996, one out of every four people aged 20–24 was unemployed. Furthermore, women do not compete with men for all jobs. After the revolution, market segmentation according to gender increased, and female employment shifted toward the service and public sectors (mainly health and education) and away from industry and the private sector. In 1976, 53 percent of working women were employed in industry and 23 percent in services, compared to 33 percent and 46 percent in 1996. The concentration of women in the public sector is evident from the fact that in 1976 about 30 percent of women worked there, compared to 42 percent in 1996. Future growth is very unlikely to boost labor demand in the already bloated service and public sectors. Added to an adverse economic environment is an unfavorable cultural environment that emphasizes the role of women as mothers and homemakers and does not look favorably on outside work (Karshenas, 2001). This is particularly difficult for women with lower levels of education, who are unlikely to end up with white-collar jobs in the public and service sectors, which are generally more tolerated in Iran's traditional culture. These norms are not permanent; they can change, as they did in Tunisia and Morocco, where an increase in the employment of less-educated women in the export industry was substantial (Shaban et al 2001). However, for at least the next 10 years, the impediments to female employment in Iran are serious enough to suggest that the vast majority of women with reduced fertility will end up using their free time some other way.

Given this constraint, for many women the remaining choices are limited to how this time at home is spent. From a growth perspective, the choice to invest in child human capital is the most productive. In the long run, however, a strategy that relies heavily on women's role at home at the expense of increasing their opportunities to work outside may be economically and socially costly. There are drawbacks to women staying home, even if the time at home is spent on the education and health of children. Women with independent incomes may influence the intrahousehold distribution of resources in favor of girls (Strauss and Thomas, 1995; Behrman, 1997), and they are good role models to encourage younger women to seek education. Furthermore, because women are not paid for home schooling, the benefits of female education may not be obvious to parents, who may therefore underestimate the benefit of female education.[7]

## *The Role of the Family in Human Capital Accumulation*

Before children enter school at age 6, their education depends on what their parents teach them. The accumulation of human capital begins even before they are born. There is strong evidence, from biological to sociological, linking parental investment during the period of early childhood to the ability to learn later in life: "Scientific evidence indicates that 50 percent of the variance in intellectual development is established by age four" (Young 1995). Better nutrition, health, and childrearing raise the child's ability to learn in school and later on the job (World Bank, 1996). Thus human capital accumulation in school depends on the quality of pre-school care a child receives. Even after children enter school, parents continue to play an important role by monitoring the child's activities away from school, supervising homework, and monitoring the quality of school itself.

The level of human capital of parents influences the human capital of their children for two reasons. First, as decision-makers, their education affects the opportunity cost of their time, their desired fertility, and the level of investment in each child as they substitute quality for quantity. Second, as teachers and mentors of their children, their education determines how effective they are in creating the child's human capital at home, and thereby their willingness to do so. Various empirical studies in many different economic and cultural settings have shown that parental characteristics in general, and education in particular, are highly correlated with child education (Strauss and Thomas, 1995). Similar micro evidence for Iran is presented in Salehi-Isfahani (2001a). Regressions of child educational attainment on parents' education, holding other household characteristics constant, show that increasing the average schooling of both parents by one year raises child schooling from 0.5 to 1.5 years depending on rural or urban residence.

If the results from the micro studies are to be believed, the family in Iran can be a particularly positive force in human capital accumulation, because it is an important unit of social organization and because parents' education has been on the rise. About 80 percent of all women are married by age 25, divorce rates are very low, and having children is at the center of family life. Nearly all marriages result in a child within the first five years. The Islamic revolution promoted this sense of the family by encouraging early marriage and childbearing. In addition, expansion of female education in the last twenty years has created the potential for a more effective parental role. Nearly all women who married in the late 1990s are literate, can read to their children, and monitor schoolwork.

**Table 6.2: Literacy Rates, 1976–96 (population 6 years and older)**

| Census year | Urban | | Rural | |
|---|---|---|---|---|
| | Male | Female | Male | Female |
| 1976 | 74 | 56 | 44 | 17 |
| 1986 | 81 | 66 | 60 | 37 |
| 1991 | 88 | 78 | 73 | 55 |
| 1996 | 90 | 82 | 77 | 62 |

*Source:* Statistical Center of Iran, *Yearbook*, various years.

Gender plays an important role in the dynamics of human capital accumulation within the family. Although evidence is far from conclusive, micro studies have shown that in many settings the intergenerational transfer of human capital is not gender-neutral, that mothers have an absolute advantage in the education of their children, while fathers have a comparative advantage in boys' education (Strauss and Thomas, 1995). According to these studies, the transfer of human capital between generations happens primarily through the female. Thus the centrality of the role of female education to long-run growth is due not just to its effect on fertility, but also to its effect on child education. Fortunately, in Iran in the last two decades the educational achievement of women, at least in the urban areas, has grown rapidly and, significantly, faster than for men (Table 6.2). Data from household surveys show that mean educational attainment of males and females has increased, and that urban women's education has accelerated for cohorts born after the 1960s, so that the gender gap in schooling has narrowed in recent years (Salehi-Isfahani, 2001a). The proportion of females among high school graduates has increased rapidly from one-third in the 1970s to 50 percent in 1990s. Women now equal men in number in universities.

The educational attainment of rural women lags well behind urban women. To the extent that families may become more influential as a channel of human capital transfer between generations, in the long run this asymmetry can lead to a deepening of the rural-urban gap in income. The likelihood that rural women will find it optimal to increase their investment of time in their children is lower. Because they are less educated, the returns to their time spent in home production of human capital may be lower than in agriculture and other informal sector activities.[8] Still, the majority of rural women entering childbearing years in 1996 were literate, and therefore able at least to read to their children, improve child nutrition and health, and follow teacher directions for working with their children at home. Proper incentives and policies to help rural women invest more in their children's human capital may induce them in the direction of greater investment in children.

The market for private tutors that flourished within urban Iran in the last ten years suggests a high level of parental commitment to the success of their children. In 1998 most private tutors charged an hourly fee of US$5–US$10, which is very high compared to their monthly salaries in their regular jobs of less than US$200.[9] At the same time, this may be seen as evidence that parents themselves do not want to, or cannot, contribute to the education of their children. The reason for resorting to private teachers may include the highly competitive entrance examinations for universities, a topic to which I will return later.

## 6. The Educational System and Incentives for Human Capital Accumulation

Parents may reap the rewards of investing in their children in terms of support during old age or the child's own welfare. In either case they care about their children's success as adults. The kind of investment they undertake depends largely on what they believe is rewarded by the labor market.[10] But since success in the labor market depends mainly on success in the formal educational system, parental incentives are shaped by the system of formal schooling.

Home production of human capital is influenced by the opportunity cost of parents' time and the signals that the system of formal education and the labor market provide concerning the benefits of parental intervention. If the argument of this chapter regarding the demographic opportunity is correct, taking advantage of it depends crucially on the incentives for human capital accumulation generated by the educational system and the labor market. Historically, the government of Iran has played a dominant role in the provision of formal education. Article 3 of the Constitution of the Islamic Republic of Iran declares education at all levels, from elementary to higher education, free. Budgetary pressures forced the government in 1993 to allow private (non-profit) schools to compete with public schools at the elementary level, but their numbers are still quite small. At the higher education level, Iran's only private university, Azad University, with over 100 campuses across Iran, has nearly as many students as all the public institutions of higher education combined.

The baby boom that followed the revolution (Salehi-Isfahani 2001b) presented the government with a serious shortage of teachers and schools. In the mid-1980s, when the baby boomers started to arrive in schools, the government was not able to increase its expenditures to maintain education quality. The country was in the midst of a costly war with Iraq and oil prices had collapsed. The government responded to the greater needs in education by increasing the share of education expenditures in the budget, but could not prevent a decline in its share relative to GNP (Figure 6.6). Most schools had to go to two and even three shifts, causing a decline in the quality of schooling. However, the drop in fertility that started sometime in the mid-1980s does not seem to have initiated a change in the reverse direction, to increase education quality. The share of expenditures in the budget declined in the 1990s (Figure 6.6), indicating that the government is unwilling to increase quality when enrollments are on the decline.

East Asian economies that started their fertility transition in the 1960s substantially increased the amount of public resources spent per pupil in basic education. For example, Korea increased its per pupil expenditure in primary education from US$51 in 1975 to US$390 in 1985, and US$610 in 1989 (World Bank, 1996). In Iran, at the peak of primary enrollment in 1993–94, government expenditures averaged about 50,000 rials (US$30) per primary student (World Bank, 1996), which is very low. Will the government be able to increase its expenditure per child in the future as the number of students in elementary schools declines, or will it maintain the quality at the same level and use the sav-

**Figure 6.6: Public Expenditures on Education**

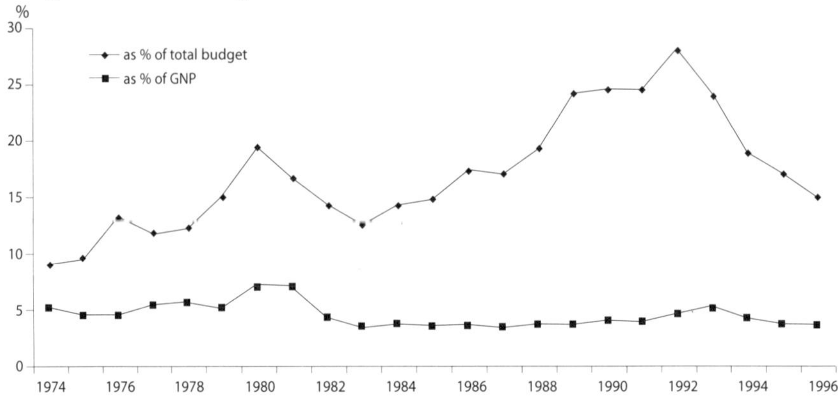


*Source:* Statistical Center of Iran, *Yearbook*, various years.

ings elsewhere? The spread of private, non-profit, elementary schools provides the more well-off parents with access to higher school quality, but, given the distribution of income in Iran, only a small percentage of families can take advantage of these schools.

Most parents in Iran have a simple yet ambitious educational objective for their children—to enter university. Since the 1960s, there has been a huge imbalance between the number of high school graduates and those who can enter university (never less than ten to one). Nearly 1.5 million students took part in the entrance examination in 2000, of whom 150,000, or 10 percent, passed the test (60 percent of the successful candidates were women!). The Islamic government expanded public higher education after the revolution, but the real increase in enrollments has come from the private Azad University, which, as noted, now has as many students as all public universities combined. Despite its high tuition fees, those who aspire to enter Azad University must also pass a competitive exam.

Although competitive entrance exams increase student effort, exclusive attention to preparation for the entrance examinations (the dreaded *concour*) can be at the expense of human capital development. As a result, the vast majority of students who do not succeed in passing the exam fail to acquire the basic skills for productive employment. The entire school system has responded to the challenge set by the *concour* by tilting the curriculum in favor of teaching skills that enable students to perform well on a multiple-choice exam once they graduate from high school. The problem with this system is not so much that it has only few winners, but that it concentrates student effort too much on the acquisition of knowledge and too little on the development of other productive skills that are not easily testable, such as creativity, teamwork, and dependability. In doing so, it also ignores the education of the majority of students, who need not go to university in order to be more productive. Under this system, parents, the vast majority of whom have not themselves had a university education, feel that the only effective role they can play is to enforce harsh study habits and pay exorbitant fees to private tutors.[11] In the mad rush to prepare their children for the 'big test,' parents neglect the teaching of skills that they could best teach, such as instilling confidence and developing teamwork. For the few who pass the exam, the competition comes to an end, and learning slows down. In a pattern that resembles other countries with 'the big test,' Iranian students work much harder than their counterparts in the west in grade school, but less after entering college. The inevitable result of studying only to pass a test is less effort when the pressure is removed. For the more than one million who fail the test each year, there lies ahead another year of study for yet another attempt at passing the exam or a long shot at landing a job.

Parents and commentators have voiced criticism of this system. According to one critic, the "few thousands who pass the entrance examinations are not the products of the formal educational system; rather they are the products of the harsh response of parents who have realized the gravity of the economic conditions and are convinced that their children must be equipped with a degree." He goes on to draw distinctions between the institutions of education in Iran and those of the advanced countries, noting that Iran's consist of "large and small classes for *concour*, highly paid private tutors ... depriving their children of all forms of relaxation, even bathing." The result "is that they produce real and steady researchers and we produce unsteady and fleeting geniuses" (Hassouri, 1998).

To remedy this situation, in the early 1980s the government embarked on an ambitious program to reform secondary education, which was first introduced in the academic year 1992–93.[12] The program aimed to separate the college-bound, early on, from the rest, so as to allow these others a more appropriate training for productive work. Most observers now agree that this reform has not succeeded (Moazzami, 1998; World Bank, 1996). The most often cited reason is the high cost of vocational training, which limits the scope of the program. Less often noted, but more important in my view, is the fact that labor market signals continue to indicate a low value for such training. Both public and private employment rewards are still based on degrees rather than skills.

## 7. Labor Market Signals and Incentives for Human Capital Accumulation

In a well-functioning labor market, firms reward productive traits and skills and thereby send signals to schools, families, and individuals that induce investment in those traits and skills. When these signals are distorted, often due to heavy government intervention, the wrong mix of investments in human capital may be produced. In Iran, public intervention in the labor market and in formal education has resulted in greater emphasis on the acquisition of degrees than on productive skills. Both public and private employers face rigid pay scales that are linked not to individual productivity but to formal education. The lack of flexibility in hiring, retention, and compensation of workers creates a specific set of incentives for firms and households which affects human capital accumulation. While lack of labor market flexibility is a problem in any economy, it can be a tragedy for a country facing the demographic window of opportunity.

The labor market is where economic returns to education are realized. Government policies that alter incentives to demand or supply effort affect parental decisions to invest in the human capital of their children. Two types of interventions exist in Iran. First, as the largest employer of trained workers (about 15 percent of all employment), rules governing employment in the public sector influence the decisions of a large proportion of the population to accumulate different types of human capital. Most civil service jobs require a university degree and carry *de facto* tenure. Historically, the security associated with these jobs has raised their value, and encouraged most parents to push their children in the direction of university education in the hope of landing a government job. As a consequence, the university degree has become more important than the actual skills learned in higher education, and technical and vocational education has become less desirable because it does not qualify one for a public sector job. The only skills worth accumulating in high school are those that increase the chances of passing university entrance examinations. These skills are by and large useful, but fall short of an optimal mix for employment.

Second, the government intervenes in the labor market by inserting itself as a mediator in the employer-employee relation. The Labor Law passed in 1993 has many provisions that make it very difficult for employers to lay off workers, short of closing plants (Tabatabai and Salehi-Isfahani, 2001; Salehi-Isfahani, 1999; World Bank, 1996).[13] The push to increase job security in both public and private employment has resulted in a situation in which workers regard finding a job as much more important than holding on to it. The former emphasizes external signals such as degrees, whereas the latter depends on the quality of the human capital.

The role of incentives on parental behavior in child education can best be illustrated by contrasting two extremes. At one extreme, jobs are permanent and are therefore assigned on the basis of *ex ante* signals of worker quality. In this case, an effective signal is a university degree because it is the most competitively allocated. If, additionally, the number of new jobs barely exceeds the number of university graduates, which has been the case in Iran, it makes sense for employers to hire only university graduates. In this system, parents will make their investments in such way as to maximize their child's chances of entering the university. Thus in Iran, where most exams, including the national university entrance examination, are based on multiple choice and require speed in answering questions, memorization has dominated learning. Many worker characteristics that would be desirable and productive are not worth accumulating because they are not tested and are therefore difficult to signal. For example, self-confidence, perseverance, teamwork, respect for authority, and the like, which are skills that parents teach well, no longer receive the emphasis they deserve. Indeed, some parents may actively promote certain types of behavior that maybe undesirable in production, such as non-cooperative behavior, but may help the child get ahead in the competitive educational system. A more acute problem arises in promoting self-confidence in children, when the risks of failure in the selection process are so great—more than 90 percent—and fear of failure is therefore an effective tool for motivation. At the other extreme, consider a situation in which employers can, with impunity, lay off unproductive workers and keep those who demonstrate high productivity. In this case, a university degree serves the bearer only if it increases his/her ability to perform on the job. Parents would then be motivated to inculcate in their children skills that would benefit them on the job rather than on the way to it.

In Iran, lack of labor market flexibility has resulted in a situation where hiring, in both public and private enterprise, is based more on diplomas as *ex ante* signals of productivity than on information on other worker characteristics, such as creativity and character, that can best be observed after employment. The inflexibility reveals itself in part in low worker turnover, which prevents employers from signaling the type of worker characteristics that they need for production. At the receiving end of these signals from the labor market, teachers, parents, and students are persuaded to invest in characteristics that do not maximize the productivity of the rising generation of workers, thus preventing the country from taking advantage of its demographic window of opportunity.

## 8. Concluding Remarks

In this chapter I have examined the implications of the demographic transition in Iran for long-term economic growth. It presents an optimistic scenario for growth in Iran, based on the well-known idea of the demographic window of opportunity, but with emphasis on human capital and its production at home. I have argued that lower fertility provides families with the opportunity to raise the quality of many aspects of their children's upbringing. Today, thanks to increased education, all young parents are at least literate, and are therefore in a position to play a key role in the intergenerational transfer of human capital. I have also argued that lower fertility is unlikely to lead to greater labor force participation in the near future, essentially leaving increased leisure and home production of human capital as the only other options for women with fewer children. The great obstacles that remain in the promotion of human capital are the distorted incentives provided by the system of formal education and the labor market.

Government policy is the chief determinant of how generous Iran's demographic gift will prove to be. The changing age structure poses an opportunity as well as a challenge for the economy. To meet the challenge, the country needs properly functioning labor and financial markets, as well as an effective educational system. Unfortunately, the ideological barriers to creating a competitive labor market are immense. President Khatami's election platforms, which have won him with more than 70 percent of the popular vote in the 1997 and 2001 elections, extended the needs of youth to include political participation but not participation in the economy. Five years after his election to office, he is still unable to articulate the economic base on which to build his promised 'civil society,' in part because of his strong association with the left, which places a much higher value on the protection of existing jobs than on job creation. Failure to enact reforms that can help Iran take advantage of the demographic opportunity may lead to a demographic nightmare of increased unemployment and social discontent. Already one in four young high school graduates is unemployed, which is three times the national average rate of unemployment. Unfortunately, fears of rising unemployment may cause policy makers to take the wrong turn and further intervene in the economy. The temptation to protect jobs in times of high unemployment may prove too strong, causing the government to further tighten, rather than loosen, restrictions in the already inflexible labor market of Iran. On the other hand, once it sees the great potential, it could well be persuaded to take the bold steps necessary for reform.

## Notes

* I wish to thank Ismail Sirageldin and Jeffrey Williamson for helpful comments on the original paper, which was first presented at the ERF conference on "Population Challenges for the Middle East and North Africa," Cairo, November 1998.

1 For an evaluation of the role of natural resources in growth, see Sachs and Warner (1995); for the role of human capital in growth, see Lucas (1988) and Barro (1991).

2 Although the size of this age group is rarely reported accurately, the phenomenal increase in the later intercensal period shows up in school enrollments.

3 This scenario in not the worst case, as I am implicitly assuming that fertility will not rise in the future, but it is consistent with the hypothesis of intertemporal substitution as noted above.

4 I assume zero rural-urban migration. Allowing for a certain percentage of rural population to move to the urban areas complicates the projections, and it would change the ratios depending on the assumptions made about the fertility of those who move.
5 This may not be a good projection for the future parent-child ratio in the urban sector, as these projections ignore rural-urban migration.
6 The 'Plan and Budget Organization' projects a more bleak picture: to maintain unemployment at its current rate, the economy must create 3.6 million new jobs in the next five years, more than it created for the ten-year period 1986–96 (*Hamshahri*, 21 April 1999).
7 Behrman *et al.* (1999) show that in rural India female education is valued in the marriage market, more highly educated women being preferred precisely because they can better educate future sons.
8 Studies of the rate of return to education in Iran are sorely lacking. In particular, we do not know how it varies by rural and urban origin of the child.
9 Personal observations. I use the exchange rate of 3000 rials per dollar.
10 Rewards for human capital are determined mainly in the labor and the marriage markets. But, to the extent that matching in marriage is based on human capital, the markets for marriage and labor produce the same signals.
11 Private tutors, especially those who teach at grades 11 and 12, easily rake in hourly rates in excess of a day's pay at their regular jobs. A World Bank (1999) study estimates that Egyptian parents spend seven billion Egyptian pounds (US$2 billion), or six percent of private expenditures, a year on private tutors.
12 For a review of the planning process, see Moazzami (1998).
13 Article 21 of the Labor Law recognizes quits, deaths, or retirement as reasons for ending a labor contract. All other reasons require government approval. Employers who lay off workers for lack of productivity risk being overruled on appeal to government councils and face penalties.

## References

Aghajanian, A. 1991. "Population Change in Iran: A Stalled Demographic Transition?," *Population and Development Review*, 17: 703–15.

———. 1995. "A New Direction in Population Policy and Family Planning in the Islamic Republic of Iran," *Asia-Pacific Population Journal*, Vol. 10, No. 1.

Barlow, R. 1994. "Population Growth and Economic Growth: Some More Correlations," *Population and Development Review*, 20: 153–65.

Barro, R. J. 1991. "Economic Growth in a Cross Section of Countries," *Quarterly Journal of Economics*, 106: 407–43.

———, and G. S. Becker. 1992. "Fertility Choice in a Model of Economic Growth," *Econometrica*, 57: 481–501.

Becker, G. S. 1992. "Fertility and the Economy," *Journal of Population Economics*, 5: 185–95.

———, K. M. Murphy, and R. Tamura. 1990. "Human Capital, Fertility, and Economic Growth," *Journal of Political Economy*, October 98.5, Part 2, pp. S12–S37.

Behrman, J. R. 1997. "Intrahousehold Distribution and the Family," in M. R. Rosenzweig and O. Stark (eds.), *Handbook of Population and Family Economics*, pp. 125–87. Amsterdam: Horth Holland.

———, Andrew D. Foster, Mark R. Rosenzweig, and Prem Vahsishtha. 1999. "Women's Schooling, Home Teaching, and Economic Growth," *Journal of Political Economy* 107: 682–714.

Bloom, D., and J. Williamson. 1998. "Demographic Transitions and Economic Miracles in Emerging Asia," *World Bank Economic Review*, 12(3): 419–55.

Cinotta, Richard P., and Robert Engelman. 1997. *Economics of Rapid Change: The Influence of Population Growth*, Population Action International, Occasional Paper No. 3.

Galore, O., and D. N. Weil. 1996. "The Gender Gap, Fertility and Growth," *American Economic Review*, 86: 374–87.

Hassouri, Ali. 1998. "The Condition We Are In," *Jamee Salem*, No. 40, Spring, Tehran (in Persian).

Hill, Kenneth. 1994. *Towards a Unified System of Demographic Estimates for the Islamic Republic of Iran*, United Nations Children's Fund (UNICEF), Tehran.

Karshenas, Massoud. 2001. "Economic Liberalization, Competitiveness and Women's Employment in the Middle East and North Africa," in D. Salehi-Isfahani (ed.), *Labor and Human Capital in the Middle East: Studies of Markets and Household Behavior*, Reading, England: Ithaca Press.

King, Elizabeth M., and M. Anne Hill. 1993. "Women's Education in Developing Countries: An Overview," in Elizabeth King and M. Anne Hill (eds.), *Women's Education in Developing Countries*, Baltimore, MD: Johns Hopkins University Press.

Lucas, R. E. 1988. "The Mechanics of Economic Development," *Journal of Monetary Economics*, 22: 3–42.

Malekafzali, H. 1995. "An Evaluation of the Family Planning Program in 1374 (1993/94)." Paper presented at the Tehran Population Seminar, June 1995.

Mankiw, Gregory N., Romer, David, and Weil, David N. 1992. "A Contribution to the Empirics of Economic Growth," *Quarterly Journal of Economics*, 107(2): 407–37.

Mehryar, Amir H. 1995. "The Rise and Fall of Fertility ates of Iranian Population after the Islamic Revolution of 1979," Institute for Research in Planning and Development, Tehran, Research Group in Population and Social Policy, Working Paper No. 3.

Moazzami, A. 1998. "The New Educational System and Teaching in the New System," *Goftegu*, 19, Spring (in Persian).

Plan and Budget Organization. 1998. *Tarh-e Samandehi-e Eqtesadi* ("Plan for Economic Reorganization"), The Plan and Budget Organization of Iran (renamed in 2000 "Management and Planning Organization"), Tehran, Iran.

Sachs, J., and A. Warner. 1995. "Natural Resource Abundance and Economic Growth," Working Paper 5398, Cambridge: National Bureau of Economic Research.

Salehi-Isfahani, D. 1999. "Labor and the Challenge of Restructuring in Iran," *Middle East Report*, 28: 34–37.

———. 2000. "Demographic Factors in Iran's Economic Development," *Social Research*, 67(2): 599–620.

———. 2001a. "Intergenerational Transfer of Human Capital: Evidence for the Role of Gender in Iran," in D. Salehi-Isfahani (ed.), *Labor and Human Capital in the Middle East: Studies of Markets and Household Behavior*, Reading, England: Ithaca Press.

———. 2001b. "Fertility, Education, and Household Resources in Iran," in E. M. Cinar (ed.), *The Economics of Women and Work in the Middle East and North Africa*, Research in Middle East Economics, Vol. 4, Amsterdam: JAI/Elsevier.

———, and A. Tandon. 1998. "Fertility Transition or Intertemporal Substitution: Evidence from Household Data," mimeo, VPI&SU Department of Economics.

Shaban, R., R. Assaad, and S. Al-Qudsi. 2001."Employment Experience in the Middle East and North Africa," in D. Salehi-Isfahani (ed.), *Labor and Human Capital in the Middle East: Studies of Markets and Household Behavior*, Reading, England: Ithaca Press.

Shafiq, Nemat. 1997. "Rents, Reform and Economic Malaise in Middle East and North Africa," in *Research in Middle East Economics*,. 2: 221–45.

Strauss, John, and Duncan Thomas.1995. "Human Resources: Empirical Modeling of Household and Family Decisions," in Jere R. Behrman and T. N. Sriniviasan (eds.), *Handbook of Development*, 3A: 1883–2024. Amsterdam: North Holland.

Tabatabai, Hamid, and Djavad Salehi-Isfahani. 2001. "Population, Labor, and Employment in Iran," in Djavad Salehi-Isfahani, (ed.), *Labor and Human Capital in the Middle East: Studies of Markets and Household Behavior*. Reading, England: Ithaca Press.
Taheripour, F. 1996. "Projection of Population," Institute for Research in Planning and Development Working Paper, Tehran, Iran.
Tunalı, Insan. 1996. "Labor market implications of the demographic window of opportunity," *The Forum*, 3(2). Cairo: Economic Research Forum for the Arab Countries, Iran, and Turkey.
World Bank. 1995. *Claiming the Future: A Long-Term Prospective Study of the Middle East and North Africa*. Washington DC: World Bank.
———. 1996. *Islamic Republic of Iran: Education, Training, and the Labor Markets*, Report No. 13233-IR. Washington DC: World Bank.
———. 1999. Education in the Middle East and North Africa: A Strategy Toward Learning for Development, Washington DC: World Bank.
Young, Mary E. 1995. *Investing in Young Children*, World Bank Discussion Paper No. 275. Washington, DC: World Bank.
Yousef, Tarek. 1998. "Demography, Capital Dependency, and Growth in MENA," ERF Working Paper No. 9801. Cairo: Economic Research Forum for the Arab Countries, Iran, and Turkey.

# 7

# Econometric Analysis of Fertility Dynamics in Turkey

*Ali C. Tasiran**

## 1. Introduction

'Demographic transition' is a term used to describe the process of change that a population experiences when it shifts from high mortality and fertility to low mortality and fertility. A historical association between this process and economic growth has been observed in developed countries. In general, economic and demographic development can be said to go hand in hand. Turkey has undergone major demographic and economic change since World War II. The total fertility rate (TFR)[1] has declined since 1950, reaching 2.7 in 1993, with an extrapolated level of 2.1 for the year 2000. Declining death rates, better health, and longer life expectancy have resulted in lower fertility nationally (SIS Report, 1995), although the population continues to grow owing to population momentum.[2] The population growth rate fell from 2.2 in 1976–77 to 1.8 in 1993–94. The age structure of the population is also changing. The population below age 15 is diminishing, while the productive population, those between 15 and 64 years, is increasing; it was 62.5 percent in 1994 compared to 55.1 in 1960. The composition of the total age dependency ratio[3] is also changing as a result of changes in age structure. The proportion of the population that is very young is declining, while the proportion that is very old is increasing. Despite some problems, Turkey is showing high economic growth rates—over 5 percent on average, except in 1994. Overall, Turkey has been experiencing a 'demographic transition,' accompanied by economic growth, since the 1950s. This process may not be taking place as rapidly as in East and Southeast Asian countries, but it is happening faster than in Latin American countries.

This chapter is a study of Turkish fertility determinants. Dynamic hazard rate fertility models are estimated using the 1993 Demographic and Health Survey data set, and the causes of these demographic changes are investigated utilizing duration models. The 1993 Turkish Demographic and Health Survey was conducted by the Institute of Population Studies, Hacettepe University, Ankara, and contains retrospective life history information for 3259 married women between ages 15 and 49. Thus we have women's childbirth histories, including partner and household relationships, and would like to establish fertility determinants for them. What roles do women's individual characteristics play in their reproductive behavior? Is it possible to distinguish different ethnic group responses on childbearing behavior? Does childbirth risk decline with increasing education levels? What role does a woman's occupational status play? Do partners' characteristics affect the outcomes? Which household and regional properties are important? Has involuntary internal migration resulting from the armed conflict with the Kurds affected the childbearing behavior of women? By studying childbirth dynamics, we are able to discover not only the factors affecting today's fertility results but also those that will affect future developments.

Basic fertility models in economics have a static structure. In this study of Turkish fertility determinants, a dynamic approach, applying models based mainly on duration analysis, is used. Duration analysis presents a more natural empirical specification of the timing of births than the usual regression analysis. Compared to traditional time-series or panel data, event histories are often better suited to the dynamic character of fertility, since the statistical methods in duration analysis can be used to analyze time intervals between childbirths. For each woman, event histories provide information about the exact interval before a birth occurs as well as the occurrence and sequence of other related events. Transition rate models use all available information in the data and correct censoring bias without generating selectivity bias.

Some of the important findings of this chapter are as follows. Duration dependency of first-birth risk shows an inverted U-shape, the birth risk is monotonically decreasing for the second child. Ethnicity is important, but not in the way it is typically believed to be and widely accepted. Kurdish women do not have higher fertility than Turkish women. In fact, the opposite is true, since armed conflict and involuntary migration have had destructive effects on their fertility. Voluntary migration increases first-birth risk in the larger cities but not second-birth risk. Women with higher education postpone the birth of their first child and also have lower risks of giving birth to subsequent children. Involuntary migration from the armed conflict regions of eastern Turkey to large cities in western Turkey leads to an increase in first births but a decline in second births.

The chapter is divided into six sections. After this introduction, background information about Turkish fertility development is given in section 2. Section 3 reports economic fertility models—first static, then dynamic models. Both structural and reduced-form dynamic models are explained in the second part of the section. Data and variables are presented in section 4. First, the sampling process in the 1993 Turkish Demographic and Health Survey is discussed; after which, the variables used in the analysis are explained. Descriptive statistics for individuals and birth spells are also reported in this section. Section 5 includes estimated parameters for univariate models, using the partial likelihood approach of a Cox model. Parameters of a multivariate hazard model are estimated for the first childbirth by using a Piecewise Constant Exponential (PCE) duration dependency. Estimation results of both first and second childbirths (jointly), using the same flexible PCE approach, are also displayed in this section. The last section, section 6, offers some concluding remarks and briefly discusses the findings.

## 2. Population Dynamics in Turkey

Turkey's population experienced many changes in its reproductive regimes before the establishment of the Republic in 1923. Population in Anatolia did not always follow traditional reproduction patterns; for example, there was low fertility in Istanbul as early as the turn of the nineteenth century. Modern demographic development can be dated back to 1923, and this period can be studied in three stages.

The first stage took place between 1923 and 1955. During the early years of the

Republic, there were serious shortages of adults due to conditions following World War I. Peace and normal life led to the steady decline of death rates. Fertility increased from around 5.5 children to 7.0. This lasted until World War II. Death rates fell and population almost doubled, increasing from 13 to 24 million between 1923 and 1955.

The second stage began in 1955 and continued until 1985. During the 1950s, fertility started to decline but population continued to grow, owing to much lower levels of infant mortality. During this period, population doubled again, from 24 to 51 million. Another important development of this period was rapid urbanization. The proportion of urban areas with populations of 10,000 and over rose rapidly after the 1950s. Following migration from rural areas to urban areas, young adults chose lower rates of reproduction. Economic, educational, and consumption opportunities of the cities have depressive effects on childbirths.

The third stage started in 1985 and continues today. During this period, mortality and fertility have declined even further. Interestingly, a decline in the rate of population growth was observed for the first time. The growth rate decreased to 2.2 percent between 1985 and 1990. By 1990, the annual rate of natural increase was 1.8 percent. By 1994, it was estimated at 1.6 percent. Two things are expected to be realized at the end of the current stage: the Total Fertility Rate should fall to a level of 2.1 children per woman, and population growth should stop. Population projections show that Turkey is now approaching a replacement level fertility situation.

## 3. Economic Models for Fertility Analysis

In this section, we look at the fertility model in economic analysis. Schultz (1992) gives a detailed analysis of fertility behavior in developing countries; Danish economist Ester Boserup (1990) explores the connections between economic growth and demographic trends. The important issues she discusses are the relationship between agriculture and population, varying constraints on food supply and agricultural productivity, the economic activities of women and the changing family, and the environmental determinants of desired fertility in low-income countries. (For a discussion of the woman's role in economic development, see Boserup, 1970.) Another important topic in Boserup's work is the complicated relationship between population and technological change. It is generally agreed that successive changes in technology have an important influence on population size (Boserup, 1981).

The issues of population growth or decline cannot be separated from questions of economic and social development or from environmental concerns related to the management of resources on a global level. In a volume edited by Kiessling and Landberg (1994), several authors present their own views on these issues and attempt to illuminate the population, environment, and development nexus from a number of interrelated perspectives. The message is clear: the issues of population, development, natural resources, and environment must be considered together.

The demand for children depends on a number of economic conditions, such as the cost of raising children, the return from their labor on the household farm or from collecting fuel-wood, the need for old-age security, and so on. The demand for children and family-planning techniques available to households are important sets of determinants in fertility change. Demographic and economic transitions in previous macro studies are explained mainly by cross-country comparison of aggregate data plus some time-series models.

In the simplest version of the macroeconomic explanation, it is assumed that every 'advanced country' that has successfully achieved a high standard of living has undergone such a demographic transition. According to Engel's Law, productivity change throughout the economy increases per-capita income and tends to reduce both the fraction of income accounted for by agricultural output and the fraction of the labor force in the agricultural sector. Engel's Law implies that economic growth will tend to increase the relative demand for skilled labor, since the agricultural sector employs the least educated labor. This development causes an associated increase in the demand for education and on-the-job training. Increases in the optimal level of human capital per child and in the relative cost of female time cause desired fertility to decline and the average quality of workers to increase, which, in turn, tends to promote economic growth and development.

## *Microeconomic Fertility Models*

### *Static fertility models*

Economists have developed tools to analyze childbirths, in particular to explain decreasing family sizes and increasing incomes after World War II. Applying the principles of consumer demand theory, they made the analysis of fertility in an economic framework possible by utilizing recent developments in the economic theory of human capital, allocation of time, and non-market household behavior. Economic fertility models at micro levels can be grouped as static and dynamic models.

The first models of fertility were static (Becker, 1960, 1965; Mincer, 1963; Schultz, 1973; Willis, 1974; and Butz and Ward, 1979.) In these models, lifetime marital fertility was analyzed, and family size was seen as a result of parental choice under financial and time constraints. The opportunity cost of parental time in child-care was the determining argument observed by fertility patterns in modern industrial societies. The most important work along these lines was done by Willis (1974).

The economic model of the family describes the demand for children as an outcome of the optimizing decisions of parents, whose objective is to maximize the utility function. But static models of fertility do not capture all important aspects of reproductive behavior. First, such models ignore the durable and irreversible nature of children as consumption goods. Second, the heterogeneity in fecundity is not taken into account. Fecundity—the ability to bear children—is not the same for all women, nor is it constant throughout a woman's lifetime. Third, even for couples who demand the same number of children, their range of wages and income affects the timing and spacing of births. (Examples of dynamic fertility models can be found in papers by Heckman and Willis, 1975; Wolpin, 1984; Moffit, 1984; Cigno and Ermisch, 1988; and Newman and McCulloch, 1984.)

### *Dynamic fertility models*

The focus of dynamic models of fertility behavior has shifted from completed family size to the timing and spacing of births. (For a detailed review of both static and dynamic fertility models in economics, see Tasiran, 1995.) Dynamic, probabilistic models of fertility have been used in demographic studies since the 1960s. Family-formation models are constructed to study the effects of variations in fecundity and contraceptive practices on the timing and number of births over a woman's reproductive life. This process is divided into distinct, mutually exclusive states—such as fecundity, pregnancy, miscarriage, or live birth—and the duration of a particular state, as well as transitions between states, are studied as random variables. This can be viewed as a stochastic process by specifying distribution functions for the waiting-time random variables between states. Family-formation models are exclusively biologically determined; therefore, such models are frequently applied to explain population growth in developing countries.

*a) Structural models*

Structural approach models observe fertility as part of the solution for an explicit dynamic programming problem, and derives estimable relationships from this solution. In the general framework of a structural model, couples are assumed to receive utility from the flow of child services proportional to the stock of children and the flow of a composite commodity representing all non-child-related sources of satisfaction. They maximize an expected lifetime utility function subject to lifetime resource constraints. It is assumed that couples intentionally space births, having children when income is relatively high, and that the household's income and costs of child services are known with certainty. In these types of models, human-capital and child-quality considerations are excluded. The latter are almost wholly absent in dynamic models and have no predictive content in such models. These equations are reformulated and solved as a dynamic programming problem.

In such a dynamic model, the decision-making process is sequential: in each period the couple must first decide whether to use contraception; if so, they must then select the amount of protection. The supply of births is then stochastically determined with an expected waiting time before conception equal to the inverse of the effective probability of conception. If it is assumed that all conceptions result in a live birth, then the decision rule is to determine the contraceptive behavior. An index for contraceptive behavior can be used, and the sequence of choices is determined by time, parity, and the outcomes of previous choices as well as by the current and future values of wages, incomes, and prices. In such a model, income and wages affect the timing and spacing of births in two ways: (1) capital market imperfections provide an incentive to time births when income is high, implying a positive relationship between income and the probability of a birth; and (2) intertemporal substitution opportunities provide an incentive to time births when the relative price of child-related services is low, implying a negative relationship between female wages and the probability of a birth.

*b) Reduced-form models*

The estimation of structural models is complex, since such models need computationally demanding dynamic programming solutions. Non-structural or reduced-form models are therefore useful and are more tractable alternatives. Reduced-form models have also a basis in the solution of some dynamic programming problems, but they do not rely heavily on specifying estimating equations, including stochastic elements. These models typically use the underlying theory to posit variables and possible error structures. The main variable of interest is birth likelihood. When this variable is regarded as continuously varying, all reduced-form dynamic fertility models adopt a hazard-rate approach to estimation. (For a recent survey about dynamic fertility models, see Arroyo and Zhang, 1997.)

Newman and McCulloch (1984) were the first to apply a hazard-rate approach to the study of fertility, where behavioral factors affect parental goals, which in turn determine the likelihood of a birth. The uncertainty of the occurrence is rooted in the uncertain nature of the biological process. While the demographic literature has stressed biological aspects, the economic literature has emphasized the behavioral nature of fertility decisions. The hazard-rate approach includes the behavioral component. It typically enters as a deterministic element, with the stochastic element of the model supplied by the process generating the births, where intervals between births are assumed to follow a certain distribution and the mean being a function of explanatory variables.

The hazard-rate approach maintains the static decision-making framework of the household production model, but assumes that parents make decisions with regard to the timing as well as the number of births. In these models, the length of the mean uncensored birth interval (the average time between births) enters positively into the family's utility function. It is frequently assumed that longer birth intervals augment the quality of the child. The length of the average closed birth interval is then treated as the quality component of child services in a typical quality-quantity interaction model. Newman postulates that longer mean intervals increase the cost of raising children, based on the assumption that children who are born closer together are more likely to have similar needs that can be met with economies of scale. The assumption that, *ceteris paribus*, longer birth intervals would be preferred by parents can also be justified by another option, namely, a balanced-consumption pattern. In the absence of perfect capital markets, spacing births may permit a more balanced pattern of consumption of non-child-related goods over time. If goods consumed in different time periods are imperfect substitutes, a more balanced consumption pattern would increase utility.

Assuming the distribution between births to be the same, and the waiting periods before each birth to be independent random variables, a complete representation of a woman's fertility history can be formulated in a likelihood function describing interval lengths. This is a product of the density functions of the waiting times before the first and all subsequent births and the probability that there will be no birth in the censored (open) interval.

## A Transition Rate Model as a Continuous-Time Birth Process Model for Turkish Fertility

In this chapter, we therefore use duration models to estimate childbirths in Turkey. A transition rate model is continuous-time and defines a stated 'space' as well as the set of feasible transitions between parities characterizing both the associated waiting-time random variables and the underlying explanatory covariates.

A hazard function can represent the instantaneous probability of a woman's giving birth, provided that she has not given birth before. The length of a spell is its duration. Time is measured at intervals and is continuous while status is discrete, in contrast to time-series models. This type of analysis is therefore called event-history analysis and/or duration analysis. The important monographs of these models are by Kalbfleisch and Prentice (1980), Cox and Oakes (1984), and Lancaster (1990).

The transition rate model can be written as a proportional rate model, denoting waiting time for a childbirth with T as a non-negative random variable:

$$h(t) = h_b(t;\alpha)\, e^{[\beta' x]} \tag{1}$$

Here the hazard rate, $h(t)$, is a product of two parts. The first, $h_b(t;\alpha)$, is called the baseline transition rate and depends on time and on a parameter vector $\alpha$. The second part links the transition rate to individual specific explanatory variables $\boldsymbol{x}$ with associated parameters $\beta$. $\exp(\sum_{i=1}^{k} x_i \beta_i)=\prod_{i=1}^{k} h_i (x_i)$ shows the relative risks. Such models are called proportional hazard rate models because the effect of individual specific explanatory variables is independent of time. Only the baseline hazard rate is dependent on time; different individual specific variables lead only to proportional shifts of the baseline rate. If the baseline hazard rate's parameters are linked to individual specific variables, the model is no longer a proportional hazard rate model.

The simple transition rate model is exponential, where it is assumed that the transition rates can vary with different groups of explanatory variables but do not depend on time. The duration variable $T$ can be described by an exponential distribution with hazard, survivor, and density functions, respectively:

$$\begin{aligned} h(t) &= a \quad \text{where} \quad a>0 \\ S(t) &= \exp(-at) \\ f(t) &= a\exp(-at) \end{aligned} \tag{2}$$

Obviously, it is implied that the transition rates are constant, not varying with the duration of the spell. In the application of childbirths this might not be realistic. The basic formulation with explanatory variables can be written:

$$h(t) = e^{(\alpha_0)}\, e^{\beta' x} \tag{3}$$

In this case, the baseline hazard rate does not depend on time; it is just $\exp(\alpha_0)$, and the relative risks, $h_i(t_i)$, just shift this constant function.

With a small modification, the exponential model becomes very flexible. The basic idea is to split the time axis into time periods and to assume that the transition rates are constant in each of these intervals but can change between them. This model is also called a Piecewise Constant Exponential model.

If there are some m periods, then the distribution of durations has m parameters. To include variables we assume only a baseline hazard rate, given by period-specific constants; it can vary across periods but the variables have the same proportional effects in each period. Note that with this model the vector of variables must not contain a separate constant.

$$h(t) = \exp\left\{\bar{\alpha_l} + \beta' x\right\} \; if\, t \in I_l \tag{4}$$

where $l$ shows the time period, by splitting points on the time axis $0 = \tau_1 < \tau_2 < \tau_3 \ldots < \tau_m$ with $\tau_{m+1} = \infty$, one gets $m$ time periods $I_l = \{t \mid \tau_l \le t \le \tau_{l+1}\}$ $l = 1, 2, \ldots$ m and for each transition, the constant $\alpha_l$ is a coefficient associated with the $l$ th time period. $\boldsymbol{x}$ is a row vector of explanatory variables and $\beta$ is an associated vector of coefficients assumed not to vary across time periods.

The parameters of the model are estimated with the maximum-likelihood estimation method, since some of observations are censored. We have two types of contributions to the likelihood: a censored part and an uncensored part. Under certain mild restrictions on the admissible class of hazard functions, these parameters are consistently estimated and asymptotically normal.

For each woman $i$, $i = 1, 2, 3, \ldots, n$ the following information was given:

$t_i$ = duration of the spell
$\delta_i$ = censoring indicator for births (0 Yes, 1 No)
$\boldsymbol{x}_i$ = explanatory variables, both time invariant and time varying variables.

The likelihood function is formulated as

$$L(\theta; x) = \prod_{i=1}^{n} [f_i(t|x_i; \theta)]^{\delta_i} [S_i(t|x_i; \theta)]^{1-\delta_i} \tag{5}$$

and the log likelihood function is

$$\ln L = \ln L(\theta; x) = \sum_{i=1}^{n} \delta_i \ln h_i(t_i|x_i; \theta) - \int_0^{t_i} h_i(u|x_i; \theta)du \tag{6}$$

The likelihood function can be maximized with respect to parameters, $\theta$. This is done by applying a modified Newton method. The inverse information matrix is evaluated at estimated parameter estimates as an estimation of the asymptotic covariance matrix of estimated parameters.

We use the spell-splitting approach to treat the time-varying variables. Introducing time-varying explanatory variables into the model requires some changes to the formulation of likelihood functions. It is generally assumed that the variables were measured at the beginning of a spell and their values did not change over the course of the spell. In many applications, however, variables may depend upon time. Some variables are realizations of some stochastic process, as external and internal time-dependent variables. In the former, the path of explanatory variables is not influenced by the duration but may affect it. In the latter, internal time-dependent variables are the outputs of a stochastic process that is generated by the unit. This implies that the value of the explanatory variable, and its path, carries information about the duration time. Being the realization of an internal stochastic process, or being expressed as previously determined, depends on the event we study.

The likelihood derivations in this chapter use the spell-splitting approach for the time-dependent variables. Designating $\boldsymbol{x}(t)$ as the variable vector at time $t$, the hazard rate is defined by

$$h(t|x(t)) = \lim_{\Delta t \to 0} \frac{1}{\Delta t} P(t \leq T < t + \Delta t \mid T \geq t, x(t)) \tag{7}$$

The survivor function and density function may also be defined, as in the case of time invariant explanatory variables. The calculation of the survivor function may be difficult due to the integration of the time paths of the variables. If the paths of these variables follow a step function over time and are piecewise constant functions over subperiods, then the cumulative hazard rates may be segmented into a sum of integrals. Designating $t_0 < t_1$

$< \ldots < t_s$ as the points of change of the explanatory variable vector within the duration interval $(0,t)$ and given $t_{s+1} = t$, the survivor function is

$$S(t|\mathrm{x}(t)) = \exp\left\{\sum_{r=1}^{s+1} \int_{t_{r1}}^{t_r} h\,(u|\mathrm{x}(t_{rl}))du\right\} = \prod_{r=1}^{s+1} S(t_r|t_{rl}, \mathrm{x}(t_{rl})) \tag{8}$$

By using hazard and survivor functions, we can construct the likelihood function. If the changes in the explanatory variables over time are continuous, cumulative hazard rates can be calculated by using numerical integrations. If they are discrete, then the step functions above will be used.

In the spell (episode)-splitting approach we substitute each period with the actual values of the time variant explanatory variables. The observed duration $t_i$ based upon the $s_i$ time points of change may be split into $s_i + 1$ independent subspells. The hazard rate is estimated as in the case of time invariant variables. Thus, for each of these spells in which the explanatory variable vector remains unchanged the data set may now be treated in the same way as described for time invariant variables, where the hazard rate is as follows:

$$h_k(t|\mathrm{x}_k(t)) = e^{[\beta'\mathrm{x}_k(t)]} \qquad k = 1,2,\ldots \tag{9}$$

Conventional statistical model-selection procedures require that all competing models are nested versions of a general model. When alternative models are nested, if they are limiting forms of each other, then likelihood-ratio tests can be used to decide among competing models. Another measure is the $R$-values. The $R$-value is the square root of a 'pseudo-$R^2$,' adjusted for degrees of freedom. More specifically,

$$R^2 = \frac{2\log\left(\frac{L_0}{L_m}\right) - 2k}{2\log(L_0)} \tag{10}$$

and $R = \sqrt{R^2}$, where $L_0$ is the value of the likelihood function when the model includes only an intercept; $L_m$ is the value of the likelihood function when the model includes explanatory variables with parameters; and k is the dimension of the parameters (i.e. the number of explanatory variables).

## 4. Data and Variables

### *1993 Turkish Demographic and Health Survey*

1993 Turkish Demographic and Health Survey (DHS) data files are obtained from Macro International Inc. The data set includes both individual and household records. The DHS Report III, Version 1.1 (with differences from DHS II), describes records from December 21, 1995. The executing agency of the survey was the Ministry of Health/Hacettepe University Institute of Population Studies. [For a detailed analysis, see Turkish Demographic and Health Survey (TDHS), 1993 (1994) and results of further analysis of the 1993 TDHS: *Fertility Trends, Women's Status, and Reproductive Expectations in Turkey* (1997).] The interviews took place at the national level in 1993 and include 8619 households with 6519 ever married women. Individual data records were arranged for 3259 women who were eligible, i.e., women were married and aged 15–49. All women, including those never married for this age group, can be calculated as 4844 women by using inflation factors in the survey.

Tables 7.1 and 7.2 show the distribution of 3259 women according to their ages and marital status in 1993. The age distribution of women is even between age cohorts; the smallest age cohort is between ages 15 and 19 (Table 7.1). The other age groups are more equally distributed. We see in Table 7.2. that 96 percent of women are still married in 1993; the rest were widowed, divorced, or not living together during this period.

**Table 7.1: Age Cohorts of Women in 1993 Turkish Demographic and Health Survey**

| Ages in 1993 | Number | Percent |
|---|---|---|
| 15–19 | 169 | 5.19 |
| 20–24 | 501 | 15.37 |
| 25–29 | 618 | 18.96 |
| 30–34 | 619 | 18.99 |
| 35–39 | 564 | 17.31 |
| 40–44 | 429 | 13.16 |
| 45–49 | 359 | 11.02 |
| Total | 3259 | 100.00 |

**Table 7.2: Marital Status of Women in 1993 Turkish Demographic and Health Survey**

| Marital Status in 1993 | Number | Percent |
|---|---|---|
| Married | 3137 | 96.26 |
| Widowed | 68 | 2.09 |
| Divorced | 38 | 1.17 |
| Not living together | 16 | 0.49 |
| Total | 3259 | 100.00 |

Almost all women in Turkey marry. The 1990 census shows that 95 percent of women in the age group 30–34 had married at least once. In the age group 50–54, the proportion is 99 percent. Virtually all reproduction occurs within marital unions (SIS Report, 1995), but we observe that the timing of marriage is changing. Each successive cohort of young people marries later, and more young people are remaining single into their 30s, but so far there is no indication of an increase in the proportion who never marry over the life course. Therefore, the statistical simplification of collecting births of married women is acceptable, and a sample of married women aged 15–49 is appropriate for fertility analysis. Women who give birth in Turkey are in general married, either in religious or in civil marital unions. Most religious marriages are followed by civil marriages over time. Non-marital unions are not so common, these types of unions are very new and can be seen among young people in the large cities. Childbirths in non-marital unions are not usual. We therefore think that the sample of married women provides appropriate data for the study of determinants of childbirth in Turkey.

*Variables and Descriptive Statistics of Individuals and Birth Spells*
Tables 7.2a and 7.2b give descriptive statistical results of the time invariant and time varying explanatory variables. The tables are arranged for the first spell by reporting the mean values of the covariates separately for censored and uncensored spells and then all together. This type of reporting should reveal any selection mechanism that exists in the data.

One of the advantages of the transition rate model is that one can use different types of time measures in the analysis. Here we have birth cohort and time trend as two different measures of time, and each of them has a different interpretation.

Women are grouped in five birth cohorts according to their own birth dates: women who were born before and up to 1954 (bcle54), between 1955 and 1959 (bc5559), between 1960 and 1964 (bc6064), between 1965 and 1969 (bc6569), and in 1970 or later (bc70ge). The proportion of women in the oldest age cohort is largest in the uncensored spells, while the proportion in the youngest is largest in censored spells (i.e., most older women have already given birth, while most younger women have not). The proportion of women born between 1965 and 1969 is also high among women without children. Except for the oldest and youngest groups the other birth cohorts have equal distributions among women.

**Table 7.2a: Descriptive Statistics of Time-invariant Variables for the First Spell**

| Time Constant Variables | (Labels) | Censored First Spell | Uncensored First Spell | Total First Spell |
|---|---|---|---|---|
| Birth Cohorts | | | | |
| | bcle54 | 0.092 | 0.297 | 0.279 |
| | bc5559 | 0.062 | 0.195 | 0.183 |
| | bc6064 | 0.089 | 0.197 | 0.187 |
| | bc6569 | 0.216 | 0.187 | 0.19 |
| | bc70ge | 0.541 | 0.123 | 0.162 |
| Ethnicity | | | | |
| | eturk | 0.865 | 0.873 | 0.872 |
| | ekurd | 0.095 | 0.101 | 0.101 |
| | eothe | 0.039 | 0.026 | 0.027 |
| Mother's Mother Tongue | | | | |
| | mturk | 0.833 | 0.852 | 0.85 |
| | mkurd | 0.125 | 0.11 | 0.111 |
| | mothe | 0.043 | 0.037 | 0.038 |
| Father's Mother Tongue | | | | |
| | fturk | 0.823 | 0.849 | 0.846 |
| | fkurd | 0.131 | 0.112 | 0.114 |
| | fothe | 0.046 | 0.039 | 0.039 |
| Migration | | | | |
| | mbfc | 0 | 0.86 | 0.779 |
| | mtcbfc | 0 | 0.343 | 0.311 |
| Education | | | | |
| | eduno | 0.151 | 0.278 | 0.266 |
| | edupr | 0.613 | 0.555 | 0.561 |
| | eduse | 0.17 | 0.134 | 0.137 |
| | eduhi | 0.066 | 0.032 | 0.035 |
| Experience | | | | |
| | wbmno | 0.55 | 0.65 | 0.641 |
| | wbmye | 0.449 | 0.35 | 0.359 |
| Occupation | | | | |
| | ocnowo | 0.669 | 0.65 | 0.652 |
| | ocagse | 0.157 | 0.217 | 0.211 |
| | ocothe | 0.157 | 0.117 | 0.121 |

Table continued overleaf

## Table 7.2a: continued

| Time Constant Variables | (Labels) | Censored First Spell | Uncensored First Spell | Total First Spell |
|---|---|---|---|---|
| Social Security | | | | |
| | ssno | 0.236 | 0.282 | 0.278 |
| | sssk | 0.033 | 0.024 | 0.025 |
| | sses | 0.052 | 0.035 | 0.037 |
| | ssot | 0.01 | 0.009 | 0.009 |
| Health Insurance | | | | |
| | hino | 0.584 | 0.466 | 0.477 |
| | hisk | 0.269 | 0.314 | 0.31 |
| | hies | 0.095 | 0.124 | 0.121 |
| | hibk | 0.023 | 0.07 | 0.066 |
| | hipr | 0.013 | 0.009 | 0.009 |
| | hiot | 0.016 | 0.016 | 0.016 |
| Partner's Education | | | | |
| | peduno | 0.029 | 0.079 | 0.074 |
| | pedupr | 0.551 | 0.579 | 0.577 |
| | peduse | 0.298 | 0.26 | 0.264 |
| | peduhi | 0.121 | 0.081 | 0.085 |
| Partner's Occupation | | | | |
| | poctech | 0.105 | 0.099 | 0.099 |
| | poccler | 0.023 | 0.04 | 0.039 |
| | pocsale | 0.105 | 0.076 | 0.079 |
| | pocagse | 0.118 | 0.169 | 0.164 |
| | pocskma | 0.108 | 0.103 | 0.103 |
| | pocusma | 0.311 | 0.277 | 0.28 |
| Partner's Mother's Mother Tongue | | | | |
| | pmturk | 0.82 | 0.841 | 0.839 |
| | pmkurd | 0.125 | 0.115 | 0.116 |
| | pmothe | 0.056 | 0.043 | 0.044 |
| Partner's Father's Mother Tongue | | | | |
| | pfturk | 0.816 | 0.84 | 0.839 |
| | pfkurd | 0.121 | 0.114 | 0.115 |
| | pfothe | 0.062 | 0.045 | 0.047 |
| Relation to the Household Head | | | | |
| | rehead | 0.007 | 0.034 | 0.032 |
| | rewife | 0.538 | 0.78 | 0.757 |
| | redaug | 0.059 | 0.031 | 0.033 |
| | redail | 0.354 | 0.13 | 0.151 |
| | reothe | 0.043 | 0.024 | 0.026 |
| Region | | | | |
| | rwest | 0.262 | 0.29 | 0.288 |
| | rsout | 0.229 | 0.195 | 0.199 |
| | rcent | 0.19 | 0.229 | 0.226 |
| | rnort | 0.17 | 0.152 | 0.154 |
| | reast | 0.147 | 0.132 | 0.134 |
| Region | | | | |
| | urban | 0.652 | 0.631 | 0.633 |
| | rural | 0.348 | 0.369 | 0.367 |
| City | | | | |
| | reglc | 0.226 | 0.204 | 0.206 |
| | regsc | 0.302 | 0.268 | 0.271 |
| | regto | 0.125 | 0.158 | 0.155 |
| | regco | 0.347 | 0.369 | 0.367 |
| Number of Spells | | 305 | 2954 | 3259 |

**Table 7.2b: Descriptive Statistics of Time-variant Variables for the First Spell**

| Time Varying Variables | Censored First Spell | | Uncensored First Spell | | Total First Spell | |
|---|---|---|---|---|---|---|
| | Values | Numbers | Values | Numbers | Values | Numbers |
| Civil armed conflict: armed conflict = 0 if time ≤ ((8.1984); armed conflict = 1 otherwise. | 0.213 | 1434 | 0.403 | 2954 | 0.340 | 4388 |
| Involuntary migration: mig = 0 if time ≤ (6.1991); mig = 1 otherwise. | 0.101 | 1037 | 0.028 | 2954 | 0.047 | 3991 |

The second variable in Table 7.2a shows the ethnic background of eligible women in the sample. In general, the correlation between a woman's own language and her parent's and her partner's parents' is high. We choose therefore the woman's own language as her ethnic indicator. Turkish women constitute 87 percent of the sample, while the proportion of Kurdish women is 10 percent. The remainder is spread over other ethnic minorities. The censored and uncensored parts of the sample have almost the same proportions. It is generally accepted that Kurds in Turkey have higher fertility rates than Turks.

The migration variable shows the voluntary internal migration before the birth of a first child. This value was not observed for women who did not give birth prior to 1993. The data show that 86 percent of women who had given birth at least once migrated before their first-born child, 34 percent of them to cities. Urbanization began to climb rapidly in the 1950s and it continues to grow. Gender ratios confirm that urbanization was to some extent male-selective up until about 1970. After 1970, the pattern changed, with women becoming almost as mobile as men. Women usually migrate with men or under the social control of their families, who migrate with or ahead of them. Young adults from villages and small towns make decisions to move, marry, and establish families in cities. Because of the economic, educational, and consumption opportunities in cities, young couples choose lower rates of reproduction and focus more on improving their standard of living after migration. This results in migrants bringing 'children not yet born,' who will be born after they settle in large cities, and their fertility is higher than the non-migrant population in these cities (SIS Report, 1995.) We expect second generation migrants in large cities to have similar fertility rates, generally below replacement level. As an empirical prediction, we can say that the birth risk of a first child, and to a certain extent of a second, after voluntary migration will not decrease, but it can be expected to decline after the second child.

Women's education was classified into the following categories: no education (illiterate); primary (0–5 years); secondary (6–8 years); and high (9 years or more). The opportunity to have an education comes at certain stages of the life course. It is very seldom that a woman in Turkey continues to study after her marriage; instead, marriage and childbirth come after school studies.

The majority of eligible women have a low level of education; this proportion is high both in censored and in uncensored groups of women. When education is used as an indicator of social class, it can be said that more than three fourths of the women belong to low social classes. Women with a low education also make a substantial contribution to the number of children being born. Fertility is lower at higher education levels. This is a prediction of the economic models as well; one expects birth risk to decrease with increasing educational levels. Level of education can also be used as an indicator of female wage earnings, which likewise contributes to lower childbirth risks. One significant disadvantage of the 1993 Turkish Demographic and Health Survey Data set is that it does not include any information on female wage rates and household incomes; we therefore used a proxy for the female wage rate.

The proportion of women who worked before marriage is only 35 percent; the majority did not. The distribution of women with working experience who did not have children is higher, at 45 percent. A woman's work experience before marriage can be thought of as an endogenous variable to her decision to give birth. Although she postpones giving birth by choosing to work first, the proportions of women with work experience and those who continue work after their first child are not very high. Working before the first child does nothing to guarantee her social security rights, since most women still have no such rights. Having work experience before the first childbirth does not appear to be a significant event in these women's lives. Since most of them have little opportunity to work either before or after the first childbirth, the decision to work is not a large obstacle for women giving birth.

The majority of women with children are housewives: 65 percent have no occupation. This number is a little bit higher among women without children: 67 percent. Only 22 percent of women working in agriculture are self-employed after the birth of the first child. The proportion of women who have other occupations is only 12 percent among those who work. They include skilled and unskilled manual work, services, clerical work, and sales.

The data concerning whether or not women pay social security are not reliable, since there is no information for about 65 percent of women. This may reflect underreporting, or it may represent a real case of workers not having any social security. Among those women whose social security payments are reported, women without any social security constitute about 28 percent of all women. The total proportion of women who make any form of social security payment is not more than 8 percent.

Information regarding health insurance payment is more reliable. We think this is because health insurance payments are more closely related to the partner's working conditions than the women's own health insurance payments. For this reason it makes sense to treat this variable as one of the partner's characteristics. However, the state of health insurance is alarming; almost half (48 percent) of all women have no health insurance. Women who pay health insurance to the Social Insurance Agency (SSK) as workers constitute 31 percent of all women. About 22 percent of women make other forms of insurance payments as civil servants or in other occupations. The social security and health insurance variables, together with a woman's educational level, can be used as indicators of her wage rate.

The classification for a partner's education follows that for a woman: no education, primary, secondary, and high. There are almost twice as many men with higher education than women. The group of illiterate men is twice as small as illiterate women, only 8 percent of all men. The partner's education, together with his occupation, can be used as a proxy for the male's income. Information about a partner's occupation alone is not as good; it tends to be as underreported as a woman's social security payments in the sample. Occupation information is available for about 66 percent of the partners.

A partner's mother's and father's native languages have the same sub-groups as for women: Turkish, Kurdish, and others. Its distribution, as we saw earlier, is similar to the distribution of a woman's own ethnic background.

The variable which shows a woman's relation to the household head is grouped as head, wife, daughter, daughter-in-law, and other. The proportion of women who are housewives is dominant at 76 percent. The second largest group consists of daughter-in-laws. This figure shows that an important proportion of young women are still living in their husband's parental houses after marriage. Although the small nuclear family type is a common living arrangement in the cities, large families can still be found in the countryside. The other groups can be treated as one group in the analysis.

Descriptive statistics of deaths of newly born children are not reported in this table, since values of these variables are used mainly for second and higher spells.

The three other variables are related to the residential area of women. The first one comprises the groups west, south, center, north, and east. Most of the women in the sample come from the western and central regions. Fewest women come from eastern Turkey, only 13 percent. The second variable consists of the groups urban and rural. The majority of eligible women are living in urban areas, 63 percent. The third is grouped by size of residential area: large cities, small cities, towns, and others. Women who are living in urban areas are residents of small and large cities.

Table 7.2.a reports descriptive statistics for two time-varying variables: the first one is a dummy for the armed conflict, having a value of one after August 1984 and zero before; and the second is involuntary internal migration, which has a value of one after June 1991 and zero before. The mean values for these variables give only a relative measure of the variation. For example, the proportion of civil armed conflict is higher than the proportion of involuntary migration. Similar information can be found also in the columns that give total censored spells. Uncensored spells have the same number as the original ones, but the number of censored spells increases as the original ones are split into sub-spells. The total number of spells increases most when we split spells for the armed conflict along the first spell, from 3259 to 4388. A lesser rise occurs when involuntary migration is defined, the number increasing from 3259 to 3991.

### *The Distribution of Childbirths*

In the sample there is a total of 3259 eligible women; 305 of them never gave birth. The schematic picture of women and their born children is given by the following arrows. Thus, 503 women had only one child, 818 had two children, 593 had three, 351 had four, and so on. One woman had 15 children, and another one 16, which was the highest number in the sample. The numbers under the child number at the right-hand side of the arrows show women who continued to give birth. For example, 2954 women out of 3259 had only one birth, 2451 of 2954 had two births, 1633 out of 2451 had three births, and so on. The 3259 women have the following birth spells:

0 → 1<br>
3259 305 2954<br>
1 → 2<br>
503 2451<br>
2 → 3<br>
818 1633<br>
3 → 4<br>
593 1040<br>
4 → 5<br>
351 689<br>
5 → 6<br>
245 444<br>
6 → 7<br>
160 284<br>
7 → 8<br>
102 182<br>
8 → 9<br>
59 123<br>
9 → 10<br>
49 74<br>
10 → 11<br>
31 41<br>
11 → 12<br>
20 21<br>
12 → 13<br>
8 13<br>
13 → 14<br>
7 6<br>
14 → 15<br>
4 2<br>
15 → 16<br>
1 1

### *The Distribution of Birth Years*

The first six births appear interesting enough to be investigated further. We will look at, and describe, all six, but we will concentrate on the determinants of only the first two. The distribution of first births shows that a total of 2954 births occur between calendar years 1966 and 1993. The number of first births increases each year, reaching a maximum of 354 in 1992. First births are negatively skewed and the trend indicates that they will increase in number over the coming years.

Second births also show an asymmetric distribution; it is also negatively skewed and mode values lie between years 1986 and 1990. The first two of all 2451 second children were born in 1961 and the last one in 1993. The general shape of the distribution of second-born children begins as close to a normal distribution.

The distribution of third births is even closer to a normal distribution, and by the fourth birth we observe an approximately normal distribution. Mode years go back for each child born: years 1979–83 for third births, 1976–79 for fourth births, 1974–78 for fifth, and 1974–77 for sixth births. These shapes indicate that there will be no additional births for women in the sample. (Figures for the distribution of childbirths between the years 1960 and 1993 are not displayed here.)

### *The Distribution of Women's Ages at Different Spells*

Another interesting distribution is the woman's age at different spells. We look at the ages of women during birth spells, including women who did not contribute a birth to the spell. This treatment gives a general picture of age distribution of women at different life stages. Women's age at time of childbirth, as an age-level variable, will be taken into consideration in the estimation of fertility models in the next section.

The mode age at the first childbirth spell is 19 years old. The shape of the distribution is close to normal with a longer tail on the right-hand side. During the second spell, the mode age is concentrated at age 21. It is 24 for the third and fourth spells, 28 for the fifth spell, and 29 for the sixth spell. As can be seen, the women in the 1993 Turkish Demographic and Health Survey sample are generally young during these spells. This is a different picture from the ones seen in developed western countries. In each figure, the positively skewed picture of ages at the various spells becomes clearer when we look at the increasing number of spells: more concentration on the young ages, fewer childbirths at older ages. (Figures for women's age distribution during the different spells are not displayed here.)

### *The Distribution of Birth Spells*

In the following table, Table 7.3, we report the number of first six birth spells and their mean and median values, measured as months. Central measures are given for both uncensored and censored spells (i.e., for spell totals).

**Table 7.3: First Six Spells with Central Measures**

| Spell Numbers | Number of Spells (months) | Mean Lengths (months) | Median Lengths |
|---|---|---|---|
| 1 | 3259 | 107.84 | 100.33 |
| 2 | 2954 | 33.18 | 26.98 |
| 3 | 2451 | 50.67 | 37.18 |
| 4 | 1633 | 55.34 | 37.94 |
| 5 | 1040 | 55.49 | 36.52 |
| 6 | 689 | 57.25 | 35.06 |

Except the first spell, the average waiting times of the spells increase by increasing parity. The mean length of the first spell is longest, since we begin to measure it from age 13. One could measure this from the marriage age or from age 15, or from another age. As we will see below, we think that age 13 is a good departure value for the births in Turkey, since it indicates the early start of the reproductive period of women in such a young society. Median values are smaller than the mean values of the spells. This means that all birth spells are right-skewed, which is usual in the transition data context.

Table 7.4 shows the distribution of the first two spells. The first spell starts at age 13. The mean age for those women who gave birth to a first child is 20.53; the median age for the same group is 20.36. If we start the first spell from the marriage date, then the mean age at first birth is still 20.53. We get the same values whether we start the first spell at age 13 or at the marriage date. Most women can be assumed to give birth after marriage and either of the start dates can be used. In the following analysis, age 13 is used for the start of first spell. In both cases, there are women who gave birth before age 13 and before marriage. There were three women who had their first child before age 13, and 29 who gave birth before they married.

**Table 7.4: First Two Spells with Central Measures**

| Spell Numbers | State of Spells | Number of Spells | Mean Lengths (months) | Median Lengths (months) |
|---|---|---|---|---|
| 1 | Censored | 305 | 161.12 | 100.33 |
| | Uncensored | 2954 | 102.34 | |
| | Sum | 3259 | 107.84 | |
| 2 | Censored | 503 | 42.28 | 26.98 |
| | Uncensored | 2451 | 31.31 | |
| | Sum | 2954 | 33.18 | |
| Sum | Censored | 808 | 87.14 | 65.45 |
| | Uncensored | 5405 | 70.13 | |
| | Sum | 6213 | 72.34 | |

For the censoring date, we use 1993, which is the year that the interviews took place in the Turkish Demographic and Health Survey. Age 49 is an upper limit for censoring dates, but we do not place any restriction on this age, since the eligible women in the survey are defined as women between ages 15 and 49; there are no women older than 49 in the sample.

## 5. Results

### *Non-parametric Empirical Life Table Estimates of First and Second Births*

We begin this section by reporting Life Table hazard rates and survivor functions of first and second births. These are non-parametric raw estimates of the transition risks and survivor probabilities. No assumptions are made about the shape of the curves; they are empirical values calculated directly from sample observations. Life Table hazard risks for the first and second births shed light on the form of birth risks during the waiting periods and give guidance for the appropriate parametric hazard forms.

The other non-parametric methods that we will use in this chapter are Product-Limit, or so-called Kaplan-Meier, estimators. These approaches are used to determine the time dependence. They are important because the available theory rarely suggests the qualitative shape of the baseline hazard rate and precise functional form. An incorrect choice of functional form risks misspecification bias. But these non-parametric estimates, without parametric assumptions about the distribution of childbirth waiting times, help us obtain estimators for the hazard functions, survivor probabilities, and integrated hazards.

In the four panels of Figures 7.1 and 7.2, the survivor function and hazard rates of the first and second births are displayed. The first panel, Figure 7.1a, shows the proportion of women who still have not given birth to their first child. After age 18 (50 months), this probability is very high, 95 percent, but it decreases drastically after age 25.5 (150 months)

**Figure 7.1a: Survival Probabilities of First Birth**

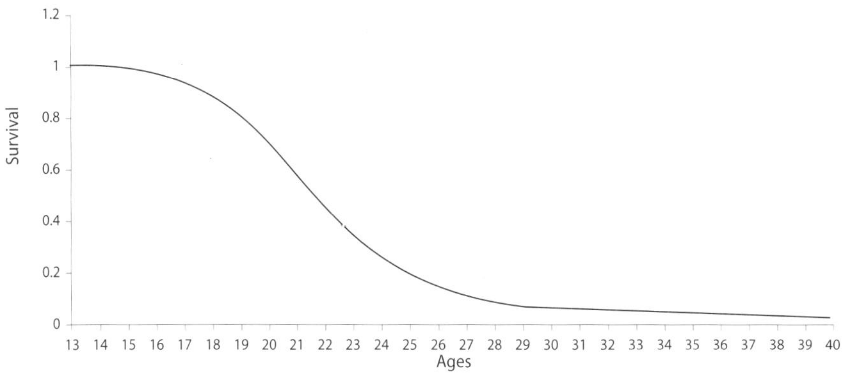


**Figure 7.1b. Hazard Risks of First Birth**

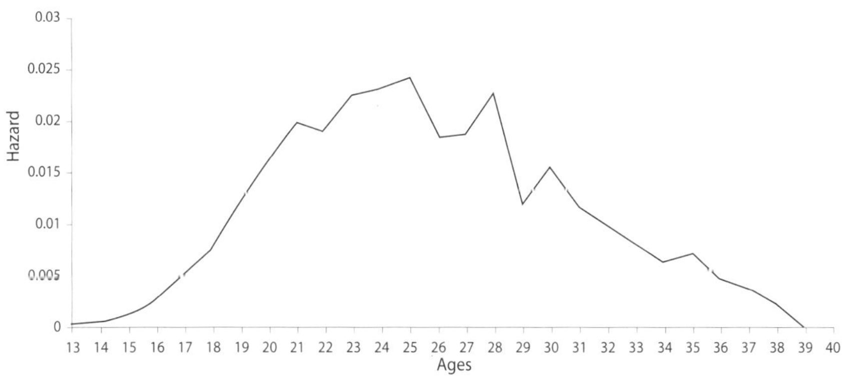


to about 15 percent. The probability of a woman not giving birth to her first child after age 21 (100 months) is 50 percent. By about age 32, almost all women in the risk set have already given birth.

The second panel, Figure 7.1b, shows the hazard risks for first births. For a smoothed version of this hazard, we can see that an inverted U-shape is appropriate, since the birth risk first increases and reaches a maximum at age 25.5 and then decreases gradually to zero at age 40.

For second-birth risk, we can see that the survivor probabilities decrease subsequently, to 10 percent at year 6 in Figure 7.2a. The probability of not having a second birth is very high 10 months after the first birth, but it decreases to 50 percent after 30 months, and is 20 percent after about 50 months. The survival probability goes to zero when time approaches 90 months after the first birth.

In Figure 7.2b, the second-birth hazard rates are plotted. The chance of having a second child increases drastically from 2 to 42 percent in months 5 to 30, then decreases

**Figure 7.2a. Survival Probabilities of Second Birth**

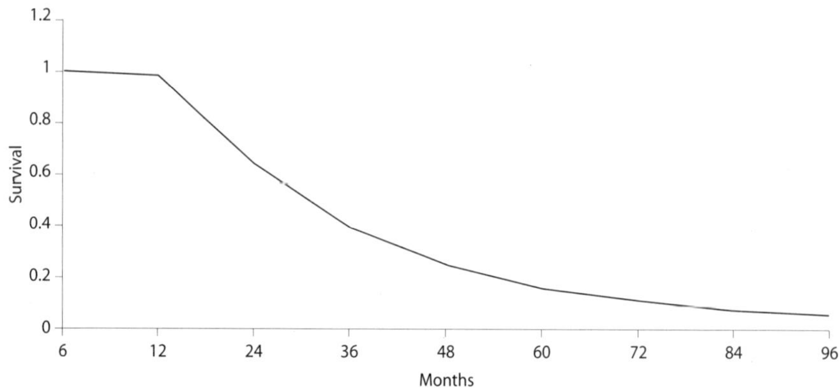


**Figure 7.2b Hazard Risks of Second Birth**

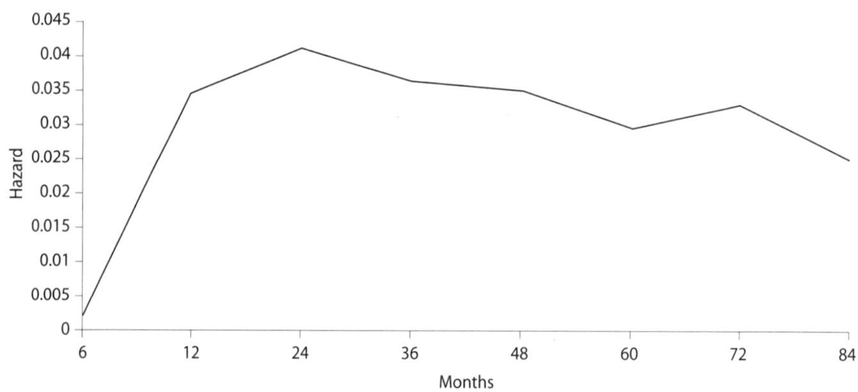


somewhat to 25 percent at 90 months. It is still a very high level in comparison to its start value. Again, it seems that an inverted U-shape for the hazard risk of second childbirth is appropriate. Except for the very first part of the duration, it seems a monotonic declining curve.

We do not display hazard and survivor function figures for more than two births in this study, but we would like to know whether or not there are significant differences between the first and the subsequent five survivor functions. If they have similar characteristics, then we can combine second and higher spells with the first and do analysis for general births. From the four panels of Figures 7.1 and 7.2, we know that the hazard shapes are similar for first and second births. To test the same thing statistically for the first and subsequent five birth spells, we calculated product limit estimates of the survivor functions for the six births. $\chi^2$ test statistics indicate that there are significant differences between product limit estimates of survivor functions for six births. Therefore, we cannot combine the first and the subsequent five spells in the analysis of childbirths in Turkey. Each birth has to be investigated separately by estimating model parameters only for the transition in question. Table 7.5a shows Log-Rank (Savage) and Wilcoxon (Breslow) $\chi^2$ test statistic results.

$H_0$: There are no differences between product limit survivor functions of first and subsequent five birth spells. $H_M$ : $H_0$ is not valid.

**Table 7.5a: Log-Rank (Savage) and Wilcoxon (Breslow) Test Statistics of First and Subsequent Five Childbirth Survivor Functions**

| Test Statistics | Survivor Functions of First and Subsequent Five Births |
|---|---|
| Tabulated at | |
| (5 dof and 5 % significance) | 11.07 |
| (5 dof and 0.5 % significance) | 16.75 |
| Observed | |
| Log-Rank (Savage) | 2021.38 |
| Wilcoxon (Breslow) | 2837.59 |

We also tested whether or not there are significant differences between the three different ethnic groups (Turks, Kurds, and others) in their first-birth spells. Table 7.5b gives $\chi^2$ test statistic results which indicate that women who are Turkish, Kurdish, or of other ethnic origin have to be studied separately, since there are significance differences between their survivor functions in the first-birth spell.

**Table 7.5b: Log-Rank (Savage) and Wilcoxon (Breslow) Test Statistics of Survivor Functions of Ethnic Groups in the First Birth Spell**

| Test Statistics | Survivor Functions of Ethnic Groups in the First Birth Spells |
|---|---|
| Tabulated at | |
| (5 dof and 5 % significance) | 11.07 |
| (5 dof and 0.5 % significance) | 16.75 |
| Observed | |
| Log-Rank (Savage) | 30.16 |
| Wilcoxon (Breslow) | 50.11 |

Table 7.5c gives the distribution of first-birth spells among different ethnic groups of women. As can be seen, the number of spells is few—especially for the 'other' group. It is impossible to study this group separately from the other two groups. Furthermore, the number of observations in the group of Kurdish women are few, which does not provide opportunity for investigating various explanatory factors.

**Table 7.5c: Distribution of First Spells among Different Ethnic Groups of Women**

| Ethnic Groups | Uncensored Spells | Censored Spells | Total Spells |
|---|---|---|---|
| Turkish women | 2578 | 264 | 2842 |
| Kurdish women | 300 | 29 | 329 |
| Other women | 76 | 12 | 88 |
| Total | 2954 | 305 | 3259 |

It was therefore decided to do an analysis combining the three groups into one spell by using ethnic background-specific dummies. This was a compromise that made it possible to study specific ethnic background effects on first- and second-birth risks.

We prefer a flexible approach without making any parametric assumptions about the hazard shape. This is a Piecewise Constant Exponential Model. The empirical Life Table hazard estimates indicated that a second degree polynomial would be appropriate for the data. We selected specific sub-periods for the spell durations and estimated a constant exponential hazard risk for each sub-period. By combining the fixed period estimates, we got a flexible shape that resembles a second degree polynomial for the hazard rates.

Piecewise Constant Exponential Model estimates will be reported below in detail. We first checked the sensitivity of the models for time-varying variables before time-invariant and time-variant variables were estimated. It is well known that parametric hazard rate estimates are sensitive for the coefficients of time-varying variables. The other variables, those with fixed values during spell lengths, have generally robust parameter estimates.

Two different models were developed using just time-varying variables; a Cox type proportional hazard rate estimate and a Piecewise Constant Exponential Model estimate with five time periods. We do not report the details of the results here, since similar findings are obtained from the estimates below.

In Table 7.6, we report stepwise PCE model estimates using other explanatory variables. Column 1 gives estimation results with demographic and social characteristics of women. These are birth cohorts, ethnicity, and internal voluntary migration. In column 2, we add the respondent's educational and economic characteristics into the model in column 1. The additional variables comprise educational level, work experience before marriage, occupational status, and health insurance payments. In column 3, we add the partner's educational level. The other characteristics of the partner are highly correlated to those of the respondent and are therefore disregarded. In column 4, the household and regional characteristics are added into the model in column 3; these are the woman's relation to the household head and her current residential area. Another interesting variable in column 4 is the death of a first-born child, which naturally is not included in the variables in the first spell. Column 5 differs from column 4 in that it has the additional variable involuntary migration.[4] The last column (6) adds the variable of armed conflict into the model in column 5. Such a stepwise estimation strategy makes it possible to trace parameter changes, if any, when introducing new control variables into the model. Some additional interaction models are also estimated for the interactions between ethnicity, region, armed conflict, and involuntary migration. The likelihood ratio test statistics indicate that the hypothesis that the interaction effects are equal to zero cannot be rejected. All interaction effects were estimated insignificantly and did not change the results of column 6.

### *Model Evaluation*

Beyond parameter estimates, other model-related information is reported in the last rows in Table 7.6. These are: negative likelihood value, number of parameters, likelihood ratio test, and square root of Pseudo $R^2$.

The likelihood ratio test statistic has the following form:

$$\Lambda = 2(\ln L(\theta \text{ of unrestricted model}) - \ln L(\theta \text{ of restricted model})) \quad (11)$$

for the hypothesis that multiple parameters are equal to zero. If $H_0$ is true, the test statistic has a central $\chi^2$ distributed asymptotically with a degree of freedom which is equal to the rank of the restriction matrix.

$\chi^2$ test results do not penalize the increasing number of parameters in the model, so their values increase for the models in columns 1–6. The more parameters in a model, the higher the value of the $\chi^2$ test statistic. Tabulated values for the $\chi^2$ test statistic at a five percent significance level with varying degrees of freedom (dof) are: 38.885 for 26 dof, 58.124 for 42 dof, 67.505 for 50 dof, 80.232 for 61 dof, 82.529 for 63 dof, and 84.821 for 65 dof. We reject the null hypothesis for all models in Table 8. The model with highest likelihood ratio test value is the best model.

The same conclusion can be drawn from the results of Pseudo $R^2$ and its square root, which also show that the model in the last column is the best. $R^2$ in a normal regression is a measure for the explained variation, where Pseudo $R^2$ expresses the relative decrease of the likelihood function of the present model by taking into account the contribution of an increasing number of explanatory variables, as opposed to the model without covariates. This can be easily seen from the Pseudo $R^2$ formula if it is written as

$$\text{Pseudo } R^2 = [1 - ((\ln L_M + k) / \ln L_0))] \quad (12)$$

We therefore use the model in the last column of Table 7.6 as the main model for our interpretations in the sequel.

*Effects of Explanatory Variables*

Duration dependency is non-monotonic for first-birth risk, and shows an inverted U-form but a declining monotonic for second-birth risks. These results are robust in the six models. In the last column of Table 7.6, the relative risk for the first-birth hazard is 0.1 percent during ages 13–17, one percent during ages 17–21, and 2 percent during ages 21–25; then it reaches a maximum of 2 percent during ages 25–31, decreasing to 0.5 percent after age 31. We get the same picture of hazard risks as in the models without time-invariant variables. First increasing and then decreasing the shape of the hazard risk for the first birth is the same in the other columns. A similar shape of the hazard risk for the second birth is also observed. It appears that the hazard risk is highest during the first eight years after the first birth and decreases gradually after that.

We see in Table 7.6 that women belonging to various birth cohorts do not have a significant estimated first-birth risk except the youngest cohort. When we add armed conflict into the model, the youngest women lose their high fertility. After armed conflict in eastern Turkey and following involuntary migration, younger women are no longer willing to have their first child, and they postpone their first birth. This can be a result of the young people's lack of optimism for the future because of armed conflict. Similar cohort effects are also estimated for the second births.

**Table 7.6: Stepwise Piecewise-Exponential Model Estimates of First and Second Births**

| Variables<br>Transition 0 → 1 | 1 | 2 | 3 | 4 | 5 | 6 |
|---|---|---|---|---|---|---|
| *Time periods (months)* | | | | | | |
| 0–48 | -7.061* | -7.017* | -6.963* | -6.866* | -6.796* | -6.784* |
| | (0.139) | (0.144) | (0.156) | (0.170) | (0.170) | (0.170) |
| 48–96 | -4.957* | -4.894* | -4.838* | -4.738* | -4.707* | -4.703* |
| | (0.122) | (0.128) | (0.141) | (0.156) | (0.156) | (0.156) |
| 96–144 | -4.160* | -4.037* | -3.980* | -3.873* | -3.898* | -3.904* |
| | (0.121) | (0.128) | (0.140) | (0.156) | (0.156) | (0.156) |
| 144–216 | -4.180* | -3.994* | -3.936* | -3.817* | -3.898* | -3.919* |
| | (0.126) | (0.132) | (0.144) | (0.159) | (0.160) | (0.162) |
| 216– | -5.314* | -5.143* | -5.093* | -4.982* | -5.163* | -5.214* |
| | (0.180) | (0.184) | (0.193) | (0.205) | (0.207) | (0.215) |
| *Birth Cohorts* | | | | | | |
| -1954 | 0.0 | 0.0 | 0.0 | 0.0 | 0.0 | 0.0 |
| 1955–59 | -0.032 | 0.016 | 0.023 | 0.036 | 0.034 | 0.028 |
| | (0.054) | (0.054) | (0.054) | (0.055) | (0.054) | (0.055) |
| 1960–64 | -0.012 | 0.029 | 0.045 | 0.071 | 0.048 | 0.023 |
| | (0.054) | (0.055) | (0.056) | (0.056) | (0.056) | (0.063) |
| 1965–69 | -0.057 | -0.007* | 0.010 | 0.059 | -0.051 | -0.105 |
| | (0.055) | (0.056) | (0.057) | (0.059) | (0.061) | (0.086) |
| 1970– | 0.313* | 0.371* | 0.389* | 0.470* | 0.152* | 0.085 |
| | (0.064) | (0.067) | (0.067) | (0.071) | (0.085) | (0.113) |
| *Ethnicity* | | | | | | |
| Other | 0.0 | 0.0 | 0.0 | 0.0 | 0.0 | 0.0 |
| Turk | 0.220* | 0.231* | 0.223* | 0.176 | 0.176 | 0.178 |
| | (0.117) | (0.117) | (0.117) | (0.118) | (0.118) | (0.118) |
| Kurd | 0.460 | 0.337* | 0.323* | 0.294* | 0.292* | 0.294* |
| | (0.129) | (0.131) | (0.132) | (0.138) | (0.137) | (0.137) |
| *Migrated to large city* | 0.231* | 0.281* | 0.278* | 0.277* | 0.296* | 0.296* |
| | (0.039) | (0.041) | (0.041) | (0.041) | (0.042) | (0.042) |
| *Education* | | | | | | |
| None | | 0.0 | 0.0 | 0.0 | 0.0 | 0.0 |
| Primary | | -0.076 | -0.060 | -0.076 | -0.077 | -0.077 |
| | | (0.047) | (0.049) | (0.049) | (0.049) | (0.049) |
| Secondary | | -0.311* | -0.239* | -0.261* | -0.260* | -0.260* |
| | | (0.070) | (0.075) | (0.076) | (0.076) | (0.076) |
| High | | -0.798* | -0.661* | -0.684* | -0.686* | 0.686* |
| | | (0.122) | (0.136) | (0.137) | (0.137) | (0.137) |
| *Worked before marriage* | | -0.278* | -0.280* | -0.277* | -0.273* | -0.273* |
| | | (0.045) | (0.045) | (0.046) | (0.046) | (0.046) |
| *Occupation* | | | | | | |
| None | | 0.0 | 0.0 | 0.0 | 0.0 | 0.0 |
| Agriculture self employed | | 0.439* | 0.430* | 0.476* | 0.476* | 0.477* |
| | | (0.055) | (0.055) | (0.058) | (0.058) | (0.058) |
| Other | | -0.027 | -0.027 | -0.019 | -0.025 | -0.026 |
| | | (0.064) | (0.065) | (0.065) | (0.065) | (0.065) |
| *Health insurance* | | | | | | |
| None | | 0.0 | 0.0 | 0.0 | 0.0 | 0.0 |
| "SSK" | | -0.041 | -0.031 | -0.035 | -0.314 | -0.031 |
| | | (0.044) | (0.045) | (0.046) | (0.046) | (0.046) |
| Other | | 0.069 | 0.102* | 0.089* | 0.093* | 0.094* |
| | | (0.052) | (0.054) | (0.054) | (0.054) | (0.054) |
| *Partner's education* | | | | | | |
| None | | | 0.0 | 0.0 | 0.0 | 0.0 |
| Primary | | | -0.055 | -0.053 | -0.052 | -0.051 |
| | | | (0.075) | (0.076) | (0.076) | (0.076) |
| Secondary | | | -0.135 | -0.123 | -0.119 | -0.119 |
| | | | (0.085) | (0.085) | (0.085) | (0.085) |
| High | | | -0.241* | -0.254* | -0.252* | -0.253* |
| | | | (0.111) | (0.112) | (0.112) | (0.112) |

| **Variables**<br>Transition 0 → 1 (continued) | 1 | 2 | 3 | 4 | 5 | 6 |
|---|---|---|---|---|---|---|
| *Relation to household head* | | | | | | |
| Other | | | | 0.0 | 0.0 | 0.0 |
| Wife | | | | 0.085 | 0.087 | 0.087 |
| | | | | (0.066) | (0.066) | (0.066) |
| Daughter-in-law | | | | -0.108 | -0.125 | -0.127 |
| | | | | (0.083) | (0.083) | (0.083) |
| *Region (current residence)* | | | | | | |
| Central | | | | 0.0 | 0.0 | 0.0 |
| West | | | | -0.119* | -0.119* | -0.118* |
| | | | | (0.053) | (0.053) | (0.053) |
| South | | | | -0.232* | -0.239* | -0.239* |
| | | | | (0.058) | (0.058) | (0.058) |
| North | | | | -0.207* | -0.213* | -0.213* |
| | | | | (0.064) | (0.064) | (0.064) |
| East | | | | -0.169* | -0.175* | -0.174* |
| | | | | (0.073) | (0.073) | (0.073) |
| *Involuntary migration* | | | | | | |
| mig=0 if time ≤ (6.1991) | | | | | 0.508* | 0.507* |
| mig=1 otherwise | | | | | (0.070) | (0.070) |
| *Armed conflict* | | | | | | |
| armed conflict=0 if time ≤ (8.1984) | | | | | | 0.063 |
| armed conflict=1 otherwise | | | | | | (0.071) |
| **Transition 1 → 2** | | | | | | |
| *Time periods (months)* | | | | | | |
| 0–48 | -3.493* | -3.344* | -3.281* | -3.394* | -3.399* | -3.398* |
| | (0.130) | (0.136) | (0.149) | (0.169) | (0.169) | (0.169) |
| 48–96 | -3.181* | -2.954* | -2.887* | -2.947* | -2.931* | -2.936* |
| | (0.138) | (0.145) | (0.157) | (0.177) | (0.177) | (0.177) |
| 96–144 | -4.133* | -3.849* | -3.784* | -3.837* | -3.799* | -3.812* |
| | (0.209) | (0.214) | (0.223) | (0.236 | (0.236) | (0.238) |
| 144–216 | -6.007* | 5.726* | -5.661* | -5.715* | -5.668* | -5.689* |
| | (0.516) | (0.519) | (0.523) | (0.528) | (0.528) | (0.576) |
| 216– | -6.673* | -6.425* | -6.368* | -6.429* | -6.334* | -6.360* |
| | (1.008) | (1.009) | (1.011) | (1.015) | (1.015) | (1.017) |
| *Birth cohorts* | | | | | | |
| -1954 | 0.0 | 0.0 | 0.0 | 0.0 | 0.0 | 0.0 |
| 1955–59 | 0.041 | 0.054 | 0.059 | 0.047 | 0.053 | 0.048 |
| | (0.055) | (0.055) | (0.055) | (0.056) | (0.056) | (0.057) |
| 1960–64 | -0.049 | -0.0045 | 0.008 | -0.017 | -0.002 | -0.017 |
| | (0.055) | (0.057) | (0.058) | (0.058) | (0.058) | (0.067) |
| 1965–69 | -0.128 | -0.095 | -0.082 | -0.116* | -0.050 | -0.075 |
| | (0.061) | (0.063) | (0.063) | (0.064) | (0.069) | (0.087) |
| 1970– | -0.459* | -0.452* | -0.433* | -0.500* | -0.357* | -0.382* |
| | (0.098) | (0.099) | (0.100) | (0.104) | (0.117) | (0.128) |
| *Ethnicity* | | | | | | |
| Other | 0.0 | 0.0 | 0.0 | 0.0 | 0.0 | 0.0 |
| Turk | -0.209 | -0.157 | -0.161 | -0.149 | -0.153 | -0.151 |
| | (0.128) | (0.129) | (0.129) | (0.130) | (0.130) | (0.130) |
| Kurd | 0.060 | -0.072 | -0.088 | -0.219 | -0.230 | -0.228 |
| | (0.141) | (0.143) | (0.144) | (0.149) | (0.149) | (0.149) |
| *Migrated to large city* | 0.0051 | 0.021 | 0.021 | -0.041 | -0.039 | -0.049 |
| | (0.043) | (0.044) | (0.044) | (0.045) | (0.045) | (0.047) |
| *Education* | | | | | | |
| None | | 0.0 | 0.0 | 0.0 | 0.0 | 0.0 |
| Primary | | -0.119* | -0.099* | -0.045 | -0.043 | -0.041 |
| | | (0.050) | (0.052) | (0.055) | (0.052) | (0.045) |
| Secondary | | -0.530* | -0.473* | -0.410* | -0.398* | -0.401* |
| | | (0.079) | (0.086) | (0.087) | (0.087) | (0.087) |
| High | | -0.757* | -0.679* | -0.599* | -0.580* | -0.586* |
| | | (0.147) | (0.167) | (0.167) | (0.167) | (0.167) |
| *Worked before marriage* | | -0.101* | -0.099* | -0.084* | -0.079 | -0.080 |
| | | (0.050) | (0.050) | (0.050) | (0.050) | (0.050) |

Table continued overleaf

**Table 7.6 (continued)**

| **Variables** Transition 1 → 2 (continued) | 1 | 2 | 3 | 4 | 5 | 6 |
|---|---|---|---|---|---|---|
| *Occupation* | | | | | | |
| None | | 0.0 | 0.0 | 0.0 | 0.0 | 0.0 |
| Agriculture self employed | | 0.094 | 0.084 | 0.043 | 0.037 | 0.038 |
| | | (0.060) | (0.060) | (0.062) | (0.062) | (0.062) |
| Other | | -0.040 | -0.038 | -0.020 | -0.023 | -0.027 |
| | | (0.070) | (0.070) | (0.071) | (0.071) | (0.070) |
| *Health insurance* | | | | | | |
| None | | 0.0 | 0.0 | 0.0 | 0.0 | 0.0 |
| "SSK" | | -0.055 | -0.046 | -0.031 | -0.027 | -0.027 |
| | | (0.049) | (0.049) | (0.050) | (0.050) | (0.050) |
| Other | | -0.071 | -0.045 | -0.076 | -0.079 | -0.077 |
| | | (0.056) | (0.058) | (0.059) | (0.059) | (0.059) |
| *Partner's education* | | | | | | |
| None | | | 0.0 | 0.0 | 0.0 | 0.0 |
| Primary | | | -0.072 | -0.048 | -0.047 | -0.048 |
| | | | (0.077) | (0.077) | (0.077) | (0.077) |
| Secondary | | | -0.153 | -0.148 | -0.142 | -0.144 |
| | | | (0.089) | (0.089) | (0.089) | (0.089) |
| High | | | -0.171 | -0.190 | -0.183 | -0.187 |
| | | | (0.126) | (0.126) | (0.126) | (0.126) |
| *Relation to household head* | | | | | | |
| Other | | | | 0.0 | 0.0 | 0.0 |
| Wife | | | | 0.107 | 0.109 | 0.109 |
| | | | | (0.074) | (0.074) | (0.074) |
| Daughter-in-law | | | | 0.116 | 0.123 | 0.122 |
| | | | | (0.099) | (0.099) | (0.099) |
| *First-born child is dead* | | | | -0.079 | -0.078 | -0.077 |
| | | | | (0.098) | (0.098) | (0.098) |
| *Region (current residence)* | | | | | | |
| Central | | | | 0.0 | 0.0 | 0.0 |
| West | | | | -0.200* | -0.201* | -0.203* |
| | | | | (0.058) | (0.058) | (0.058) |
| South | | | | 0.066 | 0.067 | 0.065 |
| | | | | (0.063) | (0.063) | (0.063) |
| North | | | | 0.100 | 0.101 | 0.101 |
| | | | | (0.069) | (0.069) | (0.069) |
| East | | | | 0.295* | 0.293* | 0.293* |
| | | | | (0.078) | (0.078) | (0.078) |
| *Involuntary migration* | | | | | | |
| mig=0 if time ≤ (6.1991) | | | | | -0.191* | -0.196* |
| mig=1 otherwise | | | | | (0.075) | (0.075) |
| *Armed conflict* | | | | | | |
| armed conflict=0 if time ≤ (8.1984) | | | | | | 0.030 |
| armed conflict=1 otherwise | | | | | | (0.064) |
| **Negative log likelihood** | 27279.58 | 27108.23 | 27102.97 | 27061.96 | 27033.07 | 27032.56 |
| **Number of parameters** | 24 | 40 | 46 | 59 | 61 | 63 |
| **Likelihood ratio test** | 2766.43 | 3109.13 | 3119.65 | 3201.68 | 3259.45 | 3260.48 |
| **Square root of Pseudo $R^2$** | 0.49096 | 0.05563 | 0.05602 | 0.05791 | 0.05899 | 0.05907 |
| **Number of spells** | | 6213 | | | 7325 | 8799 |

Although Kurdish women have higher first-birth risks, they do not have—in contrast to the widely accepted idea—higher second-birth risks. The coefficients of ethnicity are estimated insignificantly negative for both Kurdish and Turkish women for second-birth risks. Effects were more expressive in a model where age at marriage is used.

Though involuntary migration to large cities has a negative effect on first-birth risk, voluntary migration to large cities before marriage increases the risk. This is in accordance with the findings of the SIS Report (1995). According to our study, voluntary migration to large cities loses its positive effect on second births. This point is different from the SIS Report, where second children are likely to be born, for example, to the new migrants to Istanbul. First-generation migrant women in Istanbul had a replacement level of fertility which was higher than that of the non-migrant women in the city. It appears that migrant women in this study have a fertility level lower than the replacement level of fertility of the new migrants. We think such a result is more appropriate than the projections of State Institute of Statistics in Turkey.

A woman's level of education as an indicator of her wage rate lowers the birth risks. Education turns out to have a positive effect on first-birth risk for primary level education. Lower-educated women have higher fertility rates. Women with secondary and higher education have longer spells than the others, meaning that they have a tendency to postpone their first birth. This is a very understandable result, since women with higher education are more oriented to the economic opportunities they qualify for. The effects are similar for the second-birth risk.

Women working in agriculture as self-employed have higher first-birth risks than other women. Most of these women are living in the countryside and are generally considered housewives, although they are working in both households and agriculture. This is in line with the findings of Kasnakoglu (1993). She studied female occupation, income, and fertility and observes significant differences with respect to the mean number of child ever born (CEB) between different economic activity groups for 1978 and 1988 for all of Turkey and the urban and rural areas. The rankings of occupations from the highest to the lowest mean CEB for Turkey in 1988 was unpaid and paid agricultural workers, housewives, industry and trade, and services.

The other factors are less important for explaining the birth risks. Exceptions are armed conflict and involuntary migration in both transitions, and regional dummies for second births. There is a negative significant effect of work experience before marriage on the first-birth risk. Women with health insurance payments have a higher first-birth risk. This may be attributed to the fact that women in the health insurance group of 'SSK' are working, while women in the health insurance payment group ('others') have payments because of their husbands, i.e. are not working. This indicates the positive effect of male income on the first-birth risk.

A high level of education of the partner has a clear negative effect on birth risk. We cannot find any evidence that death of first-born child will increase the birth risk of another child. This parameter estimate is very robust in the models.

The current residence of the woman affects negatively the risk of first birth except in the central areas. For the second child, the situation differs by region. Women who live in western Turkey have significantly lower second-birth risks, while women who are still living in eastern Turkey have higher chances of having another child after the first.

The last two are time-varying variables of armed conflict and involuntary migration. The effect of armed conflict is insignificant on first- and second-birth risks. Involuntary migration increases first-birth risk but decreases second-birth risk. This finding accords with our earlier reasoning on these points.

*Unobserved Heterogeneity and Estimation*

We know that unobserved heterogeneity is a serious problem in transition data analysis. If unobserved heterogeneity has not been taken into consideration in an estimated model, then both estimated parameters of covariates and duration dependency terms will be biased. Neglecting important covariates leads to model misspecification and one can get a spurious duration dependency. Parameters for a negative duration dependency can be estimated instead of the 'true' ones. Such biases do not disappear by increasing the number of spells in the sample.

We suspect that unobserved heterogeneity may be present in the models above due to the lack of information about economic variables in the sample. Although a PCE form of hazard risk is flexible and a non-monotonic duration dependency guarantees against the danger of spurious duration dependency, neglected heterogeneity still can affect the parameters of explanatory variables. Therefore, we test below unobserved heterogeneity with an asymptotically standard normal distributed test statistic. For the details of the test statistic, see Blossfeld, Hamerle, and Mayer (1989) and Lancaster (1990).

We conduct the test for the neglected heterogeneity on the first births. Test results indicate that there is an unobserved heterogeneity in the model, with an observed test value 3.5197 on a one-tailed standard normal distributed variable. We use a one-tailed test because the alternative hypothesis is $\sigma^2 > 0$; where $\sigma^2$ is the variance of unobserved term, $\varepsilon$ and $Var(\varepsilon)=0$, there is no unobserved heterogeneity in the null hypothesis. When the variance of the heterogeneity is small, it is a score test for neglected heterogeneity.

To remedy this problem, we estimated a model with a Sickle parametric assumption for duration dependency and a Gamma type of mixture for the unobserved heterogeneity. This model includes the same explanatory variables as the model of column 6 in Table 7.6. It was not possible to estimate other types of non-monotonic parametric hazard models as log-logistic, log-normal, and quadratic together with a Gamma assumption about neglected heterogeneity. Results of a Sickle type of duration dependency with a Gamma type of unobserved heterogeneity are reported in Table B.2 in the longer version of this study. Estimated individual specific unobserved heterogeneity parameters for first and second transitions depress the birth risks. These unobserved factors which lower women's risks of giving first and second birth are probably related to the family's economic environment. Very tough living conditions in the cities may dictate that women have to find a job. Economic difficulties for families in the large cities, women's search for a job, and the lack of child-care possibilities, all unobserved in the data set, can decline women's risks of giving birth.

Although a Sickle Model with a Gamma type unobserved heterogeneity sheds light on the sign of unobserved factors roll in birth risks, we do not prefer it to the PCE model—for two reasons. The first is that the implied distribution of waiting time in a Sickle model is defective, meaning that there is a certain proportion of women who will never experience childbirth. There might be such women in reality, but their proportion is not so high in the sample and such a defective distribution is not appropriate for the sample we use. A plot of estimated Sickle hazard rate gives maximum birth risks for ages from 21.3 to 25.3. This is in accordance with the picture we get from Life Table Estimates and the PCE model. But the plotted hazard risk of the Sickle model also shows relatively high birth risks at the ages 38 and more, which is unrealistic.

We know that a strong theory is needed for the empirical specification of duration dependence. It is really difficult to evaluate whether an estimated parametric model of time-dependence is appropriate without a strong theory. In this context, we prefer the PCE model to the Sickle model, since the PCE model fits the data better than the Sickle model does.

**Table 7.7: Criteria for Non-nested Models**

| Criteria | PCE | Sickle with Gamma |
|---|---|---|
| AIC | 0.2076839 | 0.1483737 |
| SC | -26555.537 | -32166.443 |

The second reason is that most factors that are significantly estimated in the PCE model are no longer significant in the Sickle model except constants, age, and involuntary migration in the first transition. This happens because of a bad fit of the Sickle model to the data. To understand this feature, we calculated—Table 7.7—Akaike's Information Criteria (AIC) and Schwartz's Criteria (SC), which make it possible to compare non-nested models with each other. (For formulas of measures, see, for instance, Tasiran, 1995). Both measures indicate that PCE is a better model than the Sickle model to the 1993 Turkish Demographic and Health Survey Data Set.

## 6. Concluding Remarks

Turkey has been experiencing a demographic and economic transition since the 1950s. Even more important is the decline in population growth since 1985. Projections indicate that the Total Fertility Rate is approaching replacement level. This paper studied fertility determinants in Turkey for the first time using a dynamic fertility approach of economic theory and utilizing a transition rate model framework on a contemporaneous data set, the 1993 Turkish Demographic and Health Survey conducted by Hacettepe University. The following are a set of general conclusions that emerge from this study:

- The duration dependency of first-birth risk shows an inverted U-shape, the birth risk decreasing monotonically for the second child.
- Ethnicity is important, but not in the widely accepted sense. Kurdish women do not have higher second-birth risks than Turkish women.
- Voluntary migration rises only with the birth of the first child in the larger cities but not with the birth of second child.
- Higher-educated women postpone the birth of their first child and also have lower risks giving birth to another child.
- Involuntary migration from the armed conflict regions of eastern Turkey to the large cities in western Turkey leads to an increase in first births but a decline in the second births.

### *Future Research*

To provide a better explanation for fertility behavior and be able to predict future fertility outcomes in Turkey, an analysis of the third and subsequent births needs to be carried out. Furthermore, there is room for improved data sets with information on the economic conditions of women and their families. To use only dynamic approaches for fertility is insufficient. In future studies, researchers need to obtain information about women joining the workforce, their wage rates, household income (including the partner's income), and childcare facilities in residential areas.

## Notes

* Funding from the Swedish Council for Humanities and Social Science Research (HSFR) is gratefully acknowledged. I am grateful, too, to Insan Tunalı for his many valuable suggestions on an earlier version of this paper. I thank Heba Handoussa, Aysit Tansel, Ismet Koc, and the participants at the ERF conference "Population Challenges in the Middle East and North Africa," Cairo, November 1998, for their comments. Earlier versions of the paper were also presented at the 51st Session of the International Statistical Institute, Istanbul, 18–26 August 1997; at the Third National Demography Conference, Hacettepe University, Ankara, 2–5 December 1997, and at the Middle East Economic Association Session in the American Economic Association Winter Meeting, Chicago, January 2–5, 1998. Any errors that may remain are my own.

1 Total Fertility Rate (TFR) refers to the average number of children born to a woman during her fecund childbearing period, generally between 15 and 49 years old. Replacement Level Fertility is 2.1 live births per woman, which is slightly above two births per woman to allow for the fact that not all children born will survive to childbearing age.

2 Population momentum is primarily a result of low death rates at the young end of the population age spectrum. Young adults of the present generation survive in greater numbers than did those of the previous generation and thus contribute to an increased total population over their lifetimes. As this generation ages and eventually dies out, the population birth rate and death rate gradually reach an equilibrium and population growth slows and eventually stops.

3 The Total Age Dependency Ratio is equal to the ratio of [(Population aged 0–14) + (Population aged 65 and older)] / (Population aged 15–64).

4 We also tested another model with variable armed conflict instead of involuntary migration, but it did not give any significant result.

## References

Arroyo, C.R., and J. Zhang. 1997. "Dynamic Micro-economic Models of Fertility Choice: A Survey," *Journal of Population Economics*, 10: 23–65.

Becker, G.S. 1960. "An Economic Analysis of Fertility," in *Demographic and Economic Change in Developed Countries*, Universities-National Bureau Conference Series 11. Princeton, NJ: Princeton University Press.

———. 1965. "A Theory of the Allocation of Time," *The Economic Journal*, 70: 493–517.

Blossfeld, H.-P., A. Hamerle, and K.U. Mayer. 1989. *Event History Analysis, Statistical Theory and Application in the Social Sciences*. Hillsdale: Lawrance Erlbaum Associates.

Boserup. E. 1970 *Woman's Role in Economic Development*. New York: St. Martin's Press.

———. 1981. *Population and Technological Change, A Study of Long-Term Trends*. Chicago, IL: The University of Chicago Press.

———. 1990. *Economic and Demographic Relationships in Development*, Essays selected and introduced by T. Paul Schultz. Baltimore, MD: The Johns Hopkins University Press.

Butz, W.P., and M.P. Ward. 1979. "The Emergence of Countercylical U.S. Fertility," *American Economic Review*, 69: 318–28.

Cigno, A., and J. Ermisch. 1989. "A Microeconomic Analysis of the Timing of Births," *European Economic Review*, 33: 737–60.

Cox, D.R., and D. Oakes. 1984. *Analysis of Survival Data*. London: Chapman and Hall.

DHS III. 1995. *Description of the Demographic and Health Surveys Individual and Household Recodes, Data File*, Version 1.1 (with differences from DHS II), Macro Inc.

Hancioglu, A., B.A. Ergocmen, and T. Unalan T, (1997) *Fertility Trends, Women's Status, and Reproductive Expectations in Turkey, Results of Further Analysis of the 1993 Turkish*

*Demographic and Health Survey*. Ankara: Hacettepe University, Institute of Population Studies.
Heckman, J., and R. Willis. 1975. "Estimation of a Stochastic Model of Reproduction: An Econometric Approach," in N. Terleckj (ed.), *Household Production and Consumption*. New York: Columbia University Press.
Kalbfleisch, J.D., and R.L. Prentice. 1980. *The Statistical Analysis of Failure Data*. New York: Wiley.
Kasnakoglu, Z. 1993. "An Empirical Analysis of Female Occupation, Income and Fertility in Turkey," in Aykut Toros (ed.), *Population Issues in Turkey*. Ankara: Hacettepe University Institute of Population Studies.
Kiesling, K.L., and H. Landberg (eds). 1994. *Population Economic Development and the Environment, The Making of Our Common Future*. New York: Oxford University Press.
Lancaster, T. 1990. *The Econometric Analysis of Transition Data*. Econometric Society Monographs, 17. Cambridge: Cambridge University Press.
Mincer, J. 1963. "Market Prices, Opportunity Costs and Income Effects," in C. Christ *et al.*(eds.), *Measurement in Economics: Studies in Mathematical Economics and Econometrics in Memory of Yehuda Grunfeld*. Stanford, CA: Stanford University Press.
Moffit, R., 1984. "Profiles of Fertility, Labour Supply and Wages of Married Women: A Completed Life-Cyle Model," *Review of Economic Studies*, 51: 263–78.
Newman, J., and C. McCullogh. 1984. "A Hazard Rate Approach to the Timing of Births," *Econometrica*, 52: 939–962.
Schultz, T.P.1973. "A Preliminary Survey of Economic Analyses of Fertility," *American Economic Review*, 63: 71–87.
———. 1992. "Demand for Children in Low Income Countries, in M.R. Rosenzweig and O. Stark (eds.), *Handbook of Population Economics*. Amsterdam: Elsevier Science.
SIS Report. 1995. *The Population of Turkey 1923–1994, Demographic Structure and Development*, Report by Center for Population and Demographic Analysis in SIS, Ankara.
Tasiran, A.C. 1995. *Fertility Dynamics: Timing and Spacing of Births in Sweden and the United States*. Contributions to Economic Analysis. Amsterdam: North-Holland.
Turkish Demographic and Health Survey, 1993 (TDHS). 1994. Hacettepe University, Institute of Population Studies. Ankara.
Willis, R.J. 1974. "Economic Theory of Fertility Behavior," in T. W. Schultz (ed.), *Economics of the Family*. Chicago, IL: University of Chicago Press.
Wolpin, K. 1984. "An Estimable Dynamic Stochastic Model of Fertility and Child Mortality," *Journal of Political Economy*, 92: 852–71.

# Part III

# Labor Markets

# 8

# Globalization and Unemployment in MENA

*Jalaleddin Jalali and Farzaneh Roudi**

## Introduction

The process of economic globalization refers to the increasing freedom and ability of individuals and firms to undertake voluntary economic transactions with residents of other countries. Key features of the process include a progressive reduction in official obstacles to conducting cross-border transactions, and a convergence of the transaction costs associated with doing business with foreigners and those associated with doing business at home. Cross-border transactions fall into four categories of international trade: the exchange of goods and services across national boundaries; foreign direct investment (the establishment and operation of a business in one country that is substantially controlled by residents of another); financial integration (the purchase and sale of financial assets either through portfolio investment or through lending and borrowing); and labor migration (the offer of labor services in one country by residents of another). Any development or phenomenon that facilitates such transactions accelerates the globalization process. Thus, economic globalization could be considered complete if and when all prices equalize across the globe.

This chapter will analyze the magnitude and scope of economic globalization and its consequences for economic growth and demand for labor. It will focus on the Middle East and North Africa (MENA) and compare this region to other developing regions in terms of its participation in economic globalization. It will then discuss the effects of MENA's rapid population growth on its labor supply and address the risks associated with the high rates of unemployment prevailing in the region.

## Extent and Spread of Economic Globalization

Barriers to international trade have been eliminated progressively over the years. Broadly, barriers include official border barriers on trade (tariff and non-tariff barriers); official border barriers on foreign direct investment (FDI) or financial flows; and international transportation and communications costs. In the last group of barriers, some are due to technology or geography, such as being landlocked, and others are the result of policies—for example, the adverse effects of inadequate provision and management of port infrastructure.

Following a series of GATT agreements, tariff rates in the industrial countries have declined to a very low level. The average Most Favored Nation (MFN) import tariffs in large developing countries has also declined, from 34 percent in 1984–87 (prior to the Uruguay Round negotiations) to 24 percent in 1991–93 (following the conclusion of the Uruguay Round negotiations), and are scheduled to decline further to 14 percent by the year 2004. (See Appendix, Figure 8.A1.) By the year 2004, developing countries would have undertaken in twenty years what the industrial countries have done in fifty. Nevertheless, developing countries' tariff rates in 2004 will still be about as high as those in industrial countries were a hundred years ago.

Natural barriers to trade—such as high costs of transportation and communications—have also been falling rapidly. Between 1980 and 1996, the real cost of sea freight fell by 70 percent while air freight fell by 3 to 4 percent a year. Similarly, since 1990 the real cost of international telephone calls has fallen by 4 percent a year in developing countries and 2 percent a year in the industrial countries. The cost of a one-minute telephone call from Washington to London has fallen from about US$20 in the 1950s to a current average of under 10 cents.

As barriers decline and globalization proceeds, international transactions in goods and finance increase faster than the economy itself so that the ratio of cross-border trade to Gross Domestic Product (GDP) and finance increases. Helped by the decline in trade and investment barriers as well as in transportation and communication costs, the ratio of trade to GDP has been rising for the industrial countries since 1970 (Figure 8.A2). This ratio for the developing countries as a whole has begun rising by a faster rate since just over a decade ago. However, not all developing countries have participated in trade expansion. The rise of the trade ratio for the group of the developing countries has been mainly due to trade expansion in the developing countries of East Asia, Latin America, and the former Eastern bloc of countries of Europe and Central Asia (Figures 8.A3 and 8.A4).

One should be careful with the use of this ratio for comparing the extent of globalization across countries. The ratio of trade to GDP is typically higher for smaller countries, which usually have a less diverse set of resources. Moreover, trade volumes for many developing countries are closely linked to international commodity prices—which are often determined largely independently of the developing country policies. Consequently, a country's trade ratio may oscillate independently of the degree of its integration in the global economy.

Cross-border finance has also been expanding fast as a result of the decline in barriers to trade and the liberalization of the regulations governing international finance. Figure 8.A5 illustrates the rise in the volume of net private transfers to the developing countries; and Figure 8.A6 shows that FDI as a share of income has been rising, especially for the developing countries during the past decade. As with trade, however, not all developing countries have benefited from this phenomenon equally. In particular, as Figure 8.A7 illustrates, MENA has not been as successful as certain other developing regions in attracting foreign investment. Indeed, much of the FDI in the 1990s has flowed to Turkey alone. Thus, judged by the FDI criterion, too, MENA integration in the global economy can be considered low.

## Globalization and Economic Growth

Economists have long stressed the role of trade openness as a means of improving economic welfare. A variety of channels linking openness to growth have been proposed, perhaps the most influential of which are the so-called 'static gains' to be derived from reallocating existing resources according to comparative advantage (the Heckscher-Ohlin theorem). Adam Smith stressed that "the division of labor is limited by the size of the market," from which it follows that the more open economies producing for the larger world market have more incentives to innovate and exploit economies of scale. These incentives can generate stronger investment growth, which is associated with higher growth rates.

Trade openness also provides greater exposure to the world stock of knowledge, and therefore to more knowledge spillovers, leading to improvements in total factor productivity. One channel through which knowledge transmission could occur is FDI—which is shown to be positively related to trade openness in several studies. Additionally, open policies provide incentives for policy makers to pursue more virtuous macroeconomic policies—for example, to provide a supportive environment for domestic firms engaged in international competition.

There have been numerous empirical studies in recent years that document the existence of a positive association between open trade policies and income growth. One of the earliest and most influential of these is Sachs and Warner (1995), who, in a cross-country regression study of per capita income growth in the 1970s and the 1980s, found that being open was associated with, on average, 2.5 percent a year faster growth. Since then, a series of papers by other researchers has documented the same point. Among them, Edwards (1998) studies the openness/growth relation, using eight different policy-based measures of openness, and documents the existence of "a significantly positive relation between openness and productivity growth."

Other studies have looked at the link between FDI and income growth, with ballpark estimates suggesting that each percentage point increase in the ratio of FDI to GDP is associated with around 0.3 of a percentage point faster growth. There is some evidence that the magnitude of the FDI effect is conditional on the degree of trade openness and on employment policies. The more open the recipient market and the more flexible its employment policies, the greater the incentives for the affiliates to transfer technology—and therefore the higher the likelihood for recipient countries to draw spillovers and other benefits of FDI.

## Globalization and Unemployment

In spite of the positive effects on economic growth of open trade and FDI policies, policy makers are sometimes hesitant to pursue them for a variety of reasons. Perhaps the most important of these is a fear of the increase in unemployment that is likely to occur as firms in the import-substituting sectors and other inefficient firms downsize or go bankrupt. At the same time, however, firms open up in areas of new comparative advantage and create new employment opportunities, although the required skills may well be different. Depending on the skill mix of the labor force and the type of outgoing and new technologies, the net effect on employment could go either way. Many authors have studied the employment effect of liberalization efforts, though most have simply looked at what happened to employment or unemployment in the aftermath of trade liberalization, without controlling for other influences. This makes it difficult to evaluate the counterfactual case of what would have happened without trade liberalization. Such as it is, the evidence indicates that in most cases employment continued to rise after trade liberalization, unless the liberalization was accompanied by a macroeconomic crisis or a major systemic shift—as in the case of transition economies. Where data is available for unemployment, there is no indication of clear or systematic relations between net unemployment and trade liberalization. Depending on the skill mix of the redundant and the newly demanded labor, the distribution of income will also change.

To policy makers, the political costs of unrest in the interim by potential losers may outweigh the large welfare gains in the long run. This fear is especially serious in MENA, given its already high rates of unemployment (Appendix, Table 8.A1), which are exacerbated by high rates of increase in working-age population (15–65 years of age). MENA's current total population growth rate of 2.2 percent per annum is the second highest of all geographical regions (next only to the sub-Saharan Africa region's rate of 2.8 percent per annum). MENA's high fertility has created a very young age structure, as illustrated by the population age pyramid of the region in the mid-1990s (Figure 8.A8). Comparisons of the MENA population age pyramid with that of the OECD countries (Figure 8.A9) illustrates the extreme youth of the MENA population.

Table 8.A2 shows the ratio of population in the 0–14 year age group to that in the 50–64 year age group, in the mid-1990s. This ratio is positively correlated to fertility rates in the preceding 15 years and indicates the impact of a given age structure on the future size of the working-age population. Over time, the population in the 0–14 age group moves into the working-age group as those in the 50–64 age group exit it. The number of new entrants to MENA working-age population is now greater than ever. These ratios show that, on average, for every 100 that exit the working-age population during 1995–2010, 525 enter it in MENA, compared to 167 in the United States and only 84 in Japan. The number of new entrants to the working-age population group for every 100 that exit it are as high as 944 for Iraq, 933 (nationals) for Saudi Arabia, 860 for Yemen, and 851 for Oman. In countries whose fertility rates are lower and/or in which a decline in fertility rates started earlier, these numbers are smaller but still quite high when compared to regions other than sub-Saharan Africa: Turkey, 325; Lebanon, 402; Tunisia, 427; Egypt, 476; and Iran, 554.

It is primarily as a result of such dynamics in the working-age population that the size of MENA's labor force will expand from 130 million in 1996 to over 194 million in 2010—an increase of 2.7 percent per annum or 49 percent in cumulative terms (Table 8.A3). One implication of such a high rate of labor force expansion is that MENA economies will need to create, by the year 2010, half as many additional jobs as those already existing in 1996 in order merely to prevent the region's unemployment rate from increasing above its current rate of about 14 percent (assuming unchanged labor participation rates). Assuming an employment elasticity of GDP of 0.6, MENA output will need to expand by 4.5 percent per annum in order for the regional unemployment rate not to rise beyond its current level. A reduction of the overall unemployment rate to 10 percent by the year 2010 requires a GDP growth rate of 5.1 percent per annum. Given average annual GDP growth rates of only 0.4 percent in the 1980s and 2.8 percent in the early 1990s, such growth rates are formidable and unlikely to come about if policies remain unchanged.

What makes the task of reining in unemployment particularly formidable is that most of the higher fertility occurs in poorer countries, which usually have a harder time creating new jobs. Yemen, for instance, with a per-capita income of only US$380 in 1996 is a country where women on average give birth to 7.2 children (World Bank, 1998b, Table 2.5)—one of the highest fertility rates in the world.

Another important demographic factor that contributes to the rapid expansion of the labor force is the increasing participation of women—a reflection of both economic pressures on families and improvements in women's education. Women's share of the labor force in MENA, which stood at only 27 percent in 1980 and 28 percent in 1996 (Table 8.A4), is expected to rise greatly by the year 2010—to 33 percent according to ILO forecasts (United Nations, 1997). Note that the low share of women in the labor force—ranging from 14 percent in Saudi Arabia and UAE to about one-third in Tunisia, Morocco, and Turkey—has been an important factor in containing MENA unemployment rates in the past (World Bank, 1998b).

On the positive side, there are certain encouraging trends on the supply side of the labor force in MENA. Results of the recent demographic and health surveys in the region indicate that demographic transition is well underway and that fertility is declining. The average total fertility rate of the region (the average number of children per woman) has dropped from 5.7 in 1980 to 3.6 in 1996 (Table 8.A5). The fastest declines have occurred in Algeria, Iran, Libya, and Syria, where the average number of children per woman has fallen by more than three. The effect of these fertility declines on the age distribution of the populations is evident in population age pyramids in Figures 8.A8 and 8.A9. Fertility decline in some countries has been so rapid that the base of the population pyramids is becoming narrower than some of the upper layers—that is, there are beginning to be fewer children in the 0–4 year age groups than in some of the adjacent five-year age groups. Accordingly, it is likely that for some countries—as well as for the entire region—the ratios in the last column of Table 8.A2 are at their historic peaks. In other words, after about 2010 MENA's working-age population is likely to become increasingly older.

Unlike trade policy reforms, which could quickly affect employment and labor demand, policies aiming at fertility reduction would start to affect labor supply only in 15–20 years. The long time lag should not detract from the urgency of tackling the population problem as an integral part of economic development policies. The governments of Algeria, Bahrain, Egypt, Iran, Jordan, Morocco, Tunisia, Turkey, and Yemen have already adopted this view. Iran serves as a good example of how macroeconomic considerations influenced policy makers to reverse their fertility policy. In the aftermath of the 1980–88 Iran-Iraq war, policy makers' focus turned to the reconstruction and development of the war-torn country. High fertility was soon recognized as an important factor impeding economic development efforts. Consequently, the National Family Planning Program was revitalized and, among other things, free family planning services were expanded throughout the country.[1] As a result of these policies, the United States Census Bureau projects that Iran's dependency ratio[2] will decline from 78 in 1996 to 49 in 2006 and 47 in 2016. Further, the median age of the population will increase from 19 years in 1996 to 24 in 2006 and 29 in 2016. While such impacts of fertility policies on the labor force will become apparent only in the long run, benefits such as reduction in maternal death are already evident.[3]

## Conclusions and Policy Recommendations

This chapter has documented the fact that economic globalization is proceeding and contributing to faster economic growth. The MENA region as a whole is not fully participating in this process, thereby forgoing the potential economic benefits of increased trade and FDI that both theory and empirical observations indicate would enhance income growth and reduce unemployment. While policy makers' hesitation in adopting open economic policies may be understandable on short-term stability grounds, long-term growth considerations make it imperative that they should address the issue of globalization head on, especially in light of the region's dangerously high unemployment rates and the rapid expansion of its labor supply.

The region has a low level of exports and attracts too little FDI outside of the energy sector. Liberalizing trade and exchange policies and freeing of prices is a prerequisite of any boost to non-energy exports and FDI attraction. MENA wage rates are considerably above those of high population countries such as China and India, which are opening up and pushing global wage rates down. Hence, MENA economies will need to increase the flexibility of their labor market by improving the quality of training and education, relaxing rigid labor laws, and allowing wage rates to adjust to market-determined equilibrium levels. A number of MENA countries also suffer from the existence of large and inefficient public sectors, which tend to slow down the pace of economic reform. It is therefore important that public sector downsizing should be a focus of adjustment efforts in the region, as it has been in China and several Eastern European countries. Finally, population policy needs to be an integral part of any state social and economic development plans in the region.

## Appendix

**Table 8.A1: Unemployment Rates in MENA (%)**

| | |
|---|---|
| **MENA (ERF)** | **13.7** |
| Algeria ('92) | 23.8 |
| Bahrain ('96) | 15.0 |
| Egypt ('95) | 10.4 |
| Iran ('96) | 11.0 |
| Iraq ('92) | 33.0 |
| Jordan ('91) | 18.8 |
| Kuwait ('85) | 2.5 |
| Lebanon ('93) | 18.0 |
| Morocco ('92) | 16.0 |
| Oman ('93) | 5.1 |
| Saudi Arabia ('96) | 15.0 |
| Sudan ('86) | 13.1 |
| Syria ('91) | 6.8 |
| Tunisia ('93) | 16.1 |
| Turkey ('95) | 14.0 |
| West Bank and Gaza ('96) | 35.0 |
| Yemen ('92) | 12.3 |

*Sources*: ERF, 1996, and Filmer, 1995.

**Table 8.A2: MENA Population in the 0–14 and 50–64 Age Groups in 1995–96**

| Country | 1. Pop. 0–14 yrs (1000s) | 2. Pop. 50–64 yrs (1000s) | 1 as % of 2 |
|---|---|---|---|
| MENA (ERF) | 125,441 | 23,874 | 525 |
| Algeria | 11,016 | 1,881 | 586 |
| Egypt | 23,588 | 4,952 | 476 |
| Gaza/WB | 1,162 | 132 | 884 |
| Iran | 23,726 | 4,279 | 554 |
| Iraq | 10,137 | 1,074 | 944 |
| Jordan | 1,692 | 275 | 616 |
| Lebanon | 1,026 | 255 | 402 |
| Morocco | 9,637 | 1,966 | 490 |
| Oman | 786 | 92 | 851 |
| Saudi Arabia | 7,043 | 755 | 933 |
| Syria | 6,372 | 811 | 786 |
| Tunisia | 3,140 | 736 | 427 |
| Turkey | 18,972 | 5,836 | 325 |
| Yemen | 7,144 | 831 | 860 |
| Canada | 6,009 | 4,076 | 147 |
| Italy | 8,566 | 10,270 | 83 |
| Japan | 20,243 | 24,225 | 84 |
| USA | 59,140 | 35,463 | 167 |

*Source:* United Nations, ESCWA, 1997a, and United Nations, 1997b.

**Table 8.A3: MENA Labor Force (in millions) in 1996 and Projection for 2010**

| Country/Region | 1996 | 2010 | Growth Rate (percent) Annual avg | Cumulative |
|---|---|---|---|---|
| MENA (ERF) | 129.7 | 194.3 | 2.7 | 49 |
| Algeria | 9.0 | 15.4 | 3.6 | 71 |
| Egypt. | 21.6 | 31.5 | 2.5 | 46 |
| Iran | 18.9 | 30.9 | 3.3 | 64 |
| Iraq | 5.7 | 9.3 | 3.3 | 64 |
| Jordan | 1.2 | 2.0 | 3.8 | 76 |
| Kuwait | 0.8 | 1.0 | 1.7 | 30 |
| Lebanon | 1.4 | 2.0 | 2.5 | 46 |
| Libya | 1.5 | 2.1 | 2.4 | 43 |
| Morocco | 10.5 | 14.9 | 2.4 | 42 |
| Oman | 0.6 | 1.0 | 4.1 | 85 |
| Saudi Arabia | 6.4 | 10.4 | 3.2 | 61 |
| Sudan | 10.1 | 14.6 | 2.4 | 43 |
| Syria | 4.1 | 6.5 | 3.1 | 60 |
| Tunisia | 3.4 | 4.9 | 2.4 | 44 |
| Turkey | 28.6 | 37.6 | 1.8 | 31 |
| UAE | 1.2 | 1.5 | 1.8 | 31 |
| Yemen | 4.8 | 8.5 | 3.8 | 77 |

*Source:* World Bank, 1998b, Table 2.3.

**Table 8.A4: Women's Percentage of the Labor Force in 1980 and 1996**

| Country/Region | 1980 | 1996 |
|---|---|---|
| MENA (ERF) | 27 | 28 |
| Algeria | 21 | 25 |
| Egypt | 26 | 29 |
| Iran | 20 | 25 |
| Iraq | 17 | 18 |
| Jordan | 15 | 22 |
| Kuwait | 13 | 29 |
| Lebanon | 23 | 28 |
| Libya | 19 | 21 |
| Morocco | 34 | 35 |
| Oman | 7 | 15 |
| Saudi Arabia | 8 | 14 |
| Sudan | 27 | 29 |
| Syria | 23 | 26 |
| Tunisia | 29 | 31 |
| Turkey | 35 | 36 |
| UAE | 5 | 14 |
| Yemen | 33 | 29 |
| France | 40 | 44 |
| Italy | 33 | 38 |
| Japan | 38 | 41 |
| Spain | 28 | 36 |
| US | 42 | 46 |

*Source:* World Bank, 1998b, Table 2.3.

**Table 8.A5: Total Fertility Rates in MENA (number of children per woman)**

| Country/Region | 1980 | 1996 | Difference |
|---|---|---|---|
| MENA (ERF) | 5.7 | 3.6 | 2.1 |
| Algeria | 6.7 | 3.4 | 3.3 |
| Bahrain | 5.2 | 3.1 | 2.1 |
| Egypt | 5.1 | 3.3 | 1.8 |
| Iran | 6.1 | 2.8 | 3.3 |
| Iraq | 6.4 | 5.3 | 1.1 |
| Israel | 3.2 | 2.6 | 0.6 |
| Jordan | 6.8 | 4.4 | 2.4 |
| Kuwait | 5.3 | 2.9 | 2.3 |
| Lebanon | 4.0 | 2.7 | 1.3 |
| Libya | 7.3 | 4.0 | 3.3 |
| Morocco | 5.4 | 3.3 | 2.1 |
| Oman | 9.9 | 7.0 | 3.0 |
| Qatar | 5.6 | 3.8 | 1.8 |
| Saudi Arabia | 7.3 | 6.2 | 1.1 |
| Sudan | 6.5 | 4.7 | 1.8 |
| Syria | 7.4 | 4.0 | 3.4 |
| Tunisia | 5.2 | 2.8 | 2.4 |
| Turkey | 4.3 | 2.6 | 1.7 |
| UAE | 5.4 | 3.5 | 1.9 |
| Yemen | 7.9 | 7.2 | 0.7 |

*Source:* Based on data in World Bank, 1998b, Tables 2.3 and 2.15, except for Iran (1996).

**Table 8.A6: Population in Thousands**

| Age | under 5 | 5 to 9 | 10 to 14 | 15 to 19 | 20 to 24 | 25 to 29 | 30 to 34 | 35 to 39 |
|---|---|---|---|---|---|---|---|---|
| Algeria 1995 | | | | | | | | |
| Males | 1962 | 1853 | 1806 | 1626 | 1395 | 1197 | 1056 | 794 |
| Females | 1880 | 1778 | 1737 | 1570 | 1323 | 1169 | 1040 | 768 |
| Egypt 1995 | | | | | | | | |
| Males | 3995 | 4169 | 3893 | 3259 | 2723 | 2528 | 2241 | 2090 |
| Females | 3836 | 4012 | 3683 | 3057 | 2538 | 2356 | 2090 | 1991 |
| Iran 1996 | | | | | | | | |
| Males | 3164 | 4324 | 4622 | 3580 | 2566 | 2366 | 2013 | 1818 |
| Females | 2999 | 4158 | 4458 | 3536 | 2656 | 2343 | 1967 | 1754 |
| Iraq 1996 | | | | | | | | |
| Males | 2189 | 1740 | 1219 | 1094 | 1031 | 834 | 591 | 456 |
| Females | 2093 | 1643 | 1252 | 1129 | 978 | 785 | 588 | 486 |
| Jordan, Nationals 1996 | | | | | | | | |
| Males | 309 | 287 | 271 | 252 | 224 | 181 | 141 | 101 |
| Females | 293 | 274 | 258 | 235 | 207 | 170 | 135 | 98 |
| Lebanon 1995 | | | | | | | | |
| Males | 189 | 175 | 158 | 147 | 156 | 151 | 108 | 73 |
| Females | 182 | 168 | 154 | 145 | 153 | 147 | 123 | 105 |
| Morocco | | | | | | | | |
| Males | 1721 | 1629 | 1559 | 1539 | 1349 | 1153 | 938 | 844 |
| Females | 1653 | 1569 | 1506 | 1480 | 1297 | 1110 | 975 | 854 |
| Oman, Nationals 1996 | | | | | | | | |
| Males | 155 | 130 | 115 | 97 | 77 | 57 | 43 | 32 |
| Females | 149 | 127 | 110 | 92 | 73 | 55 | 42 | 32 |
| Saudi Arabia, Nationals 1996 | | | | | | | | |
| Males | 1440 | 1194 | 976 | 776 | 639 | 529 | 424 | 324 |
| Females | 1372 | 1139 | 922 | 728 | 619 | 547 | 436 | 317 |
| Syria 1995 | | | | | | | | |
| Males | 1074 | 1156 | 1008 | 822 | 671 | 584 | 481 | 347 |
| Females | 1035 | 1119 | 980 | 798 | 650 | 551 | 458 | 343 |
| Tunisia 1995 | | | | | | | | |
| Males | 535 | 545 | 534 | 489 | 438 | 409 | 368 | 312 |
| Females | 506 | 515 | 505 | 464 | 422 | 394 | 350 | 300 |
| Turkey 1995 | | | | | | | | |
| Males | 3213 | 2992 | 3496 | 3520 | 3125 | 2545 | 2400 | 2063 |
| Females | 3097 | 2851 | 3323 | 3298 | 3019 | 2486 | 2348 | 1962 |
| West Bank & Gaza 1996 | | | | | | | | |
| Males | 242 | 192 | 162 | 131 | 110 | 94 | 73 | 50 |
| Females | 232 | 181 | 154 | 125 | 107 | 91 | 72 | 49 |
| Yemen 1995 | | | | | | | | |
| Males | 1497 | 1173 | 951 | 846 | 762 | 657 | 527 | 256 |
| Females | 1449 | 1153 | 921 | 780 | 655 | 545 | 449 | 352 |
| Canada 1995 | | | | | | | | |
| Males | 1044 | 1015 | 1018 | 989 | 1014 | 1126 | 1355 | 1304 |
| Females | 990 | 970 | 972 | 945 | 985 | 1107 | 1319 | 1281 |
| Italy 1995 | | | | | | | | |
| Males | 1393 | 1447 | 1565 | 1899 | 2255 | 2409 | 2338 | 2033 |
| Females | 1312 | 1366 | 1483 | 1804 | 2158 | 2341 | 2290 | 2020 |
| Japan 1995 | | | | | | | | |
| Males | 3160 | 3359 | 3861 | 4418 | 5101 | 4457 | 4075 | 3954 |
| Females | 2994 | 3193 | 3676 | 4198 | 4856 | 4321 | 3989 | 3891 |
| United States 1995 | | | | | | | | |
| Males | 10338 | 10163 | 9758 | 9087 | 9090 | 9955 | 11458 | 11538 |
| Females | 9858 | 9706 | 9317 | 8683 | 8773 | 9692 | 11119 | 11268 |

*Sources:* United Nations, ESCWA, 1997a (for Iraq, Jordan, Oman, Saudi Arabia, and West Bank and Gaza); United Nations, 1997c (for Algeria, Egypt, Lebanon, Morocco, Syria, Tunisia, Turkey, Yemen, Canada, Italy, Japan, and United States); and Iran Statistical Center (for Iran).

| 40 to 44 | 45 to 49 | 50 to 54 | 55 to 59 | 60 to 64 | 65 to 69 | 70 to 74 | 75 to 79 | 80 and over | Total |
|---|---|---|---|---|---|---|---|---|---|
| 673 | 490 | 328 | 304 | 269 | 205 | 123 | 81 | 66 | 14228 |
| 629 | 479 | 347 | 331 | 302 | 228 | 150 | 87 | 67 | 13885 |
| 1757 | 1277 | 920 | 797 | 678 | 525 | 358 | 198 | 115 | 31523 |
| 1723 | 1288 | 957 | 853 | 747 | 599 | 425 | 254 | 164 | 30573 |
| 1431 | 990 | 769 | 717 | 754 | 577 | 463 | 193 | 148 | 30495 |
| 1381 | 1023 | 760 | 649 | 629 | 499 | 383 | 171 | 146 | 29514 |
| 352 | 271 | 226 | 177 | 127 | 102 | 68 | 43 | 40 | 10562 |
| 419 | 316 | 217 | 175 | 152 | 121 | 92 | 59 | 50 | 10556 |
| 69 | 62 | 57 | 47 | 38 | 25 | 16 | 9 | 5 | 2094 |
| 70 | 61 | 54 | 44 | 35 | 23 | 15 | 10 | 6 | 1989 |
| 64 | 51 | 39 | 40 | 40 | 34 | 22 | 10 | 10 | 1467 |
| 80 | 58 | 47 | 45 | 44 | 38 | 25 | 13 | 14 | 1541 |
| 657 | 471 | 321 | 313 | 262 | 228 | 135 | 98 | 61 | 13278 |
| 657 | 491 | 375 | 404 | 291 | 277 | 136 | 101 | 70 | 13246 |
| 26 | 22 | 19 | 16 | 13 | 10 | 7 | 4 | 4 | 826 |
| 27 | 22 | 18 | 15 | 12 | 9 | 6 | 4 | 5 | 798 |
| 243 | 164 | 135 | 123 | 98 | 73 | 50 | 29 | 24 | 7242 |
| 244 | 179 | 151 | 139 | 108 | 75 | 51 | 30 | 24 | 7081 |
| 251 | 197 | 145 | 132 | 114 | 91 | 55 | 34 | 21 | 7183 |
| 252 | 202 | 155 | 143 | 122 | 96 | 55 | 38 | 25 | 7022 |
| 230 | 141 | 114 | 127 | 111 | 84 | 56 | 34 | 27 | 4554 |
| 236 | 161 | 128 | 139 | 117 | 88 | 56 | 32 | 20 | 4433 |
| 1748 | 1379 | 1066 | 922 | 906 | 670 | 378 | 171 | 187 | 30781 |
| 1678 | 1340 | 1057 | 995 | 890 | 770 | 443 | 232 | 270 | 30059 |
| 38 | 28 | 22 | 17 | 15 | 15 | 12 | 8 | 9 | 1219 |
| 40 | 33 | 28 | 26 | 22 | 18 | 13 | 7 | 6 | 1204 |
| 183 | 160 | 139 | 122 | 100 | 73 | 49 | 26 | 13 | 7534 |
| 282 | 236 | 192 | 156 | 122 | 89 | 61 | 34 | 17 | 7493 |
| 1154 | 1038 | 799 | 639 | 590 | 525 | 426 | 278 | 263 | 14577 |
| 1152 | 1024 | 792 | 644 | 612 | 590 | 544 | 401 | 498 | 14826 |
| 1876 | 1919 | 1694 | 1698 | 1552 | 1377 | 1118 | 544 | 692 | 27809 |
| 1892 | 1949 | 1758 | 1821 | 1747 | 1662 | 1542 | 855 | 1391 | 29391 |
| 4553 | 5268 | 4395 | 3885 | 3583 | 2944 | 1917 | 1260 | 1217 | 61407 |
| 4511 | 5248 | 4481 | 4037 | 3844 | 3368 | 2718 | 2013 | 2316 | 63663 |
| 10247 | 8900 | 6893 | 5525 | 4874 | 4592 | 3902 | 2707 | 2572 | 131599 |
| 10186 | 8977 | 7066 | 5793 | 5312 | 5341 | 4985 | 3941 | 5498 | 135515 |

**Figure 8.A1: Average MFN Import Tariff Rates in Large Developing Countries (%)**

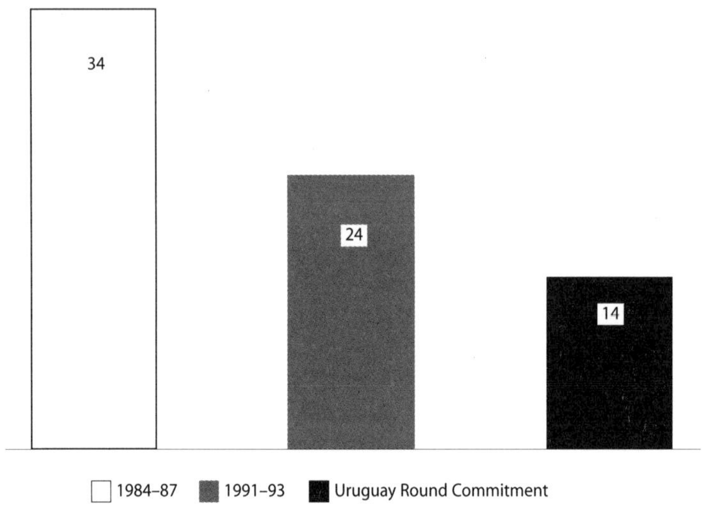


*Source:* World Bank, 1998b, and internal DECPG database of the World Bank.

**Figure 8.A2: Trade to GDP Ratios (export plus import as a percentage of GDP)**

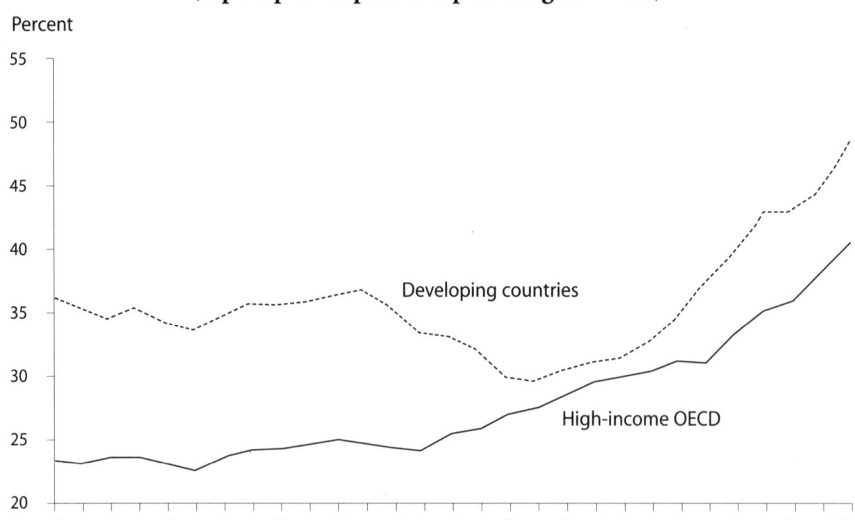


*Sources:* As for Figure 8.A2.

**Figure 8.A3: Trade Integration (exports plus imports of merchandise as % of GDP)**

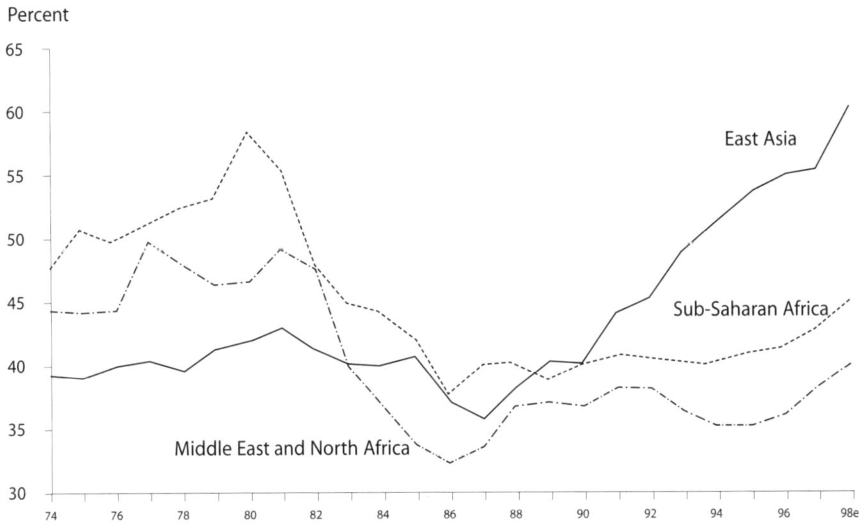


*Sources:* As for Figure 8.A2.

**Figure 8.A4: Trade Integration (exports plus imports of merchandise as % of GDP)**

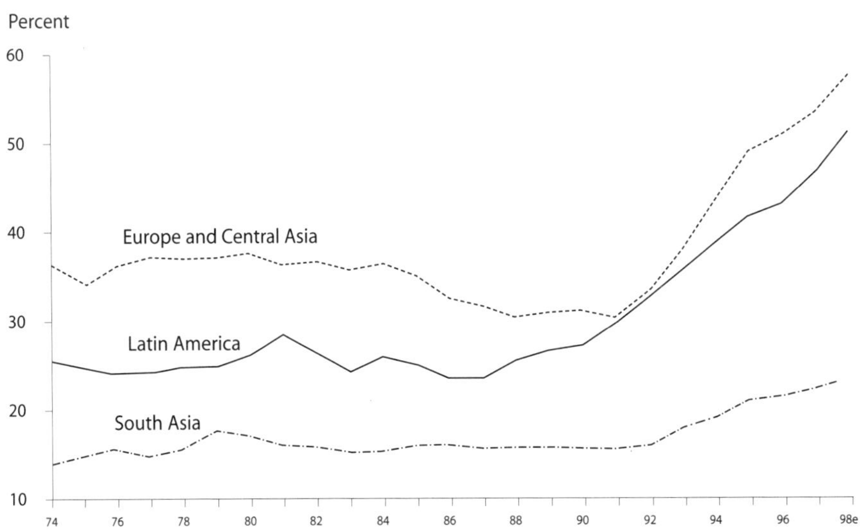


*Sources:* As for Figure 8.A2.

**Figure 8.A5: Net Private Flows to Developing Countries, 1990–98 (US$ bn)**

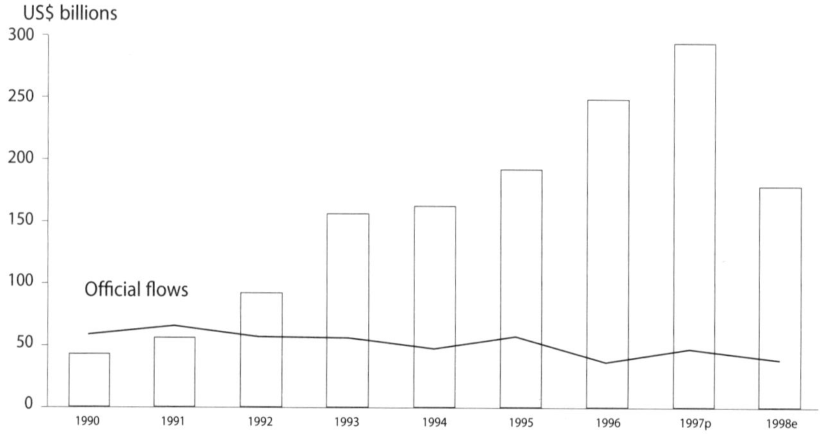


*Note:* p = preliminary; e = estimate
*Sources:* As for Figure 8.A2.

**Figure 8.A6: Ratio of FDI to GDP (%) 1970–96**

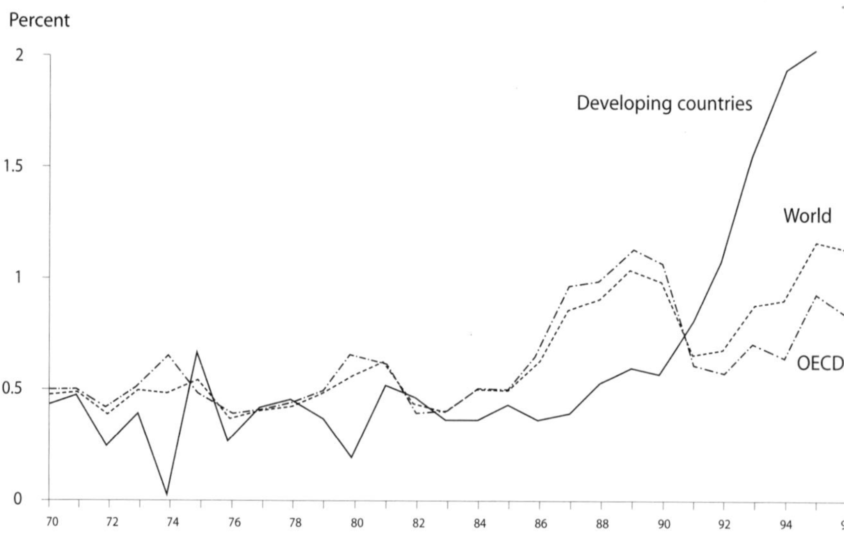


*Sources:* World Bank, 1998a and 1998b.

**Figure 8.A7: Average FDI Share of GDP, 1981–96**

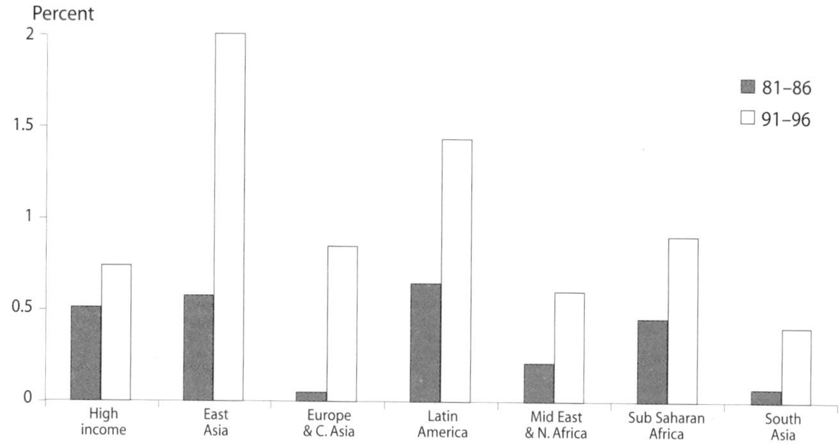


*Sources:* As for Figure 8.A6.

**Figure 8.A8: MENA Population Age Pyramid, 1995**

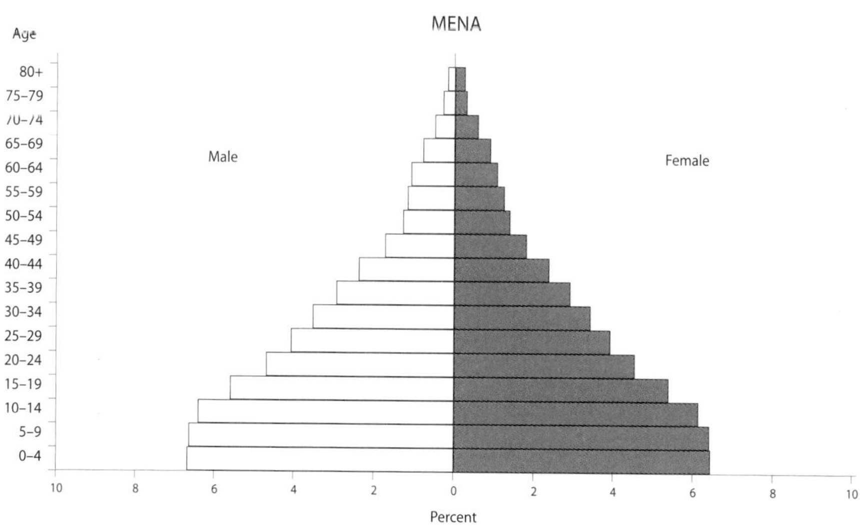


*Sources:* United Nations, ESCWA, 1997a, and United Nations, 1997c.

**Figure 8. A9: OECD Population Age Pyramid, 1995**

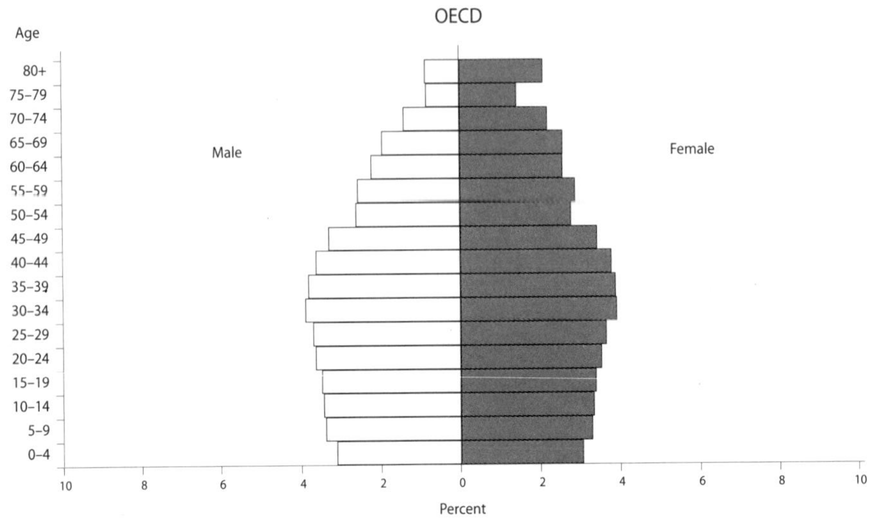


*Source:* United Nations, 1997b.

## Notes

* The authors would like to thank Milan Brahmbhatt of the World Bank and Professor Ismail Sirageldin of Johns Hopkins University for valuable discussions and comments, and Laura Kealy of the Population Reference Bureau, Washington, DC, for assistance with population age pyramids. The chapter has also benefited from comments by discussants Samir Radwan and Massoud Karshenas, as well as other participants at the ERF conference on "Population Challenges in the Middle East and North Africa," Cairo, 1998, for which the authors are grateful. The views expressed in this chapter are the authors' own and should not be attributed to the institutions to which they are affiliated.

1 A sign on a busy street in Shiraz, where one would expect to see traffic signs, reads, "Population control reins in unemployment and eliminates illiteracy."

2 Dependency ratio is defined as the ratio of the number of people in the 0–14 and 65+ age groups to those in the 15–64 age group, expressed in percentage points.

3 For instance, as a direct outcome of these policies, the ratio of pregnancy-related deaths in Iran has dropped from 140 (per 100,000 live births) in 1985 to 40 in 1995 (Ministry of Health, February 1998).

## References

Economic Research Forum for the Arab Countries, Iran and Turkey (ERF). 1996. *Economic Trends in the MENA Region*. Cairo: ERF.

Edwards, Sebastian. 1998. "Openness, Productivity and Growth: What Do We Really Know?" *The Economic Journal*, 108: 383–98.

Filmer, Deon L. 1995. "Estimating the World at Work," background paper for *World Development Report, 1995*. Washington, DC: World Bank.

Ministry of Health, Islamic Republic of Iran. 1998. *Country Report on Population, Reproductive Health and Family planning in the Islamic Republic of Iran*. Tehran. February.

Sachs, Jeffrey, and Andrew Warner. 1995. "Economic Reform and the Process of Global Integration," *Brookings Papers on Economic Activity*, Vol. 1, pp. 1–118.
United Nations, Economic and Social Commission for Western Asia (ESCWA). 1997a. *Demographic and Related Socio-Economic Data Sheets for Countries of the Economic and Social Commission for Western Asia as Assessed in 1996.* Beirut: United Nations.
United Nations, Department for Economics and Social Information and Policy Analysis. 1997b. *Report on the World Social Situation*, Table 7.2. New York: United Nations.
United Nations. 1997c. *World PopulationProspects: The 1996 Revision.* New York: United Nations.
United States Census Bureau. Web site: www.census.gov.
World Bank. 1998a. *Global Development Finance.* Washington, DC: World Bank.
———. 1998b. *World Development Indicators.* Washington, DC: World Bank.

# 9

# Female Labor Supply in Egypt: Participation and Hours of Work

*Ragui Assaad and Fatma El-Hamidi*

## Introduction

The objective of this chapter is to investigate how female labor supply in Egypt responds to market wages, unearned income, and other individual and household-level characteristics, such as educational attainment, age, and family structure. We investigate both dimensions of labor supply at the individual level, namely the decision to participate in paid work and the hours spent in such work once that decision has been made. As far as we can tell, this is the first attempt at undertaking a full-fledged female labor supply analysis in the Middle East and North Africa that uses individual-level data.

According to the standard theory of labor supply, the participation decision is based on a comparison of the market wage a woman can obtain and her reservation wage (see Killingsworth, 1983; Killingsworth and Heckman, 1986). The reservation wage is related to the opportunity cost of a woman's time spent at home (or in unpaid work), to her unearned income, and to other factors that may affect her preference for paid work relative to other time uses. Once a decision to participate is made, the decision on the number of hours of paid labor to supply depends on the marginal utility of consuming market goods and services, purchased with wage income, relative to that derived from additional 'leisure' time. Although the standard model is formulated in terms of the utility of leisure, it can be more realistically expressed in terms of the marginal utility derived from goods and services produced at home or bought with income derived from self-employment, as well as leisure time. This chapter investigates the twin decisions of participation in paid work and the hours spent in such work within the framework of this standard theoretical model of labor supply.

In Egypt, as in other developing countries, paid work is not the primary form of participation in economic activity among women. Participation in economic activity, as defined by international conventions, takes a variety of forms, such as self-employment outside the home, work in family enterprises, home production for purposes of market exchange, and production for purposes of household consumption in primary activities, such as subsistence agriculture and animal husbandry (Anker, 1990).

It is highly unlikely that the determinants of labor supply for these various forms of employment are similar. For instance, a woman who is engaged in animal husbandry for home consumption clearly has more in common with one that engages only in household tasks, such as child rearing, cleaning, and cooking, than with one who is a wage earner outside the home. It is therefore necessary to study the determinants of participation in each of these types of employment separately. Thus, in this chapter we focus on participation in paid work and its determinants.[1]

To set the stage for the empirical section of the chapter, we begin by reviewing existing studies of female labor supply in a developing country context and discuss the various econometric approaches used in the literature to model female labor supply decisions. The empirical analysis is based on data from a special round of the Egyptian Labor Force Sample Survey (LFSS) carried out in October 1988. We begin the empirical analysis by estimating a selectivity-corrected reduced-form wage equation, which we use to predict wages for all women in the sample. We also estimate a reduced-form hours equation for the wage workers in the sample. Because the survey does not provide a full measure of unearned income or income from self-employment, we use the wage earnings of male household members as our exogenous income measure, on the assumption that, in Egypt, male employment decisions are exogenous to those of their female kin. We then go on to estimate structural versions of the hours equation, which allows us to obtain estimates of the wage and income elasticities of labor supply. We go a step further than most studies of female labor supply by estimating a structural version of the participation equation, which allows us to determine how the probability of participation in paid work responds to market wages and household income for various subgroups of women.

## Review of the Literature

Although female labor supply studies of the United States and other advanced countries are quite numerous, they have produced a wide-range of conflicting estimates of labor supply elasticities with respect to wages and income. In their comprehensive survey of this literature, Killingsworth and Heckman (1986) conclude that estimates of female labor supply elasticities in these contexts are large, both in absolute terms and relative to male elasticities, but they worry that the range of estimates is "dauntingly large." The wage elasticity estimates vary widely from -0.85 to over 14, depending on the data source, the sub-populations studied (which vary by age group, marital status, and race) and the statistical methodology used. The literature emphasizes the critical importance of methodological issues, especially the need to correct for selectivity bias, as discussed in the subsequent section. It also underscores the need to conduct more studies and more sensitivity analyses across different model specifications (Killingsworth and Heckman, 1986: 197).

Studies of female labor supply in developing countries, on the other hand, generally focus on the labor force participation decision rather than the hours-of-work decision. To our knowledge, ours is the first study attempting a full-fledged labor supply framework for the Middle East and North Africa region that produces estimates of wage and income female labor supply elasticities.

Sahn and Alderman (1988) estimate a labor supply function for Sri Lankan men and women using 1980–81 data. They explain to what extent the wage offer is sensitive to productivity endowments, and whether there is a relationship between nutrition and productivity. They estimate a labor force participation function and a labor supply function for wage workers. However, they use the number of weeks worked instead of hours worked as their measure of the quantity of labor supplied. They found that the elasticity of labor supply with respect to wages is positive, and lower in urban than in rural areas (0.14 for rural men, 0.07 for urban men; 0.15 for rural women, and 0.03 for urban women). They found that more labor market experience tends to increase labor supply but at a decreasing rate. Ownership of agricultural land reduces the supply of wage labor for both men and women, and marriage reduces the market labor supply for women in rural areas but has no significant effect in urban areas. They also found that the number of children under six years old has no significant effect on the decision to join the paid labor force. Finally, they found that the presence of male workers in the household has a negative but statistically insignificant effect on women's decision to engage in paid work and that higher levels of non-labor income reduce the probability of female participation in paid work.

Another study, by Shah and Al-Qudsi (1990) on Kuwait, notes the problem of undercounting female economic activities in informal and household-based activities. Using census data for the 1965–85 period, these authors looked at the sociocultural and demographic characteristics of female labor force participation, and the extent of wage discrimination in the labor market. They found that 60 percent of single women aged 25–29, and 63 percent aged 30–39, were in the labor force compared to 27 and 30 percent for married women in the same age groups. They also found that education increases the participation rate of Kuwaiti women, and financial need is an important factor in joining the labor force.

Eltigani (1990) also found low levels of female participation in the labor force in rural Gezira in Sudan. He looked at the effect of agricultural development on female labor force participation. Using a sub-sample of a 1987 survey of married women aged 15–55, he found that 25 percent of the ever-married women in the sample were working. He attributed this low female participation rate to the increased use of modern agricultural machinery, which tends to displace female labor in favor of male labor. Other factors that he found to influence the probability of female labor force participation include the number of young children in the household, the woman's level of education, and the socioeconomic status of the head of the household.

Connelly, DeGraff, and Levison (1997), using 1985 household survey data, compared the determinants of participation in employment with the determinants of hours worked for urban Brazilian women. They found substantial differences between the factors affecting the two decisions. Factors such as the predicted wage, the ages of a woman's young children, her years of education, and the presence of a care provider in the household strongly affect the participation decision but not the hours-of-work decision, and that both are affected by the presence of pre-school-aged children. The woman's age, the presence of other household income, and the presence of a self-employed husband were all found to be significant determinants of a woman's hours of work. Moreover, because there is a large proportion of households headed by unmarried females in Brazil, these authors divided their sample into women whose husband was present and single female heads of households. They found that the unobservable factors that increase the likelihood of employment of single female heads actually cause their hours of work to decrease, once employed. For women with spouses, unobservable factors tended to operate in the same direction for both participation and hours worked.

In summary, the existing research points to low rates of participation and low elasticities of female labor supply with respect to wages in developing countries. The studies also indicate that the factors that affect the decision to participate need not be the same as the factors that affect the hours of work supplied by those who decide to participate. This implies that there should be separate equations for participation and hours of work, allowing for different sets of explanatory variables.

## The Econometric Model and Estimation Methodology

Killingsworth (1983) classifies empirical studies of labor supply into first and second generation studies. First generation studies, which began in the 1930s and continued into the 1970s, estimate the parameters of the labor supply using ordinary least squares. The typical specifications used by these first generation studies were as follows:

$$H = a + bW + cV + \varepsilon \tag{1}$$

$$H_i = a_i + \sum_{j=1}^{m} b_{ij} W_j + c_i V + \varepsilon_i \tag{2}$$

$$H_i = a_i + b_i W_i + c_i (V + \sum_{j \neq i}^{J} W_j H_j) + \varepsilon_I \tag{3}$$

where, $H$ is the hours of work, $W$ is the real wage rate, $V$ is per period real property income, $\varepsilon$ is a stochastic term, and the $i$ and $j$ subscripts are for different household members. Although it is not always explicitly stated, $H$ is the number of hours of paid work and therefore does not include any unpaid work performed for a family enterprise or in the form of self-employment.

Equation 1 refers to the labor supply of a given individual, ignoring interpersonal effects among individuals within the same household. Equation 2 refers to the labor supply of a given household member (in an $m$-member household). In this specification, cross-substitution effects are not constrained to equal zero, so that $i$'s labor supply is affected by $j$'s wage. Equation 3 constrains these intrahousehold substitution effects to zero, so that $i$'s labor supply depends only on $i$'s own wage and the income effect from other family members' earnings, which are lumped with property income.

According to the standard neoclassical labor supply model, the elasticity of labor supply $H_i$ with respect to unearned income $V$ should be negative if leisure is a normal good. The same applies to other family members' income $W_j$, especially if intrahousehold substitution effects can be neglected. The elasticity of labor supply with respect to own wage $W_i$,—usually called the gross or uncompensated wage elasticity—could be either positive or negative because it is made up of two opposing effects. If leisure is a normal good, a wage change will have a negative income effect on labor supply, which will be counteracted by a positive own-substitution effect as market time becomes more valuable relative to time in non-market pursuits. The latter effect is termed the compensated wage elasticity of labor supply.

First generation studies generally assumed that the observations included in the sample of paid workers were drawn from a random population. They did not take into consideration the problem of sample selection bias, which became an important issue in second generation studies. First generation studies predicted wages for all individuals in the sample, using wage equations estimated by the ordinary least squares (OLS) method and data on paid workers only. They then used the predicted wages to estimate some variant of equations 1–3 on a random sample of the population with the labor supply of non-working individuals set at zero. This method, which is termed estimation procedure I by Killingsworth and Heckman (1986), yielded inconsistent estimates of the parameters owing to model mis-specification. Alternatively, they predicted wages for the working sample in the same way, and estimated a structural labor supply (hours) equation on workers only (estimation procedure II). This also yielded inconsistent estimates of the parameters due to selectivity bias.

Second generation studies are characterized by attempts to deal with these problems by taking into account the fact that individuals are not randomly selected into the working sample. A number of studies used some variant of the Tobit estimation technique to account for the fact that a large number of observations have exactly zero hours of labor supply. These studies typically specify individual labor supply functions as:

$$H_i = x_i'\beta + u_i \quad \text{if } W_i > W_{ir} \tag{4}$$

$$H_i = 0 \qquad \text{otherwise}$$

where $x_i'\beta = a_i + b_i W_i + c(V + W_j H_j)$ plus additional control variables, and $W_{ir}$ is the reservation wage—the wage below which no paid labor is supplied.[2] Like first generation studies, wages are predicted for all individuals from OLS wage equation estimates on the working sample, and Tobit estimation is used on all individuals to obtain structural labor supply estimates (estimation procedure III). The problem with this method is that it does not allow the determinants of participation to differ from those of labor supply.

Heckman (1980) suggested that a solution can be found by identifying two equations: the selection equation, which models the probability of engaging in paid work, and the outcome equation, which applies only to those who are observed in paid work.[3] The model thus takes the form:

$$z_i^* = W_i - W_{ir} \tag{5}$$

$z_i = 1$ if $z_i^* > 0$, i.e., the individual is observed in paid work

$z_i = 0$ if $z_i^* \leq 0$, i.e., the individual is not observed in paid work;

$$H_i^* = x_i'\beta + u_I \tag{6}$$

$$H_i = H_i^* \quad \text{if } z_i = 1$$

$H_i^*$ not observed if $z_i = 0$.

where $z^*$ is an unobserved (or latent) continuous variable, $z$ is a categorical variable, which is the observed realization of the latent variable $z^*$. If $z=1$, we observe $H$ (hours of paid work), which is the observed realization of a second latent variable, $H^*$. In the reduced-form version of the participation equation, we assume that both the market wage and the reservation wage, which make up $z^*$, are linear functions of a vector of individual and household characteristics $w$ so that:

$$z_i^* = w_i'\alpha_i + e_i \tag{7}$$

The two error terms $e$ and $u$ are assumed to have a bivariate normal joint distribution with zero means and constant variances $\sigma_e^2$ and $\sigma_u^2$, respectively and correlation $\rho$ between them. In order to ensure that identification does not depend exclusively on functional form assumptions, some of the explanatory variables in $w$ must not be included in $x$.

Heckman's procedure—which has become known as 'Heckit'—consists of first using the parameter estimates from the participation equation to compute a variable $\lambda$ (called the selection term), which is then included, in a second step, as an additional regressor in the outcome equation to correct for sample selection bias. The first step, the participation equation, is a probit model for the probability of $z=1$, which is estimated using all the observations in the sample:

$$Pr(z_i = 1) = Pr(z_i^* > 0) = Pr(e_i > -w_i'\alpha_i) = \Phi(w_i'\alpha_i). \tag{8}$$

where $\Phi$ is the cumulative normal distribution function. Because the model parameters $\alpha$ and $\sigma_e$ are not separately identifiable in the probit model, we normalize $\sigma_e$ to 1.

The outcome equation consists of estimating the expected value of hours of work (or hourly wage), conditional on $z=1$ and on the vector of characteristics $x$:

$$E(H_i | z_i = 1, x_i) = x_i'\beta + E(u_i | z_i = 1) \tag{9}$$

$$x_i'\beta + E(u_i | e_i > -w_i'\alpha)$$

$$x_i'\beta + \rho\,\sigma_u \lambda_i$$

where $\lambda_i = \phi(w_i'\alpha) / \Phi(w_i'\alpha)$ is the inverse Mills ratio. Consistent estimates of the parameters $\beta, \alpha, \rho$, and $\sigma_u$. can either be obtained by a two-stage estimation method or by Full Information Maximum Likelihood (FIML) simultaneous estimation of the two equations, the approach pursued here. We can also obtain an estimate of $\theta = \rho\sigma_u$, the coefficient of the selection term $\lambda$. An insignificant $\theta$ parameter indicates that there is no significant sample selection based on unobservables.

Once selectivity-corrected reduced-form wage and hours equations are obtained, structural versions of the labor supply equations can be estimated by introducing predicted wage as a regressor in the hours equation. This is referred to as estimation procedure VII by Killingsworth and Heckman (1986). A slight variation on this estimation method is the use of structural rather than reduced-form, wage equations to predict wages for inclusion in the structural version of the hours equation (estimation procedure VIII). This procedure also relies on identifying the hours equation by excluding some variables that enter into the determination of wages. Our analysis relies primarily on estimation procedure VII, but we also conduct sensitivity analyses using estimation procedure VIII.

## Data and Empirical Results

The analysis employs data from the October 1988 special round of the Egyptian Labor Force Sample Survey (referred to hereafter as the October 1988 LFSS). This round of the survey used a much more detailed questionnaire than the usual rounds to inquire about earnings and individual and household characteristics than the regular rounds. The analysis was restricted to women 12 years of age or older, comprising 67 percent of all females and 33 percent of all individuals in the overall sample, which is a stratified random sample of the population. The working sample on which the analysis is based consists of 18,645 females ages 12 and above, of which 1778 individuals are wage workers with a positive number of working hours in the reference year.

The October 1988 LFSS collected data on hours and earnings for a long reference period of one year. For regular workers (defined as continuously employed workers), annual hours of work were estimated by multiplying the average number of hours per day and the average number of days per week by the actual number of weeks worked per year. The wages of these workers were then estimated by dividing annual earnings by this estimate of annual hours. For irregular workers with more intermittent employment, the reference year was divided into four quarters and the workers were asked about the number of months worked per quarter, the average number of days worked per month, the average number of hours worked per day and the average wage per day each quarter. An estimate of the number of hours worked per year was then obtained by adding the estimated quarterly hours. The hourly wage was obtained by dividing the average daily wage over the four quarters by the average length of the working day across the four quarters. In contrast to the number of days worked per month, neither of these two variables vary much across quarters, resulting in fairly reliable estimates of the hourly wage for irregular workers. There is, however, a significant room for measurement error in the estimation of work hours for irregular workers using this method because of recall problems and possibly some desire on the part of such workers to under-report the number of hours they supply. However, the low proportion of irregular workers among female wage workers (16 percent) makes such measurement problems less important.

In what follows, we briefly describe the general characteristics of the study population, as measured by the October 1988 LFSS.[4] The overall female participation in economic activity is 38.3 percent, of which 34.5 percent are working and 3.9 percent are unemployed. Nearly half of the working females work for family at no wage, while 27 percent are wage workers (9.1 percent of the study population).[5]

As shown in Table 9.1, female wage workers tend to work longer hours than non-wage workers and tend to be younger than either non-wage workers or non-workers. They are also much more educated on average. Whereas only 20 percent of female wage workers are illiterate, nearly 85 percent of non-wage workers and 55 percent of non-workers are. Conversely, 70 percent have secondary education or above, compared to 1.9 percent for non-wage workers and 13 percent for non-workers. These dramatic differences in educational attainment across employment states point to the well-established fact that achieving secondary education is one of the most powerful determinants of participation in paid labor in Egypt. As discussed in more detail below, this is in large part due to the long-standing but currently suspended public employment guarantee for graduates, which comes into effect at that level.

As expected, female wage workers tend to be highly concentrated in the two metropolitan regions, the greater Cairo region and Alexandria and the Suez Canal cities, which are taken together as one region for purposes of this analysis. Non-wage workers, by contrast, are concentrated in rural Lower and Upper Egypt because of the importance of women's participation in farming and animal husbandry as family labor in rural areas. We note, however, that rural Lower Egypt has a much higher concentration of wage workers than the more socially conservative rural Upper Egypt. Non-workers appear to be distributed across regions in similar proportions as the population as a whole.

An examination of household characteristics reveals that female wage workers are just as likely as other females to be heads of households. They are less likely to be married than non-wage workers, but, surprisingly, more likely to be married than non-workers. This is probably due to the fact that non-workers include a large number of young females who have not yet married. Female wage workers, however, have, on average, a lower number of young children in either the 0–2 or the 3–6 age groups, than non-wage workers or non-workers, with the contrast being greatest with non-wage workers.

**Table 9.1: Means and Standard Deviations of the Variables Used in the Analysis, Females Age 12 and above**

| Variables | All Individuals | Wage Workers | Non-wage Workers | Non-workers |
|---|---|---|---|---|
| Hourly wage | | 0.615 | | |
| | | (0.580) | | |
| Hours of work | 1610 | 1770 | 1501 | # |
| | (940) | (792) | (1015) | |
| Age (in years) | 32.8 | 30.7 | 32.7 | 33.1 |
| | (16.5) | (10.1) | (14.3) | (18.0) |
| Experience (in years) | 6.1 | 10.2 | 17.6 | 1.2 |
| | (11.2) | (9.5) | (13.5) | (5.6) |
| **Educational Attainment** | | | | |
| Illiterate (Reference) | 0.588 | 0.204 | 0.846 | 0.545 |
| | (0.492) | (0.403) | (0.361) | (0.498) |
| Ability to read and write* | 0.094 | 0.030 | 0.056 | 0.118 |
| | (0.292) | (0.170) | (0.231) | (0.322) |
| Primary* | 0.090 | 0.031 | 0.050 | 0.114 |
| | (0.286) | (0.175) | (0.218) | (0.318) |
| Preparatory* | 0.071 | 0.034 | 0.028 | 0.093 |
| | (0.257) | (0.181) | (0.165) | (0.290) |
| General secondary* | 0.027 | 0.023 | 0.003 | 0.037 |
| | (0.163) | (0.150) | (0.057) | (0.190) |
| Technical secondary* | 0.075 | 0.347 | 0.012 | 0.060 |
| | (0.264) | (0.476) | (0.110) | (0.237) |
| Technical institute* | 0.016 | 0.103 | 0.001 | 0.009 |
| | (0.124) | (0.305) | (0.029) | (0.092) |
| University* | 0.037 | 0.214 | 0.003 | 0.024 |
| | (0.188) | (0.410) | (0.051) | (0.153) |
| Postgraduate* | 0.002 | 0.014 | 0.000 | 0.001 |
| | (0.043) | (0.118) | (0.015) | (0.026) |
| **Region of Residence** | | | | |
| Greater Cairo (Reference) | 0.220 | 0.337 | 0.049 | 0.268 |
| | (0.414) | (0.473) | (0.215) | (0.443) |
| Alexandria and Suez Canal Cities* | 0.094 | 0.138 | 0.018 | 0.117 |
| | (0.292) | (0.345) | (0.134) | (0.321) |
| Urban Lower Egypt* | 0.137 | 0.153 | 0.073 | 0.160 |
| | (0.344) | (0.360) | (0.259) | (0.366) |
| Urban Upper Egypt* | 0.098 | 0.099 | 0.059 | 0.113 |
| | (0.297) | (0.299) | (0.236) | (0.316) |
| Rural Lower Egypt* | 0.272 | 0.213 | 0.483 | 0.200 |
| | (0.445) | (0.410) | (0.500) | (0.400) |
| Rural Upper Egypt* | 0.178 | 0.059 | 0.318 | 0.142 |
| | (0.383) | (0.236) | (0.466) | (0.349) |
| **Household Characterisitics** | | | | |
| Head of household* | 0.096 | 0.106 | 0.109 | 0.090 |
| | (0.295) | (0.308) | (0.311) | (0.287) |
| Currently married* | 0.546 | 0.557 | 0.670 | 0.497 |
| | (0.498) | (0.497) | (0.470) | (0.500) |
| No. of children 0–2 | 0.533 | 0.346 | 0.727 | 0.487 |
| | (0.786) | (0.607) | (0.865) | (0.764) |
| No. of children 3–6 | 0.793 | 0.534 | 1.069 | 0.725 |
| | (1.032) | (0.812) | (1.121) | (1.005) |
| Presence of other females 12–64* | 0.742 | 0.620 | 0.763 | 0.752 |
| | (0.438) | (0.486) | (0.425) | (0.432) |
| Male wage worker in household* | 0.570 | 0.665 | 0.487 | 0.588 |
| | (0.495) | (0.472) | (0.500) | (0.492) |
| Male agric. non-wage worker in household* | 0.343 | 0.138 | 0.667 | 0.249 |
| | (0.475) | (0.345) | (0.471) | (0.432) |
| Male non-agric. non-wage worker in household* | 0.405 | 0.182 | 0.681 | 0.333 |
| | (0.491) | (0.386) | (0.466) | (0.471) |
| Total male wage earnings (in 000s LE) | 0.998 | 1.438 | 0.647 | 1.068 |
| | (1.468) | (1.932) | (0.976) | (1.517) |
| Number of Observations | 18,645 | 1,778 | 4,661 | 12,206 |

*Notes:* Standard deviations are in parentheses.
* Indicates a dummy variable. # Hours estimated on the basis of 2,616 observations with non-missing data.
*Source:* Authors' calculations.

Finally, the presence of male wage workers in the household, together with higher male wage earnings, increases the probability of female participation in paid work. This suggests that the income effect of higher male earnings is more than counteracted by the help women can get in finding paid employment from their male relatives. Conversely, the presence of male non-wage workers in the household appears to discourage women from engaging in paid work. It remains to be seen whether or not the patterns identified here from descriptive statistics will carry over to the multivariate analysis.

### *The Reduced-form Wage and Hours Equations*

As mentioned in the 'Econometric Model and Estimation Methodology' section above, the first step is to estimate a selectivity-corrected reduced-form wage and hours equation on the sample of wage workers. The reduced-form wage equation will be used to predict wages for all individuals in the sample and the reduced-form hours equation is estimated primarily for purposes of comparison with the structural version. We specify a standard Mincerian wage equation in which log-hourly wage is regressed against experience (calculated as the number of years since entering the labor market for the first time), experience squared/100, educational attainment and regional dummies. We include a variety of regressors that would affect wages indirectly through their effect on labor supply behavior. These include: age and age squared/100, marital and headship status, number of children aged 0–2 and 3–6, presence of other adult females in the household who could act as potential alternative care providers, the presence of male wage workers in the household and male wage earnings—which are intended to capture the income effect on female labor supply. The reduced-form hours equation has exactly the same log-linear specification. To account for selectivity in both equations we include a selection term calculated from probit estimates of a reduced-form participation equation as explained above. Parameter estimates from simultaneous FIML estimation of the reduced-form wage/participation and the hours/participation equations are shown in Table 9.2.[6]

Before discussing the specific results for each of the two equations, we note that selectivity does not appear to be an issue in this sample in either the reduced-form or the structural equation estimates. All the selection term parameters are statistically insignificant and the estimated correlation between the error term of the participation equation and that of the wage and hours equations, respectively, are small. Thus it appears that women are not systematically selected into paid work based on unobservables. This is in line with previous work on the same sample that found no significant selection into the female wage workers sample (Assaad, 1997b). OLS estimates of these equations would have in fact been sufficient.[7]

The reduced-form wage equation estimates conform to expectations and do a good job explaining the variation in the sample.[8] The experience coefficients indicate the usual concave wage profile, but the peak wage is reached at levels of experience way beyond the sample range (108 years). The returns to experience are much higher in this sample than is typical, but this can be attributed to the fact that most female wage workers in Egypt work for the public sector, and that public-sector-pay rules place a lot of emphasis on seniority. Once experience is taken into account, the effect of age is mostly insignificant.

**Table 9.2: Selectivity-corrected Wage and Hours Equations, Females Age 12 and above Full Information Maximum Likelihood Heckman Selection Model[#]**

| Variables | Reduced-form Wage Equation ln (hourly wage) | Reduced-form Hours Equation ln (annual hours) | Structural Wage Equation ln (hourly wage) | Structural Hours Equation ln (annual hours) |
|---|---|---|---|---|
| Constant | -1.237 *** | 5.546 *** | -2.030 *** | 6.334 *** |
| | (0.224) | (0.335) | (0.742) | (0.429) |
| Predicted log hours | | | 0.056 | |
| | | | (0.101) | |
| Predicted log hourly wage | | | | 0.650 *** |
| | | | | (0.172) |
| Age (in years) | -0.015 | 0.086 *** | | -0.102 *** |
| | (0.009) | (0.017) | | (0.016) |
| Age squared/100 | 0.034 ** | -0.118 *** | | -0.153 *** |
| | (0.013) | (0.024) | | (0.021) |
| Experience (in years) | 0.047 *** | 0.033 *** | 0.057 *** | |
| | (0.004) | (0.008) | (0.006) | |
| Experience squared/100 | -0.086 *** | -0.076 *** | -0.083 *** | |
| | (0.011) | (0.022) | (0.016) | |
| **Educational Attainment** | | | | |
| Ability to read and write | -0.091 | 0.024 | -0.090 | 0.084 |
| | (0.069) | (0.137) | (0.070) | (0.138) |
| Primary | 0.189 *** | -0.208 | 0.213 *** | -0.328 ** |
| | (0.069) | (0.135) | (0.073) | (0.137) |
| Preparatory | 0.255 *** | 0.021 | 0.255 *** | -0.142 |
| | (0.069) | (0.134) | (0.070) | (0.139) |
| General secondary | 0.589 *** | -0.245 | 0.681 *** | -0.615 *** |
| | (0.084) | (0.160) | (0.085) | (0.182) |
| Technical secondary | 0.402 *** | 0.249 ** | 0.537 *** | -0.003 |
| | (0.075) | (0.108) | (0.071) | (0.119) |
| Technical institute | 0.510 *** | 0.121 | 0.681 *** | -0.197 |
| | (0.092) | (0.134) | (0.087) | (0.151) |
| University | 0.749 *** | 0.109 | 0.945 *** | -0.364 ** |
| | (0.083) | (0.122) | (0.079) | (0.160) |
| Postgraduate | 1.011 *** | 0.128 | 1.275 *** | -0.505 * |
| | (0.132) | (0.225) | (0.130) | (0.278) |
| **Region of Residence** | | | | |
| Alexandria and Suez Canal Cities | -0.103 *** | 0.041 | -0.106 *** | 0.106 |
| | (0.036) | (0.070) | (0.036) | (0.073) |
| Urban Lower Egypt | -0.099 *** | -0.103 | -0.123 *** | -0.045 |
| | (0.035) | (0.069) | (0.037) | (0.071) |
| Urban Upper Egypt | -0.165 *** | -0.010 | -0.182 *** | 0.092 |
| | (0.041) | (0.080) | (0.041) | (0.086) |
| Rural Lower Egypt | -0.172 *** | -0.179 ** | -0.190 *** | -0.077 |
| | (0.038) | (0.073) | (0.043) | (0.074) |
| Rural Upper Egypt | -0.226 *** | -0.308 *** | -0.229 *** | -0.174 |
| | (0.053) | (0.104) | (0.063) | (0.111) |
| **Household Characteristics** | | | | |
| Head of Household | 0.036 | -0.049 | | -0.084 |
| | (0.044) | (0.085) | | (0.084) |
| Currently married | 0.122 *** | -0.029 | | -0.134 ** |
| | (0.037) | (0.069) | | (0.069) |
| No. of children 0–2 | -0.011 | 0.014 | | 0.022 |
| | (0.021) | (0.040) | | (0.040) |
| No. of children 3–6 | 0.013 | -0.034 | | -0.042 |
| | (0.015) | (0.030) | | (0.030) |
| Presence of other females 12–64 | -0.016 | 0.044 | | |
| | (0.028) | (0.055) | | |
| Presence of male wage workers | -0.120 *** | -0.055 | | 0.024 |
| | (0.031) | (0.059) | | (0.064) |
| Total male wage earnings (in 000s LE) | 0.042 *** | 0.018 | | -0.009 |
| | (0.007) | (0.014) | | (0.016) |
| Selection Term (λ) | -0.015 | 0.051 | 0.079 | 0.058 |
| | (0.054) | (0.066) | (0.053) | (0.065) |
| Correlation of disturbance with that of the participation equation | -0.032 | 0.056 | 0.165 | 0.063 |
| Log Likelihood | -4955.0 | -6205.8 | -4993.7 | -6207.0 |
| Number of Observations | 1758 | 1778 | 1758 | 1778 |

*Notes:* Standard errors are in parentheses. Statistical significance at the 1% (***), 5% (**), and 10% (*) levels is marked. [#] Each of the three equations shown is estimated simultaneously with the reduced-form participation equation shown in Table 9.3.
*Source:* Authors' calculations.

Merely being literate has no effect on wages, but, expectedly, higher levels of formal education result in higher wages. The returns to education implied by these results are quite low, about 3 percent per year at the primary and preparatory level. General secondary graduates seem to fare better in the labor market than both technical secondary graduates and graduates of post-secondary technical institutes, who receive two more years of schooling after the secondary level.[9] The return to each year of schooling up to the general secondary degree is 4.9 percent compared to 3.3 percent per year for technical secondary degrees. The returns to university and postgraduate education are also relatively high at 4.7 and 5.6 percent per year, respectively.

The regional pattern of wages is also predictable, with Greater Cairo (the reference category) having the highest wages, followed by Alexandria, the Suez Canal cities, and urban Lower Egypt at about 10 percent lower wages, followed by rural Lower Egypt and urban Upper Egypt at 16 percent lower. Rural Upper Egypt, the poorest part of the country, trails with wages 20 percent lower than in Greater Cairo. The remaining variables are generally insignificant, except marital status and the presence of male wage workers in the household, whose effects mostly cancel each other out.

The reduced-form hours equation does a much poorer job than the wage equation in explaining the variation in the dependent variable, with only six significant coefficients among 24 regressors.[10] Both age and age squared and experience and experience squared show a sharply concave age/hours profile. Once the decision to participate in paid work has been made, education has generally no effect on the number of hours supplied except for technical secondary school graduates, who appear to work longer hours than other female wage workers. Women in rural areas generally spend fewer hours in wage work than their urban counterparts, with the difference being greatest for rural Upper Egypt. Surprisingly, marital status, number of children in different age categories, the employment status of male household members, or the level of their earnings have no effect on hours once the decision to participate has been made.

## *The Labor Supply Model:*

### *The structural hours equation*

Following Killingsworth and Heckman's estimation procedure VII, the parameters of the reduced-form wage equation were used to predict wages for the entire sample. The predicted log wage was then included as a regressor in the structural hours equation, shown in column 4 of Table 9.2. The structural hours equation is identified by the exclusion of the experience and experience squared variables, which appear in the wage equation. The remaining variables are educational attainment and region, which are hypothesized to influence the preference for, and social attitudes toward, paid work. Household-level variables, such as headship and marital status, the number of children in two separate age groups, and the presence of other adult (ages 12–64) women who can act as alternative child care providers in the home, are hypothesized to affect the opportunity cost of time at home, and therefore labor supply.[11] Finally, we include male earnings as the income variable. However, since earnings are available only for male wage workers, we also include a male wage worker dummy. Hence, the income effect is only estimated across households with male wage earners.[12] The income effect from the male's earnings would be expected to reduce a woman's labor supply.

The first thing to note is the highly significant coefficient on predicted wage, which gives the uncompensated elasticity of hours supplied with respect to own wage. For each one percent increase in wages, women increase their supply of paid labor by 0.69 percent—conditional on already being engaged in paid employment. The elasticity estimate we obtain is quite large compared to that found in other studies on developing countries, for instance Sahn and Alderman (1988) and Connely, DeGraff, and Levison (1997). In fact, the latter authors found that wages in Brazil, although a significant determinant of participation, are not a significant determinant of hours.

Age continues to be an important determinant of hours supplied even after wage is taken into account, indicating that labor supply has a life-cycle dimension. Keeping wages constant, educated workers appear to work fewer hours and therefore show a higher preference for leisure than less educated workers, with the exception of those with technical secondary degrees. As expected, being married tends to reduce the hours of paid labor supplied, but, unexpectedly, having children in either the 0–2 or the 3–6 age groups has no discernible effect. The presence of male wage workers and the size of male wage earnings has no significant effect either. We therefore fail to detect the expected negative income effect on labor supply.

*Participation equations*

As mentioned previously, we estimate binomial probit reduced-form and structural participation equations. The reduced-form equation was used to correct the wage and hours equations for selectivity using the Heckit procedure. The specification of the reduced-form participation equation is based on the standard neoclassical labor supply model and is therefore very similar to that of the hours equation. The main difference is the inclusion of dummy variables for male non-wage workers in and out of agriculture who reside in the woman's household. These variables indicate the presence of a family farm or other family enterprise and are therefore expected to negatively affect a woman's decision to engage in paid work outside the home. However, once the decision to engage in paid work has been made, the presence of male non-wage workers is not expected to affect the number of hours of paid work a woman supplies.

Rather than show the probit coefficients in Table 9.3, we show the marginal effect on the probability of participation of a change in each variable, evaluated at the overall sample means and the means for the wage workers sub-sample. This allows us to immediately ascertain the magnitude of the effect at these points. Whereas, in case of continuous variables, the effect shown is the partial derivative of the probability with respect to the relevant variable, in the case of dummy variables it is the effect of a discrete change from zero to one.

The reduced-form estimates, shown in the first and third columns of Table 9.3, reveal the following. The probability of participating follows the same life-cycle pattern observed for hours, with participation peaking at the age of 37. Education has no effect on participation up to the secondary level. At the overall sample means, the probability of participation increases by 0.035 for general secondary graduates, but jumps by as much as 0.36 for technical secondary graduates.[13] This essentially means that the probability of participation of technical secondary school graduates is ten times higher than that of illiterates, whose other characteristics reflect the sample means. This big jump in participation at the

## Table 9.3: Determinants of the Probability of Participation in Paid Work, Reduced-form and Structural Estimates

(Maximum Likelihood Probit Estimates, Dependent Variable: 1 = wage worker, 0 = otherwise)

| | Marginal Effects Evaluated at Sample Means for: | | | |
|---|---|---|---|---|
| | Overall Sample | | Wage Workers | |
| **Variables** | Reduced Form | Structural | Reduced Form | Structural |
| Predicted Probability at Relevant Sample Means | 0.042 | 0.0230 | 0.328 | 0.423 |
| ***Marginal Effect of a Unit Change in:***[#] | | | | |
| Predicted log hourly wage | | 0.162 *** | | 1.161 *** |
| | | (0.008) | | (0.043) |
| Age (in years) | 0.010 *** | 0.003 *** | 0.039 *** | 0.024 *** |
| | (0.001) | (0.001) | (0.003) | (0.004) |
| Age squared/100 | -0.013 *** | -0.008 *** | -0.054 *** | -0.058 *** |
| | (0.001) | (0.001) | (0.004) | (0.005) |
| **Educational Attainment** | | | | |
| Ability to read and write | -0.004 | 0.026 *** | -0.015 | 0.142 *** |
| | (0.006) | (0.007) | (0.024) | (0.031) |
| Primary | 0.006 | -0.019 *** | 0.025 | -0.183 *** |
| | (0.007) | (0.002) | (0.026) | (0.025) |
| Preparatory | 0.010 | -0.020 *** | 0.039 | -0.210 *** |
| | (0.007) | (0.002) | (0.027) | (0.024) |
| General secondary | 0.035 *** | -0.024 *** | 0.117 *** | -0.360 *** |
| | (0.013) | (0.002) | (0.036) | (0.018) |
| Technical secondary | 0.358 *** | 0.038 *** | 0.558 *** | 0.184 *** |
| | (0.017) | (0.007) | (0.015) | (0.024) |
| Technical institute | 0.572 *** | 0.052 *** | 0.662 *** | 0.220 *** |
| | (0.031) | (0.014) | (0.013) | (0.038) |
| University | 0.457 *** | -0.013 *** | 0.626 *** | -0.115 *** |
| | (0.024) | (0.003) | (0.016) | (0.034) |
| Postgraduate | 0.694 *** | -0.021 *** | 0.655 *** | -0.292 *** |
| | (0.079) | (0.002) | (0.017) | (0.061) |
| **Region of Residence** | | | | |
| Alexandria and Suez Canal Cities | 0.006 | 0.033 *** | 0.025 | 0.169 *** |
| | (0.005) | (0.007) | (0.020) | (0.025) |
| Urban Lower Egypt | -0.005 | 0.012 *** | -0.020 | 0.076 *** |
| | (0.004) | (0.004) | (0.019) | (0.023) |
| Urban Upper Egypt | -0.006 | 0.028 *** | -0.027 | 0.149 *** |
| | (0.005) | (0.007) | (0.021) | (0.027) |
| Rural Lower Egypt | 0.030 *** | 0.032 *** | 0.111 *** | 0.183 *** |
| | (0.005) | (0.005) | (0.018) | (0.021) |
| Rural Upper Egypt | -0.007 | 0.023 *** | -0.027 | 0.134 *** |
| | (0.005) | (0.006) | (0.022) | (0.028) |
| **Household Characteristics** | | | | |
| Head of Household | 0.013 ** | -0.001 | 0.048 ** | -0.005 |
| | (0.006) | (0.004) | (0.022) | (0.027) |
| Currently married | -0.035 *** | -0.055 *** | -0.139 *** | -0.330 *** |
| | (0.004) | (0.004) | (0.017) | (0.020) |
| No. of children 0–2 | -0.009 *** | -0.003 ** | -0.037 *** | -0.023 *** |
| | (0.002) | (0.002) | (0.010) | (0.011) |
| No. of children 3–6 | 0.00003 | -0.004 *** | 0.000 | -0.028 *** |
| | (0.002) | (0.001) | (0.007) | (0.008) |
| Presence of other females 12–64 | -0.006 | -0.004 | -0.023 | -0.025 |
| | (0.004) | (0.003) | (0.014) | (0.017) |
| Male wage worker in household | 0.008 ** | 0.025 *** | 0.032 ** | 0.183 *** |
| | (0.004) | (0.003) | (0.015) | (0.018) |
| Male agric. non-wage worker | -0.013 ** | -0.018 *** | -0.052 ** | -0.134 *** |
| in household | (0.006) | (0.004) | (0.024) | (0.028) |
| Male non-agric. non-wage worker | -0.025 *** | -0.013 *** | -0.102 *** | -0.095 *** |
| in household | (0.005) | (0.004) | (0.021) | (0.027) |
| Total male wage earnings | -0.0003 | -0.008 *** | -0.001 | -0.058 *** |
| (in 000s LE/yr) | (0.0010) | (0.001) | (0.004) | (0.006) |
| Log likelihood | -3836.4 | -3316.5 | -3836.4 | -3316.5 |
| Pseudo-$R^2$ | 0.346 | 0.435 | 0.346 | 0.435 |
| Total No. of observations | 18,645 | 18,645 | 18,645 | 18,645 |

Standard errors are in parentheses

secondary level is probably an underestimate of the extent to which labor supply increases at this level because it does not take into account the sharp increase in unemployment that also occurs at this level (see Assaad, 1997a). At the sample mean for wage workers, the increase is even larger at 0.558. The probability of participation continues to increase at higher levels of education, with a marginal effect at the postgraduate level of 0.694 and 0.655 at the overall sample means and the wage workers sample means, respectively.

The big jump in participation for technical secondary degree holders is explained by the fact that it is at this level that the public sector employment guarantee for graduates kicks in. Although the guarantee is now suspended, it clearly continues to have a powerful effect on the labor market decisions of educated females.[14] It remains to be seen whether, in the absence of further public sector hiring, participation in paid work among educated females will remain this high.

Although the descriptive statistics showed the largest concentration of female wage workers to be in the metropolitan regions of Cairo and Alexandria, the multivariate results indicate that the only region that appears to have significantly higher rates of participation in paid work is rural Lower Egypt. Cairo and Alexandria simply have a higher proportion of educated females, who tend to have a higher probability of participation irrespective of region. Rural Lower Egypt, by contrast, is characterized by the presence of medium to large farms that provide paid employment opportunities for uneducated women. There are few such employment opportunities for uneducated women in urban areas, and the more conservative social setting of rural Upper Egypt precludes such a role for women there.

Household characteristics appear to have the expected effect on participation in paid work. Being currently married has a large and highly significant effect. At the overall sample means, marriage reduces the probability of participation by 3.5 percentage points or by nearly 85 percent in relative terms. At the sample mean for wage workers, marriage reduces participation by 14 percentage points or 42 percent in relative terms. Female heads of household, who have more limited access to a spouse's earnings, however, are slightly more likely to engage in paid work than other women. The presence of children under the age of 3 in the household provides an additional deterrent for participation, but the magnitude of the effect is much smaller than that of marriage. Each child under 3 reduces participation by 0.9 percentage points at the overall sample means, and by 3.7 percentage points at the sample means for wage workers. The presence of children ages 3–6 has no detectable effect in the reduced-form equation. The positive effect on participation of the presence of a male wage-worker in the household, and the negative effect of the presence of male non-wage workers noted from the descriptive statistics, is confirmed here. The presence of male non-wage workers outside farming has the largest deterrent effect, probably because it indicates the presence of a family enterprise, which raises the opportunity

*Notes to Table 9.3:* Statistical significance at the 1% (***), 5% (**), and 10% (*) levels is marked.
[#] Marginal effects are computed as the partial derivative of the probability with respect to the relevant variable for continuous variables, and the change in the probability as the value of the variable goes from 0 to 1 for dummy variables. The constants of proportionality for recovering the original probit coefficients are 11.26 and 18.31 for the reduced form and structural equations at the overall sample means and 2.77 and 2.55 for the reduced-form and structural equations at the sample means for wage workers. These constants of proportionality apply only to continuous variables.
*Source:* Authors' calculations.

cost of a woman's time. Finally, as in the case of hours, we fail to detect a negative income effect on participation in the reduced-form equation.

The structural participation equation, shown in the second and fourth columns of Table 9.3, is obtained by including predicted log wage as a regressor. As in the case of the hours equation, it is identified by the exclusion of the experience and experience squared variables. Predicted log hourly wage has the expected sign and is highly significant. It also has a numerically large effect on the probability of participation in paid work. At the overall sample means, a one percent increase in wage increases the probability of participation from 2.30 percent to 2.46 percent, which translates into an elasticity of about 7. At the sample means for wage workers the effect of a one percent increase in wages on participation is numerically larger but the implied elasticity is smaller (2.75).

Once wage is accounted for, most of the education variables now have negative coefficients, indicating a greater preference for leisure as education level rises. The main exceptions are technical secondary and technical institute graduates, who participate at higher than expected rates, probably because of the powerful effect of the public sector employment guarantee at these threshold levels. The difference between the effect of education in the structural and reduced forms is informative. Although, the reduced form shows that educated women have a much higher probability of participation than uneducated women, the structural form indicates that this higher participation is entirely due to the higher wages they can obtain as a result of their education or to the greater access they have to paid jobs in the public sector.

All regional dummies are now positive and significant, indicating that females in Greater Cairo have the lowest participation rate when their higher wages have been taken into account. The family structure variables have similar effects in the structural equation as in the reduced-form equation discussed above. The main difference is the fact that the deterrent effect of marriage is now even larger, and the coefficient of children ages 3–6 is now significant and has the expected negative sign.[15] The structural participation equation finally yields the expected negative income effect predicted by theory. However, its magnitude is relatively small. A LE1000 increase in the annual earnings from wages of male household members (which represents a doubling of such earnings) lowers the probability of female participation by 0.8 percentage points at the overall sample means and 5.8 percentage points at the sample means for wage workers.

*Sensitivity analysis*

The literature on female labor supply in developed countries has shown that labor supply elasticities vary widely across studies, making it necessary to test the sensitivity of the results obtained to changes in methodology and to the sub-sample of women used. We conduct such a sensitivity analysis to ascertain the robustness of our results to the estimation methods used and to the way we defined our sample. First, we start by noting that our results are not sensitive to the use of selectivity-corrected estimation methods because selectivity turned out to be insignificant in all cases. Two-stage least squares estimation of the hours equation yielded virtually identical elasticities to the ones discussed above. Second, we tested whether our results are sensitive to the way wages are predicted. In contrast to estimation method VII, which we used, estimation method VIII predicts wages from structural rather than reduced-form wage equations. The method also calls for over-identifying the hours equation through the exclusion of more than the experience variable from the hours equation. We do so by excluding the region variables, which turned out to be mostly insignificant in the structural version of the hours equations. Third, we tested the robustness of our results to changes in the sample by first restricting the sample to women ages 20–44 and then to married women ages 20–44.

The comparison of results obtained from estimation methods VII and VIII are shown in Table 9.4. As reported by Killingsworth and Heckman (1986), estimation method VIII tends to produce lower wage elasticities of labor supply, but the difference in our case is not dramatic. The uncompensated wage elasticity of hours drops from 0.65 to 0.47, a 27 percent change. The uncompensated wage elasticity of participation drops from 2.8 to 1.9, at the sample means for wage workers, and from 7 to 4.9 at the overall sample means, a 30 percent change.[16]

**Table 9.4: Labor Supply Elasticities According to Different Estimation Methods**

| | Formula | At Means of Wage Workers Sample | | At Overall Sample Means | |
|---|---|---|---|---|---|
| | | VII# | VIII | VII# | VIII |
| **Hours of Paid Work** | | | | | |
| Uncompensated Wage Elasticity | $\frac{dH/H}{dW/W}$ | 0.65 | 0.47 | N/A | N/A |
| Compensated Wage Elasticity | $\frac{dH/H}{dW/W} - \frac{dH/H}{dY/Y}$ | 0.66 | 0.44 | N/A | N/A |
| Income Elasticity | $\frac{dH/H}{dY/Y}$ | -0.01 | 0.03 | N/A | N/A |
| **Participation in Wage Work** | | | | | |
| Uncompensated Wage Elasticity | $\frac{dP/P}{dW/W}$ | 2.75 | 1.92 | 7.04 | 4.87 |
| Compensated Wage Elasticity | $\frac{dP/P}{dW/W} - \frac{dP/P}{dY/Y}$ | 2.95 | 1.95 | 7.39 | 4.92 |
| Income Elasticity | $\frac{dP/P}{dY/Y}$ | -0.20 | -0.03 | -0.35 | -0.05 |

*Notes:* # Baseline estimate. VII and VIII refer to Killingsworth's and Heckman's (1986) estimation methods VII and VIII. Estimation procedure VII relies on a reduced-form wage equation to predict wages, whereas estimation procedure VIII predicts wages using structural versions of the wage equation.
H = Hours of Paid Work; W = Wage; Y = Earnings of male household member; P = Probability of Participation in Paid Work.
*Source:* Authors' calculations.

**Table 9.5: Labor Supply Elasticities for Different Subgroups of Women**

| | Formula | At Means of Wage Workers Sample | | | At Overall Sample Means | | |
|---|---|---|---|---|---|---|---|
| | | All Women 12+[#] | All Women 20–44 | Married Women 20–44 | All Women 12+[#] | All Women 20–44 | Married Women 20–44 |
| **Hours of Paid Work** | | | | | | | |
| Uncompensated Wage Elasticity | $\frac{dH/H}{dW/W}$ | 0.65 | 0.73 | 0.15 | NA | N/A | N/A |
| Compensated Wage Elasticity | $\frac{dH/H}{dW/W} - \frac{dH/H}{dY/Y}$ | 0.66 | 0.75 | 0.14 | N/A | N/A | N/A |
| Income Elasticity | $\frac{dH/H}{dY/Y}$ | -0.01 | -0.03 | 0.02 | N/A | N/A | N/A |
| **Participation in Wage Work** | | | | | | | |
| Uncompensated Wage Elasticity | $\frac{dP/P}{dW/W}$ | 2.75 | 3.67 | 2.00 | 7.04 | 6.17 | 6.50 |
| Compensated Wage Elasticity | $\frac{dP/P}{dW/W} - \frac{dP/P}{dY/Y}$ | 2.95 | 3.93 | 2.16 | 7.39 | 6.48 | 6.84 |
| Income Elasticity | $\frac{dP/P}{dY/Y}$ | -0.20 | -0.26 | -0.17 | -0.35 | -0.31 | -0.34 |

*Notes:* [#]Baseline estimate. H=Hours of Paid Work; W=Wage; Y=Earnings of male household members; P= Probability of participation in Paid Work.
*Source:* Authors' calculations.

The results we obtain by limiting the sample to all women ages 20–44 and to married women ages 20–44 are shown in Table 9.5. The uncompensated wage elasticity of hours supplied increases from 0.65 to 0.72 when the age range is restricted to 20–44, but when the sample is restricted to married women in that age range it drops to 0.15. The uncompensated wage elasticity of participation increases by a third when only the age range is restricted and declines by a fourth when we both restrict the age range and limit the sample to married women.

## Conclusions

This chapter focused on estimating female labor supply behavior in Egypt, both in terms of participation in paid work and of the hours supplied in such work. Our estimates of the elasticity of female labor supply in Egypt are quite high relative to those found in other studies on developing countries. According to our baseline estimates, a one percent increase in wages results in a 0.65 percent increase in hours supplied and a 7 percent (relative) increase in participation at the overall sample means. The wage elasticity of participation at the sample mean for wage workers was somewhat lower, at 2.75. Assuming that new entrants will be closer in attributes to existing wage workers than the average woman, we use the latter estimate to come up with an estimate of the overall elasticity of female labor supply that takes both participation and hours of work into account. According to that estimate, a one percent increase in wages, would result in a 3.4 percent increase in the aggregate hours of female labor supplied in the economy.

To illustrate how large these elasticities are, we can compare the effect of an increase in wages with that of household characteristics and family structure. For instance, a 20 percent increase in wage can offset the negative effect of marriage on hours supplied, conditional on participation. A 35 percent increase in wage can offset marriage's negative effect on participation. Similarly, a 10 percent increase in wage can offset the negative effect of having two children under age 3 and two children ages 3–6.

Labor supply elasticities with respect to income, measured here as income from wages to male household members, were found to be very small and mostly insignificant. In our baseline estimate, the income elasticity of the supply of hours was -0.01 and statistically insignificant. The income elasticity of participation was -0.20 at the overall sample means and -0.35 at the sample means for wage workers and statistically significant at the one percent level. Although these results must still be considered preliminary because of the absence of a good measure for unearned income, they are suggestive that any income effect from increased female wages is swamped by the positive substitution effect of more valuable market time relative to home time.

Our estimates of labor supply elasticities proved to be fairly robust to changes in estimation methodology and to changes in the universe of women studied. Changing the estimation methodology as suggested in the literature resulted in a 25 to 30 percent change in the estimated elasticities. These changes are modest compared to those reported in the literature. Changing the universe of women from all women age 12 and above to women ages 20–44 resulted in a modest increase in estimated wage elasticities—a margin of about 10 percent for hours and 30 percent for participation. However, when the sample was restricted to married women in the 20–44 age range, the estimated wage elasticity of hours supplied dropped by 76 percent and that of participation by about 25 percent. Thus, being married not only has a dampening effect on the level of female labor supply, but also reduces the extent to which labor supply responds to market wages.

We detected a strong dependence of participation in paid work on educational attainment, with a big jump occurring at the technical secondary level. When we controlled for wages, however, most of the education effects turned negative, with the exception of the technical secondary and technical institute effects. These results show that most of the observed increase in participation at higher levels of education is due to the increase in the value of women's time in market work, which more than compensates for a greater preference for leisure at higher education levels. The higher than expected participation rates among technical secondary and technical institute graduates can probably be attributed to the lingering effect of the employment guarantee for graduates, which is expectedly strongest at these threshold levels.

The policy implications of these findings are far-reaching. Previous work has shown that female wages in the private sector are not only significantly lower than those of males, but also much lower than female wages in the public sector (Assaad, 1997b). The virtual suspension of public sector hiring of graduates, in effect since the mid-1980s, is therefore likely to have had an adverse impact on female labor supply by significantly reducing the wage offers available to female new entrants. The rising unemployment rates of female graduates relative to male graduates in the 1990s attest to the fact that these women would rather withhold their labor than accept very low-paying jobs in the private sector. Since large parts of the Egyptian private sector are virtually closed to female new entrants, they tend to crowd into a few occupations and job niches, in which, as a consequence, wages get depressed. In the long run, policies should aim at breaking down the barriers that contribute to the segregation of the labor market along gender lines. Since, in the short run, this may be difficult to achieve quickly, policies should aim at enhancing labor demand in activities that make heavy use of female labor, such as export-oriented, labor-intensive manufacturing.

## Notes

1 We examine the determinants of participation in other forms of work in Assaad and El-Hamidi (2001).

2 We assume here and in the ensuing empirical analysis that cross-substitution effects among different members of the household are equal to zero.

3 In our case, the observed outcomes for those who engage in paid work are either hours or wage. Although the Heckman sample selection model is written in terms of hours of work H, the same equations apply equally well to the wage W.

4 The percentages cited here will differ slightly from those implied in the descriptive statistics of Table 9.1 because the latter take sample weights into account.

5 The October 1988 LFSS produces a much higher rate of female participation in economic activity for Egypt than the regular rounds of the LFSS. The difference can be attributed largely to the strict application in October 1988 of the ILO definition of economic activity, which considers individuals economically active even if they are employed in the production and processing of primary goods for their own use. Thus most of the difference shows up for women who are self-employed or working for the family at no wage in agricultural activities. The proportion of women ages 12 and above in paid work (9.1 percent) is fairly similar to that obtained from regular rounds of the survey, which averaged 8.3 percent in the 1990 rounds, for instance.

6 The estimated parameters for the participation equation are suppressed in the table. However, the specification of the participation equation is shown in the first column of Table 9.3. The parameter estimates resulting from the simultaneous estimation are in fact very close to those of the independent estimation of the participation equation shown in Table 9.3.

7 We in fact ran OLS versions of these equations, which produced parameter estimates that were nearly identical to those shown in Table 9.2.

8 The $R^2$ from OLS estimate, which is not shown here, is 0.496.

9 However, the wage difference between technical institute graduates and general secondary graduates is not statistically significant.

10 $R^2 = 0.10$ in the OLS version.

11 The survey does not allow us to relate the number of children in the household to a particular woman. Therefore, we assumed that child care is shared among the adult female members of the household.

12 We assume that in Egypt, the labor market decisions of males, and therefore their earnings, are not affected by those of their female kin, this allowing us to treat male employment status and earnings as exogenous.

13 Because the general secondary diploma is not a terminal degree as is the case with the technical secondary diploma, many of those who hold general secondary degrees may be pursuing further studies.

14 For a discussion of the effect of the employment guarantee on the labor market prospects of graduates, see Assaad (1997b).

15 The findings on children are in line with findings in other studies that showed a negative effect of children under 6 on participation (Nakamura and Nakamura (1994), Shaw (1994), and Hill (1989).

16 Since income elasticities are generally very low and statistically insignificant, we limit ourselves to a discussion of uncompensated wage elasticities. Compensated wage elasticities are simply the difference between uncompensated wage elasticities and income elasticities.

## References


Anker, R. 1990. "Methodological Considerations in Measuring Women's Labor Force Activity in Developing Countries: The Case of Egypt," in Ismail Sirageldin (ed.), *Research in Human Capital and Development*, 6: 26–58. Baltimore, MD: Johns Hopkins University Press.

Assaad, Ragui. 1997a. "The Employment Crisis in Egypt: Current Trends and Future Prospects," in K. Pfeifer (ed.), *Research in Middle East Economics*, Vol. 2. Greenwich, CT: JAI Press.

———. 1997b. "The Effects of Public Sector Hiring and Compensation Policies on the Egyptian Labor Market," *World Bank Economic Review*, Vol. 11, No. 1 (January).

———, and Fatma El-Hamidi. 2001. "Is All Work the Same? A Comparison of the Determinants of Female Participation and Hours of Work in Various Employment States in Egypt," in Mine Cinar (ed.), *The Economics of Women and Work in the Middle East and North Africa*, Vol. 2 of *Research in Middle East Economics*. Greenwich, CT: JAI Press.

Central Agency for Public Mobilization and Statistics. 1996. *Labor Force Sample Survey. Combined Annual Rounds for 1995*. Cairo: CAPMAS.

———. 1988. *Egyptian Labor Force Sample Survey* (LFSS). Cairo: CAPMAS.

Connely, Rachel, Deborah S. DeGraff, and Deborah Levison. 1997. "Women's Hours of Employment: Determinants and Implications for Child Care Arrangements in Urban Brazil." Paper presented at the annual meetingsof the Population Associates of America. Washington, DC, 27–29 March.

Dixon-Muller, R., and R. Anker. 1988. *Assessing Women's Economic Contribution To Development*. Geneva: International Labor Organization (ILO).

Eltigani, Eltahir. 1990. "The Mode of Agricultural Production and Female Labor Force Participation: The Case of Gezira Scheme, Sudan," in Ismail Siregeldin (ed.), *Research in Human Capital and Development*, 6: 247–68. Baltimore, MD: Johns Hopkins University Press.

Fergany, Nader. 1996. *Review of Labor Force Sample Survey in Egypt, Estimates of Employment and Unemployment, and Proposals for Improvement*. Cairo: ILO.

Heckman, James J. 1980. "Sample Selection Bias as a Specification Error," in James P. Smith (ed.), *Female Labor Supply Theory and Estimation*, pp. 206–48. Princeton, NJ: Princeton University Press.

Hill, M. Ann. 1989. "Female Labor Supply in Japan: Implications of the Informal Sector for Labor Force Participation and Hours of Work," *The Journal of Human Resources*, 24: 143–61.

Killingsworth, Mark. 1983. *Labor Supply*. Cambridge: Cambridge University Press.

———, and James Heckman. 1986. "Female Labor Supply: A Survey," in O. Ashenfelter and R. Layard (eds.), *Handbook of Labor Economics, Volume I*. Amsterdam: Elsevier Science Publishers.

Lee, L. F. 1983. "Generalized Econometric Models with Selectivity," *Econometrica*, 51: 507–12.

Nakamura, Alice, and Masao Nakamura. 1994. "Predicting Female Labor Supply: Effects of Children and Recent Work Experience," *The Journal of Human Resources*, 29: 302–27.
Sahn, David E., and Harold Alderman. 1988. "The Effects of Human Capital on Wages and The Determinants of Labor Supply in a Developing Country," *Journal of Development Economics*, 29: 157–83.
Shah, Nasra M., and Sulayman S. Al-Qudsi. 1990. "Female Work Roles in Traditional Oil Economy: Kuwait," in Ismail Serageldin (ed.), *Research in Human Capital and Development*, 6: 213–46. Baltimore, MD: Johns Hopkins University Press.
Shaw, Kathryn. 1994. "The Persistence of Female Labor Supply: Empirical Evidence and Implications," *The Journal of Human Resources*, 29: 349–77.

# 10

# Differentials in Income-generating Activities and Consumption Expenditures between Female- and Male-headed Households in Turkey

*İsmet Koç*

## Introduction

The past two decades have witnessed an increased focus on the role of women in developing countries. Within this context, an interest has arisen in documenting and analyzing the circumstances of a particular subset of women: namely, female-headed households.

Although female-headed households have historically constituted a relatively small proportion of households in the developing world, they are becoming increasingly common, as divorce, and temporary and long-term out-migration, increase, and as kinship systems, economic opportunities, and attitudes toward women change in conjunction with changing macroeconomic structure and social relations. The household is considered to be the basic social and/or economic unit of society. Changes at the household level therefore have repercussions at the aggregate level of the country. For instance, changes in household composition and structure have an impact on the distribution of goods and services, and on the planning of community institutions—the requirements for schools, housing, health, and infrastructure. Recently, policy makers have become more and more interested in studying households and their heads; moreover, they have come to regard the gender of the head as one of the household's most important characteristics. Traditionally, in most countries, households have been predominantly headed by men. When they are headed by women, it is generally thought that they are more likely to be deprived, particularly in the developing countries (Buvinic, 1990; Folbre, 1990; DeGraff and Bilsborrow, 1992; Lloyd and Brandon, 1993; Barros *et al.*, 1994; Lloyd and Blanc, 1996). For this reason, female-headed households have been classed among the most vulnerable groups by the United Nations, together with migrants, the disabled, and the elderly (United Nations, 1991).

Already two decades ago, policy attention was called to the alarming number of female-headed households throughout the world. It was estimated at the time that the percentage of households in developing countries that were headed by women varied between 4 percent and 48 percent (Buvinic *et al.*, 1978). This assessment intensified policy interest in female-headed households as a special socioeconomic category in developing countries. Turkey is no exception, the proportion of households headed by women having doubled over the past 45 years, from 6.1 percent of total households in 1950 to 11 percent in 1994. This proportion implies that approximately 4.2 million people were living in such households in Turkey in the mid-1990s (Koc, 1997; Koc, 1998). Within this context, the present chapter focuses on three separate but closely interrelated policy issues concerning household welfare. The first pertains to the identification of vulnerable households: Are female-headed households more likely to be impoverished than male-headed households? The second concentrates on the patterns of income and consumption: Do households headed by females generate/use their resources differently than households headed by males? And the third, once these questions have been addressed, asks: Do female-headed households warrant extra government attention?

## Data and Definition of Key Concepts

### *Sources of Data*

The data used in this study come mainly from the *1994 Household Income and Consumption Expenditures Survey* (HICES), conducted by the State Institute of Statistics (SIS). The survey covered the entire country, and was applied to 26,256 households (18,264 in urban areas and 7,992 in rural areas) between January 1 and December 31, 1994. It was based on a nationwide representative sample selected by multi-stage, stratified cluster sampling. The obtained sample results were weighted by using generalization factors in order to reflect the Turkish population projected for mid-1994. The weighted number of households was 13,342,055 (7,487,766 households in urban areas and 5,854,289 in rural areas). The survey defines settlements with a population of 20,000 or under as rural, and those with a population of 20,001 or over as urban.

Two additional sources of data can be used in analyzing female-headed households in Turkey: censuses and surveys. The first census in Turkey was carried out in 1927; after that, starting from 1935, censuses were undertaken at five-year intervals up to 1990. Censuses conducted before 1950 have no information on the gender of household heads, while those conducted between 1950 and 1990 do include such information. Information included in censuses carried out between 1950 and 1970 is not comparable to information included in censuses conducted between 1975 and 1990. A methodological change,[1] deriving from the definition of female-headed households, caused an underestimation of female-headed households in the post-1970 censuses. For this reason, censuses conducted between 1950 and 1970 are used in the present study as an important supplementary source of data.

The surveys conducted by the Hacettepe University Institute of Population Studies (HIPS) every five years, beginning in 1968, are the second and most important source of data on female-headed households. Although both the first survey, "The 1968 Social Survey on Family Structure and Population Problems in Turkey," and the second, "The 1973 Survey on Population Structure and Problems in Turkey," contain important information on headship status, they cannot be used in computer analysis owing to technical problems related to raw data. The following, therefore, have been used as further supplementary sources of data in this study: "1978 Turkish Fertility Survey" (TFS), "1983 Turkish Fertility and Health Survey" (TFHS), "1988 Turkish Population and Health Survey" (TPHS), and "1993 Turkish Demographic and Health Survey" (TDHS).

### *Definitions of the Key Concepts*

In the literature, the words household and family are typically used interchangeably and are sometimes combined in the one term family household (Kuznets, 1978). However, in the parlance of demographers, household refers to a co-residential unit, whereas family refers to a group of individuals related by blood. *The United Nations Multilingual Demographic Dictionary* defines a household as a socioeconomic unit consisting of individuals who live together, and a family primarily in terms of relationships associated with the reproductive process which are regulated by law or custom (United Nations, 1992). The concept of a household is based on arrangements made by persons, individually or in a group, to provide themselves with food and other essentials for living. A household may be either a one-person household, that is a person who buys his or her provisions or other essentials for living, or a multi-person household, that is a group of two or more persons living together who buy their provisions or other essentials for living. Persons in the group may pool their incomes and have a common budget to a greater or lesser extent; they may also be related or unrelated or a combination of both. The concept of family is accepted as more restricted than the concept of household in that a household may consist of only one person but a family must contain at least two members, and the members of a multi-person household need not be related to each other, whereas members of the family must be.

Depending on the perspective adopted, a household has been defined in many different ways. For instance, Harris (1981) asserts that a household is a common form of social organization and often represents the primary site for the restructuring of gender relations and women's specific experience. Becker (1981) defines a household as an economic unit where resources are equally shared and distributed among members by an altruistic head. However, there is increasing evidence to suggest that resources are often distributed unequally or unfairly among the household members. Townsend and Momsen (1987), adopting a Marxist-feminist paradigm, identify a household as an "arena of subordination." Braydon and Chant (1989), by contrast, define the household as a residential unit whose members share domestic functions and activities, "a group of people who eat out of the same pot" or "share the same bowl." They aptly point out that the household is crucial as a unit of analysis because it is "the point at which productive and reproductive relations meet." Demographic surveys performed by HIPS and income distribution surveys (IDS) carried out by SIS, on the other hand, define a household as "a dwelling where a person or a group of people usually live and eat together" (SIS, 1997a; SIS, 1997b; HIPS, 1994), regardless of whether they are related or unrelated. For the purpose of this study, the household denotes a common unit of social organization combining both shared residence and shared reproduction—that is, income generation, consumption, and domestic activities such as cooking and eating. Therefore, by virtue of this definition, those members of the household who make some contribution to household resources but do not reside in the household are not considered part of the household in question. Despite its currency in demographic literature, the concept of a head of household remains quite problematic. First, countries use different and therefore non-comparable definitions of both the term household and the term head of household in their census and survey instruments. The United Nations (1992) reviewed population censuses and household surveys carried out in developing countries and showed that there are essentially three different types of headship definition:

- Self-definition: that is, classifying as head of household the person who nominates him- or herself as the head; or other-definition: that is, identifying as head the person who is so designated by other household members;

- Identification of the person in authority: that is, the person who controls the maintenance of the household and exercises the authority to run the household;
- Identification of the economic supporter of the household: that is, the chief earner or the main supporter of the household's economy.

Second, there is ambiguity inherent in the term head of household when the assignment of headship is left to the judgment of household members. Members may use different criteria to make this assignment, rendering in-country comparisons invalid. The third and perhaps most serious limitation, pointed out by Folbre (1990), is that the term head of household is not neutral. It is loaded with additional meanings that reflect a traditional emphasis on households as undifferentiated units with a patriarchal system of governance and no internal conflicts in the allocation of resources. In response to the definition and measurement problems, some experts would prefer to use a more specific term than female-headed household. Some suggested terms are 'reference person' (United Nations, 1992), 'woman-maintained household' (Lloyd and Brandon, 1991), 'woman-led household', 'mother-centered household' (De Vos, 1992), and 'male-absent household' (Hetler, 1983). These terms, however, may more accurately describe different household structures. The problem relating to the meaning of the term head of household, and the consequent identification of the head, has been addressed in some countries, especially in developed countries, by the introduction of another concept, 'reference person.'

In determining headship, the present study employs the concept of reported head. That is, the head of household is the person acknowledged as such, either spontaneously or by the other household members. The term 'household head' was originally introduced in censuses and surveys to avoid the double-counting of household members in household rosters, and it does not necessarily reflect any of the dimensions which the concept of headship can assume: regular presence in the household, moral authority within the group, or primary economic contribution. Thus, in the absence of an ideal demographic, social, and economic concept of headship, headship in this study simply represents the cultural norm of headship among household members. In addition, although it is recognized that headship can be joint or multiple, we assume for the purposes of the study that only one person undertakes headship in the household.

It is sometimes asserted that 'reported head' in the survey/census reflects the norms of the household members questioned or of the interviewer, rather than a person's relative economic importance within the household, and that this bias can result in an underreporting of female-headed households. There are two definitions of headship employed in the literature, one using the measure of income, and the other an hours worked criterion. The first definition identifies the household head as the person who has the highest income (Youssef and Hetler, 1983; Barros et.al., 1994); the second definition, proposed by Rosenhouse (1988), considers the head to be the person who contributes most by way of "efforts on behalf of and commitment to the household." In this definition, effort is measured by the number of market-oriented hours worked. Because of the limitations of the data sets used in the study, there is no way of systematically checking whether the declared heads of household do in fact contribute more income or more hours of work to the household welfare than the non-heads, and what sort of influence they have on the decision-making process. Rosenhouse (1988) shows that using a definition of headship based on hours of market labor provided almost double the percentage of Peruvian households classified as female-headed. Barros *et.al.* (1994) show that in Brazil there is virtually no difference. They also show that use of an income criterion rather than reported headship raises female headship only slightly. Since these two approaches do not seem to have substantial advantages over the reported head approach, and since censuses and surveys, which are the data sources for this study, do not allow the use of these alternative measures, we have used the reported head approach.

## Changing Trends in the Prevalence of Female Headship

As seen in Table 10.1, the proportion of households headed by women has increased by approximately 64 percent over a 45-year life span, from 6.1 percent in 1950 to 10.0 percent in 1993. However there have been considerable fluctuations in the proportion of female headship during this period. Thus, in the years 1950–78, the percentage of female headship increased by about 70 percent, from 6.1 percent in 1950 to 10.4 percent in 1978, when it reached its peak in the extended 1950–93 period. After 1978, the percentage tended to decline until 1988. After this decline, female headship increased by 14 percent, from 8.6 percent in 1988 to 10.0 percent in 1993. The figure observed in 1993 indicates that the level of female-headed households nearly reached the level observed in 1978. When looking at female headship rates obtained from 1978 TFS and 1993 TDHS, we see that the percentage of female headship decreased by 4 percent, from 10.4 percent in 1978 to 10.0 percent in 1993.

**Table 10.1: Trends in Female-headed Households and Some Other Indicators, 1950–94**

| Census/ Survey Years | % Female-headed Hsehlds (FHHs) [1] | % Married Female-headed Hsehlds: All FHHs[1] | Gender Ratio at Prime Wrkg Age (25–59) [1] | % Extended Family[2] in Turkey | % Extended Family: Rural[3] Turkey | Differences in $e^0$ between Male & Female[4] |
|---|---|---|---|---|---|---|
| 1950 | 6.1 | — | 0.931 | — | — | 2.8 |
| 1955 | 7.4 | 9.6 | 0.975 | — | — | 3.3 |
| 1960 | 7.8 | 11.6 | 1.010 | — | — | 3.5 |
| 1965 | 8.7 | 32.2 | 0.955 | — | — | 5.5 |
| 1970 | 9.9 | 35.1 | 0.917 | 32.1(5) | 38.7(5) | 6.1 |
| 1978 | 10.4 | 25.7 | 0.901 | 28.5(6) | 36.9(6) | 6.3 |
| 1983 | 9.7 | 19.5 | 1.033 | 27.9(7) | 36.7(7) | 6.5 |
| 1987 | 8.6 | — | 1.029 | — | — | 6.7 |
| 1988 | 8.7 | 14.9 | 1.033 | 22.0(8) | 33.8(8) | 6.7 |
| 1993 | 10.0 | 12.1 | 0.965 | 19.4(9) | 30.1(9) | 4.6 |
| 1994 | 11.7 | — | 0.951 | — | — | 4.9 |

*Sources and Notes:* (1) Percentages for 1950–70 are obtained from Population Censuses performed by the State Institute of Statistics (SIS) percentages for 1978, 1983, 1988, and 1993 are derived from Surveys carried out by HIPS; percentages for 1987 and 1994 are obtained from the Household Income and Consumption Expenditures Survey performed by SIS.
(2) 'Extended family' refers to a group of kin beyond the nucleus of husband, wife, and/or their children.
(3) 'Rural' refers to settlements with a population less than 2,000 for 1968 and 1978 and 1983, less than 10,000 for 1988 and 1993.
(4) Koç and Toros (1997); (5) Timur (1973); the figure refers to the year of 1968 (6) Hancioglu (1985); (7) Unalan (1986); (8) Koç (1996); Koç (1997).

Although the percentages of female headship observed in the last decades may at first glance seem low relative to some African and Latin American countries, they might be regarded as quite high for a country like Turkey, where the historical/cultural background is based on a patriarchal social structure. On the other hand, again, in the light of the intensive emigration of male workers to European countries from the beginning of the 1960s, they seem rather low—even the 10.4 percent found in 1978. Consistent with this argument, Buvinic, Youssef, and Von Elm (1978) argued that the main cause for the rise in female-headed households observed in the 1970s is precisely the emigration of male labor from Turkey, as well as from Algeria, Morocco, and Italy, to the industrial centers of Europe. For this reason, it may be worth looking at Turkish emigration patterns during this period.

### *Migration History of Turkish Workers*

Turkish labor migration to European countries, which has no colonial roots, gained momentum quickly. Within the context of bilateral agreements, the migration of Turkish workers to European countries snowballed in the early 1960s and early 1970s, so that by the early 1970s over 100,000 people were going abroad annually for employment. Turkey signed a bilateral recruitment agreement with the former Federal Republic of Germany (FRG) in 1961, with Austria, Belgium, and the Netherlands in 1964, and with France in 1967 (Gokdere, 1978; Abadan-Unat, 1976; Akgunduz, 1995). Between 1963 and 1966, the number of Turks recruited to work in the FRG, the Netherlands, Belgium, and Austria increased significantly. By the end of 1966, there were about 180,000 Turkish workers in European countries. The 1966–67 economic recession then reduced Turkish employment in Europe, especially in the FRG. The Turkish Employment Service (TES) handled the transfer of 520,000 workers to European nations between 1968 and 1973, 80 percent of them going to the FRG. About one-fourth of these migrants were women (Abadan-Unat, 1976; Kiray, 1976), three-fourths of whom were from rural areas (Gokdere, 1978). Between 1961 and 1975, about 810,000 people were sent to work through the TES. Gitmez (1984) makes the point that another 120,000 to 150,000 emigrated illegally within the same period. Some other observers, (e.g. Penninx and van Velzen, 1976), too, reported that about 20 percent of Turkish migrants at this time went to European nations illegally. In the mid-1970s, the estimated number of unauthorized workers in the FRG was anywhere from 40,000 to 100,000. After the mid-1970s, host countries' policy strongly affected the migration of Turkish workers to European nations as a result of world economic recession. For this reason, from 1974 until the end of the 1980s, migration slowed considerably.

In the 1970s, when Europe began to lose its appeal, another workers' migration began. Migration to Arab countries started with a labor-force agreement signed by Turkey with Libya in 1975. This agreement marked the opening of a new phase in the history of Turkish migration and diverted migration from Europe to North Africa, and then to the Middle East (Gokdere, 1994). Migration to the oil-exporting Arab countries increased very rapidly and reached its peak in 1981–83, when there were nearly 300,000 workers in Arab countries. After the collapse of the USSR, another important wave of outward migration appeared in Turkey. Some members of the Commonwealth of the Independent States (CIS), as well as other newly emerging countries, launched reconstruction programs. This provided new opportunities for project-tied and job-specific migration, though on a more modest scale than the one to oil-exporting countries. These movements to Arab countries and to the CIS, however, never reached the dimensions and the scope of the previous movement. The increase in the number of workers sent by the Turkish Employment Service after the 1980s appears to relate mainly to the these two waves of migration.

The data for female-headed households during the period of intensive migration from Turkey to European countries shows that the outward migration process has a considerable effect on the prevalence of female-headed households (Table 10.1). The high proportion of households headed by currently married females, and the low gender ratios at the prime working age (25–59) for the period 1965–78, further confirm this effect. Conversely, the decline in the proportion of households headed by married women, and the increase in the gender ratio at prime working age after the period of intensive outward migration, may be explained both by the decline in the emigration of Turkish workers and by the rise of family reunifications, which happened immediately after the intensive migration period. The relatively low level of female-headed households (compared to African and Latin American countries) that followed the period of intensive migration in 1960–74 can be explained by two main factors: first, the extent of family reunification, and, second, the existence of extended families. As noted, the recruitment of new workers by European nations essentially ceased in the middle of the 1970s, but there remained the issue of Turkish workers reuniting with their families in the European host countries. In this respect, after 1974, the migration of Turks for work purposes was replaced by migration for family reunification. There were, however, some difficulties in the reunification process (Martin, 1990). The FRG, for example, stopped issuing work permits to newly migrated spouses and dependants of foreign workers at the end of 1974, thereby discouraging them from entering the country.

The Turkish population in Europe rose to about 2 million in 1980, and has remained stable since then. About 40 percent, or 800,000, of this population were in one country, the Federal Republic of Germany. The changing composition of Turkish population in the FRG is striking. In 1973, two-thirds of its Turkish population was in the labor force; by 1980, the proportion was only one-third (Martin, 1990). A study in 1964 found that less than one-third of the migrants had their families with them in the FRG (Abadan, 1964). By contrast, Penninx (1982), commenting on the situation in 1972, reported that over half the migrants had their families with them. He stated further that, by 1974, there were one million Turks in the FRG: 60 percent workers, 20 percent children, and 20 percent non-working spouses and other dependants.

It may also be useful to look at the position of women in the emigration process in order to understand the impact of family reunification on female headship. According to Abadan-Unat (1976) and Kudat (1974), women became a large part of the Turkish migrant workforce. Thus 13 percent of all Turkish migrants recruited through the TES in 1961, and approximately 20 percent of officially recruited Turkish migrants in the early 1970s, were women. The proportion of adult women residents in Europe who were employed rose from one-third in 1961 to almost two-thirds in the early 1970s, and then fell abruptly. The women who emigrated from Turkey after 1975 often joined their spouses abroad, but did not or could not work upon their arrival in Europe (Akgunduz, 1995). This information suggests that, in addition to intensive family reunification, the significant number of women recruited to European countries to join the labor force was another important factor in reducing the prevalence of female headship in Turkey in the period of intensive outward migration of males.

### *Other Factors Affecting Female Headship in Turkey*

The spread of extended families may be used as yet another explanatory variable in the analysis of the impact of outward migration on the prevalence of female-headed households in Turkey. The proportion of extended families in Turkey was 31.0 percent in 1978 and decreased to 19.4 percent in 1993. These figures imply that extended families are still one of the major family types in Turkey. The argument here is that although male outward migration from Turkey to Europe created many left-behind families in their country of origin, these were absorbed by Turkey's traditional extended family system. This male-dominant system prevents household members from reporting a woman as the head if an adult-male is left in the household. Research done by Gokdere (1978), which shows that most of the emigrants were married males and came from rural areas, makes the picture clearer, since the number of extended families was relatively higher in the rural areas of Turkey, especially in the late 1970s.

A further influence on the change of female headship may be mortality differences observed between males and females. The increase in differences in life expectancy at birth between males and females in favor of females within the period 1950–78 appears to be consistent with the increase in the prevalence of female headship for the same period. Although the gap in the life expectancy at birth continued to enlarge in 1983 and in 1988, a decline is observed in female headship for the same years. This contrast leads us to the conclusion that there were some other factors which had stronger effects on female headship than differences in mortality levels, such as an increase in family reunification and the declining intensity of male outward migration. Between 1988 and 1993, there was an increase in female headship, which cannot be explained by emigration or mortality level differences, since the percentage of households headed by married women and the level of mortality differences between males and females decreased between 1988 and 1993. The increase in female headship observed in these five years seems to be due to the rise in urbanization and the erosion of the extended family system, rather than male outward migration and mortality level differences (Table 10.1). In sum, it may be said that the large-scale international outward migration of males observed in the 1970s (a gradual weakening of the extended family system due to urbanization in the last decade), and an increase in the level of mortality differences between males and females (specially in the 1970s), resulted in the emergence of a significant number of female-headed households in Turkey.

## Demographic, Social, and Economic Profiles of Female-headed Households

### *Demographic Profile*

Consistent with the finding that female heads are older than male heads, the members of female-headed households, comprising 6.7 percent of the total population in 1993, were found to be older than the members of male-headed households by approximately five years. The total adult gender ratios confirm the imbalance between the sexes that is observed in the age-gender structure of female-headed households. The total gender ratio in male-headed households is 103.7, which is very close to the gender ratio of the total population, whereas in female-headed household it is only 49.4. The extent of male emigration can be proposed as a plausible explanation for the relative excess of females over males in Turkey. This emigration process seems to have had an important impact on the prevalence of female-headed households and, at the same time, on the age-gender structure of the female-headed households.

A second reason for the distortion in the age-gender structure of female-headed households is that they house more elderly people, in particular elderly females. Female-headed households, at the same time, include fewer children and fewer adults and therefore tend to be smaller than male-headed households in terms of average household size. The dependency ratio shows the economic burden of people in the non-productive age groups (-15 and/or 65+) on people from the economically active age group (15–64), who support them. It is seen that the distortion in the age-gender structure of female-headed households has an important effect on dependency ratios. The total and young dependency ratios in male-headed households are found to be higher, while only the elderly dependency ratio is higher in female-headed households than in male-headed households (Table 10.2). The figures related to dependency ratios provide strong evidence that the higher dependency burden of female-headed households in 1978 originates primarily from the shortage of adult males in these households. This may be attributed to the intensive male outward migration that occurred of the 1970s. In that a similar pattern in male dependency ratios for male-headed households can be observed, we obtain new information on the impact of the intensive population movement on the age-gender structure of households.

**Table 10.2: Demographic Characteristics of Households by Gender of Household Heads**

| Variables | Male-headed Households | Female-headed Households |
|---|---|---|
| Average Age | 27.39 | 32.28 |
| **Gender Ratios** | | |
| Child | 106.5 | 89.7 |
| Adult | 100.4 | 49.7 |
| Elderly | 130.0 | 5.8 |
| Total | 103.7 | 49.4 |
| **Dependency Ratios** | | |
| Young | 53.1 | 37.4 |
| Elderly | 8.1 | 19.7 |
| Total | 61.2 | 57.1 |
| **Household Size** | | |
| Child | 1.57 | 0.72 |
| Adult | 2.94 | 1.91 |
| Elderly | 0.24 | 0.38 |
| Total | 4.74 | 3.01 |

*Source:* 1993 TDHS.

The decrease in the last decades in the percentage of currently married female heads, together with the increase in the average age of female heads, has had an important effect on the child and elderly dependency ratios in female-headed households in 1993. Since the proportion of children found in the total population of female-headed households has decreased considerably, and since a shortage of males in female-headed households continues to exist, the young dependency ratio in these households is found to be lower than that of male-headed households. The child dependency ratios are found to be 53.1 and 37.4 for female- and male-headed households respectively. The average number of elderly people in female-headed households is higher than that in male-headed households, and the members of the household in general tend to be older. This situation leads female-headed households to have a much higher elderly dependency ratio than male-headed households. This result suggests that female-headed-households have a serious problem with the elderly dependency ratio and could use a special intervention program, which would target and support elderly people found in these households. In regard to the total dependency ratio, although female-headed households have a lower ratio than male-headed households, the figures show that no significant differentials exist. It seems, then, that the shortage of adult and elderly males is compensated by the high number of elderly females, and this compensation creates an increase in the total dependency ratio, which comes largely from the excess of elderly females in female-headed households.

### *Social Profile*

Table 10.3 shows some of the social characteristics of the female- and male-headed households for 1993. Although there have been marked improvements in the level of education in Turkey in the last decades for both men and women, the illiteracy rate in female-headed households is higher than that in male-headed households. However, focusing on the illiteracy rate alone, for the purposes of this analysis, may in fact be misleading, since the proportion of household members who have a secondary or higher level of education is actually higher in female-headed households. This situation seems to create a balance in the educational levels of the two types of household. In terms of the marital status, the table shows that married people account for the majority in male-headed households, whereas single and formerly married people account for the majority in female-headed households. Thus 62.5 percent of the people living in male-headed households are married, as against only 20.0 percent in female-headed households. The proportion of single people in female-headed households is also much higher, as is the number of widowed people: nearly one-third of the people in female-headed households are widowed. The proportion of divorced people likewise is higher in female-headed households. Finally, although the percentage of formerly married people in male-headed households remained quite stable in the last decades, it has increased considerably in households headed by females during the same period. This may help to explain the increase in the distortion of the age structure of people living in female-headed households in the 1990s.

When family patterns[2] are considered, as expected, male-headed households are more likely to live in a man-wife-children family. The man-wife-children family structure accounts for more than half of these households. When man-wife families and man-wife-children families are taken into account together under the rubric nuclear family, we observe that they predominate in male-headed households. The percentage of nuclear families increased during the last two decades for both types of household. On the other hand, broken families (one-person families and mono-parental families) are dominant in female-headed households. The percentage of mono-parental families in female-headed households has decreased by 22.3 percent, whereas the percentage of the one-person families has increased by 83.9 percent in the last two decades. This can be explained by the family reunification process, which saw a surge in the mid-1970s and a weakening of the extended family system. The high level of broken families within female-headed households implies that these households contain fewer males and tend to be smaller. When the distortion in the age structure of female-headed households is taken into account, it is seen that the majority of children in female-headed households have to live with an elderly mother in mono-parental households. The most striking finding is that the proportion of extended families in female-headed households is considerably higher than in male-headed households. This situation may be explained by the finding that approximately 90 percent of female heads seem to be the oldest person in their households. If a woman is the oldest member of the household, she can be reported as the head of household, even in an extended family situation. The Complexity Index[3] shows that households headed by males are likely to be more complex than those headed by females.

**Table 10.3: Social Characteristics of Households by Gender of Household Heads**

| Variables | Male-headed Households | Female-headed Households | Total |
|---|---|---|---|
| **Education** (%) | | | |
| No Education | 18.7 | 24.6 | 19.1 |
| Primary Incomplete | 17.6 | 14.8 | 17.4 |
| Primary | 43.9 | 38.0 | 43.5 |
| Secondary + | 19.8 | 22.6 | 20.0 |
| **Marital Status** (%) | | | |
| Single | 33.9 | 42.9 | 34.6 |
| Married | 62.5 | 20.0 | 59.4 |
| Widowed | 3.1 | 31.8 | 5.2 |
| Divorced/Separated | 0.5 | 5.3 | 0.8 |
| **Family Patterns** (%) | | | |
| Man-Wife Families | 12.8 | 0.8 | 11.7 |
| Man-Wife-Children | 61.7 | 1.6 | 55.9 |
| Mono-parental Families | 1.4 | 32.0 | 4.3 |
| One-person Family | 0.4 | 38.8 | 4.1 |
| Extended Families | 11.9 | 21.5 | 12.8 |
| Multiple Families | 11.6 | 1.9 | 10.7 |
| Unrelated | 0.2 | 3.4 | 0.5 |
| **Complexity Index** | 1.224 | 1.134 | 1.215 |

*Source:* 1993 TDHS.

## *Economic Profile*

In terms of the number of working people in households, Table 10.4 shows that approximately 51 percent of female-headed households do not house any people who are in the workforce, while the corresponding figure for male-headed households is only 10.5 percent. Approximately half the male-headed households include one person who works, and one-fifth of them have at least three people in work; the figures for female-headed households are approximately one-third, and slightly below one-tenth, respectively.

As seen in Table 10.4, the average number of working people within a household is found to be under 2 (1.98 and 1.12) for both types of household. Consistent with this finding, the workforce participation rate is likely to be lower in female-headed households. Although the percentage of the working-age population (ages 15–64) is roughly the same for both types, the distortion in the age-gender structure leads female-headed households to have a lower level of workforce participation. The lower level of workforce participation of women in Turkey (SIS, 1988; SIS, 1992; World Bank, 1993), and the female-dominant gender structure of households headed by females, are the underlying reasons for this lower level of participation. In fact, the overall percentage of people who are not in the workforce in Turkey is quite high, partly because of the intensity of rural-urban migration, and partly on account of the increase in schooling, based in years (Gokdere, 1978; Martin, 1990). The tendency to take education to a higher level seems to be more pronounced for households headed by males. In relation to working status, the percentage of people who work for wages in male-headed households is much higher than in female-headed households. The main reasons behind the increase in the percentage of non-wage workers in female-headed households may be the considerable increase in the percentage of the elderly population, and the decrease in the number of working-age males in these households.

**Table 10.4: Economic Characteristics of Households by Gender of Household Heads**

| Variables | Male-headed Households | Female-headed Households | Total |
|---|---|---|---|
| **Number of People in Workforce** | | | |
| 0 | 10.5 | 51.1 | 14.5 |
| 1 | 51.4 | 26.9 | 49.0 |
| 2 | 23.2 | 14.4 | 22.3 |
| 3+ | 14.9 | 7.6 | 14.2 |
| Mean Number of Working People | 1.98 | 1.12 | 1.92 |
| **Working Status (%)** | | | |
| Not in the Workforce | 60.6 | 70.2 | 61.2 |
| Wage-Worker | 24.6 | 14.6 | 23.9 |
| Non-Wage Worker | 14.8 | 15.2 | 14.8 |
| Average Number of Income Earners | 2.12 | 1.70 | 2.09 |
| Number of Earners per Worker | 1.07 | 1.52 | 1.09 |
| Number of Dependents per Earner | 1.33 | 0.76 | 1.29 |
| **Social Security Status of the Hsehld (%)** | | | |
| No Security | 31.6 | 42.4 | 32.7 |
| Only Indirect | 2.9 | 24.9 | 4.8 |
| Only Direct | 18.4 | 13.2 | 18.0 |
| Direct and Indirect | 47.1 | 21.0 | 44.5 |

*Source:* 1988 TPHS; 1994 HICES.

The average number of breadwinners in male-headed households is significantly higher than in female-headed ones as a result of the lower average number of working people in female-headed households. The increase observed in the number of earners may be due to the increase in the percentage of wage workers, but this is not borne out by the data used by this study. Although the labor-force participation rate in female-headed households is lower than in male-headed households, the earner-worker ratio is higher. This result implies two important characteristics of female-headed households. First, the majority of working people in female-headed households work as wage-workers; and, second, female-headed households have a larger number of people who are out of the workforce, but who have a certain income in the form of a pension or remittance. The 1994 HICES results show that there is an excess in the number of earners over the number of workers, which appears to be connected with the increase in the number of persons who have unearned-income, such as interest-dividend, rents, and transfers. This process seems to be more pronounced for female-headed households, where the dependent-earner ratio is 0.76, compared to 1.33 for male-headed households. This indicates that the economic burden on earners in male-headed households is considerably heavier than in female-headed ones.

In terms of the structure of social security in these households, there are significant differences. Approximately one-fourth of female-headed households house people who have only indirect social security. This figure implies that about 25 percent of female-headed households depend on people who have direct social security and who do not live in the same household. In male-headed households, the corresponding figure is only 2.9 percent. Approximately half of male-headed households include people who have direct and indirect social security (whereas the corresponding figure for female-headed households is only 21.0 percent).

## Differentials in Income-generating Activities and Consumption Expenditures

### *Income-generating Activities*

In terms of the level of income, a simple comparison of the average household income[4] leads us to conclude that female-headed households have a lower household income than male-headed households. Overall, the mean household income of male-headed households is approximately 32 percent higher. Although the differential in household incomes shows a decrease in terms of the standardized household income,[5] it also confirms that the average household income of female-headed households is 15 percent lower than that of households headed by males. On the other hand, the results of the average adjusted household income, which were calculated by using per capita income and standardized per capita income measures, lessen the impact of the conclusion reached with the average household income. When adjusted household income measures are taken into account, we note, surprisingly, that the income levels in female-headed households are considerably better adjusted than those in male-headed households (Table 10.5). Moreover, the standardized per capita income in female-headed households, which was standardized by the household size distribution of male-headed households, is much higher than that of male-headed households.

**Table 10.5: Mean Household Income and Per capita Income by Gender of Household Heads[6]**

| Variables | Male-headed Households | Female-headed Households | Total |
|---|---|---|---|
| **Household Income** | | | |
| TL | 14,065,562 | 10,650,024 | 1.32 |
| USD | 366.1 | 277.2 | 1.32 |
| **Household Income (Standardized)** | | | |
| TL | 14,065,562 | 11,841,044 | 1.15 |
| USD | 366.1 | 308.2 | 1.15 |
| **Per capita Income** | | | |
| TL | 2,843,080 | 3,523,114 | 0.81 |
| USD | 74.0 | 91.7 | 0.81 |
| **Per capita Income (Standardized)** | | | |
| TL | 2,843,080 | 4,053,310 | 0.70 |
| USD | 74.0 | 105.5 | 0.70 |

*Source:* 1994 HICES.

When the patterns of income-generating activities are examined in two separate groups, as income in cash and income in kind[7] (Table 10.6), the share of income in cash of total income is much higher than the percentage of income in kind for both types of household. The share of cash income is approximately 91.1 percent for male-headed households, as against approximately 81.8 percent for female-headed households. The share of income in kind for female-headed households (18.2 percent) is thus approximately two times higher than that of male-headed households (8.9 percent). As seen in Table 10.6, rent money represents the highest proportion of income in kind for both types of household. The reason for this is that imputed rents,[8] applicable to the dwelling unit occupied by the household, are assumed to be the rental charges and are therefore shown in kind income. The considerably higher percentage of income earned in kind observed for female-headed households, on the other hand, seems to be related to the higher percentage of housing ownership.

**Table 10.6: Percentage Distribution of Income Types by Gender of Household Heads**

| Variables | Male-headed Households | Female-headed Households | Total |
|---|---|---|---|
| Income Types | | | |
| Income in Cash | 91.08 | 81.76 | 90.45 |
| Wages and Salaries | 23.79 | 15.83 | 23.26 |
| Entrepreneurial | 53.30 | 22.27 | 51.21 |
| *Agriculture* | *23.36* | *14.64* | *22.77* |
| *Trade* | *13.76* | *2.56* | *13.00* |
| *Services* | *7.56* | *3.00* | *7.26* |
| *Non-Agric.* | *8.62* | *2.07* | *8.18* |
| Rent | 3.20 | 7.67 | 3.50 |
| Interest-dividend | 1.75 | 2.82 | 1.82 |
| Transfers | 9.04 | 33.16 | 10.67 |
| *Government* | *7.52* | *16.22* | *8.10* |
| *Abroad* | *0.82* | *11.40* | *1.54* |
| *Other* | *0.70* | *5.54* | *1.03* |
| Income in Kind | 8.92 | 18.24 | 9.55 |
| Wages and Salaries | 0.82 | 0.66 | 0.81 |
| Entrepreneurial | 0.24 | 0.16 | 0.24 |
| *Agriculture* | *0.06* | *0.07* | *0.06* |
| *Trade* | *0.08* | *0.00* | *0.08* |
| *Services* | *0.04* | *0.05* | *0.04* |
| *Non-agric.* | *0.06* | *0.04* | *0.06* |
| Rent | 7.72 | 17.05 | 8.35 |
| Transfers | 0.14 | 0.37 | 0.16 |

*Source:* 1994 HICES.

In terms of income in cash, the percentage of cash earned from factor incomes[9] is the highest source of income in both types of household. The results indicate that the highest factor income for both types of household is the entrepreneurial group, followed by wages and salaries. Of total income in cash, 90.1 percent for male-headed households and 59.4 percent for female-headed households consists of factor incomes. This finding implies that female-headed households have a considerably lower level of factor incomes. When the pattern of factor incomes is examined, the share of entrepreneurial incomes[10] in total income has a tendency to be much higher for male-headed households. The proportion of this type of income out of the total is 53.3 percent for households headed by males, as opposed to 22.3 percent for female-headed households. The percentages of entrepreneurial incomes that are obtained from agriculture, trade, services, and non-agricultural activities are also found to be higher in male-headed households.

Within the entrepreneurial group, agricultural incomes come first for both types of household, while services for male-headed households and non-agricultural incomes for female headed households come last. It is interesting to note that the proportions of rent and interest-dividend incomes are much higher for female-headed households. This tendency is more pronounced for income obtained from rent. The lower level of wages and salaries observed for female-headed households appears to stem from the lower level of workforce participation in members of these households. The proportion of transfer incomes[11] in cash for female-headed households (33.2 percent) is much higher than for male-headed households (9.0 percent). The transfers from the government represent the highest proportion, while transfers from other sources represent the lowest proportions out of income received from transfers. When the proportion of transfers from abroad is considered, we see that 11.4 percent of income generated by female-headed households is obtained from abroad, while the corresponding figure is found to be less than one percent for male-headed households. This finding shows that an important part of income received by households headed by females comes from abroad. This testifies to the fact that the male outward migration that occurred between the 1960s and 1970s had a considerable effect on the prevalence and welfare status of female-headed households.

Table 10.7 gives the percentage distribution of income types (regardless of whether in cash or in kind) for both types of household. The percentage of wages and salaries, agriculture, trade, services, and non-agricultural incomes in male-headed households has a tendency to be higher than in female-headed ones. Incomes obtained from rent, interest-dividends, and especially transfers (from government, from abroad, and from other sources) are, on the other hand, much higher in female-headed households. The higher percentage of transfer income out of their total income shows that women are dependent on the transfers from government and especially from abroad. It is seen that the combination of cash and kind incomes has no significant effect on the differences in the distribution of income sources for either type of household. However, the amount of income received by female-headed households from rent and transfers is significantly higher, and differences in the source of the income seem to be much clearer, as a result of the combination of cash and kind incomes.

Table 10.7 also provides a clearer picture of the differentials in income-generating activities between the two types of household. It indicates that more than one-third of the total income generated by female-headed households is received from transfers, the corresponding figure being only 9.2 percent for male-headed households. When incomes obtained from transfers, interest-dividends, and rent are examined together, the proportion of these non-earned incomes, out of the total income, increases to approximately 61.1 percent for female-headed households, whereas the figure is only about 21.9 percent for male-headed ones. The reasons behind the higher level of non-earned income in female-headed households may be partly due to differences in the level of workforce participation rates between the two types of household, and to the dominance of elderly people in these households, as discussed earlier. The typical female head must manage to provide an income and carry out welfare-enhancing household activities. With only one person fulfilling both roles, time constraints are likely to limit the number of hours devoted to either category of activity. As we have already shown (Koç, 1997), female heads are less likely to be employed than their male counterparts (20.5 percent versus 80.8 percent in 1994). Income-generating activities in households headed by females are thus less common. The data suggest that the need for female heads to work is lessened by the higher remittances that they receive: non-earned income reduces workforce participation. Moreover, households headed by females receive more in the form of non-earned income than earned income, as Tables 10.6 and 10.7 show.

**Table 10.7: Percentage Distribution of Income Types (Cash or Kind) by Gender of Household Heads**

| Variables | Male-headed Households | Female-headed Households | Total |
|---|---|---|---|
| **Income Types** | | | |
| Wages and Salaries | 24.61 | 16.49 | 24.07 |
| Entrepreneurial Income | 53.53 | 22.43 | 51.45 |
| *Agriculture* | *23.41* | *14.71* | *22.83* |
| *Trade* | *13.84* | *2.56* | *13.08* |
| *Services* | *7.60* | *3.05* | *7.30* |
| *Non-agricultural* | *8.68* | *2.11* | *8.24* |
| Rent | 10.92 | 24.71 | 11.85 |
| Interest-dividend | 1.75 | 2.82 | 1.80 |
| Transfers | 9.19 | 33.53 | 10.83 |
| *From government* | *7.52* | *16.22* | *8.10* |
| *From abroad* | *0.83* | *11.40* | *1.54* |
| *Other* | *0.84* | *5.91* | *1.19* |
| **Total** | 100.0 | 100.0 | 100.0 |

*Source:* 1994 HICES.

### *Consumption Expenditures*

Thus far, we have considered whether the economic resources available to female-headed households differ from those of male-headed households. We now focus on how the heads use the resources available to them, and seek to answer our second question: "Do households headed by females use their resources differently than households headed by males"? There are two types of resources: time and money. This section examines the use of the second. In particular, it assesses the extent to which female- and male-headed households show different consumption levels and patterns.

**Table 10.8: Average Propensity to Consume and Per capita Consumption by Gender of Household Heads**

| Variables | Male-headed Households | Female-headed Households |
|---|---|---|
| Propensity to Consume | 77.8 | 87.9 |
| Propensity to Consume (Standardized) | 77.8 | 82.7 |
| Per capita Consumption (USD) | 57.6 | 80.6 |
| Per capita Consumption (Standardized) | 57.6 | 87.2 |

*Source:* 1994 HICES.

The average propensity to consume[12] is found to be higher in female-headed households (87.9 percent) than in male-headed ones (77.8 percent), whereas the average propensity to save is likely to be higher in male-headed households (22.2 percent) than in female-headed ones (12.1 percent), as seen in Table 10.8. This implies that households headed by females use more of their available resources in order to maintain a certain standard of living. When a standardization procedure was applied to the consumption level of female-headed households, it was observed that the average propensity to consume increased by 6 percent. As discussed above, female-headed households have a higher mean per capita income relative to male-headed households. Consistent with this finding, mean per capita consumption[13] is also found to be higher in female-headed households, even after a standardization procedure. When a comparison is made between whole figures, it is striking to note that the consumption level of female-headed households is approximately 1.4 times higher than that of the male-headed households (Table 10.8). Although most poverty experts (Ravallion, 1992; Lustig, 1993) give more credence to the per capita consumption index than to the per capita income index as an indicator of household welfare, it is hypothesized that consumption indicators are likely to be subject to gender biases that result in underestimating the poverty of female-headed households. This happens for one important reason: since female heads are often the chief earners as well as being responsible for the whole household, they are more likely to report accurate information about the household's consumption expenditures. Females in male-headed households, on the other hand, may not have complete information about household expenditures, especially about expenditures incurred by the male heads themselves. This tends to inflate the consumption level in households headed by females, and understate that of male-headed households (Horton and Miller, 1989; Louat *et al.*, 1992).

**Table 10.9: Percentage Distribution of Consumption Expenditures[14] by Gender Household Heads**

| Variable | Unadjusted | | Adjusted | |
|---|---|---|---|---|
| | Male-headed Households | Female-headed Households | Male-headed Households | Female-headed Households |
| **Consumption Expenditures** | | | | |
| Food | 32.4 | 27.5 | 36.2 | 33.0 |
| Expenditures in Restaurants | 3.6 | 2.3 | 4.0 | 2.8 |
| Clothing | 12.3 | 12.4 | 13.7 | 14.9 |
| House Furnishings | 9.5 | 9.3 | 10.6 | 11.2 |
| Goods/Services for HH Operation | 2.0 | 2.8 | 2.2 | 3.4 |
| Health | 2.6 | 2.1 | 2.9 | 2.5 |
| Personal Care | 0.8 | 1.0 | 0.9 | 1.2 |
| Transportation and Communication | 9.9 | 4.9 | 11.1 | 5.9 |
| Education, Culture, & Entertainment | 4.6 | 4.8 | 5.1 | 5.8 |
| Housing | 21.0 | 30.1 | 10.5 | 16.6 |
| Other | 3.2 | 2.9 | 3.6 | 3.5 |
| **Total** | 100.0 | 100.0 | 100.0 | 100.0 |

*Source:* 1994 HICES.

As Table 10.9 demonstrates, male- and female-headed households display different patterns of consumption. In addition, we observe a marked difference in the percentage distribution of available sources. The table shows that, in 1994, in terms of the percentage distribution of unadjusted consumption expenditures,[15] expenditure on food in male-headed households holds first place (32.4 percent), whereas housing occupies that position in female-headed households (30.1 percent). However, when adjusted consumption expenditures[16] are examined, housing expenditures are relegated to second place in households headed by females (16.6 percent), and food expenditures hold first place for male-headed and female-headed households alike (36.2 percent and 33.0 percent, respectively).

The unadjusted and adjusted consumption expenditures indicate that food expenditure is considerably higher in male-headed households, whereas housing expenditure is much higher in female-headed ones. Expenditure on clothing, which holds second place for male-headed households with 13.7 percent and third place for female-headed households with 14.9 percent, and expenditure on household furnishings, which holds fourth place for both types of household with 10.6 percent and 11.2 percent, respectively, are likely to be slightly higher in female-headed households. Expenditure on transportation and communication is in third place with 11.1 percent, and that on housing in fifth place with 10.5 percent, for male-headed households. Expenditures for personal care are in last place with approximately 1 percent for both types of household.

As seen in Table 10.10,[17] male- and female-headed households have very similar consumption patterns. Expenditures for both types may be arranged, in order of importance, as follows: food (food goods, restaurants, and other similar places); housing (household furnishings, goods and services for the maintenance of the household); clothing; transportation/communication; education/culture/entertainment; other household expenditures; health; and personal care. Since the imputed rents have not been included in the housing charges, the exclusion of this item relegates these expenditures to the second rank with 31.2 percent for female-headed households. Although a similar consumption pattern is observed, the proportion of consumption expenditures out of total expenditures is considerably different for the two types of household.

Expenditures on food, health, and transportation/communication are likely to be higher in male-headed households (Table 10.10). The relatively lower share of food expenditures observed in female-headed households may stem from the underreporting of home-made foods in these households, a tendency noted by Lauat (1992) with respect to Latin American countries. Lauat found that the amount of home-made foods out of the total food consumption tended to be higher for female-headed households, and that these households generally understated these consumption expenditures. For this reason, it may be useful to examine the coverage of food expenditures. When these are examined in detail, it can be seen that expenditures for cigarettes and alcoholic beverages are included in it. Once these two items are excluded, as Table 10.10 reveals, the share of expenditure on food, as a proportion of total expenditure, is slightly higher (32.7 percent) in households headed by females is than in households headed by males (31.9 percent).

The lower share of transportation/communication expenditures in female-headed households may relate to the mobility constraints that their members experience as a result of the lack of adult males and an excess of elderly people (Koç, 1997). On the other hand, these households tend to spend more on clothing, housing, personal care, education, culture, and entertainment. The higher percentage of expenditures on, in particular, food, clothing, housing, and education observed in female-headed households (32.7 percent,

14.9 percent, 31.2 percent, and 5.8 percent as opposed to 31.9 percent, 13.7 percent, 23.3 percent, and 5.1 percent) clearly indicates that the needs of the household and of children are more likely to receive priority in female-headed households.

**Table 10.10: Percentage Distribution of Adjusted Consumption Expenditures and their Rank Order by Gender of Household Heads**

| Variable | Male-headed Households | Rank Order | Female-headed Households | Rank Order |
|---|---|---|---|---|
| Consumption Expenditures | | | | |
| Food | 40.2 | 1 | 35.8 | 1 |
| *Food* | *31.9* | | *32.7* | |
| *Cigarettes and alcoholic beverages* | *9.3* | | *3.1* | |
| Clothing | 13.7 | 3 | 14.9 | 3 |
| House | 23.3 | 2 | 31.2 | 2 |
| Health | 2.9 | 7 | 2.5 | 7 |
| Personal Care | 0.9 | 8 | 1.2 | 8 |
| Transportation and Communication | 11.1 | 4 | 5.9 | 4 |
| Education, Culture, and Entertain. | 5.1 | 5 | 5.8 | 5 |
| Other | 3.6 | 6 | 3.5 | 6 |
| **Total** | 100.0 | - | 100.0 | - |

*Source:* 1994 HICES.

## Conclusion and Policy Implications

In this chapter, we have examined the considerable increase in female-headed households that Turkey has experienced over the past 45 years. During a 45-year life span, the proportion of households headed by women rose by approximately 65 percent, from 6.1 percent of the total households in 1950 to 11 percent in 1994. Within this context, our aim has been to examine three different, but closely interrelated, policy issues concerning female headship. The first addresses the economic circumstances of households headed by females: Are female-headed households more likely to be impoverished than male-headed households? The second looks at the patterns of income sources and consumption expenditures: Do households headed by females generate/use their resources differently than households headed by males? And the third, arising out of concerns about the targeting process, asks: Do female-headed households warrant extra government attention?

In relation to the welfare status of a household, a simple comparison of unadjusted average household incomes of female- and male-headed households leads us to conclude that households headed by females have a considerably lower household income than households headed by males. If, however, we compare adjusted household incomes, calculated by using standardized and per capita measures, the force of the earlier conclusion is greatly diminished. In fact, when the average adjusted household income is taken into account, households headed by females would not generally be considered poor.

Results show that the pattern of generation and use of the economic resources available to them differ markedly in the two types of household. In terms of income generation, although cash income represents the majority of the total income for both types, households headed by females are less likely to have a large income in cash. When all economic resources are examined, regardless of income types, it is observed that households headed by females have lower incomes from wages/salaries and entrepreneurial activities and higher incomes from rent, interest-dividends, and especially transfers. The lower level of incomes from wages/salaries and entrepreneurial activities is related primarily to the lower level of workforce participation in female-headed households. This appears to be the result of a lower level of education, the generally older age of female heads, and the time constraints under which they operate. The higher portion of income from rent, interest-dividends, and transfers seems to originate from the elderly-dominant age structure of female-headed households. The extremely high level of transfer incomes in female-headed households shows that these households are dependent on transfers from the government and from abroad.

In relation to the use of the resources, as revealed by the adjusted consumption expenditures, female- and male-headed households have very similar patterns of consumption. However, the proportions of consumption expenditures differ considerably. The proportion of consumption expenditures on food, clothing, housing, personal care, and education/culture/entertainment is likely to be higher in female-headed households—an indication that the needs of households and children are more likely to be prioritized in these households. This emphasis is reflected in the higher levels of housing quality and welfare status of children observed in households headed by females. As regards consumption levels, the average propensity to consume is likely to be higher in female-headed households, since females tend to invest in their households and children. Thus, the level of per capita consumption in households headed by females is found to be approximately 1.4 times higher than in households headed by males.

These important welfare differentials between the two types of household, and the higher level of unmet needs in terms of access to education, social security, employment, and income in female-headed households, have certain policy implications, which may be worth taking into consideration within the context of this study:

- It should be recognized that large-scale programs that fail to take into account the differentials in household levels may not reach those in need. Five-year development plans that were designed implicitly for male-headed households will not give the desired results. Female-headed households should also be considered as an integral part of future programs.
- Our findings suggest that the gender of household heads could be used as a policy tool to identify vulnerable groups in society. Since a major problem in the targeting process is to identify the vulnerable groups, particularly in the context of developing countries (O'Laughlin, 1994), policy makers concerned with ending poverty might like to consider singling out female-headed households as a key target group, deserving of added attention, by using the findings of this study.
- The study shows, further, that female-headed households are not a homogeneous group. Some female-headed households are not only as well-off as male-headed households, but are even better-off because of a particularly important economic supplement: remittances. This finding suggests that female-headed households are, on average, a vulnerable group, but that some of them are relatively well provided for (i.e., households headed by currently married women). Others, the majority, are very poor indeed (i.e., households headed by formerly married women), and this subset is quite vulnerable. This situation should also be taken into account in

the targeting process, because focusing only on the gender of the individual identified as the household head may in fact be misleading.

- The evidence shows that there are differences between the welfare status of children in female- and male-headed households in terms of the children's level of education and their workforce participation. Children in female-headed households have higher school attendance records, and lower workforce participation rates, even though households headed by women need to earn extra money. Although the worse-off situation of children living in male-headed households may be of some policy concern, the main policy implication of the study is that a special intervention for girls in both types of household is needed, given their tendency to stay out of school. This is important in the long-run development of Turkey, as a means of human capital formation.
- Female-headed households are a heterogeneous group also in terms of the welfare status of children. Children living in households headed by currently married women have a better level of education than children living in households headed by formerly married women. Since it is likely that women's desire to invest in their children does not vary according to marital status, the negative impact of female headship on children's welfare in households headed by formerly married female heads may be due to the fact that these women heads face greater constraints to realize their preferences. In order to minimize these obstacles, women need to be equipped with the means to achieve autonomy, such as a higher level of education and of participation in the workforce, which in turn would have an impact on the welfare status of their households and their children.
- Female-headed households have lower social security and a higher elderly dependency ratio than male-headed households. This finding suggests that female-headed households need a special social security intervention program, which would target and support the elderly people found within their households.
- In the literature, three main approaches are proposed for raising the welfare of vulnerable groups (Hollis, 1974). The first is to redirect investment to vulnerable groups in the form of education and access to credit and public facilities; the second is to redistribute income to vulnerable groups through the fiscal system or through the direct allocation of consumer goods; and the third is to transfer existing assets to vulnerable groups to make them more productive. The advantages and limitations of each strategy will vary according to the circumstances of the country concerned. In relation to Turkey, some elements of each of these approaches may be applicable, depending on the initial economic and social structure. The approach of the redistribution of income to vulnerable groups can be used for short-term purposes, but it is known that female-headed households in Turkey also need long-term investment. Particular emphasis should therefore be given to directing public investment to raise the productive capacity and income of female-headed households in the long run.
- In view of the increase in the percentage of female headship in Turkey in the period 1988–94, we may assume that this trend will continue. In fact, projections[18] show a percentage increase of approximately 15 percent at the beginning of the twenty-first century. The increased frequency of female headship, together with the

higher level of women's unmet needs as regards access to education, employment, social security, and income, makes clear the need for further studies on the determinants of female headship in Turkey. This chapter has presented a profile of the lives, characteristics, and problems of such households. Further studies are required in order to shed more light on other important aspects of these women's lives. For example, future studies should seek to determine the level of support needed both on a national level and locally. Finally, a household database is required so as to provide information on family formation patterns and to facilitate the follow-up of changing living conditions and household structures over time. In this way, it would be possible to assess the success of social policies and programs aimed at assuring welfare, security, and stability for these households, and to adjust such policies as necessary.

## Notes

1 Information on the gender of household heads included by censuses conducted during 1950–70 was based on the usual residents, while information on the gender of household heads included by censuses conducted during 1975–90 was based on both usual residents and non-usual residents. Since the person named as head of the household was not necessarily a usual member of the household in the censuses conducted between 1975 and 1990, the number of households headed by females was underestimated in the censuses carried out in this period.

2 Our study uses a modified version of the household typology suggested by Hammel and Laslett (1974). Family patterns are classified as follows: simple family, extended family, multiple family, one-parent family, solitary, and no family. Simple family refers to the nuclear family, which means man-wife family or man-wife-child(ren) family. Extended family and multiple family refer to a group of kin beyond the nucleus of husband, wife, and/or their children. The extended family and the multiple family are differentiated by the number of marital units in the household, a multiple family comprising more than one marital unit. One-parent consists of a widowed, divorced, unmarried, or married (partner absent) mother or father with his/her child(ren). Solitary refers to a one-person household of either gender. No family consists of unrelated persons.

3 The Complexity Index is a measure that refers to the marital units per household, where the number of marital units is defined as the number of married males, plus the number of widowed and divorced males and females. The reasoning behind this measure is as follows: if all persons marry, and all married couples are represented by the number of married males, and all widowed and divorced persons maintain separate residences, the number of marital units would be equal to the number of households and their ratio would be one. A ratio of marital units greater than one indicates doubling up and thus household complexity.

4 Household income includes all incomes received monthly by household members, irrespective of their working status or occupation.

5 In view of the differences in household size and household composition between male- and female-headed households, two adjustment procedures were employed in the study: the direct standardization technique and adult equivalence scales. Household size distribution of male-headed households is taken as a standard distribution, and direct standardization technique, which is commonly used in demographic literature, is used in order to make comparison possible between the household incomes of these two groups. In the absence of adult equivalence scales developed for Turkey, adult equivalence scales suggested by Deaton and Muellbauer (1986) are used in the present study, on the assumption that this procedure can reflect the

consumption patterns of the Turkish population. This scale assumes that additional household members, particularly children, are less costly, in the sense of requiring less additional consumption to maintain the welfare level of the household. In these measures, the 'cost' of additional members is defined in terms of fractions of adults. They assign a weight of 0.2 to children 0–6 years, 0.3 to children 7–12 years, and 0.5 to children 13–17 years. Persons over age 17 have a weight of one. Since both the techniques produced very similar results, the results obtained by the direct standardization technique are the ones we have used in the study (Table 10.5).

6 One USD was equivalent to 38,420 TL in 1994 (SIS, 1995).

7 Income in cash is the income received in terms of cash by the household members; income in kind is the income received in kind by the household members. The sales price at the nearest market to the household is used for the valuation of the latter. All definitions used in this chapter are obtained from 1994 Household Income and Consumption Expenditures Survey (SIS, 1997b).

8 Imputed rent is the amount of rent which would normally be paid by a household regardless of the fact that it owns the residence that it occupies or is living in a free lodging.

9 Factor incomes consist of wages and salaries, profits (entrepreneurial incomes), rental (real estate incomes), and interest (share and bonds) incomes.

10 Entrepreneurial income is the income obtained by the entrepreneurs from agriculture, trade, services, and non-agricultural activities.

11 Transfer incomes refer to non-earned incomes received in cash or in kind by any member of the household, from the state, private sector enterprises, or abroad.

12 Average propensity to consume, a ratio of total consumption expenditures to total income, shows the percentage of total income used for consumption expenditures. The inverse of the average propensity to consume equals the average propensity to save.

13 Mean per capita consumption (PCC) is calculated by using the following equation. PCC=(PCI × APTC)/100; where PCI refers to the mean per capita income (Table 10.5), where APTC refers to the average propensity to consume (Table 10.8).

14 Household consumption covers all purchases paid in cash or on installments during the month in which the survey was conducted for goods and services in terms of food, restaurants, clothing, maintenance, health, transportation, communication, culture, education, entertainment, housing, and other needs. Definitions of these expenditures are as follows:

- Food expenditures comprise expenditures incurred by the household for: bread and cereals; meat, fish and poultry; fats, oils, milk, dairy products and eggs; pulses, dried fruits; fresh vegetables; fresh fruits; processed food products; tobacco products, and liquors and beverages.
- Expenditures in restaurants and similar places cover meals and drinks (alcoholic and non-alcoholic beverages) consumed outside the household. Foods purchased from restaurants, pastry shops, and similar places and consumed at home are also in this category.
- Clothing expenditures are divided into four main groups: men's clothing, ladies' clothing, children's clothing, and fabrics. These groups include all fabrics, tailoring, and clothing accessories.
- Household furnishings and goods and services for household operation cover electrical and non-electrical appliances, furniture, cleaning materials, kitchen and household utensils, and other goods and service for the maintenance of the household.
- Health expenditures are the expenditures for medical goods and services including medical insurance. Medical services and assistance covered by the employer are not included in this group.

- Personal care expenditures cover all goods and services for personal care.
- Transportation and communication expenditures cover transportation expenditures (local, inter-city, and abroad) and communication expenditures. The expenditures for private motor vehicles are also included in this group.
- Cultural, educational, and entertainment expenditures encompass all expenditures incurred by household members for their cultural, educational, and entertainment needs.
- Housing expenditures cover expenditures of the household for rent (including imputed rent), electricity, gas, water, and heating.
- Other expenditures are the expenditures other than those listed above. All financial documentation charges, death and burial costs, tuition fees to associations, out-of-pocket payments, and religious payments (other than sacrificial and votive ones) are in this category.

15 Unadjusted consumption expenditures include the imputed rent.

16 Adjusted consumption expenditures exclude the imputed rent.

17 In Table 10.10, expenditures on food and for restaurants and similar places are put into one category under the heading food expenditures; and expenditures on house furnishings, and goods and services for household and housing, are put together as house expenditures in order to provide a clearer picture of the pattern of consumption expenditures.

18 The projection of percentage shares of households by gender of heads is done by using a modified exponential formula which was suggested by Kono (1981):

$$p_{(j,t+m)} = 1 - [1 - p_{(j,\,t-n)}] \cdot \left[\frac{1 - p_{(j,t)}}{1 - p_{(j,\,t-n)}}\right]^{\frac{(t+m)-(t-n)}{n}}$$

Where *p (j, t+m)* denotes the percentage share of the households by gender of head *j* in year *t+m*, *m* years after *t* of the last survey; *p (j, t)* denotes the percentage share in year *t*, the year of the last survey; *p (j, t-n)* denotes the percentage share in year *t-n*, and *n*, years before the last survey.

## References


Abadan, N. 1964. *Bati Almanya'daki Turk Iscileri ve Problemleri* (Turkish Workers and Their Problems in FRG). Published by State Planning Organization, Ankara.

Abadan-Unat, N. 1976. "Turkish Workers to Europe," in N. Abadan-Unat (ed.), *Turkish Workers in Europe 1960–1975*. Leiden: E.J. Brill.

Akgunduz, A. 1995."Labour Migration from Turkey to Western Europe." *Revue Européenne des Migrations Internationales*, Vol. 11, No. 1.

Barros, R., L. Fox, and R. Mendonca. 1994. "Female-headed Households, Poverty and the Welfare of Children in Urban Brazil," Policy Research Working Paper No. 1275. Washington, DC: The World Bank Policy Research Department Office.

Becker, G. 1981. *A Treatise on the Family*. Cambridge: Harvard University Press.

Braydon, L., and S. Chant. 1989. *Women in the Third World: Gender Issues in Rural and Urban Areas*. Cheltenham, England: Edward Elgar.

Buvinic, M. 1990. "The Vulnerability of Women-headed Households: Policy Questions and Options for Latin America and the Caribbean." Paper presented at Conference on Vulnerable Women, United Nations, Economic Commission for Latin America and the Caribbean, Vienna, 26–30 November.

———, N.H. Youssef, and B. Von Elm. 1978. "Women-headed Households: The Ignored Factor in Development Planning." Working Paper No. 1593. International Center for Research on Women, Washington, DC.

Deaton, A., and J. Muellbauer. 1986. "On Measuring Child Cost: with Application to Poor Countries," *Journal of Political Economy*, Vol. 94, No. 4, 33–42.

DeGraff, D.S., and R.E. Bilsborrow. 1992. "Female-headed Households and Family Welfare in Rural Ecuador." Paper presented at the meeting of the Population Association of America. Denver, CO, 30 April–2 May.

De Vos, S. 1992. "A Preliminary Demographic View of Change 1970–1980 in Unmarried Mothers 15–49 Heading their Own Households in Brazil." Paper presented at the meeting of the Population Association of America. Denver, CO, 30 April–2 May. Folbre, N. 1990. "Families Maintained by Women Alone: Policy Issues for Developing Countries." Report prepared for "Project on Female Headship," Population Council/International Center for Research on Women (mimeo).

Gitmez, A. 1984. "Geographical and Occupational Re-integration of Returning Turkish Workers," in D. Kubat (ed.), *The Politics of Return*. New York, N.Y: Center for Migration Studies.

Gokdere, A. 1978. The Labor-Force Flow to Foreign Countries and its Impact on Turkish Economy. Ankara: Türkiye Is Bankasi, 29–56.

———. 1994. "An Evaluation of Turkey's Recent Migration Flows and Stocks," *The Turkish Journal of Population Studies*, Vol. 16.

Hacettepe University Institute of Population Studies. 1980. "Turkish Fertility Survey, 1978, First Report." *Vol. I: Methodology and Findings*. Ankara: HIPS.

———. 1987. *1983 Turkish Population and Health Survey*. Ankara: HIPS.

———. 1989. *1988 Turkish Population and Health Survey*. Ankara: HIPS.

———. 1994. *1993 Turkish Demographic and Health Survey*. Ankara: HIPS.

Hammel, E.A., and P. Laslett. 1974. "Comparing Household Structure Over Time and Between Cultures." *Comparative Studies in Society and Culture*, Vol. 16, No. 1, 11–26.

Hancioglu, A. 1985. "Family Types and Household Size in Turkey in 1978." M.A. thesis, Hacettepe University Institute of Population Studies, Ankara.

Harris, O.1981. "Households as Natural Units" in K. Young, C. Wokowitz and R. McCullagh (eds.), *Of Marriage and Market*. London, U.K.: Routledge and Kegan Paul.

Hetler, C.B. 1983. "Establishing the economic Condition of Women-headed Households in the Third World: A New Approach," in M. Buvinic, M.A. Lycette, and W.P. McGreevy (eds.), *Women and Poverty in the Third World*. Baltimore, MD: Johns Hopkins University Press.

Hollis, C. 1974. *Redistribution with Growth*. Oxford: Oxford University Press.

Horton, S., and B.D. Miller. 1989. "The Effect of Gender of Household Head on Food Expenditures: Evidence from Low-Income Households in Jamaica." Paper presented at Conference on Family, Gender Differences, and Development, Yale University. 13–15 July.

Kiray, M. 1976. "The Family of the Immigrant Worker," in N. Abadan-Unat (ed.), *Turkish Workers in Europe 1960–1975*. Leiden: E.J. Brill.

Koç, İ. 1996. "Changing Family Patterns and Living Arrangements in Turkey (1978–1993)." Paper presented at 30th Annual Conference of German Society for Population Studies, Luxembourg, 11–12 April.

———. 1997. "Analysis of Female-headed Households in Turkey with Special Emphasis on the Welfare Status of these Households." Ph.D. thesis, Hacettepe University Institute of Population Studies, Ankara (unpublished).

———.1998. "Welfare Status of Households Headed by Women: Policy Implications in Turkey." *Forum*, Vol. 5. No.1, 18–20.

Koç, İ, and A. Toros. 1997. "A Historical Analysis of the Life Expectancy at Birth in Turkey, 1900–1993." (unpublished manuscript).

Kono, S. 1985. "The Headship Rate Method for Projecting Households," in J Bongaarts, T. Burch, and K. Wachter (eds.), *Family Demography: Methods and Their Applications*. Oxford and New York: Oxford University Press.

Kudat, A. 1974. "The Changing Composition of Europe's Guestworker Population," *Monthly Labor Review*, 103: 10–17.
Kuznets, P. 1978. "Size and Age Structure of Family Households: Exploratory Comparisons," *Population and Development Review*, Vol. 5, No. 4, 15–28.
Lloyd, C.B., and A. Brandon. 1991. "Women's Role in Maintaining Households: Family Welfare and Gender Inequality in Ghana." Working Paper No. 26. Washington, DC: Population Council/International Center for Research on Women.
———. 1993. "Women's Role in Maintaining Households: Family Welfare and Sexual Inequality in Ghana," *Population Studies*, Vol. 47, No. 1, 47–56.
———. 1996. "Children's Schooling in Sub-Saharan Africa: The Role of Fathers, Mothers and Others," *Population and Development Review*, Vol. 22, No. 2, 51–64.
Louat, F., M.E. Grosh, and J. van der Gaag. 1992. "Welfare Implications of Female Headship in Jamaican Households." Paper presented at International Food Policy Research Institute Workshop on "Interhousehold Resource Allocation: Policy Issues," Washington, DC, 21–23 April.
Lustig, N. 1993. "Measuring Poverty in Latin America: The Emperor Has No Clothes." Paper presented at the conference "Poverty: New Approaches to Analysis and Policy," International Institute for Labor Studies, Geneva, 22–24 November.
Martin, P.L. 1990. "An Assessment of Turkish Labor Migration to Western Europe." Working Paper No. 45. International Labor Organization World Employment Program. Geneva: ILO.
O'Laughlin, B. 1994 "Targeting the Poor under Structural Adjustment: The Case of Food Subsidies." Teaching text, Population and Development Program. The Hague: Institute of Social Studies/Netherlands Interdisciplinary Demographic Institute.
Penninx, R. 1982. "A Critical Review of Theory and Practice. The Case of Turkey," *International Migration Review*, Vol. 16, 21–34.
———, and Velzen, L. 1976. *A Contribution to the Theory on International Migration: The Export of Manpower from a Rural District in Central Turkey*. Report prepared for the Netherlands Universities Foundation for International Cooperation, Institute for Social Research in Developing Countries, The Hague.
Ravallion, M. 1992. "Poverty Comparisons: A Guide to Concepts and Methods," *Living Standards Measurement Study*, World Bank Working Paper No. 88. Washington, DC: World Bank.
Rosenhouse, S. 1988 "Identifying the Poor: Is Headship A Useful Concept?" Paper presented at seminar on "Determinants and the Consequences of Female–Headed Households," International Center for Research on Women/Population Council, New York, 12–13 December.
State Institute of Statistics (SIS). 1961a. *1950 Census of Population*, Publication No. 410. Istanbul: SIS.
———. 1961b. *1955 Census of Population*, Publication No. 399. Istanbul: SIS.
———. 1963. *1960 Census of Population*, Publication No. 452. Ankara: SIS.
———. 1969. *1965 Census of Population: Social and Economic Characteristics of Population*, Publication No. 568. Ankara: SIS.
———. 1977. *1970 Census of Population: Social and Economic Characteristics of Population*, Publication No. 756, Ankara: SIS.
———. 1988. *Statistical Yearbook 1987*, Publication No. 143. Ankara: SIS.
———. 1992. *Statistical Yearbook 1991*, Publication No. 210. Ankara: SIS.
———.1995. *Turkey in Statistics 1996*, Publication No: 1983. Ankara: SIS.
———.1997a. *Results of the Household Income Distribution Survey 199*. Publication No: 2051. Ankara: SIS.

———.1997b. *Household Consumption Expenditures Survey Results 1994*. Publication No. 2030. Ankara: SIS.

Timur, S. 1973. *Family Structure in Turkey*. Publication D-15. Ankara: Hacettepe University.

Townsend, J., and J. Momsen. 1987. "Toward the Geography of Gender in the Third World," in J. Momsen and J. Townsend (eds.), *Geography and Gender in the Third World*. London: Hutchinson.

United Nations. 1991. *World's Women: 1970–1990 Trends and Statistics*. New York: United Nations.

———. 1992. *1990 Demographic Yearbook*. New York: United Nations.

Unalan, T. 1986. "Some Social and Economic Characteristics of the Family Types in Turkey with Special Reference to Black Sea and Mediterranean Regions." M.A. thesis, Hacettepe University Institute of Population Studies, Ankara.

World Bank. 1993. *Turkey: Women in Development*. A World Bank Country Study. Oxford and New York: Oxford University Press.

Youssef, N.H., and C.B. Hetler. 1983. "Establishing the Economic Condition of Women Headed Households in the Third World: A New Approach" in M. Buvinic, M.A. Lycette and W.P. McGreevy (eds.), *Women and Poverty in the Third World*. Baltimore, M.D.: Johns Hopkins University Press.

# 11

# General versus Vocational High Schools and Labor Market Outcomes in Turkey

*Aysıt Tansel**

## Introduction

Recently, policy makers in Turkey have been advocating an increase in the number of vocational high schools and a streamlining of students to vocational high school training. This is seen as the panacea for the ever-growing numbers of general high school graduates who cannot be placed in a university program and must turn to the labor market without applicable work skills. As yet, there is no study that compares either the costs and benefits of vocational versus general high school education, or the labor market outcomes in terms of earnings and employment for graduates of the two programs.

The World Bank's recent policy recommendation has been in support of general secondary education (World Bank, 1995). Psacharopoulos (1987) provided evidence that the rates of return to investments in general curricula are much higher than those in vocational programs. In a later paper (Psacharapoulos, 1994), he reviewed studies where returns to general secondary schools are higher than to the vocational track and stressed that the difference in social rates of return is more dramatic because of the much higher unit cost of vocational education. Bennell (1996) challenged this view by critically examining the relative social profitability of general and vocational schooling in developing countries. He pointed out a number of more recent studies that provide evidence contrary to the established view. Moock and Bellew (1990) found that, in Peru, returns to investment in vocational schooling are comparable to those in general schooling while there were no cost differentials in their provision. Chung (1990) found higher earnings for vocational than for general education in Hong Kong. The World Bank (1990) found higher social rates of return to vocational than to general secondary schooling in Thailand. Neuman and Ziderman (1991) found, in Israel, that vocational high school graduates who are in training-related occupations earn more than general high school graduates. There is no significant difference in the earnings of vocational school graduates in occupations unrelated to the course of study and those of general school graduates. Similarly, Arriagada and Ziderman (1992) found, in Brazil, that earnings differentials favored vocational school graduates in matched occupations by 16–18 percent. The World Bank (1994) found, in rural Chile, higher returns to vocational skills than to general secondary education. The World Bank (1995) also found, in Indonesia, that although the returns to vocational and general education are about the same, the former is more expensive than the latter.

This study examines how individuals are selected into general high school, vocational high school, or other schools and the wage determination in these choices. The main objective is to provide evidence on the extent of wage differentials between general and vocational high school graduates who do not go on to higher education. The analysis is carried out for men and women separately. Individual-level survey data from the Turkish 1994 Household Expenditure Survey are used. A three-way multinominal logit model is estimated for school selection. Mincerian wage equations are estimated for each group taking school selection into account. The results obtained in this chapter reinforce recent studies in developing countries. First, when controlled for observed characteristics and sample selection, the wages of vocational high school graduate men are higher than the wages of general high school graduate men. It was not possible to make a similar comparison for women due to poor wage equation estimates for vocational high school graduate women. Second, the unemployment rate is lower among the vocational high school graduates than among the general high school graduates. Third, it is observed that, for men, private returns to vocational high schooling are higher than to general high schooling. Thus, in Turkey, vocational high schools provide greater benefits than general high schools in terms of labor market outcomes such as private rates of return to schooling, unemployment rates, and wages.

This chapter is organized as follows. First, background information on the Turkish educational system is given, together with a review of the evidence on returns to schooling. There follows an explanation of the model and the empirical specifications. The data used in the study are then described, followed by the estimation results. Implications for population policy are discussed in the penultimate section. The chapter ends with some concluding remarks.

## Turkish Educational System

The formal educational system consists of eight years of primary school, and three or four years of high school followed by various tertiary levels. Until the educational reform of August 1987, five years of compulsory primary school was the only compulsory education. In August 1997, compulsory education was extended from five to eight years to include three years of middle school. High schools include general, vocational, and technical high schools. General high schools give three or four years of training, vocational high schools three years, and technical high schools four years. Tertiary levels of schooling take place at institutions offering two-year programs or at universities offering four- to six-year programs. Formal education is provided by the government free of charge in public schools. There are private schools at all levels and in all categories except for vocational and technical high schools.

Enrollments at all levels have increased substantially during the past three decades. The primary school gross enrollment ratio was over 100 percent for both males and females in 1993. As for secondary school gross enrollment, the ratio was 50 percent for females and 74 percent for males in 1993. The tertiary gross enrollment ratio was 16 percent in 1993 (World Bank, 1997). The enrollment ratio at the general high school level is higher than that at the vocational high school level. In 1995, the enrollment ratio was 31 percent in general high schools versus 22 percent in vocational and technical high schools (State Planning Organization, 1995: 28). This indicates that students prefer general high schools to vocational and technical schools.

### *General, Vocational, and Technical High Schools*

General high schools prepare students specifically for university. Vocational and technical high schools (hereafter referred to as vocational high schools) provide vocational training whose main objective is to impart specific marketable skills. Their graduates are also eligible to participate in the university entrance examinations. There is excess demand for tertiary level schooling, and supply is restricted by two-tier competitive entrance examinations. Recently, only about 20 percent of applicants gained admittance to a program. A follow-up study of vocational high school graduates indicated that about 40–53 percent of them were attending a tertiary level of study, while 30–40 percent were preparing for the competitive examinations prior to admittance (Ministry of Education, 1997).

**Table 11.1: Distribution of High Schools, 1997–98 Academic Year**

| Characteristics | General High Schools | Vocational High Schools |
|---|---|---|
| Number of Schools | 2,555 | 3,369 |
| Number of students(in ths.) | 1,313,90 | 949.5 |
| Percent Male | 57.3 | 61.5 |
| Percent Female | 42.7 | 38.5 |
| Number of Teachers | 70,454 | 72,518 |
| Student-Teacher Ratio | 18.7 | 13.1 |

*Source:* Ministry of Education (1998: 17).

**Table 11.2: Structural Distribution of High Schools, 1997–98 Academic Year**

| | Distribution of Schools (%) | Distribution of Students (%) | Student-Teacher Ratio |
|---|---|---|---|
| **General High Schools:** | | | |
| General High School | 62.9 | 70.7 | 19.2 |
| Anadolu High School | 15.3 | 4.3 | 6.2 |
| Science High School | 1.5 | 0.6 | 12.3 |
| Fine Arts High School | 0.6 | 0.2 | 8.2 |
| Evening High School | 0.3 | 0.03 | 11.7 |
| Anadolu Teachers HS | 3.1 | 1.8 | 15.6 |
| Private High School | 16.4 | 4.3 | 5.4 |
| Distance High School | — | 18.2 | — |
| **Total** | **100** | **100** | **18.7** |
| **Total in Numbers** | **2,555** | **1,313.90 (ths.)** | — |
| **Vocational and Technical High Schools:** | | | |
| Men's Technical High School | 32.4 | 39.0 | 15.9 |
| Women's Tech. High School | 18.9 | 10.8 | 7.9 |
| Trade and Tourism High School | 19.3 | 25.0 | 22.3 |
| Religious Vocation High School | 18.0 | 18.8 | 9.5 |
| Other Vocational High School | 11.4 | 6.4 | 9.0 |
| **Total** | **100** | **100** | **13.1** |
| **Total in Numbers** | **3,369** | **949.5 (ths.)** | — |

*Source:* Ministry of Education (1998: 18–21).

Table 11.1 gives information about the distribution of general and vocational high schools. The number of schools and teachers is higher in vocational schools, while the number of students is higher in general high schools. About 42 percent of all high school students are registered in vocational high schools. Table 11.2 gives the structural distribution of the high schools. It is noteworthy that 71 percent of total high school students are in 'general high schools,' and 18 percent are in distance-learning high schools. Student-teacher ratios are lowest at the private high schools and in Anadolu high schools (see below). Of the vocational high school students, almost 40 percent are in men's technical high schools and almost 20 percent are in religious vocational high schools.

Anadolu high schools are special schools in which instruction in some courses is in a foreign language—usually English or German. In Anadolu schools students spend a preparatory year in studying the foreign language of instruction of the school. There are Anadolu vocational high schools also. Such schools comprise about 25 percent of men's technical high schools, 22 percent of women's technical high schools, 31 percent of trade and tourism high schools, and 18 percent of the religious vocational high schools (Ministry of Education, 1998).

### *Private Returns to Schooling in Turkey*

Table 11.3 provides the private rates of return to general and vocational high school graduate men and women in Turkey compiled from different sources. For men, we observe that in all cases the private rates of return to vocational high schooling are higher—by substantial margins—than those of general high schooling. The results for women are less clear-cut. Only in the case of the 1994 survey are vocational high school returns markedly higher than general high school returns. These returns are computed over a middle school education. In both the general and the vocational high school computations, training is assumed to take three years, although in both cases some programs take four years. International evidence presented by Psacharopoulos (1994) reports higher social returns to general secondary school curricula than to vocational curricula, which is due mainly to the higher unit costs of vocational school programs.[1]

**Table 11.3: Private Rates of Return to General and Vocational High Schools**

| | General High School | | Vocational High School | |
|---|---|---|---|---|
| **Kind of Survey Used** | Men | Women | Men | Women |
| **Turkish Household Budget Survey 1987**[a] | | | | |
| Wage Earner | | | | |
| All Ages | 8.6 | 6.5 | 13.0 | 2.0 |
| Under 25 years of age | 11.5 | — | 37.0 | — |
| 25–44 years of age | 7.7 | — | 11.0 | — |
| Over 44 years of age | 15.8 | — | 15.0 | — |
| **Turkish Household Labor Force Survey 1989**[b] | | | | |
| Wage Earner | 10.1 | 11.7 | 13.0 | 12.5 |
| Self Employed | 3.2 | 12.3 | 6.7 | 2.1* |
| **Turkish Household Expenditure Survey 1994**[c] | | | | |
| Public Administration | 11.1 | 8.8 | 16.3 | 16.1 |
| State-Owned Enterprises | 8.5 | — | 14.1 | — |
| Covered Private Sector[d] | 13.6 | 11.4 | 15.3 | 20.9 |

*Notes:* * Insignificant at 5 percent level.

a, b, c: In both the general and the vocational high school computations, training is assumed to take three years.

d: Covered Private Sector includes those wage earners who are covered by social security.

*Source:* a. Tansel (1994); b. Tansel (2001); c. Tansel (1999).

## The Model

The distribution of individuals between general and vocational high schools is not random. Ignoring this, potential biases could result in estimates of the wage equations (Heckman, 1974). In addressing this, then, I assume that individuals face three mutually exclusive choices: not joining high school ($j$=0), going to general high school ($j$=1), or going to vocational high school ($j$=2). The perceived net differentials in the wage or non-wage compensations determine the school choice. Individual tastes, preferences, and other characteristics will further influence the school choice. At this point, I also note that while general high school students are specifically trained for pursuing a university education, vocational high school students are trained for a vocation. However, vocational high school students are also allowed to take part in the competitive university entrance examinations—albeit with a lesser chance of succeeding.

I assume a conditional logit model for the probability that the individual chooses alternative $j$ as follows:

$$P_j = \exp(Z\alpha_j) / (1 + \sum \exp(Z\alpha_j)) \tag{1}$$

where $Z$ is a vector of explanatory variables affecting school choice, $\alpha_j$ is a vector of unknown parameters of the alternative $j$, and the summation is over $j$ = 1, 2, 3. I adopt a two-step method in estimating the wage equations (Lee, 1983; Trost and Lee, 1984). In the first stage, I estimate the school choice probabilities by the maximum likelihood logit method and construct the selection term for the alternative $j$ as follows:

$$\lambda_j = \phi(H_j) / \Phi(H_j) \text{ where } H_j = \Phi^{-1}(P_j) \tag{2}$$

where $\phi$ and $\Phi$ are the standard normal density and distribution functions respectively. In the second stage, I estimate by OLS Mincerian wage equations, including the estimated $\lambda_j$ among its explanatory variables. In the Mincerian wage equations (Becker, 1975; Mincer, 1958 and 1974), log wages are explained by human capital characteristics and locational factors ($X$), and the estimated $\lambda_j$:

$$\ln W_j = \beta_{oj} + X_j\beta_j + \theta_j\lambda_j + \upsilon_j \tag{3}$$

where $\beta_o$ is the unknown intercept term, $\beta$ is the vector of other unknown parameters, $\theta = p_j\sigma_j$, and $\upsilon$ is the random disturbance term. This method provides consistent estimates of $\beta_o$, $\beta$ and $\theta$.

### *Empirical Specification*

The explanatory variables considered are as follows. Experience and a quadratic term in experience are included in both the multinominal logit and the wage equations. Experience is computed as age minus the number of years of schooling minus six—the age of entry into school (Mincer, 1974). A dummy variable indicates whether the individual resides in an urban location. Settlements with a population of over 20,000 are defined as an urban location. Further, dummy variables for regions of residence are included to control for the differential in labor market conditions. Marmara was the reference region.

Interviews were conducted in different months throughout 1994. To control for seasonal factors, if any, seasonal dummy variables are included.

The unearned income of the individual, the unearned income of the other household members, and the amount of land owned are other variables included in the multinomial logit equations of school choice. These variables are expected to increase the probability of an individual's attendance at a general or a vocational high school. Unearned income is defined to include rental income and interest income.

## Data

I use the results of the 1994 Household Expenditure Survey conducted by the State Institute of Statistics of Turkey,[2] and restrict the sample to individuals 15 to 65 years of age. I focus on those individuals who terminated schooling with general high school or vocational high school.[3] It was not possible to identify the type of high school completed by those who went on to higher education. Details of the subject of study for vocational high school graduates were not asked for in the survey. The main characteristics of the data are given in Appendix Table 11.A1. For both men and women, the hourly wages of vocational high school graduates are higher than those of general high school graduates. However, in both samples, vocational high school graduates are about two years older and have two more years' job experience than general high school graduates.

Wages are the sum of cash earnings, bonuses, and the value of income in kind. Wages are considered only for the primary job. For secondarily employed individuals, earnings from the second job are disregarded, since information on these hours of work was not collected. Two kinds of information about wages were collected. One was the wage earnings for the month of the interview, and the other was the wage earnings for the previous year. I used wage earnings for the month of the interview, assuming that it involves fewer errors of recollection than the wage earnings for the previous year. The survey also asked for the usual hours of work per week. I imputed the monthly hours of work by multiplying the weekly by 4.3—since no information was collected on the number of weeks worked per month. I obtained the hourly wage by dividing the reported monthly wage by the imputed monthly hours of work.[4]

Appendix Table 11.A1 also shows the regional distribution of individuals. The percentage of general and vocational high school graduate men and women are about the same in all regions except in East and Southeast Anatolia—where the percentages of general high school graduates are twice that of vocational high school graduates in the men's sample.

### *Unemployment Rates*

Table 11.4 shows the occupational distribution of vocational and general high school graduate men and women in the sample. It is noteworthy that a larger percentage of men are working, while a larger percentage of women are housewives. Percentages of working men and women are higher among vocational high school graduates than among general high school graduates. For both men and women, unemployment rates are lower among vocational high school graduates than among general high school graduates. Skills acquired in vocational high schools may be helpful in finding jobs in the labor market. Further, it was found that almost twice as many general high school graduates are college students as compared to vocational high school graduates. This confirms the hypothesis that while vocational high schools prepare students for employment, general high schools prepare students for further study.

**Table 11.4: Occupational Distribution of General and Vocational High School Graduates, 1994**

| Occupation | Men | | Women | |
|---|---|---|---|---|
| | General High School | Vocational High School | General High School | Vocational High School |
| Working | 70.8 | 78.0 | 28.1 | 38.2 |
| Unemployed | 12.8 | 8.8 | 12.1 | 9.7 |
| Student | 10.8 | 4.8 | 13.2 | 6.2 |
| Housewife | — | — | 43.0 | 36.9 |
| Retired | 3.6 | 5.8 | 1.9 | 7.2 |
| Other | 2.0 | 2.6 | 1.7 | 1.8 |
| Total | 100 | 100 | 100 | 100 |
| Total in Numbers | 4,972 | 703 | 3,067 | 390 |

*Source:* Author's computations using the 1994 Household Expenditure Survey.

## Estimation Results: Multinominal Logit Estimates

Multinominal logit estimates of school choice for men and women are shown in Tables 11.5 and 11.6 respectively. The tables provide the marginal effects and the associated asymptotic t-ratios. The marginal effects of each variable on the probability of school choice are calculated at the mean values of the variables.

**Table 11.5: Maximum Likelihood Multinominal Logit Estimates of Secondary School Choice of Men, 1994**

| Variables | General High School | | Vocational High School | |
|---|---|---|---|---|
| | Marginal Effect | t-Ratio | Marginal Effect | t-Ratio |
| Constant | -0.1248 | 450.00 | -0.0425 | 10.00 |
| Experience (× $10^{-2}$) | -0.2956 | 157.00 | -0.0892 | 4.28 |
| Experience Square (× $10^{-4}$) | -0.8374 | 183.00 | 0.0260 | 0.57 |
| Unearned Income (× $10^{-4}$) | 0.3077 | 299.00 | 0.0487 | 4.14 |
| Unearned HH Income (× $10^{-4}$) | 0.3639 | 40.00 | 0.0525 | 0.54 |
| Land (× $10^{-4}$) | 0.1382 | 16.80 | 0.0081 | 0.09 |
| Urban location | 0.0648 | 390.00 | 0.0100 | 4.99 |
| **Regions:** | | | | |
| Aegean | -0.0002 | 1.02 | -0.0010 | 0.40 |
| Mediterranean | 0.0119 | 48.40 | -0.0098 | 3.58 |
| Central Anatolia | 0.0142 | 72.10 | 0.0017 | 0.79 |
| Black Sea | 0.0280 | 126.00 | -0.0042 | 1.78 |
| East Anatolia | 0.0536 | 203.00 | -0.0098 | 3.41 |
| Southeast Anatolia | -0.0180 | 50.90 | -0.0259 | 5.33 |
| - Log Likelihood | | 11,474 | | |
| Chi-Squared | | 2,835 | | |
| Sample Size | | 26,035 | | |

*Source:* As Table 11.4.

**Table 11.6: Maximum Likelihood Multinominal Logit Estimates of Secondary School Choice of Women, 1994**

| | General High School | | Vocational High School | |
|---|---|---|---|---|
| **Variables** | Marginal Effect | t-Ratio | Marginal Effect | t-Ratio |
| Constant | -0.0411 | 909.00 | -0.0161 | 2.46 |
| Experience (× $10^{-3}$) | -0.8934 | 420.00 | 0.0691 | 0.50 |
| Experience Square (× $10^{-4}$) | -0.2574 | 463.00 | -0.0982 | 1.49 |
| Unearned Income (× $10^{-4}$) | 0.1725 | 587.00 | 0.0367 | 1.56 |
| Unearned HH Income (× $10^{-7}$) | -0.1445 | 1.03 | -1.0420 | 0.12 |
| Land (× $10^{-3}$) | 0.1327 | 358.00 | -0.0339 | 1.27 |
| Urban location | 0.0365 | 1906.00 | 0.0072 | 2.37 |
| **Regions:** | | | | |
| Aegean | 0.0020 | 103.00 | 0.0007 | 0.59 |
| Mediterranean | -0.0004 | 18.60 | -0.0014 | 1.01 |
| Central Anatolia | -0.0015 | 70.40 | 0.0004 | 0.30 |
| Black Sea | 0.0032 | 176.00 | 0.0012 | 1.06 |
| East Anatolia | 0.0010 | 45.50 | 0.0016 | 1.20 |
| Southeast Anatolia | -0.0065 | 195.00 | -0.0014 | 0.70 |
| - Log Likelihood | | 2,728 | | |
| Chi-Squared | | 1,924 | | |
| Sample Size | | 9,908 | | |

*Source:* As Table 11.4.

The multinominal logit estimates for men indicate that experience has a negative effect on the probability of high school choice. The unearned income of the individual, the unearned income of the other household members, and the landholdings all increase the probability of the choice of general high school. They also increase the probability of the choice of vocational high school, but are statistically significant only for individual unearned income. In the case of the multinominal logit estimates for women, experience similarly decreases the probability of high school choice but is insignificant in the case of vocational high school. As in the case of men, individual unearned income, household unearned income (statistically insignificant), and landholdings all increase the probability of choosing general high school. However, all these terms are statistically insignificant in the case of vocational high schools. In all cases, an urban location increases the probability of choosing vocational high school.

### *Wage Equations*

Selectivity corrected estimates of the general and vocational high schools' wage equations are given in Tables 11.7 and 11.8 for men and women respectively. The wage equations are overall statistically significant, as indicated by the F-statistics. However, in the case of women, the vocational high school wage equation has a poor fit and most of the individual coefficients are statistically insignificant. Therefore, in the ensuing discussion, it is not possible to make a true comparison between the wages of general and vocational high school women graduates.

**Table 11.7: Selectivity Corrected Estimates of Wage Equations of Men, 1994**

| Variables | General High School Coefficient | General High School t-Ratio | Vocational High School Coefficient | Vocational High School t-Ratio |
|---|---|---|---|---|
| Constant | 0.0127 | 0.03 | 0.9657 | 0.50 |
| Experience | 0.1069 | 15.10 | 0.1125 | 5.81 |
| Experience Square | -0.0027 | 14.70 | -0.0025 | 8.57 |
| Urban location | 0.4110 | 4.23 | 0.4367 | 2.04 |
| **Regions:** | | | | |
| Aegean | -0.2870 | 4.06 | -0.2257 | 1.53 |
| Mediterranean | -0.3153 | 4.81 | -0.0135 | 0.05 |
| Central Anatolia | -0.0092 | 0.14 | -0.0715 | 0.55 |
| Black Sea | -0.1660 | 2.34 | -0.0181 | 0.10 |
| East Anatolia | 0.0432 | 0.47 | 0.1879 | 0.64 |
| Southeast Anatolia | -0.0817 | 1.05 | -0.1013 | 0.17 |
| Selection term | 0.2773 | 1.09 | 0.0928 | 0.10 |
| R-Square | 0.1504 | | 0.2120 | |
| F (K, N-K-1) | 47.70 | | 11.58 | |
| SER | 1.00 | | 1.11 | |
| Sample Size | 3,520 | | 548 | |

*Source:* As Table 11.4.

**Table 11.8: Selectivity Corrected Estimates of Wage Equations of Women, 1994**

| Variables | General High School Coefficient | General High School t-Ratio | Vocational High School Coefficient | Vocational High School t-Ratio |
|---|---|---|---|---|
| Constant | 0.3906 | 0.77 | 2.9086 | 2.08 |
| Experience | 0.0771 | 6.68 | -0.0713 | 3.57 |
| Experience Square | -0.0017 | 4.10 | -0.0021 | 2.95 |
| Urban location | 0.5672 | 2.18 | -0.1085 | 0.32 |
| **Regions:** | | | | |
| Aegean | -0.0047 | 0.05 | -0.1699 | 0.85 |
| Mediterranean | -0.0031 | 0.03 | -0.0281 | 0.12 |
| Central Anatolia | 0.1400 | 1.41 | -0.1245 | 0.58 |
| Black Sea | -0.0531 | 0.63 | -0.1271 | 0.68 |
| East Anatolia | 0.0560 | 0.56 | -0.0469 | 0.22 |
| Southeast Anatolia | 0.3191 | 1.98 | 0.4504 | 1.68 |
| Selection term | 0.1236 | 0.47 | -0.5095 | 0.98 |
| R-Square | 0.2079 | | 0.2580 | |
| F (K, N-K-1) | 17.14 | | 3.61 | |
| SER | 0.7640 | | 0.7465 | |
| Sample Size | 863 | | 149 | |

*Source:* As Table 11.4.

Linear and quadratic terms in experience have the expected positive and negative signs, respectively, in all cases except in the vocational high school estimates for women. For general high school male graduates, wages peak at about 20 years of experience and for vocational high school male graduates, at about 23 years of experience. For general high school female graduates, wages peak at 23 years of experience. In all cases, urban wages are higher than rural wages. Regional wage differentials are, for the most part, statistically insignificant.

The coefficient estimates of the selection terms are, in all cases, statistically insignificant. Thus, the OLS estimates of the wage equations would also be unbiased and consistent.

Table 11.9 shows the expected wages for general and vocational high school graduates at different levels of experience. At all levels of experience, the wages of vocational high school graduate men are higher than those of general high school graduate men. For both groups, wages start to decline after about 20 years of experience. It is not possible to make a similar comparison for women owing to poor wage equation estimates for vocational high school graduate women.

**Table 11.9: Expected Wages at Different Levels of Experience by School of Choice and Gender, 1994**

(Turkish Lira per hour)

| Experience | Men[b] | | Women[a,b] |
|---|---|---|---|
| (years) | General High School | Vocational High School | General High School |
| 5 | 1.81 | 4.18 | 2.86 |
| 10 | 2.53 | 6.07 | 3.70 |
| 15 | 3.09 | 7.77 | 4.40 |
| 20 | 3.31 | 8.77 | 4.80 |
| 25 | 3.10 | 8.73 | 4.81 |
| 30 | 2.54 | 7.66 | 4.43 |
| 35 | 1.83 | 5.92 | 3.74 |

*Notes:* [a] Expected wages for women vocational high school graduates are not presented, since the wage equation estimates for this group were unsatisfactory.
[b] In the computation of expected wages the selection terms are ignored. Therefore, they represent the expected wages for a randomly drawn individual from the population. For each high school category, the expected wages are computed at the means of the variables.
*Source:* Author's calculations based on wage equation estimates in Tables 11.7 and 11. 8.

### *Oaxaca-Blinder Decomposition*

Table 11.10 provides the decomposition of wage differentials for general and vocational high school graduates. Such decompositions are based on Oaxaca (1973) and Blinder (1974). I decompose the total mean log wage differential for general and vocational high school graduates into four components as follows:

$$\ln W_j - \ln W_i = (\beta_{oj} - \beta_{oi}) + 0.5(\beta_j + \beta_i)(X_j - X_i) + 0.5(X_j + X_i)(\beta_j - \beta_i) + (\theta_j\lambda_j - \theta_i\lambda_i) \qquad (4)$$

where the last two terms refer to the differentials caused by the selectivity bias (Idson and Feaster, 1990). Variables are evaluated at their means; $j$ denotes general high school and $i$ denotes vocational high school. The first component is the difference in the intercept terms. It is commonly interpreted as the premium or pure rent from being in a given sector (Terrell, 1993). The second component is due to the differences in endowments of the individuals. The third component is due either to differences in coefficients or to market returns to endowments. The last component is due to the difference in selection terms. The differentials due to the intercept terms and the coefficients are often referred to as unexplained differentials. The decomposition in Table 11.10 indicates that for men, the wage differential in favor of vocational high school graduates is due largely to the differential in intercept terms—a small part resulting from the differential in coefficients. Thus, we can talk about pure rent in the case of vocational high school graduate men. The results for women are not interpreted owing to poor wage equation estimates for vocational high school graduate women.

**Table 11.10: Decomposition of Wage Differentials for General and Vocational High School Graduates by Gender, 1994**

| | Mean Log Wage Differential between General and Vocational High School Graduates (%) | |
|---|---|---|
| Wage Differential | Men | Women[a] |
| Total Mean Differential | -29.99 | -45.85 |
| Component Attributed to: | | |
| Intercept term | -95.30 | -251.82 |
| Selection | 60.75 | 130.42 |
| Endowments | 53.10 | -9.04 |
| Coefficients | 0.74 | 84.57 |
| Total Unexplained Differential | -96.05 | -167.23 |

*Notes:* [a] Results for women are not reliable due to poor wage equation estimates for women vocational high school graduates.
*Source:* Author's calculations based on the wage equation estimates in Tables 11.7 and 11.8. Each of the components are evaluated at the sample means of the variables.

## Population Policy Implications

Demographers agree that Turkey has recently passed into the third phase of the demographic transition. The population growth rate, which was at its highest (2.8 percent per year) during the 1950s and 1960s, declined to 2.2 percent during the 1980s (SIS, 1995). It had dropped to 1.6 percent by 1995 and was projected to be 1.4 percent by 2000. (At the time of writing, no confirmation of the figure was yet available.) The total fertility rate (TFR) has been declining since the 1950s, reaching 2.5 children per woman in 1995. Declining mortality, longer life expectancy, and better health contributed to nationwide lower fertility (SIS, 1995). Although the population continues to grow due to population momentum (Shorter, 1995), the age structure of the population is expected to change dramatically. The population will stabilize at 98 million by the mid-twenty-first century. The youth population (0–14), which was increasing up to the 1990s, is projected to stabilize, while the elderly population (65 and over) is projected to register a slight increase and the so-called producer population (20–54) is projected to show a large increase (SIS, 1995). The argument of the 'demographic window of opportunity' suggests that fast rates of growth of the producer population can factor in a faster economic growth (Barlow, 1994). However, the current quality of the labor force is poor. According to the 1990 Census, about three-fifths of the literate population had only primary schooling (SIS, 1993). To take advantage of the demographic window of opportunity, it will be necessary to raise the educational levels of the producer population. Until recently, high fertility rates and population growth meant rising numbers of youth to educate. This required an expansion of the educational system. With the stabilization of the youth population, it will be possible to concentrate on improving the quality of education and expanding the higher levels of schooling, including both general and vocational high schools and universities.

Since fertility rates have fallen substantially over the past decade, the size of the high school age cohort (15–19) has already stabilized, while the size of the university age cohort (20–24) is projected to increase by 18 percent by 2005 before it stabilizes (Shorter, 1995). Thus, although the high school age population will not change, the enrollments at the high school level will expand due to improvements in the enrollment ratios at this level. The seventh five-year development plan targets universal enrollments for eight-year schooling and a 75 percent enrollment rate at the high school level (SPO, 1995). In the future, income growth, a higher level of education on the part of parents, and urbanization will all contribute to higher demand for schooling (Tansel, 2002).

This means that provision of university education must also be expanded to accommodate the high school cohort as it moves through the system. Since the highest rates of return to schooling in Turkey are observed at the university level, a large proportion of the high school graduates will want to obtain a university degree. There will be an ever-increasing accumulation of students at the doors of the universities. This is why it is particularly important for high school graduates to be equipped with skills demanded by the labor market—in the event that they do not succeed in gaining entrance to a university. Such skills can apparently be better provided at vocational high schools than at general high schools, since the labor market wages of vocational high school graduates are found to be higher than the wages of general high school graduates. To take this into account, planners should pay special attention to the provision of vocational high schools in the future.

## Conclusion

This chapter examines the school choice and wage differentials of general and vocational high school graduates in Turkey. For this purpose, I use the individual level 1994 Household Expenditure Survey data of the State Institute of Statistics. High school choice is explained by means of a three-way logit model. Selectivity corrected wage equations for the general and vocational high school graduates are estimated for men and women separately. The results obtained reinforce recent studies of developing countries. When controlled for observed characteristics and sample selection, the wages—for men—of the vocational high school graduates are larger than the wages of the general high school graduates. For women, it was not possible to make a comparison due to poor wage equation estimates for vocational high school graduates. Further analysis using Oaxaca-Blinder decomposition indicates that this differential is a premium or pure rent to the skills of vocational high school graduates. It is also observed that the unemployment rate is lower among the vocational than among the general high school graduates. Further, previous studies show that private rates of return to vocational schooling are higher than those to general high schools for men. Thus, vocational high schools are superior to general high schools in terms of several indicators of efficacy in enhancing labor market outcomes in Turkey.

## Appendix

**Table 11:A1: Means and Standard Deviations of Variables by High School and Gender, 1994**

| Variables | Men | | Women | |
|---|---|---|---|---|
| | General High School | Vocational High School | General High School | Vocational High School |
| Hourly Wage[a] | 6.06 | 8.25 | 5.42 | 7.72 |
| | (9.32) | (10.96) | (5.25) | (4.72) |
| Log Hourly Wage | 1.29 | 1.59 | 1.38 | 1.84 |
| | (1.08) | (1.11) | (0.85) | (0.75) |
| Age | 32.20 | 33.95 | 27.89 | 30.25 |
| | (8.88) | (10.60) | (7.33) | (8.00) |
| Experience | 14.19 | 15.95 | 9.90 | 12.26 |
| | (8.87) | (10.60) | (7.32) | (8.00) |
| Experience Square | 280.40 | 365.90 | 151.60 | 213.80 |
| | (321.00) | (451.00) | (192.00) | (241.00) |
| Unearned Income[a] | 92.09 | 89.53 | 33.81 | 36.87 |
| | (1164.00) | (438.00) | (217.00) | (125.00) |
| Unearned HH Income[a] | 3352.00 | 39.50 | 92.91 | 88.52 |
| | (196170.00) | (180.00) | (361.00) | (319.00) |
| Land(dekar)[c] | 9.19 | 9.34 | 4.27 | 4.93 |
| | (101.00) | (73.20) | (22.80) | (25.10) |
| Urban Location[b] | 0.81 | 0.80 | 0.87 | 0.83 |
| Regions[b]: | | | | |
| Marmara | 0.13 | 0.21 | 0.17 | 0.16 |
| Aegean | 0.10 | 0.15 | 0.17 | 0.17 |
| Mediterranean | 0.14 | 0.11 | 0.16 | 0.11 |
| Central Anatolia | 0.16 | 0.24 | 0.12 | 0.13 |
| Black Sea | 0.18 | 0.16 | 0.23 | 0.25 |
| East Anatolia | 0.20 | 0.10 | 0.11 | 0.15 |
| Southeast Anatolia | 0.09 | 0.04 | 0.03 | 0.03 |
| Selection term | 1.42 | 2.29 | 1.34 | 2.24 |
| | (0.31) | (0.25) | (0.42) | (0.29) |
| Sample Size | 3520.00 | 548.00 | 863.00 | 149.00 |

*Notes:* [a] Measured in 1987 Turkish liras.
[b] These are dummy variables. Their standard deviation(sd) are not reported for brevity but may be computed from their reported means (m) as sd= $(m(1-m))^{1/2}$.
[c] One dekar is 1,000 square meters or 0.247 acres.
*Source:* Author's computations using the 1994 Household Expenditure Survey.

## Notes

* I would like to thank the president of the State Institute of Statistics of Turkey, Ömer Gebizliolu and the vice-president, Nurgül Öğüt, who helped to implement this study. Thanks are also due to Abda El-Mahdi and Heba Handoussa for helpful comments. Any errors are mine alone.

1 There is no study on the relative costs of general and vocational high schools in Turkey. However, international evidence in Psacharopoulos (1987) shows that the costs of vocational programs are considerably higher than those of general schooling.

2 The survey was administered to 26,256 households. Interviews covered 58 provinces out of the total of 76 provinces in the country. There were 281 clusters that were selected with strati-

fied, multistage sampling. The stratification was on seven geographical regions, and according to the rural-urban settlements in each region and the size of each region's population. Further stratification was according to the socioeconomic status of the settlements as developed, developing, and undeveloped. Household was the sampling unit. Each household was interviewed ten times a month. A different series of households was interviewed in each month throughout 1994. Details may be found in the State Institute of Statistics (1997).

3 Since the highest rates of return to schooling in Turkey are observed at the tertiary levels of study, there is a high demand for university education and most general and vocational high school graduates would like to continue studying in a university program. As the sample used in this study is restricted to general and vocational high school graduates who did not continue studying at a tertiary level institution, it is possible that some of these individuals were not successful in gaining entry to a university program. As such, they may identify as academically less able individuals.

4 The annual inflation rate was about 90 percent during 1994. Since the households were interviewed at different months throughout 1994, I deflated the wages and unearned income figures by the local monthly consumer price index (CPI). Households located in 16 major cities were assigned the monthly CPIs for those cities. Households in other locations were assigned either a rural or an urban regional monthly CPI according to their region of location and whether this was a rural or an urban location. A location is considered urban if its population is over 20,000. The base for the CPI was 1987. The data was obtained from the State Institute of Statistics (1994).

## References


Assaad, R. 1994. "The Effects of Public Sector Hiring and Compensation Policies on the Egyptian Labor Market," *World Bank Economic Review*, 11(1): 85–118.

Arriagada, A.M., and A. Ziderman. 1992. *Vocational Secondary Schooling Occupational Choice and Earnings in Brazil.* Population and Human Resources Department Working Paper No. 1037. Washington, DC: World Bank.

Barlow, R. 1994. "Population Growth and Economic Growth: Some More Correlations," *Population and Development Review,* 201 (1): 133–65.

Becker, G.S. 1975. *Human Capital,* Second edition. New York, NY: Columbia University Press/National Bureau of Economic Research.

Bennell, P. 1996. "General versus Vocational Secondary Education in Developing Countries: A Review of the Rates of Return Evidence," *Journal of Development Studies,* 32 (2): 230–47.

Blinder, A.S. 1974. "Wage Discrimination: Reduced Form and Structural Estimates," *Journal of Human Resources,* 8 (4): 436–55.

Chung, Y.P. 1990. "Educated Misemployment: Earnings Effects of Employment in Unmatched Fields of Work," *Economics of Education Review,* 1, (4): 331–42.

Heckman, J.J. 1974. "Shadow Prices, Market Wages and Labor Supply," *Econometrica,* 42: 679–94.

Idson, T., and D. Feaster. 1990. "A Selectivity Model of Employer-Size Wage Differentials," *Journal of Labor Economics,* 8 (1): 99–122.

Lee, L.F. 1983. "Generalized Econometric Models with Selectivity" *Econometrica,* 51: 507–12.

Middleton, J., A. Ziderman, and A.van Adams. 1993. *Skills for Productivity: Vocational Education and Training in Developing Countries.* New York, NY: Oxford University Press.

Mincer, J. 1958. "Investments in Human Capital and Personal Income Distribution," *Journal of Political Economy,* Vol. 56: 281–302.

———. 1974. *Schooling, Experience and Earnings.* National Bureau of Economic Research. New York, NY: Columbia University Press.

Ministry of Education. 1997. *Endüstriyel Teknik Öğretim Okul ve Kurumlarının 1997–1998 Öğretim Yılı Bilgi Dökümanı* (*Documentation of Information for the 1997–1998 Academic Year of the Industrial and Technical Schools*). Ankara: Milli Eğitim Bakanlığı.

———. 1988. *Milli Eğitim ile İlgili Bilgiler* (*Information Related to National Education*). Ankara: Milli Eğitim Bakanlığı.

Moock, P., and R. Bellew. 1990. "Vocational and Technical Education in Peru," *Economics of Education Review*, 9 (4): 365–75.

Newman, S., and A. Ziderman. 1991. "Vocational Schooling, Occupational Matching and Labor Market Earnings in Israel," *Journal of Human Resources*, 26 (2): 256–81.

Oaxaca, R. 1973. "Male-Female Wage Differentials in Urban Labor Markets." *International Economic Review*, 14 (3): 693–709.

Psacharopoulos, G. 1987. "To Vocationalize or not to Vocationalize : That is the Curriculum Question," *International Review of Education*, 33 (2): 187–211.

———. 1994. "Returns to Investment in Education: A Global Update," *World Development*, 22 (9): 1325–43.

Shorter, F.C. 1995. "The Crisis of Population Knowledge in Turkey," *New Perspectives on Turkey*, 12 (1): 1–31.

State Institute of Statistics (SIS). 1993. *1990 Population Census: Social and Economic Characteristics of the Population*. Ankara: SIS, Turkish Republic Prime Ministry.

———. 1994. *Monthly Bulletin of Statistics*. Ankara: SIS, Turkish Republic Prime Ministry.

———. 1995. *The Population of Turkey, 1923–1994*. Ankara: SIS, Turkish Republic Prime Ministry.

———. 1997. *Household Consumption Expenditures Survey Results, 1994*. Ankara: SIS, Turkish Republic Prime Ministry.

State Planning Organization (SPO). 1995. *Seventh Five Year Development Plan, 1995–2000*. Ankara: SPO, Turkish Republic Prime Ministry.

Tansel, A. 1994. "Wage Employment, Earnings and Returns to Schooling for Men and Women in Turkey," *Economics of Education Review*, 13 (4): 305–20.

———. 1999. "Public-Private Employment Choice, Wage Differentials and Gender in Turkey." Economic Growth Center Discussion Paper 797. New Haven, CT.: Yale University.

———. 2001. "Self Employment, Wage Employment and Returns to Schooling by Gender in Turkey," in D. Salehi-Isfahani (ed.), *Labor and Human Capital in the Middle East*, pp. 337–367. Reading, UK: Ithaca Press.

———. 2002. "Determinants of School Attainment of Boys and Girls in Turkey: Individual, Household and Community Factors," *Economics of Education Review*. Forthcoming.

Terrell, K. 1993. "Public Private Wage Differentials in Haiti: Do Public Servants Earn a Rent?" *Journal of Development Economics*, 42: 293–314.

Trost, R., and L.F. Lee. 1984. "Technical Training and Earnings: A Polytomous Model with Selectivity," *Review of Economics and Statistics*, 66: 151–56.

World Bank. 1990. *Thailand's Education Sector at the Crossroads: Selected Issues*. Washington, DC: World Bank.

———. 1994. *Chile: Strategy for Rural Areas, Agricultural Competitiveness and Alleviating Rural Poverty*, Report 12776-Chile. Washington, DC: World Bank.

———. 1995. *Training and the Labor Market in Indonesia: Policies for Productivity Gains and Employment Growth*. Population and Human Resources Division, Country Department III, East Asia and Pacific Regional Office. Washington, DC: World Bank.

———. 1997. *World Development Report 1997*. Washington, DC: Oxford University Press.

# Part IV

# Migration and Urbanization

# 12

# Rationality of Migration*

*İnsan Tunalı*

## 1. Introduction

Conventionally, statistical formulations of the migration decision rely heavily on the paradigm of a rational individual acting upon the earnings-enhancing benefits of migration (Sjaastad, 1962). Under conditions of uncertainty, the decision will be based on expectations regarding earnings opportunities. Since realized earnings depend on an individual's locational choices, which in turn depend on that person's expectations regarding earnings differentials, the augmentation in earnings that is attributed to migration might actually reflect the researcher's failure to take account of the sorting out (self-selection) of individuals (Antel, 1980; Nakosteen and Zimmer, 1980; DaVanzo and Hosek, 1981; Robinson and Tomes, 1982; Islam, 1985; Borjas, 1990; Lanzona, 1998).

The self-selection problem is typically resolved by adopting a joint decision/outcome model of the type popularized by Heckman (1974, 1976, 1978) and Lee (1978, 1979). The choices available to the individual are expressed as a pair of earnings equations that characterize the stochastic outcome at both the origin and the destination. Individuals sort themselves into migrant and non-migrant categories on the basis of the potential earnings gain resulting from a move, net of migration costs. A reduced-form equation that mimics this selection mechanism quantifies the influence of the explanatory variables on the migration decision and provides a ranking of individuals by likelihood of migration. This information is used in adjusting the earnings equation for unobserved heterogeneity. Lee (1982), Heckman and Sedlacek (1985), and Heckman and MaCurdy (1986) pointed out that the joint Normality assumption that underlies the conventional method used for estimating models that are subject to selectivity could be too strong and have offered less restrictive alternatives. Subsequent developments in semi-parametric and non-parametric estimation methods broadened the range of alternatives, but the new techniques have yet to make significant inroads in the empirical literature.

In this paper, I examine the migration/earnings link using a rich micro-data set from Turkey. I rely on Lee's (1982) modification of the popular two-step procedure, which is robust to deviations from Normality. My findings add to the evidence against the conventional method. I test the rationality hypothesis by using several measures of the impact of the migration decision on earnings consistent with the decision rule. While the hypothesis holds up, a significant segment of the migrant subpopulation is seen to experience a small negative return. I seek explanations for this and other patterns that emerge with the help of recent contributions to the literature. By treating the means of the migration effect measures as functions of the migration probability, I obtain informative *ex post* assessments of the manner in which unobserved heterogeneity influenced the earnings outcome. The key findings and the main arguments used in reconciling theory with the facts are summarized in the last section.

## 2. A Model of Rational Migration

I begin by establishing a simple framework for examining the implications of rational migration, in which moves are triggered by the prospect of higher earnings. To make matters simple, I assume that there are no observed differences between individuals, except that some are seen to move while others choose to stay. Complications introduced by other observables are handled in section 3, when I present the econometric model.

Consider an individual who anticipates two earnings prospects $y_1^*$ and $y_2^*$ (expressed in present value terms) under the move ($M$ = 1) and stay ($M$ = 0) options respectively, and a one-time anticipated cost of migration $c^*$. Letting

$$\delta^* = y_1^* - y_2^*, \tag{1}$$
$$y^* = \delta^* - c^*, \tag{2}$$

the migration decision is carried out according to

$$M = \begin{cases} 1, \text{ “move” iff } y^* > 0 \\ 0, \text{ “stay” iff } y^* \leq 0 \end{cases} \tag{3}$$

Here and below the superscript asterisk ($^*$) denotes that the quantity involved is the individual's anticipation, and is therefore known to the individual.[1] According to (1), the individual will move if the anticipated earnings gain $\delta^*$, net of anticipated costs $c^*$, is positive and stay if it is not. Thus $\delta^* > 0$ is a necessary, but not a sufficient, condition for migration to take place.

In the absence of perfect foresight, actual earnings (= $y$) will differ from the individual's anticipations according to

$$y_m = y_m^* + f_m, \; m = 0,1 \tag{4}$$

where $f$'s denote random forecast errors. I assume that anticipations exploit all the information available to the individual at the time of the migration decision, and are unbiased in the sense that $E(f_m \mid y^*) = 0$ for m = 0,1. As I show below, this assumption is crucial in the tests of rationality. Without loss of generality, anticipations may be expressed as

$$y_m^* = \mu_m + v_m, \; m = 0,1 \tag{5}$$
$$c^* = \kappa + v_c \tag{6}$$

where $\mu$'s and $\kappa$ denote population means, and $v$'s denote zero mean random variables. Substitution of (5) in (4) yields a similar decomposition for actual earnings:

$$y_m = \mu_m + u_m, \; m = 0,1 \tag{7}$$

where $u_m = v_m + f_m$, m = 0,1.

Since the move and stay options are mutually exclusive, actual earnings are observed under the chosen option only:

$$y = \begin{cases} y_0 & \text{iff } M = 0 \\ y_1 & \text{iff } M = 1 \end{cases} \tag{8}$$

We therefore exploit the economic (and subsequently the statistical) content of the model to assess the consequences of migration. Using (7) and defining $\delta = \mu_1 - \mu_0$, $u = (1 - M)\, u_0 + M\, u_1$, we obtain

$$y = \mu_0 + \delta M + u \tag{9}$$

The systematic sorting that (3) accomplishes has two implications in our model of rational migration. First, self-selection has to be taken into consideration when estimating the parameters of equation (9).[2] Second, $\delta$ does not have a straightforward interpretation as "the effect of migrant status on earnings." In fact, $\delta > 0$ is not even a necessary condition for migration to take place. This may be seen by substituting (5) in (1) and recalling $\delta = \mu_1 - \mu_0$ to obtain

$$\delta^* = \delta + v_1 - v_0 \tag{10}$$

With $\delta < 0$, $v_1 - v_0 > |\delta|$ is sufficient for $\delta^* > 0$.

What, then, does $\delta$ capture? Taking expectations conditional on migration status, we get

$$E(\delta^* \mid M) = \delta + E(v_1 \mid M) - E(v_0 \mid M) \tag{11}$$

Self-selection in migration implies $E(\delta^* \mid M) \neq \delta$. Thus $\delta$ is not the expected value of the difference in anticipated earnings that figures in the migration decision.[3] Taking unconditional expectations, we find that $E(\delta^*) = \delta$. Thus (consistently estimated) $\delta$ has an interpretation as the *average* realizable earnings gain across *all* individuals. Based on this interpretation, $\delta$ is the average price attached to migrant status in the labor market. A negative $\delta$, for example, would imply that on balance being a migrant is regarded as a negative attribute.

**Table 12.1: Expected Earnings under Alternative Scenarios**

| Observed Decision | Expected earnings option at the 'best' destination | Expected earnings option at the origin |
|---|---|---|
| Stay ($M = 0$) | $E(y_1 \mid M = 0) = \mu_1 + E(v_1 \mid M = 0)$ | $E(y_0 \mid M = 0) = \mu_0 + E(v_0 \mid M = 0)$ |
| Move ($M = 1$) | $E(y_1 \mid M = 1) = \mu_1 + E(v_1 \mid M = 1)$ | $E(y_0 \mid M = 1) = \mu_0 + E(v_0 \mid M = 1)$ |

To construct meaningful measures of the migration effect at the level of the individual, we need to recognize the fact that individuals *are not randomly assigned* their migration status, but instead *choose* their migration status. The expressions compiled in Table 12.1 become relevant for constructing such measures. These have been derived from (7), taking expectations conditional on $M$ (observed outcome of the migration decision) for m =1 (best destination) and m = 0 (origin), upon invoking the assumption that anticipations are unbiased (in the sense defined above). In the northwest and southeast cells of Table 12.1, expected earnings have been calculated under the *actual* outcome of the migration decision (m = $M$). In the other two cells, the respective *counterfactual* earnings calculations have been carried out (m $\neq M$).

Suppose we had all four quantities in hand.[4] We focus on the respective rows in Table 12.1 first. This allows us to compare the expected earnings of a given individual under the actual (*ex ante* optimal) choice with that under the counterfactual (*ex ante* non-optimal) choice. For migrants, we obtain what may be termed the "returns to migration":[5]

$$\delta_1 = E(y_1 \mid M = 1) - E(y_0 \mid M = 1) = \delta + E(v_1 \mid M = 1) - E(v_0 \mid M = 1) \tag{12}$$

In analogous fashion, for stayers we obtain the "returns to staying":

$$\delta_0 = E(y_0 \mid M = 0) - E(y_1 \mid M = 0) = -\delta + E(v_0 \mid M = 0) - E(v_1 \mid M = 0) \tag{13}$$

From (10), we see that $\delta_1 = E(\delta^* \mid M = 1)$ and $\delta_0 = -E(\delta^* \mid M = 0)$, and can therefore be used to assess whether the individual behaved rationally. The counterfactual route for measuring the migration effect was proposed by DaVanzo and Hosek (1981). I will follow these authors and call the variable components of equations (12)-(13), $\theta_1 = E(v_1 \mid M = 1) - E(v_0 \mid M = 1)$ and $\theta_0 = E(v_0 \mid M = 0) - E(v_1 \mid M = 0)$, respectively, the "sorting gains" to migration and staying. Measured *ex post*, positive sorting gains and positive returns would lend strong support for *ex ante* rationality. When assumptions about the nature of the forecast errors are maintained, negative values would constitute evidence against rationality.

A second test of rationality may be based on a different contrast of the (*ex ante*) optimal choices with the (*ex ante*) non-optimal choices. This time we focus on the respective columns of Table 12.1 and obtain a pair of measures based on the comparison of the average values of the unobservables in the subpopulations of migrants and non-migrants. These in turn inform us about the "selection of migrants,"

$$\psi_1 = E(y_1 \mid M = 1) - E(y_1 \mid M = 0) = E(v_1 \mid M = 1) - E(v_1 \mid M = 0), \tag{14}$$

and the "selection of stayers,"

$$\psi_0 = E(y_0 \mid M = 0) - E(y_0 \mid M = 1) = E(v_0 \mid M = 0) - E(v_0 \mid M = 1 \tag{15}$$

Rationality implies that the average mover anticipated higher earnings at the destination than the average stayer, and that the average stayer anticipated higher earnings at the origin than the average mover. This measure has been used by Borjas (1990) and Pessino (1991). It is implicit in the interpretations offered by Nakosteen and Zimmer (1980), Robinson and Tomes (1982), Islam (1985), and Lanzona (1998).

Although it does not provide a test of rationality, a third informative contrast based on the actual (*ex ante* optimal) outcomes is available. Using the northwest and southeast cells of Table 12.1 we may measure the "earnings differential in favor of migrants" as

$$\varepsilon_1 = E(y_1 \mid M = 1) - E(y_0 \mid M = 0) = \delta + E(v_1 \mid M = 1) - E(v_0 \mid M = 0) \tag{16}$$

This measure compares the experience of an average migrant with that of an average non-migrant. It is an improvement over $\delta$, because unobserved heterogeneity figures in the calculation. A companion measure may be exploited to carry out a similar comparison in terms of the foregone (*ex ante* non-optimal) options:

$$\varepsilon_0 = E(y_1 \mid M = 0) - E(y_0 \mid M = 1) = \delta + E(v_1 \mid M = 0) - E(v_0 \mid M = 1) \tag{17}$$

Since Table 12.1 contains four different entries, some redundancy is present. The measures in (12)–(17) are related through:

$$\varepsilon_1 = \psi_1 - \delta_0 = \delta_1 - \psi_0, \tag{18}$$

$$\varepsilon_0 = \psi_0 - \delta_0 = \delta_1 - \psi_1 \tag{19}$$

## 3. Econometric Issues

In the typical cross-section data set, we have information on a vector of explanatory variables ($\underline{z}$), migration status ($M$), and earnings ($y$) which is observed either at the origin ($M = 0$), or at the destination ($M = 1$). Coupled with assumptions about the statistical properties of the model, this information is sufficient to test the implications of rational migration presented above. Toward that end, suppose that earnings depend on a subset $\underline{x}$ of the explanatory variables and costs depend on a subset $\underline{w}$, so that $\underline{z} = \{\underline{x} \cup \underline{w}\}$. The population means ($\mu_0$, $\mu_1$ and $\kappa$) defined for the anticipations may be expressed as linear functions of the observables to capture the systematic components of earnings and costs. After some algebra, we obtain the Switching Regression (SR) version of the model as[6]

$$y^* = \underline{\xi}'\underline{z} + v \tag{20}$$

$$M = \begin{cases} 1, \text{ iff } y^* > 0 \\ 0, \text{ iff } y^* \leq 0 \end{cases} \tag{21}$$

$$y_0 = \underline{\pi}'\underline{x} \qquad\quad + u_0 \tag{22}$$

$$y_1 = \underline{\pi}'\underline{x} + \underline{\delta}'\underline{x} + u_1 \tag{23}$$

$$y = \begin{cases} y_0 & \text{iff } M = 0 \\ y_1 & \text{iff } M = 1 \end{cases} \tag{24}$$

The estimation techniques I use in this paper build on a popular two-step procedure developed by Heckman (1974, 1976, 1978) and Lee (1978, 1979), which assumes that the disturbances $v$, $u_0$, $u_1$ are independent of $\underline{z}$, and are trivariate Normally distributed with zero expectations and positive definite covariance matrix:

$$\begin{bmatrix} \sigma_v^2 & \sigma_v\gamma_{01} & \sigma_v\gamma_{11} \\ \sigma_v\gamma_{01} & \sigma_0^2 & \omega \\ \sigma_v\gamma_{11} & \omega & \sigma_1^2 \end{bmatrix} \tag{25}$$

At the first step, the migration equation is estimated using probit analysis. At the second step, the earnings equations are estimated using linear regression, by including generated regressors (so-called inverse Mill's ratios) that adjust for selectivity.

I will refer to the simpler version of the model, which imposes the testable restriction $\underline{\delta}'\underline{x} = \delta$, as the Additive Shift (AS) model. This restriction has an important implication: In the AS model, it is heterogeneity in the systematic costs of migration alone that makes the systematic component of $y^*$ depend on the individual's characteristics.

Regardless of the distributional assumption invoked, there is broad agreement in the findings from reduced-form equations that examine the determinants of the migration decision. This suggests that survey data typically satisfy the mild restrictions under which slope coefficients of index-function models will be estimated consistently (up to a factor of proportionality) using any one of the commonly used techniques such as logit and probit, even ordinary least squares (Ruud, 1983; Stoker, 1986). When the earnings outcome of the migration decision is examined, however, the results appear to be sensitive to the specification of the model (Tunalı, 1985, 1986). Research done in other contexts suggests two possible explanations: (i) violation of the joint Normality assumption (Lee, 1982;

Heckman and Sedlacek, 1985; Heckman and MaCurdy, 1986); (ii) improper representation of the selection rule (Heckman and Robb, 1986; Heckman, Hotz and Dabos, 1987; Heckman and Hotz, 1989).

To deal with the first issue, I use Lee's (1982) extension of the original Heckman-Lee framework. Lee's generalization is based on an expansion of the joint density of the selection and outcome equations as a series in the derivatives of the standard bivariate Normal density function. If the disturbance of the selection equation ($v$) is Normally distributed, computations simplify considerably. In this case, Lee's modification of the second step yields a convenient polynomial specification that nests the conventional Heckman-Lee correction for selectivity within a linear regression framework. I follow this route and thereby maintain the assumption that $v$ is Normally distributed throughout the paper.[7]

Since the model entertained here does not satisfy the requirements for non-parametric identifiability of the extended Roy model (see Heckman, 1990), it does not circumvent the vulnerability of the conventional Heckman-Lee framework to the criticism that identification is achieved through parametric assumptions. On the other hand, in the typical migration study, exclusion restrictions arise naturally because the migration decision precedes the assessment of the income consequences by several years. Additional exclusions from the outcome equation can be justified because of the dependence of the migration decision on the costs of moving. Given the nature of the data I had, alternative approaches favored by Heckman and his colleagues could not be employed; thus the second issue could not be addressed convincingly.[8] The specific identifying assumptions are discussed in the next section.

**Table 12.2: Measures of the Migration Effect[#]**

| | |
|---|---|
| Returns to migration: | $\delta_1 = E(y_1 \mid M = 1) - E(y_0 \mid M = 1) = \delta + (\underline{\gamma}_1 - \underline{\gamma}_0)'\underline{\lambda}_1$ |
| Returns to staying: | $\delta_0 = E(y_0 \mid M = 0) - E(y_1 \mid M = 0) = -\delta + (\underline{\gamma}_0 - \underline{\gamma}_1)'\underline{\lambda}_0$ |
| Sorting gains to migration: | $\theta_1 = (\underline{\gamma}_1 - \underline{\gamma}_0)'\underline{\lambda}_1$ |
| Sorting gains to staying: | $\theta_0 = (\underline{\gamma}_0 - \underline{\gamma}_1)'\underline{\lambda}_0$ |
| Selection of migrants: | $\psi_1 = E(y_1 \mid M = 1) - E(y_1 \mid M = 0) = \underline{\gamma}_1'(\underline{\lambda}_1 - \underline{\lambda}_0)$ |
| Selection of stayers: | $\psi_0 = E(y_0 \mid M = 0) - E(y_0 \mid M = 1) = \underline{\gamma}_0'(\underline{\lambda}_0 - \underline{\lambda}_1)$ |
| Earnings differential in favor of migrants: | $\varepsilon_1 = E(y_1 \mid M = 1) - E(y_0 \mid M = 0) = \delta + \underline{\gamma}_1'\underline{\lambda}_1 - \underline{\gamma}_0'\underline{\lambda}_0$ |

*Notes:* [#] The elements of the 3×1 vectors $\underline{\lambda}_j$ (j = 0,1) that correct for unobserved heterogeneity (selectivity) are: $\lambda_{j1} = \phi(\xi)[j - \Phi(\xi)] / \{\Phi(\xi)[1 - \Phi(\xi)]\}$, $\lambda_{j2} = -\xi\, \lambda_{j1}$, $\lambda_{j3} = (\xi^2 - 1)\, \lambda_{j1}$, where $\xi = \underline{\xi}'\underline{z}$, and functions $\phi(.)$, $\Phi(.)$ respectively denote the standard univariate Normal pdf and cdf.

My objective in the empirical part of this chapter is to confront the model of rational migration with the data, by exploiting the measures of the migration effect discussed in section 2. In the implemented version of the model, the assumption that anticipations are unbiased may be restated as the requirement that the forecast errors have zero means independently of migration status and the covariates: $E(f_m \mid M, \underline{z}) = 0$, m = 0, 1. The analytical expressions for the measures are compiled in Table 12.2. In the interest of brevity, conditioning arguments other than $M$ and possible dependence of $\delta$ on $\underline{x}$ (as in the SR model) have been suppressed. Unobserved heterogeneity is captured by the $\lambda$'s, which are the generated regressors included in the earnings equations estimated in the second step. The expressions for the elements of the $\lambda$'s are given in the note to Table 12.2.

## 4. Data and Empirical Strategy

The empirical work is based on data from a 1973 nationwide survey done by Hacettepe Institute of Population Studies (HIPS), Ankara, Turkey. The working sample consists of 2429 employed male household heads in the 18–65 age bracket in 1973, for whom complete internal migration and employment histories for the 1963–73 period, as well as information on other variables of interest, were available. For the purposes of this study, migration is defined as a change in the 1963 residence, providing the move took the individual at least across a village boundary. According to this definition 28 percent of the males in the sample were classified as migrants. Because income and migration information are available for a subsample of the original sample of over 4242 households, non-reporting bias has to be accounted for. This problem is easily handled by modifying the two-step procedure.

**Table 12.3: Model Specifications#**

| | | Covariates | Date measured |
|---|---|---|---|
| Migration equation: | | human capital variables | time invariant |
| | | location variables | 1963 |
| | | occupation variables | 1963 |
| | | cost variables | 1963 |
| Sample selection equation: | | | |
| | | human capital variables | time invariant |
| | | location variables | 1973 |
| | | occupation variables | 1973 |
| Earnings equation: | | | |
| | Model I: | human capital variables | time invariant |
| | | location variables | 1973 |
| | | occupation variables | 1973 |
| | Model II: | human capital variables | time invariant |
| | | location variables | 1973 |
| | | occupation variables | 1973 |
| | | household controls | 1973 |
| Unobserved heterogeneity: | | | |
| | Model A: | none | |
| | Model B: | conventional correction for migration selectivity | 1963–73# |
| | Model C: | robust correction for migration selectivity | 1963–73# |
| | Model D: | conventional correction for migration selectivity & conventional correction for non-reporting bias | 1963–73# |
| | Model E: | robust correction for migration selectivity & conventional correction for non-reporting bias | 1963–73# |
| | Model F: | robust correction for migration selectivity & robust correction for non-reporting bias | 1963–73# |

*Notes:* # Information on 1963–73 migration status, as well as the variables in the migration equation, was used.

A second modification is introduced to account for the fact that the dependent variable in the earnings equation is the (natural) logarithm of household, rather than individual income. Self-employment and agricultural production constitute major forms of economic activity in Turkey. As a consequence, the standard earnings concept applies to a very small segment of the population. Furthermore, for households that have more than one breadwinner, the migration decision has implications for the economic activities undertaken by the entire household. These two observations suggest that household income, as opposed to individual earnings, is the appropriate concept for studying migration. There is some evidence that measurement errors on the dependent variable can not be readily ignored in models with selectivity (see Stapleton and Young, 1984). To isolate the variation associated with sources other than the earnings of the male household head, I also report estimates from a longer version of the earnings equation.

The model specifications are identified in Table 12.3. The first step consists of estimating two independent probit models: One for the endogenous migration decision, and a second for sample selection that is induced by non-reporting. To account for (the earnings implications of) unobserved heterogeneity in the migration equation, three regressors each were generated for migrants and for stayers. To account for unobserved heterogeneity in the sample selection equation, three additional regressors were generated. Model labels A through F indicate the type of correction applied to the earnings equations. Robust correction refers to Lee's (1982) generalization, which is robust against non-Normality of the regression equation disturbance. Conventional correction refers to the original Heckman-Lee method, in which case the parameter vector $\underline{\gamma}'_j = (\gamma_{j1}, \gamma_{j2}, \gamma_{j3})$, j = 0,1, is restricted to be $(\gamma_{j1}, 0, 0)$, where $\gamma$'s are the terms that appear in the covariance matrix in (25). Model labels I and II distinguish the specification of the observables in the earnings equations. Note that time-varying covariates are measured at different points in time, depending on the nature of the dependent variable.

Variable definitions and descriptive statistics are reported in Table 12.4. The differences in the mean values of the explanatory variables in the working sample and in the full sample are minor. The same list of human capital, location, and occupation variables was used in all three equations. Variables grouped under the subheading migration costs were excluded from the sample selection equation and the earnings equation. While some of these have human capital interpretations, their location specificity coupled with the fact that they have been measured at the point of origin in 1963, justify the exclusions. Turning to the earnings equation, a very rich specification was adopted to do justice to the theory in section 2, which views the migration decision as a function of anticipated earnings. In addition to the conventional measures of human capital, variables that measure quality differences were also included. Institutional features, non-pecuniary factors, and compensating differentials were captured using location and occupation dummies. Finally, in an attempt to guard against measurement-error related biases, a long list of household controls were included in the specification identified as model II.

## 5. Empirical Evidence

The emphasis in this section is on the measures of the migration effect compiled in Table 12.2, which were used to test the implications of the model of rational migration. Estimation results from the probit step, and partial results from the linear regression step, are collected in the Appendix. I begin with a brief review of these results. Heteroscedasticity-consistent standard errors are reported throughout.

### Table 12.4: Variable Definitions and Descriptive Statistics#

| | Migration eq. Mean (std.dev.) | Selection eq. Mean (std.dev.) | Earnings eq. Mean (std.dev.) |
|---|---|---|---|
| **Dependent variables:** | | | |
| Migrated during 1963–73* | 0.28 (0.45) | — | — |
| Included in the working sample* | — | 0.57 (0.49) | — |
| Log. of household income | — | — | 9.68 ( 0.87) |
| **Human capital:** | | | |
| Years of formal schooling | 4.04 (3.61) | 4.60 (4.09) | 4.04 (3.61) |
| Experience | 13.8 (10.1) | 21.2 (14.2) | 23.6 (10.5) |
| Literate* | 0.81 (0.39) | 0.81 (0.39) | 0.81 (0.39) |
| Received elementary school diploma after age 15* | 0.08 (0.27) | 0.06 (0.24) | 0.08 (0.27) |
| Vocational school diploma* | 0.03 (0.18) | 0.05 (0.22) | 0.03 (0.18) |
| Age | 30.7 (10.1) | 40.8 (14.7) | 40.7 (10.1) |
| **Location:** | | | |
| Major metropolitan area (Ankara, Istanbul, Izmir)* | 0.20 (0.40) | 0.24 (0.43) | 0.24 (0.43) |
| Other large city* | 0.17 (0.38) | 0.19 (0.39) | 0.18 (0.39) |
| Other urban area (reference)* | 0.30 (0.46) | 0.35 (0.48) | 0.36 (0.48) |
| Rural area* | 0.33 (0.47) | 0.22 (0.41) | 0.22 (0.41) |
| Northern region* | 0.14 (0.34) | 0.12 (0.33) | 0.12 (0.33) |
| Western region* | 0.33 (0.47) | 0.35 (0.48) | 0.36 (0.48) |
| Southern region* | 0.13 (0.34) | 0.13 (0.34) | 0.14 (0.34) |
| Eastern region * | 0.17 (0.38) | 0.14 (0.34) | 0.16 (0.36) |
| Central region (reference)* | 0.23 (0.42) | 0.26 (0.44) | 0.22 (0.41) |
| **Occupation:** | | | |
| Self-employed professional* | 0.005 (0.067) | 0.007 (0.082) | 0.007 (0.081) |
| Self-employed outside agriculture or employer* | 0.20 (0.40) | 0.24 (0.43) | 0.28 (0.45) |
| Manager or supervisor* | 0.043 (0.20) | 0.029 (0.17) | 0.035 (0.18) |
| Semi-autonomous worker* | 0.041 (0.20) | 0.041 (0.20) | 0.04 (0.20) |
| Non-agricultural worker* | 0.32 (0.47) | 0.31 (0.46) | 0.37 (0.48) |
| Self-employed in agriculture* | 0.28 (0.45) | 0.16 (0.37) | 0.18 (0.39) |
| Agricultural worker (reference)* | 0.11 (0.31) | 0.21 (0.19) | 0.056 (0.23) |
| **Migration costs:** | | | |
| No job-related security* | 0.57 (0.50) | — | — |
| Unemployed* | 0.075 (0.26) | — | — |
| Years of residence | 19.5 (13.6) | — | — |
| Province development index | 1.13 (0.70) | — | — |
| Number of previous moves | 1.05 (1.41) | — | — |
| **Household controls:** | | | |
| No. of breadwinners (outside ag.) | — | — | 0.93 (0.69) |
| Married (in agriculture)* | — | — | 0.23 (0.42) |
| Has working age children (in ag.)* | — | — | 0.18 (0.38) |
| Has no supplementary income* | — | — | 0.79 (0.41) |
| Has no real estate* | — | — | 0.42 (0.49) |
| Has no productive animals* | — | — | 0.071 (0.26) |
| Head intermittently employed* | — | — | 0.067 (0.25) |
| Father self-employed in ag.* | — | — | 0.57 (0.50) |
| Father literate* | — | — | 0.40 (0.49) |
| Father has more than elementary school education* | — | — | 0.031 (0.17) |
| **Sample size:** | 2429 | 4242 | 2429 |

*Notes:* # See Table 12.3 for the dates on which the variables were measured.
* Indicator variables (= 1 if the definition applies, = 0 else).

### *5.1. First step*

The probit estimates of the migration equation are reported in Appendix Table 12.A1. Based on goodness-of-fit and prediction criteria, the model fits the data very well. The results reinforce the findings of the migration literature. As the determinants of migration in Turkey during the 1963–73 period have been discussed in detail in Tunalı (1996, 1997), I do not dwell on the subject here. Turning to the probit estimates of the sample selection equation reported in Table 12.A2, we find that inclusion status is predicted extremely well using the observables. Inclusion probability decreases with years of formal schooling. It increases until 41 years of age (which is the mean value in both samples), then decreases. The pattern with respect to experience is similar, except the maximum is reached at 45 years. Coefficients on the occupation and location dummies reveal that a disproportionate number of agricultural workers, persons residing in the central region, and persons residing in large cities other than Ankara, Istanbul, and Izmir have been excluded from the working sample.

### *5.2. Second step*

Linear regression estimates of the AS version of the earnings equation under specifications I-A and II-A are reported in Tables 12.A3 and 12.A4. In Model I covariates explain 26 percent of the variation in the logarithm of household income. When household controls are added in Model II, this figure exceeds 31 percent. We find that literacy and formal schooling matter; somewhat surprisingly, labor market experience does not. However, earnings increase with age. The coefficient estimates change marginally when unobserved heterogeneity revealed by choice of migration status is accounted for. Substantial changes in the coefficients of occupation and location dummies are found when non-reporting bias is taken into consideration. The estimated return to schooling is about two percentage points higher. These changes are consistent with the patterns in Table 12.A2. To save space, detailed results from AS specifications B through F have been left out of the paper.

### *5.3. Model diagnostics*

Results from Wald tests that exploit the nesting features of the estimated models are reported in Table 12.5. Starting with the rightmost column, we see that the AS restrictions hold up. Turning to the specification of unobserved heterogeneity terms, we find that the evidence favors the robust, rather than the conventional, method of correction. If our interest is confined to the sub-population of prime-age employed male household heads represented by the working sample, tests favor models I-C and II-C. If inferences for the full population are called for, model I-C still fares well, but II-C does not. If concerns with the nature of the dependent variable are taken seriously, then at a minimum model II-E is called for.

As a further check of the adequacy of the conventional Heckman-Lee method, properties of the earnings equation residuals obtained from models A, B, and D were examined. In all the cases, the empirical distributions of the residuals were non-symmetric and heavily skewed. The tests recommended by D'Agostino, Belanger, and D'Agostino Jr. (1990) handily reject the null hypothesis of Normality.[9] In sum, the results from the regression step strongly point to the need for estimation methods that are robust against departures from Normality.

**Table 12.5: Model Diagnostics#**
**Marginal Significance of the Null Model under Alternative Specifications of Unobserved Heterogeneity**

| | Alternative Specification | | | | | |
|---|---|---|---|---|---|---|
| **Null model** | **B** | **C** | **D** | **E** | **F** | **SR** |
| AS I-A | 0.16 | 0.02 | 0.19 | 0.027 | 0.016 | 0.52 |
| AS I-B | — | 0.022 | 0.29 | 0.033 | 0.02 | 0.51 |
| AS I-C | — | — | — | 0.40 | 0.15 | 0.47 |
| AS I-D | — | — | — | 0.026 | 0.016 | 0.39 |
| AS I-E | — | — | — | — | 0.10 | 0.28 |
| AS II-A | 0.06 | 0.024 | 0.042 | 0.02 | 0.013 | 0.63 |
| AS II-B | — | 0.064 | 0.11 | 0.053 | 0.032 | 0.58 |
| AS II-C | — | — | — | 0.03 | 0.19 | 0.53 |
| AS II-D | — | — | — | 0.078 | 0.046 | 0.52 |
| AS II-E | — | — | — | — | 0.11 | 0.48 |

*Notes:* # See Table 12.3 for model definitions.

### *5.4. Evidence on δ*

The subset of parameter estimates collected in Table 12.A5 indicate that the estimated value of $\delta$ is highly sensitive to the specification of unobserved heterogeneity. As shown in section 2, $\delta$ may be interpreted as the average price attached to migrant status in the labor market. Treating migrant status as any other observable trait—such as region of origin—large negative $\delta$ values obtained in the preferred models indicate that being a migrant is viewed as a negative productivity trait in the labor market. Note, however, that no individual left to his own devices will be subjected to this earnings reduction. The estimated value of $\delta$ is a meaningful number only if migration status is exogenously determined, taking the $\underline{x}$ vector as given. This experiment amounts to breaking the structure given by (the AS version of) equations (17)-(21). When the structure is kept intact, migrant status depends on $\underline{x}$, as well as unobservables. What makes migration an interesting phenomenon is that of two individuals who otherwise look the same, one migrates, and the other does not. Thus, proper understanding of the earnings consequences of migration, calls for the incorporation of the sorting mechanism into the migration effect measure. The difference between hypothetical destination and home earnings averaged over all individuals says nothing about the very process that sets movers apart from stayers.

### *5.5. Measures of the effect of migration on earnings*

In sample means and standard deviations of the estimates of the migration effect measures are reported in Table 12.6.[10] The estimates of the parameters that enter the migration effect measures are compiled in Appendix Table 12.A5. Recall that the diagnostic tests favored model I-C, and models II-E or II-F. All three models yield a very small mean earnings differential in favor of stayers, rather than migrants. However, the magnitude of the standard deviation suggests that there is considerable variation in the individuals' experiences.

Turning to the measures that exploit the counterfactual route reported in Table 12.6, we find that the mean values of three of the four measures support the rationality hypothesis in the case of model I-C. The record is perfect when models II-E and II-F are examined. Observe that the mean of the returns to migration are minuscule (<0.02) in the case of models II-E and II-F, compared to the negative magnitude (–0.13) produced by model I-C. It turns out that large negative values are responsible for the weak support for rationality (see Table 12.A5). When we turn to the sorting gains from migration, the means are respectively 0.37 (I-C), 0.49 (II-E), and 0.45 (II-F). We conclude, then, that the sample means of the measures in the preferred models favor the rationality hypothesis. However, with the exception of the estimated magnitude for selection of migrants, none of the means exceeds zero by more than two standard deviations. This suggests that there are winners, as well as a sizable number of losers.

**Table 12.6: Estimates of the Migration Effect Measures**

Sample Means (standard deviations)

| **Measure*** | **Model#** | B | C | D | E | F |
|---|---|---|---|---|---|---|
| Returns to migration (migrant subsample) | AS I | –0.13 | –0.13 | –0.12 | –0.12 | –0.11 |
| | | (0.043) | (0.24) | (0.044) | (0.24) | (0.26) |
| | AS II | –0.10 | 0.0092 | –0.095 | 0.0077 | 0.018 |
| | | (0.065) | (0.36) | (0.068) | (0.35) | (0.36) |
| Returns to staying (stayer subsample) | AS I | 0.25 | 0.77 | 0.25 | 0.80 | 0.74 |
| | | (0.025) | (0.22) | (0.025) | (0.23) | (0.21) |
| | AS II | 0.28 | 0.61 | 0.28 | 0.65 | 0.60 |
| | | (0.038) | (0.16) | (0.039) | (0.18) | (0.16) |
| Selection of migrants (migrant subsample) | AS I | 0.25 | 1.11 | 0.25 | 1.16 | 1.07 |
| | | (0.023) | (0.45) | (0.023) | (0.47) | (0.42) |
| | AS II | 0.29 | 0.82 | 0.30 | 0.91 | 0.82 |
| | | (0.027) | (0.28) | (0.027) | (0.33) | (0.28) |
| Selection of stayers (stayer subsample) | AS I | –0.10 | 0.18 | –0.10 | 0.18 | 0.22 |
| | | (0.015) | (0.61) | (0.015) | (0.60) | (0.65) |
| | AS II | –0.060 | 0.50 | –0.053 | 0.47 | 0.51 |
| | | (0.0089) | (0.80) | (0.0079) | (0.76) | (0.81) |
| Earnings differential in favor of migrants (full sample) | AS I | 0.013 | –0.020 | 0.015 | –0.018 | –0.018 |
| | | (0.066) | (0.20) | (0.066) | (0.20) | (0.21) |
| | AS II | 0.016 | –0.010 | 0.019 | –0.0073 | –0.0071 |
| | | (0.087) | (0.21) | (0.089) | (0.20) | (0.21) |

*Notes:* * See Table 12.2 for the definitions of the measures.
# See Table 12.3 for model definitions.

To underscore the importance of heterogeneity, I turn to graphical representations of the findings and focus on model II throughout. The patterns that emerge from model I are very similar. The issue of rationality being my main concern, I begin by analyzing the returns to migration with the aid of Appendix Figure 12.A1. The two top panels in Figure 12.A1 show the empirical distributions of the estimated values of returns to migration, while the two bottom panels plot the returns to migration as a function of the move probability. The panels at the top inform us about heterogeneity in our sample. The bottom panels exploit the parametric assumptions fully and allow us to assess the broader implications of the findings by treating the migration probability as a sufficient statistic for unobserved heterogeneity.[11] Panels (c) and (d) are from our preferred model II-E. Results from model II-D, which relies on the conventional correction method, are included in panels (a) and (b) for comparison. Note that the horizontal axes of all four panels have the same scale. The dotted vertical lines in panels (b) and (d) represent the estimated value of $\delta$ in model II-A, which does not adjust for selectivity.

From panel (c), we learn that about 75 percent of the migrants in our sample realized negative returns to their decision. The distribution is heavily skewed to the right: A small segment of migrants reaped very high positive returns. Turning to panel (d), we see that individuals with very low move probabilities are the ones who realize large positive returns to migration. In terms of their observed characteristics, these individuals constitute a minority in observed migration flows. However, they have unobserved traits that render them successful as migrants. By contrast, many of the losers share characteristics that make migration highly likely. These high propensity migrants suffer, perhaps because they flood the destination labor markets.

Before we pursue the issue of rationality further, note that model II-D (which is rejected by the diagnostics) presents a more negative picture. In panel (a), the proportion of migrants who realized negative returns is close to 90 percent. The long right tail observed in panel (c) is missing. Evidently the conventional method of adjusting for selectivity fails to capture the complicated form of unobserved heterogeneity: The returns to migration function plotted in panel (b) is a very poor approximation for the pattern displayed in panel (d).

Returning to model II-E, what are we to make of the finding that a very large majority of the migrants experienced a reduction in income compared to what they would have earned at their point of origin? One possibility that comes to mind is that the losses might be of a transitory nature. I pursued this explanation by regressing the estimated returns on duration of stay in the 1973 locality, but failed to detect any relationship. It appears the losses are there to stay. Note, however, that for a broad range of move probabilities (from about 0.4 to 0.8) the predicted income loss is about 10 percent. The model predicts that a majority of migrants will end up settling for a small reduction in income. A small minority will succeed—perhaps it is this possibility that pushes individuals to seek their fortunes elsewhere. This pattern is consistent with theoretical models of migration behavior that allow for risk (see, for instance, David, 1974, Katz and Stark, 1986, and Vishwanath, 1991).[12]

As mentioned earlier, it is the large negative value of the estimated coefficient on migration status, $\delta$, which is responsible for the negative returns to migration. In fact, the estimated values of the sorting gains from migration are positive for all the migrants.[13] That is, the unobserved traits of migrants indeed give them an edge under the chosen option. This point is reinforced when we assess the nature of the selection using our second measure, which is graphed in Figure 12.A2. The frequency distribution in panel (c) indicates that migrants are indeed positively selected. Compared to observationally identical individuals who chose to stay, all migrants do better under the migration option. Recall that the move probability summarizes what we are able to infer about unobserved heterogeneity. The shape of the selection of migrants function plotted in panel (d) indicates that the counterfactual earnings gap in favor of migrants increases with migration probability, except when that probability is very low. The picture that emerges from the conventional correction method is radically different, as seen in panels (a) and (b). Once again, the functional form assumed for unobserved heterogeneity in the conventional Heckman-Lee approach is not flexible enough to track the upper tail of the distribution.

The premise of rationality is strengthened upon examination of the evidence on the stayers' side. As we see in Figure 12.A3, the estimated returns from staying are positive for all individuals in the non-migrant subsample. Obviously the same caveat about $\delta$ applies:

Large estimated negative values of $\delta$ favor stayers. When we focus on the sorting gains from staying instead, we find that about one percent of the stayers realize negative gains (model II-E).[14] When we turn to the nature of the selection at work, we see that not all stayers are positively selected (see Figure 12.A4). According to the results from model II-E, 36 percent of the stayers do worse than what observationally identical migrants would have experienced. In panel (d), we see that stayers who are indifferent about moving or staying are predicted to be negatively selected. It appears that migrants in this range have unobservable traits that would have given them an edge over stayers. Once again, the contrast between the results obtained from conventional correction [panels (a) and (c)], and robust correction [panels (b) and (d)] is striking.

### *5.6. Returns by type of migration*

The AS model treats the parameter $\delta$ as a constant across all individuals. As noted earlier, this restriction held up in all the models when tested against the unrestricted SR version. As a further check of the restrictions, I experimented with relaxing the AS constraint partially, and allowing $\delta$ to be different across migrant types. The vast literature on migration reminds us that not all migrations are the same. Some migrants move shorter distances, others longer distances. Some return to the point of origin, a small segment move again. A possible explanation for this pattern is that remigration is undertaken as a corrective measure, when realizations fall below expectations (Polachek and Horvath, 1977; DaVanzo, 1981; McCall and McCall, 1987; Pessino, 1991; Vishwanath, 1991). Since cost and information implications of different types of moves are different, we might expect to find differences in the returns to migration by type of migration undertaken.

The definition of migration used until now is a very wide one: Individuals who relocated by crossing the boundary of their village were classified as migrants. When I used successively narrower definitions that drew the boundary respectively at district and province level, the results changed marginally. Based on model II-E, the mean return from migration at the district level was about 5 percent lower, and at the province level about 5 percent higher, compared to the village level. The shapes of the frequency distributions were very similar.

When I broke down the migrant category further as one-time, repeat, and return movers, the differences in returns once again turned out to be minor.[15] When I re-examined the returns using a 2x2 classification of the origin and destination locations, however, some important differences emerged. The frequency distributions of the estimated returns to migration are graphed in Figure 12.A5 by migration type. The contrasts are remarkable. We find that individuals with rural origins (49 percent) are the ones who experience negative returns in large numbers. Individuals who originate their moves in an urban locality (51 percent) have a distinct advantage, perhaps because they have access to better information about opportunities elsewhere.

In the elaborations on the original model, the adjustment for unobserved heterogeneity was handled in the same manner for all migrant types. While the resulting estimates are still consistent, they might be inefficient. More precise and richer contrasts may be drawn when more elaborate forms of selectivity into migration types are allowed. Since the computational burden increases immensely, I chose to limit my analysis to the simplest case for the purposes of this paper.

### 5.7. Earnings differentials

Although redundancy is present, I conclude my discussion of the empirical findings with an examination of the heterogeneity in the earnings differentials. Recall that the measure I termed earnings differential in favor of migrants ($\varepsilon_1$) compares the experience of the average migrant with that of the average non-migrant. The results are given in Figure 12.A6. Beginning with panel (c), we see that the opportunities are there, but the magnitudes in question are very small for an overwhelming majority of the individuals in our sample. The plot in panel (d) suggests that the labor markets have been unkind to individuals with move probabilities in the 0.15–0.90 range. Evidently the opportunities are there for a small segment of the population, whose traits place them at the tails of the heterogeneity distribution. In fact, the frequency distribution for the migrant subgroup (not shown) indicates that the estimated earnings differential is negative for 40 percent of the individuals in this subsample. Finally, panels (a) and (b) once again forcefully demonstrate the ramifications of drawing conclusions from models based on conventional methods of correction for selectivity. A policy maker confronted with the frequency distribution in panel (a) might be alarmed that there are sizable differentials favoring individuals who have not yet exercised the migration option (low probability migrants). The picture that emerges from panel (c) is that the markets have done a pretty good job of allocating jobs and people.

## 6. Summary and Conclusions

In this chapter, I subject the paradigm of a rational individual acting upon the earnings-enhancing benefits of migration to careful statistical scrutiny, using a rich data set from Turkey. I find that the Normality assumption routinely invoked in empirical work is rejected by the income data, and that conclusions based on the conventional method of adjusting for selectivity can be seriously misleading. Results with Lee's robust selectivity correction method support the rationality hypothesis: Both migrants and non-migrants chose the option in which they had comparative advantage. However, the estimated gain from moving is found to be negative for a substantial portion of the migrants.

According to my estimates, three-fourths of the internal migrants in Turkey over the 1963–73 period have realized a negative return. The bulk of the losses are in the 10–20 percent range, and appear to be of a non-transitory nature. By contrast, a small segment of migrants reap very high returns, some in excess of 100 percent. This finding lends credence to theoretical models that view the migration decision as a risky undertaking. Under this interpretation, migrants engage in a lottery of sorts: if they are lucky, they do extremely well. However, a very large majority of them may have to settle for a loss.

Another possible interpretation is that the migrants are making mistakes, and are moving when they should not. The literature recognizes that subsequent moves take place as individuals learn from their mistakes and take corrective action. My exploratory examinations of this possibility suggests that it might be worthwhile to break migrants into subgroups which can be differentiated by the amount of information they are likely to have had at the time about the move. In fact I find that migrants originating in urban areas do much better than migrants originating in rural areas. The explorations suggest that it might be fruitful to relax the assumption of unbiased anticipations, and look for evidence of systematic differences in forecast errors across individuals.

# Appendix

Figure 12.A1: Returns to Migration: $\delta_1$ (migrant subsample)

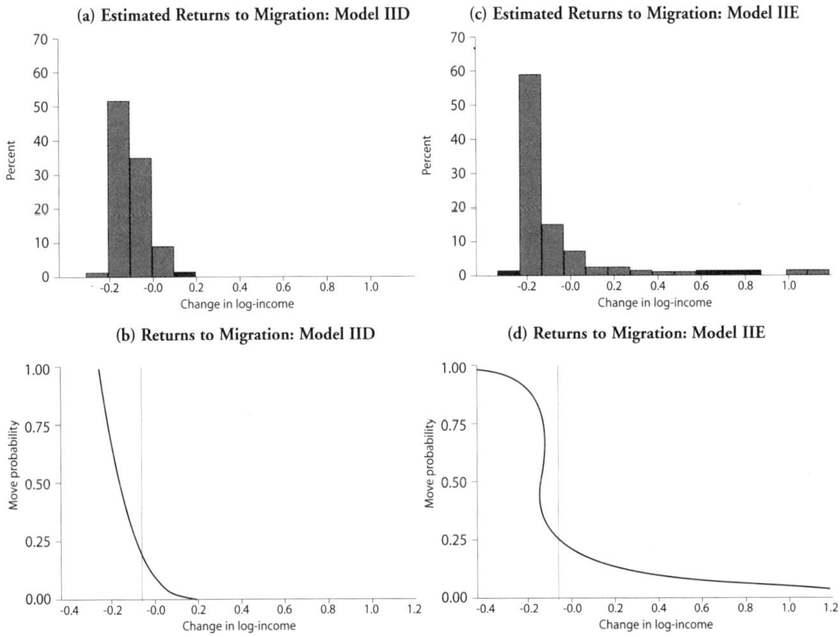


Figure 12.A2: Selection of Migrants: $\psi_1$ (migrant subsample)

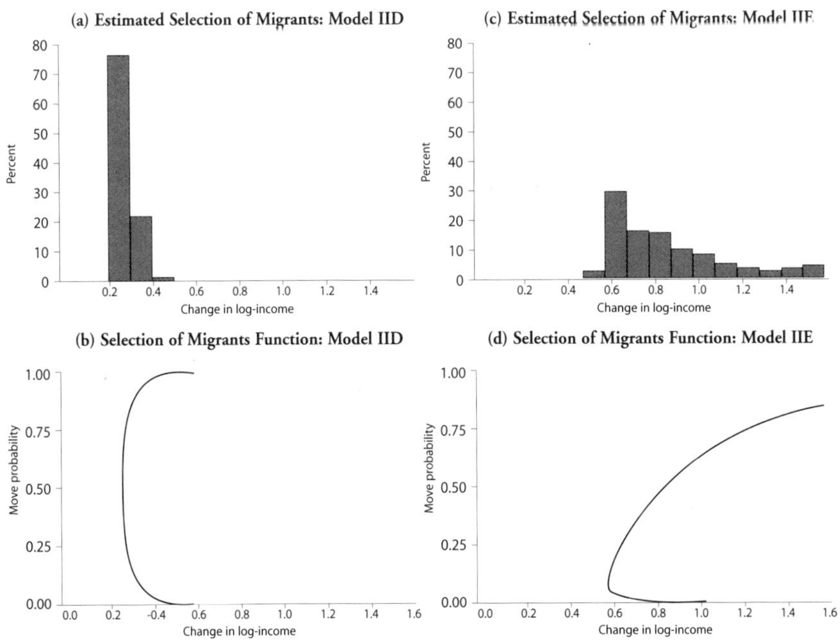

## Figure 12.A3: Returns to Staying: $\delta_0$ (stayer subsample)

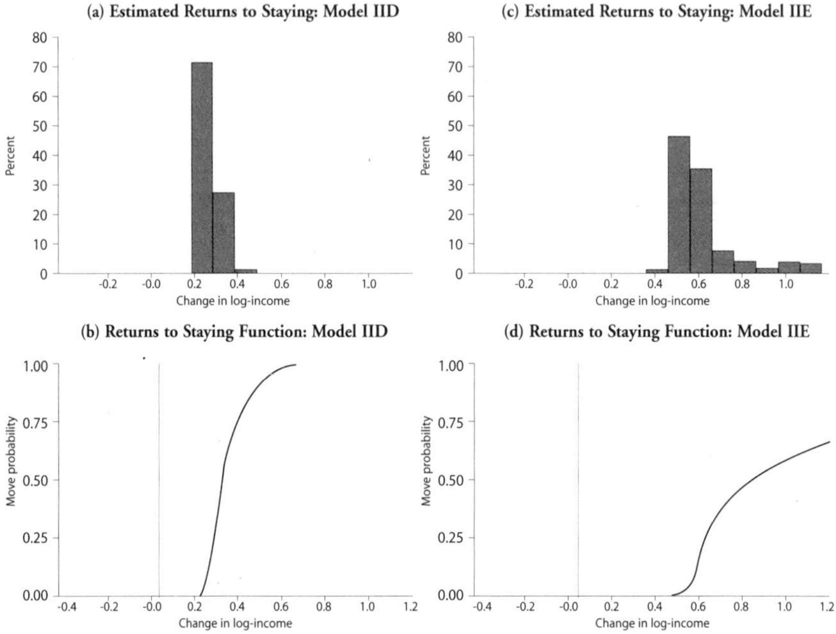


## Figure 12.A4. Selection of Stayers: $\psi_0$ (stayer subsample)

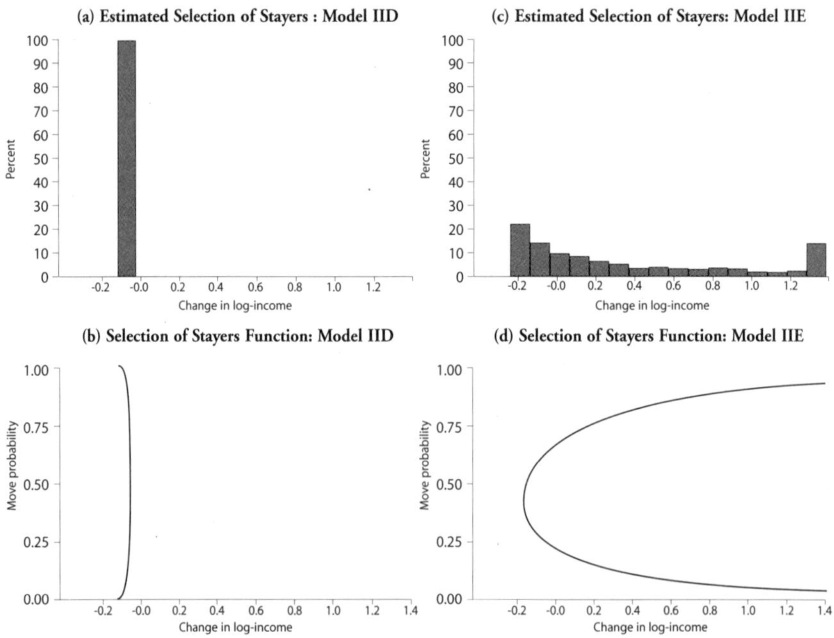

**Figure 12.A5: Returns to Migration ($\delta_1$) by Type of Move (migrant subsample)**

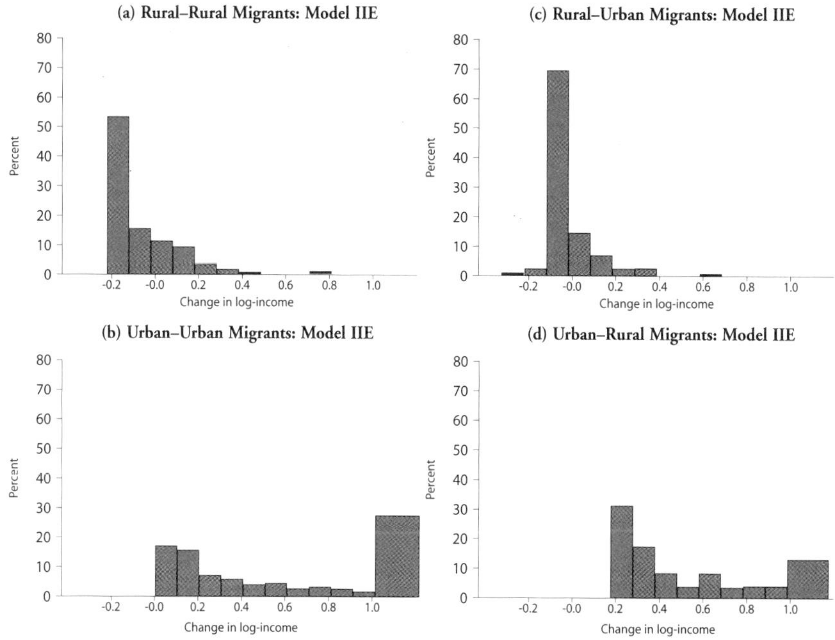


**Figure 12.A6: Earnings Differential in Favor of Migrants: $\varepsilon_1$ (full sample)**

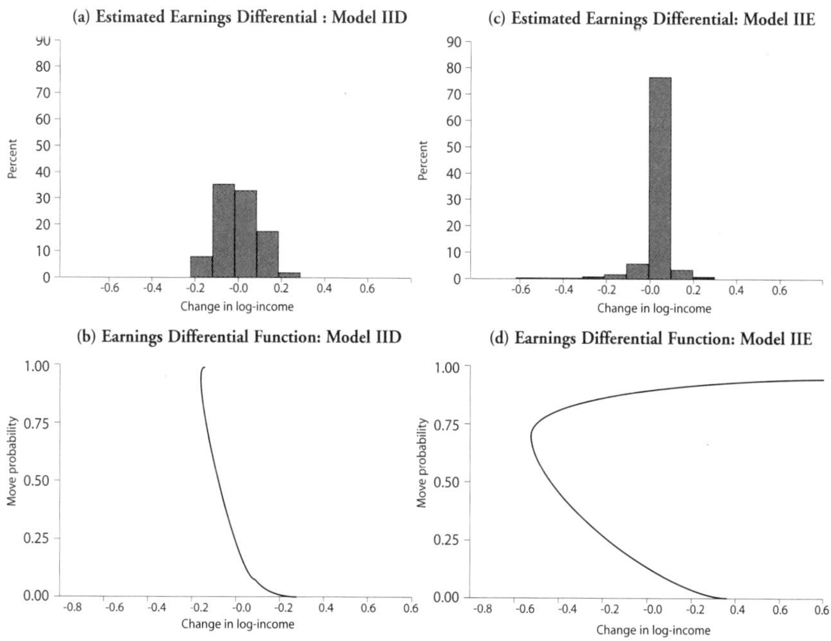

**Table 12.A1: Maximum Likelihood (Probit) Estimates of the Migration Equation[#]**
**Dependent variable: 1 = migrated during 1963–73, 0 = else.**

| | Estimate | Std. error | p-value |
|---|---|---|---|
| Constant | −1.09 | 0.46 | 0.02 |
| Years of formal schooling | 0.050 | 0.013 | <0.01 |
| Experience | −0.066 | 0.017 | <0.01 |
| Experience squared | 0.14 | 0.051 | <0.01 |
| Literate | 0.056 | 0.10 | 0.58 |
| Received elementary school diploma after age 15 | 0.27 | 0.11 | 0.01 |
| Vocational school diploma | 0.30 | 0.17 | 0.08 |
| Age | 0.035 | 0.03 | 0.26 |
| Age squared | −0.074 | 0.051 | 0.15 |
| Major metropolitan area (Ankara, Istanbul, Izmir) | −0.0078 | 0.14 | 0.96 |
| Other large city | −0.10 | 0.089 | 0.24 |
| Rural area | 1.00 | 0.096 | <0.01 |
| Northern region | −0.0093 | 0.10 | 0.93 |
| Western region | −0.076 | 0.087 | 0.38 |
| Southern region | −0.026 | 0.11 | 0.98 |
| Eastern region | −0.16 | 0.10 | 0.13 |
| Self-employed professional | 0.75 | 0.45 | 0.09 |
| Self-employed outside agriculture or employer | 0.21 | 0.18 | 0.25 |
| Manager or supervisor | 0.75 | 0.23 | <0.01 |
| Semi-autonomous worker | 0.94 | 0.24 | <0.01 |
| Non-agricultural worker | 0.52 | 0.18 | <0.01 |
| Self-employed in agriculture | 0.13 | 0.16 | 0.43 |
| No job-related security | 0.44 | 0.094 | <0.01 |
| Unemployed | 0.4 | 0.21 | <0.01 |
| Years of residence | −0.040 | 0.009 | <0.01 |
| Years of residence squared | 0.054 | 0.019 | <0.01 |
| Province development index | −0.17 | 0.086 | 0.05 |
| Number of previous moves | 0.37 | 0.31 | 0.23 |

*Notes:* [#] See Table 12.4 for variable definitions and descriptive statistics. Sample size = 2429. Log-likelihood without covariates = −1434.5. Log-likelihood with 27 covariates = −1126.0. Goodness of fit: Chi-Squared (27) = 617.0; Pseudo-$R^2$ = 0.21. Percent correctly predicted (total): migrants 73% (674), stayers 70% (1755).

**Table 12.A2: Maximum Likelihood (Probit) Estimates of the Sample Selection Equation#**
**Dependent variable: 1 = included in working sample, 0 = else.**

| | Estimate | Std. error | p-value |
|---|---|---|---|
| Constant | −6.37 | 0.33 | <0.01 |
| Years of formal schooling | −0.036 | 0.009 | <0.01 |
| Experience | 0.068 | 0.01 | <0.01 |
| Experience squared | −0.00076 | 0.00021 | <0.01 |
| Literate | 0.047 | 0.08 | 0.56 |
| Received elementary school diploma after age 15 | 0.26 | 0.10 | <0.01 |
| Vocational school diploma | −0.16 | 0.12 | 0.17 |
| Age | 0.24 | 0.019 | <0.01 |
| Age squared | −0.003 | 0.00023 | <0.01 |
| Major metropolitan area (Ankara, Istanbul, Izmir) | −0.0047 | 0.069 | 0.95 |
| Other large city | −0.20 | 0.066 | <0.01 |
| Rural area | 0.11 | 0.079 | 0.16 |
| Northern region | 0.51 | 0.086 | <0.01 |
| Western region | 0.39 | 0.062 | <0.01 |
| Southern region | 0.60 | 0.085 | <0.01 |
| Eastern region | 0.72 | 0.083 | <0.01 |
| Self-employed professional | 1.31 | 0.30 | <0.01 |
| Self-employed outside agriculture or employer | 1.32 | 0.084 | <0.01 |
| Manager or supervisor | 1.49 | 0.16 | <0.01 |
| Semi-autonomous worker | 1.24 | 0.14 | <0.01 |
| Non-agricultural worker | 1.34 | 0.084 | <0.01 |
| Self-employed in agriculture | 0.93 | 0.097 | 0.43 |

*Notes:* # See Table 12.4 for variable definitions and descriptive statistics. Sample size = 4242. Log-likelihood without covariates = −2895.4. Log-likelihood with 27 covariates = −1827.1. Goodness of fit: Chi-Squared (21) = 2136.6; Pseudo-$R^2$ = 0.37. Percent correctly predicted (total): included 82% (2429), excluded 76% (1813).

**Table 12.A3: Least Squares Estimates of the Earnings Equation, Model I-A[#]
Dependent variable: log. household income.**

| | Estimate | Std. error | p-value |
|---|---|---|---|
| Constant | 7.31 | 0.33 | <0.01 |
| Migrated during 1963–73 | −0.034 | 0.037 | 0.32 |
| Years of formal schooling | 0.073 | 0.0064 | <0.01 |
| Experience | −0.012 | 0.011 | 0.28 |
| Experience squared | 0.00036 | 0.00021 | 0.09 |
| Literate | 0.15 | 0.048 | <0.01 |
| Received elementary school diploma after age 15 | −0.065 | 0.057 | 0.26 |
| Vocational school diploma | 0.075 | 0.095 | 0.43 |
| Age | 0.078 | 0.02 | <0.01 |
| Age squared | −0.00083 | 0.00024 | <0.01 |
| Major metropolitan area (Ankara, Istanbul, Izmir) | 0.23 | 0.045 | <0.01 |
| Other large city | 0.22 | 0.043 | <0.01 |
| Rural area | −0.95 | 0.054 | 0.08 |
| Northern region | 0.082 | 0.042 | 0.05 |
| Western region | 0.082 | 0.056 | 0.15 |
| Southern region | −0.17 | 0.055 | <0.01 |
| Eastern region | −0.26 | 0.053 | <0.01 |
| Self-employed professional | 0.46 | 0.20 | 0.02 |
| Self-employed outside agriculture or employer | 0.39 | 0.072 | <0.01 |
| Manager or supervisor | 0.35 | 0.11 | <0.01 |
| Semi-autonomous worker | 0.31 | 0.11 | <0.01 |
| Non-agricultural worker | 0.17 | 0.073 | 0.02 |
| Self-employed in agriculture | 0.15 | 0.077 | 0.04 |

*Notes:* [#] See Table 12.4 for variable definitions and descriptive statistics. Sample size = 2429. Goodness of fit: $F(23, 2406) = 38.8$; $R^2 = 0.26$.

**Table 12.A4: Least Squares Estimates of the Earnings Equation, Model II-A#**
**Dependent variable: log. household income.**

| | Estimate | Std. error | p-value |
|---|---|---|---|
| Constant | 7.66 | 0.36 | <0.01 |
| Migrated during 1963–73 | −0.040 | 0.036 | 0.27 |
| Years of formal schooling | 0.063 | 0.0066 | <0.01 |
| Experience | −0.0093 | 0.01 | 0.37 |
| Experience squared | 0.00036 | 0.0002 | 0.07 |
| Literate | 0.12 | 0.048 | <0.01 |
| Received elementary school diploma after age 15 | −0.065 | 0.056 | 0.24 |
| Vocational school diploma | 0.089 | 0.092 | 0.33 |
| Age | 0.068 | 0.019 | <0.01 |
| Age squared | −0.00079 | 0.00023 | <0.01 |
| Major metropolitan area (Ankara, Istanbul, Izmir) | 0.18 | 0.044 | <0.01 |
| Other large city | 0.19 | 0.042 | <0.01 |
| Rural area | −0.035 | 0.057 | 0.53 |
| Northern region | 0.05 | 0.055 | 0.36 |
| Western region | 0.048 | 0.041 | 0.24 |
| Southern region | −0.19 | 0.053 | <0.01 |
| Eastern region | −0.25 | 0.052 | <0.01 |
| Self-employed professional | 0.30 | 0.25 | 0.23 |
| Self-employed outside agriculture or employer | 0.31 | 0.16 | 0.05 |
| Manager or supervisor | 0.24 | 0.18 | 0.19 |
| Semi-autonomous worker | 0.22 | 0.18 | 0.24 |
| Non-agricultural worker | 0.092 | 0.17 | 0.58 |
| Self-employed in agriculture | 0.14 | 0.087 | 0.12 |
| No. of breadwinners (outside agriculture) | 0.26 | 0.028 | <0.01 |
| Married (in agriculture) | 0.059 | 0.14 | 0.41 |
| Has working age children (in agriculture) | 0.094 | 0.083 | 0.25 |
| Has no supplementary income | −0.17 | 0.042 | <0.01 |
| Has no real estate | −0.17 | 0.034 | <0.01 |
| Has no productive animals | −0.43 | 0.086 | <0.01 |
| Head intermittently employed | −0.15 | 0.06 | 0.01 |
| Father self-employed in agriculture | −0.009 | 0.033 | 0.78 |
| Father literate | 0.11 | 0.0034 | <0.01 |
| Father has more than elementary school education | 0.13 | 0.094 | 0.17 |

*Notes:* # See Table 12.4 for variable definitions and descriptive statistics. Sample size = 2429. Goodness of fit: $F(29, 2400) = 34.3$; $R^2 = 0.31$.

**Table 12.A5. Least Squares Estimates of the Parameters of the Migration Effect Measures in Table 12.2**

| Model[#] | Estimate (standard error) | | | | | | |
|---|---|---|---|---|---|---|---|
| | $\delta$ | $\gamma_{01}$ | $\gamma_{11}$ | $\gamma_{02}$ | $\gamma_{12}$ | $\gamma_{03}$ | $\gamma_{13}$ |
| AS I-A | −0.047<br>(0.033) | — | — | — | — | — | — |
| AS I-B | −0.26<br>(0.10) | 0.071<br>(0.12) | 0.18<br>(0.063) | — | — | — | — |
| AS I-C | −0.50<br>(0.21) | −0.16<br>(0.32) | 0.57<br>(0.29) | 0.14<br>(0.16) | −0.23<br>(0.19) | −0.30<br>(0.23) | 0.055<br>(0.067) |
| AS I-D | −0.26<br>(0.10) | 0.069<br>(0.12) | 0.18<br>(0.063) | — | — | — | — |
| AS I-E | −0.54<br>(0.21) | −0.15<br>(0.32) | 0.63<br>(0.29) | 0.13<br>(0.16) | −0.27<br>(0.20) | −0.28<br>(0.23) | 0.063<br>(0.068) |
| AS I-F | −0.50<br>(0.21) | −0.17<br>(0.32) | 0.57<br>(0.29) | 0.14<br>(0.16) | −0.23<br>(0.19) | −0.30<br>(0.23) | 0.052<br>(0.068) |
| AS II-A | −0.040<br>(0.033) | — | — | — | — | — | — |
| AS II-B | −0.23<br>(0.11) | 0.032<br>(0.12) | 0.17<br>(0.065) | — | — | — | — |
| AS II-C | −0.44<br>(0.21) | −0.21<br>(0.32) | 0.54<br>(0.29) | 0.12<br>(0.16) | −0.22<br>(0.19) | −0.29<br>(0.23) | 0.051<br>(0.068) |
| AS II-D | −0.23<br>(0.11) | 0.028<br>(0.12) | 0.17<br>(0.065) | — | — | — | — |
| AS II-E | −0.48<br>(0.21) | −0.20<br>(0.32) | 0.60<br>(0.29) | 0.11<br>(0.16) | −0.25<br>(0.20) | −0.28<br>(0.23) | 0.061<br>(0.069) |
| AS II-F | −0.44<br>(0.21) | −0.22<br>(0.32) | 0.53<br>(0.29) | 0.12<br>(0.16) | −0.22<br>(0.20) | −0.30<br>(0.23) | 0.049<br>(0.068) |

*Notes:* [#] See Table 12.3 for model definitions.

## Notes

* This paper first appeared in *International Economic Review*, Vol. 41, No.4, pp. 893–920, and is reprinted by kind permission of the Editor and the Publisher. Some editorial changes have been made in the present version.

1 I adopt the term "anticipations" to distinguish the individual's expectations from the use of the mathematical expectation operator. The distinction emerges because the individual typically knows more about the problem than does the researcher.

2 The classic paper on the manifestations of self-selection is by Roy (1951). A mathematical formulation of Roy's model may be found in Maddala (1983: 257–60). The version that applies in the migration context is known as the extended Roy model, because selection is based on broader considerations than earnings maximization. The first published account of self-selection in the context of migration is that of Nakosteen and Zimmer (1980).

3 If $E(v_1|M) = E(v_0|M)$, then $E(\delta^*|M) = \delta$. In this case there is no selection on unobservables, and $\delta$ can be interpreted as the effect of migrant status on individual earnings, in the sense that it is the magnitude that drives the migration decision. A general discussion that applies to models of the type being entertained here may be found in Heckman and Robb (1985). For the important distinction between selection on observables vs. unobservables, see Barnow, Cain and Goldberger (1980), and Heckman and Hotz (1989).

4 The challenges that emerge in the estimation of the four entries is the subject of the next section.
5 This measure is the counterpart of the widely used "effect of treatment on the treated" in the literature on program evaluation.
6 We let $\mu_0 = \underline{\pi}'\underline{x}$, $\mu_1 = (\underline{\pi} + \underline{\delta})'\underline{x}$, $\delta - \kappa = \underline{\delta}'\underline{x} - \underline{\kappa}'\underline{w} = \underline{\xi}'\underline{z}$, $v_1 - v_0 - v_c = v$.
7 The Normality assumption is easily defended in light of the consistency results in Ruud (1983) and Stoker (1986). For a summary argument, see Heckman and MaCurdy (1986), note 12. Vella (1993) shows that the correction adopted here is equivalent to the use of a polynomial function of the generalized residuals from the probit step. Alternatively, the correction terms may be viewed as functions of $P(M = 1 \mid \underline{z})$, the so-called propensity score which figures in matching based approaches (Rosenbaum and Rubin, 1983). Deaton (1997) guides practitioners to the polynomial specification on the grounds that the distribution-free methods are still experimental (p.105).
8 The identifying assumptions of the alternative approaches have not gone uncontested; see Imbens and Angrist (1994).
9 The tests are based on functions of the third and fourth sample moments and compare favorably with competing tests in terms of power.
10 Except for $\varepsilon_1$ these have been calculated on the appropriate subsample. In light of (18), the value of $\varepsilon_1$ which compares the average migrant in our migrant subsample with the average non-migrant in the non-migrant subsample is easily obtained as the difference $\psi_1 - \delta_0$ or $\psi_0 - \delta_1$. The average value of $\varepsilon_1$ reported in Table 12.6 sweeps over the full sample instead.
11 Heckman, Smith, and Clements (1997) underscore the value of arriving at a distribution of program impacts in the evaluation context.
12 A related literature views migration as a sequential process. Individuals take corrective action if realizations fall below expectations. I briefly examine the subject of corrective action in section 5.6 below. A detailed assessment may be found in Tunalı (1996, 1997).
13 The frequency distribution for the sorting gains to migration is obtained by shifting the distribution in Figure 12.A1, panel (c), to the right by $-\delta$.
14 The frequency distribution for the sorting gains to staying is obtained by shifting the distribution in Figure 12.A3, panel (c), to the left by $\delta$.
15 Strictly speaking, return migration does not fit into the two-way comparison that the model is based on. An extension along the lines of Tunalı (1986) would be appropriate. Since return migrants constituted less than 4 percent of the working sample, the problem is ignored here.

## References


Antel, J.J. 1980. "Returns to Migration: Literature Review and Critique." N-1480-NICHD, The Rand Corporation, Santa Monica, CA.

Barnow, B., G. Cain, and A.S. Goldberger. 1980. "Issues in the Analysis of Selection Bias," *Evaluation Studies*, 5: 42–59.

Borjas, G.J. 1990. "Immigration and Self-selection," in R.B. Freeman and J.M. Abowd (eds.), *Immigration, Trade, and the Labor Market*. Chicago, IL: University of Chicago Press.

D'Agostino, R.B., A. Belanger, and R.B. D'Agostino Jr. 1990. "A Suggestion for Using Powerful and Informative Tests of Normality," *The American Statistician*, 44: 316–21.

DaVanzo, J. 1981. "Repeat Migration, Information Costs, and Location Specific Capital," *Population and Environment*, 4: 45–73.

———, and J.R. Hosek 1981. "Does Migration Increase Wage Rates? An Analysis of Alternative Techniques for Measuring Wage Gains to Migration," Rand Note, N-1582-NICHD, The Rand Corporation, Santa Monica, CA.

David, P.A. 1974. "Fortune, Risk and the Microeconomics of Migration," in P.A. David and M.W.Reder (eds.), *Nations and Households in Economic Growth*, pp. 21–88. New York: Academic Press.

Deaton, A. 1997. *The Analysis of Household Surveys: A Microeconomic Approach to Development Policy*. Baltimore and London: The Johns Hopkins University Press.

Heckman, J.J. 1974. "Shadow Prices, Market Wages, and Labor Supply," *Econometrica*, 42: 679–94.

———. 1976. "The Common Structure of Statistical Models of Truncation, Sample Selection and Limited Dependent Variables and a Simpler Estimator for Such Models," *Annals of Economic and Social Measurement*, 5: 475–92.

———. 1978. "Dummy Endogenous Variables in a Simultaneous Equations System," *Econometrica*, 46: 931–59.

———. 1990. "Varieties of Selection Bias," *American Economic Review*, 80: 313–18.

———, and V.J. Hotz. 1989. "Choosing Among Alternative Nonexperimental Methods for Estimating the Impact of Social Programs: The Case of Manpower Training," *Journal of the American Statistical Association*, 84: 862–74.

Heckman, J.J., V.J. Hotz, and M. Dabos. 1987. "Do We Need Experimental Data to Evaluate the Impact of Manpower Training on Earnings?" *Evaluation Review*, 11: 395–427.

Heckman, J.J., and T. MaCurdy (1986) "Labor Econometrics," in Z. Griliches and M.D.Intriligator (eds.) *Handbook of Econometrics*, Volume III. Amsterdam: North-Holland.

Heckman, J.J. and R. Robb, Jr. 1985. "Alternative Methods for Evaluating the Impact of Interventions," in J.J. Heckman and B. Singer (eds.), *Longitudinal Analysis of Labor Market Data*, pp. 156–245. Cambridge, England: Cambridge University Press.

Heckman, J.J., and G. Sedlacek. 1985. "Heterogeneity, Aggregation, and Market Wage Functions: An Empirical Model of Self-Selection in the Labor Market," *Journal of Political Economy*, 93: 1077–1125.

Heckman, J.J., J. Smith, and N. Clements. 1997. "Making the Most Out of Programme Evaluations and Social Experiments: Accounting for Heterogeneity in Programme Impacts," *Review of Economic Studies*, 64: 487–535.

Imbens, G.W., and J.D. Angrist. 1994. "Identification and Estimation of Local Average Treatment Effects," *Econometrica*, 62: 467–75.

Islam, M.N. 1985. "Self-selectivity Problems in Interregional and Interindustry Migration in Canada," *Environment and Planning A*, 17: 1515–32.

Lanzona, L.A. 1998. "Migration, Self-selection and Earnings in Philippine Rural Communities," *Journal of Development Economics*, 56 (1): 27–50.

Lee, L.F. 1978. "Unionism and Wage Rates: A Simultaneous Equation Model with Qualitative and Limited Dependent Variables," *International Economic Review*, 19: 415–33.

———. 1979. "Identification and Estimation in Binary Choice Models with Limited (Censored) Dependent Variables," *Econometrica*, 47: 977–96.

———. 1982. "Some Approaches to the Correction of Selectivity Bias," *Review of Economic Studies*, 49: 355–72.

Maddala, G.S. 1983. *Limited-dependent and Qualitative Variables in Econometrics*. Cambridge, England: Cambridge University Press.

McCall, B.P., and J.J. McCall.1987. "A Sequential Study of Migration and Job Search," *Journal of Labor Economics*, 5: 452–76.

Nakosteen, R.A. and M. Zimmer. 1980. "Migration and Income: The Question of Self-Selection," *Southern Economic Journal*, 46: 840–51.

Katz, E., and O. Stark. 1986. "Labor Migration and Risk Aversion in Less Developed Countries," *Journal of Labor Economics*, 4: 134–49.

Pessino, C. 1991. "Sequential Migration Theory and Evidence from Peru," *Journal of Development Economics*, 36: 55–87.

Polachek, S.W., and F.W. Horvath. 1977. "A Life-cycle Approach to Migration: Analysis of the Perspicacious Peregrinator," in R. Ehrenberg (ed.), *Research in Labor Economics*, 1: 103–49. Greenwich, CT: JAI Press.

Robinson, C., and N. Tomes. 1982. "Self-selection and Interprovincial Migration in Canada," *Canadian Journal of Economics*, 3: 474–502.

Rosenbaum, P., and D.B. Rubin. 1983. "The Central Role of the Propensity Score in Observational Studies for Causal Effects," *Biometrika*, 70: 41–55.

Roy, A.D. 1951. "Some Thoughts on the Distribution of Earnings," *Oxford Economic Papers*, 3: 135–46.

Ruud, P.A. 1983. "Sufficient Conditions for the Consistency of Maximum Likelihood Estimation Despite Misspecification in Multinomial Discrete Choice Models," *Econometrica*, 51: 225–28.

Sjaastad, L. 1962. "The Costs and Returns of Human Migration," *Journal of Political Economy*, Vol. 70, Part 2, pp. 80–93.

Stapleton, D.C., and D.J. Young. 1984. "Censored Normal Regression with Measurement Error in the Dependent Variable," *Econometrica*, 52: 737–60.

Stoker, T.M. 1986. "Consistent Estimation of Scaled Coefficients," *Econometrica*, 54: 1461–81.

Tunalı, İ. 1985. "Migration, Earnings and Selectivity: From Theory to Fact—Evidence from Turkey, 1963–73." Unpublished Ph.D. Thesis, University of Wisconsin, Department of Economics.

———. 1986. "A General Structure for Models of Double Selection and an Application to a Joint Migration/Earnings Process with Remigration," in R. Ehrenberg (ed.), *Research in Labor Economics*, Vol. 8, Part B, pp. 235–82. Greenwich, CT: JAI Press.

———. 1996. "Migration and Remigration of Male Household Heads in Turkey, 1963–73," *Economic Development and Cultural Change*, 45 (October): 31–67.

———. 1997. "Migration and Remigration as Interdependent Decisions: A Bivariate Probit Formulation," *The Turkish Journal of Population Studies*, 19: 101–26.

Vella, F. 1993. "A Simple Estimator for Simultaneous Models with Censored Endogenous Regressors," *International Economic Review*, 34: 441–57.

Vishwanath, T. 1991. "Information Flows, Job Search and Migration," *Journal of Development Economics*, 36: 313–35.

# 13

# A Macroeconometric Model of the Effects of Migrant Remittances in Mediterranean Countries

*Nicholas P. Glytsos**

## Introduction

In many of the labor-exporting countries, migrant remittances represent a very high proportion of foreign exchange proceeds and an indispensable source for covering balance-of-payments deficits, as well as being a generator of high demand in their domestic economies. Therefore, knowledge about the effects of these remittances is vital. In Egypt, remittances have been at times higher than the sum of foreign exchange from oil exports, Suez Canal dues, and tourism, and have considerably exceeded merchandise exports (by 45 percent in 1993). In Morocco, remittances reached almost 8 percent of gross domestic product (GDP) in 1990, and in Tunisia almost 5 percent of GDP. As a proportion of merchandise exports, remittances in some countries have reached very high levels indeed in recent years: Jordan 83.3 percent, Morocco 52.8 percent, Syria 19.0 percent, and Tunisia 15.5 percent. In all the labor-exporting countries mentioned in this chapter, the volume of remittances has increased greatly over the past 25 years (Tables 13.1a–c).[1]

**Table 13.1a: Volume of Remittances (in current US$ million)**

| | Algeria | Egypt | Greece | Jordan | Morocco | Portugal | Syria | Tunisia |
|---|---|---|---|---|---|---|---|---|
| 1970 | 211.0 | 29.0 | 333.0 | 20.7[1] | 63.0 | 523.0 | 7.0 | 29.0 |
| 1993 | 993.0 | 4,960.0 | 2,360.0 | 1,066.4[2] | 1,945.0 | 3,844.4 | 600.0 | 589.8 |

**Table 13.1b: Remittances as a Proportion (%) of GDP**

| | 1970 | 1973 | 1976 | 1979 | 1982 | 1985 | 1986 | 1990 | 1993 |
|---|---|---|---|---|---|---|---|---|---|
| Algeria | 0.04 | 0.03 | 0.02 | 0.01 | 0.01 | 0.01 | 0.01 | 0.01 | 0.02 |
| Egypt | 0.45 | 1.46 | 6.59 | 7.04 | 8.85 | 11.42 | 8.92 | 10.03 | 12.24 |
| Greece | 3.38 | 4.40 | 3.37 | 3.40 | 2.58 | 2.24 | 2.34 | 2.75 | 3.39 |
| Jordan | 3.17 | 6.33 | 29.33 | 28.28 | 25.75 | 26.25 | 29.52 | — | — |
| Morocco | 1.57 | 3.23 | 5.32 | 4.85 | 5.01 | 6.99 | 7.99 | 7.68 | 7.44 |
| Portugal | — | 9.03 | 5.10 | 6.26 | 9.33 | 8.60 | 7.71 | 6.40 | 4.71 |
| Syria | 0.71 | 0.97 | 0.72 | 9.95 | 2.59 | 2.28 | 2.41 | 2.96 | — |
| Tunisia | 2.04 | 3.32 | 2.93 | 3.07 | 4.75 | 3.23 | 3.96 | 4.75 | 3.96 |

**Table 13.1c: Remittances as a Proportion (%) of Merchandise Exports (*X*)**

| | 1970 | 1973 | 1976 | 1979 | 1982 | 1985 | 1986 | 1990 | 1993 |
|---|---|---|---|---|---|---|---|---|---|
| Algeria | 20.9 | 14.5 | 7.1 | 3.0 | 2.8 | 1.4 | 3.2 | 2.5 | 9.8 |
| Egypt | 3.5 | 11.7 | 34.8 | 61.3 | 54.1 | 89.0 | 83.1 | 119.0 | 145.1 |
| Greece | 54.4 | 58.1 | 34.9 | 28.9 | 24.5 | 18.0 | 20.9 | 27.9 | 46.9 |
| Jordan | — | 60.6 | 188.7 | 134.5 | 129.9 | 129.3 | 161.8 | 47.0 | 83.3 |
| Morocco | 12.9 | 22.6 | 40.0 | 45.4 | 39.7 | 44.3 | 57.4 | 47.4 | 52.8 |
| Portugal | 54.7 | 61.8 | 50.6 | 69.1 | 63.3 | 36.8 | 35.8 | 26.1 | 25.5 |
| Syria | 3.5 | 10.4 | 5.0 | 54.7 | 20.5 | 18.8 | 31.1 | 9.3 | 19.0 |
| Tunisia | 15.3 | 21.5 | 17.0 | 17.4 | 18.2 | 15.3 | 19.9 | 16.8 | 15.5 |

*Notes:* (1): 1972. (2): 1986.
(Remittances / GDP) × 100, at constant 1987 prices in local currencies.
(Remittances / *X*) × 100, at current US dollars.
*Source:* World Bank, *World Tables*, 1991, 1994, 1995.

Are remittances a stable source of finance? Evidence shows that those coming from migrants in the oil-rich Gulf countries are more volatile, since they are sensitive to oil price shocks, affecting host countries' economies and entailing massive movements of migrants between host and home countries. Such, for instance, was the case in the oil windfalls of 1973 and 1979 and during price drops in 1982 and 1986, which generated very serious problems of adjustment in the labor-exporting countries of the Middle East (Appendix Figure 13.A1). The gradual switch of demand in the Gulf countries from large numbers of unskilled laborers to smaller numbers of skilled and well-educated workers with easier family unification has had an additional dampening effect.

North African and Southern European labor-exporting countries—with larger proportions of permanent migrants, mostly in the Western European countries France and Germany—have not been exposed to similar extreme experiences, because of the relative stability of the host countries' economies. These countries, however, did suffer from mild economic setbacks which, analogously, affected the employment of migrants and often, but not always, their remitting capacity. In fact, there is some evidence that during the economic recession in France, Moroccans and Tunisians increased their remittances (Garson, 1994).

Despite their importance, only in the last dozen or so years has the literature given some attention to remittances. Theoretical studies concentrate on their impact on poverty and income distribution (for example, Lundahl, 1985; Djajic, 1986; Kirwan and Holden, 1986; Rivera-Batiz, 1986; Stark, Taylor, and Yitzhaki, 1986; and Stark, 1991), with a large part of the work being qualitative, assessing different countries or presenting general surveys (for example, Richards and Martin, 1983; Russell, 1986, 1992; Keely and Tran, 1989; Appleyard, 1992; Glytsos, 1996; Farrag, 1996; and Wahba, 1996). Systematic quantitative or econometric work is very limited (see Oberai and Singh, 1980; Kandil and Metwally, 1990; Looney, 1990; Adams, 1991; Glytsos, 1993; and Taylor and Wyatt, 1996 and places emphasis on income distribution and welfare effects.

Qualitative studies that draw on the experiences of particular countries—although illuminating—do not offer estimates of the relative effects of remittances and their time distribution on different sectors of the economy, or of macroeconomic variables that have a bearing on development. Further, they are largely contradictory. The question is: to what extent could differences among countries be justified by different conditions, and to what extent could they result from the lack of concrete empirical analysis, hiding perhaps some uniformity among countries and leaving enough room for speculation and judgmental propositions?

This chapter will try to respond empirically to these questions and to draw some conclusions about the overall impact of labor remittances on development. The tool of our analysis is a macroeconometric model, which will be applied to a number of countries on both sides of the Mediterranean basin, with the great majority of their migrants being either in the oil-rich Arab countries or in Europe.

## The Model

Labor-exporting developing economies are primarily concerned with long-run growth and structural change, their major objectives being to widen the basis of economic activity, raise competitiveness, and reduce their dependence on foreign resources. At the same time, these countries have to worry about short-run fluctuations in their economies, since their persistence hinders long-run development. Changing remittance flows, having both short- and long-term implications, may be one source of such disturbances (e.g. Handoussa, 1991)—which is what this chapter will try to evaluate. The aim is to estimate the effects of the demand generated by remittances on certain macroeconomic variables that are related to short-run economic changes and to determine how these changes move the economy toward long-run growth and development.

For our purposes, a very simple linear macroeconometric model, comprising four major features, would be appropriate. It must: be demand-oriented; be aggregate enough to have room for a number of different countries in order to be able to offer comparable estimates; satisfy—setting aside detailed individual or sectoral characteristics—a certain minimum of accepted econometric standards; and, last but not least, make good theoretical sense in terms of compatibility with the kind of economies to which it will be applied. The model adopted along these lines is essentially Keynesian, but with a dynamic perspective consisting of three behavioral equations: namely, a consumption function, an investment function, and an imports function, together with a national income identity—through which remittances are introduced as an exogenous variable into the model. The focal point of the model is to determine the effects of an exogenous shock of remittances on these four endogenous variables, which is the minimum required to determine the short-run effects and in addition trace their long-run impact on the economic trajectory.

There are three phases in our analysis. The first is the construction and estimation of the econometric model, with time series data for eight Mediterranean countries. The second concerns the use of the estimates of the model to obtain short- and long-run multipliers of the endogenous variables, with respect to remittances. Finally, the third is to apply these multipliers to the series of data for each country, in order to determine the actual effects of remittances on their economies over time.

### *Consumption Function*

Two major hypotheses, with some variant expressions in each case, have been tested. The first is the permanent income hypothesis, which has a sound theoretical basis (see Friedman, 1957; Ando and Modigliani, 1963). The second is the more modern error correction model, whose structure is empirical (Davidson, Hendry, Srba, and Yeo, 1978; and Davis, 1984). These studies found that the 'best' performance for almost all countries was the following consumption equation:

$$C_t = \alpha_0 + \alpha_1 Y_t + \alpha_2 C_{t-1} \tag{1}$$

where $C$ = Private Consumption, $Y$ = GDP + Remittances, subscript $t$ stands for time, and the $\alpha$'s are parameters to be estimated.

This is a dynamic long-run consumption equation that is backed by two different distributed-lag hypotheses: an adaptive expectations model and a partial adjustment model.[2] The equation can produce estimates of short- and long run effects of income on consumption. It seems to satisfy our criterion for a model suitable for developing countries, where various uncertainties are present concerning income changes and with the component of remittances generating considerable income fluctuations, as noted earlier. This is more true for MENA countries undergoing transition, given their efforts to move toward the privatization and liberalization of their economies—having joined the World Trade Organization and having signed agreements with the European Union for liberalizing trade.

*Investment Function*

According to certain theoretical views, there is some desired stock of capital toward which businessmen orient their investment activity. This means that gross investment is generally inhibited by the existing capital stock. Investment, however, is positively correlated with business profits, property income, and business output, whereas profits are positively related to national income (Christ, 1966: 582–3; Duesenberry, 1958). Accordingly, in our model, profits are assumed to be a positive function of income ($Y_t$), which enters as an argument in our investment equation, along with lagged capital stock ($K_{t-1}$), which allows some time for investment to adjust to that stock. Thus, the expected signs are respectively positive and negative. A similar equation, used by others, has yielded good results (see, for example, Pavlopoulos, 1966: 63–64). Our investment equation, therefore, is:

$$I_t = \beta_0 + \beta_1 Y_t + \beta_2 K_{t-1} \tag{2}$$

Capital stock is approximated by cumulative investment, which in linear models like the above do not have any bearing on the capital coefficient (Pavlopoulos, 1966: 63). The $\beta$s are parameters to be estimated.

*Import Function*

The import equation comes straight from the life-cycle hypothesis as developed for consumption by Ando and Modigliani, among others (see Davidson, Hendry, *et al.*, 1978), incorporating the influence of income and wealth.[3] It is of the form:

$$M_t = \gamma_0 + \gamma_1 Y_t + \gamma_2 Y_{t-1} + \gamma_3 M_{t-1} \tag{3}$$

This theoretical approach for imports, which performed well when tested, can be justified by the great need for imported goods in the countries investigated. Variable $M_{t-1}$ carries the effect of past incomes on current imports, indicating adaptive expectations. The coefficients of equation (3) may be expressed in terms of the theoretical parameters in note 3 as follows: $\gamma_1 = \lambda$, $\gamma_2 = (\delta - r) - \lambda$ and $\gamma_3 = 1 - (\delta - r)$, over-identifying the value of $(\delta - r)$.

By construction of the import function, $(\delta - r) > 0$, therefore $\gamma_2 >< 0$, depending on $(\delta - r) >< \gamma_1$. In other words, lagged income will affect imports positively (negatively) if the marginal propensity to import with respect to current wealth $(\delta - r)$ is higher (lower) than the marginal propensity to import with respect to current income $(\gamma_1)$. The lagged imports coefficient $\gamma_3$ will be positive, since $(\delta - r) < 1$.

To summarize, the structural model consists of equations (1), (2), and (3), and an income identity,[4] that is:

$$C_t = \alpha_0 + \alpha_1 Y_t + \alpha_2 C_{t-1} \quad (1)$$
$$I_t = \beta_0 + \beta_1 Y_t + \beta_2 K_{t-1} \quad (2)$$
$$M_t = \gamma_0 + \gamma_1 Y_t + \gamma_2 Y_{t-1} + \gamma_3 M_{t-1} \quad (3)$$
$$Y_t = C_t + I_t + G_t + X_t - M_t + R_t \quad (4)$$

*List of variables:*

Endogenous variables:

$C$ = private consumption expenditure

$I$ = gross domestic investment (private and public), including change in stocks

$M$ = imports of goods and non-factor services

$Y$ = a kind of national disposable income, made up of GDP and the volume of migrant remittances

Exogenous variables:

$K$ = cumulative gross domestic investment $\sum_{1969}^{1993} I_t$ (as proxy of capital stock)

$G$ = general government consumption expenditure

$X$ = exports of goods and non-factor services

$R$ = migrant remittances deflated by the domestic absorption price index

$t$ = time.

The model is estimated by two-stage least squares (TSLS) and is applied individually to eight countries: Algeria, Egypt, Greece, Jordan, Morocco, Portugal, Syria, and Tunisia. These countries can be classified into three groups, with different characteristics regarding migration. The Middle East countries—Egypt, Jordan, and Syria—generally have temporary migrants in the oil-rich Gulf states. The North African countries—Algeria, Morocco, and Tunisia—have predominantly permanent migrants in Europe, particularly in France. The Southern European countries—Greece and Portugal—are members of the European Union and have more-or-less permanent migrants in Germany and France.

The data used are annual data for the period 1969–93, except for Jordan, which is covered only for the period 1970–88. All figures are expressed in local currencies at constant 1987 prices, except for Jordan, for which the price index base is 1980 (see Appendix 13.A2 for sources and details). The estimates of the model are presented in Tables 13.2a-c.

**Table 13.2a: Structural Regression Coefficients (TSLS Estimates): Consumption ($C$)**

| | Const | $Y_t$ | $C_{t-1}$ | $\bar{R}^2$ | DW |
|---|---|---|---|---|---|
| Algeria | 2.837 | 0.248 | 0.460 | 0.963 | 2.18 |
| | (0.416) | (2.349) | (2.345) | | |
| Egypt | 2,762.47 | 0.158 | 0.713 | 0.981 | 1.44 |
| | (2.768) | (1.525) | (4.141) | | |
| Greece | -187.81 | 0.162 | 0.823 | 0.985 | 1.88 |
| | (-0.647) | (1.294) | (6.299) | | |
| Jordan | 32.78 | 0.479 | 0.325 | 0.957 | 1.87 |
| | (0.714) | (4.433) | (2.185) | | |
| Morocco | 7.50 | 0.376 | 0.356 | 0.973 | 1.78 |
| | (2.279) | (3.546) | (2.007) | | |
| Portugal | 350.00 | 0.165 | 0.654 | 0.952 | 1.34 |
| | (2.198) | (2.471) | (5.900) | | |
| Syria[1] | 2.836 | 0.151 | 0.779 | 0.895 | 2.33 |
| | (0.448) | (1.037) | (3.958) | | |
| Tunisia | 30.527 | 0.229 | 0.648 | 0.991 | 2.49 |
| | (0.235) | (2.248) | (4.241) | | |
| Expected sign | | + | + | | |

**Table 13.2b: Structural Regression Coefficients (TSLS Estimates): Investment ($I$)**

| | Const | $Y_t$ | $K_{t-1}$ | $\bar{R}^2$ | DW |
|---|---|---|---|---|---|
| Algeria | -68.260 | 0.883 | -0.067 | 0.889 | 1.95 |
| | (-5.415) | (12.66) | (-9.871) | | |
| Egypt | -3,293.13 | 0.409 | -0.070 | 0.927 | 1.35 |
| | (-3.757) | (9.671) | (-5.692) | | |
| Greece | -845.68 | 0.545 | -0.057 | 0.203 | 1.19 |
| | (-0.859) | (2.384) | (-2.561) | | |
| Jordan | -252.02 | 0.665 | -0.103 | 0.796 | 1.11 |
| | (-3.155) | (6.291) | (-3.845) | | |
| Morocco | -23.767 | 0.548 | -0.073 | 0.691 | 1.12 |
| | (-1.293) | (2.515) | (-1.715) | | |
| Portugal | -1,471.01 | 0.642 | -0.037 | 0.644 | 0.68 |
| | (-1.549) | (2.643) | (-1.317) | | |
| Syria | -23.832 | 0.580 | -0.086 | 0.697 | 1.97 |
| | (-3.377) | (6.686) | (-5.227) | | |
| Tunisia | -3,172.56 | 1.220 | -0.174 | 0.838 | 1.33 |
| | (-4.605) | (6.648) | (-5.736) | | |
| Expected sign | | + | - | | |

**Table 13.2c: Structural Regression Coefficients (TSLS Estimates): Imports (*M*)**

| | Const | $Y_t$ | $M_{t-1}$ | $Y_{t-1}$ | $\bar{R}^2$ | DW |
|---|---|---|---|---|---|---|
| Algeria | 6.329 | 0.375 | 0.804 | -0.374 | 0.727 | 2.14 |
| | (0.754) | (1.338) | (5.502) | (-1.477) | | |
| Egypt | 2,475.30 | 0.776 | 0.562 | -0.710 | 0.867 | 1.79 |
| | (2.323) | (2.734) | (3.811) | (-2.653) | | |
| Greece | -477.11 | 0.614 | 0.982 | -0.524 | 0.980 | 1.83 |
| | (-2.059) | (3.272) | (13.66) | (-2.959) | | |
| Jordan | 58.622 | 0.270 | 0.853 | -0.160 | 0.966 | 2.38 |
| | (0.659) | (0.992) | (3.498) | (-0.718) | | |
| Morocco | 2.140 | 0.025 | 0.807 | 0.025 | 0.906 | 1.56 |
| | (0.687) | (0.124) | (5.767) | (0.122) | | |
| Portugal | -613.40 | 0.754 | 0.948 | -0.633 | 0.976 | 2.22 |
| | .(-3.370) | (5.099) | (11.79) | (-4.381) | | |
| Syria | 12.239 | -0.286 | 0.779 | 0.259 | 0.611 | 2.12 |
| | (2.245) | (-1.698) | (4.296) | (1.724) | | |
| Tunisia | -109.15 | 0.476 | 0.674 | -0.321 | 0.948 | 1.82 |
| | (-0.514) | (1.409) | (4.009) | (-0.970) | | |
| Expected sign | | + | + | + / - | | |

*Notes:* (1): The consumption equation for Syria is the OLS estimates, because of a negative income coefficient in the TSLS run. T-values in parentheses underneath the coefficients.
*Source:* Author's calculations.

## Empirical Results of the Structural Model

The model seems to fit the data of all eight countries rather well—with all signs (except one) as theoretically expected and with very significant coefficients in most cases. The lagged dependent variables in the consumption and imports equations, expressing the dynamic nature of the model, are all highly significant, as is the lagged capital in the investment equation. These findings confirm the hypothesized permanent income behavior in all countries, but with different degrees of adaptability to consumer spending in the face of income increases. The presence of time distribution effects of income on consumption and imports is also detected. We may therefore observe a remarkably uniform performance in these differing—in several respects—countries, with their particularities reflected in the magnitude and not the nature of the various structural responses to the model.

Egypt, Greece, and Portugal, with very similar and very low short-run marginal propensities to consume (MPC) (respectively, 0.158, 0.162, and 0.165), experience the highest short-run marginal propensities to import (respectively, 0.776, 0.614, and 0.754). This suggests that the immediate concern of consumers in these countries, when their income increases, is to buy imported goods rather than domestically produced ones. Businessmen, similarly, are anxious to buy investment goods from abroad as soon as they can afford to. In contrast, Jordan and Morocco, with the highest short-run MPC (0.479 and 0.376, respectively), have the lowest marginal propensities to import (0.270 and 0.025, respectively)—indicating an urge to satisfy immediate consumption needs from domestic production rather than from imports. Thus, these two groups of countries, although overlapping in earlier stylized classification based on the nature and destination of migration, are clearly different in this respect.

The consistently negative sign of lagged income in the import equation is statistically significant and with relatively high coefficients for Egypt, Greece, and Portugal. As we argued during the discussion of the import function, the coefficient of $Y_{t-1}$ would be negative if the marginal propensity to import with respect to income is higher than the marginal propensity to import with respect to wealth. This means that these three countries more than the others, despite the urgency of their demand for imports, are hesitant to liquidate assets for that purpose; rather, they wait for an increase in their income to satisfy suppressed demand for imports. In the rest of the countries, this reaction—as also the reaction to current income changes—is insignificant; they are more influenced by past levels of imports—an indication of a stronger effect of adaptive expectations in the purchase of imports.

The estimated investment equation behaves uniformly in almost all countries, with highly significant and similar size coefficients in most of them. Exceptions are Algeria and Tunisia, with substantially higher income coefficients (0.883 and 1.220, respectively), compared to the rest of the countries (0.409 - 0.665). Recalling that income in the investment function represents profits, it appears that Algeria and Tunisia—more than the other countries—respond very promptly to investing profits or other additional income in private or public capital goods and housing. Finally, the investment-restraining factor of the capital stock seems to work as expected with negative and statistically significant coefficients.

## Dynamic Remittance Multipliers from the Model

The dynamic nature of the model allows the possibility of estimating short- and long-run effects of a change in one exogenous variable—all other exogenous variables remaining unchanged on the endogenous variables of the model, tracing the time path and the speed of these effects. The relationship between an endogenous variable and all the predetermined variables of our system of equations—the reduced-form expression of the structural equations (1)–(4)—is of the form:

$$X_{it} = \pi_0 + \pi_1 C_{t-1} + \pi_2 Y_{t-1} + \pi_3 M_{t-1} + \pi_4 K_{t-1} + \pi_5 G_t + \pi_6 X_t + \pi_7 R_t \qquad (5)$$

where $X_{it}$ stands for any of our endogenous variables $C, I, M, Y$.

The parameters $\pi$'s are the partial derivatives of the endogenous variable $X_{it}$ with respect to any predetermined variable $Z$, that is: $\frac{\partial X_{it}}{\partial Z_{it}} = \pi_i$

Estimates of the $\pi$'s may be obtained either directly by Ordinary Least Squares (OLS) from equation (5), or by solving the TSLS expressions of $\pi$'s in terms of the estimated structural parameters. In discrete variable notation, the partial derivatives of equation (5) are equivalent to $\Delta X = \pi \, \Delta Z$, which indicates that $\pi$ is a multiplier, called an 'impact multiplier,' that represents the magnitudes of direct and indirect effects of a unit change in any predetermined variable $Z$ on any endogenous variable $X$ of the system, in the first year of the change in $Z$. Subsequent effects during the years 2, 3, ..., $n$ come as a result of the dynamic nature of the model, through the lagged dependent variables in the form of time-distributed interim multipliers, from which the cumulative or truncated multiplier of long-run effects may be calculated (Appendix 13.A3).

Based on best results (signs of coefficients and their long-run convergence to zero), we choose for calculations of impact and interim multipliers the reduced-form estimates for all countries except Portugal, for which the solved TSLS estimates are used. Algeria is left altogether out of further discussion, since neither method gave acceptable estimates of interim multipliers.[5] Given the objective of this chapter, the exogenous variable whose effects will be studied is remittances. In equation (5), $\pi_7$ is the short-run or impact multiplier of a change of remittances by one unit $\Delta R = 1$, sustained for subsequent years, that is, with no further increase ($\Delta R = 0$) in years 2, 3, ... , $n$, all other predetermined variables in the equation remaining unchanged for $t = 1, 2, ..., n$ years. Naturally, in the same way, the other $\pi$'s in the equation have analogous meaning for any of the exogenous variables.

The calculated figures for a maximum of six years, during which most of the multipliers converge to zero, are given in Table 13.3. Looking at the size of the impact and interim multipliers, we observe that in the Middle Eastern countries the effects of additional income from remittances on consumption are delayed more than in other countries—perhaps because recipients are more uncertain about the sustainability of the increase, given the volatility of remittances in these countries, as noted earlier. In contrast, Greeks and Tunisians, are more anxious to raise their consumption immediately after an increase in remittances—probably due to an experience of more stable flows of remittances from their migrants in Germany and France. Egypt, Syria, and Morocco peak additional spending in the second year, whereas Jordan's highest interim multiplier comes in the third year. Finally, Greece and Tunisia almost exhaust their additional spending on consumption in the first year, while in Portugal remittance effects peak, but are not exhausted, in the first year.

Some of the countries with low short-run consumption multipliers—such as Egypt, Jordan, Morocco, and Portugal—have high short-run investment multipliers, indicating some kind of trade-off in the first-year effect of a remittance increase. As for Syria and Tunisia, they have negative short-run multipliers for investment, and Tunisia, but not Syria, ends up with a negative long-run multiplier, after a positive spell in the second year. Most of the countries of low short-run consumption multipliers—such as Egypt, Morocco, Portugal, and Syria—have not only high investment but also high import multipliers. This points to a relatively strong immediate effect on imports of capital goods. Finally, the short-run income multiplier as the sum of the multipliers of the income components is high in Greece, Jordan, and Portugal, and relatively low in Egypt and Morocco. It is negative for Syria and Tunisia, because of the high negative investment multipliers in these two countries.

The time distribution of remittance effects, as expressed by the interim multipliers, traces a path that is converging rather smoothly to long-run equilibrium, for all four variables, in Egypt, Jordan, and Syria. Except for imports, Greece's increasing remittance effects wear out after the second year, with negative multipliers afterward. Morocco demonstrates some oscillatory movements for investment and imports, with a final convergence, whereas Portugal converges smoothly for consumption and imports but exhausts the effects on investment and income in the second year. In Tunisia, the strong negative short-run multiplier prevails throughout the years, giving a negative long-run effect on investment and income, which does not seem to be very convincing. This could be attributed to a number of factors that are beyond the scope of this chapter.

**Table 13.3: Time Distribution of the Effects of Remittances on Certain Macroeconomic Variables**

(impact and dynamic multipliers)

| Countries and Equations | Impact Multipliers* (short-run effect) | Interim (dynamic) Multipliers* Years | | | | | Truncated Total Multipliers (long-run effects) (sum of the six yrs) |
|---|---|---|---|---|---|---|---|
| | Year 1 | 2 | 3 | 4 | 5 | 6 | |
| **Egypt** | | | | | | | |
| Consumption | 0.159 | 0.800 | 0.725 | 0.652 | 0.599 | 0.557 | 3.492 |
| Investment | 0.385 | 0.306 | 0.167 | 0.119 | 0.095 | 0.082 | 1.154 |
| Imports | 0.708 | 0.503 | 0.274 | 0.159 | 0.104 | 0.076 | 1.824 |
| Income | 0.835 | 0.602 | 0.618 | 0.612 | 0.591 | 0.564 | 3.822 |
| **Greece** | | | | | | | |
| Consumption | 0.737 | 0.081 | -0.020 | -0.001 | 0.018 | 0.023 | 0.838 |
| Investment | 2.429 | 1.466 | 0.364 | -0.001 | -0.061 | -0.046 | 4.151 |
| Imports | 1.655 | 0.859 | 0.364 | 0.169 | 0.106 | 0.084 | 3.237 |
| Income | 2.511 | 0.689 | -0.021 | -0.170 | -0.149 | -0.107 | 2.753 |
| **Jordan** | | | | | | | |
| Consumption | 0.096 | 0.267 | 0.390 | 0.361 | 0.276 | 0.194 | 1.584 |
| Investment | 0.410 | 0.664 | 0.208 | 0.037 | -0.005 | -0.008 | 1.306 |
| Imports | 0.023 | 0.478 | 0.287 | 0.119 | 0.042 | 0.015 | 0.964 |
| Income | 1.483 | 0.453 | 0.311 | 0.280 | 0.230 | 0.171 | 2.926 |
| **Morocco** | | | | | | | |
| Consumption | -0.427 | 1.022 | 0.520 | 0.014 | -0.056 | 0.016 | 1.089 |
| Investment | 0.962 | 0.214 | -0.018 | 0.182 | 0.219 | 0.136 | 1.695 |
| Imports | 0.851 | 0.038 | 0.369 | 0.474 | 0.317 | 0.165 | 2.214 |
| Income | 0.683 | 1.197 | 0.132 | -0.278 | -0.153 | -0.013 | 1.568 |
| **Portugal** | | | | | | | |
| Consumption | 0.175 | 0.119 | 0.077 | 0.045 | 0.022 | 0.005 | 0.443 |
| Investment | 0.679 | 0.019 | 0.004 | -0.020 | -0.030 | -0.035 | 0.609 |
| Imports | 0.797 | 0.109 | 0.079 | 0.056 | 0.038 | 0.025 | 1.104 |
| Income | 1.056 | 0.029 | -0.007 | -0.031 | -0.046 | -0.054 | 0.947 |
| **Syria** | | | | | | | |
| Consumption | 0.031 | 0.416 | 0.304 | 0.292 | 0.245 | 0.211 | 1.499 |
| Investment | -0.768 | 0.359 | 0.190 | 0.170 | 0.133 | 0.113 | 0.197 |
| Imports | 0.816 | 0.127 | 0.250 | 0.167 | 0.153 | 0.126 | 1.639 |
| Income | -0.554 | 0.648 | 0.245 | 0.295 | 0.227 | 0.199 | 1.060 |
| **Tunisia** | | | | | | | |
| Consumption | 0.714 | -0.479 | 0.158 | -0.075 | 0.038 | -0.010 | 0.346 |
| Investment | -2.644 | 0.762 | -0.263 | 0.165 | -0.041 | 0.034 | -1.987 |
| Imports | 0.510 | -0.159 | 0.133 | -0.014 | 0.031 | -0.001 | 0.500 |
| Income | -1.440 | 0.443 | -0.237 | 0.103 | -0.034 | 0.024 | -1.141 |

*Notes:* * Assuming $\ddot{A}R = 1$, sustained over the years.
*Source:* Author's calculations.

This discussion of multipliers is summarized for each of our four endogenous variables in Figures 13.A2, 13.A3, 13.A4 and 13.A5, depicting for each country the time path of truncated multipliers. As Figure 13.A5 shows, remittances constitute a rather strong propagating force of output growth for the three Middle Eastern countries—Egypt, Jordan, and Syria. In contrast, for Greece, Portugal, and Morocco whose remittances come largely from

Europe, remittance effects reach a maximum point in the second or third year, after which they shrink toward zero. Tunisia stays permanently in the red, below zero.

## Macroeconomic Effects of Remittances

### *Effects on Consumption, Investment, and Imports*

In this section, the estimated interim multipliers are applied to the actual annual changes of remittances to calculate the corresponding quantitative effects on consumption, investment, imports and output. The overall direct and indirect change on the endogenous variables $X_t = (C, I, M, Y)$ at time t of a sustained change in remittances over time can be expressed by:

$$\Delta X_t = \sum_{j=0}^{j=n} \frac{\partial X_t}{\partial R_{t-j}} \times \Delta R_{t-j} \tag{6}$$

where $\frac{\partial X_t}{\partial Z_{t-i}} = \pi_j$ is the multiplier of year $j$, $\Delta R_{t-j}$ is the actual change in remittances between year $(t\text{-}j)$ and $\{(t\text{-}j)\text{-}1\}$, and $X_t$ is any of our four endogenous variables: $C$, $I$, $M$ and $Y$. Then, the proportional contribution of remittances in year $t$ on any of the $X$'s is calculated as $(\Delta X_t / X_t) \times 100$.

For our six-year time distribution of remittance effects the following analytical expression is applied:

$$(X_t - X_{t-1}) = \Delta X_t = \frac{\partial X_t}{\partial R_t} \times dR_t + \frac{\partial X_t}{\partial R_{t-1}} \times dR_{t-1} + \frac{\partial X_t}{\partial R_{t-2}} \times dR_{t-2} +$$

$$\frac{\partial X_t}{\partial R_{t-3}} \times dR_{t-3} + \frac{\partial X_t}{\partial R_{t-4}} \times dR_{t-4} + \frac{\partial X_t}{\partial R_{t-5}} \times dR_{t-5} \tag{7}$$

The results of the calculations for C, I, M, and Y for each year of the period 1975–93 (five years are lost from our original 1969–93 period due to lags), together with the corresponding actual growth rates of the variables, are presented in Tables 13.4–13.7.

An overview of our findings shows that remittances have generally a strong positive influence in the economies of Egypt and Jordan, and a much weaker positive or negative influence in the rest of the countries. The induced changes in consumption, investment, and imports in these two countries are much higher than in any other country. At some distance follows Morocco—with much lower, mostly positive, contributions of remittance changes to consumption and contributions to investment and imports, which are consonant with Egypt and Jordan. Remittances in Syria, however, demonstrate relatively strong effects on consumption, investment, and with imports—exceeding those of Morocco, but not those of Egypt and Jordan. Tunisia has experienced both strong positive and strong negative contributions to investment, although these may apply largely to housing.

Finally, Greece and Portugal display a roughly similar behavior, having, with some exceptions, low growth rates, mostly below one percent for all three variables in question, and a fifty-fifty division between positive and negative spells for different time periods. The exception for Greece is a high incidence on investment during the later years of the period, while for Portugal it is a high incidence on investment and imports during the early years. The two countries are particularly differentiated for all three variables in the early 1990s, giving positive induced values for Greece and negative ones for Portugal.

One common characteristic of our findings is the great temporal fluctuation of the induced magnitudes for all three variables and all countries, but with different time patterns. This seems to suggest a dependence of the remittance effects on different conditions and policies in the home rather than in the host countries, given that the latter are common (the Gulf countries, or France and Germany) for some of the different recipient countries.

**Table 13.4: Rate of Growth (%) of Consumption Induced by Remittances***

| Year | Egypt | Greece | Jordan | Morocco | Portugal | Syria | Tunisia |
|---|---|---|---|---|---|---|---|
| 1975 | 1.81 | 0.18 | — | 1.40 | — | 0.07 | 0.39 |
| | *0.13* | *7.5* | — | *5.2* | — | *6.1* | *15.4* |
| 1976 | 3.30 | 0.41 | 5.64 | 2.77 | — | 0.12 | -0.30 |
| | *4.0* | *6.7* | *28.6* | *9.7* | — | *8.9* | *4.1* |
| 1977 | 5.10 | 0.22 | 8.41 | 1.51 | -0.10 | 0.11 | 0.39 |
| | *15.7* | *6.1* | *13.2* | *3.1* | *-1.7* | *8.1* | *9.6* |
| 1978 | 6.13 | -0.26 | 8.59 | -0.46 | 0.55 | 0.54 | 0.51 |
| | *6.1* | *4.7* | *13.3* | *7.0* | *-1.3* | *9.1* | *5.7* |
| 1979 | 9.56 | -0.01 | 5.77 | 0.19 | 1.14 | 3.79 | 0.33 |
| | *18.3* | *1.0* | *21.2* | *5.7* | *1.2* | *-1.6* | *6.2* |
| 1980 | 9.37 | -0.31 | 4.47 | 0.99 | 0.73 | 3.72 | -0.29 |
| | *12.1* | *-0.4* | *-5.4* | *6.7* | *2.7* | *10.8* | *12.5* |
| 1981 | 7.43 | 0.23 | 3.87 | 0.09 | 0.42 | 1.64 | 0.97 |
| | *2.3* | *8.1* | *-4.1* | *-4.1* | *1.5* | *8.4* | *6.8* |
| 1982 | 3.50 | -0.22 | 2.43 | 1.38 | 0.18 | 0.06 | -0.17 |
| | *3.2* | *6.8* | *18.0* | *5.9* | *2.5* | *-5.9* | *2.4* |
| 1983 | 2.87 | -0.05 | 3.39 | -0.95 | -0.13 | -0.08 | 0.02 |
| | *4.5* | *0.8* | *19.1* | *-0.8* | *1.3* | *-2.8* | *4.5* |
| 1984 | 3.50 | 0.11 | 4.79 | 0.82 | 0.01 | -1.98 | -0.47 |
| | *8.1* | *1.6* | *3.3* | *3.4* | *-0.7* | *-10.2* | *5.7* |
| 1985 | 3.24 | -0.28 | 5.06 | 0.62 | -0.13 | -2.12 | -0.32 |
| | *6.0* | *4.3* | *-0.2* | *0.5* | *1.5* | *21.6* | *2.4* |
| 1986 | 0.78 | 0.11 | 3.59 | 0.98 | -0.22 | -1.07 | 1.04 |
| | *0.6* | *2.5* | *15.0* | *12.3* | *3.5* | *-11.6* | *1.7* |
| 1987 | 0.21 | 0.57 | 1.71 | 2.92 | -0.01 | -0.07 | 0.82 |
| | *0.3* | *4.5* | *-3.4* | *-0.7* | *4.1* | *26.4* | *1.6* |
| 1988 | 1.06 | 0.50 | -0.30 | 2.48 | -0.10 | 0.26 | -0.34 |
| | *-6.3* | *-0.4* | *-11.2* | *8.7* | *3.8* | *14.0* | *1.6* |
| 1989 | 0.73 | -0.54 | — | -2.43 | 0.02 | 0.72 | -0.52 |
| | *2.6* | *8.2* | — | *6.1* | *3.6* | *-8.1* | *-1.6* |
| 1990 | -0.92 | 0.13 | — | -2.50 | -0.04 | 0.77 | 0.60 |
| | *6.0* | *4.5* | — | *1.2* | *5.9* | *10.2* | *10.2* |
| 1991 | 1.08 | 0.52 | — | 2.90 | -0.12 | 0.10 | -0.62 |
| | *1.3* | *3.0* | — | *11.0* | *4.3* | *5.9* | *2.0* |
| 1992 | 4.72 | 0.15 | — | 1.27 | -0.29 | — | -0.15 |
| | *0.8* | *0.8* | — | *-3.1* | *2.3* | — | *7.2* |
| 1993 | 6.28 | 0.19 | — | 0.61 | -0.30 | — | 0.73 |
| | *4.2* | *-0.5* | — | *-6.2* | *0.8* | — | *3.2* |

*Notes:* * The figures in italics underneath the estimates of induced growth rates are the overall rates of growth, calculated from World Bank, *World Tables*, 1991, 1994, 1995.
*Source:* Author's calculations.

Comparatively high is the induced consumption in Egypt and Jordan, and particularly low (positive or negative) in Greece and Portugal, affecting only slightly their standard of living. Both the magnitude and the fluctuations of induced consumption are much larger in Morocco and Syria (Table 13.4). In other words, with the exception of Egypt and Jordan, and to some extent Morocco, the overall effect on consumption is rather modest. Remittances often pull down the consumption level, at least in five of the countries of our sample. This is the case, despite the high proportion of remittances spent by recipients on consumption, according to ample empirical evidence (for examples, see Keely and Tran, 1989; Adams, 1991).

Our findings shed some light on the much-debated issue of whether or not remittances help investment and, consequently, economic development. Most of the literature seems to take a negative view, and concludes that remittances are spent unproductively on consumption, land, and housing, and cannot therefore contribute to development (see references in Russell, 1992; Glytsos, 1993, 1998a). This chapter cannot provide a clear answer to the question, owing to the fact that our gross investment variable includes public and private fixed investment, changes in stocks and also residential housing construction, which makes for a complicated picture. Nevertheless, the analysis of the effects of remittances—even in this gross variable—offers some insights. Our estimates suggest that changes in remittances affect gross investment considerably, and in some cases even strongly, in various direct and indirect ways (Glytsos, 1998).

A relatively wide range of effects, positive or negative, is observed for Egypt, where, in all but three years (1982, 1986, 1987), remittances raised investment between 1.5 percent and 13.1 percent (Table 13.5). These estimates may be contrasted to some pieces of conflicting evidence for Egypt, such as a corresponding 25 percent rate given for the same years by Lesch (1990); Feiler's (1987) contention that remittances influence Egyptian investment negatively; or Farrag's (1996) claim that investment financed by remittances is limited. In Jordan, remittance-induced investment is also high, but, in contrast to Egypt, there are very wide fluctuations in its growth.

Narrower ups and downs are to be found in Morocco, with negative effects in the years 1982, 1988, 1992, and 1993. Tunisia's case is similar, but with negative spells in more than half the years. Syria displays a much wider and more unstable range of influences, but with fewer years of negative effects. The comparison between the high induced growth rates of investment with the low induced growth rates of consumption in 1980, 1981, 1990, and 1991, in Syria, supports the view that, at least in these years, remittances went considerably to productive uses (Wahba, 1996, referring to Al-Ashakar, 1992). Quite moderate in width, but of significant size, are the induced investment changes in Greece and Portugal. In roughly half the years, the rates are positive while in the other half negative—the two countries coinciding for their negative growth rates in 1982, 1983, 1985, 1986, and 1990.

Exceptionally 'bad' years—with negative rates of induced investment for almost all countries, but probably for different reasons in each—were 1982 and 1986. This declining trend of induced investment continued until 1987. Exceptions are Jordan, in the first year, and Morocco, in the second, having positive and high rates (8 percent each). In these two years, there was a considerable drop in oil prices, which probably directly affected some oil-exporting countries, such as Tunisia, and indirectly affected others through a reduction in the size of their migrants in the oil-rich Gulf countries. In counterpart, 'good' years for most countries, except Syria and Tunisia, were 1977 and 1988; and for Egypt, Jordan, and Morocco, 1983 and 1984.

**Table 13.5: Rate of Growth (%) of Investment Induced by Remittances***

| Year | Egypt | Greece | Jordan | Morocco | Portugal | Syria | Tunisia |
|---|---|---|---|---|---|---|---|
| 1975 | 3.4 | -3.9 | — | 5.9 | — | 0.1 | -2.2 |
| | *56.4* | *-1.3* | — | *65.6* | — | *27.7* | *-1.1* |
| 1976 | 7.3 | 1.5 | 32.8 | 2.4 | — | 0.2 | 1.2 |
| | *-0.3* | *2.1* | *48.8* | *17.4* | — | *34.8* | *10.3* |
| 1977 | 6.6 | 2.6 | 31.1 | 0.5 | 3.1 | -1.2 | -2.3 |
| | *12.7* | *1.1* | *22.8* | *15.5* | *34.0* | *13.6* | *2.0* |
| 1978 | 13.1 | -0.6 | 7.4 | 4.0 | 4.9 | -17.1 | -4.2 |
| | *11.3* | *8.1* | *4.7* | *-25.9* | *6.6* | *-13.4* | *10.8* |
| 1979 | 13.1 | -0.3 | -0.5 | 4.1 | 6.5 | 0.9 | -3.8 |
| | *11.8* | *9.8* | *10.4* | *1.3* | *7.5* | *1.0* | *6.3* |
| 1980 | 8.8 | -2.4 | 2.4 | 1.5 | 0.0 | 13.4 | 0.8 |
| | *-1.4* | *-4.5* | *30.8* | *4.6* | *10.7* | *21.9* | *0.9* |
| 1981 | 1.5 | 0.5 | 6.0 | 3.1 | -0.4 | 10.1 | -6.6 |
| | 8.2 | -14.2 | 39.7 | 0.3 | 3.6 | 2.4 | 15.0 |
| 1982 | -0.7 | -1.5 | 8.0 | -0.8 | -0.6 | -0.8 | -1.2 |
| | *12.6* | *-6.4* | *2.1* | *16.4* | *1.3* | *2.9* | *-0.7* |
| 1983 | 6.3 | -1.2 | 10.9 | 4.5 | -2.3 | 0.4 | -0.5 |
| | *3.8* | *-0.8* | *-18.9* | *-17.0* | *-19.1* | *6.1* | *-2.2* |
| 1984 | 7.6 | 0.7 | 15.8 | 3.6 | 1.2 | -1.3 | 3.4 |
| | *10.2* | *-7.9* | *-6.1* | *7.3* | *-20.4* | *1.3* | *8.7* |
| 1985 | 1.1 | -2.4 | 5.5 | 4.8 | -1.5 | -4.1 | 4.4 |
| | *-1.9* | *12.7* | *-1.3* | *12.4* | *-2.0* | *4.9* | *-12.6* |
| 1986 | -3.5 | -0.1 | -1.6 | 8.0 | -1.5 | -1.3 | -9.5 |
| | *-4.1* | *-7.0* | *-8.1* | *-2.1* | *17.9* | *-11.0* | *-18.7* |
| 1987 | -2.6 | 8.0 | -4.4 | 3.4 | 1.2 | -2.3 | -13.2 |
| | *-17.8* | *-12.2* | *-11.9* | *-8.3* | *24.1* | *-32.1* | *-1.7* |
| 1988 | 3.4 | 8.6 | -22.6 | -6.3 | -0.7 | -2.7 | -1.2 |
| | *32.0* | *22.4* | *-13.6* | *5.3* | *20.4* | *-4.0* | *-12.2* |
| 1989 | 1.7 | -2.7 | — | 1.0 | 0.6 | 0.8 | 4.9 |
| | *-0.02* | *3.5* | — | *14.5* | *6.0* | *-25.2* | *31.7* |
| 1990 | 0.4 | -0.7 | — | 10.2 | -0.4 | 8.6 | -3.9 |
| | *-0.9* | *-1.2* | — | *10.5* | *5.8* | *7.2* | *19.3* |
| 1991 | 4.9 | 5.7 | — | 1.1 | -0.7 | 5.3 | 4.4 |
| | *-4.6* | *5.9* | — | *-3.9* | *3.8* | *-10.6* | *2.0* |
| 1992 | 11.2 | 4.2 | — | -0.4 | -1.6 | — | 2.8 |
| | *-9.8* | *2.9* | — | *-4.1* | *7.2* | — | *19.3* |
| 1993 | 2.5 | 3.5 | — | -0.5 | -0.9 | — | -5.3 |
| | *1.4* | *1.2* | — | *7.8* | *-4.0* | — | *0.4* |

*Notes:* * The figures in italics underneath the estimates of induced growth rates are the overall rates of growth, calculated from World Bank, *World Tables,* 1991, 1994, 1995.
*Source:* Author's calculations.

Finally, this chapter offers some findings regarding induced imports. It was found that new income from remittances raised imports in Egypt at the rates of 11–12 percent, in 1978, 1979, and 1992, but it also damped imports, at much lower rates, in 1982, 1986, and 1987 (Table 13.6). The peak of induced imports for Jordan was 1977, with a 9.3 percent rate, and the years of decline were 1986 and 1988, which overlap with the years of decline for Egypt.

The positive and relatively high growth rates of imports in Jordan, for most of the time, seem to be compatible with Keely and Saket's (1984) findings of a substantial contribution of remittances to imports in this country, for several years, 1976–1978 and 1982–1985. Recall that, in most of these years, induced investment (which consists largely of imports) increased at even faster rates, making for a correspondingly high contribution of remittances to GDP. This is perhaps an argument for supporting the view that spending remittances on imports can be beneficial, rather than harmful, to development, through imports of machinery and other intermediate goods that increase domestic production (Russell, 1992: 274).

**Table 13.6: Rate of Growth (%) of Imports Induced by Remittances***

| Year | Egypt | Greece | Jordan | Morocco | Portugal | Syria | Tunisia |
|---|---|---|---|---|---|---|---|
| 1975 | 2.53 | -1.52 | — | 5.66 | — | 0.10 | 0.56 |
| | *20.7* | *6.3* | — | *30.5* | — | *46.5* | *9.8* |
| 1976 | 5.85 | 1.53 | 4.20 | 3.09 | — | 0.13 | -0.13 |
| | *-5.4* | *6.1* | *49.0* | *21.6* | — | *-4.0* | *11.4* |
| 1977 | 5.33 | 1.72 | 9.34 | 2.64 | 3.16 | 0.99 | 0.40 |
| | *5.4* | *8.0* | *21.8* | *12.4* | *12.0* | *40.7* | *15.2* |
| 1978 | 12.16 | -0.89 | 4.71 | 4.72 | 5.78 | 12.82 | 0.61 |
| | *3.4* | *7.1* | *14.1* | *-12.9* | *0.2* | *-13.9* | *8.4* |
| 1979 | 11.00 | -0.34 | 0.96 | 3.07 | 8.05 | 7.05 | 0.52 |
| | *16.2* | *7.2* | *27.3* | *3.3* | *12.6* | *11.8* | *15.1* |
| 1980 | 6.29 | -1.96 | 0.53 | 1.55 | 1.13 | -0.73 | -0.01 |
| | *8.1* | *-8.0* | *-6.0* | *-7.9* | *6.9* | *-0.3* | *4.5* |
| 1981 | 0.15 | 0.65 | 1.23 | 3.32 | 0.71 | -3.68 | 0.96 |
| | *5.3* | *3.6* | *18.9* | *1.9* | *2.3* | *-8.2* | *13.0* |
| 1982 | -1.78 | -1.25 | 2.40 | -0.21 | 0.45 | 0.27 | 0.18 |
| | *-13.2* | *7.0* | *6.7* | *3.1* | *3.9* | *-15.7* | *0.9* |
| 1983 | 6.44 | -0.77 | 2.37 | 5.24 | -1.54 | -1.74 | 0.22 |
| | *1.0* | *6.6* | *2.8* | *-11.3* | *-6.1* | *-1.3* | *-2.2* |
| 1984 | 7.88 | 0.32 | 3.41 | 2.44 | 1.41 | -3.71 | -0.35 |
| | *14.8* | *0.2* | *-0.7* | *4.5* | *-4.4* | *-1.2* | *5.7* |
| 1985 | 0.93 | -1.50 | 3.84 | 5.20 | -1.44 | -1.32 | -0.49 |
| | *3.0* | *12.8* | *1.8* | *0.03* | *1.4* | *36.4* | *-13.0* |
| 1986 | -4.04 | 0.07 | -0.42 | 7.43 | -1.53 | -1.85 | 1.00 |
| | *-12.7* | *3.8* | *5.2* | *7.9* | *16.9* | *-34.8* | *-2.1* |
| 1987 | -3.44 | 2.83 | 1.24 | 3.74 | 0.78 | 1.39 | 1.31 |
| | *-15.6* | *16.6* | *3.6* | *7.9* | *20.2* | *26.0* | *-3.4* |
| 1988 | 3.92 | 3.41 | -2.77 | -0.93 | -0.76 | 3.15 | 0.15 |
| | *12.5* | *8.0* | *0.5* | *6.8* | *16.4* | *-16.3* | *16.1* |
| 1989 | 2.05 | -1.07 | — | 3.92 | 0.48 | 2.45 | -0.27 |
| | *2.1* | *10.8* | — | *7.3* | *7.9* | *6.3* | *14.6* |
| 1990 | 1.08 | 0.25 | — | 6.04 | -0.41 | -1.28 | 0.54 |
| | *8.3* | *12.0* | — | *12.6* | *13.7* | *7.0* | *9.0* |
| 1991 | 5.65 | 2.02 | — | -1.58 | -0.65 | -2.55 | -0.49 |
| | *-0.7* | *13.2* | — | *1.6* | *5.4* | *-24.7* | *-5.1* |
| 1992 | 11.10 | 1.30 | — | 1.74 | -1.30 | — | -0.26 |
| | *-2.8* | *5.7* | — | *7.7* | *11.1* | — | *14.8* |
| 1993 | 1.31 | 1.28 | — | 1.14 | -0.93 | — | 0.56 |
| | *2.7* | *-1.9* | — | *0.4* | *-3.2* | — | *3.2* |

*Notes:* * The figures in italics underneath the estimates of induced growth rates are the overall rates of growth, calculated from World Bank, *World Tables*, 1991, 1994, 1995.
*Source:* Author's calculations.

Similar mixed results are obtained for Syria. For several years in the period 1975–91, remittances tended to reduce imports, with a particularly strong impact in 1981 and 1991, coinciding with a considerable contribution of remittances to investment (10.1 and 5.3 percent, respectively) and a negligible contribution to consumption. In 1978 and 1979, however, remittances increased imports at very high rates (12.8 and 7.0 percent), with respectively high negative or zero induced investment growth. This kind of trade-off indicates a competitive situation for Syria between induced imports and induced investment, in contrast to a corresponding complementarity for Jordan—in the sense that Jordan's investment goods are extensively purchased abroad. Unless one refers to particular time periods, these findings can neither support nor refute the argument that remittances in Syria raise imports and augment, rather than alleviate, its balance-of-payments problems (Wahba, 1996, referring to Al-Ashakar, 1992).

The induced rates of imports in Morocco were considerable, although much lower than in Egypt and Jordan, in almost all years—growth rates ranging between 1.1 percent and 7.4 percent, with slightly negative rates in 1982, 1988, and 1991. In Tunisia, both positive and negative growth rates were generally below one percent. In Greece and Portugal, as in all other countries, we observe positive and negative contributions of remittances, the former being higher than the latter. In other words, the demand for imports with respect to remittances is, in these two countries, downward inelastic and upward elastic, which perhaps reflects the theoretical life-cycle hypothesis, which is behind our import equation. Particularly good' (or 'bad'?) years of high induced imports in all countries, except Greece, were 1977, 1978, and 1979, and particularly 'bad' (or 'good'?) years of very low or negative induced imports growth rates for all countries, except Morocco, were 1982, 1985 (save Jordan), 1989, and 1990.

### *Growth Effects of Remittances*

The changes in consumption, investment and imports brought about by remittances are reflected in GDP changes. Our findings on this, for Egypt and Jordan, seem to be consistent with the arguments favoring the view that remittances are a significant positive factor in the economic development and growth of these two countries. At different years of the period 1976–84, remittances raised the Egyptian GDP between 2.7 percent and 7.5 percent annually, and the Jordanian GDP between 4.3 per cent and 11.5 percent, generating in both cases a very large portion of the overall rate of growth of GDP (Table 13.7). Particularly good years for Jordan were 1976–84, when the country had a high proportion of its labor force working outside the country (40 percent in 1984) (Samha, 1992). In fact, the potential contribution of remittances to GDP peaked for Jordan in 1984 (11.5 percent growth rate), which, as shown, was also a year of high induced investment (15.8 percent). These high rates were generated in the face of a 70–80 percent average expenditure on consumption out of remittance income (Samha, 1992). This apparent contradiction can be explained by the indirect effects of remittances on output through induced consumption (our estimated total multiplier for Jordan is 2.9 percent).

The situation changed substantially for Egypt from 1985 onward, and for Jordan from 1986, when the two countries experienced mostly negative rates of induced output. Egypt recovered in 1991 and continued with positive rates in 1992 and 1993. Farrag (1996) points out that, during the invasion of 1990, half a million Egyptian workers were deported from Kuwait, leaving behind their savings and their unpaid earnings. This, according to her, led to a decline in remittances. However, official remittances increased greatly in 1991 and 1992—perhaps as a result of the devaluation of the Egyptian pound by 25 percent in 1990 and 1991, which, among other things, shifted remittances from the black market to official channels, thus making up any loss from deported migrants and substantially raising investment and output. Remittances almost doubled between 1989 and 1991 (from 6.8 million Egyptian pounds to 12.3 million) and increased further by 50 percent in 1992, to 18.2 million Egyptian pounds.

**Table 13.7: Rate of Growth (%) of GDP Induced by Remittances***

| Year | Egypt | Greece | Jordan | Morocco | Portugal | Syria | Tunisia |
|---|---|---|---|---|---|---|---|
| 1975 | 2.43 | -0.48 | — | 2.56 | — | 0.06 | -0.46 |
| | *10.1* | *6.1* | — | *6.7* | — | *4.5* | *7.1* |
| 1976 | 4.55 | 0.58 | 28.98 | 1.82 | — | 0.08 | 0.22 |
| | *15.4* | *6.5* | *29.4* | *11.0* | — | *13.0* | *8.1* |
| 1977 | 4.37 | 0.61 | 10.52 | -0.07 | 1.44 | -0.26 | -0.42 |
| | *13.1* | *3.6* | *4.8* | *4.9* | *5.6* | *-4.3* | *3.8* |
| 1978 | 8.92 | -0.34 | 4.31 | -0.39 | 2.33 | -3.14 | -0.76 |
| | *7.7* | *2.7* | *9.1* | *2.9* | *3.0* | *10.2* | *6.5* |
| 1979 | 9.30 | 0.01 | 5.40 | 0.67 | 3.10 | 2.60 | -0.69 |
| | *7.9* | *7.8* | *9.1* | *4.6* | *6.2* | *3.0* | *6.7* |
| 1980 | 7.47 | -0.71 | 6.66 | 0.71 | 0.00 | 4.34 | 0.11 |
| | *10.8* | *1.5* | *19.0* | *9.1* | *4.4* | *13.5* | *7.3* |
| 1981 | 4.55 | 0.35 | 9.35 | 0.58 | -0.23 | 2.17 | -1.27 |
| | *4.0* | *0.0* | *4.7* | *-2.8* | *1.1* | *10.7* | *5.4* |
| 1982 | 2.71 | -0.41 | 5.97 | 0.26 | -0.33 | -0.43 | -0.20 |
| | *10.7* | *0.4* | *7.4* | *9.6* | *2.2* | *3.6* | *0.0* |
| 1983 | 5.54 | -0.13 | 9.91 | 0.05 | -0.97 | 0.17 | -0.15 |
| | *7.7* | *0.6* | *5.9* | *-0.5* | *0.0* | *1.8* | *4.7* |
| 1984 | 4.00 | 0.23 | 11.47 | 1.21 | 0.43 | -0.77 | 0.59 |
| | *6.1* | *2.7* | *5.8* | *4.2* | *-1.8* | *18.7* | *5.7* |
| 1985 | 0.44 | -0.57 | -2.78 | 1.41 | -0.49 | -1.69 | 0.63 |
| | *4.1* | *3.1* | *2.3* | *6.3* | *2.8* | *-15.8* | *5.6* |
| 1986 | -0.66 | 0.16 | 8.13 | 2.12 | -0.55 | -0.51 | -1.13 |
| | *5.1* | *1.6* | *5.4* | *7.8* | *4.1* | *-2.7* | *-1.4* |
| 1987 | 0.48 | 1.45 | -8.50 | 1.88 | 0.50 | -0.35 | -1.42 |
| | *2.5* | *-0.4* | *3.2* | *-2.2* | *5.5* | *-0.9* | *6.6* |
| 1988 | 2.68 | 1.40 | -4.20 | -1.09 | -0.34 | -0.13 | -0.14 |
| | *4.2* | *4.4* | *-11.8* | *10.2* | *5.7* | *0.1* | *0.2* |
| 1989 | 0.06 | -1.09 | — | -2.45 | 0.30 | 0.48 | 0.53 |
| | *3.0* | *3.5* | — | *2.3* | *5.8* | *-10.1* | *1.7* |
| 1990 | -0.69 | 0.07 | — | 1.02 | -0.20 | 1.16 | -0.58 |
| | *2.4* | *-0.8* | — | *3.8* | *4.2* | *7.6* | *7.6* |
| 1991 | 2.12 | 1.17 | — | 2.64 | -0.37 | 0.31 | 0.64 |
| | *2.1* | *3.1* | — | *5.9* | *2.1* | *9.7* | *3.8* |
| 1992 | 5.01 | 0.49 | — | 0.56 | -0.83 | — | 0.39 |
| | 0.3 | *1.0* | — | *-4.0* | *1.1* | — | *8.0* |
| 1993 | 2.21 | 0.54 | — | -0.47 | -0.45 | — | -0.77 |
| | 0.5 | -0.5 | — | -1.1 | -1.1 | — | 2.2 |

*Notes:* * The figures in italics underneath the estimates of induced growth rates are the overall rates of growth, calculated from World Bank, *World Tables*, 1991, 1994, 1995.
*Source:* Author's calculations.

As a result, the contribution of remittances to GDP growth increased from zero in 1989 to 2.1 percent in 1991 and 5.0 percent in 1992. The corresponding Egyptian actual overall rate of growth of GDP was 2.4 percent in 1990, 2.1 percent in 1991, and 0.3 percent in 1992. These rates are much lower compared to the rates of previous years. Comparing the relative magnitudes of induced and actual growth rates of output for Egypt and Jordan in the earlier (1976–84) and the later part of the period (after 1985), one may realize that changes in remittances have a strong impact on changes in economic growth of these two countries. It is particularly evident that remittances did indeed contribute to the high growth rates of the earlier period.

As Table 13.7 shows, our model gives moderate growth rates of induced output in Morocco (1.8–2.5 percent, in 1975, 1976, 1986, 1987, and 1991), and Syria (2.2–4.3 percent, during the period 1979–81). The rest of the countries experienced either very low positive rates (mostly below one percent) or very low negative rates of induced GDP growth in all years. Evidence presented for Morocco (Wahba, 1996: 19) testifies to a raised standard of living for remittance recipients and to a negative impact on agricultural output, since some farmers can afford to live from remittances and abandon cultivation. Other evidence indicates that remittance spending on housing is extremely high in Morocco. In some regions—those with heavy migration to the European Union—about 75–80 percent of the new houses belong to migrants (Bencherifa, *et al.*, 1992: 99).

Our findings for Morocco seem to support this evidence on both counts. Induced imports and induced gross investment are rather high for most of the period 1975–93, whereas induced rates of GDP growth are very low or negative. Taken together, these developments most probably signify that imports concern primarily consumer goods, and investment concerns primarily housing, whereas the low or negative rates of output reflect an induced drop in agricultural production, especially when the actual growth (as in years 1981, 1983, 1987, 1992, and 1993) was negative.

As an oil-exporting country, Tunisia was favored by rising oil prices in the early 1970s, which helped investment activity. In turn, however, it was harmed by the drop of oil prices in the early 1980s, depriving the country of substantial foreign exchange. This loss was probably made up to a limited extent by a moderate increase in remittances. After the oil price hike and up until 1992, Tunisia generally managed to sustain a high rate of output growth (5.4–7.3 percent), apparently without the help of remittances. A particularly bad year with a negative growth rate (-1.4 percent) was 1986, when Tunisia underwent a severe crisis in foreign exchange. It immediately recovered in the next year (6.6 percent growth rate), following a successful stabilization and structural reform policy, at a time when remittances had a negative contribution to investment and output. A concise picture of the effects of remittances on GDP is given for each country in Figure 13.A6, which depicts the close relationship between remittances and the growth of the Egyptian and Jordanian economies and the limited, if any, influence for the remaining countries.

Our findings in this section may help answer the question put by several authors and reiterated by Adams (1991: 12): Can remittances secure the resources needed for the development of the Third World or not? It seems that for periods of time and for some countries the answer is affirmative. This may also partly justify Looney's (1990) argument about a marginal impact of remittances on development in Egypt (we found it to be true only for the second half of the 1980s). Our results may also put in question Wahba's (1996: 19) rather general statement, resulting from a review of the literature for the Middle East, that "evidence shows that remittances have not helped the development process."

## Concluding Remarks

Our model's creation is motivated by the uncertainties surrounding the role of remittances in the economic development of labor-exporting countries. Much of the literature claims that remittances are spent on consumption or leak to imports and are not channeled to investment activity, which would generate growth and help the development of these countries. This study has attempted to illuminate these issues. Experimenting with a model of simultaneous equations, separately for eight developing countries having different migratory characteristics and migrant destinations, we found some common ground for discussion but also expressions of the particularities of the countries involved.

The distributed-lag feature of the model was able to determine the time distribution of the effects of remittances on the endogenous macroeconomic variables and to trace their growth path over time. The estimated model demonstrated a great structural uniformity in the experiences of different countries and gave very illuminating results regarding the growth-generating power of remittances and the determination of their actual effects on the macroeconomic variables, by country and for different periods of time.

The findings reveal a rather unstable situation in all countries, with remittances having fluctuating positive and negative effects. A trade-off between investment and imports is found in some countries and a complementarity in others. This seems to indicate different priorities of induced spending, following changes in remittances.

Some general and rather self-evident policy objectives from this analysis include: (1) strengthening the growth-generating power of remittances; (2) reducing the temporal instability of remittance effects and eliminating their negative impact; (3) motivating remittance recipients to spend according to the growth objectives of the government; and finally (4) integrating any policies on remittances in the long-term strategies of the economies concerned. As for individual countries, one would need, before being able to draw specific policy conclusions, to interpret the findings of our analysis against the experience of each country—keeping in mind the above objectives.

## Appendix 13.A1

### Figure 13.A1: Change of Workers' Remittances as a Proportion of Merchandise Exports in Selected Mediterranean Countries, 1973–93 (Index 1973 = 100)

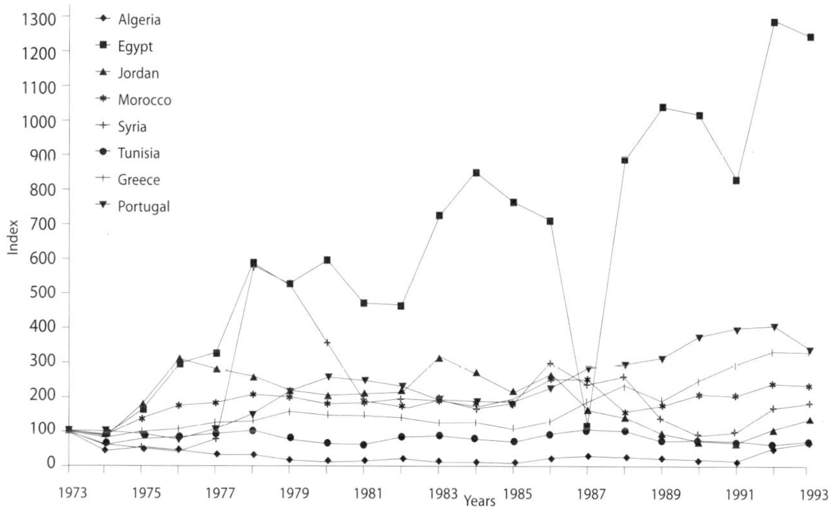


*Source:* World Bank, *World Tables*, 1994, 1995.

### Figure 13.A2: Time-path of Cumulative Effects on Consumption of One Unit Increase in Remittances ($\Delta R = 1$), (Sustained over Time), during a Period of Six Years

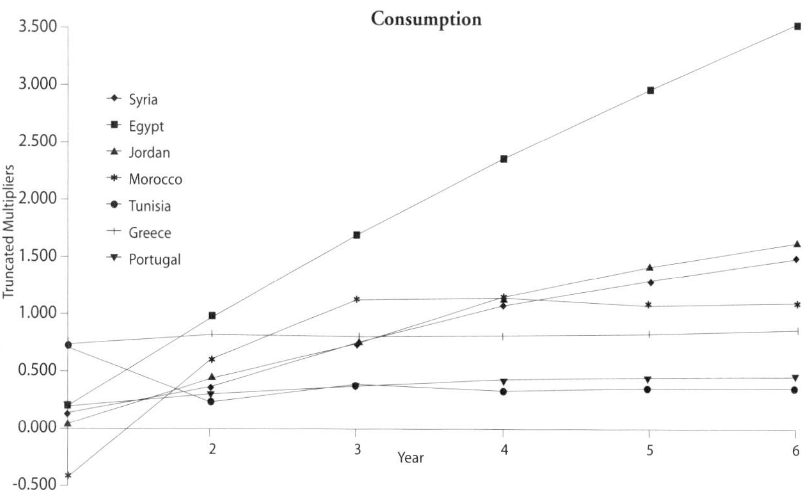


*Source:* Author's calculations.

**Figure 13.A3: Time-path of Cumulative Effects on Investment of One Unit Increase in Remittances ($\Delta R = 1$), (Sustained over Time), during a Period of Six Years**

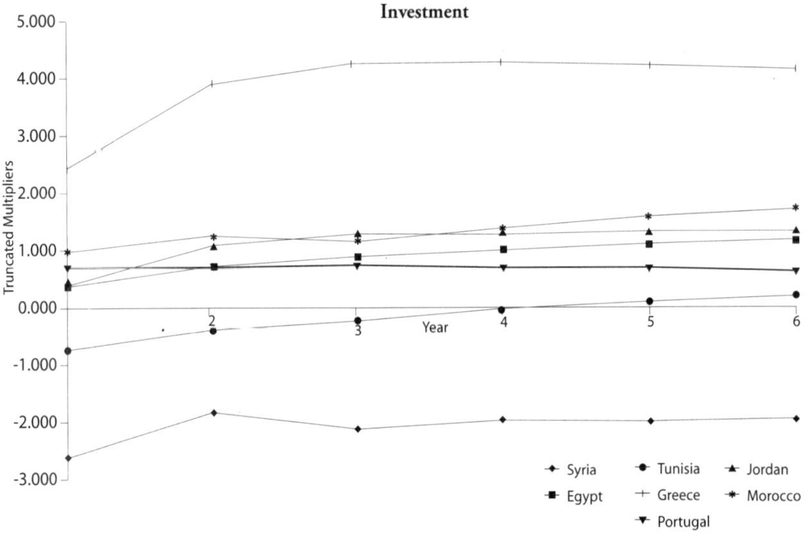


*Source:* Author's calculations.

**Figure 13.A4: Time-path of Cumulative Effects on Imports of One Unit Increase in Remittances ($\Delta R = 1$), (Sustained over Time), during a Period of Six Years**

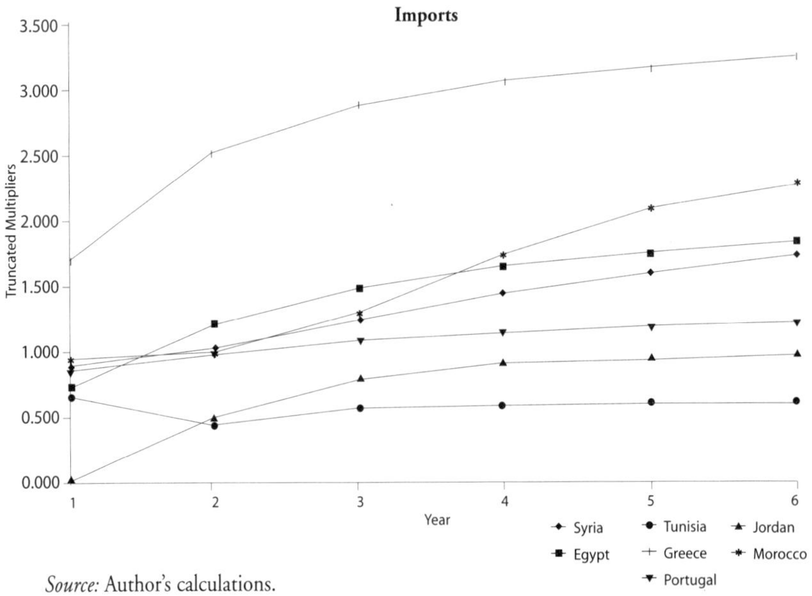


*Source:* Author's calculations.

**Figure 13.A5: Time-path of Cumulative Effects on GDP of One Unit Increase in Remittances ($\Delta R$ = 1), (Sustained over Time), during a Period of Six Years**

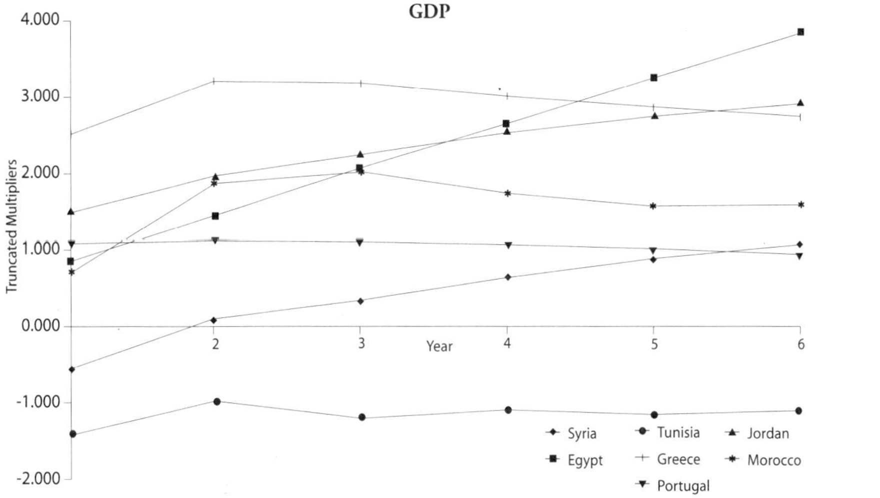


*Source:* Author's calculations.

**Figure 13.A6: Rates of Growth of GDP Induced by Remittances and Overall Rates of Growth of GDP, 1975–93**

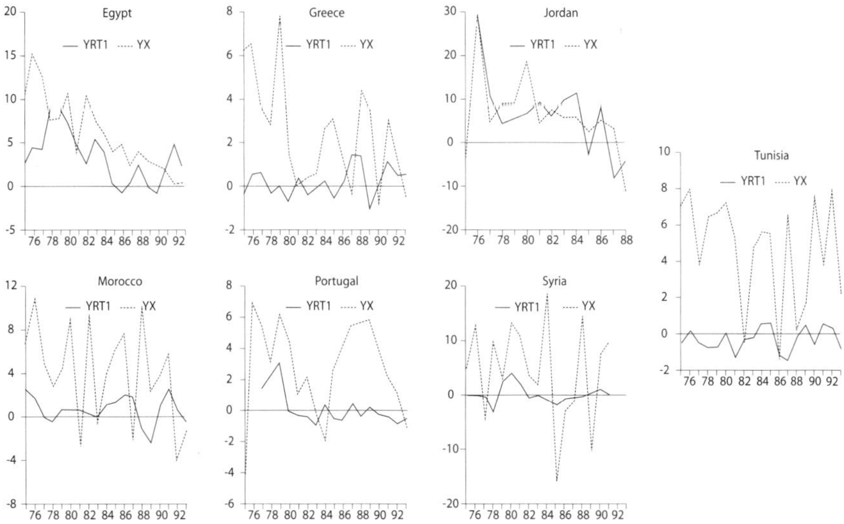


*Notes:* The vertical axis depicts rates of growth; the horizontal axis, years.
YRT1 = Rate of growth of GDP induced by Remittances.
YX = Overall rate of growth of GDP.
*Sources*: (a) Author's calculations (for induced GDP). (b) Calculations from World Bank, *World Tables*, 1991, 1994, and 1995 (for overall rates of growth).

## Appendix 13.A2

### Data

The data refer to the period 1969–93 and are taken from the World Bank, *World Tables*, 1991, 1994, and 1995. They are expressed at constant 1987 values, except for the figures of Jordan, which are expressed at 1980 constant prices. All values are in local currencies. The values in US dollars have been converted using the conversion index of the World Bank *Tables*.

Egypt: Consumption and government expenditures for the period 1969–73 are estimates by the author, as follows:

$$C_t = \left(\frac{DA_t}{DA_{t+1}}\right) \times C_{t+1} \text{ and } G_t = DA_t - C_t - I_t$$

where $DA$ = domestic absorption, $C$ = private consumption, $G$ = general government consumption, and $I$ = gross domestic investment.

Jordan: All data for Jordan refer to the period 1970–88.

Morocco: The 1969 remittances are "corrected" by the author.

Portugal: $C$, $I$, $G$, $X$, and M for 1960 and 1970 are author's estimates based on the 1971 ratio of variables expressed in 1987 and 1980 prices.

Syria: Remittances for 1969–71 are taken from the UN's *Balance of Payments Statistics Yearbook*, 1976. All data for Syria refer to the period 1969–91.

Tunisia: Remittances for 1969 are taken from the UN's *Balance of Payments Statistics Yearbook*, 1976.

## Appendix 13.A3

A system of simultaneous equations is presented in the form of matrix notation, that is, $BX + \Gamma Z = 0$, where $X$ is a vector of endogenous variables, $Z$ a vector of predetermined variables, and $B$ and $\Gamma$ respective matrices of endogenous and predetermined variables parameters. Shifting terms and pre-multiplying by $B^{-1}$, gives $X = (-B^{-1}\,\Gamma)\ Z$. This is a reduced-form expression of the system of equations, with matrix: $\Pi = -B^{-1}\,\Gamma$ containing the reduced-form coefficients $\pi$'s as non-linear functions of the structural parameters estimated by TSLS. A typical row of such coefficients is the $\pi_1, \pi_2, \pi_3, \pi_4, \ldots \pi_7$, in the above reduced-form equation (5) (see, for instance, the textbooks by Christ, 1966, and Johnston, 1972; and empirical applications by Goldberger, 1959, and Pavlopoulos, 1966).

The interim multipliers for the 2nd, 3rd, 4th, ... and $n^{th}$ years are calculated by partitioning matrix $\Pi$, into three sub-matrices: $\Pi_1$ with the current exogenous variables; $\Pi_2$ with the lagged exogenous variables and $\Pi_3$ with the lagged endogenous variables. The interim multipliers are obtained as follows:

$$\begin{aligned}
\text{second year multipliers} &= (\Pi_2 + \Pi_3\Pi_1)\\
\text{third year multipliers} &= \Pi_3(\Pi_2 + \Pi_3\Pi_1)\\
\text{fourth year multipliers} &= \Pi_3^2(\Pi_2 + \Pi_3\Pi_1)\\
&\vdots\\
n^{th}\text{ year multipliers} &= \Pi_3^{n-2}(\Pi_2 + \Pi_3\Pi_1)
\end{aligned}$$

The total multipliers are given by the matrix $\Pi_1 + \sum_{t=2}^{t=n} \Pi_3^{t-2}(\Pi_2 + \Pi_3\Pi_1)$.

It is obvious from these expressions that matrix $\Pi_3$ of the lagged endogenous variables is the pushing factor, moving the system forward toward long-run equilibrium if certain conditions of convergence exist.

## Notes

* The assistance of Yulie Papakonstantinou is gratefully acknowledged.

1 It should be noted that particularly in the MENA countries very large amounts of remittances do not go through official channels, because the black market premium in foreign exchange is very profitable. For instance, during the period 1977–89 this premium was 270 percent in Algeria, whereas in Morocco and Tunisia it was very low, turning higher proportions of remittances to official channels. A cross-section econometric analysis that included Algeria, Morocco, Portugal, Tunisia, Turkey, and former Yugoslavia found a minus 0.3 elasticity of official remittances with respect to black market exchange rate premium (Elbadawi and Rocha, 1992).

2 Either we assume a permanent income ($Y_t^*$) determining current consumption ($C_t$), i.e. $C_t = \beta_1 + \beta_2 Y_t^* + u_t$, or a long-run desired consumption ($C_t^*$) as a function of current income, i.e. $C_t^* = \gamma_1 + \gamma_2 Y_t + u_t$, where $u_t$ the error term, entailing correspondingly adaptive expectations of income or partial adjustment of consumption, the estimable equation is the same and will appear with a lagged consumption, although the statistical issues of efficiency and reliability are different. Coefficient $\beta_2$ is the MPC on permanent income and $\gamma_2$ the long-run MPC. It is therefore an empirical matter how to interpret the estimated coefficients in different countries. In cases where "habit persistence or inertia" in the behavior of consumers prevails, the partial adjustment model is involved. If consumption is "forward-looking," however, adaptive expectations are involved (see, among others, Duesenberry, 1949: 87; Brown, 1952; Davis, 1984: 800; and Gujarati, 1988: 532).

3 Assume that imports, as other writers assume for consumption (see Davidson *et al.*, 1978), are a function of current income and current wealth ($A$) i.e., $M_t - \lambda Y_t + (\delta - r)A_t$, where $r$ = rate of return on assets, and $A_t = A_{t-1} + Y_{t-1} - M_{t-1}$. With a proper manipulation, these two expressions give our import equation (3).

4 An effort to introduce remittances directly as an exogenous variable into equations (1), (2), and (3), along with GDP, gave economically unjustified results. Therefore we choose to demonstrate its influence through a kind of national disposal income ($Y_t$), made up of GDP + $R$.

5 For Algeria, the solved TSLS impact multipliers (short-run) are: for consumption 1.017, for investment 3.615, for imports 1.537, and for income 4.095. Solved TSLS interim multipliers are extremely explosive and reduced-form estimated impact and interim multipliers are all negative. For Egypt and Greece, solved TSLS impact and interim multipliers are also good and converge through time, but with different distribution patterns ending in much smaller total multipliers. For Portugal, reduced-form estimated impact and total multipliers for consumption and imports are negative. For Tunisia, although the findings of reduced-form estimated impact and total multipliers are generally not very satisfactory, being negative for investment and income, the solved TSLS multipliers are even worse (very high impact multipliers, 9.0–46.0, and an extremely explosive time distribution).

## References

Adams, Richard, H. 1991. *The Effects of International Remittances on Poverty, Inequality and Development in Rural Egypt.* Research Report No. 96. Washington, DC: International Food Policy Research Institute.

Ando, A., and F. Modigliani. 1963. "The Life-Cycle Hypothesis of Saving: Aggregate Implications and Tests," *American Economic Review*, March, pp. 54–84.
Appleyard, R.T. 1992. "International Migration and Development: An Unresolved Relationship." *International Migration*, 30 (3/4 Special Issue): 251–66.
Bencherifa, A., M. Berriane, and M. Refass. 1992. *Etude des Mouvements Migratoires du Maroc vers la Communauté Européene*. Etude pour la Commission. Rapport Final, Group d'Etudes et de Recherches Appliquées. Faculté des Lettres et des Sciences Humaines, Rabat (mimeo).
Brown, T.M. 1952. "Habit Persistence and Lags in Consumer Behaviour," *Econometrica*, 20: 355–71.
Christ, Carl, F. 1966. *Econometric Models and Methods*. New York: John Wiley.
Davidson, J.E.H., D.F. Hendry, F. Srba, and S. Yeo. 1978. "Econometric Modelling of the Aggregate Time Series Relationship between Consumers' Expenditure and Income in the U.K," *Economic Journal*, 88: 661–92.
Davis, E.P. 1984. "The Consumption Function in Macroeconomic Models: A Comparative Study," *Applied Economics*, 16: 799–838.
Djajic, S. 1986. "International Migration, Remittances and Welfare in a Dependent Economy," *Journal of Development Economics*, 21: 229–34.
Duesenberry, J.S. 1958. *Business Cycles and Economic Growth*. New York: McGraw-Hill.
Elbadawi, Ibrahim A., and Robert de Rezende Rocha. 1992. "Determinants of Expatriate Workers' Remittances in North Africa and Europe." Policy Research Working Paper, WPS 1038. Washington, DC: World Bank.
Farrag, Mayar. 1996. "Emigration Dynamics in Egypt." Paper presented at the Policy Workshop on Emigration Dynamics in the Arab Region, International Organization of Migration/United Nations Fund for Population Activities (IOM/UNFPA). Paper No 1. Geneva, Switzerland, 7–8 October (mimeo).
Feiler, G. 1987. "Scope and Some Effects of Remittances of Egyptian Migrant Workers in the Arab Oil-Producing Countries: 1973–1984," *Asian and African Studies*, 21: 305–25.
Friedman, M. 1957. *A Theory of the Consumption Function*. Princeton, NJ: National Bureau of Economic Research (NBER).
Garson, Jean-Pierre. 1994 "The Implications for the Maghrebian Countries of Financial Transfers from Emigrants," in *Migration and Development: New Partnerships for Co-operation*: 255–287. Paris: Organization for Economic Cooperation and Development (OECD).
Glytsos, Nicholas P. 1993 "Measuring the Income Effects of Migrant Remittances: A Methodological Approach Applied to Greece," *Economic Development and Cultural Change*, 42 (1): 131–68.
———. 1996. "Migration as a Key Factor in Regional Integration: The Case of Remittances." Paper presented at the OECD Seminar on Migration, Free Trade and Regional Integration in the Mediterranean Basin. Athens, 31 October/1 November. (Mimeo.)
———. 1998. "Migrant Remittances in the MENA Region: Issues and Policies for Consideration," *Forum*, Vol. 5, No. 1, May: 25–27.
———. 1998a. "La Migration comme Moteur de l'Intégration Régionale: L'Exemple des Transfers de Fonds," in (ed.), *Migration, Libre Échange et Intégration Régionale dans le Bassin Méditerranéen*, pp. 173–86. Paris: Organization de Cooperation et Developpement Economiques (OCDE).
Goldberger, A.S. 1959. *Impact Multipliers and Dynamic Properties of the Klein-Goldberger Model*. "Contributions to Economic Analysis" series, No. 19. Amsterdam: North-Holland.
Gujarati, D. N. 1988. *Basic Econometrics*. Second edition. New York: McGraw-Hill.
Handoussa, Heba. 1991. "Crisis and Challenge: Prospects for the 1990s," in H. Handoussa and G. Potter (eds.), *Employment and Structural Adjustment: Egypt in the 1990s*. Cairo: The American University in Cairo Press.

Johnston, J. 1972. *Econometric Methods.* Second edition. New York: McGraw-Hill.
Kandil, M., and M.F. Metwally. 1990. "The Impact of Migrants' Remittances on the Egyptian Economy," *International Migration*, 28: 159–79.
Keely, C. and B.N. Tran. 1989. "Remittances from Labor Migration: Evaluations, Performance and Implications," *International Migration Review*, 23: 500–525.
———, and B. Saket. 1984. "Jordanian Migrant Workers in the Arab Region: A Case Study of Consequences for Labour Supplying Countries," *The Middle East Journal*, 38: 685–98.
Kirwan, F., and D. Holden. 1986. "Emigrants' Remittances, Non-Traded Goods and Economic Welfare in the Source Country," *Journal of Economic Studies*, 13: 52–58.
Lesch, A. M. 1990. "Egyptian Labour Migration," in I.M. Oweiss (ed), *The Political Economy of Contemporary Egypt*. Washington, DC: Georgetown University Press.
Looney, R.E. 1990. "Macroeconomic Impacts of Worker Remittances on Arab World Labour Exporting Countries," *International Migration*, 28: 25–44.
Lundahl, Mats. 1985. "International Migration, Remittances and Real Incomes: Effects on the Source Country," *Scandinavian Journal of Economics*, 87: 647–57.
Oberai, A.S., and H.K.M. Singh. 1980. "Migration, Remittances and Rural Development: Findings of a Case Study in the Indian Punjab," *International Labour Review*, 119 (No. 2): 229–41.
Pavlopoulos, P. 1966. *A Statistical Model for the Greek Economy, 1949–1959*. "Contributions to Economic Analysis" series, No. 44. Amsterdam: North-Holland.
Richards, A., and P.L. Martin. 1983. "The Laissez-faire Approach to International Labor Migration: The Case of the Arab Middle East," *Economic Development and Cultural Change*, 31: 455–74.
Rivera-Batiz, F. 1986. "International Migration, Remittances and Economic Welfare in the Source Country," *Journal of Economic Studies*, 13: 3–19.
Russell, Sharon Stanton. 1986. "Remittances from International Migration: A Review in Perspective," *World Development*, 14: 677–96.
———. 1992. "Migrant Remittances and Development," *International Migration*, 30 (3/4 Special Issue): 267–87.
Samha, M. 1992. "The Impact of Migratory Flows on Population Changes in Jordan: A Middle Eastern Case Study," *International Migration*, Vol. 30, No. 2
Stark, Oded. 1991. *The Migration of Labor.* Cambridge, Mass.: Basil Blackwell.
———, J. E. Taylor, and S. Yitzhaki. 1986. "Remittances and Inequality," *Economic Journal*, 96: 722–40.
Taylor, J. E., and T. J. Wyatt. 1996. "The Shadow Value of Migrant Remittances, Income and Inequality in a Household-farm Economy," *The Journal of Development Studies*, 32: 899–912.
Wahba, J. 1996. "Remittances in the Middle East: A Review." Paper presented at the conference on Labor Markets and Human Resource Development, sponsored by the Economic Research Forum for the Arab Countries, Iran and Turkey. Kuwait, 16–18 September (mimeo).
World Bank. Various years. *World Tables.* Washington, DC: World Bank.

# 14

# Big Cities and Migration: Evidence from Egypt

*Barry McCormick and Jackline Wahba*

## Introduction

Whereas half a century ago large cities were found mainly in developed countries, many of the world's largest cities are now in developing countries. By the year 2000, it is estimated that 17 of the 22 mega-cities, with 10 million or more inhabitants, will be in the developing world. The rapid pace of urbanization in developing countries, and in particular that of the large cities, is a source of considerable concern for policy makers, given the potential market failures in congestion and pollution, and the problems of infrastructure development.

Middle Eastern countries are no exception. The Middle East has long been dominated by its cities. Even in 1800, cities were focal points of the extensive international trade system linking Europe to Asia. Landlords and rulers alike lived in the cities, not in the countryside, as had their European feudal counterparts. Today, cities in the Middle East and North Africa (MENA) region are still the center of gravity of economics, politics, and intellectual life. In 1990, 57 percent of the total population lived in urban areas in the MENA region, compared to 27 percent in 1950. In some MENA countries—Bahrain, Kuwait, Qatar, the United Arab Emirates, Saudi Arabia, Iraq, and Lebanon—the proportion of the population living in urban areas is more than three-quarters. In many MENA countries, the urban population is concentrated in one or two very large cities—over 40 percent of urban Moroccans live in Casablanca and Rabat; Baghdad contains more than half of all urban Iraqis.

The MENA region has three of the world's largest cities: Cairo, Tehran, and Istanbul. They ranked 15th, 26th, and 27th, respectively, in 1990. However, during the last two decades, a small group of MENA countries—Egypt, Morocco, Algeria, and Tunisia—have experienced a relative stabilization of growth of their largest cities (Karoufi, 1996). Nonetheless, Cairo is still the region's largest city, with more than a quarter of MENA's urban population and one of the world's highest population densities—the average being 40,000 per square kilometer, while in some areas in Cairo it exceeds 100,000 per square kilometer (Omran and Roudi, 1993).

Natural population growth and rural-urban migration are seen as the main causes of urbanization and city growth in developing countries. To understand the growth of cities, we need to explore not only rural-big city migration but also urban-big city migration. Whereas rural-urban migration flows have received considerable attention in the literature, intra-urban flows, which are at least as significant, have been less emphasized (see, for examples: Mazumdar, 1987, and Yap, 1977). We study whether internal migration has contributed to the growth of Egypt's three largest cities—Cairo, Giza, and Alexandria—and whether migration has altered the skill and human capital composition of the labor force of these cities. We will use a three-way distinction between rural areas, large cities, and other urban areas. This enables us to examine separately the determinants of rural and urban migration into and out of large cities.[1] Consequently, our econometric work explores separately the flows of male workers between large cities and (a) less dense urban areas, and (b) rural areas. The chapter is organized as follows. The next section discusses the literature on migration to large cities; there follows an introduction to the data; we then present the findings concerning migration to and from large cities in Egypt; and, finally, we give our conclusions.

## Migration and Large Cities

Although there is an enormous literature on migration in developing countries, there have been few studies of the nature of this migration into large cities. Fuller *et al.* (1985) study migration characteristics to Bangkok from rural areas, while Mazumdar (1981) examines the characteristics of migrants to Kuala Lumpur by origin. Likewise, very few attempts have been made at examining the nature of migration out of large cities—Pessino (1991) studies out-migration from a large city, Lima. However, we are not aware of any attempts to use individual data to study the pattern of flows both into and out of a large city in a less developed country (LDC). Thus, in consequence, little is known, for example, about how migration alters the composition of net labor skills in large cities, which is important in the analysis of the role of cities in economic growth.

A primary concern of this chapter is to examine how migration alters the human capital and skill composition of workers in large cities by studying the selectivity of migration by education. We will explore whether this selectivity applies not only to migration from rural areas and small towns but also to migration out of big cities. Several studies (e.g., Yap, 1977, and Mazumdar, 1987) find that educated workers tend to have a higher propensity to migrate than the less educated. In particular, educated workers are more likely to migrate from rural to urban areas. Development economists—for example, Williamson (1988)—have been concerned that education leads to more rural-urban migration and hence affects rural development. Already in the 1890s, economists like Alfred Marshall were arguing that educated labor is drained out of rural areas and smaller cities, and into large cities.[2] Thus Henderson (1986 and 1988), for example, argues that in most developing countries there is a strong positive correlation between city size and the skill composition of the workforce, with skilled labor being drawn out of the smaller cities.

There are two suggested main reasons for the draining of educated workers into large cities. First, on the demand side, it is hypothesized that skill requirements in production rise as city size rises. The types of goods produced in large cities require relatively high skill inputs. Industries with high skill requirements tend to locate in the larger urban areas because of the external economies of scale in production that these areas provide. Second, on the supply side, educated people are attracted to large cities because of amenities and services: the 'bright lights' hypothesis. The disproportionate distribution of educated and skilled workers in large cities relative to smaller cities and other areas has a variety of important implications. When regions are under-endowed with educated workers, and therefore with educated decision-makers, this affects local public policy and quality of life. Also, disparities in the educational attainments of the labor force in large and small cities, make large cities more attractive for advanced industries to locate in. When large cities are better endowed with skills, they tend to offer a more sophisticated service infrastructure for both producers and consumers relative to other areas (Henderson, 1988). Thus, in this chapter we examine whether educated workers are absorbed from small urban areas as well as from rural areas into Egypt's large cities. In addition, we study whether Egypt's largest cities retain their educated workers.

## The Egyptian Context and Data

### *City Growth in Egypt*

Egypt has been cited as an over-urbanized developing country: town dwellers make up approximately 45 percent of the total population, with the main part of the densely populated urban network in a patchwork arrangement along the length of the Nile. The 1986 census published by the Central Agency for Public Mobilization and Statistics (CAPMAS) shows that the population of Egypt's three largest cities—Cairo, Giza, and Alexandria—as a percentage of both total and urban population has stabilized over the last two decades, while the most recent census of 1996 shows a slight decline between 1986 and 1996. The annual urban population growth rate is still rising, but at a declining rate (see Table 14.1). Nonetheless, Cairo, Giza, and Alexandria, with approximately 13 million inhabitants (that is 21.5 percent of the total population and 50 percent of the urban population), continue to dominate the national urban system. Alongside, there has been a growth of small and medium-sized towns during the last three decades (see Karoufi, 1996).[3]

**Table 14.1: Population Trends in Cairo, Giza, and Alexandria**

| | Cairo | Giza | Alexandria | Other Urban | Total |
|---|---|---|---|---|---|
| Annual Urban Population Growth Rate[1] | | | | | |
| 1960–76 | 2.60 | 7.4 | 2.7 | — | 3 |
| 1976–86 | 1.8 | 4.5 | 2.4 | — | 2.8 |
| 1986–96 | 1.59 | 2.73 | 1.59 | — | 2.1 |
| Population (thous)[2] | | | | | |
| 1976 | 5074 | 1378 | 2318 | 16037 | 36626 |
| 1986 | 6069 | 2140 | 2927 | 21216 | 48254 |
| 1996 | 6789 | 2590 | 3328 | 25471 | 59272 |
| Population as Percent of Urban Population[2] | | | | | |
| 1976 | 31.64 | 8.59 | 14.45 | — | — |
| 1986 | 28.6 | 10.10 | 13.80 | — | — |
| 1996 | 26.66 | 10.17 | 13.07 | — | — |
| Population as Percent of Total Population[2] | | | | | |
| 1976 | 13.85 | 3.76 | 6.33 | 43.78 | — |
| 1986 | 12.60 | 4.44 | 6.10 | 43.97 | — |
| 1996 | 11.45 | 4.37 | 5.62 | 42.97 | — |

*Sources:* 1. National Institute of Planning Egypt Human Development Report 1994.
2. CAPMAS, Egypt Statistical Yearbook, various years.

Small cities and towns have been fulfilling an increasing number of functions due to the development of service activities, including administration, education, and health. Through decentralization and the downward migration of civil servants and managerial personnel, these small cities and towns have acquired the position of administrative, commercial, and even manufacturing centers (Karoufi, 1996). We shall study whether this is reflected in a complementary composition of migrants to these areas, or whether these developments have occurred despite the attractions of migration presented by Cairo and Alexandria.

## *The Data*

This study uses individual-level data from the October 1988 round of the Labor Force Sample Survey (LFSS) carried out by CAPMAS in Egypt, which was the first to include questions regarding mobility and earnings. The individual-level data set used is from the survey's labor mobility module, which provides detailed information on approximately 10,000 individuals. With respect to mobility information, the 1988 LFSS reports residential and work locations in 1988 (the year of the survey) and retrospective information concerning October 1981.[4] For the purposes of this chapter, a migrant is a person who has moved from one labor market to another between 1981 and 1988 (inclusive). Our spatial framework comprises 26 governorates, each with a rural and an urban labor market.[5] We examine migration between the largest three cities in Egypt—Cairo, Giza, and Alexandria—and (i) the rural areas and (ii) the urban areas of the other governorates. These three cities—Cairo, Giza, and Alexandria—accounted for 52.5 percent of the total urban population in 1986 and are located in northern Egypt. The analysis is confined to male workers in the labor force who are aged between 15 and 64.

Table 14.2a displays the distribution of educated individuals (secondary and university degree holders) of different age categories across large cities, urban areas (small cities and towns), and rural areas in Egypt. The distribution of age groups (15–34, 35–54, and 55–64), both for the total working population and for the educated workers, is examined. Large cities have more educated workers than other urban areas; 23 percent of the large cities' working population have secondary or higher levels of education compared to 18 percent in other urban areas and 6 percent in rural areas. Large cities appear to have slightly more (3 percent) young persons relative to smaller cities and towns, and slightly more (2 percent) educated workers below the age of 35. There appears to be a sizable gap in the distribution of the middle-age group (35–54) between large cities and smaller cities and towns among the educated. Among the educated, the share of the large cities is 5 percent higher. The most interesting age difference between large cities and other urban areas is that of the older workers: large cities have fewer 55–64 year-olds, but among the educated, the share is 6 percent higher than in other urban areas. Thus, in terms of labor stocks, the large cities would appear to have a disproportionate share of those who are both educated and experienced.

Table 14.2b provides evidence concerning the contribution of migration selectivity to the age pattern in large cities. Over 80 percent of migrants to large cities are under 35 years old, whereas less than 40 percent of migrants from large cities are under 35. Whilst migration is concentrated among the young, this is largely for migration into

Cairo, Alexandria, and Giza, and less so for migration out of these densely populated areas.

**Table 14.2a: Distribution of the Working Population by Age and Education**

| Percentage that are Age: | Large Cities (Cairo, Giza & Alexandria) | | Other Urban Areas | | Rural | |
|---|---|---|---|---|---|---|
| | Total Sample | Sec & Higher (23% of Area Total)* | Total Sample | Sec & Higher (18% of Area Total)* | Total Sample | Sec & Higher (6% of Area Total)* |
| 15–34 | 53 | 24 | 50 | 22 | 56 | 6 |
| 35–54 | 39 | 23 | 39 | 18 | 33 | 4 |
| 55–64 | 8 | 13 | 11 | 7 | 11 | 1 |
| Sample Size | 1582 | 364 | 1531 | 243 | 2102 | 126 |

*Note:* Percent of area population with secondary or higher education in given age category.

**Table 14.2b: Age Composition of Migrants to and from Large Cities (%)**

| | Labor Force in Large Cities | | Labor Force in Other Areas[1] | |
|---|---|---|---|---|
| Age | Migrants to Rural & Other Urban Areas | Total Sample | Migrants to Large Cities | Total Sample |
| 15–21 | 2.17 | 8.34 | 18.18 | 16.41 |
| 22–26 | 8.70 | 16.43 | 25.97 | 13.57 |
| 27–34 | 27.17 | 22.12 | 37.66 | 21.00 |
| 35–44 | 33.70 | 21.87 | 6.49 | 18.99 |
| 45–54 | 16.30 | 17.07 | 6.49 | 15.58 |
| 55–64 | 11.96 | 12.77 | 5.19 | 9.80 |

*Note:* 1. Labor Force in rural and urban areas excluding large cities.
*Source:* Authors' calculations based on the 1988 LSSS.

Table 14.3 highlights an important finding: namely, that net internal migration of male workers to Egypt's three largest cities has been close to zero between 1981 and 1988.[6] There are several explanations for this. First, Vining (1985) has hypothesized that "Cairo has reached a state of absolute diseconomies of urban scale and density leading to reversal or slowdown of coreward migration." Cairo has become one of the most densely populated urban areas in the world, has one of the lowest provisions of road space per capita, and has become one of the most polluted cities. Second, industries are no longer attracted to locate in Egypt's largest cities. The percentage of the labor force engaged in industry in Cairo and Alexandria, respectively, was 32.7 and 34.3 in 1976, and 31.3 and 33.2 in 1986. However, the percentage of the total labor force engaged in industry increased from 16.4 to 18.2 between 1976 and 1986 (National Institute of Planning, 1994: 132). Third, the development of new towns close to Cairo and Giza (for example, Sixth of October and Tenth of Ramadan cities) has attracted both manufacturing firms and workers. The number of new towns and cities rose from nine in 1986 to 19 by 1996 (CAPMAS, yearbooks). Fourth, there is also scattered evidence that internal migration has slowed down. During 1976–86, Cairo experienced a 50 percent decline in net in-migration rates compared to the previous ten-year inter-census period. Also, the rate of rural-urban migration decreased by one percent between 1986 and 1996 (CAPMAS, yearbooks). Fifth, the public sector has played an important role in reallocating workers across regions. However, the slowdown of the government's guaranteed employment scheme and the stabilization of the share of public sector employment may have weakened that role, and hence ameliorated the reallocation of workers across regions (McCormick and Wahba, 1999). Finally, during the 1970s and 1980s, the increase in international migration has correspondingly slowed down internal migration. In addition, unlike many developing countries, studies have shown that the majority of return overseas migrants have gone back to their region of origin (see, for example, Nasser, 1994, and Fergany, 1988) and, thus, have not contributed to the growth of the large cities in Egypt.

**Table 14.3: Descriptive Statistics**

| | Rural | | Other Urban | | Large cities | | |
|---|---|---|---|---|---|---|---|
| | Migrants to Large Cities | Total Sample | Migrants to Large Cities | Total Sample | Migrants to Oth. Urban | Migrants to Rural | Total Sample |
| Age in 1981 | 23.7 | 31.4 | 26.9 | 32.7 | 27.33 | 30.13 | 31.63 |
| **Educational Level** | | | | | | | |
| Illiterate | 36.59 | 58.04 | 16.67 | 29.7 | 17.31 | 25.00 | 23.40 |
| Less than secondary | 48.78 | 35.89 | 47.22 | 51.87 | 46.15 | 62.50 | 54.08 |
| Secondary & higher | 14.63 | 6.07 | 36.11 | 18.35 | 36.54 | 12.50 | 22.50 |
| Public sector in '81 | 9.76 | 14.46 | 33.33 | 43.11 | 46.15 | 47.50 | 45.76 |
| **Industry in '81** | | | | | | | |
| Agriculture | 34.15 | 65.56 | 5.56 | 10.12 | 1.92 | 7.50 | 4.55 |
| Manufacturing | 9.76 | 7.04 | 13.89 | 19.20 | 25.00 | 25.00 | 26.04 |
| Construction | 14.63 | 4.23 | 22.22 | 6.99 | 17.31 | 20.00 | 11.00 |
| Services | 41.46 | 23.17 | 58.33 | 63.69 | 55.77 | 47.50 | 58.41 |
| **Origin Region** | | | | | | | |
| Rural Lower | 41.46 | 60.42 | — | — | — | — | — |
| Rural Upper | 58.54 | 39.58 | — | — | — | — | — |
| Canal cities | — | — | 22.22 | 7.71 | — | — | — |
| Urban Lower | — | — | 55.33 | 57.28 | — | — | — |
| Urban Upper | — | — | 19.45 | 35.01 | — | — | — |
| Cairo | — | — | — | — | 69.23 | 47.50 | 55.97 |
| Giza | — | — | — | — | 13.46 | 30.00 | 18.03 |
| Alexandria | — | — | — | — | 17.31 | 22.50 | 26.00 |
| **Average Distance**[1] | 237.80 | 254.44 | 208.13 | 271.55 | 221.54 | 183.56 | — |
| Sample size | 42 | 2102 | 36 | 1531 | 52 | 40 | 1582 |

*Note:* [1] Average distance is in kilometers.
*Source:* Authors' calculations.

Although we find that net internal migration of male workers to these three largest cities has been close to zero, it is interesting to examine whether internal migration has altered the skill composition and human capital of the labor force of these cities. Characteristics of migrant workers, non-migrants, and those of the total sample included in the analysis are shown in Table 14.3. First, it is significant to note that the percentage distribution of these educational groups among the urban migrants to large cities (col. 3) is very similar to the percentage of the educated among the large city migrants to other urban areas (col.5). However, the percentage of the more educated among the rural migrants to large cities is slightly greater than the percentage of the educated among the migrants from large cities to rural areas. Given that only 6 percent of the workers in rural areas are educated compared to about 23 percent in large cities, these statistics seem to show that the educated workers in rural areas are much more likely to migrate. Given that the migration rates to big cities from rural areas are very similar to those from urban areas, big cities seem to get the majority of the illiterate migrants from rural areas—36.6 percent of the rural migrants are illiterates compared to 16.7 percent of the urban migrants. First, the bulk of the educated migrants from other urban areas—36.1 percent of the urban migrants—are highly educated compared to 14.6 percent from rural areas. Second, rural migrants to large cities tend to be on average younger not only than non-migrants, but also than other migrants.

We also find that rural individuals migrate on average longer distances to large cities than those migrating from urban origins. This is because, interestingly, most of the rural migrants to large cities tend to be from the south of Egypt (Upper Rural), 59 percent, and not from the north of the country (Lower Rural). In contrast, 55 percent of urban migrants to large cities come from the urban north of Egypt. Also, migrants out of large cities to other urban areas move longer distance than migrants to big cities from urban areas. However, migrants from big cities to rural areas tend to move shorter distances, not only than migrants from big cities, but also than all other migrants. Finally, large cities seem to be losing manufacturing workers rather than attracting them from other urban areas, a finding that is consistent with the growth of Egyptian manufacturing based outside the largest cities.

## Empirical Evidence from Egypt

### *Modeling Framework*

Our strategy is to estimate models of the probability of migrating into the large cities from (i) rural areas and (ii) urban areas. We then estimate a model of a worker in a large city migrating to a rural area, a small city or town, or another large city, or remaining in the origin large city. To implement this, first we estimate two separate binomial logit models. The probability of migration is a variable bounded by zero and one, and it is assumed that this probability may be described as a logistic function of various socioeconomic variables. This implies that the probability of an individual of type $i$ is characterized by a vector $Z_I$

$$P_i = \exp(\beta' Z_i) \,/\, (1 + \exp(\beta' Z_i)) \qquad (1)$$

Where $\beta' > 0$ is a vector of parameters obtained by maximum likelihood estimation and $P_i = 1$ for migrants and 0 for non-migrants. The dependent variable is the logit of the probability of migrating. Column 1 in Table 14.4 shows the probability of migration to a large city from rural areas, while column 2 shows the probability of migration to a large city from other urban areas.

**Table 14.4: Logit Models of Probability of Migration to Large Cities: From (i) Other Urban and (ii) Rural Areas**

| Variables | Other Urban to Large Cities | Rural to Large Cities |
|---|---|---|
| Constant | -4.27 | -2.54 |
| | (-3.34) | (-1.82) |
| **Educational Levels** | | |
| Less than secondary | 0.53 | 0.43 |
| | (1.06) | (1.10) |
| Secondary & higher | 1.51 | 1.08 |
| | (2.56) | (1.64) |
| **Age Group Dummies** | | |
| 26 and under | 0.07 | -0.33 |
| | (0.16) | (-0.93) |
| 35 and over | -0.97 | -1.53 |
| | (-1.24) | (-1.81) |
| Distance | -0.09 | -0.10 |
| | (-0.92) | (-1.57) |
| **Occupational Dummies** | | |
| Public sector = 1 | -0.26 | -1.37 |
| | (-0.60) | (-2.24) |
| **Economic Conditions** | | |
| Relative unemployment rate | 0.04 | -0.62 |
| | (0.05) | (-0.47) |
| Relative wage rate | 0.47 | -0.03 |
| | (0.48) | (-0.03) |
| **Industry Dummies** | | |
| Agriculture = 1 | -0.03 | -1.32 |
| | (-0.04) | (-3.14) |
| Manufacturing = 1 | -0.11 | -0.42 |
| | (-0.21) | (-0.70) |
| Construction = 1 | 1.55 | 0.38 |
| | (3.26) | (0.71) |
| Regional dummy (Upper = 1) | -0.50 | 1.15 |
| | (-0.91) | (3.00) |
| Log-likelihood | -151.32 | -170.50 |
| Chi-squared | 31.00 | 55.47 |
| DF | 12 | 12 |
| Sample size (no of migrants) | 1531 (36) | 2102 (42) |

*Notes:* $t$-statistics are in parentheses. Reference group: 27–34 year-olds, illiterate, employed in the services industry.
*Source:* Authors' calculations.

Next, we study the determinants of migration out of a large city. The destination choice model is estimated using a multinomial logit model. Let $j$ be the choice of region of destination in 1988. For workers in large cities in 1981, $j = 0$ is staying in large city; $j = 1$ is migrating to an urban area; and $j = 2$ is migrating to a rural area. Let $Z_i$ be a vector of attributes of $i$ type of individual. We assume that

$$P_{ij} = \exp(\beta'_j Z_i) \,/\, (1 + \Sigma_j \exp(\beta'_j Z_i)) \qquad (2)$$

The parameter estimates of the migratory choice model are given in Table 14.5. This provides estimates of the relative probability of choosing each listed destination relative to the probability of remaining in the large city of origin.

**Table 14.5: Multinomial Model of Migration Probability from Large Cities**

| Variables | Large Cities to | |
|---|---|---|
| | Other Urban | Rural |
| Constant | 1.57<br>(0.48) | 3.52<br>(-1.01) |
| **Educational Levels** | | |
| Less than secondary | 0.18<br>(0.44) | 0.02<br>(0.06) |
| Secondary & higher | 1.06<br>(1.93) | -0.77<br>(-1.16) |
| **Age Group Dummies** | | |
| 26 and under | -0.76<br>(-2.09) | -0.16<br>(-0.36) |
| 35 and over | 0.61<br>(0.70) | 0.55<br>(0.65) |
| **Occupational Dummies** | | |
| Public Sector = 1 | -0.02<br>(-0.06) | 0.32<br>(0.89) |
| **Economic Conditions** | | |
| Relative unemployment rate | -1.36<br>(-1.85) | -0.72<br>(-1.05) |
| Relative wage rate | -2.70<br>(-1.02) | 0.37<br>(0.13) |
| **Industry Dummies** | | |
| Manufacturing = 1 | 0.18<br>(0.53) | 0.01<br>(0.04) |
| Construction =1 | 0.63<br>(1.54) | 0.76<br>(1.75) |
| **Regional Dummy** | | |
| Alexandria = 1 | -0.71<br>(-1.21) | 0.10<br>(0.16) |
| Giza = 1 | -0.77<br>(-1.37) | 0.74<br>(1.43) |
| Log-likelihood | -396.76 | |
| Chi-squared | 34.415 | |
| DF | 22 | |
| Sample size (no of migrants) | 1582 | ( 52, 40) |

*Notes: t*-statistics are in parentheses. Reference group: 27–34 year-olds, illiterate, employed in the services industry and working in Cairo.
*Source:* Authors' calculations.

These models can be thought of as reduced-form equations in which the factors influencing the expected gain from migration are included. Individual characteristics—education and age—are used to explain the determinants of migration. In addition, we control for other characteristics such as employment characteristics, distance, regional characteristics, and economic conditions in region of origin. In the rest of this section, we discuss the variables we have used.

*Education*

Since we are interested in examining whether internal migration has altered the skill composition and human capital of the labor force of large cities, we begin by looking at education and age. Education is an important determinant of migration. Evidence from most LDCs shows that the propensity to migrate is generally higher for the more educated (Mazumdar, 1987). Even when age is controlled for, migration rates by education group increase with the level of education. There are several possible explanations why migration propensities rise with education. First, education, being general human capital, is easily transferable to different locations. Higher levels of education may also reduce the risks of migration by contributing to a person's ability to collect and process information. Also, the higher migration rate of the educated may be due to the relatively higher responsiveness of educated individuals to wage incentives (see Fields, 1982, and Schultz, 1982), as well as to the higher growth rate of jobs requiring educational qualifications in the urban economy (see Mazumdar, 1987). Another reason for the much higher rates of migration among the educated is that they may be attracted by non-monetary advantages of urban jobs, such as job security (Speare and Harris, 1986). Thus, one would expect the educated to be more mobile and to be attracted to cities. We distinguish between three educational groups: those with no education, those with less than secondary education (i.e., less than primary, primary, and preparatory levels), and those with secondary or higher education (i.e., secondary, university, and postgraduate levels).

*Age*

Age is one of the most consistently noted differences between migrants and non-migrants. Younger persons are more mobile than older persons because the lifetime income gains to moving are larger for the young. In contrast, older individuals have higher moving costs from accumulated assets and larger families, and have more locational family ties. In most developing countries, migration is concentrated in the 15–30 age group, with a substantial portion in the 15–24 sub-group. It is to be expected that large cities would attract younger individuals. Three age group dummies—26 and under, 27–34, and 35 and over—are used.

*Distance and regional location*

Most migration studies—including those for LDCs—find that the distance between origin and destination is an important deterrent to migration. The distance coefficients in migration functions are typically negative and very significant when included with, for example, employment, wage, education, and urbanization variables (Yap, 1977). The likelihood that with increased distance the psychic costs of migration rise, and the availability of information about labor markets falls, has provided the primary explanation for the deterrent effect of distance. However, Mazumdar (1987) has pointed out that, in the case of migration to large cities, distance may not be a deterrent; the distance variable, therefore, may not show the usual negative impact on migration. In this chapter, the distance variable measures the distance between the area of the rural or urban governorate of origin and Cairo.

Also, regional dummies are used to control for the specific characteristics of the region of origin. Two regional dummies are used: Upper is the south and Lower is the north.

*Economic conditions*

Various studies show that migrants respond to economic incentives. Individuals move for economic gains, from poorer areas to wealthier areas. Differences in average wage rates between two places are significant variables affecting migration between two locations. Several migration functions in LDCs have found that destination wage is much more important in determining the migration rate than the wage at origin (see the survey by Mazumdar, 1987). In addition, employment is another important factor affecting an individual's incentives to migrate. Unemployment rates or employment rates, at origin and destination, are used in migration functions. However, the results are mixed. Several studies have found the unemployment rate to be insignificant in migration function (see, for example, Fields, 1982, and Schultz, 1982).

Our study examines migration between a large city, and distributions of (i) urban areas and (ii) rural areas. We shall explore how the relative wage and unemployment rates in these urban and rural areas, in turn, explain the likelihood of migration to one of the large cities. Since the latter is the sole destination and we have a single cross-section, we are able to eliminate the destination conditions from our models and express both urban and rural wages and unemployment relative to the national average.[7] To add specificity to these variables, we (i) differentiate the hourly wage at origin by educational category, and relative to the national average hourly wage, and (ii) differentiate the unemployment rate at origin by age category.

*Employment characteristics*

Given the different opportunities for migration afforded by the public sector in Egypt, we allow for being a public sector employee. We also differentiate by sector of employment: agriculture, manufacturing, construction, and services. All the employment characteristics used refer to 1981—that is, before migration. We expect agricultural workers to be the least mobile, given that their sector specific skills are not easily used in urban areas (for recent evidence, see Tunalı, 1996). Manufacturing workers are often found to be less mobile than service workers in studies of developed countries, but this may not hold in countries where manufacturing skills are scarce. Construction workers are also often found to be highly mobile.

## *Empirical Results*

The estimates of the logits model of migration to large cities are given in Table 14.4. Column 1 provides the estimates of urban migration to large cities, while column 2 provides the estimates of rural migration to large cities. The estimates of the multinomial model of migration from large cities are given in Table 14.5. The estimates of the relative probabilities of migration to another urban area (column 1) or to a rural area (column 2) relative to staying in a large city and not migrating are displayed in Table 14.5. Table 14.6 and 14.7 report the marginal effect of each independent variable, the increment in the probability of migration, evaluated at the reference set of individual characteristics and sample mean. The reference group is individuals with no education, aged 27–34 employed in the private sector and in the services industry in Lower Egypt. Also, it is worth noting that insignificant t-statistics indicate that the probability of migration is not significantly affected by that variable.

**Table 14.6: Predicted Probabilities of Migration to Large Cities: Marginal Effects**

| Variables | Other Urban to Large Cities | Rural to Large Cities |
|---|---|---|
| Constant | -0.062 | -0.024 |
| | (0.022) | (0.014) |
| **Educational Levels** | | |
| Less than secondary | 0.008 | 0.004 |
| | (0.007) | (0.004) |
| Secondary & higher | 0.022 | 0.010 |
| | (0.009) | (0.006) |
| **Age Group Dummies** | | |
| 26 and under | 0.001 | -0.003 |
| | (0.006) | (0.003) |
| 35 and over | -0.014 | -0.014 |
| | (0.011) | (0.007) |
| **Distance** | -0.001 | -0.001 |
| | (0.001) | (0.001) |
| **Occupational Dummies** | | |
| Public sector = 1 | -0.004 | -0.013 |
| | (0.006) | (0.006) |
| **Economic Conditions** | | |
| Relative unemployment rate | 0.005 | -0.006 |
| | (0.009) | (0.013) |
| Relative wage rate | 0.007 | -0.0003 |
| | (0.014) | (0.011) |
| **Industry Dummies** | | |
| Agriculture = 1 | -0.0004 | -0.012 |
| | (0.011) | (0.004) |
| Manufacturing = 1 | -0.002 | -0.004 |
| | (0.008) | (0.004) |
| Construction =1 | 0.023 | 0.004 |
| | (0.007) | (0.005) |
| **Regional Dummy** | | |
| Upper=1 | -0.007 | 0.011 |
| | (0.008) | (0.006) |

*Notes:* The standard error of the marginal effect is reported in parentheses.
Reference group: 27–34 year-olds, illiterate, employed in the services industry.
*Source:* Authors' calculations.

Education increases the probability of migration of both rural and urban workers to large cities (Table 14.4). Highly educated workers are more likely than illiterate workers to migrate to large cities from both rural areas and urban ones. Table 14.5 shows that the highly educated workers are more likely to migrate out of large cities, provided their destination is to other urban areas. Education has a symmetric effect on the probability of migration between big cities and other urban areas. However, we find no tendency for education to increase out-migration from large cities to rural areas. In other words, there is no migration selectivity by education for large cities to rural moves. Pessino (1991) finds that migrants out of the Peruvian capital Lima are not more likely to move if they are educated. Thus we can confirm Pessino's findings, but only for out-migration to rural areas. Although large cities attract the educated from other urban areas, large cities also tend to lose their educated, and at a similar rate, to other urban areas. However, there is evidence that large cities attract educated workers from rural areas but tend not to lose their educated to rural areas.

**Table 14.7: Predicted Probabilities of Migration from Large Cities: Marginal Effects**

| Variables | Large Cities to | |
|---|---|---|
| | Other Urban | Rural |
| Constant | -0.043 | -0.078 |
| | (0.002) | (0.078) |
| **Educational Levels** | | |
| Less than secondary | 0.005 | 0.001 |
| | (0.0002) | (0.009) |
| Secondary & higher | 0.028 | -0.018 |
| | (0.0004) | (0.016) |
| **Age Group Dummies** | | |
| 26 and under | -0.019 | -0.003 |
| | (0.0003) | (0.010) |
| 35 and over | 0.015 | 0.012 |
| | (0.0005) | (0.019) |
| **Occupational Dummies** | | |
| Public sector = 1 | -0.001 | 0.007 |
| | (0.0002) | (0.008) |
| **Economic Conditions** | | |
| Relative unemployment rate | -0.035 | -0.015 |
| | (0.0004) | (0.016) |
| Relative wage rate | -0.070 | 0.010 |
| | (0.002) | (0.061) |
| **Industry Dummies** | | |
| Manufacturing = 1 | 0.005 | 0.0002 |
| | (0.0002) | (0.009) |
| Construction = 1 | 0.016 | 0.016 |
| | (0.0003) | (0.011) |
| **Regional Dummy** | | |
| Alexandria = 1 | -0.018 | 0.003 |
| | (0.0004) | (0.013) |
| Giza = 1 | -0.020 | 0.017 |
| | (0.0003) | (0.012) |

*Notes:* The standard error of the marginal effect is reported in parentheses.
Reference group: 27–34 year-olds, illiterate, employed in the services industry and working in Cairo.
*Source:* Authors' calculations.

Table 14.4 shows, further, that persons who are between 27 and 34 years of age are the most likely to migrate. Large cities attract younger persons from other areas. The probability of migration to large cities drops after the age of 34. The likelihood of migration to large cities is high among the young and low among the old. Table 14.5 indicates that migration to rural areas from large cities is not age-selective. However, being young (26 or under) decreases the likelihood of migration out of large cities to urban areas. Being 35 or over increases the probability of migration out of large cities more than that into large cities; see Table 14.8, where the predicted probabilities of migration by age and education are shown.

Although there is a negative relationship between distance and migration, the probability of migration to large cities seems to be not significantly affected by distance, in particular in the case of migration from urban areas.

**Table 14.8: Predicted Probabilities of Migration by Age and Education**

| | Rural-Large Cities | Oth. Urban-Large Cities | Large Cities-Oth. Urban | Large Cities-Rural |
|---|---|---|---|---|
| **No Education** | | | | |
| Less than 26 | 0.008 | 0.007 | 0.004 | 0.006 |
| 27– 34 | 0.011 | 0.006 | 0.009 | 0.006 |
| 35 or more | 0.002 | 0.002 | 0.016 | 0.010 |
| **Less than Secondary** | | | | |
| Less than 26 | 0.014 | 0.011 | 0.006 | 0.009 |
| 27– 34 | 0.019 | 0.011 | 0.012 | 0.008 |
| 35 or more | 0.005 | 0.004 | 0.023 | 0.014 |
| **Secondary & Higher** | | | | |
| Less than 26 | 0.024 | 0.030 | 0.012 | 0.008 |
| 27– 34 | 0.033 | 0.028 | 0.025 | 0.008 |
| 35 or more | 0.007 | 0.011 | 0.046 | 0.014 |

*Source:* Authors' calculations.

Origin average regional unemployment and relative wage rates appear to have no significant impact on migration to large cities.[8] This may be simply because the range of economic incentives includes more than income and employment opportunities. One possible argument is that when the destinations are cities, especially large cities, better living conditions, better access to services, or a wider variety of social and recreational activities may also be important motivating factors: the 'bright lights' hypothesis. If the bright lights were the main influence on migration to big cities, migrants would be attracted to big cities regardless of their origin. However, the unequal regional dummies appear to show quite a different effect. Individuals from rural Upper Egypt are more likely to migrate to big cities than individuals from rural Lower Egypt. This may reflect that there is also a strong push factor at work in addition to the pull of the bright city lights: people are pushed from rural Upper Egypt, where there is a lack of public services and facilities. In other words, people may well be pushed out to the big cities by the comparatively 'dim lights' in their region of origin. Our data is consistent with this view.

Employment in the public sector seems to encourage workers to remain in their area of origin—especially in rural areas. The likelihood of migration of a public sector worker from a rural area is less than for a private sector worker. Being employed in the public sector, however, has no significant impact on workers in large cities migrating to urban and rural areas. One explanation may be the fact that it is not uncommon to transfer public sector workers from large cities to smaller cities and rural areas.

Industry seems to play a certain role in determining migration in and out of large cities. Rural workers attached to the agriculture sector are less likely to migrate to large cities. Urban workers in the construction sector have higher rates of migration than the service sector workers who comprise the reference group. Large city workers in the construction sector are more mobile than workers in the service sector.

## Conclusion

This chapter examines the pattern of migration to and from large cities. It uses evidence from the three largest cities in Egypt: Cairo, Giza, and Alexandria. The main findings are as follows. Net internal migration of male workers to these three largest cities has been close to zero between 1980 and 1988. Being educated increases the likelihood of migration from small towns to big cities as much as the likelihood of leaving the big cities to go to smaller towns. In other words, education has a symmetric effect on the probability of migration between big cities and other urban areas. However, being educated increases the likelihood of migrating from rural areas to large cities, but not from large cities to rural areas. Also, being young increases the tendency of migration to big cities from all other areas, but not from big cities to other areas. Being 35 or over increases the likelihood of migration out of big cities more than that it does into big cities. However, the over 35s have a greater tendency to migrate out of the big cities than to migrate to big cities. Thus, although internal migration did not contribute to the growth of Egypt's largest cities in the 1980s, it had the effect of not only raising the skill composition of the labor force, but also reducing the mean age of the labor force in these cities. If, as seems likely, this trend continues, the gap in the productivity of the labor force between the largest cities and the rest of the country, rural areas in particular, will widen.

## Notes

1 We do not study intra-large city migration in this chapter.
2 Alfred Marshall's (1890) observations are cited in Glaeser (1997: 2–3).
3 Between 1976 and 1986, the inter-census period, the urban population grew by 10 percent and the number of towns having more than 100,000 inhabitants rose from 20 to 24.
4 October 1981 was chosen because President Sadat was assassinated in that month.
5 Cairo, Alexandria, and the Canal cities are urban only governorates.
6 In a sample of 1582 workers in Cairo, we found a net out-migration of 14 male workers. This gives a net-out-migration rate of less than one percent.
7 Figures for 1988 are used. Unemployment rates for males by age group and region are used. Hourly wage rates are calculated from the earnings module of the 1988 October round of the LFSS.
8 Several studies find that the origin wage rate in LDCs is not as important a determinant of migration as the destination wage rate, and also that the unemployment rate produces mixed results (Mazumdar, 1987).

## References

Bairoch, P. 1988. *Cities and Economic Development.* Chicago: University of Chicago Press.
Bienen, H. 1980. "Urbanisation and Third World Stability," *World Development*, 12: 661–91.
Central Agency for Public Mobilization and Statistics (CAPMAS). Various years. *Egypt Statistical Yearbook.* Cairo: CAPMAS.
Fergany, N. 1988. *In Pursuit of Livelihood.* Beirut: The Center for Arab Unity Studies.
Fields, G. 1982. "Place-to-Place Migration in Colombia," *Economic Development and Cultural Change*, 30: 539–58.
Fuller, T.D., P. Lightfoot, and P. Kamnuansilpa. 1985. "Rural-Urban Mobility in Thailand: A Decision-Making Approach," *Demography*, 22: 565–79.
Glaeser, E. 1997. "Learning in Cities." National Bureau of Economic Research (NBER) Working Paper No. 6271. Cambridge, MA: National Bureau of Economic Research.
Ghatak, S., P. Levine, and S.W. Price. 1996. "Migration Theories and Evidence: An Assessment," *Journal of Economic Surveys*, 10: 159–98.
Greenwood, M. J. 1969. "The Determinants of Labor Migration in Egypt," *Journal of Regional Science*, 9: 283–90.

Henderson, J.V. 1986. "Urbanization in a Developing Country: City Size and Population Composition," *Journal of Development Economics*, 22: 269–93.

———. 1988. *Urban Development: Theory, Fact and Illusion*. Oxford: Oxford University Press.

Karoufi, M. 1996. "Urbanization and Urban Research in the Arab World." Management of Social Transformations (MOST) Discussion Paper No. 11. Paris: UNESCO.

Lucas, R.E.B. 1985. "Migration Amongst the Botswana," *The Economic Journal*, 95: 358–82.

———. 1997. "Internal Migration in Developing Countries," in M. Rosenzweig and O. Stark (eds.), *Handbook of Population and Family Economics*, Vol. 1B. The Amsterdam: Elsevier.

Maddala, G. 1983. *Limited Dependent Variables and Qualitative Variables in Econometrics*. Cambridge: Cambridge University Press.

Marshall, Alfred. 1890. *Principles of Economics*. London: Macmillan.

Mazumdar, D. 1981. *The Urban Labor Market and Income Distribution: A Study of Malaysia*. New York: Oxford University Press.

———. 1987. "Rural-Urban Migration in Developing Countries," in E.S. Mills (ed.), *Handbook of Regional and Urban Economics*, Vol. 2. Amsterdam: Elsevier .

McCormick, B., and J. Wahba. 1999. "Has Public Employment Fuelled Agglomeration in LDCs? Evidence from Egypt." Southampton, UK: University of Southampton. Mimeo.

Moomaw, R., and Shatler, A. 1996. "Urbanization and Economic Development: A Bias Toward Large Cities," *Journal of Urban Economics*, 40: 13–37.

Nassar, H. 1994. *Final Report: Return Migration*. Cairo: CAPMAS.

National Institute of Planning. 1994. *Egypt Human Development Report 1994*. Cairo: National Institute of Planning.

Omran, A.R., and F. Roudi. 1993. "The Middle East Population Puzzle," *Population Bulletin* 48. Washington, DC: Population Reference Bureau.

Pessino, C. 1991. "Sequential Migration Theory and Evidence from Peru," *Journal of Development Economics*, 36: 55–87.

Schultz, P. 1982. "Lifetime Migration within Educational Strata in Venezuela: Estimates of a Logistic Model," *Economic Development and Cultural Change*, 30: 559–93.

Speare, A. Jr., and J. Harris. 1986. "Education, Earnings and Migration in Indonesia," *Economic Development and Cultural Change*, 34: 223–43.

Tunalı, İ. 1996. "Migration and Remigration of Male Household Heads in Turkey: 1963–1973," *Economic Development and Cultural Change*, 45: 31–67.

Vining, D.R. Jr. 1985. "The Growth of Core Urban Regions in Developing Countries," *Population and Development Review*, 11: 495–514.

Williamson, J. 1988. "Migration and Urbanization," in H. Chenery and T.N. Srinivasan (eds.), *Handbook of Development Economics*, Vol. 1. Amsterdam: Elsevier.

Yap, L. 1977. "The Attraction of Cities: A Review of Migration Literature," *Journal of Development Economics*, 4: 239–64.

# Index

In this series:

*Institutional Reform and Economic Development in Egypt*
Edited by Noha El-Mikawy and Heba Handoussa

*The Egyptian Labor Market*
Edited by Ragui Assaad

*Economic Trends in the Middle East and North Africa Region, 2002*
Edited by The Economic Research Forum for the Arab Countries, Iran and Turkey.

*Employment Creation and Social Protection in the Middle East and North Africa*
Edited by Heba Handoussa and Zafiris Tzannatos